Communication Yearbook / 14

Communication
Yearbook / 14

edited by
JAMES A. ANDERSON

 Published Annually for the
International Communication
Association

 **SAGE PUBLICATIONS**
The International Professional Publishers
Newbury Park London New Delhi

For information address:

SAGE Publications, Inc.
2455 Teller Road
Newbury Park, California 91320

SAGE Publications Ltd.
6 Bonhill Street
London EC2A 4PU
United Kingdom

SAGE Publications India Pvt. Ltd.
M-32 Market
Greater Kailash I
New Delhi 110 048 India

Printed in the United States of America

Library of Congress: 76-45943

ISBN 0-8039-3543-9
ISSN 0147-4642

FIRST PRINTING, 1991

Sage Production Editor: Astrid Virding

CONTENTS

THE INTERNATIONAL COMMUNICATION ASSOCIATION

The International Communication Association was formed in 1950, bringing together academicians and other professionals whose interest focused on human communication. The Association maintains an active membership of more than 2,200 individuals, of which some two-thirds are teaching and conducting research in colleges, universities, and schools around the world. Other members are in government, the media, communication technology, business law, medicine, and other professions. The wide professional and geographical distribution of the membership provides the basic strength of the ICA. The Association is a meeting ground for sharing research and useful dialogue about communication interests.

Through its Divisions and Interest Groups, publications, annual conferences, and relations with other associations around the world, ICA promotes the systematic study of communication theories, processes, and skills.

In addition to *Communication Yearbook,* the Association publishes *Human Communication Research, Communication Theory,* the *ICA Newsletter,* and *ICA Directory.* Several divisions also publish newsletters and occasional papers.

PREFACE

Once again, and for the last time under this editor's stewardship, *Yearbook* authors have prepared a rich sampling of the subjects and perspectives of communication. As is our tradition, authors have offered rugged claim up for comment in a robust critical activity. Chapters are coupled with commentaries that critique, support, and extend, but always engage the primary issues. These are lively exchanges. This volume is divided into four sections. In the paragraphs that follow, I present a brief overview of each section and its articles.

Klaus Bruhn Jensen opens this volume with yet another assault on the centrality of text in media analyses and participates in what appears to be a widespread rediscovery of Charles Sanders Peirce as well as the rehabilitation of pragmatism in the project of empowering the audience. Jensen empowers the audiences of media by granting them interpretive rights supported in social action. For his comment on Jensen, John Fiske examines the fit between the social action perspective and Peircean semiotics and finds it wanting. He argues that Saussurean semiology is more appropriate to the social action perspective. For his part, Horace Newcomb proclaims Jensen's argument noble but flawed and, more important, limited by its own moment of appearance.

Karl Erik Rosengren takes advantage of the 15-year history of a media research program conducted with both panel and cross-sectional methodologies to produce an analysis of the structural invariants of media use as explained by development, social class, and socialization processes. The power of this analysis is shown as consistent patterns emerge despite an era of great technological introduction and change. Commentator Cecilia von Feilitzen takes up particular methodological issues in the manner of measurement and in the comparison of panel and cross-sectional data collections. She argues for even stronger conclusions concerning consistency. John Murray, on the other hand, cautions against the conclusions that Rosengren does draw, noting the considerable instability that his own research shows. For my own part, this set of three arguments shows the contributions that different methodological approaches make to the knowledge claims advanced.

In this era, when cultural studies seem intent on capturing center stage of social issues in media analysis, Denis McQuail offers an approach from the perspective of traditional social science by creating a "hybrid of the the social responsibility and empiricist schools of criticism." Working from the normative principles of freedom, equality, and order, McQuail argues that objective measures of performance can be applied to media assessment and provides specific examples of this application. But for commentator Douglas Birkhead, McQuail's work is much too sanitized — too far removed from the political, ideological, moral, and historical engagement that successful criticism requires. Birkhead claims that objective measures become assessment criteria only in the push and shove of social and moral interaction. Jan Servaes finds the value of McQuail's analysis in the study of the rationalistic issues of the news. Such issues do not capture the heart of the ideation process of which news is a part, however. The analysis of that process must also press against the nonrational — the issues of subjectivity, ethnicity, and cultural mythology, as well as ideology.

The chapter by Jeremy Tunstall and the companion piece by James Danowski work a special form to enlarge the industrial view of media production and organizational activity. Tunstall wants us to consider the intraorganizational character and the extraorganizational structure of media industries as ways of understanding the media product distributed. In his principal argument, Tunstall claims that national industries are remarkably different from one another (differences most often not properly understood) and at the same time moving toward a global market. Danowski takes Tunstall's analysis and casts it as a specific example in his theory of organizations' media behavior. Time- and space-shifting media are organizational resources which are put to different work depending on the organization's inward or outward orientation. The media industries, with their domestic peculiarities and global commonalities, offer a profitable site of analysis.

J. Michael Sproule begins the section on propaganda and public opinion with a second look at the American critical impulse in media studies. He contrasts Marxist critical interests in class and the state with American interests in private institutions and their professional propagandists. He traces the history of propaganda studies as they moved from the critical to the rational and from being called *propaganda* studies to being called *communication* studies to their present redeployment in a post-Vietnam, postmodern mode of critique. He argues that the present critical movement is unknowing of its active American past and could benefit from that knowledge. Garth Jowett works the history of the American progressives' response to the introduction of the movies to provide for an examination of the value of European critical thought for the analysis of American institutions. He, like Sproule, finds the application strained. Raymie McKerrow, on the other hand, finds difficulties in the application of progressive criticism. For him, the progressives were propagandists in their own right, practicing what they preached against, which prevents their critical approach from being useful in the postmodern project of the analysis of the discourse of power.

Chapters 6 and 7 complete a project on public opinion and agenda-setting begun in *Communication Yearbook 11*. In Chapter 6, Elisabeth Noelle-Neumann provides a comprehensive statement on the spiral of silence as a theory of the public opinion process. In this extension of her seminal work, Noelle-Neumann presents new evidence from her ongoing research program in support of the central tenets of the theory. She includes a discussion of the role of media in opinion formation and concludes with an analysis of the design requirements for opinion research. Mihaly Csikszentmihalyi enlarges Noelle-Neumann's analysis by examining the prior issues of social integration and individual conformity. His analysis examines how value resources and agents of action vary across cultures and how individuals within cultures differentially assimilate public opinion into personal action. Serge Moscovici contrasts Noelle-Neumann's emphasis on the manner by which common opinions emerge with his question of why deviant positions sometimes overcome common ones. Referencing the remarkable recent changes in Eastern Europe, he postulates sturdy dissident positions that survive even under the dominant ideological cover and emerge opportunistically when that cover cracks.

Stephen Reese's chapter reaches back to Rogers and Dearing's review of agenda-setting research that appeared in volume 11 of the *Yearbook* to answer their call for an analysis of the process that sets the media's agenda. At the top of the process, he argues for a symbiotic relationship in which elite media and the political elite are resources for one another, neither consistently dominant over the other. Elite media, rather than the political elite, however, are more likely to set the agenda for the less elite of the industry. He also notes that the present is a time of restructuring of the media industry, with signs abounding of loss of power among its elite, particularly broadcast media. Both of Reese's commentators move aggressively to deconstruct the concept of agenda-setting. Lee Becker begins by calling our understanding of the agenda concept into question. For him, the concept serves no good purpose, particularly in the study of content creation. D. Charles Whitney would appear to agree. He rejects the idea of an orderly arrangement of agenda-setting and advances the notion that content creation occurs in a set of contingent relations. On the other hand, both commentators commend Reese's use of power as the primary explanatory device.

Sara Newell and Randall Stutman move us into the realm of interpersonal studies in their investigation of social confrontation. Taking both interactionist and cognitivist perspectives, Newell and Stutman provide a description and examples of the roles and structures of this type of conversational episode. In his engagement of Newell and Stutman's piece, Joseph Folger considers the role that culturally shared interpretations play in the development of claims about conversational structure. He contrasts this approach with one requiring an intimate knowledge of the participants' world. Taken from the latter perspective, episodic boundaries of confrontation can disappear into an ongoing practice of a relationship. G. H. Morris seeks to place Newell and Stutman's analysis in his larger construct of "alignment talk." For him, social confrontation is an attempt to achieve an appropriate definition of proper conduct. Morris also believes that we can best study these attempts in the close reading of their actual performance.

Actual performances are also the "right stuff" for Mary Louise Willbrand and Richard Rieke in their analysis of logic in use and strategies of reasoning. Focusing on reason giving as a discursive performance in support of some action, Willbrand and Rieke develop a grounded typology of reasons from the performances of young children, teenagers, and adults. Commonalities and developmental changes are identified. These typologies are compared across other respondent groups, including cross-cultural and mentally impaired subjects. As might be expected, substantial differences were found between the grounded taxonomies of all respondent groups and the formal categories of logic or compliance-gaining theories. Donald Tibbits compares these reason-giving performances with the constructs of critical thinking. He finds in critical thinking an underlying understanding for the strategies motivating the reasons given. Stephen Toulmin, on the other hand, points out that the procedures used by Willbrand and Rieke are not as clearly connected to "reasoning" per se as may appear. Reason giving is a language game governed not only by cognitive processes but also by, among other influences, the cultural rules of discursive performance; in fact, some reason giving may not be reasoning at all.

Michael Sunnafrank examines the time-honored claim that similarity—birds of a feather—is the basis for initiating and continuing relationships. His conclusion is that there is little support for this claim when similarity is considered a trait—rather than a practice—of the relation. His counterclaim is that it is discursive strategies that function to encourage and maintain relationships by managing the potentials for attraction and repulsion. He argues further that there are but a few critical areas in any relationship where similarity or dissimilarity is crucial to relationship survival and encourages research focus on communication practices and the critical areas of agreement in a relationship.

Arthur Bochner's reply is that even this enlightened view saves too much of the attraction paradigm. To Bochner, it is clear that the evidence in favor results from experimental protocols with little mundane validity. He rejects the individualistic and rationalistic ideology that the attraction paradigm seems to embrace. Steven McDermott takes a different tack altogether, by looking at similarity and dissimilarity as different engines of attraction in intra- and intercultural settings. His review would support their strategic management in attraction and repulsion.

In the sole chapter in the final section of this volume, Mark Peterson and Ritch Sorenson provide an extensive review of the cognitive/contextual literature on leadership in the service of developing an overarching model. They work their way through the evidence in support of 13 propositions in which leadership behavior is explained by a combination of the cognitive scripts and schemata of the leader and the traits, practices, and resources of the organizational setting. Their argument is very much a hybrid that poaches from traditional and nontraditional claims in an attempt to build a predictable world on a foundation of contingencies. G. Lloyd Drecksel argues that Peterson and Sorenson's argument is premature, and that they have jumped into an epistemic explanation with inadequate ontological footing. She asks, "What is leadership, and where would we find it? By what metaphors and to what ends is our research directed?" Beverly Davenport Sypher undercuts the cognitive and causal basis of Peterson and Sorenson's position by arguing that interpretation and its practices are at the center of an adequate explanation of leadership. It is not in the study of cognitive states but of communication strategies by which we will come to an understanding of leadership.

Sypher's comment brings us back to the beginning of this volume and Jensen's concern for meaning production. In the main, the thrust of this volume is toward discursive practices—the strategic and tactical production and interpretation of text. And it moves some distance closer to the position that both production and interpretation are themselves best understood as discursive practices. It is a move that for me brings into clearer focus the proper phenomena of communication study.

ACKNOWLEDGMENTS

This volume is dedicated to Chris Metts, an associate of the *Yearbook*, whose courage in facing death both humbled and inspired. It is also dedicated to the 150 or so authors and dozens of reviewers who created the four volumes of my editorship. Together we experienced the human struggle of scholarship. Julie Brown experienced that struggle a bit more than others by serving her second term as the *Yearbook*'s editorial associate. She did so superbly. The staff and scholarly community of the Department of Communication at the University of Utah contributed to this volume and to each of the three preceding volumes in immeasurable ways, particulary Ann Castleton, Jennifer Duignan, and Leonard Leckie. Finally, I am delighted that the *Yearbook* is being passed into the capable hands of Stan Deetz.

James A. Anderson
University of Utah

SECTION 1

MEDIA STUDIES: AUDIENCES, INDUSTRIES, AND ASSESSMENT

1   When Is Meaning?
Communication Theory, Pragmatism,
and Mass Media Reception

KLAUS BRUHN JENSEN
University of Copenhagen

This chapter offers an outline of a social semiotics of mass communication and defines meaning simultaneously as a social and as a discursive phenomenon. The argument draws its concepts of signs, discursive differences, and interpretive communities from the philosophical pragmatism of Charles Sanders Peirce in order to move beyond the essentialistic notions of meaning that characterize much previous communication theory, both in the social sciences and in cultural studies. Mass-mediated signs give rise *not* to a transmission of entities of meaning, but to specific processes of reception that are performed by the audience acting as cultural agents or interpretive communities. As audiences engage in socially specific practices of reception, mass media come to function as institutions-to-think-with. Empirical research has served to question notions of mass media as a relatively autonomous cultural forum in which polysemic messages lend themselves to diverse audience uses and pleasures. The polysemy of audience discourses, indeed, suggests the prevalence of contradictory forms of consciousness that tend to reproduce a dominant construction of social reality. Critical social theory in a pragmatic mode, emphasizing the interested and future-oriented character of scientific analysis, can help to indicate how and to what extent audiences may make a social difference.

T HROUGH reference to the category of *reception*, mass communication studies of the 1980s began to reexamine some fundamental issues concerning the nature and origins of meaning in human communication. Whereas audiences have been the object of continuous and substantial study since

AUTHOR'S NOTE: Research for this chapter was conducted, in part, during 1988-89, when I was a Fellow of the American Council of Learned Societies at the Annenberg School of Communications, University of Southern California; I wish to acknowledge the support of both the ACLS and colleagues at the Annenberg School. Part of the chapter was presented as a paper to the Charles Sanders Peirce Sesquicentennial International Congress, Harvard University, September 5-10, 1989. Other sections were given as lectures at the University of Utah, University of Wisconsin—Madison, Pennsylvania State University, and University of Kentucky during February 1989.

Correspondence and requests for reprints: Klaus Bruhn Jensen, Department of Film, TV, and Communication, University of Copenhagen, Njalsgade 80, DK-2300 Copenhagen S, Denmark.

Communication Yearbook 14, pp. 3-32

the beginnings of the field, current work implies a reconceptualization of mass communication processes as everyday practices producing and circulating meaning in society, particularly emphasizing the constitutive role of audiences as interpretive agents. The attention given to the decoding and social uses of media content has been apparent both in empirical research on audience responses and in cultural studies about media discourses. Further, it has entailed a dialogue across the critical-empirical, qualitative-quantitative boundaries of the field (Jensen, 1987; Jensen & Rosengren, in press; Schröder, 1987). The turn toward reception is, perhaps, most distinctively articulated in the recent tradition of qualitative empirical audience studies (Ang, 1985; Jensen, 1986; Katz & Liebes, 1984; Lindlof, 1987; Lull, 1988b; Morley, 1980, 1986; Radway, 1984), which have accumulated evidence that mass media audiences make their own sense of media content in complex and unexpected ways. Audiences may, to a significant degree, modify or oppose the specific meanings that appear to be proffered by mass media, and may, furthermore, appropriate those meanings for alternative ends as they engage in a questioning and reconstruction of social reality.

Behind this reconceptualization lies the as yet undeveloped assumption that meaning is simultaneously a *social* and a *discursive* phenomenon. On the one hand, meaning may be defined as the outcome of an interest-driven, situated act of interpretation performed by a social agent. This definition locates meaning in the real world of people, power, and pleasures. On the other hand, meaning traditionally is associated with particular vehicles — texts or other discursive forms. Discourse theory may be said to suggest that subjects and social realities are primarily functions of the operations of discourse, so that, for analytical purposes, media audiences should also be conceptualized as discourses or, perhaps, discursive strategies of interpretation. It is this duality of the concept of meaning that may, in part, account for the major ambiguities and conflicts over how to approach communication, both theoretically and methodologically, that have emerged in some recent attempts to take stock of reception analysis (for instance, see *Critical Studies in Mass Communication*, vol. 5, no. 3, 1988; and *Cultural Studies*, vol. 2, no. 3, 1988). (The reader may also wish to see Jensen, 1986, chap. 10, which offers a model of discourses and further serves to introduce the focus of my argument.)

Levels of Discourse

While recognizing the distinction between media discourses, such as television programs, and various types of audience discourses, such as decodings of or conversations about television, empirical reception studies have challenged the assumption that media discourses are somehow primary and that they narrowly constrain the meanings voiced in audience discourses. Instead, both forms of discourse can be said to represent moments or manifestations of the wider category of social meaning production. Even if studies have shifted the relative empirical emphasis toward the audience, the perspective has been one of audience-cum-content analysis, incorporating the discourses of empirical media users, which have often been absent in critical and cultural studies, as well as the structures of content, which, at least in the sense of culturally coded discourses, fall outside the scope of most social scientific research. Thus reception analysis seeks to account for mass media as social resources of meaning that may lend a sense of purpose to political, cultural, and other practices.

How to study the multiple *discourses* of mass communication with reference to an analytical level of discourse where evidence can be categorized and reflected upon is perhaps the main point of contention in recent debates. According to Lull (1988a), one of the foremost tasks for audience research is to develop *metadiscourses*, in the sense of systematic descriptive procedures that specify research designs, forms of evidence, and bases of inference. His underlying concern is with the social aspect of meaning, with people who engage a material and political reality through cultural forms of understanding that, significantly, are accessible for scientific analysis. In the next procedural step, the evidence may be assigned explanatory value from the perspective of a particular *theoretical discourse*, which is the third discursive level of reception analysis. In the words of Anderson and Meyer (1988), "It is method that generates the facts that become evidence within theory" (p. 292).

In contrast, some cultural theorists suggest that the above approach tends to reify particular conceptions of media, recipients, and discourses (Allor, 1988; Grossberg, 1988). They want to shift the focus of the debate to a further, fourth level of *epistemological discourse*. From this perspective, a continuous process of self-reflection may come into play regarding the precise status of audience discourses and media discourses, the interrelations among multiple discourses, as well as the analytical stance of the researcher who also works in and through discourses. Emphasizing the discursive aspect of meaning, such an enterprise would aim constantly to deconstruct and reconstruct the subject positions within discourse from which media might be said to make sense, either for "audiences" or for "researchers."

However, whereas the level of epistemological discourse represents an important feedback mechanism in a discourse-based approach to reception analysis, analysts who insist on staying within the epistemological loop jeopardize their claim to a discursive position from which they might address mass communication as an aspect of social reality. For example, Grossberg's (1988) advance reservations about the validity of Radway's (1988) proposal to study the cultural practices of a single heterogeneous community to move beyond predefined notions of popular cultural forms, historical subjects, and their modes of engagement are indicative of an epistemological anxiety before the social aspects of discourse. By definition, studies of mass communication and other meaning production require researchers to take discursive positions in their analytical metadiscourse as well as in theoretical discourse. An interesting intervention in the debates has been made by Hartley (1988), who notes that one implicit aim of reception analysis is, and must be, to "*persuade* audiences to take up, unproblematically or otherwise, those positions that our critical analysis suggests are *better* than others" (p. 238).

Because the activity of reception has major implications for issues of power and cultural identity, a theory of mass media reception would have to explain how the discourses of audiences, as well as of analysts, might make a concrete difference in the social construction of reality.

To sum up, the argument of this essay will focus on the level of theoretical discourse, while assuming that any specific theoretical perspective must be checked and balanced against other levels of discourse. In particular, I suggest that the framework of pragmatism and semiotics, as originally outlined by Charles Sanders Peirce, can help to integrate the social and discursive aspects of reception analysis.[1] Semiotics may, in fact, be contrasted with Saussurean semiology, the applications of which to mass media and popular culture have often neglected or misconstrued the reception aspect because of a particular philosophical legacy. Building on the Peircean framework, I characterize reception as a socially situated, semiotic practice through reference to the concept of interpretive communities. Finally, I introduce findings from empirical reception analysis in order to reinterpret the notion of polysemy, with implications for the analysis of mass media as social institutions and for the political conclusions that may be drawn from work with mass media audiences.

WHERE IS MEANING?

A Cartesian Legacy

Like history, theory tends to repeat itself. Communication theory, in its quest for the foundations or origins of meaning, has reiterated the quest for some incorrigible foundation of knowledge that has preoccupied professional philosophy since Descartes (Rorty, 1979). Descartes, having hypostatized the distinction between the knowing subject and its objects in reality, committed philosophy to the project of reestablishing a symmetry between the subjective and objective realms as a foundation of human enterprise. Central to the Cartesian project was, of course, the definition of the subjective and objective poles of the universe. At the center of the modern mental universe emerged the solitary, but perspicacious, individual, just as in the areas of economic enterprise and political activity the individual presumably now reigned supreme (Lowe, 1982). The knowing subject was seen to have, potentially, the powers of introspection and self-awareness. Similarly, the objects of knowledge were seen to have positive existence. The crucial link between the realms — the correlate of external reality in human experience — was defined, following Locke, as the data of sense perception. Accordingly, eyesight entered philosophical discourse as the major metaphor for the activity of knowing. By pointing to sense data as objective correlates of individuals' subjective knowledge, early modern philosophy arrived at a spatial and essentialist conception of reality and was thus able to address the question, Where is reality?

By analogy, the first few decades of communication theory have addressed the question, Where is meaning? Whereas Cartesian philosophy searched for means of gaining access to and representing aspects of reality, communication theory seeks to identify the means by which one mind is able to represent its own understanding (representation) of reality in a form that is understandable or meaningful to another mind. The question of meaning, admittedly, has received a variety of answers (McQuail & Windahl, 1981), but a common feature of several classic theories is the transmission metaphor, assuming that meaning is an essence of message content that can be located in spatial terms. In Lasswell's (1948/1966) formulation of "Who/Says What/In Which Channel/To Whom/With What Effect?" (p. 178), the "what" of communication is conceived of as a message entity that maintains a rather simple presence in the world and links two minds with reference to a shared reality. Reception is said to involve a selection of certain building blocks of meaning, so that any communicant who "performs a relay function can be examined in relation to input and output" (p. 186).

Other classic communication theories approach the question — Where is meaning? — in a way that is reminiscent specifically of twentieth-century philosophy. As part of the general shift toward a philosophy based in the analysis of language (Hartnack, 1965; Wittgenstein, 1958), the procedures of knowing came to be seen as dependent upon formal and later natural languages, and philosophy may be said to have retreated to a position that observes reality from within language. Similarly, some communication theories focus their analysis on the manifest vehicles of meaning. The mathematical theory of communication (Shannon & Weaver, 1949), for one, suggests that meaning resides in the signal of communication. This theory attempts to dissolve the question by reducing meaning to information or stimuli. While recognizing the semantic and pragmatic aspects of communication, the vocabulary of the book defines also the recipients in technical terms when arguing that a general theory of communication "will surely have to take into account not only the capacity of the channel but also (even the words are right!) the capacity of the audience" (p. 27). Whether or not these are the right words is precisely the issue. By assigning meaning and information to distinct categories of reality and by assuming the hegemony of technical reality, the mathematical model begs the question and ultimately fails to consider the *reference* of communication to some social reality and its *reception* by interpretive agents.

A similar delimitation of meaning has been made within semiology, and it has provided the framework for much research on the reception of media discourses. From a semiological perspective, meaning may be said to reside in structures of discourse.

Discourses of Semiology

By distinguishing between the code of communication and the channel, or contact, Jakobson's (1960/1981) model makes the important point that meaning production is dependent upon culturally specific forms of encoding and decoding. A transmission via cable radio of, say, a symbolist poem by Baudelaire activates numerous codes of linguistic and cultural form even though the vehicle may be a digital signal. However, while Jakobson refers to the addresser and addressee who communicate through a message with reference to a context, he proposes to stay within the bounds of the language code, examining linguistic structures that may underscore a particular element of the model and hence a particular function of communication, for example, an expression of emotion, a command, or a poetic use of language. Indeed, the elements of Jakobson's model have no status outside of language; reality and recipients are conceived of as linguistic traces. Jakobson wants to refrain from addressing "the question of relations between the word and the world" (p. 19).

While Saussure (1916/1959), like Jakobson, originally emphasized an imma- nent analysis of linguistic structures, some later semiological research, especially from a critical perspective, has developed the argument that the use of particular structures of media discourse may be a sufficient condition for an ideological impact, hence implying that the primary locus of ideology is in media discourses, rather than in their contextual uses by audiences (Jensen, 1988b). It may have been tempting to conclude further that ideological impact is due to a false or, at least, historically and situationally inadequate representation of reality in discourse that gives rise to false consciousness. In fact, the elementary sign, as defined by Saussure (1916/1959), consisting of signifier (sound-image) and signified (con- cept), recalls the subject-object, mind-matter dualism of the Cartesian legacy.[2] The importance attached to the structure of media discourse, moreover, grows out of the long hermeneutic tradition in the West of studying religious and other canonical works. Thus, whereas a great deal of credit is due to semiological work within anthropology, literary criticism, and cultural studies (Culler, 1975; Eagleton, 1983; Fiske & Hartley, 1978) for initiating and legitimating a systematic study of popular culture, the theoretical framework has focused attention on media discourses as meaning *products*, and has not been able to accommodate the analysis of meaning production as *process* or social practice. By reformulating the question of meaning in temporal and relational terms, semiotics offers a contrast and an alternative to semiology.

WHEN IS MEANING?

Applying a pragmatist mode of analysis to the arts, Goodman (1978) has argued that "What is art?" is the wrong kind of question, and should be restated as "When is art?" (p. 57). No object is permanently or inherently a work of art: In a specific context an object may be assigned the function of whatever the word *art* implies. Meaning, by analogy, is not an essential feature of discourse, but is a quality assigned to discourse by interpretive agents. This line of argument may be substantiated with reference to Peirce's conceptualization of signs, interpretants, and interpretive communities.

Signs

In contrast to the Saussurean dualism of signifier and signified, Peirce (1931-1958) proposes a basic configuration of three elements — sign, object, and interpretant:

> A sign, or *representamen*, is something which stands to somebody for something in some respect or capacity. It addresses somebody, that is, creates in the mind of that person an equivalent sign, or perhaps a more developed sign. That sign which it creates I call the *interpretant* of the first sign. The sign stands for something, its *object.* (vol. 2, p. 228)

While my argument focuses on the interpretation of discursive meaning, to Peirce all cognition and indeed all perception is thus mediated by signs: Through the senses, we do not have access to any brute reality of facts. Peirce's objects include physical things, ideas, and acts, as well as discourses, and may be thought of as grammatical objects. Interpretants, in their turn, are signs by which people may orient themselves toward and interact with a reality of diverse objects, events, and discourses. Significantly, the interpretant is neither identical with the interpretive agent nor an essence representing the content of that person's thoughts. Positing that "every thought must be interpreted in another, or that all thought is in signs," Peirce (1958, p. 34) suggests that interpretation is a continuous process, rather than one act that, once and for all, internalizes external phenomena through a medium of signs.

This is not to imply that the interpretive agent is forever separated from social or material reality. Nothing, in fact, could be further from Peirce's argument than the nominalist position that we can know "only" signs; Peirce consistently defines himself as a realist.[3] To Peirce, then, signs are not *what* we know, but *how* we come to know what we can justify saying we know. Signs constitute a primary human mode of interacting with reality.

Specifically regarding the interpretation of discursive meaning, this suggests shifting the analytical emphasis from the structures of discourse to the processes of interpretation and their bases in social contexts. While the sign remains the central explanatory concept, meaning comes to be defined in *relational* rather than essential terms: The meaning of signs is determined not by their inherent characteristics, but by their position within the system of meaning production as a whole. Saussure (1916/1959), to be sure, advanced a similar argument, namely that, within the language system, "units are not positive entities but the nodes of a series of differences" (Culler, 1975, p. 11). However, by emphasizing the relations of difference *within* the language system and leaving aside the uses of language in social practices, the semiological paradigm has become preoccupied with the potential, immanent meaning of discursive relations. In contrast, semiotics offers a framework for studying meaning production with reference to those concrete discursive relations that are actualized by socially situated interpretive agents. How the interpretive strategies of specific audience-publics address and assimilate particular media and genres would seem to be a central question for any "science that studies the life of signs within society" (Saussure, 1916/1959, p. 16).

Interpretants

The continuous and practice-oriented aspects of interpretation may be specified through reference to Peirce's notion of the interpretant. Whereas interpretants can be characterized as signs constituting the steps of a continuous interpretive process, Peirce (1958) distinguishes three levels or kinds of interpretants. First, his Immediate Interpretant is "the total unanalyzed effect that the Sign is calculated to produce, or naturally might be expected to produce" (p. 413). In the context of mass communication, this level may be said to refer to the potential meaning of media content. The fact that media discourses have proven to be relatively open structures that can accommodate a variety of messages may be explained, in part, by the status of media discourses as complex relations of difference. While it may be possible to determine the potential or *structural* meaning of these relations of difference for purposes of a textual or historical analysis, it is important to keep in mind that such meaning is the construct of an interpretive act with particular theoretical assumptions. Meaning always involves an interpretive stance, whether of a researcher or another interpretive agent.

Peirce's second level of interpretation is the Dynamical Interpretant, which "consists in direct effect actually produced by a Sign upon an Interpreter of it" (p. 413). Again, this may be said to refer to the actualized meaning that audiences arrive at as they interact with mass media in the immediate context of media use, thus establishing specific relations of difference between structures of media content and available strategies of interpretation. Thus interpretive agents literally make a difference in the process of meaning production, and the process of interpretation results in the production of *situated* meaning. Interpretation is not oriented primarily toward media discourses, but toward the setting in which media discourses attain relevance. It should perhaps be added that the "effect" referred to by Peirce is not primarily behavioral. While some later research has appropriated Peircean concepts in a behaviorist version of semiotics (Morris, 1971), it is in keeping with Peirce's own mode of analysis to think of meaning effects as dispositions, or discursive differences, that may be actualized as action or consciousness.

Third, what Peirce calls the Final Interpretant is "the effect the Sign *would* produce upon any mind upon which circumstances should permit it to work out its full effects" (p. 413). Whereas Peirce appears to subscribe to a notion of Truth — the Sign to end all signs — one interesting implication of this third level of interpretation is that the interpretive process unfolds over time, so that, for instance, media discourses may be reactivated outside the immediate context of media use. As a result, interpretations of media content, to some degree, orient the consciousness and action of audience-publics. For want of a better term, we may label this interpretive dimension of everyday experience as *performative* meaning; it is the result of specific relations of difference being worked out between media discourses and the diverse discourses through which people position themselves in contexts of social life. Because performative meaning represents a discursive difference that, if enacted, may have a concrete effect on individual as well as social action, it is of special interest for assessing the political implications of reception.

The idea that interpretation may constitute an enactment of specific discursive differences in social practice has been developed by other research: Meaning is a difference that makes a difference (Bateson, 1972, p. 242; Goodman, 1976, p. 227). It was W. I. Thomas who stated the principle that the social construction of reality has practical consequences: "If men define situations as real, they are real in their consequences" (quoted in Rochberg-Halton, 1986, p. 44). Accordingly, information about and perspectives on political and everyday reality that are assimilated from mass media help to shape and are in turn shaped by current social practices. The concrete difference made by mass media reception in social life depends, further, on the discursive and institutional structures within which interpretation is situated. Interpretation, in many respects, is the accomplishment not of individuals, but of collectives or communities.

Communities

Rejecting the Cartesian, individual subject as a foundation of knowledge, Peirce instead introduces communities of knowers as the only possible public sanction of knowledge. While he does not credit individuals with any power of introspection or immediate self-awareness, Peirce (1958) suggests that the sense of self might be the indirect and cumulative result of numerous other cognitions whose consistency suggests a subjective center, what is referred to as a "man-sign" (p. 71). However, any discursive position remains open to challenge and revision as part of an ongoing interpretive social process. Consequently, Peirce argues, true knowledge must be arrived at by some public procedure:

> Unless truth be recognized as *public* — as that of which *any* person would come to be convinced if he carried his inquiry, his sincere search for immovable belief, far enough — then there will be nothing to prevent each one of us from adopting an utterly futile belief of his own which all the rest will disbelieve. (p. 398)

In the areas of logic and science, at least, the communities of inquiry must subject themselves to certain public procedures of interpretation that determine what will count as true knowledge. Being public, moreover, the interpretive procedures are subject to constant reformulation. Hence scientific communities perform the socially central function of developing interpretive principles for examining particular aspects of reality, sometimes with major social implications (Kuhn, 1970; Lowe, 1982). Even if scientific communities have no essential attributes in the form of special insight, authority, or power, they nevertheless may make a difference also beyond scientific practice by asserting and legitimating particular procedures and practices of knowing, or performative meanings.

Two points may serve to specify the explanatory value of the concept of interpretive communities in relation to mass media reception. First, the *macrosocial* functions of mass media are comparable, in some respects, to those of science as characterized by Peirce. Both institutions serve to place reality on a public agenda, and they operate through practices that presuppose some degree of consensus regarding interpretive procedures. Furthermore, whereas the specific organizational hierarchies admittedly differ, as do access to and participation in the interpretive communities of science and mass communication, respectively, both communities are increasingly important agents for maintaining the political, cultural, and material structures of society. In Peirce's terminology, science is a context for negotiating the Final Interpretant of knowledge. Mass communication, similarly, may provide a forum for negotiating particularly those performative meanings that are contested, because meanings might be enacted through some form of concerted, socially sanctioned action.

Second, the Peircean framework suggests the constitutive role of discursive, or *microsocial*, acts of interpretation in communicative practices at the macrosocial level of organization. In other words, the reproduction of many forms of social life depends not just on the availability of specific institutions of communication, but also on the existence of interpretive communities that crisscross other social formations as they serve to orient the process of meaning production toward particular contexts and purposes. Interpretive communities thus may be a strategic juncture between micro- and macrosocial levels of analysis.

What distinguish interpretive communities of mass media reception from Peirce's scientific communities are, perhaps, diversity and complexity. While communities in the scientific world are relatively delimited, both professionally and institutionally, Peirce also implies that their interpretive procedures, ideally, would be homogeneous and, if not simple, at least explicit and conscious, progressing toward clarity and consensus. In contrast, there are multiple approaches to interpreting and using mass communication that, further, grow out of and bear witness to a complex and conflictual social reality. Mass media reception, being codetermined by and integrated with other social practices, thus may be analyzed as a socially situated, semiotic practice.

RECEPTION AS SOCIAL PRACTICE

Despite some previous research stressing the interrelatedness of media with other social practices (Ball-Rokeach, 1985), few studies, from either critical or mainstream perspectives, have given much attention to the contexts and purposes of media use, compared to the texts and production strategies of media as such (Anderson & Meyer, 1988). Yet, for most people most of the time, mass communication could hardly be the factor overdetermining their orientations and actions. Instead, a complex set of social practices with political, economic, and cultural purposes generally circumscribes the reception of mass communication. Whereas some earlier studies have suggested ways of combining a discursive with a social perspective of communication (Hodge & Kress, 1988; Rochberg-Halton, 1986; Volosinov, 1973), social semiotics is still in the making.

Interpretive Communities

The concept of interpretive communities may help to reestablish the links between reception analysis and the analysis of mass media as social *institutions.* If the generalized social function of mass media is the production and circulation of meaning in society, then, evidently, a variety of social factors set the general conditions of reception. As noted by Schudson (1987), the recent interest in reception implies a certain sentimentality in academia concerning the empowered role of individuals in mass communication processes that may deflect attention from structural issues regarding the distribution of cultural resources in society. It would seem to be an overstatement, for example, that mass media recipients performing oppositional decodings engage in "semiotic 'guerilla warfare' " (Eco, 1976, p. 150). Interpretive communities, instead, can be seen as forms of cultural agency to which individuals are socialized and that generate discursive strategies for making sense of the institutions with which individuals interact on a regular basis.

Whereas the concept of interpretive communities originates in recent literary theory, particularly the work of Fish (1979), most research in the literary tradition has not addressed the concrete social uses of literature and rarely has examined readers in any empirical sense (Holub, 1984; Suleiman & Crosman, 1980; Tompkins, 1980). Recently, however, the term has been used in communication research (Jensen, 1987; Lindlof, 1988) as a means of linking hermeneutic and social scientific modes of analyzing meaning production. Media audience groups may be defined not just by their formal social roles, but, more important, by the strategies of understanding by which they engage mass media content and other cultural forms. Three general features seem to characterize such interpretive communities: They are multiple, overlapping, and potentially contradictory.

First, different audience groups may apply *multiple* interpretive strategies to the same media discourse and still make sense of it. An obvious example would be the studies of the reception of *Dallas* in different cultures (Katz & Liebes, 1984), which imply that the series can be assimilated by various modes of interpretation to make a statement on family or social issues in many cultural settings. More important, perhaps, the same recipient may draw on multiple interpretive strategies, depending on the purpose or context of reception. A radio listener may act as member of a subculture (Hebdige, 1979) when listening to certain programs (for example, music) while, perhaps, merging with a more general audience for other programs (for example, news). Second, then, interpretive communities should also be seen as *overlapping* each other in that a group of recipients may share some but not all interpretive strategies with other groups. Even within what might be taken as one subculture, for example, the punk culture of San Francisco, Lull (1987) suggests that there are subtle but significant distinctions between the outlooks of self-defined skinheads and those of punks.

Third, and perhaps most important, interpretive strategies that are employed by the same individual or group may be mutually inconsistent, or *contradictory*, because they derive from different contexts or represent the orientations of different social formations that may be in conflict. While this last point is elaborated below, it begins to identify the conflictual aspect of much interpretation that works out specific perspectives on social reality.

Without aiming for a typology at this stage, the sections below examine some of the social forces structuring interpretive strategies. Three types of factors may be thought of as conditions of existence for interpretive communities: discourses and genres, practices, and social institutions.

Discourses and Genres

It is important, first of all, to recognize the discursive organization of everyday experience. For one thing, it appears evident that the mastering not just of a language code, but of particular forms of communicative interaction and interpretation, is a prerequisite of social competence. For another thing, it is normally agreed that twentieth-century mass media, especially television (National Institute of Mental Health, 1982), have contributed to a new kind of totalized media environment that envelops media recipients in an unprecedented fashion, dissolving previously separate categories and levels of reality (Meyrowitz, 1985). Ratings and readership figures, at any rate, suggest that the mass media provide an intense and continuous training in skills for decoding communication. Similarly, the narrative conventions of music videos (Kinder, 1984) imply a perceptual readiness on the part of a young generation of viewers that may be the cumulative result of being socialized to particular visual discourses.

Genres, more specifically, invite recipients to take particular stances with implied social roles (Williams, 1977), thus contributing to the building of specific interpretive communities. The classic examples in communication history are the novel (Watt, 1957) and the mass press (Habermas, 1962; Schudson, 1978), which bear witness to the rise of new cultural and political publics. What needs to be emphasized, perhaps, is the efficacy of socioeconomic forces in the process of change. As Hall (1980a) notes, there is a tendency in some discourse theory to assume that discursive structures stake out a narrow range of positions and practices for recipients, leaving little scope for the activity of historical, social subjects, and providing little explanation of how social practices change. Presumably, in a contemporary perspective as well, it is reformers and revolutionaries who create pamphlets, not vice versa.

One example of interpretive communities constituting themselves around specific genres might be fan groups for music and even for individual texts, such as the cult following of movies like *The Rocky Horror Picture Show*. At one level, these groups are comparable to religious congregations centered in holy scriptures. In both cases, of course, the texts may be seen as means of orienting the religious or cultural practices of the group.

Finally, and more generally, much education might be thought of as the social creation of certain canonical strategies of interpretation that, further, are often centered in a particular body of texts. This is not to deny the general relevance of critical interpretive skills, but to raise the question of which social purposes are served by a specific interpretive canon. The social purposes of interpretive strategies may be assessed with reference to practices.

Practices

The concept of practice serves to emphasize the processual aspect of much social interaction. As Hall (1980b) suggests, a great deal of work in cultural studies integrates *structuralist* assumptions, seeing society as a structured totality of interrelated sectors, with *culturalist* assumptions, pointing to the indeterminacies of the social structure and underlining the role of human consciousness and cultural forms generally in the reproduction of social life. Whereas the social roles of individuals are, to a great extent, predefined by structural factors, these roles nevertheless may be negotiated and reconstructed as part of the ongoing activities of either work or leisure. Building on Peirce (1958, p. 71), one could say that social practices create a wo/mansign, or a sense of identity. Practices may be defined as socially meaningful activities. One example of how meaning production applies to material, economic activities is advertising, which, while serving fundamental purposes of exchange and distribution, simultaneously invites recipients to take particular discursive positions in relation to a particular economic system. Advertising may be "capitalism's way of saying 'I love you' to itself" (Schudson, 1984, p. 232).

Mass media, then, provide occasions for negotiating the practice-related roles in which people find themselves, and practices, in turn, constitute a framework that may orient not just specific interpretations, but also routines of media use. This comes out, for example, in media habits that are differentiated by gender. Morley's (1986) study of television viewing in British families of a specific socioeconomic group suggests that, at least in this microcosm, the male head of the household has special privileges for choosing which programs the family will watch together because he spends most of the day at work outside the home, which is defined for him as a locus of leisure. In cases where the male is unemployed and the female employed, however, the pattern may be reversed. For female heads of households, the home may not be so clearly defined as a sphere of leisure because they are more likely also to take care of household work there, frequently in addition to employment outside the home. Television viewing in the home context thus may be defined for women as a "guilty pleasure." Radway (1984) found a similar pattern in relation to women's romance reading, which may be a means of claiming time for oneself, and might be construed as a "declaration of independence." In general, then, media may become *resources* for coping with particular realities of everyday practices.

In other respects, the family is an important site of practices that have a bearing on media use. Lull (1980) suggests that television schedules are used, for example, to establish firm bedtimes, and the portrayal of daily family life, for instance in fictional television series, may be used as a source of arguments in disputes about family matters. Moreover, this points to a specific socializing impact of television as it portrays families to family audiences across a variety of genres. By offering, for private consumption, public images of private lives, television may redraw the boundaries between private and public spheres (Meyrowitz, 1985). The family is one of the social institutions serving as a point of reference for the interpretation and use of mass communication.

Institutions

The perceived relevance of mass communication may be explained, in part, by the reference of media content to major social institutions that are subject to negotiation in contemporary society. Mass communication highlights aspects of political, cultural, and economic institutions with which the members of the audience-public interact on a regular basis, thus providing a context for the interpretation of everyday reality. The institutions can be said, generally, to lend orientation to the activity of interpretation; they are thus another condition of existence for interpretive communities.

Though mass communication addresses a wide variety of social institutions, certain genres tend to thematize particular institutions. For example, programs using the format of a law court serve to thematize the judicial system. Similarly, television soap operas and situation comedies construct different perspectives on family life and the private sphere in general. And certain talk shows on American television can be said to trace the border between private and public areas by offering public perspectives on private issues, or vice versa.

Perhaps the most obvious nexus is that between the news genre and the institutions of political democracy. The news genre constitutes a resource for political participation and action, at least in principle. In order to explore the interrelations among institutions, discursive forms, and political agents, I propose to examine briefly the reception of news and the role of interpretive communities in political processes. Drawing on qualitative empirical research about American television news (Jensen, in press), I discuss the explanatory value of the present theoretical discourse for the audience discourses of a concrete study. Specifically, I suggest that one may detect several contradictory constructions of political institutions that emerge as ambiguity, or polysemy, in audience discourses. Whereas some previous research has employed the concept of polysemy to explain the finding that audiences can derive different meanings from the same *media* discourses, polysemy may also be a feature of *audience* discourses that serves to question the legitimacy of a particular political order.

POLYSEMY: THE CASE OF NEWS

Polysemy of Media Discourses

The most detailed account of polysemy has been offered by Fiske (1986, 1987), who argues that polysemy is the source not only of the popularity and pleasure of watching television, but of a progressive political potential in television as well. While emphasizing the active role of television audiences, Fiske focuses attention on the discursive structures of media that may explain the variability of actual interpretations. Television discourses, he suggests, must be polysemic in order to be popular with a heterogeneous mass audience, and he supports his point with some insightful readings of television programs. In addition, whereas the pleasure of reception may function either as a "motor of hegemony" or as an essential component of "the ability to shake oneself free from its constraints" (Fiske, 1987, p. 234), "its typical one is the playful pleasure that derives from, and enacts, that source of all power for the subordinate, the power to be different" (p. 236). Thus his conclusion is that television discourses are not only potentially, but tendentiously, progressive in political terms because they provide audiences with the means to resist the dominant social order.

The argument is not persuasive, however, primarily because resistance is not related specifically to those other social practices and institutions through which the dominant order is enforced. Instead, resistance is referred to in the abstract or defined in discursive terms. Resistance, in order to be a manifestation of power in any socially relevant sense, must be seen to make a difference beyond that immediate context of media use and those individual decodings that are most often invoked by Fiske. Even if a thousand oppositional decodings of media discourses are performed in a thousand homes employing a common interpretive strategy, that does not add up to resistance.

Fiske (1987) is careful to qualify his argument at various points lest he be thought to overestimate what might be called a "pseudo-power" (p. 318). Still, while it is certainly true that "social or collective resistance cannot exist independently of 'interior' resistance, even if that is given the devalued name of 'fantasy' " (p. 318), this makes fantasy a necessary, but not sufficient, condition of social change. When Fiske deduces the further point that "paradoxically, diversity of readings may best be stimulated by a greater homogeneity of programming" (p. 319), he implies a defense of whatever programming proves economically most profitable, thus entrusting cultural policy to market forces. Whereas there may be no populist intention behind the argument, the analysis tends to lose sight of the forest of political implications amid all the polysemic trees. There is, in fact, no evidence from actual comparative studies of more or less "homogeneous" types of programming to support Fiske's conclusion, because most recent studies have not been comparative and have most often focused on programs that have been popular in market terms.

Finally, it is somewhat surprising to find, a few pages later, the suggestion that a very different argument applies to reception in the context of developing nations:

> A lot more work needs to be done on the international reception of both news and entertainment programs and ways that the developed nations can help the less developed to produce their own cultural commodities that can genuinely challenge Hollywood's in the arena of popular taste rather than of political or economic policy. (p. 323)

While more international research certainly is needed, and while the tribute to cultural specificity elsewhere is a nice gesture, it is not clear why the argument from polysemy would not apply here, or why the subcultures of the so-called developed nations do not need "their own cultural commodities" but are well served by those of Hollywood. Ultimately, though popular cultural forms may offer resources for resistance, in part because of their polysemic structure, the implications of polysemy need to be assessed by social standards. Resistance is always resistance to something, for a purpose, and in a context.

Polysemy of Audience Discourses

The context of the empirical study of television news reception was the United States; the aim was to examine how viewers conceive of the relevance of the information. Television has emerged, over the last three decades, as a major source of political information for Americans. Even if television may not be the main source of news in terms of information recalled (Robinson & Levy, 1986), it is perceived in opinion polls as the most credible and comprehensive source (Roper, Inc., 1985), and television, moreover, may have become a cultural common denominator, or forum (Newcomb & Hirsch, 1984), where major social issues are negotiated. Accordingly, television newscasts were used as points of departure for in-depth interviews about the political use value of the news genre. On the one hand, news may be seen as an *account* that covers political events and issues so that the audience may keep up as citizens and voters. News thus functions as an agent of representative democracy, legitimating and documenting that this political system really works. On the other hand, news may be seen as a *resource* in a more participatory form of democracy. Ideally, political communication might become the starting point of political intervention. In this model, news and political democracy are constitutive elements of the same social practice, and it is a familiar notion from the political revolutions of the Western world that today survives in the rhetoric of political discourse. If polysemy is located in such audience conceptions of political institutions, rather than in media discursive structures, this may call into question the legitimacy of the encompassing political system.

It generally has been assumed by critical (Holzer, 1973) as well as mainstream (Blumler, 1979) researchers that media content may have at least three different types of relevance. First, media may be a means of surveillance and a source of specific information about the social context, suggesting, if not action, at least a readiness for action. News, of course, may be the basis of opinion formation as well as political activity in some form. Second, media content may provide a sense of identity or self-legitimation, of belonging to a community, a subculture, or, perhaps, a political order. Third, media are a source of entertainment or diversion, offering relief for anxiety and escape from boredom. While referring to particular stories as well as stylistic features of various news formats, the interviews thus focused on issues relating to these three experiential dimensions, including the instrumental uses of news in an everyday context or in political life, the credibility of the information, and the aesthetic qualities particularly of the visual discourse.

Without entering into details of the methodology (Jensen, in press), it may be noted that a total of 12 news programs, representing network news as well as the programs of a local commercial station and a local public television station, and 24 interviews were recorded in an urban area of the northeastern United States. After a particular program was recorded on the night it aired, it was shown the following day, individually, to two respondents, who were subsequently interviewed individually. The days were selected randomly; the respondents were men drawn from the directory of a local university, representing a range of educational and occupational backgrounds.

A linguistic discourse analysis of the verbatim transcripts served to identify particular structures in these audience discourses. Specifically, the linguistic structures point to the simultaneous presence of several different, perhaps contradictory, assumptions concerning the use value of news, which may be interpreted, with reference to the theoretical discourse of semiotics, as polysemy deriving from contradictions in the practices and institutions of politics. While it is interesting to note the relative homogeneity of audience discourses across the spectrum of respondents, implying that the contradictions are systemic, the main issue here is the three dimensions of the news experience.

The respondents attributed the relevance of news, first of all, to its factual information regarding political issues and events. Among their arguments for watching television news was a need to check information, both over time and with reference to several media. However, when discussing how to resolve actual conflicts between sources, the respondents implied that this was hardly a relevant concern in practice. Asked whether he would actually seek more evidence in case of conflicting information, one respondent said:

> I would probably seek more evidence. You've got, it's kind of an interesting idea that, that two news, news sources, two, two medias who are in conflict in their reporting. It would be kind of interesting to see how, you know, how it works out, how it comes out.

The implication of his main point — that it is an interesting question — is that this is also an unfamiliar issue. In practice, it seems, this respondent is not likely to seek further evidence. A conflict is something that "works out" or "comes out," rather than something that is actively resolved.

One explanation may be that news is not, after all, perceived as an instrument or resource in any concrete sense. Talking about the possible uses of news in politics, respondents expressed frustration as well as embarrassment. With reference to editorials in newscasts, for which contributions from the public are often solicited, a respondent suggested that it would be relevant for him to contribute, and yet, "it could be done, but I don't do it [laughs]." Another respondent mentioned that as a young person he wanted to get into politics, "I guess deep in the back of my mind I still want it too, [but now] I guess the opportunity will have to arise. . . . I feel I'm just the average person out here." In sum, there may no precedent and no institution for such participatory uses of the information, even if this is the implicit promise of the news genre.

Legitimation, instead, emerges as a major use value of television news: News viewing provides a sense of belonging to a specific social and political order. Whereas the respondents appear to enact a legitimation of their own role in the political order, they may also, in doing so, attribute legitimacy to that order as it currently exists. In particular, two concepts — *control* and *distance* — lend structure to this aspect of the news experience. Even though viewers may have no control over political events, the news, particularly concerning local political matters, can give them a *sense* of control over events that would otherwise appear distant:

> Sometimes on the local level it's, if you can't do anything about it, at least it's more, it's closer to you, you know, and, you know, you feel like you can do something more about it maybe when it comes to voting or to some other activity.

The concept of legitimacy does not imply that the respondents necessarily endorse the legitimacy of specific political positions. As shown by previous work on news decoding, there is relatively great scope for selective and oppositional interpretations of particular news *accounts* (Jensen, 1988a; Morley, 1980). Moreover, the respondents presented a variety of criticisms of news media, including reference to the "glittering generalities" of local television news. The point is that while television news is a convenient mechanism, in the context of everyday life, for keeping up with political information, it does not acquire the status of a *resource* in political practice.

The third use value — diversion or entertainment — presents itself as a specific, integrated aspect of news reception. In particular, the performance of the anchorpeople and the extensive use of video coverage contribute to a dimension of "sparkle" in the news discourse. Whereas, for example, gratifications research tends to assume that entertainment might be as prominent an aspect of the news experience as any other (McQuail, Blumler, & Brown, 1972), these respondents suggest rather that it is an integrated dimension that, while important, is subordinated to other use values. Television news is, indeed, recognized as a political genre. Thus, while a number of narrative conventions and interpretive strategies associated with genres of entertainment may enter into news viewing, they can be said to constitute a subdiscourse of news reception. One respondent suggested the complexity of what may be expected from television news when he described his ideal news program: "It would be more in the direction of something like Mac-Neil/Lehrer but with more pizzazz to it, with more visuals."

In conclusion, while television news provides a daily forum for the viewers' reassertion of their political competence, it is not conceived of as a resource to be applied in the organizations and institutions of political life, even though the respondents argued that this is, in principle, possible and relevant. The contradictory aspects of news reception may bear witness to a divided form of everyday consciousness that derives from contradictions at the macrosocial level of social institutions, where the social uses of news are not institutionalized and do not have any precedent in political practice. It may, then, be a contradictory *social* definition of news that manifests itself at the level of audience discourses as polysemy. News audiences remain interpretive communities, rather than becoming communities of political practice.

Like the news genre, a variety of fictional genres also address issues of power relating to social institutions. In the perspective of pragmatism, mass media may be seen generally as institutions-to-think-with about other institutions.

POLITICS OF PRAGMATISM

Institutions-to-Think-With

While anthropologists sometimes speak of objects-to-think-with (Schudson, 1987, p. 56), mass media can be thought of as industrialized institutions-to-think-with. Even if the media environment of the late twentieth century may be, in certain respects, blurring the boundary between everyday reality and mass-mediated reality, media institutions still serve to bracket reality and place it on a public agenda. Traditionally, this function has been associated with the press and other news media that have been labeled the Fourth Estate (Cater, 1959; Siebert, Peterson, & Schramm, 1956). The assumption, again, is that the press may serve as a vehicle of political information and debate, keeping voters informed and ready to act, while holding politicians accountable.

Recently, this aspect of mass communication has been reconceptualized as a *cultural forum* (Newcomb & Hirsch, 1984) that extends its area of application beyond narrowly political processes. The argument is that mass media that are consumed by practically the entire public in a culture (e.g., American television) make up a special social site or forum. In particular, Newcomb and Hirsch (1984) imply that the cultural forum may be rather indeterminate in its effects and quite liberal in the range of perspectives it may accommodate, since "the raising of questions is as important as the answering of them" (p. 63). Drawing on the anthropological framework of Victor Turner, the authors suggest that television programming constructs a *liminal* or in-between realm whose functions in American culture may be comparable to those of ritual. Whereas much television fare might be seen as escapist, it also allows for a culture to trace its beliefs and test its boundaries as well as for individuals to explore alternative identities and realities. Thus the social role of television may not be one of presenting ready-made ideological conclusions; rather, it *"comments on* ideological problems" (p. 64). Initiating a negotiation of social reality, then, television may invite audience participation by leaving a significant scope for interpretation and reconstruction.

The cultural forum model is sometimes combined with the concept of polysemy to suggest similar political implications: Audiences are powerful, and television programs are valuable resources for the reconstruction of social reality. Recognizing that they may seem to overstate the critical potential of television, Newcomb and Hirsch (1984) do note that the cultural forum "is an effective pluralistic forum only insofar as American political pluralism is or can be" (p. 64). In other words, American political pluralism may not be pluralistic in any meaningful sense of that term. Yet, the authors also ascribe to television a capacity "to monitor the limits and effectiveness of this pluralism" (p. 64), implying that television can indeed perform its role of political and cultural watchdog, on which much of the faith in pluralism rests. Among the references to attempts at criticism and reform that have been initiated by television is mentioned the emergence of diverse special interest groups (presumably ranging from, for example, Action for Children's Television to the Moral Majority) that may support their case regarding particular social issues with reference to their (mis)representation on television. By identifying " 'fault lines' in American society" (p. 69), television could be said to empower its audience-publics.

The main limitation of the analysis is that it represents a perspective from only one type of social institution, namely, mass media. What is not considered are the relations of feedback between the mass media and other institutions, in the present case TV news media and political institutions. Unlike geological faults, social fault lines, once identified, might be acted upon. Which sectors of society, first of all, are likely never to be subject to any television representation and hence to any form of negotiation? What impact, if any, could the cultural forum be said to have had on a particular institution in a specific respect? Which factors will explain why certain social groups have little or no access to the cultural forum? And which factors will explain the existence of knowledge gaps among participants in the cultural forum? In essence, while the cultural forum model takes an important step beyond some previous simplified conceptions of effects, it stops short of a model that might account for the specific social and cultural differences made by mass media, and by their recipients, including the difference that consists of maintaining the status quo. Some elements of such a model may be found in the tradition of pragmatism following Peirce.

Elements of Pragmatism

While I could not hope to cover in any detail here the development of pragmatism (Ogden & Richards, 1923/1946; Rorty, 1966; White, 1973), it is interesting to note the social implications of Peirce's thinking as developed by some later work in a pragmatic mode (Bernstein, 1986). The epochal shift from a philosophy of the human subject to a philosophy of language that was, in certain respects, signaled by Peirce may be taken as one condition for the development of a new conception of truth that is linked to communication and practice. First, then, Peirce's characterization of knowledge as processual and mediated by signs begins to reevaluate the acts of communication and interpretation that construct knowledge. Second, despite his ambiguity concerning the historicity of knowledge, Peirce implies, through reference to interpretive communities, that the validation of knowledge must be accomplished in public. Knowledge and truth thus might be seen as historical constructions, representing a consensus that is socially validated and has practical consequences. Accordingly, knowledge that derives from media use is the outcome of historically situated interpretive strategies that interact with contemporary social practices. The third implication of pragmatism, which may be emphasized especially by current work, is that the institutions of knowledge and communication are crucial in any process of social change. Pragmatism may also inform a critical theory of communication and society.

While Peirce appears to insist on the purity of science, arguing against a notion of applied research (Skagestad, 1981, p. 199), other early proponents of pragmatism, particularly John Dewey, have pointed to the practical, social implications of knowledge. In contrast to earlier forms of philosophy, Dewey suggests, pragmatism implies a specific orientation toward the future, toward difference and action:

> Whereas, for empiricism, in a world already constructed and determined, reason or general thought has no other meaning than that of summing up particular cases, in a world where the future is not a mere word, where theories, general notions, rational ideas have consequences for action, reason necessarily has a constructive function. (Rorty, 1966, p. 210)

In other words, principles of social and political action are related to and, perhaps, deducible from a particular form of rationality. Dewey himself, however, remained vague in his analyses, for example, of how to increase public participation in political life (Dewey, 1927). In his attempts to deconstruct the contemporary philosophical tradition, Dewey tended to stay within the form of abstract conceptual analysis that characterized that tradition (Rorty, 1982, p. 35).

"Pragmatism survived as a philosophical position from the time of John Dewey to the late 1970s, but it did not flourish" (Prado, 1987, p. 1). In European thought, it might be added, even though ideas concerning the social construction of subjectivity, which are similar especially to those of Mead (1934), run through much Continental sociology, psychology, and semiotics, the relevance of pragmatism rarely has been explored. Recently, however, the discourse of pragmatism has reasserted itself on both sides of the Atlantic in a form that often seeks to combine a philosophy of language with a critical theory of society (Bernstein, 1986; Goodman, 1976; Goodman & Elgin, 1988; Habermas, 1981, 1984; Rorty, 1979, 1982, 1989). Working out a theory of communication that addresses the historical origins and social uses of meaning may, indeed, be a common agenda for writers such as Hans-Georg Gadamer, Jürgen Habermas, and Richard Rorty (Bernstein, 1986, p. 58).

Perhaps the most sustained attempt to develop a social theory of communication that integrates institutional and discursive levels of analysis is the work of Jürgen Habermas. A few of the main concepts of his theory of communicative action (Thompson, 1984) may suggest his articulation of pragmatism. Language, Habermas notes, is a distinctive feature of humans, and it is the use of language in various contexts that makes complex social structures possible. Linguistic intercourse, however, is not by nature a neutral means of coordinating social life: Language is also a source of power and control. It would be important, then, for a critical theory of society to determine the general conditions under which language may serve communicative ends of understanding, as opposed to strategic ends of domination.

In order to define what might be ideal conditions of communication generally, Habermas (1984) adopts the common strategy of twentieth-century philosophy of grounding himself in linguistic structures: A theory of communication must "start from the structure of linguistic expressions rather than from speakers' intentions" (p. 275). His analytical strategy is one of deducing the ideal conditions of communication at the macrosocial level from the micro level of dialogue where individuals interact. Reformulating the speech-act theory of Austin (1962), Habermas distinguishes between two aspects of the communicative acts individuals perform, namely, "illocutionary acts (the act performed *in* saying something) and perlocutionary acts (the act performed *by* saying something)" (Thompson, 1984, p. 295). Whereas perlocution has some ulterior purpose, illocution essentially works to achieve intersubjective understanding. From this distinction at the level of interpersonal discourse, Habermas generalizes to other social modes of communication, and he suggests that illocution may be constitutive of a privileged, natural form of communication. With reference to this standard, then, it might be possible to evaluate the practices and institutions of communication in a given historical setting, since, in general,

> the use of language with an orientation to reaching understanding is the *original mode* of language use, upon which indirect understanding, giving something to understand or letting something be understood, and the instrumental use of language in general, are parasitic. (Habermas, 1984, p. 288)

This dualism appears indicative of an essentialist ontology that dichotomizes the world into a secondary social structure and a primary level of reality constituting natural forms of existence and interaction. The dichotomy recurs at the macroso-cial level, where Habermas divides social reality into *system* (the dimension maintaining the material and institutional structures of society) and *lifeworld* (the dimension of collective and largely implicit premises of understanding that sustain everyday life). In Habermas's strategy, the primary level of the lifeworld is used to justify particular communicative procedures as the legitimate means of reaching a social consensus, even if communicative reason is defined in counterfactual terms, as an unrealized potential that might motivate changes in the prevailing social forms of communication. It is not clear, however, what purpose is served by hypostatizing dialogue as an ideal-type forum that exists outside of history. Changes in the *social* forms of communication, by definition, are enacted and legitimated in social and historical context. Indeed, the most controversial issues in a politics of communication have to do not with the abstract, inalienable rights of individuals to engage in social dialogue, but with the practices and institutions for *ending* dialogue, making decisions, and transforming decisions into action.

What Habermas develops, then, may be a last-ditch articulation of the question, Where is meaning? The implied answer is that meaning is inherent in certain natural conditions for the use of language: It is the original mode of language use that may make possible not only an incorrigible understanding of other individuals, but also the determination of certain fundamental principles of human community and social action. Even if neither the introspective subject nor the structure of language itself may be considered a reliable guide to the structure of social reality, it might be possible, according to Habermas, to deduce specific rules of interaction from human communication that would, then, constitute a forum where communi-cative reason might at last guide understanding and social action. How this production of meaning might be structured and legitimated in a particular social and historical context, however, remains an open question in Habermas' (1981, 1984) articulation of pragmatism. It is this question, finally, that a pragmatist theory of mass communication would have to address.

Toward a Pragmatist Theory of Mass Communication

The outline of such a theory may be specified with reference to three concepts: signs, purposes, and contexts. Meaning production may be defined in simple terms as the use of signs for a specific purpose in a particular context. Elsewhere, Habermas addresses several aspects of this definition. First, when examining the role of *signs* in social interaction, Habermas (1984) emphasizes the importance of a *"three-term model"* of sign use that goes back to Bühler and, from the very start, relates the analysis of linguistic meaning to the 'idea' of participants in communi-cation coming to an understanding about something in the world" (p. 397). This formulation, while crediting another philosopher, recalls Peirce's configuration of sign, object, and interpretant, and it further suggests the orientation of most communication toward social practice. Peirce's general theory of signs might be a productive framework for the concrete analysis of communication and conscious-ness as developed by, among others, Habermas.[4]

Second, Habermas further has identified the constitutive role of *purposes* in social practices. With reference to different forms of science — human, natural, and social — Habermas (1971) suggests that their organization and procedures are characterized by particular purposes or *knowledge interests*. Whereas for the humanities the purpose of inquiry is contemplative understanding, and for the natural sciences predictive control, the purpose of the social sciences is defined as a liberating critique that can suggest alternatives to the forms of social organization that may appear inevitable when encountered in everyday life. Similarly, the knowledge interests of mass media are inscribed in their genres and institutional forms. A particular media content gives rise to particular applications by the recipients within the historical context of specific social institutions.

Third, then, the reception of mass communication takes place with reference to a *context* of social institutions, which, further, are premised on particular worldviews. Habermas (1962), in an early work, traces the historical development of the worldview associated with industrial capitalism, which assigns political, economic, and cultural aspects of reality to separate and relatively autonomous spheres: private versus public, the state versus individual economic enterprise, politics versus culture, and so on. The mass media may contribute to reproducing this worldview, in part, because it is implicit in the total configuration of media genres and institutional forms. Mass communication, in the aggregate, may serve to segregate or compartmentalize social reality in a specific form, thus fragmenting audiences' understanding of interrelations within the social structure. Addressing a particular range of issues, mass media are institutions-to-think-with for particular purposes that may have ideological implications.

Whereas it will take further theoretical work to explore the implications for the study of mass communication processes, pragmatism may offer a relevant framework for the field of communication research. By reformulating the question of meaning and developing the concept of difference, pragmatism begins to reconcile social and discursive aspects of communication. In particular, a social semiotics may produce models for relating a social-institutional level of analysis with analyses of the interpretive strategies of individual communicants. After a decade where much empirical attention has been given to the microsocial level of reception and to the discursive aspect of meaning production, it may be time to refocus on their interrelations with the macrosocial level of institutions and classes. What is at stake in mass communication, after all, is control over an important means of inquiry into social reality.

For a politics of communication, pragmatism may help to theorize the interrelations of mass media with other institutions of socialization, particularly educational institutions. Whereas one general aim of education is to acquaint students with the prevailing genres and institutions of meaning production, much less attention is paid to the *conditions* of meaning production, the social contexts and purposes of particular forms of culture and communication. One example is a favored assumption in much educational discourse about the so-called information society, namely, that communication technologies may make information available on an unprecedented scale, further implying numerous uses of the information in a variety of political and cultural practices. There is, however, little or no precedent for such uses of communications media, in part because this has not been considered a major purpose of formal education, which still emphasizes literacy and other basic instrumental skills as well as the acquisition of knowledge as such — meaning products that represent the cultural tradition as articulated by, for example, Bloom (1987). If, instead, schools were to emphasize looking for information with a purpose and the uses of information in social and cultural processes, they might help to reactivate interpretive strategies and social uses of mass communication.

To sum up, meaning may be when social agents interact through the use of signs for a specific purpose in a particular context, even if the difference made by signs may not be explicit or conscious; reflection, as practiced in schools and outside, may occur when the purpose of interaction is to specify the meaningfulness of the first level of signs in relation to their context. In discourse terms, reflection consists of establishing specific relations of difference between an analytical discourse and media discourse in order to assess the difference that media discourses may make in other social practices. In social terms, one aim of education, as it applies to the area of communication and culture, must be to bring about the condition of reflexivity in students, empowering them outside the educational forum to assess the knowledge interests of current forms of meaning production. Reflexivity need not imply an ideal-type forum of the Habermasian kind, involving a detached form of understanding, but rather might entail a socially situated analysis in a context and for a purpose. Whether such analyses may come to orient social action and change will depend, eventually, on the audience-publics who may enter into social institutions to enact a different system of mass communication.

CONCLUSION

Though the audience has been said to exist either nowhere, except as a discursive trace (Allor, 1988), or everywhere, in all of social reality (Lull, 1988a), this essay has argued that both perspectives are, in effect, correct, applying to different levels of analysis. Mass media audiences are both social and discursive phenomena. Whereas communication researchers gain access to media and recipients methodologically through discourses, and while the theoretical framework of analysis may be conceptualized as a discursive construct, this does not deny the existence of a social reality in which power, pleasure, pain, and injustice are important ingredients, and that might be changed for the better. Signs, following Peirce, are a primary human mode of interacting with reality, but that does not imply the Cartesian vision turned upside down, leaving subjects caught in a web of signs. Meaning is, indeed, constituted through a continuous process involving discursive relations of difference; it is also, however, enacted in social practices. One important role of mass media is the production and circulation of meaning in society. Their audiences, representing a complex of interpretive communities, contribute to the negotiation of polysemy and the reconstruction of social reality as participants in what may be seen as a cultural forum. Being institutions-to-think-with for particular social purposes, mass media incorporate social contradictions that, in the long term, give rise to contradictory forms of reception. In sum, mass media recipients, while being relatively autonomous interpretive agents, enter into a specific historical configuration of practices and institutions that may be given a different form not by individual interpretations, but through social action.

Mass media reception, in many ways, is an integrated aspect of the everyday practices of communities and specific cultural groups, and should be studied in its social and discursive context. Qualitative methodologies, moreover, are especially relevant for conducting focused studies of strategic junctures in meaning produc-tion — for example, the audience perception of genres addressing major social institutions. While such focused studies may also be integrated with other forms of quantitative as well as qualitative evidence within a common theoretical frame-work, much research so far has been of a generally exploratory type. In method-ological terms, moreover, reception studies still need to develop systematic procedures of analysis (Jensen, 1989). Interview statements by audiences are discursive documents that must be organized and analyzed with reference to a metadiscourse as well as theoretical and epistemological discourse, rather than being referred to for exemplification. Whereas "the best way to find out what the people think about something is to ask them" (Bower, 1973, p. vi), some reception studies have made premature conclusions about a new powerful audience, in part because systematic methodologies have been lacking in the area.

Two perspectives on reception processes — across cultures and across media — may have special explanatory value in further research. First, most studies to date have focused on Western Europe and North America (but see Lull, 1988b), normally without an explicitly comparative approach. While research on other regions is overdue, specific comparative studies may suggest the bearing of a particular cultural configuration on forms of reception and media use. Further, communication technologies such as satellite television that introduce new forms of programming across cultural boundaries are likely to give rise to specific forms of negotiation and accommodation on the part of audiences as well as national media institutions. Such developments should be studied in order to assess the relative power of cultural agencies at different levels of the international political and social structure.

Second, whereas television has been especially popular as an object of reception analysis in the 1980s, radio and various print media remain important ingredients of the media environment as a whole. Even more important, perhaps, media environments in different cultural settings increasingly constitute interrelated structures, not just from economic and institutional angles, but from the audience angle. The intertextuality of much mass communication — the references of one medium or genre to others — implies that similar meanings may be generated in the interaction between audiences and media that are in principle distinct, thus reinforcing whatever impact individual media could be said to have. While there are major theoretical and methodological problems connected with the analysis of total media environments, examining the reception and use of mass communication across several media will be an important task for the next decade of reception analysis. Though the medium may not be the message (McLuhan, 1964), an important aspect of the message is produced in the interaction between recipients and a specific configuration of media.

The social relevance of reception analysis depends, in part, on the difference it may make in relation to mass media audiences and institutions. One general implication of pragmatism for research is a challenge to make the production of knowledge public: The process of reflexivity, in certain respects, may become social and institutional. In addition to considering its forms of presentation and its own discourses (Van Maanen, 1988), communication scholars are obliged to reflect on the knowledge interests of researchers as they interact with audiences and programmers (Lindlof & Anderson, 1988). Being social agents, respondents need not shut up when the tape recorder is shut off. What I am saying, with Peirce, is, "Do not block the way of inquiry!" (Skagestad, 1981, p. 5).

NOTES

1. For an introduction to Peirce, see, for example, Skagestad (1981) and Hookway (1985). Despite an enormous body of work, which he produced under difficult circumstances and for the most part outside of any academic institution, Peirce never completed the system of logic and sciences that he envisioned. As part of an extensive correspondence between Lady Viola Welby and Peirce toward the end of his life, which may be read as the testament of an isolated and agonized scholar, he mentions that he was then "working desperately to get written before I die a book on Logic that shall attract some good minds through whom I may do some real good" (Peirce, 1958, p. 408). While the *Collected Papers* (Peirce, 1931-1958) represents the first attempt to edit his work, a chronological edition currently is being issued by Indiana University Press; the majority of the planned volumes are still in press. *Values in a Universe of Change* (Peirce, 1958) is a useful collection of central texts.

2. Assessing the ideological efficacy of signs, some analysts have suggested that particular textual structures tend to naturalize particular worldviews — signifieds — for the recipients of communication (Barthes, 1957/1973). Moreover, when considering ways of countering ideological impact, poststructuralists and deconstructionists in particular have repudiated the emphasis on the signified, pointed to the signifier as a shaper of alternative worldviews, and defined the signifier as a material force in a process of mental as well as social change. Referring to avant-garde forms of high cultural arts, Coward and Ellis (1977) suggest that audience-publics may be able to see themselves and their social contexts in a new light through the ruptures of such poetic language, since there is a "correspondence of the signifying practices of these texts and revolutionary practice" (p. 150). Whereas classic semiology may be the dream of Cartesianism, and deconstructionism its nightmare, both modes of analysis tend to hypostatize the signified-signifier, mind-matter distinction. Consequently, the specific historical relationships between structures of signification and social practices, in many respects, remain unanalyzed in theories of signs.

3. Skagestad (1981) has suggested that Peirce's thinking rests on two premises — verificationism and realism — that might be reconciled. Whereas reality manifests itself in a variety of everyday practices, scientific practices, by thematizing the conditions of knowledge whenever an aspect of reality is called into question, rely on a methodological conception of reality that implies that all knowledge

remains preliminary and, indeed, is subject to continuous challenge. Thus the *cogito* of Peircean pragmatism might have been, *Erro, ergo sum.* Again, the relevant question is not, What is reality? (that is, where, in which unitary set of phenomena, does it reside) but rather, When is reality, and for what purpose?

4. There may be an ambivalence in Habermas' position in relation to Peirce. The theory of communicative action (Habermas, 1981, 1984), while pointing to the three-term model of signs, refers to Peirce only in passing. This is despite the similarity between Habermas's ideal conditions of communication and Peirce's interpretive communities, particularly his Final Interpretant. Both authors entertain the notion of a realm of signs before or apart from social reality. While Habermas (1971) associates Peirce's philosophy with "an idealism that is not unlike Hegel's" (p. 111), the charge of German idealism thus would seem to apply equally to both positions. However, Habermas (1971) further argues that Peirce's notion of signs, ultimately, cannot solve the epistemological problem of how to infer the "out there" from the "in here"; it "does not suffice to explain how thought processes transform the *presymbolic influx* of information" (p. 107; emphasis added). Habermas, in contrast to Peirce, then, assumes a brute reality as well, a reality before or apart from signs.

REFERENCES

Allor, M. (1988). Relocating the site of the audience. *Critical Studies in Mass Communication, 5*, 217-233.

Anderson, J. A., & Meyer, T. P. (1988). *Mediated communication: A social action perspective.* Newbury Park, CA: Sage.

Ang, I. (1985). *Watching Dallas.* London: Methuen.

Austin, J. (1962). *How to do things with words.* London: Oxford University Press.

Ball-Rokeach, S. (1985). The origins of individual media-system dependency. *Communication Research, 12*, 485-510.

Barthes, R. (1973). *Mythologies.* London: Paladin. (Original work published 1957)

Bateson, G. (1972). *Steps to an ecology of mind.* London: Paladin.

Bernstein, R. (1986). *Philosophical profiles.* Cambridge: Polity.

Bloom, A. (1987). *The closing of the American mind.* London: Penguin.

Blumler, J. (1979). The role of theory in uses and gratifications studies. *Communication Research, 6*, 9-36.

Bower, R. (1973). *Television and the public.* New York: Holt, Rinehart & Winston.

Cater, D. (1959). *The fourth branch of government.* Boston: Houghton Mifflin.

Coward, R., & Ellis, J. (1977). *Language and materialism.* London: Routledge & Kegan Paul.

Culler, J. (1975). *Structuralist poetics.* London: Routledge & Kegan Paul.

Dewey, J. (1927). *The public and its problems.* Chicago: Swallow.

Eagleton, T. (1983). *Literary theory: An introduction.* Minneapolis: University of Minnesota Press.

Eco, U. (1976). *A theory of semiotics.* Bloomington: Indiana University Press.

Fish, S. (1979). *Is there a text in this class?* Cambridge, MA: Harvard University Press.

Fiske, J. (1986). Television: Polysemy and popularity. *Critical Studies in Mass Communication, 3*, 391-407.

Fiske, J. (1987). *Television culture.* London: Methuen.

Fiske, J., & Hartley, J. (1978). *Reading television.* London: Methuen.

Goodman, N. (1976). *Languages of art* (2nd ed.). Indianapolis: Hackett.

Goodman, N. (1978). *Ways of worldmaking.* Indianapolis: Hackett.

Goodman, N., & Elgin, C. (1988). *Reconceptions in philosophy and other arts and sciences.* Indianapolis: Hackett.

Grossberg, L. (1988). Wandering audiences, nomadic critics. *Cultural Studies, 2*, 377-391.

Habermas, J. (1962). *Strukturwandel der Öffentlichkeit* [Structural change of the public sphere]. Neuwied, Federal Republic of Germany: Luchterhand.

Habermas, J. (1971). *Knowledge and human interests.* Boston: Beacon.

Habermas, J. (1981). *Theorie des kommunikativen Handelns* [The theory of communicative action] (Vol. 2). Frankfurt am Main, Federal Republic of Germany: Suhrkamp.

Habermas, J. (1984). *The theory of communicative action* (Vol. 1). Boston: Beacon.

Hall, S. (1980a). Recent developments in theories of language and ideology. In S. Hall, D. Hobson, A. Lowe, & P. Willis (Eds.), *Culture, media, language* (pp. 157-163). London: Hutchinson.

Hall, S. (1980b). Cultural studies: Two paradigms. *Media, Culture & Society, 2,* 57-72.

Hartley, J. (1988). The real world of audiences. *Critical Studies in Mass Communication, 5,* 234-238.

Hartnack, J. (1965). *Wittgenstein and modern philosophy.* New York: New York University Press.

Hebdige, D. (1979). *Subculture: The meaning of style.* London: Methuen.

Hodge, R., & Kress, G. (1988). *Social semiotics.* Ithaca, NY: Cornell University Press.

Holub, R. (1984). *Reception theory: A critical introduction.* London: Methuen.

Holzer, H. (1973). *Kommunikationssoziologie* [Sociology of communication]. Hamburg, Federal Republic of Germany: Rowohlt.

Hookway, C. (1985). *Peirce.* London: Routledge.

Jakobson, R. (1981). Linguistics and poetics. In S. Rudy (Ed.), *Selected writings* (Vol. 3, pp. 18-51). The Hague: Mouton. (Original work published 1960)

Jensen, K. B. (1986). *Making sense of the news.* Aarhus, Denmark: Aarhus University Press.

Jensen, K. B. (1987). Qualitative audience research: Toward an integrative approach to reception. *Critical Studies in Mass Communication, 4,* 21-36.

Jensen, K. B. (1988a). News as social resource: A qualitative empirical study of the reception of Danish television news. *European Journal of Communication, 3,* 275-301.

Jensen, K. B. (1988b). Surplus meaning: Outline of a social theory of media reception. *SPIEL, 7,* 93-108.

Jensen, K. B. (1989). Discourses of interviewing: Validating qualitative research findings through textual analysis. In S. Kvale (Ed.), *Issues of validity in qualitative research* (pp. 93-108). Lund, Sweden: Studentlitteratur.

Jensen, K. B. (in press). Politics of polysemy: Television news, everyday consciousness, and political action. *Media, Culture & Society.*

Jensen, K. B., & Rosengren, K. (in press). Five traditions in search of the audience: Towards a typology of research on the reception, uses, and effects of mass media content. *European Journal of Communication.*

Katz, E., & Liebes, T. (1984). Once upon a time, in Dallas. *Intermedia, 12,* 28-32.

Kinder, M. (1984). Music video and the spectator: Television, ideology, and dream. *Film Quarterly, 38,* 2-15.

Kuhn, T. (1970). *The structure of scientific revolutions* (rev. ed.). Chicago: University of Chicago Press.

Lasswell, H. (1966). The structure and function of communication in society. In B. Berelson & M. Janovitz (Eds.), *Reader in public opinion and communication* (pp. 178-190). Glencoe, IL: Free Press. (Original work published 1948)

Lindlof, T. (Ed.). (1987). *Natural audiences.* Norwood, NJ: Ablex.

Lindlof, T. (1988). Media audiences as interpretive communities. In J. Anderson (Ed.), *Communication yearbook 11.* Newbury Park, CA: Sage.

Lindlof, T., & Anderson, J. (1988, July 24-29). *Problems in decolonizing the human subject in qualitative audience research.* Paper presented to the Congress of the International Association for Mass Communication Research, Barcelona, Spain.

Lowe, D. (1982). *History of bourgeois perception.* Chicago: University of Chicago Press.

Lull, J. (1980). The social uses of television. *Human Communication Research, 6,* 197-209.

Lull, J. (1987). Thrashing in the pit: An ethnography of San Francisco punk subculture. In T. Lindlof (Ed.), *Natural audiences* (pp. 225-252). Norwood, NJ: Ablex.

Lull, J. (1988a). The audience as nuisance. *Critical Studies in Mass Communication, 5,* 239-243.

Lull, J. (Ed.). (1988b). *World families watch television.* Newbury Park, CA: Sage.

McLuhan, M. (1964). *Understanding media.* New York: McGraw-Hill.

McQuail, D., Blumler, J., & Brown, J. (1972). The television audience: A revised perspective. In D. McQuail (Ed.), *Sociology of mass communications* (pp. 135-165). London: Penguin.

McQuail, D., & Windahl, S. (1981). *Communication models for the study of mass communications.* London: Longman.

Mead, G. H. (1934). *Mind, self, and society.* Chicago: University of Chicago Press.

Meyrowitz, J. (1985). *No sense of place.* New York: Oxford University Press.

Morley, D. (1980). *The 'Nationwide' audience.* London: British Film Institute.

Morley, D. (1986). *Family television: Cultural power and domestic leisure.* London: Comedia.

Morris, C. (1971). *Writings on the general theory of signs.* The Hague: Mouton.

National Institute of Mental Health. (1982). *Television and behavior* (Vols. 1-2). Washington, DC: Government Printing Office.

Newcomb, H., & Hirsch, P. (1984). Television as a cultural forum: Implications for research. In W. Rowland & B. Watkins (Eds.), *Interpreting television* (pp. 58-73). Beverly Hills, CA: Sage.

Ogden, C. K., & Richards, I. A. (1946). *The meaning of meaning* (8th ed.). New York: Harcourt, Brace & World. (Original work published 1923)

Peirce, C. S. (1931-1958). *Collected papers* (Vols. 1-8). Cambridge, MA: Harvard University Press.

Peirce, C. S. (1958). *Values in a universe of change: Selected writings.* Garden City, NY: Doubleday.

Prado, C. (1987). *The limits of pragmatism.* Atlantic Highlands, NJ: Humanities Press International.

Radway, J. (1984). *Reading the romance.* Chapel Hill: University of North Carolina Press.

Radway, J. (1988). Reception study: Ethnography and the problems of dispersed audiences and nomadic critics. *Cultural Studies, 2,* 359-376.

Robinson, J., & Levy, M. (1986). Interpersonal communication and news comprehension. *Public Opinion Quarterly, 50,* 160-175.

Rochberg-Halton, E. (1986). *Meaning and modernity.* Chicago: University of Chicago Press.

Roper, Inc. (1985). *Public attitudes toward television and other mass media in a time of change.* New York: Author.

Rorty, A. (Ed.). (1966). *Pragmatic philosophy.* Garden City, NY: Doubleday.

Rorty, R. (1979). *Philosophy and the mirror of nature.* Princeton, NJ: Princeton University Press.

Rorty, R. (1982). *Consequences of pragmatism.* Minneapolis: University of Minnesota Press.

Rorty, R. (1989). *Contingency, irony, and solidarity.* Cambridge: Cambridge University Press.

Saussure, F. de. (1959). *Course in general linguistics.* London: Peter Owen. (Original work published 1916)

Schröder, K. (1987). Convergence of antagonistic traditions: The case of audience research. *European Journal of Communication, 2,* 7-31.

Schudson, M. (1978). *Discovering the news.* New York: Basic Books.

Schudson, M. (1984). *Advertising: The uneasy persuasion.* New York: Basic Books.

Schudson, M. (1987). The new validation of popular culture: Sense and sentimentality in academia. *Critical Studies in Mass Communication, 4,* 51-68.

Shannon, C., & Weaver, W. (1949). *The mathematical theory of communication.* Urbana: University of Illinois Press.

Siebert, F., Peterson, T., & Schramm, W. (1956). *Four theories of the press.* Urbana: University of Illinois Press.

Skagestad, P. (1981). *The road of inquiry.* New York: Columbia University Press.

Suleiman, S., & Crosman, I. (Eds.). (1980). *The reader in the text.* Princeton, NJ: Princeton University Press.

Thompson, J. (1984). *Studies in the theory of ideology.* Cambridge: Polity.

Tompkins, J. (Ed.). (1980). *Reader-response criticism.* Baltimore: Johns Hopkins University Press.

Van Maanen, J. (1988). *Tales of the field.* Chicago: University of Chicago Press.

Volosinov, V. (1973). *Marxism and the philosophy of language.* New York: Seminar.

Watt, I. (1957). *The rise of the novel.* London: Penguin.

White, M. (1973). *Pragmatism and the American mind.* New York: Oxford University Press.

Williams, R. (1977). *Marxism and literature.* London: Oxford University Press.

Wittgenstein, L. (1958). *Philosophical investigations.* London: Macmillan.

Semiological Struggles

JOHN FISKE
University of Wisconsin —Madison

J ENSEN'S account of the undeserved neglect of Peircean semiotics in favor of a Saussurean semiology is timely and provocative.[1] His densely packed and thoroughly researched argument is both a critical overview of our field's current attempts to come to grips with the problem of meaning and an attempt to argue that Peirce's theories may offer a set of insights that are more incisive than those with which we are currently working.

I am full of admiration for his critical summaries of the main theorists in the field, which deserve far more discussion and elaboration than would be possible in the space available to me. So I shall focus instead on the comparative contributions of Peirce and Saussure, or semiotics and semiology. And I must make my position clear: My academic development has taken place through Saussurean semiology, none of my writing or thinking is free of his formative influence, and I have no regrets about that, for I believe Saussure's wide-reaching influence to be thoroughly deserved.

Saussure's theories have generated more developments and argument than Peirce's, and there is a far larger body of work that is Saussurean and post-Saussurean (or even anti-Saussurean) than there is Peircean. True, but why? It is not that Peirce has been capriciously overlooked, or that he never wrote a book on semiotics but scattered his arguments throughout his voluminous and disorganized writings. The fact that no one has yet been able to edit his collected papers and produce from them a "Peircean semiotics" as the equivalent of the "Cours Generale" that Saussure's students produced from his lectures can be only part of the reason for the inequality of influence of the two founding fathers of the discipline.

More productive differences must be sought in the epistemological focuses of their theories, the ways of knowing that we are invited to bring to bear upon them and to develop from them. The key difference is a very simple one: Saussure is a linguist and Peirce is a logician. It all follows from that. Logicians investigate how

Correspondence and requests for reprints: John Fiske, Department of Communication Arts, University of Wisconsin, Madison, WI 53706.

Communication Yearbook 14, pp. 33-39

sense is made by rational human beings; linguists focus on how meanings are generated and circulated socially. Peirce's *interpretant* is not a social being but a cognitive being divorced from any social or historical specificity. So, as Jensen cites him, he can define the Final Interpretant as "the effect the Sign would produce upon *any mind*" and, similarly, can define truth as "that of which *any person* would come to be convinced" (p. 10, emphases added). The idea of *any* mind or *any* person evidences an essentialist view of meaning that has quite justifiably proved unproductive, for meanings are socially produced and socially circulated: They change as they move through the social formation and as they move through history. A white, middle-class male living in the twentieth-century capitalist West lives with a very different set of meanings from those of his counterpart in the eighteenth century, or from those of a nineteenth-century African American, or from those of a contemporary woman in the so-called Third World. The examples proliferate endlessly.

Language changes over time; it differs between cultures, and even within the same society and historical period it is inflected differently by different social formations — class, race, gender, age, region, and so on. A semiotics based upon the mental processes of an essentialist, cognitive being is unable to address some of the most crucial problems of the late twentieth-century world — the problems of economic, social, and political inequality.

The understanding of reception to which Jensen claims Peirce's theory of the interpretant can lead us is a cognitive one, not a social one. When Peirce moves beyond a mentalistic account of meaning, it is to a concept of "the public" rather than "the social." The public, for Peirce, appears to be a communally consensual way of thinking that denies social difference or its historical production. His public — unlike, say, Habermas' "public sphere" — is not a historical product of the socially dominant, but rather a process that we might call one of intercognition.

Jensen's use of the term *reception* is itself significant, for it implies a stage in the process of cognition. Those working in the post-Saussurean tradition, however, tend not to use it, preferring terms such as *reading* or even *production*, which emphasize the active role of the media user in the production of socially pertinent meanings from the text. The process of watching television, for example, is not called a process of reception, but one of production, or, in earlier, more ideologically inflected accounts, of reproduction. In literary theory, the term *reception theory* is typically used when the emphasis is upon a textually determined process of reading rather than a socially determined one.

I agree with Jensen's emphasis on the *when* of meaning and would add to it both a *where* and a *whose*. In other words, I would want to understand the *when* as a historical moment that is also situated specifically within a social formation rather than as a stage in a cognitive process as would Peirce. The right sort of language theory has a social and historical dimension in the way that logic does not, and that cognitive theory tends to minimize if not ignore.

Its potential for sociohistorical specificity is not the only reason a linguistically focused semiology has proved more generative than a semiotics derived from logic or cognitive theory. Another is what we might call its homologic potential. I stress the word *potential* because I do not wish to claim that Saussure's structural account of language is either complete or adequate. It is not, but it *is* generative. In fact, Peirce's semiotics is a far more developed theory than either Saussure's semiology (which consists of no more than a widely cited embryonic paragraph) or even his theory of language itself. Although Saussure says quite firmly that language is a social fact, he expends all his investigative energy upon the linguistic system and none at all upon the social system or upon the relations between the two. But the fact that Saussure's theory is structural, rather than essentialist, has allowed Jacobsen, for example, to establish that the phonetic system is homologically equivalent to the verbal system, and Lévi-Strauss to use language as the base homologue by which to explain almost every cultural system from cooking to mythology.

The generativity of Saussure not only outweighs the incompleteness of his own work, but may actually be a product of it. Thus his insistence on the arbitrary nature of the sign has had far greater implications than any he himself envisaged. When he argued that "value" (the relationship of a sign to others in the system) rather than "significance" (the relationship of a sign to an external referent) was the prime producer of meaning he opened up a wonderful Pandora's box of theoretical possibilities. For instance, he made it possible to link a theory of ideology to a theory of language and thus to admit Marxism and structuralism into a long-lasting and productive marriage based upon a core of similarity (that knowledge is relational and that social systems, whether economic or linguistic, can be understood only structurally, not essentially) but in which each compensated for the other's deficiencies: Structural linguistics compensated for Marxism's lack of a theory of language and Marxism compensated for structuralism's lack of a theory of social difference.

Peirce's triad of sign-object-interpretant posits a sign-object relationship that, however modified by the three-storied processes of the interpretant, finally ties some part of the meaning of the sign to a positivist reality. For Peirce, therefore, there is a part of meaning that is grounded in universal, eternal nature, not in culture: It lies outside the social production of meaning and is therefore not available for the exercise of social power. The cognitivism of Peirce's interpretant is the equivalent of the objectivism of his sign — both tie the meaning-making process to ahistorical factors, the human mind or external reality.

The arbitrary nature of Saussure's sign, however, has produced theories of meaning as being entirely a social product and, therefore, as part of the distribution of power in society and as part of the social struggle which the inequities of that distribution necessarily produce. Marx's famous dictum that the ideas of the ruling class become the ideas of their time is as provocative and undeveloped as Saussure's definition of semiology as the life of signs within society. But when the two were brought together, as, for instance, in the work of Barthes and Hall, there resulted a substantial body of work that traced the social and semiotic processes by which the ideas of the ruling classes established themselves as the common sense of society and, equally, showed how the linguistic system was put to use in historically and socially specific conjunctures.

In a different but equally productive move, Lacan argued that Freud's theories of the unconscious were structuralist and were homologous to the arbitrary relationship between the signifier and the signified. His theory of the development of subjectivity as an entry into a meaning system produced a body of work that explained the development of subjectivity as the equivalent at the level of the individual to ideology at the level of the social. This enabled Marx's undeveloped theory of consciousness to be explained and elaborated psychoanalytically, in the same way structural linguists fleshed out his ideas on the social power of knowledge.

Feminists in particular have found the marriage of semiology and psychoanalysis particularly fruitful, and have given us incisive accounts of how patriarchal power is exerted through systems of representation. Indeed, the theory of representation could have evolved only within a Saussurean rather than a Peircean theory of signs, for it too depends upon arbitrariness for its thesis that what sign systems do is represent the dominant ideology rather than an external reality.

Psychoanalysis has also given us the concept of repression: As the unconscious represses certain experiences and memories in order to produce a socially functional consciousness, so signs can produce socially functional meanings only by repressing others. The significant absence or silence is a concept in both psychoanalytic and ideological theory that argues that what is not said is at least as significant as, if not more significant than, what is. Because the repressed meanings are systematically and not occasionally repressed, they can be recovered by structural analysis. The cognitivist and pragmaticist thrust of Peircean semiotics makes it almost impossible for it to include notions of repression, silence, and absence in its account of meaning, for all of these concepts contain traces of opposition or struggle that make them structuralist and not positivist.

Saussure, Marx, and Freud are arguably the three thinkers who have produced a twentieth-century epistemology that is fundamentally one of structural relativity and thus contradicts the nineteenth century's emphasis on objectivism and positivism. In the 1970s, in Britain and Europe particularly, a major body of theoretical and analytical work developed that brought together insights from these three seminal thinkers to produce a comprehensive account of the political work of meaning generation and distribution in the white patriarchal capitalist societies in which we live. It was comprehensive because it traced homologic relationships between economic and ideological structures, between the structures of consciousness and subjectivity, and between linguistic and semiotic structures. Its ability to comprehend the domains of language, consciousness, and society gave it an enormous epistemological scope. The importance of Saussure is not to be found in his own (very limited) works, but in the productive and generative relationships that they have formed with those of other major theorists of their time. It remains to be seen whether the relationship of Peirce's semiotics with pragmatism and cognitivism can be as fertile: Certainly Jensen argues convincingly for its potential.

But the generativity of Saussure's ideas has not been confined to elaborating them and relating them to others: They have spawned disagreements that have proved as valuable as the developments. Such attacks on his thought are still Saussurean because they either take place within the frame he established or use his conceptual apparatus as the starting point from which to establish contradictory ones.

For materialist linguists, Saussure's theory was not so much wrong as upside down. Volosinov (1973) and Hodge and Kress (1988), for example, argue within Saussure's framework but against his priorities. His prioritization of *langue* over *parole*, of the paradigmatic over the syntagmatic, of the synchronic over the diachronic, and finally of the signifier over the signified should, they argue, be reversed in order to understand not what the linguistic system is, but how it is used in specific social situations. For Volosinov meaning is produced not by the linguistic system alone but at its intersection with a social system at its moments of use. So the same sign in the same linguistic structures can be accented differently according to its social point of usage. Signs are signs only when they pass between socially located beings, and thus signs can best be understood as part of social relations, rather than as part of a linguistic system. Signs are "multiaccentual" because they can form different social relations according to who speaks them, and as the key social relations in capitalist societies are ones of struggle, so the multiaccentuality of signs enables and ensures their entry into that struggle. The struggle over meaning is part of the social struggle, as feminists have understood so well. The form that the struggle for meaning takes is historically specific (diachronic rather than synchronic) and is fought out in speech acts (paroles and syntagms) rather than at the structural level (langue and paradigms). But the relationship between the uses of a system and the system itself is organic, each use modifies or confirms the system, however minutely, and it is only in its uses that one can trace the mechanisms and processes of change.

Although Saussure may, according to this view, have gotten his priorities wrong, he did at least stress that meaning is not produced when a single sign comes into relationship with an interpretant and a piece of reality, but when it comes into relationship with other signs, whether paradigmatically into a relation of difference, or syntagmatically into one of combination. Saussure modeled the relationship of syntagm to paradigm and langue to parole as a symptomatic one — paroles and syntagms were the material realizations of the potential of the abstract paradigm and langue. The symptoms were the only way to study the system, and, equally, were valuable only as symptomatic of that system. For material linguists or social semiologists, however, the relationship can be antagonistic. Langue and the paradigmatic dimension are bearers of social power in a way that Saussure never realized: Their historically specific uses, however, can resist or oppose the power inscribed in them. Language's ability to play an active rather than reflective role in social change can be traced only through a focus on parole and syntagmatic specificities.

So the macrostructural studies (Saussurean-Marxian-Freudian) also produced historically and socially situated studies of the system in use. These initially centered on resistant or negotiated uses whereby subordinated groups devised their own tactics to cope with the system that subordinated them. They began to investigate the relationship between semiotic resistance and social resistance, which raised the questions of under what specific conditions the struggle for meaning could become a social struggle, and under what conditions a social struggle could move between the micro and macro levels of social relationships. The recent inflections of structuralism have tended to emphasize the practices, both semiotic and social, by which people use for their interests the resources of the system within (and against) which they live their everyday lives. But such studies are always situated within the framework whose priorities they oppose but whose structure they accept.

So, too, many of the theories that have been categorized as poststructuralist or deconstructive depend directly upon the arbitrary nature of the sign as embodied in the signifier-signified relationship. If meaning cannot be produced finally at the intersection between a sign and a fixed referent (whether an objectivist reality or a cognitivist mind), then meaning is in constant process. The signified is not a referential anchor for the signifier, but becomes itself a signifier in an unending chain of "deferral" by which meaning is never made but is always in the making.

Similarly, postmodern theories of the simulacrum rely on the arbitrariness of the sign in order to contradict the dualism of the signifier/signified concept and of the relationship of similarity and difference by which social systems and representational systems are, in structuralism, made to make sense of each other. A simulacrum and a hyperreality are "implosive" concepts that collapse into themselves the polarities of the signifier/signified and the representational/the social.

We may not be comfortable with the epistemological crisis diagnosed for us by poststructuralism, deconstructionism, and postmodernism, but we have to recognize how widely accepted it has become: It is the perhaps inevitable outcome of the structural relativity of what I have claimed to be the defining characteristic of twentieth-century thought. It is contradicted from within its own tradition by the focus on material practices rather than overarching structures or grand narratives, and from without by the sort of Peircean pragmatism promoted by Jensen. My brief account of why Saussurean semiology has, up to now at least, proved more generative than Peircean semiotics should be read historically, not essentially. Saussure's is not an inherently "better" theory, but it has proved itself better able to offer more socially powerful explanations of what it claims to be the key features of twentieth-century experience. As our historical conditions change, and change they must, maybe a more positivist and pragmatic epistemology will replace a structural relativist one: I remain to be convinced.

NOTE

1. I follow Jensen's use of the terms *semiology* and *semiotics* to refer to the Saussurean and Peircean schools, respectively. This is a useful rhetorical device for this essay, but it is not normal usage: The term *semiotics* frequently refers to the Saussurean tradition.

REFERENCES

Hodge, R., & Kress, G. (1988). *Social semiotics*. Ithaca, NY: Cornell University Press.
Volosinov, U. N. (1973). *Marxism and the philosophy of language* (L. Matejka & I. R. Titunik, Trans.). Cambridge, MA: Harvard University Press.

The Search for Media Meaning

HORACE M. NEWCOMB
University of Texas at Austin

I N his essay, Jensen focuses on one of the central questions in contemporary media studies. He is concerned with the role of media "audiences" in creating, modifying, constructing, or reconstructing (depending on one's prior assumptions) meaning from and within mass-mediated communication. He not only frames his problem in terms of the shift in media studies to conceptions of active audiences, by now a commonly accepted notion across various approaches to the study of mass communication, but asks us to consider appropriate levels of analysis within audience studies.

I agree with this general approach. Analysis remaining at the general, "structural" level assumes too much, establishes too little, and results in cynical, circular critiques of broad-scale social patterns. Most of these analyses are critiques of capitalism, or American capitalism, or BBC hegemony, or "privatization," or "media imperialism" more than they are critiques of specific media processes. As such broad-scale critiques take media content and media institutions as their focus, they may be quite useful. Still, within such analysis no answer to any problem can be sufficient without wholesale social reconstruction.

At the other end of the spectrum, generalized fervor for the power of individual appropriation of mass-mediated messages in "subverting" or "rereading" media content leads into a swamp of solipsism. Finally, no understanding is possible. Intersubjectivity disappears. Society crumbles. Culture dissolves. This approach (characterized here in extreme fashion) seems to me patently incompatible with much that we know about mass-mediated communication, particularly, for my concerns, much that we know about the generation and perpetuation of entertainment forms.

Jensen's plea is for a middle ground, though he might object, on the face of it, to my spatial metaphor. The question remains: If we cannot deduce media effectivity from theoretical constructs and if the sum of myriad individual experiences

Correspondence and requests for reprints: Horace M. Newcomb, Department of Radio-Television-Film, University of Texas, Austin, TX 78712.

Communication Yearbook 14, pp. 40-47

never coheres into any significant pattern, where do we look for media meaning and how do we study it?

Jensen's answer is to call for what he refers to as "a social semiotics." Such an approach depends, or at least benefits, in his view, from an exploration of a relatively new source for media studies, Peircean semiotics. It also recalls, especially for American scholarly communities, the significance of a Habermasian perspective on the public sphere. After exploring the assumptions of other scholars regarding the construction of meaning in and from mass media, and after introducing his distillation of these "new" sources, Jensen suggests a possible direction:

> In particular, a social semiotics may produce models for relating a social-institutional level of analysis with analyses of the interpretive strategies of individual communicants. After a decade where much empirical attention has been given to the microsocial level of reception and to the discursive aspect of meaning production, it may be time to refocus on their interrelations with the macrosocial level of institutions and classes. What is at stake in mass communication, after all, is control over an important means of inquiry into social reality. (p. 26)

As stated earlier, I tend to agree with this conclusion — insofar as I understand its terms. Unfortunately, and somewhat paradoxically, the links in Jensen's chain of argument are often weaker than his basic assumptions and his admirable conclusions. This suggests that while I, and perhaps many others, might agree with the general aspects of his approach, finding common ground on what is to be done next might be difficult. The programmatic implications of Jensen's pronouncements are thin, and, to my thinking, not all that far removed from much of the work produced in the "previous decade" he cites. Put another way, this essay, clearly designed to provoke, to critique some currently prominent approaches, to redirect, and to lead in new directions, is unlikely to alter research agendas in any major way. This is the case because many researchers, some of Jensen's "targets" among them, are already doing more of what he suggests than he allows. It is also the case because, fortunately, research communities now seem much more aware of the cumulative, even dialectical, progress we make rather than simply maintaining dependence upon the coherent, hermetic nature of research of earlier periods. In this regard, Jensen's essay makes its major contribution by reminding us of other sources for thinking that can contribute to and refine our approaches even if they do not revolutionize them. It sounds other voices, often noticed but seldom heard in meaningful ways. It enriches the discussion that constitutes — slight, halting, meandering — progress in the human sciences. This is most evident in the internal workings of Jensen's essay in the back-and-forth movement between aspects of mass communication that structure or direct interpretation and interpretive moves that may sometimes, somehow, modify those structuring devices. In spite of an attempt to make his approach into something new, Jensen's analysis does not escape this movement. Indeed, in the end, it is constrained by old, familiar questions and by an old and familiar inability to resolve them. To explore some of these issues more closely, to examine both the weaknesses and strengths of the essay, I intend to look at its parts in the order of their presentation.

EPISTEMOLOGY AND DISCOURSE

The first sections of Jensen's chapter demonstrate the difficulties encountered by any scholar wishing to redirect thinking in the field we know as communication or media research. Because we do not deal with a bounded and defined discipline, with an agreed-upon body of texts, procedures, and central questions, such an effort is too often preoccupied with recultivating ground already cleared and replanted many times. In the present case we deal with multiple applications of the term *discourse*, and wind up with a rather simple pronouncement that Jensen chooses to "focus on the level of theoretical discourse" (p. 6). By this he means he will work on explanation of data at a level that can be applied in social practice. This is in contrast, in his view, to work performed at the level of "epistemological discourse," which can trap its practitioners "within the epistemological loop" and "jeopardize their claim to a discursive position from which they might address mass communication as an aspect of social reality" (p. 5). Put another way, if we worry solely about how we know what we know, we will be unable to act.

My concern here is not with such a conclusion, but with whether or not we have to be walked through this discussion in order to reach it. Perhaps my concerns are more editorial here than substantive, but I think not. The step taken, to focus on "theoretical" discourse, hardly allows one to step outside epistemology, a clear impossibility. Instead, Jensen simply indicates that he assumes an epistemology that privileges social action rather than wallows in confusion over how to act. This privileging is clearly indicated when he cites, with approval, Hartley's (1988) claim that scholarly analysis has a clear rhetorical dimension, that one aim of scholarship, among others, is to decide that some interpretations are better than others and to attempt to "*persuade*" audiences to "take up" those more appropriate positions. A valuable idea, it is almost buried in a section bent on clarifying related matters.

INTERPRETIVE COMMUNITIES,
LEVEL OF ANALYSIS, AND AUDIENCE FREEDOMS

Jensen's next section, "Where Is Meaning," is a valuable summary of the development of assumptions about communication built on a spatial metaphor. Descartes and Locke are quickly related to "mainstream" communication theory of an earlier generation and iconic names — Lasswell, Shannon and Weaver — are invoked to suggest how we sometimes got ourselves into trouble with these unexamined assumptions. Similarly, Saussure and Jakobson, icons of another, interpretive, tradition, are also linked to the spatial concept, and, appropriately in my view, found wanting for engendering a too-narrow focus on media structures and products rather than on media processes.

Such a focus on process, Jensen suggests, necessarily shifts our dominant metaphor for communication from space to time. Thus the questions shift: No longer are we concerned with "where" meaning resides, but with "when" it occurs. As he calls up Peirce's semiotic theory, explicates, and applies it to mass communication, Jensen does indeed profitably shift emphasis to process and context, to the social and public nature of communication, to interaction, verification, and action. He moves from Peirce's notion of scientific communities of knowers, relatively homogeneous and organized, to the multiply involved interpretive communities that deal with mass communication. These latter may shift and change with regard to different media content, use, and display. The interpretive strategies they employ "may be mutually inconsistent, or *contradictory*, because they derive from different contexts or represent the orientations of different social formations that may be in conflict" (p. 14). In short, they are not nearly so clean and distinct as the Peircean communities, and because they are involved with so much mediated communication, they may be quite difficult to pin down for study.

At this point, roughly halfway through his essay, Jensen seems to be leaning toward the newer concerns for microlevel analysis. So much diversity and difference would seem to drive any reception analysis in that direction, this in spite of the hesitation he seemed to express for this sort of analysis earlier. Or perhaps it would be better to say that he leans in this direction with all the earlier reservations in mind, suggesting that a stronger form of this microanalysis is forthcoming, or that some clearer suggestion for a midlevel analysis is in the offing.

Instead, the next move is indicative of that dual thrust, oscillating between the structures of mediated content and the freedom to deflect or refract those structures. "Genres . . . invite recipients to take particular stances with implied social roles (Williams, 1977), thus contributing to the building of specific interpretive communities" (p. 14). Specific texts (e.g., *The Rocky Horror Picture Show*) orient interpretations. Education itself, while offering critical skills, nevertheless structures interpretation through canon formation and instructional strategies. Similarly, certain social practices, "socially meaningful activities" (p. 15), such as gendered behavior, social organization, or the family, can restrict or direct interpretation.

Still, because all of us are members of varied communities or groups, because we are structured by multiple discourse systems, the various restricting devices may be at odds with one another. As Jensen puts it, "One may detect several contradictory constructions of political institutions that emerge as ambiguity, or polysemy, in audience discourses" (p. 16). This statement, in addition to summarizing once again the swinging focus between structure and freedom, signals a transition into Jensen's only offer of specific analysis in his essay. It comes here, appropriately, because the essay has reached the point of asking, "Okay, which is it, structure (content, text, message), or use (audience, freedom of interpretation, individual)? If neither (or both, in some innovative mixture missed before), what is this new processual, midground, Peircean-based analysis?" And it is also at this point that Jensen is compelled to respond to other scholars who have raised some of the same issues. Thus the applied section of the essay calls for a close look.

John Fiske's arguments for the counterhegemonic aspects of popular entertainment, specifically of television, have called forth considerable response. (See, in addition to the present example, Condit, 1989.) Assertive, persuasive, synthetic in the best sense, *Television Culture* (Fiske, 1987) is the first overview of television built around the particular issues addressed here. It deals with the interactions among active audiences, complex popular texts, and political discourses. The very organization of the book tends, as Jensen suggests, toward privileging audience freedom to subvert the hegemonic structures produced by socially central institutions and governed by the yawning maw of advertising as a sociopolitical practice.

Jensen points out, of course, that "Fiske (1987) is careful to qualify his argument at various points lest he be thought to overestimate what might be called a 'pseudo-power' (p. 318)" (p. 17). This is true, and Jensen would do well to point out the different qualifications in their different contexts to do justice to Fiske, especially since he becomes the primary whipping boy for a much too lax approach to audiences' interpretive freedom. Instead, Jensen merely dismisses one of Fiske's primary arguments, and summarizes: "This makes fantasy a necessary, but not sufficient, condition of social change" (p. 17). The qualifications alluded to in Fiske's book make precisely the same point. What Jensen overlooks is exactly what he calls for in other places. He fails to see Fiske's work as a social act, performed in specific social contexts. He fails, in short, to see Fiske's book as an intervention in the same ongoing debate Jensen addresses. I am particularly interested in this issue because some of the same charges have been leveled against my own work, despite its fundamental differences from Fiske's. Indeed, to move ahead slightly, Jensen suggests something of the same critique in his discussion of the cultural forum model of network television proposed by Paul Hirsch and myself (Newcomb & Hirsch, 1984).

What Jensen fails to recognize, or wishes not to acknowledge, is that in the continuing discussion of the ideological role of mass media in general and television in particular, *necessary is enough*, and far more than many previous scholars have allowed. Indeed, it would be helpful if Jensen — or someone, anyone — would define *sufficient* conditions for social change.

But perhaps I become too harsh or too particular. Part of the problem here is that in the tradition of the humanities, in their contribution to the human sciences as opposed to the contributions of what we generally know as social science, one too often feels compelled to write "*as if*" one's claims are stronger or larger than they actually can ever be. It would be wise for many of us to write more tentatively, but editors have a way of suggesting that those who hesitate are lost already, and unworthy of serious consideration. So much for a digression on the rhetoric of scholarly analysis. Structurally, however, in his essay, Jensen's discussion of Fiske is also a digression. Ostensibly he feels compelled to discuss Fiske because Fiske's account of polysemy is "the most detailed" (p. 17). Actually, Jensen discusses not

Fiske's account of polysemy, but the suggested ideological effects of polysemic media content. He would have done better to stick with the stated purpose, for his own use of "polysemy" as a definition of multiple interpretive strategies within single audience groups or members is unwieldy and unusual. It needs defense and explanation to avoid the sort of problem caused by his own statement equating polysemy with ambiguity (p. 17).

CONCLUSIONS

Jensen's search for the midlevel in his Peircean-based analysis remains unfulfilled. His desire to make social institutions and practices, such as the actual organizations and assumptions defining "news," into the link that defines that level is not supported here. Indeed, if contradictions in consciousness (in individuals or in groups such as "interpretive communities") can "derive from" contradictions at the level of macrosocial institutions, we are back to a form of spatial description. Meaning somehow originates in one place and, in some undefined manner, is transmitted to another. While this model permits a more process-oriented analysis, that kind of analysis does not appear here. If Jensen could show the process of that transference, using Peircean terms and procedures, he would go far in convincing me that he is onto something new.

Instead he moves ahead to discuss mass media as the locus of information *about* institutions. Here he discusses my own work and I will respond briefly, passing over a number of quibbles I have long since decided are more the result of imprecise statement on my part than of misinterpretation by my critics. I will comment, then, only on the part of the argument that continues this discussion of the relations among media content, social institutions, and audiences.

> The main limitation of the [cultural forum] analysis is that it represents a perspective from only one type of social institution, namely, mass media. What is not considered are the relations of feedback between the mass media and other institutions, in the present case TV news media and political institutions. Unlike geological faults, social fault lines, once identified, might be acted upon. (p. 22)

I point out first that geologic faults can, and often must, be acted upon. But to do that, one must have a map. Indeed, because many types of maps are useful in the process, one needs as many maps as possible. One purpose of the cultural forum model is simply to provide a different type of map of content found in popular entertainment of particular sorts. Such a map is presented in terms different from prior understandings of television content and suggests that the medium might serve as a metaphor for social fault lines.

I point out next that all the questions Jensen suggests as unanswered by the forum model are in fact engendered by that model, as was intended. Prior to the promulgation of that model most media research, particularly that deriving from the hermeneutic tradition, *assumed* homogeneity in television content. The forum model at least insists that that assumption be tested empirically. Jensen's questions—for example, "Which sectors of society . . . are likely never to be subject to television representation . . . ?" (p. 22)—can be explored quite fully using this model. (His conclusion from that question, "and hence [never to be subject] to any form of negotiation" [p. 22] simply does not follow. As Fiske, among others, has often remarked, exnomination is indeed a form of cultural negotiation, quite likely to provoke just the sort of macrosocial institutional political behavior Jensen calls for. This is the point Fiske was making with his comment on homogeneous programming. And the "comparative evidence" Jensen finds lacking for this "effect" [p. 22] exists throughout the literature on special interest groups.) All this suggests that any analysis of the "where" or the "when" of meaning will be affected by our models of the "what" of meaning, a topic Jensen deals with only implicitly.

His remarks about the shortcomings of the forum model are often well taken, but there is an element in his critique that indicates he finds the work wanting merely because it does not do what it was never intended to do. As with Fiske's work, Jensen has ignored the specific social (i.e., academic, institutional, historical, and rhetorical) context in which the work appeared. Once again, his own analysis seems to violate his preferred model of communication research.

Having found all his examples wanting in forging satisfactory links among audience interpretation, media content, and social institutions, Jensen returns to Peirce to expand the discussion of applicable elements of pragmatism. And here he also turns to another major model in the work of Habermas. Especially significant is the judicious critique of Habermas. Jensen carefully points out the idealistic nature of Habermas's theory of communicative action, referring to it as a "last-ditch articulation of the question, Where is meaning?" (p. 25). But beyond this he draws on Habermas to show that we should all be aware of the interests underlying our own research. And one of the clearest statements of Jensen's aim comes in his description of the project of Gadamer, Habermas, and Rorty. It is their "common agenda," he suggests, to work out "a theory of communication that addresses the historical origins and social uses of meaning" (p. 24). Again, I agree that this aim is worthy, and any progress toward this sort of practice is urgently needed. Jensen is to be applauded for foregrounding the call.

The penultimate section of Jensen's essay, preceding a general restatement of his major points in the conclusion, is titled "Toward a Pragmatist Theory of Mass Communication" (p. 25). Here we find the clear statement of what this journey through various theories and models leads to: "In particular, a social semiotics may produce models for relating a social-institutional level of analysis with analyses of the interpretive strategies of individual communicants" (p. 26). Unfortunately, for reasons cited above, Jensen's suggestions do not add up to a workable model for analyzing these relations. In case after case he leans too far in one direction or another. Often he relies heavily on deterministic structures and institutions. Yet in his one instance of applied analysis, he goes too far in the other direction, depending on narrow readings of source interviews. By example, most likely unintended, he shows us just how difficult a goal he has set.

That goal has been a common one for the past decade. Many of the researchers Jensen criticizes have offered partial approaches for achieving it—swaying, tightroping on whatever line divides structurally determined, socioideological effects from free, multiple, solipsistic, exciting, and potentially useless individual interpretation. A model for resolving tension between the perspectives or for studying the relationship has not emerged. The flawed, struggling attempts are the best we have.

Jensen now offers his version, and takes us a step further along. His critiques of current scholarship, despite their flaws, will aid in more precise understanding. His citation of Habermas reminds us of the social interests that should drive our work. His recovery of Peirce provides a needed corrective to the limitations of other forms of semiotic/semiological analysis. It is especially important that the critiques and the new or reiterated sources should be presented in the context of qualitative audience research, currently theorized and demanded by so many and practiced by so few. I wish Jensen had shown more of his own and others' applied qualitative audience research instead of diving so deeply into theoretical discussion. His theories, as I have already suggested, are not so new, or so different. His analysis of applied work would be as valuable as what is presented here.

But this is the essay he wrote. And this is the one I have tried, after the habit, the practice, the interest of textual analysis as I know it, to wrench into my own misrestatement.

REFERENCES

Condit, C. (1989). The rhetorical limits of polysemy. *Critical Studies in Mass Communication, 6*, 103-122.

Fiske, J. (1987). *Television culture*. London: Methuen.

Hartley, J. (1988). The real world of audiences. *Critical Studies in Mass Communication, 5*, 234-238.

Jensen, K. B. (in press). Politics of polysemy: Television news, everyday consciousness, and political action. *Media, Culture & Society*.

Newcomb, H., & Hirsch, P. (1984). Television as a cultural forum: Implications for research. In W. Rowland & B. Watkins (Eds.), *Interpreting television* (pp. 58-73). Beverly Hills, CA: Sage.

Williams, R. (1977). *Marxism and literature*. London: Oxford University Press.

2 Media Use in Childhood and Adolescence: Invariant Change? Some Results from a Swedish Research Program

K A R L   E R I K   R O S E N G R E N
University of Lund

During the better part of the twentieth century, systematic studies of the character, causes, and consequences of individual mass media use have been carried out in a number of countries and have produced a multitude of sometimes contradictory results. This state of affairs raises some questions about the historical specificity versus the invariance over time and space of the phenomenon under study. A serious answer to such questions calls for systematic comparative research, preferably combining spatial and temporal comparisons, as well as cross-sectional and longitudinal data. This chapter presents the Media Panel Program, which has been carried out for some 15 years at the University of Lund in Sweden. Some 3,000 children and their parents living in two Swedish towns have been followed, in some cases from preschool to adulthood. The program is based on a combined cross-sectional/panel design, at present covering eight data collection waves. This chapter presents some central results from the program. Confronting the historical specificity of some results with the "invariant change" found in others, the question is posed whether current generalizations about individual mass media use will survive the ongoing restructuring of the European media scene.

I N 1955, while discussing the effects of television on children and adolescents, Paul F. Lazarsfeld rightly maintained that the real problem in the area concerned "the cumulative effects of television": Effects that make themselves felt "six years, not six minutes later." Today, 35 years later, a number of longitudinal projects have provided some knowledge about such effects. What we still do not know, however, is how invariant such long-term effects are over geographical and social space, and over time. Will long-term causal patterns show

AUTHOR'S NOTE: I wish to thank all members of the Media Panel Group, especially Ingrid Höjerback, Gunilla Jarlbro, Ulla Johnsson-Smaragdi, Thomas Lööv, Fredrik Miegel, and Inga Sonesson, for valuable assistance in writing this chapter.

Correspondence and requests for reprints: Karl Erik Rosengren, Department of Sociology, University of Lund, P.O. Box 114, S-22100 Lund, Sweden.

Communication Yearbook 14, pp. 48-90

long-term invariance? Will the differences in media use and effects hitherto observed between different social categories prove invariant over time? Are there invariant patterns of change? In short, to what extent are our theories valid over time and social space?

This chapter presents an overview of an ongoing Swedish research program, the Media Panel Program (MPP), which is being carried out by a research group at the Department of Sociology, University of Lund, Sweden. One aim of this program is to provide answers to some of the questions just posed.

The MPP concerns children's and adolescents' use of television and other mass media. It consists of a number of panel and cross-sectional studies that since 1975 have been conducted on some 3,000 children and adolescents altogether (in most cases their parents and teachers also participated). As a rule the children were living in the towns of Malmoe and Vaxjoe in the counties of Skåne and Småland in southern Sweden (some 230,000 and 60,000 inhabitants, respectively). The program has for many years enjoyed generous support from the Swedish Social Science Council, the Bank of Sweden Tercentenary Foundation, and the Swedish National Board of Education.

The most comprehensive presentation of the program and its results so far has appeared in a book by Rosengren and Windahl (1989). A number of other detailed reports have also been published, including seven doctoral theses appearing as books (Flodin, 1986; Hedinsson, 1981; Jarlbro, 1988; Johnsson-Smaragdi, 1983; Jönsson, 1985; Roe, 1983; Sonesson, 1979). Presentations of different waves, panels, and approaches of the program may be found, for instance, in Höjerback (1986), Johnsson-Smaragdi and Roe (1986), Rosengren (1986), Jarlbro, Lööv, and Miegel (1989), Johnsson-Smaragdi and Höjerback (1989), Sonesson (1989), and Sonesson and Höjerback (1989). The basic epistemology and the methodology behind the program are discussed in Rosengren (1989a; see also Jarlbro, 1986). Some research projects currently growing out of the program are presented in Rosengren (1988, 1989b).

MPP is not exactly the first study in its area (see Wartella & Reeves, 1987). Two excellent recent overviews of research on children and television are those by Comstock and Pail (1987) and Liebert and Sprafkin (1988). Thousands of cross-sectional studies have been conducted. Longitudinal studies of media use by children and adolescents range from classics such as Himmelweit, Oppenheim, and Vince (1958) and Schramm, Lyle, and Parker (1961) to the oft-quoted panel study by Lefkowitz, Eron, Walder, and Huesman (1972) to more recent panel and/or cohort studies by, for example, Milawsky, Kessler, Stipp, and Rubens (1982), Singer, Singer, and Rapaczynski (1984), Huesman and Eron (1986), Wiegman, Kuttschreuter, and Baarda (1986), Williams (1986), and Werner (1989). The combination of cross-sectional studies and long-term panel studies used in the MPP is, however, rare.

The overall design of the study is depicted visually in Figure 1. In the rest of this chapter, panels will be denoted by letters and figures referring to town and year of birth, respectively; for instance, panel V69 is the Vaxjoe panel born in 1969.

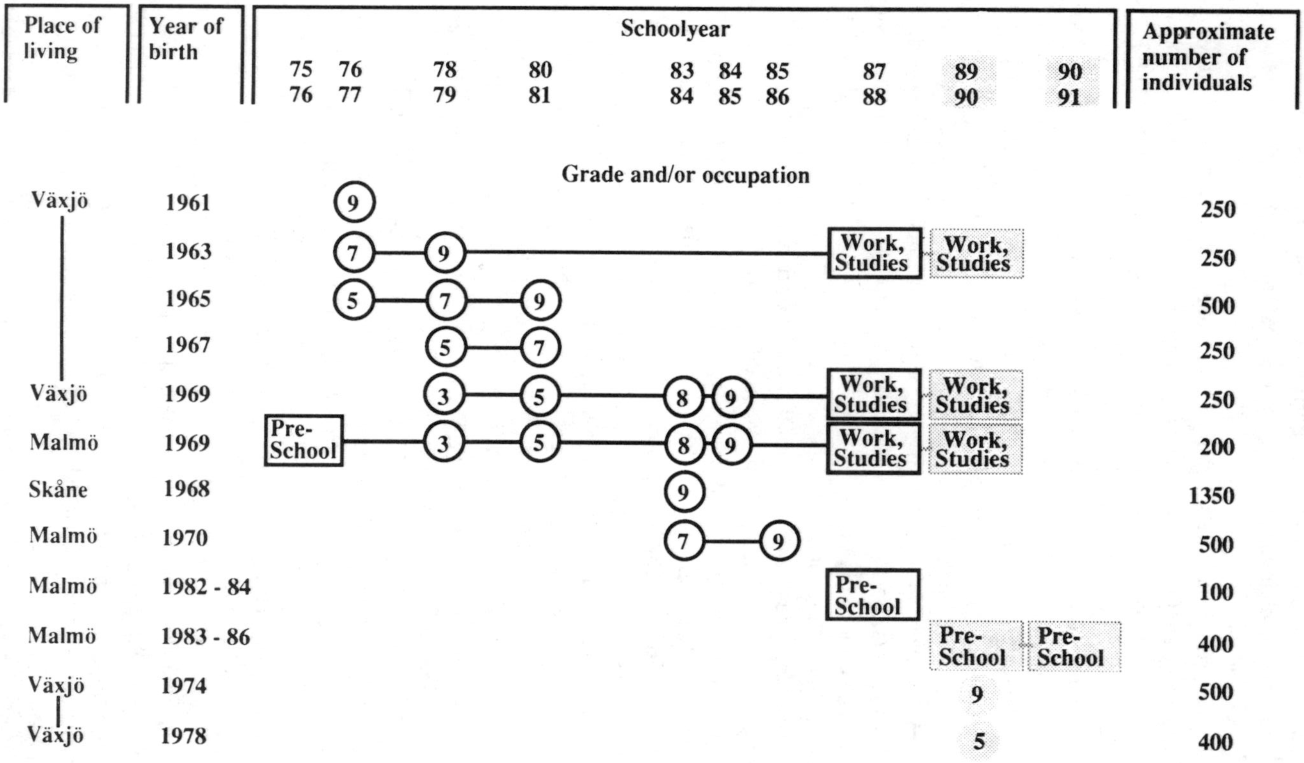

Place of living	Year of birth	Schoolyear										Approximate number of individuals
		75/76	76/77	78/79	80/81	83/84	84/85	85/86	87/88	89/90	90/91	
Växjö	1961	⑨							Work, Studies			250
	1963		⑦	⑨						Work, Studies		250
	1965		⑤	⑦	⑨							500
	1967			⑤	⑦							250
Växjö	1969	Pre-School		③	⑤	⑧	⑨		Work, Studies	Work, Studies		250
Malmö	1969			③	⑤	⑧	⑨		Work, Studies	Work, Studies		200
Skåne	1968					⑦	⑨					1350
Malmö	1970						⑦	⑨				500
Malmö	1982 - 84								Pre-School			100
Malmö	1983 - 86								Pre-School	Pre-School	Pre-School	400
Växjö	1974									9		500
Växjö	1978									5		400

Grade and/or occupation

Figure 1. Design of data collection within the Media Panel Program. Circles and squares represent surveys of individuals inside and outside the compulsory school program. Shaded squares and circles represent surveys not carried out at the time of writing. Text in circles and squares shows grade and/or occupation.

The panels are built on representative samples of the populations under study (or on practically everybody in those populations). Usual tests of representativeness, reliability, and so on have been undertaken (Rosengren & Windahl, 1989). Panel mortality is a problem, of course, but efforts have been made to keep it down, and even in the latest panel wave, tests show that the remaining groups of individuals do not significantly deviate with respect to basic demographic data from the composition of the original samples (Jarlbro et al., 1989). Since most of the panels stem from two rather different towns, and some from different communities in the countryside (the Skåne panel), we have some confidence in having caught — in addition to the temporal variation inherent in the design — a substantial part of existent geographical variation in Swedish adolescents' mass media use.

The mixed cross-sectional and longitudinal design has been applied because it is so efficient when one is looking for answers to questions about change and invariance, and about invariance in change. Actually, the many waves and panels open up the possibility of carrying out small-scale meta-analyses (Fraser, Walberg, Welch, & Hattie, 1987; Glass, 1976) based on more comparable sets of data and more intimate knowledge of those data than is usually the case. This is quite advantageous, especially when dealing with constancy and change.

Change is time-related difference. There are three types of causes of time-related differences at the individual level: maturational, situational, and generational. Maturational change is due to age-related processes (e.g., those occurring during adolescence). Situational differences are the effects of specific environmental conditions prevailing at the moment of observation (e.g., a specific media structure). Generational (or cohort) differences are the results of powerful circumstances making a lasting imprint on a given generation (e.g., the "1968 events").

The MPP design admits three types of analysis that provide information about the three types of difference and change. *Cross-sectional analyses* demonstrate differences and similarities between different age groups at the same time. These differences and similarities may be due to maturational or generational effects. *Panel analyses* demonstrate differences and similarities in the same cohort of individuals as they move through time. Such differences and similarities may be due to maturational or situational effects. *Diagonal analyses* demonstrate differences and similarities between individuals of the same age at different periods of time. Such differences and similarities may be due to situational or generational effects. By shifting among cross-sectional, panel, and diagonal analyses, we may arrive at insights into the subtle interplay among maturational, generational, and situational influences.

A basic characteristic of the MPP is that it is not limited to a given theoretical or methodological perspective, nor is it dedicated to research on one substantive mass communication problem. On the contrary, it deals with such *substantive* aspects of media use and effects as behavioral, attitudinal, and structural causes and consequences of media use. Its main focus is television (broadcast, cable, and VCR variants), but it does heed other media as well, including the medium of music.

Methodologically, its stance could be described as quantitative and qualitative studies carried out within a combined uses-and-effects approach (see Bryant & Zillmann, 1986; Rosengren, Wenner, & Palmgreen, 1985). *Theoretically*, three main perspectives have been applied: a development perspective, a class perspective, and a socialization perspective.

The broad theoretical and methodological approach of the MPP is manifest in the design of the program, and also in the basic conceptual scheme used to give some overall structure to the empirical studies. The scheme is depicted in Figure 2. Its broad character offers opportunities for studies within the various theoretical and methodological approaches mentioned above. It should be noted that the scheme rendered in Figure 2 is "timeless." In longitudinal studies, of course, relevant parts of the scheme have to be repeated diachronically, often more than once.

The main variables contained in the boxes of Figure 2 are listed in Rosengren and Windahl (1989, p. 10). The total number of variables is very large. The variables referred to in this chapter will be presented in necessary detail when they appear in the text.

One important task of the MPP is to chart the development of the mass media use of Swedish children and adolescents as the Swedish media scene is being reshaped by the so-called new media and the development they bring about in media structure, program fare, and so on. Simple as such a descriptive task may appear, it actually raises methodological and theoretical problems that are quite intriguing. Some such problems — all of which have to do, directly and indirectly, with the notions of invariance and change — will be discussed in the next section of the chapter. The basic theoretical perspective behind that section is development theory. The two sections following thereafter will offer some specific results gained within the other two theoretical perspectives applied in the MPP: class and socialization. These two sections, however, will focus on the general theme of the chapter, which is invariance in change.

In the final section of the chapter, some general problems will be discussed, primarily the possibilities of drawing general and lasting conclusions from results such as those presented.

THEORETICAL AND METHODOLOGICAL PROBLEMS
IN LONGITUDINAL STUDIES OF MEDIA USE

In this section, I will discuss some different types of stability and change, as well as some aspects of mass media use and some methodological problems encountered when measuring these phenomena. I will then turn to stability and change as found in the amount of media use observed among children and adolescents. The empirical data provide an opportunity to illuminate further different methodological and theoretical problems in the area.

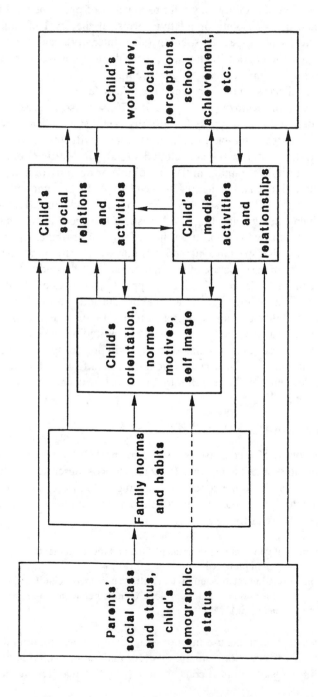

Figure 2. Conceptual scheme of the Media Panel Program. Arrows show assumed causal relationships.

The Notions of Stability and Change

The notion of stability may refer to a welter of phenomena. It may be applied, for instance, in absolute or relative terms, at the level of individual cases or aggregates, with respect to strength (size, intensity), rank, or structure, or over cases or characteristics. Technically, these distinctions would result in a typology of 24 cells, but some of these might be empty.

In their discussion of change and continuity (and continuity in change), Mortimer, Finch, and Kumka (1982, pp. 266-270; see also Johnsson-Smaragdi, 1983) are content to list four types of continuity. The list established by Mortimer et al. is no full-fledged typology, but in most cases it will suffice for our purposes, and where it does not, it will be developed slightly. In Mortimer et al.'s terminology, "level stability" is stability in the magnitude or quantity of a given phenomenon, at the individual and/or aggregate level (e.g., in the amount of TV watched). "Normative stability" is stability in individuals' ranks or differences with respect to a given phenomenon (e.g., with respect to school achievements over time). "Ipsative stability" is stability in the ordering of attributes of an individual over time (e.g., with respect to a hierarchy of interests). "Structural invariance," finally, is continuity in the structure of the phenomenon under study. An interesting aspect of structural invariance is that it may apply to processes of change.

It is not impossible to get a hunch about the actual prevalence of some of these types of stability by means of cross-sectional data. Longitudinal data are better, however, and a combined cross-sectional/longitudinal design such as the one used in the MPP is best. Later in this section, I will present some phenomena of change and invariance (and invariance in change) manifesting themselves in children's and adolescents' media use. Before doing so, however, I must clarify the notion of media use itself.

The Notion of Media Use

The notion of media use is tricky. In the MPP we have found it fruitful to conceptualize it as having four aspects (see Rosengren & Windahl, 1989, p. 18; Sonesson, 1979). In the conceptual scheme of Figure 2, all four different aspects are contained in the box named "Child's media activities and relationships." The four aspects are as follows:

- amount of consumption in terms of time and media content
- type of content preferred
- type of relation established to the content consumed (identification and the like)
- type of consumption situation (alone or together with others, primary or secondary activity, and so on)

The aspect of media use most often studied in mass communication research is amount of consumption, which in its turn may be measured in two quite different ways: in terms of habits of consumption (usually measured by means of interview

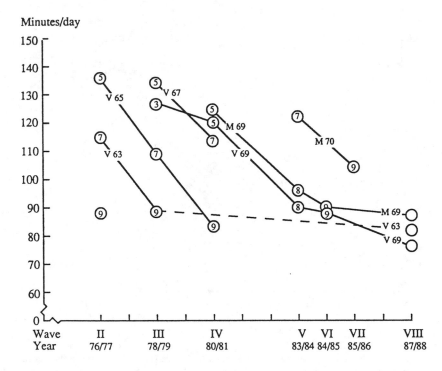

Figure 3. Amount of TV consumption in different panels and waves. Circles indicate surveys under-taken. Codes on lines show town and year of birth of given panel. Figures in circles show grade in compulsory school system. Empty circles represent panels outside the compulsory school system.

or questionnaire), and in terms of actual consumption during a given period (usually measured by means of meters or diaries, sometimes by more direct observation — for instance, televised observation — or by the so-called ESM technique, in which the individual reports his or her own activities at random intervals; Csikszentmihalyi & Kubey, 1981; Gunter & Svennevig, 1987; Lööv & Miegel, 1989; Lööv & Rosengren, 1988). The two ways of measurement tap two conceptually different phenomena that unfortunately are sometimes confused. Habits are dispositional phenomena, in principle similar to attitudes, while actual consumption is just that: actual behavior. It is well known that attitudes and actual behavior are less than perfectly correlated, and the same holds true for media habits and actual media behavior during a given period of time. Distinctions such as these should be kept in mind when comparing descriptive data from different times and countries. They are valid, of course, not only for television but also for other types of media use, such as newspaper reading or listening to music. Let's apply them to TV viewing and listening to music.

Figure 3 presents the amount of TV viewing by children, adolescents, and young adults in six panels within the MPP, covering the period 1976-1988, and ages 10/11 to 24/25. Figure 4 presents the amount of listening to popular music during the

Days/week

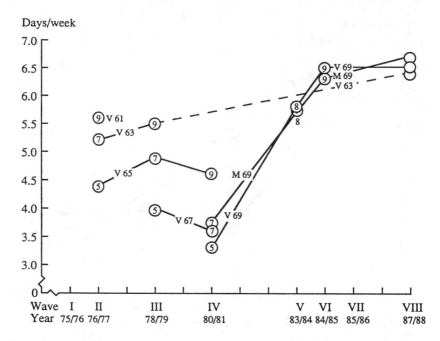

Figure 4. Amount of listening to music in different panels and waves. Circles indicate surveys undertaken. Codes on lines show town and year of birth of given panel. Figures in circles show grade in compulsory school system. Empty circles represent panels outside the compulsory school system.

same period of time, by the same panels (except panel M70). Both TV viewing and listening to music are measured as habits. Note that the units of measurement in the two figures are very different: for TV, minutes per day; for music, days per week. (For further technical details, see Rosengren & Windahl, 1989, pp. 19, 105; also see below.)

What do the two figures tell us? The first thing that strikes the eye is the high amount of variation. Take the age span 10-15, for instance (roughly corresponding to grades 3-9 of the figures). We see that during these years the habit of TV viewing is reduced from more than two hours a day to less than an hour and a half (panels V65, V69, and M69). The change in listening to music is even stronger, although in a different direction. The amount of listening to popular music is roughly doubled from grade 5 to grade 9 (panels V69 and M69). This large variation showing up within age spans that in current media statistics are often indiscriminately lumped together does provide some food for thought.

Age, Generation, and Situation

Methodologically, the variation may be understood as effects of age (maturation), generation, and situation. In this case, age effects should be theoretically interpreted primarily in terms of development theory, which is able to provide quite a convincing interpretation of the fact that in early adolescence children move away from family-oriented television to peer-oriented music (see below). Generation effects should not be expected to be very strong within the relatively short period under study (some 12 years so far). Closer analysis does reveal, however, that already within such short periods, there may be discernible differences between "generations" (Rosengren & Windahl, 1989, p. 26). According to the same analysis, on the other hand, situation effects may be quite strong, although not as strong as age effects.

A situational effect is clearly visible in Figure 4. For some unknown reason, overall listening to music is much lower in 1980/81 than in earlier and later waves. This affects the development within all four panels measured in that wave, so that they differ from the overall pattern of continually increasing listening during adolescence, a pattern most clearly discernible, perhaps, in cross-sectional analysis (see Rosengren & Windahl, 1989, p. 106). Thus panel V65 gets an A-shaped development, and the increase from grade 5 to grade 8 is much more dramatic for panels V69 and M69 than is otherwise the case. Without our combined panel/cross-sectional design, this situation effect might have been erroneously interpreted as a maturational phenomenon.

Speculating on the causes of this strong situational effect, one may think of changes in either media structure or music fashions. (For discussion of the interplay between structural change and fashion cycles, see Peterson & Berger, 1975.) We have found no structural changes relevant to the phenomenon, but are inclined to suggest that the decline in music listening may be at least partly due to the downfall of the popularity of punk reportedly taking place in Sweden around 1980.

Be that as it may, the overall methodological lesson to be drawn from Figures 3 and 4 is that when analyzing descriptive data about media use, it is preferable to have access to both narrow age categories and a combined cross-sectional/longitudinal design. Broad categories and cross-sectional or panel data alone may result in quite misleading results. In addition, it is wise to keep in mind that empirical data about the absolute level of consumption are heavily dependent on both the conceptualization and the operationalization of media use (habit versus actual consumption, type of question, and so on). Some of the data in Figure 3 offer a striking illustration of the latter truth.

It will be seen that the M70 panel in Figure 3 deviates considerably from the rest of the panels. Its values for TV consumption are some 10-20% or more above comparable values. Why is that so? Part of the difference may be ascribed to the difference in media habits between the city of Malmoe and the town of Vaxjoe. A quick comparison between panels V69 and M69, however, shows that difference to be in the order of 5-10%, while panel M70 differs much more from the rest of the panels. The difference between Malmoe and Vaxjoe, then, does not suffice as an explanation. Actually, the main reason for the difference is of quite a different character. It is methodological.

Dependence of Descriptive Results
on the Operationalization Used

As data collection within the MPP proceeded, a change in Swedish leisure habits was definitely established, a change that had really begun in the 1960s and 1970s. Due to the change from a six-day to a five-day workweek, Friday night gradually became the equivalent of the Saturday night of previous times. For children and adolescents, the real breakthrough in this respect came after 1973, when, after a fairly long transition period, all Swedish schools were closed on Saturdays.

Most members of the MPP at the time had children in school. As late as 1975, however, when the MPP started, we still must have felt that Friday was more similar to Thursday than it was to Saturday, for in the six-item battery on which we built our media consumption index, we preferred to group the days of the week that way. As always in panel studies, we then had to stick as long as possible to the original operationalizations, in order to maintain direct comparability. For the M70 panel, however — which was conceived of as a rather independent panel — we felt free to heed the change in leisure habits having meanwhile definitively taken place. Consequently, Friday, Saturday, and Sunday were treated as days of their own, while the four "real" weekdays were lumped together. The six-item battery was thus changed into an eight-item battery. As a result of all this, the level of TV consumption came to stand out as considerably higher for the V70 panel than for the others.

The short and the long of all this is a caveat with respect to figures about actual level of media consumption based on survey questions (see Comstock & Pail, 1987, p. 13). To a considerable extent, such figures are dependent on the formulation of the questions and/or the buildup of the index. In studies comparing media habits between countries, the risk of meeting with such artifactual differences should be even higher. For instance, children in the United States are reported to have a viewing time double that of Norwegian children, with Swedes coming somewhere in between (Rosengren & Windahl, 1989, p. 21). But only very careful comparisons could reveal how much of those differences is a methodological artifact and how much is due to differences in media structure and general societal structure (for instance, the difference between the commercial U.S. system of radio and TV and the Scandinavian public service type of system).

The fact that the absolute level of media consumption is a tricky thing to measure does not mean, of course, that relative levels cannot be measured. In Figures 3 and 4 the really important thing to observe is not the absolute levels but the strong dynamics observable in relative terms: the enormous increase in the importance of music during adolescence, and the corresponding reduction in the importance of television viewing. With respect to these two media, then, adolescence is really — as with respect to so many other phenomena — a period of dramatic upheaval. It should be pointed out, however, that in the midst of upheaval, there is considerable stability. Stability in consumption, however, is perhaps an even trickier concept to conceptualize and operationalize than is consumption itself. The concepts of level stability, normative stability, and structural invariance presented above will help us do just that.

Stability in Turmoil:
The Structural Invariance of Change

Looking at each one of the several MPP panels, we have already noted that the level of television use is substantially lowered during adolescence, while that of music is even more substantially heightened; strong level instability seems to be evidenced. Controlling for age by means of comparing *between* instead of *within* panels, however, we find instead strong level stability, for level differences are almost negligible within grades (excepting, of course, differences between the Malmoe and Vaxjoe panels, as well as, for reasons mentioned above, panel M70). Thus overall level stability is low; age-specific level stability is high.

One interesting aspect of *structural invariance* in the phenomena under study is illustrated by the fact that in the age span between grades 5 and 9, the rate of level change in TV consumption is almost linear, the slope being almost identical for the six panels (see Figure 3). In this connection, panel M70 is especially valuable. In spite of its somewhat different index of consumption (which gives it a higher absolute level of consumption; see above), the slope is much the same as for the five other panels. It is also interesting to note that the use of grade 8 instead of grade 7 in panels M69 and V69 only seemingly disturbs the linearity.

With respect to pop music listening, the results would have been much the same were it not for the strong situation effect observed in 1980/81. This effect, of course, has nothing to do with structural invariance per se, and it could have been controlled away, had I chosen to use the well-established control techniques developed in cohort studies for that very purpose (Glenn, 1973). It does not seem unwarranted, therefore, to conclude that for both TV viewing and music listening, our combined cross-sectional and panel design has been able to reveal considerable structural invariance, in spite of the low overall level stability observed for the same activities.

What phenomena lie behind this structural invariance? In order to provide an answer to that question we should try to find the best expression possible of the general tendency of the case of structural invariance at hand.

Behind Structural Invariance

A glimpse of the general tendency hidden behind the more or less random variations of Figures 3 and 4 may be had from Figure 5, which presents an overall picture of the dramatic changes in television viewing and listening to music that take place during teenage years (in this case, ages 12-19). The data of the figure synthesize all data presented in Figures 3 and 4, unweighted means being calculated first for Malmoe and Vaxjoe separately, then for the two towns together. In this way, cohort, situational, and geographical effects are controlled for, letting age (developmental) effects stand out as clearly as possible. The deviating values of

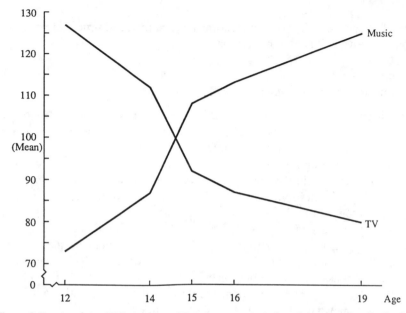

Figure 5. Development of TV viewing and listening to music during adolescence. Standardized mean during age period under study = 100.

panel M70 were not included in the calculations. (Note that the levels of the two curves are dependent on the standardization of the data. The units are no longer minutes per day and days per week, as in Figures 3 and 4, respectively. In order to facilitate comparison, the unweighted means for each of the two curves have been set at 100.)

By means of averaging and standardizing procedures the two curves have become quite smooth, calling to mind classical S curves of growth and decline, a type of curve followed by many basic developmental phenomena. The steep part of the curve in both cases falls between ages 14 and 15 — that is, toward the end of the physical growth-spurt phase that is such a visible sign of biological development in the puberty period (see Tanner, 1962). Biological development is accompanied and followed by cognitive and social development.

A basic observation of Brown, Cramond, and Wilde (1974) is that because of biological, cognitive, and social development during late childhood and early adolescence, the individual's need structure changes in that a set of intermittently felt needs ("spasmodic" needs in the expressive terminology of Brown et al.) is added to a set of more or less constant needs. These new, spasmodic needs naturally call for increased control of the adolescents' environment.

In terms of media use, all this means that mere access to a given medium is no longer enough. Adolescents feel they need to control media use themselves. Consequently, they increasingly try to escape the relatively tight control of the family, turning instead to the peer group, which provides better opportunities for satisfaction of this new set of needs. At the same time, they turn from the family medium of television to the peer medium of music, which comes to them by way of more easily controllable media (primarily radio, record player, tape recorder, and VCR).

What actually takes place is a thoroughgoing functional reorganization of adolescent media use (Brown et al., 1974). This functional reorganization is neatly illustrated by the curves of Figure 5. In the combined cross-sectional/longitudinal MPP data we find it again and again, manifesting itself as low overall level stability, high age-specific level stability, and structural invariance in the changes of media use during childhood and adolescence. Behind this structural invariance lies biological, cognitive, and social development.

How to Measure and Visualize Normative Stability

So far I have been discussing level stability and structural invariance. What about the two other types of stability mentioned above, ipsative and normative stability? To demonstrate the degree of ipsative stability (the ordering of attributes of an individual over time) would demand quite a different organization of our data than the present one. Our design does provide good information about the normative stability of the phenomena under study, however. (Normative stability, it will be remembered, is stability in individuals' ranks or differences with respect to a given phenomenon.)

Measurement of normative stability demands longitudinal analysis at the individual level: some type of correlational analysis of panel data, showing the extent to which individuals high on a given phenomenon at time 1 tend to be high also at time 2 (regardless of the amount of level stability of the phenomenon). What is the normative stability of children's and adolescents' television use, then? Before turning to an answer to the question, we should remember that "media use" is a multidimensional concept. Four important aspects of media use were listed at the beginning of this chapter (amount of consumption, content preferences, relations established to media content, situation of consumption).

Figure 6 offers a panel analysis for two of those aspects: amount of viewing (measured as habit) and relations established to television content. There are many such relations, but we chose a combination of the two most often referred to in mass communication studies: parasocial interaction (imagined interaction with personae on the screen; see Horton & Wohl, 1956; Rosengren & Windahl, 1989, pp. 38-42) and long-term and short-term identification with such personae. The combination — labeled Identification in the figure — was measured by a seven-item scale (see Rosengren & Windahl, 1989, p. 38).

The figure is the structural part of a LISREL model. The coefficients attached to the arrows are standardized beta coefficients, expressing the unique influence of one variable on another after controlling for all relevant variables in the model. (For further information about the model, see Johnsson-Smaragdi, 1983, p. 140; about the LISREL technique, see Cuttance & Ecob, 1987; Jöreskog & Sörbom, 1989; Saris & Stronkhorst, 1984).

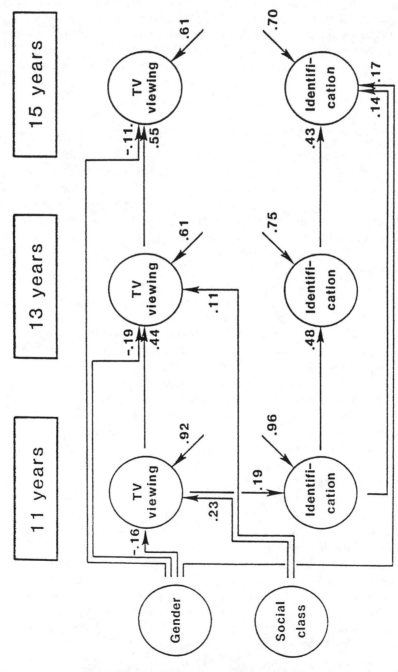

Figure 6. A LISREL model of TV viewing and TV relations, panel V65. For details of figure, see text. $N = 312$; $\chi^2 = 322$; $df = 273$; $p = .023$.

The figure may appear bewildering, but it is really quite simple. It shows, for instance, that TV viewing at the age of 13 is influenced by the viewer's gender (–.19; girls view less than boys), social class (.11; working-class kids view more than middle-class kids), and, above all, by viewing at the age of 11 (.44). In its turn, TV viewing at 13 exerts a strong influence on TV viewing at 15 (.55; note that this is after controlling for all variables in the model, for instance, gender, class, and TV viewing at 11).

Before proceeding to a short discussion of the measures of normative stability, I should note in passing that (after controlling for gender and social class) the two aspects of television used — amount of viewing and identification — do not seem to be very strongly related. That is a good argument for paying attention to more than the aspect of media use that more often than not is the only one heeded: amount of consumption. The argument is further supported by the fact that the type of media relations measured here (parasocial interaction and identification) have been shown to exert an influence of their own on other relevant phenomena, over and above the influence exerted by amount of consumption alone (see Hedinsson & Windahl, 1984; Rosengren & Windahl, 1989, p. 82; Windahl, Höjerback, & Hedinsson, 1986).

In Figure 3 we found that, as a given cohort proceeds through the turmoil of adolescence, there is a heavy reduction in TV viewing. Level stability, then, is low. In contrast, we find relatively high normative stability in Figure 6; coefficients in the .40s and .50s. (Note that the control for gender and class inherent in the model reduces the stability coefficients somewhat; part of "raw stability" depends on stable influences from gender and class.) We also note that the stability is continuously regenerated anew: The coefficients between ages 13 and 15 are about the same as those between ages 11 and 13. For comparative purposes it should be mentioned, however, that parental normative stability in TV viewing tends to be considerably higher (Johnsson-Smaragdi, 1983; Rosengren & Windahl, 1989, p. 193; see also below). Although higher than one might perhaps have expected from the low level stability, normative stability in TV viewing during adolescence, then, is not as high as during more stable periods of life, such as middle age. Presumably, that is as it should be.

In addition, it is quite interesting to note the normative stability for that other aspect of television use, relations established with the TV content consumed. Surprisingly enough, it is about as high as the normative stability for amount of viewing. Relations established to television content consumed are subtle phenomena indeed, supposedly of rather fleeting nature (identification, parasocial interaction, and the like). All the same, it is possible to measure them, it would seem, by means of conventional paper-and-pencil tests, and their normative stability is quite respectable.

The LISREL technique is a powerful instrument of analysis. In large and complex models, however, it may sometimes be difficult to get an immediate and intuitive understanding of what the many coefficients and arrows really stand for. (For instance, the size of stability coefficients depends on the degree of control for

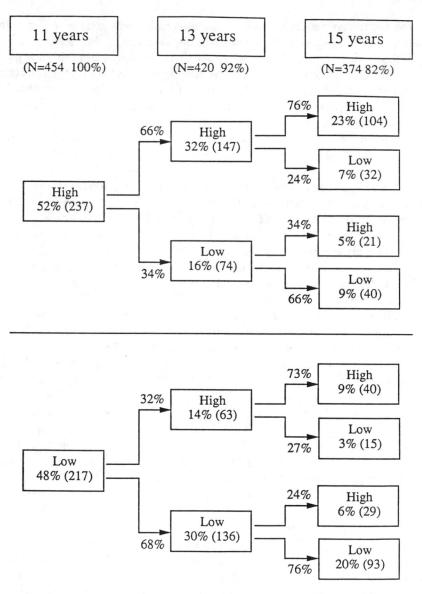

Figure 7A. Stability of TV viewing, panel V65. High and Low indicate high and low TV viewing. Percentages in squares show proportions of panels that are High and Low. Percentages on arrows show proportions of individuals in squares changing to, or staying, High or Low on TV viewing.

influence from central background variables such as gender and social class.) In order to make the presentation somewhat more concrete, Figures 7A and 7B are offered. For panels V65 and M69 (grades 5, 7, and 9 and 5, 8, and 9, respectively) they present the normative stability of amount of TV consumption in terms of what

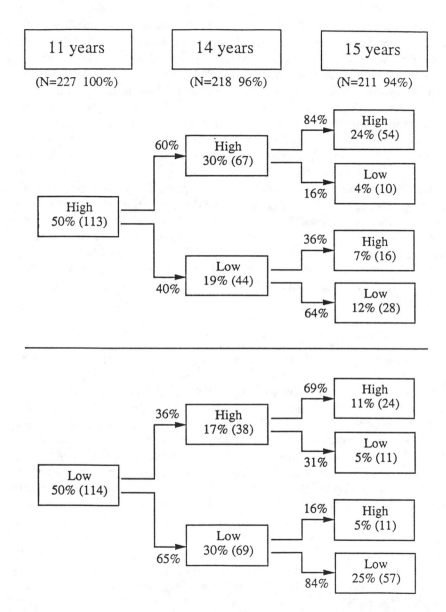

Figure 7B. Stability of TV viewing, panel M69. High and Low indicate high and low TV viewing. Percentages in squares show proportions of panels that are High and Low. Percentages on arrows show proportions of individuals in squares changing to, or staying, High or Low on TV viewing.

might be called "transition probabilities": the percentages among those high and low on TV consumption in one wave who in the next wave are high and low (*high* and *low* being defined by means of the overall median for each age category).

The transition probabilities may be said to correspond to the stability coefficients of the LISREL model. It should be noted, however, that the latter are controlled for gender and social class, something that the former are not. To complicate matters further, the transition probabilities are affected by the fact that some categories become gradually more homogeneous and others become less so. Also, in the LISREL model, measurement errors are taken care of by the outer, measurement model (not rendered here), while they cannot be separated from the transition probabilities. "True" normative stability, then, is somewhat higher than is suggested by Figures 7A and 7B. Part of that stability, on the other hand, is due to influence from various background variables.

Normative stability expressed as transition probabilities seems to be quite high. In the "pure categories" of the third waves we find proportions around 80%; in the "impure categories," around 70%. If an adolescent is watching much television one year, chances are high, then, that two years later he or she will be comparatively high, too—high, that is, at the lower level prevailing at that age. In some 20% to 30% of the cases, however, we find change from high to low and vice versa. Thus high normative stability should not be mistaken for absolute absence of individual change.

The Structural Invariance of Normative Stability

The transition probabilities of Figures 7A and 7B are interesting enough in their own right, but the figures have more to offer as well. By comparing the values of Figures 7A and 7B, we may get a notion of what might be called — applying a novel combination of the terms used by Mortimer et al. (1982) — the "structural invariance of normative stability." The similarity between the transition probabilities of the two figures is indeed striking, and the small differences between the two figures tend to agree with the fact that the distances between the waves are somewhat different in the two panels. (In Figure 7A, the first and the second waves are closer to each other; in Figure 7B, the second and the third waves are close.) The close similarity suggests that the crude figures do indeed reveal something essential and enduring. The degree of normative stability of TV viewing seems to be very stable over at least short periods of time: two to four years or so. It is indeed tempting to regard it as a structural feature of television viewing among adolescents and adults alike. Future comparisons between transition probabilities for parental TV viewing in different cohorts will likely add to our knowledge of the structural invariance of normative stability.

Micro Stability in Spite of Macro Change

Level stability in individual media use is especially interesting in periods when media structure itself is changing. What happens to level stability at the micro level when at the macro level there are substantial structural changes? In this connection it may be rewarding to take a look at that new medium entering the Swedish media scene while the Media Panels were being observed: the VCR.

The VCR came to Sweden in the early 1980s. In 1980, 3% of households had access to VCRs; in 1985, 23%; and in 1988, 41% (Alvarado, 1988; Gahlin & Nordström, 1988; Roe, 1988; von Feilitzen, Filipson, Rydin, & Schyller, 1989; see Rosengren & Windahl, 1989, p. 5). There is considerable social and geographical variation behind these overall figures, however. In 1988, for instance, the figure was 60% among 14-year-olds.

The rapid and uneven diffusion process that followed the introduction of VCRs actually released something of a moral panic in Sweden, characterized by genuine concern for children and adolescents, and, of course, also by strong group and party interests (Roe, 1985). Several government committees were looking into the new medium, which, in some circles, was considered a threat to the public service monopoly of Swedish Radio and Television. At the time of this writing, however, it may be said that by and large this moral panic over VCR use has abated. In Sweden, just as in the United States and many other countries, video viewing has found its niche somewhere between cinema and traditional television.

We first measured VCR use among our panels in 1980/81 (Rosengren & Windahl, 1989, p. 49). In 1984/85, VCR viewing had become so widespread that it was meaningful to use the same type of index as the one used for TV viewing (regarded as habit). In grade 9, average viewing time was then 2.3 hours per week in the town of Vaxjoe, and 3.1 in the city of Malmoe. Three years later, it was 3.8 and 5.0 hours per week, respectively, for the same individuals (who by then were 19 years old). In an older panel, V63 (whose members were by then 25), it was considerably lower in the same wave: 2.0 hours per week (Jarlbro et al., 1989; Sonesson & Höjerback, 1989).

VCR use, of course, does not necessarily imply VCR ownership. Nonowners often rent "boxes" and also view together with owner friends. Actually, amount of viewing was only some 10-20% higher among owners than among nonowners. Nevertheless, the better part of the increase in average amount of video viewing must have been due mainly to the increase in VCR ownership.

How did the increase in video viewing affect more traditional broadcast and cable TV viewing? Following in Figure 3 the values for TV viewing in grade 9 of the different panels from 1976/77 to 1985/86, we find no indication that the introduction of VCRs should in any considerable way have changed the overall level of regular TV viewing for this age bracket (see Sonesson & Höjerback, 1989). The levels of the curves for adolescent broadcast and cable TV viewing were basically the same in the mid-1980s as in the late 1970s. They were not changed by the introduction of VCR use. In this case, then, age-specific level stability at the micro level seems to have been more or less unaffected by structural change at the macro level.

Just as with TV viewing, of course, figures about the absolute level of video viewing are heavily dependent on conceptualization and operationalization. However, since we measured video and regular TV viewing by the same type of index, they should be roughly comparable. Regular TV viewing is still overwhelmingly larger than video viewing.

All the same, it is quite possible that VCR use may have increased the time spent before the TV screen considerably for a small minority. Such an increase has probably taken place primarily among those who were already high on television viewing. Zero-order correlations between television and videocassette viewing are moderate to strong and, in addition, we know from other MPP data that, even years before their VCR purchases, TV viewing is considerably higher among families who later become VCR owners than among other families (see Sonesson, 1989; Sonesson & Höjerback, 1989). The new medium of the VCR thus seems to have been grafted onto already existing media habits, something that no doubt is part of the explanation behind its rapid diffusion.

While the introduction of the VCR did not change the amount of traditional TV viewing very much, it did bring some changes to moviegoing. Already as a consequence of the introduction of broadcast TV in the late 1950s, moviegoing in Sweden was reduced by no less than 75% (Gahlin & Wigren, 1989). Once the initial investment was made, the on-tap medium of broadcast television proved more attractive than the movies. Young people, however, were foremost among those who stayed with moviegoing; presumably the movies offered them more choice and freedom from family control than did TV.

However, the VCR offered even more possibilities for control of time and place as well as content consumed than did broadcast TV, and moviegoing was thus further reduced. This time the reduction hit young people also. Looking at 15- to 16-year-old boys and girls in 1976, 1980, 1985, and 1986 (grade 9, panels V61, V65, V69; M69, M70), Sonesson and Höjerback (1989) found that during this decade moviegoing in this specific age group was reduced by no less than two-thirds. A considerable portion of this reduction should no doubt be ascribed to the advent of the VCR. In this case, then, macro change had effects on micro, age-specific level stability. (With respect to book reading, however, no similar changes were found.)

So far, we have been dealing with the question of how the introduction of the VCR affected level stability in individual use of old media such as broadcast and cable TV, cinema, and books. Turning now to the new medium itself, what stability can we find during the process of its introduction? Video transition probabilities corresponding to those visualized in Figures 7A and 7B tell us that only four or five years after its introduction, the new medium was able to demonstrate a normative stability only slightly lower than that of television (calculated for panels M69, V69). For video and television alike, then, the structural invariance of normative stability seems to be considerable among young people, in spite of the low overall level stability of television and video viewing found in this population category.

In this section we have been looking at invariance and change in the media use of some Swedish children and adolescents, as they grew from children to adolescents, at the same time the surrounding media structure was undergoing considerable change. In the next section I present a look at class-related differences in children's and adolescents' mass media use. By asking to what extent such class differences are stable over time, I will gradually return to the continuing theme of invariance and change.

A CLASS PERSPECTIVE

Society is stratified along a number of basic dimensions, with age, gender, and social class being, perhaps, the three most important ones. Two values on each of these three dimensions create eight different social worlds; three values on age and class, eighteen. That is more worlds than most students of mass media use care to include in their analyses. The problem is further complicated by the fact that social class is no unidimensional concept, the distinction between a Marxian notion of class and a Weberian notion of status being the first one to come to mind in this connection. In addition, temporal distinctions should be made among class of origin, class of context, and class of destination: where you come from, where you stand, and where you are going (Rosengren & Windahl, 1989, p. 114). (*Mutatis mutandis*, this distinction, of course, might be applied equally well to status.)

The notions of social class and status are relevant to communication studies for the simple reason that social class exerts an almost ubiquitous influence on a number of communication processes — for instance, on mass media use. Regardless of what conceptualization and operationalization of the notions of class and status one happens to prefer, two basic problems turn up when relating class or status to media use: What type of relationship do we find? How stable is that relationship? The latter question, of course, has a bearing on the general theme of this chapter: change and invariance. When looking at the stability of a given relationship between two variables, we are looking at what Mortimer et al. (1982) call "structural invariance."

The Media Panel Program offers an opportunity to approach these problems in empirical terms (Rosengren & Windahl, 1989, pp. 111-157). Below, I begin with a section providing some information about our way of operationalizing the central concepts of the problem at hand. Then I turn to the type of relationship existing between class and status on the one hand and mass media use on the other. In a later section I ask whether that influence is stable during childhood and adolescence. Finally, I approach the question of whether the relationship between class and media use may be affected by ongoing changes in the media structure.

Class and Status Measured

In the MPP, class of origin has been measured as a composite index of parents' occupation (based on the semiofficial classification systems used in Sweden; Rosengren & Windahl, 1989, pp. 23, 125). Class of destination has been measured as the occupational expectations of the children and adolescents under study; class of context, as the proportion of children of working- or middle-class origin in a given school class.

Status has been measured by means of a composite index of parents' education, roughly corresponding to the number of years of schooling. (Education has sometimes been used also as an indicator of "cultural capital," a metaphorical concept of some heuristic value; see Bourdieu, 1984; Rosengren & Windahl, 1989, p. 113.)

In terms of the conceptual scheme presented in Figure 2, status and class of origin are located in the far left-hand box of the figure; class of context is located in the box labeled "Child's social relations"; and class of destination is in the far right-hand box of the figure.

Class and Media Use: What Type of Relationship?

Although some dissenting voices have been heard (for instance, Morley, 1980; Piepe et al., 1975), one usually assumes and finds a linear relationship between, say, amount of TV viewing and social class or status. Looking more closely at the relationship, however, we found that curvilinear class relationships do turn up again and again in the MPP data. Status relationships, on the other hand, tend to be linear at the level of zero-order correlations (Höjerback, 1986; Roe, 1983; Rosengren & Windahl, 1989, p. 129).

In addition, we found intricate interaction effects between class (occupation) and status (education), effects that in the last analysis result in very strong differences in TV viewing among various class/status categories. For instance, even in the same grade, kids having high-class/low-status background watched an hour or more of television a day than did kids having high-class/high-status background (Rosengren & Windahl, 1989, p. 130). However, combining not class and status, but two different types of social class — namely, class of origin and class of context — we see that the pattern becomes somewhat more regular.

According to prevailing ideology, Swedish schools should be socially integrated. It is well known, however, that there is still considerable school segregation in Sweden (Arnman & Jönsson, 1983), although no schools are completely segregated. Consequently, many children belong to school classes dominated by children from a social class different from their own. This makes it possible to study the joint and separate influence of class of origin and class of context on the amount of adolescents' TV viewing. In Figure 8, this influence is illustrated for panel V65, grade 9.

As before, class of origin is represented by the index of combined parental social class. *Class of context* refers to the social composition of the school class in which the adolescent spends some 30 hours a week. As it turns out, both types of class have a curvilinear influence, and the combined result of the two curvilinearities stands out rather strikingly in the figure. There are nine columns, and the middle column is the highest of them all, representing almost five hours a week more of TV viewing than does the lowest column.

Each of the various combinations of class of origin and class of context represents interesting social psychological reactions of profilation and accommodation (among, say, working-class students in a middle-class context, or vice

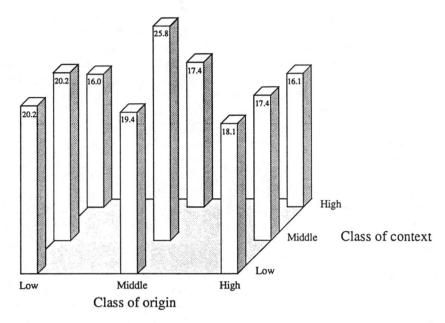

Figure 8. Class of origin, class of context, and TV viewing. For details of figure, see text.

versa) well worth closer study (Rosengren & Windahl, 1989, p. 144). The main message of the figure, however, is quite simple. Because of the curvilinear relationships between each of the two types of class and TV viewing, the combination of an origin in the middle strata of society and a class context dominated by the middle strata constitutes the heartland of television viewing. (The term *middle strata* of course, does not denote the same phenomena as the term *middle class*, used in other parts of this presentation.)

Interesting as the curvilinearity may be in itself, it also presents a technical problem, because many types of conventional statistical analysis assume linear relationships. When suspecting curvilinearity, it is wise, therefore, to apply more than one type of statistical analysis to the same problem. In the MPP we have combined, for instance, MCA analysis (giving information about curvilinearity) with techniques building on the assumption of linearity, such as, say, LISREL (see Rosengren & Windahl, 1989, p. 131).

Social Class and TV Use: Diminishing Influence?

So far I have been discussing the first of the two basic problems about social class and media use mentioned above: What type of relationship do we find? Let us now turn to the second question: How stable is that relationship? In this case we are dealing with the stability of a relationship between at least two variables — that is, in the terms of Mortimer et al. (1982) referred to above, structural invariance.

More precisely, there are two main ways in which the relationship between social class and media use may be said to be invariant or stable over time: within and between cohorts. In addition, we may be talking about stability measured cross-sectionally and longitudinally. Finally, we have the two basic distinctions between class and status on the one hand and, on the other, class of origin, context, and destination. Space permits only some illustrations of the many combinations available.

The simplest way to look empirically at the problem of diminishing or increasing influence from social class on the use of mass media is to produce some cross-sectional coefficients of association between, say, class of origin and TV consumption among different age categories. At the time of this writing, the organization of the data admitted the production of 17 MCA beta coefficients (controlling for gender), covering ages 10 to 25 and distributed within and between five different panels. The mean of those coefficients was .20, the maximum .32 and the minimum .03 (an outlier). There was no linear tendency of increasing or decreasing strength with increasing age, but ages 16 and 19 were generally low (.17 and .14, respectively). Within the period covered so far (about a dozen years), there was no discernible trend of weakening relationship between class and media use, a finding observed in other contexts and fitting in well with overall societal trends otherwise observed (e.g., Comstock & Pail, 1987, p. 6).

The tentative conclusion to be drawn from this heterogeneous set of coefficients is that in childhood, adolescence, and early adulthood, TV use may be an activity far too contingent on all sorts of age, generational, situational, and other, more or less random effects to show any very stable trend in first-order or second-order relationship to class of origin — a conclusion that does throw some light on the highly differing results about the relationship between class and mass media use by children and adolescents appearing in the literature.

The situation is similar to the one we confronted when trying to tease out the influence of development on the use of television and music. In that situation we arrived at a meaningful result by means of pooling large amounts of data (see Figure 5). This time we will choose a radically different strategy. Rather than averaging for a small number of variables over many points of observation, we will look closely at the intricate interplay of several variables. This is best done by means of the LISREL technique.

In Figure 6, the influence of gender and social class on amount of TV consumption and TV relations in grades 5, 7, and 9 (panel V65) is visualized in a LISREL model. Let's return to it for a while. To begin with, note that there is no direct class influence on TV relations (but some from gender). Presumably, the TV relations under study (parasocial interaction and identification with personae on the screen) have more to do with personality characteristics than with position in a social structure. It will be seen however, that according to this model, social class exerts a direct influence on amount of viewing in both grades 5 and 7, but none in grade

9. But absence of a direct effect does not mean absence of an indirect one, of course. Indirect effects may be obtained by multiplying direct effects over paths; total effects, by summing all direct and indirect effects. The total effect of social class on amount of viewing is .23 in grade 5, .21 in grade 7, and .12 in grade 9 (see Johnsson-Smaragdi, 1983, p. 143). According to the model, then, class influence is being reduced during adolescence.

Before jumping to any conclusions, however, we must mention that the reduced influence may be due to the simple fact that in the model, social class was measured in grade 5 only. Although the stability of social class is very high, we must suppose some attenuation due to decreasing relevance of the early measurement of class in grade 5. To heed this objection, we should have inserted social class at each one of the three points of measurement, looking at the unique influence of class at each of these three points. At present we have no such model available.

Using MCA analysis, however, we did measure (for panel V69 in grade 9) the influence of class on TV use, controlling for class as measured in grade 5 (Rosengren & Windahl, 1989, p. 134). The unique influence in grade 9 was .17, as compared with the total influence of .26 in grade 5. (At the first point of measurement — in this case, grade 5 — we cannot, of course, distinguish between direct and indirect influence.) Part of the total influence manifesting itself in grade 5 of the model in reality must have been exerted at a much earlier point in time. We thus draw the tentative conclusion that what reduction there may be during adolescence in the unique influence of class of origin on amount of TV viewing probably is not all that strong. (In addition, it should be borne in mind that we have not yet touched the question of whether in its turn the reduction, be it weak or strong, is invariant over cohorts; see below.)

Class, Gender, and Media Use: Structural Change

So far, I have been dealing primarily with the relationship between class and amount of TV consumption. Turning now to the relationship between class and use of other media as well, I start by mentioning that at least for our much-analyzed panel V65 it has been found again and again that the influence of class of origin on various aspects of media use (and also activities related to media use) is much stronger for girls than for boys. That is, class of origin and gender interact so that class has differential effects on media use among the two genders (Flodin, 1986; Johnsson-Smaragdi, 1983; Roe, 1983; Rosengren & Windahl, 1989, p. 127). Similarly but conversely, mass media use has also been found to have differential effects among different social classes (Rosengren & Windahl, 1989, p. 154). The detailed character of such structural relationships, as well as their potential invariance over time, remains to be studied, however. There is no reason to expect that the entrance upon the Swedish media scene of the so-called new media — particularly, perhaps, the VCR — should not have affected the invariance of such complex relationships.

A first grasp of these relationships may be had from simply comparing the zero-order correlations (cross-sectional and longitudinal) between amount of use of a number of different mass media for boys and girls from different social classes. A number of such correlations for working-class boys and middle-class girls in grades 5, 7, and 9 of panel V65 are graphically presented in Figures 9A and 9B: all positive correlations larger than .30, and all three negative correlations found (see Rosengren & Windahl, 1989, p. 123). The contrasts between the two categories are striking. (Middle-class boys and working-class girls fell in between.)

The conclusion to be drawn is that the media habits of working-class boys and middle-class girls are differentially structured to a very high degree. At least that was the case in our panel V65. Later MPP panels provide an opportunity to take a look at the invariance of this differential degree of structuring. Figures 10A and 10B offer parallel data from panel M69, representing a cohort that is four years younger and from another town.

On the face of it, it would seem that the contrast between the two categories showing up for panel V65 is totally lacking in panel M69: the number of significant correlations is exactly the same (10) for working-class boys and middle-class girls. (The number of significant correlations should be expected to be lower in Figures 10A and 10B than in Figures 9A and 9B, since N is much lower—some 50 individuals rather than some 100; see Figure 1.) Looking more closely at Figures 10A and 10B, however, we do find a difference between the two categories. For working-class boys, 7 of the 10 arrows have to do with the VCR; for middle-class girls, only 4. Without the VCR, then, middle-class girls would have double the number of positive correlations of the working-class boys. Similar results have been found for panel M70, and also — although admittedly less clear-cut ones — for panel V69. (It should be mentioned that in Vaxjoe, the site of that panel, the VCR penetration was not at all as strong as in Malmoe.)

Now, how can we explain this difference between later and earlier cohorts? And what does the original difference found for panel V65 between working-class boys and middle-class girls really mean, in the first place?

Direct parental control of adolescents' media use seems to be rather weak, especially for boys (Rosengren & Windahl, 1989, p. 43). At the same time, a number of MPP results rather convincingly demonstrate that parents' attitudes toward TV do influence the media behavior of their children (see Jönsson, 1986; Sonesson, 1979, 1989). Presumably, then, there is such control, and it seems to be indirect rather than direct.

Against this background, a reasonable interpretation of the original difference might be that, all in all, working-class boys probably are under looser parental control with respect to their overall media use than are middle-class girls. Consequently, their media habits should become much less structured. At least that was the case for panel V65. For somewhat later cohorts—for instance, M69, V69, and M70—something seems to have happened that started to alter this structural difference gradually. What happened?

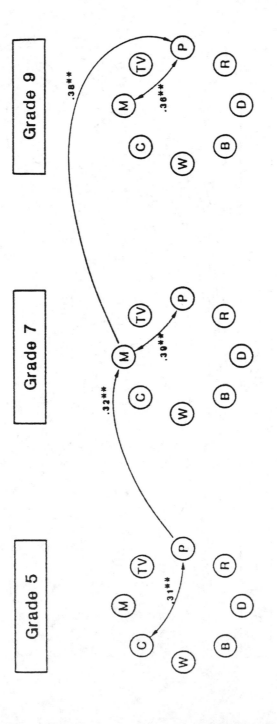

Figure 9A. Pattern of media use, working-class boys, panel V65. Coefficients on arrows include all negative correlation coefficients and all positive correlation coefficients .30 and higher. M = movies, TV = TV viewing, P = pop, R = radio, D = dailies, B = books, W = weeklies, C = comics. $r \geq 30$.

75

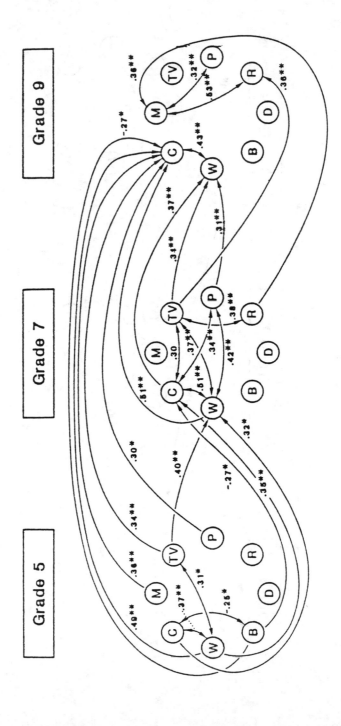

Figure 9B. Pattern of media use, middle-class girls, panel V65. Coefficients on arrows include all negative correlation coefficients and all positive correlation coefficients .30 and higher. M = movies, TV = TV viewing, P = pop, R = radio, D = dailies, B = books, W = weeklies, C = comics. $r \geq 30$; $r \leq -.25$.

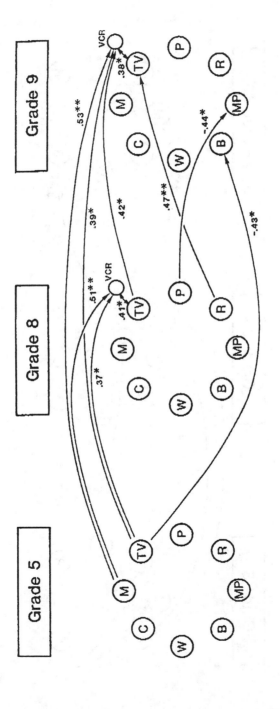

Figure 10A. Pattern of media use, working-class boys, panel M69. Coefficients on arrows include all negative correlation coefficients and all positive correlation coefficients .30 and higher. M = movies, TV = TV viewing, P = pop, R = radio, MP = morning paper, W = weeklies, C = comics. $p < .05$.

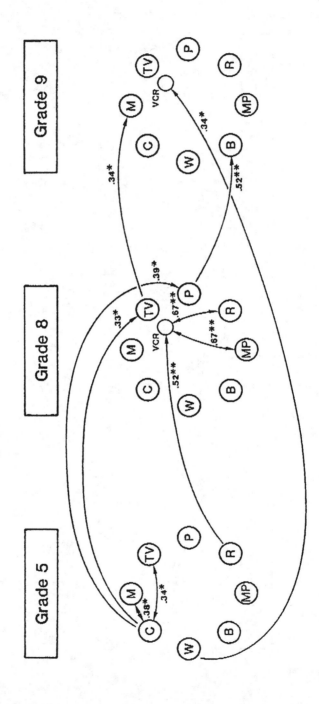

Figure 10B. Pattern of media use, middle-class girls, panel M69. Coefficients on arrows include all negative correlation coefficients and all positive correlation coefficients .30 and higher. M = movies, TV = TV viewing, P = pop, R = radio, MP = morning paper, B = books, W = weeklies, C = comics. $p < .05$.

New Medium: Emerging Functional Reorganization?

One thing that happened was that the VCR entered the scene. It is a medium easy to control for those who are sometimes left to take care of themselves (and/or believe they are able to do so) — for instance, working-class boys. They seem to have seized the opportunity that turned up, and, as a consequence, their media habits may now be in a process of getting the structure they were formerly lacking. In qualitative terms (structure in media habits) they may thus be approaching middle-class girls. (For quantitative comparisons of VCR use, see Höjerback, 1986; Johnsson-Smaragdi & Roe, 1986; Sonesson & Höjerback, 1989.)

To conclude: In a previous section we saw that the introduction of the VCR did not substantially affect the level of TV viewing (or, for that matter, age-related changes in that level). Level stability was left unchanged, and so was its structural invariance. The introduction of the VCR may have had other and more subtle effects, however. Figures 9A and 9B and 10A and 10B seem to provide a snapshot of an ongoing functional reorganization of adolescent media habits, a reorganization caused not by biological, cognitive, and social development (see above) but possibly by changes in the media structure, interacting with an already existing class/gender structure. The structural invariance of the relationships among class, gender, and media use may not have withstood the introduction of the VCR. In the long run, one might speculate, such a reorganization may even have some reverberations on that class/gender/media-use structure itself, for mass media are powerful — although sometimes rather haphazard — agents of socialization.

A SOCIALIZATION PERSPECTIVE

Socialization is the process by means of which societal culture is communicated between generations. It is also the process by means of which the delicate balance between continuity and change is upheld in society. In its turn, the process of socialization itself shows both continuity and change, and also continuity in change: structural invariance. In this section I shall discuss the process of socialization from the perspective of structural invariance. Before doing so, however, I must present some basic concepts related to socialization and socialization research.

Agents of Socialization

In modern societies, there are eight main types of socializing agents: the family, peer groups, work groups, schools, churches, judicatures, various formal organizations, and the mass media. The process of socialization always implies close interaction, not only between these agents of socialization and the individual socialized, but also among the agents of socialization themselves.

The socialization agents vary considerably with respect to both the form and content of the socialization processes in which they engage. Some focus on abstract, formal culture; others, on lived culture. Some proceed quite systematically and purposively; others act almost without knowing it themselves (something that does not necessarily make them less important as agents of socialization, of course). As agents of socialization the mass media deal with both abstract, formal culture and lived culture. They sometimes act quite purposefully as agents of socialization, and sometimes without any socializing purpose at all. For more than a century, and especially during the last few decades, their importance as agents of socialization has been constantly on the increase.

Perspectives in Socialization Research

In socialization research, two main societal perspectives and two main perspectives on the human individual have been prevalent. Society has been regarded from a perspective of consensus or conflict; the human individual, as an active subject or a passive object. The four combinations of these twin pairs of perspectives result in four main traditions of socialization research, neatly corresponding to a well-known typology for schools of sociology originally presented by Burrell and Morgan (1979) and related to mass communication research by Rosengren (1983, 1989a).

In the Media Panel Program, we believe that all societies are characterized by both consensus and conflict, and we also believe that all individuals are both subjects and objects. Indeed, some of the most interesting problems in connection with socialization by means of mass communication arise only when the different perspectives are combined. How is consensus arrived at in spite of conflict? How is conflict made palpable in spite of superficial consensus? How may seemingly passive objects of vile oppression turn into willing and acting subjects? Obviously, such grand questions cannot all be answered within one single research program. But that is no reason not to try to keep the questions alive also when dealing with less grandiose phenomena related to socialization. That is what we have tried to do in the MPP.

There is always interaction among all eight main types of socialization agents. Sometimes this interaction turns into more or less conscious, more or less open competition (for instance, between school and family, or between school and mass media). Parents sometimes denounce teachers on more or less specific points. Teachers sometimes denounce mass media content across the board, trying to substitute their own messages for those of the mass media. In such cases, agents of socialization (or their representatives) sometimes regard the individuals socialized as passive recipients, vessels to be filled to the brim with this or that type of knowledge, this or that skill, this or that view on society and the world at large. But children and adolescents certainly are not passive vessels. On the contrary, in cases of competition between different agents of socialization about domination over the supposedly passive objects of socialization, they are most adept at turning one agent against the other, to their own advantage — at least in the short run. In the long run, of course, the end result may be quite different.

Socialization Studies within the MPP

Within the MPP, the relations between the individual socialized and the four socializing agents of family, school, peer group, and the mass media have been studied in detail by means of a great number of MCA analyses, LISREL, and PLS models. Such analyses sometimes offer graphic illustrations of the abstract argumentation of socialization theory summarized above. Structural models offer especially good opportunities to combine the deterministic, causal perspective naturally prevalent when the individual is regarded as a passive object of strong internal and external forces with the voluntaristic, finalistic perspective naturally prevalent when he or she is regarded as a willing and acting subject. In terms of mass communication research they offer opportunities to combine the two sometimes antagonistic research traditions of effects research and uses and gratifications research (Bryant & Zillmann, 1986; Rosengren et al., 1985).

The analyses and models produced within the MPP cover a wide array of socialization phenomena, including the following:

(1) the interplay between social class and family communication climate in shaping the use made of TV by children and adolescents (Jarlbro, 1986, 1988)
(2) the relations among school, family, peer group, and popular music, in which school grades seem to influence music preferences rather than the other way around (Roe, 1983)
(3) the (unexpectedly small) role of TV in shaping both vertical and horizontal dimensions of adolescents' work expectations (Flodin, 1986)
(4) the interplay among family, school, and television in influencing school achievement, constituting "good spirals" and "bad spirals" (Jönsson, 1986)
(5) the interaction over time of TV use and personal characteristics such as aggressiveness, anxiety, and lack of concentration, finally resulting in nonnegligible aggressiveness by a small group of boys and girls (Sonesson, 1989)

Among themselves, these analyses cover the four basic value orientations — instrumental, expressive, cognitive, and moral — that may be said to define the societal culture created, stored, reshaped, and transmitted by the various agents of socialization (Rosengren, 1985, 1988). Space does not permit any detailed presentation of all these results. I shall concentrate, therefore, on two of the most powerful agents of socialization: TV and the family.

Stability in Family Communication Patterns

Logically, before asking questions about the ways and means by which mass media act as agents of socialization for our children and adolescents, one should ask how children and adolescents come to use the media, and how that use is shaped by other agents of socialization. An obvious answer to questions such as these is that — in this case as in so many others — the family, that primordial agent of socialization, acts as the prime mover.

In an oft-quoted chapter, McLeod and Brown (1976) discuss three modes in which socialization may take place: modeling, reinforcement, and interaction. As socializing agents, all families draw on all three of these modes. Yet we know that the pattern of socialization may be radically different in different families. The explanation most often used for this differentiation, of course, is social class. Another reason is that — over and above class differences — differentiation in the general family communication pattern is quite considerable. This fact, in its turn, has important consequences for the role played by other agents of socialization, not least for the role of TV.

In the first waves of the MPP we measured the parents of our children and adolescents by means of the well-known scale for family communication patterns developed by Chaffee, McLeod, and their associates. Built on two basic, dichotomized dimensions, "socio-orientation" and "concept orientation," the scale classifies families into four different types of communication patterns (Chaffee, McLeod, & Atkin, 1971; Tims & Masland, 1985). In a number of quantitative analyses, Jarlbro (1988) has shown the importance of family communication patterns for the use and effects of television, demonstrating that under certain conditions the family communication pattern may actually neutralize the influence of social class. (For instance, working-class kids tend to be high on TV use, but this does not apply to the same extent for kids from strongly and purely concept-oriented families.) Jarlbro thus provides some information about the structural invariance over space (United States-Sweden) of the relationship between family communication patterns and mass media use. She has also done more than that, however.

Five years after the latest measurements of panel V65, Jarlbro returned to some of those adolescents (who by then had become young adults, 20 years old) and carried out long informal interviews with them about their childhoods, their present situations, and their plans for the future (Jarlbro, 1986, 1988). After having carried out some preliminary interviews, Jarlbro, using a double-blind test without any error, located 16 out of 16 young adults into the correct cells of the fourfold family communication pattern typology (the cells to which their families had been shown to belong five years earlier, by means of the formalized quantitative Likert scale responded to by the parents in a mail survey). In the terms of Mortimer et al. (1982), Jarlbro convincingly demonstrated normative stability with respect to a two-dimensional typology. Formalized, quantitative techniques and informal, qualitative techniques thus proved able to bridge a gap stretching over five years and between two generations. This is a result that has some general methodological implications with respect to the old debate between proponents of quantitative and qualitative methods (a debate, incidentally, that to no small extent could be characterized as a pseudodebate; see Rosengren, 1989a).

While Jarlbro's results are impressive, they call for further theoretical elaboration and specifications by means of more powerful techniques of analysis, such as structural modeling. It will be an important task in the continued work within the MPP to explicate these and other results in terms of structural models. In this way we will be able to provide more explicit theories and more precise assessments of the degree of stability of that important phenomenon, the family communication climate, and its effects on mass media use. We will then know whether the relations between family communication patterns and mass media use — so important for the general socialization of children and adolescents — are structurally invariant not only over space, but also over time.

The Invariance of Causal Structures

At present we do not have available any longitudinal structural models of the role played by the family communication climate in the socialization process. (For a tentative cross-sectional model, see, however, Hedinsson, 1981.) Suppose we had. What then?

The logical next step would then be to look into the stability of such models between different panels and cohorts. The important question will thus become: How stable is a longitudinal LISREL model? To reformulate the question in the terms used by Mortimer et al. (1982): What is the structural invariance of longitudinal causal structures as mapped by means of a LISREL model? In yet other words: How generally valid are our theories?

In some disciplines and research traditions — for instance, in the sociology of work and class — series of increasingly better structural models are accumulating as researchers build upon and gradually refine each other's models, as well as the conceptualizations and operationalizations behind them. Because of the cost in time and money, however, only a few models have been replicated within precisely the same theoretical, methodological, and empirical surroundings. Actually, we have been able to find only one such replication with at least some relation to substantive problems dealt with in the MPP: two cross-sectional LISREL models of schooling in the first grade, 10 years apart (Entwisle, Alexander, Cadigan, & Pallas, 1986).

Structural models built on panel data are rarer than cross-sectional models. A number of longitudinal models have been presented in different communication studies, two well-known examples being those of Milawsky et al. (1982) and Huesman and Eron (1986). As for replications of longitudinal models, so far we have been unable to find even one. The Media Panel Program, however, with its store of longitudinal models already built and under construction, offers rich potential for such replications (e.g., Johnsson-Smaragdi, 1983; Roe, 1983; Rosengren & Windahl, 1989). As a matter of fact, two such replicative longitudinal models have already been presented in a recent report from the program (Johnsson-Smaragdi & Höjerback, 1989), and more are on their way (Johnsson-Smaragdi, in press).

Figures 11A and 11B show two different LISREL models of the interplay between the individual socialized and two agents of socialization, family and television, within the structural framework established by gender and social class (the latter variable in both cases being measured — for technical reasons — by maternal occupation; see Johnsson-Smaragdi & Höjerback, 1989). More specific-

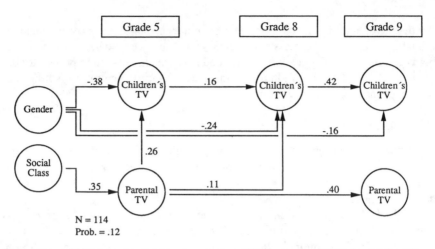

Figure 11A. A LISREL model of children's and parents' TV viewing, panel V69. For details of figure, see text.

ally, for two Malmoe and Vaxjoe panels (M69 and V69) the two models show how and to what extent the amounts of children's and parents' TV consumption are mutually influential.

The two models are replications of a model presented in Johnsson-Smaragdi (1983, p. 161), building on data from panel M65. The interested reader may compare the original model with the two replications, finding basic structural similarities. For the sake of simplicity, however, we restrict our discussion to the two models presented here.

The structures of the two models are by no means identical, but there are considerable similarities. Both similarities and dissimilarities have their interest. In both models, gender exerts a considerable influence on children's viewing, and so does social class — on children's and parents' TV viewing alike. In panel V69, there is a direct, unique influence from gender in all three waves, while in M69, that influence is found only in the first two waves. In panel V69, the influence from social class on children's TV viewing is only indirect (relayed by the parental TV habits), while in M69 there is also a direct influence. In addition to such qualitative differences, there are also quantitative differences in the size of coefficients expressing the strength of the causal influence.

The main difference between the two models, however, lies in the relationships between children's and parents' viewing in grade 9. In both panels, there is considerable influence from parental viewing to children's viewing in grades 5 and 8 (although in the Malmoe panel that influence is direct only in grade 5). In the Malmoe panel, however, there is also a significant causal influence on parental viewing from children's viewing in grade 9. In the Vaxjoe panel there is no such thing.

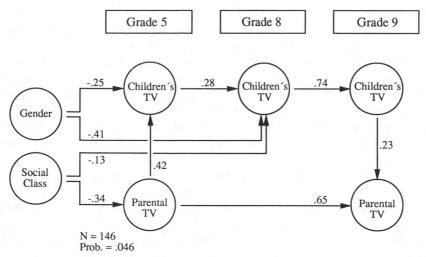

Figure 11B. A LISREL model of children's and parents' TV viewing, panel M69. For details of figure, see text. $N = 146$; $p = .046$.

Parental influence on children's viewing has been much discussed. It may be interpreted, for instance, in terms of reinforcement, modeling, and interaction. Influence in the other direction has been less discussed, but the very interesting possibility of "reversed modeling" has been recognized, and the phenomenon has been empirically observed (Johnsson-Smaragdi, 1983, pp. 154ff.; Rosengren & Windahl, 1989, p. 194). Figure 11A graphically depicts this possibility. The phenomenon would no doubt deserve a discussion of its own (see Johnsson-Smaragdi, in press). Interesting as the substantive interpretations of specific similarities and dissimilarities between the two models may be, however, our concern here and now is more with the general formal similarity and/or difference between the models.

In the most general terms, what Figures 11A and 11B present is the fact that structural invariance is a matter of degrees. Actually it is so in at least two ways. In the first place, even if most arrows are identical in the two models, the coefficients attached to the arrows are by no means identical. As a rule the difference is small, but sometimes it may be considerable. That is a quantitative difference. Second, the structures themselves, the two patterns of arrows between latent variables, although similar, are far from identical. As we have seen, some arrows may be found only in one of the figures. That is a qualitative difference. There are at least two types of structural invariance, then: quantitative and qualitative. Intuitively, the latter stands out as more important than the former.

Figures 11A and 11B show some lack of both quantitative and qualitative invariance. This is so in spite of the fact that we are dealing with two equally old samples measured three times in exactly the same way at about the same time, differing only in the place of residence. (The differences grow even stronger, of course, if we compare with the model offered in Figure 6 above, only part of which is directly comparable with the models of Figures 10A and 10B.)

Part of the differences may be due to the heavy and uneven reduction in sample size caused by missing answers on one or more of the many variables of the models. Missing answers are dealt with by either listwise or pairwise deletion. In this case, we used listwise deletion, which has its advantages but results in heavier reduction than the other technique. Systematic comparisons based on the two techniques may shed some light on the problem. Building on previous experiments of that type (e.g., Flodin, 1986; Rosengren & Windahl, 1989, p. 266), we are fairly convinced, however, that this is no serious cause of difference between the two models.

Continued work with replication of longitudinal structural models will show the extent of quantitative and qualitative structural invariance to be expected in cases like these. It has been mentioned already that within the MPP, work in this direction is on its way. Since the relevance of all research rests on the assumption of structural invariance (or reliable knowledge about the lack of such invariance) the outcome of such studies must be considered to be of some interest.

What outcome may we expect? Personally, I expect the amount of both quantitative and qualitative structural invariance to be less than has implicitly been taken for granted. If that is so, it may have some consequences—in communication research as well as in the general debate. Cases in which structural invariance is lacking will point to the need for renewed theoretical and methodological efforts. Cases of structural invariance will provide strong support for existing theory and methodology.

CONCLUDING DISCUSSION

The Media Panel Program was inaugurated with a view to (a) describing the mass media use of children and adolescents, and (b) arriving at some reasonably safe conclusions about its causes and effects. To the extent that we did know it beforehand, it did not take us very long to realize that our descriptive data were completely dependent on two contingencies: the state of the media structure at the time of the measurement, and the conceptualizations and operationalizations used. Neither of these dependencies, of course, represents any good argument against the production of descriptive data about media use.

On the contrary, since the media structure is gradually changing all the time (the rate of change — as well as the media structure itself — differing considerably from time to time, and from society to society), the dependence of descriptive data on the surrounding media structure is a very strong argument for the continuous collection of such data. The fact that — like all data — these data are contingent on the conceptualizations and operationalizations behind them could be regarded as trivial. However, it is probably best looked upon as a challenge, a demand for methodological development, in its turn calling for basic theoretical research about various aspects of media use and its relationship to social structure in general, and to media structure in particular.

As work within the MPP continued, it wasn't long before we realized that not only descriptive results, but also results about the causes and effects of media use might be bound to specific situations and structures. We soon found out, for instance, that whereas among Anglo-American children of the early 1950s high TV viewing seems to have been related to low social interaction, that was not so among Swedish children of the late 1970s and early 1980s. (Actually, it was the other way around.) Causes and effects of the use of a relatively new medium in one society, we concluded, were not necessarily the same as causes and effects of the use of a well-established medium in another society — even if, superficially, that medium was one and the same in the two cases (Rosengren & Windahl, 1989, p. 189; see also Johnsson-Smaragdi, 1983; Sonesson, 1979, 1989).

This may be a rather trivial insight, too. But it does point to the fact that now that a number of American and European longitudinal studies have provided some answers to Lazarsfeld's 30-year-old question about the long-term effects of TV use, we may generalize his question. Which — if any — causes and effects of social phenomena are independent of the surrounding social structure? More specifically: Is the structural invariance of media use (including causes and effects of that use) strong enough to survive the change of the media structure currently going on in Sweden and many other European countries?

Looking around for specific answers to questions such as these forms an important part of the activities going on right now within the Media Panel Program. Some preliminary attempts in that direction have been presented in this chapter. Others will follow. The "specified lack of knowledge" is certainly large. We do not know what the answers will be, but we do believe that some of them will be rather unexpected. After all, that is what makes the game worthwhile.

REFERENCES

Alvarado, M. (Ed.). (1988). *Video world-wide: An international study.* Paris: UNESCO.

Arnman, G., & Jönsson, I. (1983). *Segregation och svensk skola.* Lund: Studentlitteratur.

Bourdieu, P. (1984). *Distinction.* London: Routledge & Kegan Paul.

Brown, J. R., Cramond, J. K., & Wilde, R. J. (1974). Displacement effects of television and the child's functional orientation to media. In J. Blumler & E. Katz (Eds.), *The uses of mass communications* (pp. 93-112). Beverly Hills, CA: Sage.

Bryant, J., & Zillmann, D. (Eds.). (1986). *Perspectives on media effects.* Hillsdale, NJ: Lawrence Erlbaum.

Burrell, G., & Morgan, G. (1979). *Sociological paradigms and organisational analysis.* London: Heineman.

Chaffee, S. H., McLeod, J. M., & Atkin, C. K. (1971). Parental influences on adolescent media use. *American Behavioral Scientist, 14*, 323-340.

Comstock, G., & Pail, H. J. (1987). *Television and children: A review of recent research.* Syracuse, NY: ERIC.

Csikszentmihalyi, M., & Kubey, R. (1981). Television and the rest of life. *Public Opinion Quarterly, 45*, 317-328.

Cuttance, P., & Ecob, R. (Eds.). (1987). *Structural modeling by example.* Cambridge: Cambridge University Press.

Entwisle, D., Alexander, K., Cadigan, & Pallas, A. (1986). The schooling process in first grade: Two samples a decade apart. *American Educational Research, 23*, 587-613.

Flodin, B. (1986). *TV och yrkesförväntan: En longitudinell studie av ungdomars yrkessocialisation.* Lund: Studentlitteratur. (With a summary in English)

Fraser, B., Walberg, H., Welch, W., & Hattie, J. (Eds.). (1987). Syntheses of educational productivity research. *International Journal of Educational Research, 11*(2).

Gahlin, A., & Nordström, B. (1988). *Video i Sverige.* Stockholm: Sveriges Radio/PUB.

Gahlin, A., & Wigren, G. (1989). *Långfilmdags. En analys av TV-publiken, biobesöken och videotittandet.* Stockholm: Sveriges Radio/PUB.

Glass, G. V (1976). Primary, secondary and meta-analysis of research. *Educational Researcher, 5*, 3-8.

Glenn, N. D. (1973). *Cohort analysis.* Beverly Hills, CA: Sage.

Gunter, B., & Svennevig, M. (1987). *Behind and in front of the screen.* London: John Libbey.

Hedinsson, E. (1981). *TV, family and society: The social origins and effects of adolescents' TV use.* Stockholm: Almqvist & Wiksell International.

Hedinsson, E., & Windahl, S. (1984). Cultivation analysis: A Swedish illustration. In G. Melischek, K. E. Rosengren, & J. Stappers (Eds.), *Cultural indicators: An international symposium* (pp. 389-406). Vienna: Akademie de Wissenschaften.

Himmelweit, H., Oppenheim, A. N., & Vince, P. (1958). *Television and the child.* London: Oxford University Press.

Höjerback, I. (1986). *Video i Malmö* (Lund Research Papers in the Sociology of Communication, 3). Lund, Sweden: University of Lund.

Horton, D., & Wohl, R. R. (1956). Mass communication and para-social interaction. *Psychiatry, 19*, 215-229.

Huesman, L. R., & Eron, L. D. (Eds.). (1986). *Television and the aggressive child: A cross-national comparison.* Hillsdale, NJ: Lawrence Erlbaum.

Jarlbro, G. (1986). *Family communication patterns revisited: Reliability and validity* (Lund Research Papers in the Sociology of Communication, 4). Lund, Sweden: University of Lund.

Jarlbro, G. (1988). *Familj, massmedier och politik.* Stockholm: Almqvist & Wiksell International. (With a summary in English)

Jarlbro. G., Lööv, T., & Miegel, F. (1989). *Livsstil och massmedieanvändning: En deskriptiv rapport* (Lund Research Papers in the Sociology of Communication, 14). Lund, Sweden: University of Lund.

Johnsson-Smaragdi, U. (1983). *TV use and social interaction in adolescence: A longitudinal study.* Stockholm: Almqvist & Wiksell International.

Johnsson-Smaragdi, U. (in press). *Structural invariance in media use: Some longitudinal LISREL models replicated.*

Johnsson-Smaragdi, U., & Roe, K. (1986). *Teenagers in the new media world* (Lund Research Papers in the Sociology of Communication, 2). Lund, Sweden: University of Lund.

Johnsson-Smaragdi, U., & Höjerback, I. (1989). *Replikation av en LISREL-modell på ett nytt urval. Likheter i barns och föräldrars TV-konsumtion* (Lund Research Papers in the Sociology of Communication, 13). Lund, Sweden: University of Lund.

Jönsson, A. (1985). *TV—ett hot eller en resurs för barn?* Lund: CWK Gleerup. (With a summary in English)

Jönsson, A. (1986). TV: A threat or a complement to school? *Journal of Educational Television, 12*(1), 29-38.

Jöreskog, K. G., & Sörbom, D. (1989). *LISREL 7: A guide to the program and applications* (2nd ed.). Chicago: SPSS.

Lazarsfeld, P. F. (1955). Why is so little known about the effects of television on children, and what can be done? *Public Opinion Quarterly, 19*, 243-251.

Lefkowitz, M. M., Eron, L. D., Walder, L. O., & Huesman, L. R. (1972). Television violence and child aggression: A follow-up study. In G. A. Comstock & E. A. Rubinstein (Eds.), *Television and social behavior, III* (pp. 35-135). Washington, DC: Government Printing Office.

Liebert, R. M., & Sprafkin, J. (1988). *The early window* (3rd ed.). New York: Pergamon.

Lööv, T., & Miegel, F. (1989). *Vardagsliv, livsstilar och massmedieanvändning. En studie av 12 malmöungdomar* (Lund Research Papers in the Sociology of Communication, 16). Lund, Sweden: University of Lund.

Lööv, T., & Rosengren, K. E. (1988). *The experience sampling method (ESM)* (Lund Research Papers in the Sociology of Communication, 9). Lund, Sweden: University of Lund.

McLeod, J., & Brown, J. D. (1976). The family environment and adolescent television use. In R. Brown (Ed.), *Children and television* (pp. 199-234). London: Collier Macmillan.

Milawsky, J. R., Kessler, R. C., Stipp, H. H., & Rubens, W. S. (1982). *Television and aggression: A panel study.* New York: Academic Press.

Morley, D. (1980). *Reconceptualizing the media audience.* Birmingham: Centre for Contemporary Cultural Studies.

Mortimer, J. T., Finch, M. D., & Kumka, D. (1982). Persistence and change in development: The multidimensional self-concept. In P. B. Baltes & O. G. Brim (Eds.), *Life-span development and behavior* (Vol. 4). New York: Academic Press.

Peterson, R. A., & Berger, D. G. (1975). Cycles in symbol production: The case of popular music. *American Sociological Review, 40,* 158-173.

Piepe, A., et al. (1975). *Television and the working class.* Farnborough: Saxon House.

Roe, K. (1983). *Mass media and adolescent schooling: Conflict or co-existence?* Stockholm: Almqvist & Wiksell International.

Roe, K. (1985, June). The Swedish moral panic over video 1980-1984. *Nordicom Review of Mass Communication Research,* pp. 20-25.

Roe, K. (1988). *Adolescent's VCR use: How and why?* Gothenburg: University of Gothenburg, Unit of Mass Communication.

Rosengren, K. E. (1983). Communication research: One paradigm or four? *Journal of Communication, 33,* 185-207.

Rosengren, K. E. (1985). Media linkages of culture and other societal systems. In M. L. McLaughlin (Ed.), *Communication yearbook 9* (pp. 19-56). Beverly Hills, CA: Sage.

Rosengren, K. E. (Ed.). (1986). *På gott och ont. TV och video, barn och ungdom.* Stockholm: Liber.

Rosengren, K. E. (1988). *The study of media culture: Ideas, actions and artifacts* (Lund Research Papers in the Sociology of Communication, 10). Lund, Sweden: University of Lund.

Rosengren, K. E. (1989a). Paradigms lost and regained. In B. Dervin, L. Grossberg, B. O'Keefe, & E. Wartella (Eds.), *Paradigm dialogues: Theories and issues* (pp. 21-39). Newbury Park, CA: Sage.

Rosengren, K. E. (1989b). Medienkultur: Forschungsansatz und Ergebnisse eines schwedischen Langzeitprojekts. *Media Perspektiven, 6,* 356-372

Rosengren, K. E., Wenner, L. A., & Palmgreen, P. (Eds.). (1985). *Media gratifications research: Current perspectives.* Beverly Hills, CA: Sage.

Rosengren, K. E., & Windahl, S. (1989). *Media matter: TV use in childhood and adolescence.* Norwood, NJ: Ablex.

Saris, W., & Stronkhorst, H. (1984). *Causal modelling in non-experimental research.* Amsterdam: Sociometric Research Foundation.

Schramm, W., Lyle, J., & Parker, E. B. (1961). *Television in the lives of our children.* Stanford, CA: Stanford University Press.

Singer, J. L., Singer, D. G., & Rapaczynski, W. (1984). Family patterns and television viewing as predictors of children's beliefs and aggression. *Journal of Communication, 34*(2), 73-89.

Sonesson, I. (1979). *Förskolebarn och TV.* Stockholm: Esselte Studium.

Sonesson, I. (1989). *Vem fostrar våra barn? Videon eller vi?* Stockholm: Esselte.

Sonesson, I., & Höjerback, I. (1989). *Skolungdomars medievanor före och efter videon* (Lund Research Papers in the Sociology of Communication, 12). Lund, Sweden: University of Lund.

Tanner, I. M. (1962). *Growth at adolescence.* Oxford: Basil Blackwell.

Tims, A. R., & Masland, J. L. (1985). Measurement of family communication patterns. *Communication Research, 12,* 35-57.

von Feilitzen, C., Filipson, L., Rydin, I., & Schyller, I. (1989). *Barn och unga i medieåldern. Fakta i ord och siffror* [Children and young people in the media age: Facts in words and figures]. Stockholm: Rabén & Sjögren.

Wartella, E., & Reeves, B. (1987). Communication and children. In C. R. Berger & S. H. Chaffee (Eds.), *Handbook of communication science* (pp. 619-650). Newbury Park, CA: Sage.

Werner, A. (1989). Television and age-related differences. *European Journal of Communication, 4*, 33-50.

Wiegman, O., Kuttschreuter, W., & Baarda, B. (1986). *Television viewing related to aggressive and prosocial behaviour.* The Hague: SVO/THT.

Williams, T. M. (Ed.). (1986). *The impact of television: A natural experiment.* Orlando, FL: Academic Press.

Windahl, S., Höjerback, I., & Hedinsson, E. (1986). Adolescents without television: A study in media deprivation. *Journal of Broadcasting and Electronic Media, 30*, 47-63.

Children's and Adolescents' Media Use: Some Methodological Reflections

CECILIA von FEILITZEN
Stockholm University

K ARL Erik Rosengren's chapter presents an overview of an ongoing Swedish research program, the Media Panel Program (MPP). His chapter displays a sample of thoughts, methods, and results from the research program, a compressed selection of what I presume are some of the clearest and "best" examples. The numerous snapshots of lines of thought, methodology, and empirical results are connected by a theme — the question of "invariant change" or "the possibilities of drawing general and lasting conclusions from results such as those presented" (p. 52).

What I appreciate most about the MPP are, among other things, (a) its chronological order of the panel observations, which facilitates causal conclusions and the study of *long-term media influences*; (b) its knowledge of *how the same individuals change over time* (i.e., the gross amount of individual change and trends within samples); (c) its *multitude of variables* about the child, the family, school, and peer groups, rendering possible comprehensive analyses of differences and similarities between media use of various groups, and of media influences; and (d) its *advanced statistical methods* that have ameliorated the basis of conclusions.

As most of Rosengren's chapter is devoted to media use, I shall in this commentary offer some methodological reflections of import for the question of "invariant change" concerning media use — both media use at a given point in time and media use over time.

Correspondence and requests for reprints: Cecilia von Feilitzen, Unit of Media and Cultural Theory, Department of Journalism, Media and Communication, Stockholm University, S-106 91 Stockholm, Sweden.

Communication Yearbook 14, pp. 91-101

MEASURING MEDIA USE
AT A GIVEN POINT IN TIME

In the MPP, media use, of which television use is the focus, has been conceptualized as having four aspects: amount of consumption in terms of time and media
content, type of content preferred, type of relation established to the content
consumed (identification and so on), and type of consumption situation (alone or
together with others, primary or secondary activity). Obviously, there also are
many other important facets of media use, such as attention, selectivity, and
intensity of the use; emotional experience during use; reception of media content
in terms of decoding of meanings; and valuation of media content. In the case of
television, we can also add switching between channels, watching whole programs
or parts of programs, and listening to television (e.g., music television), as well as
delayed television viewing using VCRs (time shifting).

The MPP has primarily measured media use based on the amount of time used
by *habits* of media consumption. Rosengren points out that measures of habits are
different from measures of actual viewing:

> Habits are dispositional phenomena, in principle similar to attitudes, while actual
> consumption is just that: actual behavior. It is well known that attitudes and actual
> behavior are less than perfectly correlated, and the same holds true for media habits
> and actual media behavior during a given period of time. (p. 55)

That Rosengren's data are based on habits of media consumption allows them
to be profitably compared with data on children's and adolescents' *actual TV
viewing* from repeated cross-sectional studies performed by the Audience and
Programme Research Department (APRD) of the Swedish Broadcasting Corporation (Filipson & Rydin, 1989). What is presented here are merely a few illustrating
examples as a basis of discussion. Furthermore, I would like to caution that not
only do habits and actual viewing differ, but different ways of conceptualizing and
measuring actual viewing may give rise to widely divergent results also.

With those caveats in mind, Figure 1 shows the actual television viewing on an
average day in 1987/88 (based on 120 days scattered during the year) in each age
group among 3- to 20-year-olds. Because of limited space, only one year of
observation is included here, but my comparisons with the MPP are based on
similar APRD data on these age categories for several previous years. The object
of my comparisons is the habits of television viewing in the MPP demonstrated in
Rosengren's Figure 3 (summarized in Figure 5).

The comparisons suggest that in terms of the shape of the curves, the two
measures correspond quite well, but that the values for habits elevate the peak of
the curve substantially. However, questions on habits appear to agree better with
actual viewing when the latter is measured over a long time than over a short time.
Specific differences between habits and actual viewing measures may result more
from local variations. For example, Sweden has only two national television

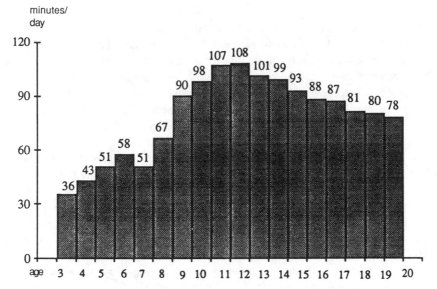

Figure 1. TV viewing (minutes) of different ages in an average day, 1987-1988.
SOURCE: Filipson and Rydin (1989). Reprinted by permission.

channels. Television viewing in Sweden is sensitive to the popularity of current television series, occurrences of sport events, and the like. Measuring actual viewing during a single week—often done in studies with diaries—may consequently exhibit quite different results for different weeks, even if the weeks are in the same month. In addition, even when actual television viewing is based on 120 days scattered during the year, the average viewing per day may, in certain age groups of children, fluctuate as much as half an hour from one year to another. These fluctuations are probably due to children's varying interest in different program series in combination with seasonal variations, as the 120 days have not been exactly the same each year (see Figure 2). These problems are not entirely avoided by means of questions on habits. Much points to the fact that questions on habits are influenced by the broadcasts during the period previous to the investigation.

Nonetheless, questions on habits are sometimes a better indicator of actual viewing over the long run than measuring actual viewing during, for example, a single week, if the week deviates from the ordinary program output. As actual viewing, for practical reasons, cannot always be studied during a long period, questions on habits are thus preferable for some purposes. Still, the comparisons seem to show that questions on habits also included an attitudinal component. (In studies on actual viewing, too, attitudes may exert an influence, so that some persons adjust their answers, but experience indicates that this happens to a low degree.) The summarizing assumption is, then, that questions on habits cannot be regarded as sheer measures of dispositions/attitudes, but that they partly comprise an actual behavioral component and partly comprise a sizable attitudinal component.

If this assumption is right, what are the consequences of this sizable attitudinal component in applying questions on habits? First, one should not, on the basis of such questions, make statements about the amount of actual television viewing in absolute terms (even careful researchers such as Rosengren easily slip in their terminology). This restriction is important for other estimates as well, such as the viewing of specific television programs and the amount of use of other media. The amount of time reported by measures of habits can be inflated or deflated by the attitude component. For example, when actual behavior and attitudes are "positively" correlated (in statistical terms), the absolute differences are "only" reinforced. This reinforcement can, perhaps, be seen in the MPP data that suggest a peak for television use rather too early and too high followed by a precipitous decline from more than two hours a day to less than an hour and a half during the age span 10-15 (p. 60 and Figure 5). Figures from APRD for all available measurements throughout the 1970s and 1980s show a much lower peak and consequently a less steep slope of decline. Thus what may be measured is a double phenomenon: a successive decline of actual viewing combined with a simultaneously more disinterested attitude toward television. As younger children have overestimated their viewing while older children and adolescents have estimated more correctly or underestimated it, the difference becomes particularly great.

Second, it is doubtful if even the relative level of media use could be properly stated, as is Rosengren's opinion (p. 61). The relative level, too, is affected by the attitudinal component. Consider the effect on relative values when actual behavior and attitudes are (statistically) "negatively" or "zero" correlated. For instance, adults with more education say they prefer certain programs (cultural ones, debates, and so on) more than their actual viewing would suggest. Their profile of program viewing is in fact similar to that of persons with less education. In other words, those with more education watch the same kinds of programs as those with less education, but they watch fewer of all kinds (Hoijer, 1972; Lund & Ulvaer, 1983). Measures of habits, therefore, may well be confounded with education and other demographic variables. One should be aware of the fact that in the subsequent analyses the values of the habits are already attitudinally affected by the persons' individual and social characteristics. Not only is age connected to the attitude toward television, but gender and sociocultural background, among other things, are as well. In Sweden, boys and men appreciate television more than do girls and women, persons with less education appreciate it more than do persons with more education, and so on (the second circumstance is true of national television but not of Anglo-American satellite television). Persons of different ages, genders, and sociocultural backgrounds also cherish different types of television programs in various ways, and their attitudes toward other media are different from their attitudes toward television. The consequence is that we do not even know if we measure a relative level of media consumption.

The contamination of actual behavior and attitudes may have consequences for the question of "invariant change," the main thread in Rosengren's chapter. For instance, structural invariance (stability of a given relationship between two variables) over time and space may, in the "positive" case above, lead to overestimated conclusions about generality, which would support erroneous theories. In sum, there is a need to examine empirically the validity of questions concerning media habits far more than has hitherto been done; their relationships with actual use and attitudes among different groups of individuals must be scrutinized.

DRAWING CONCLUSIONS
ABOUT MEDIA USE OVER TIME

Rosengren's chapter stresses that the combination of panel and cross-sectional studies has special advantages for the analysis of descriptive data about media use *over time*. Among other things, cohort, age, and period (as well as interactional) effects are considered to be evaluated best by this design: how media use varies according to the facts that (a) individuals belong to a certain "generation" (cohort), (b) individuals mature as they pass through life stages (aging), and (c) the situation or period (cultural, political, industrial) itself can change.

In theory, a combination of panel and cross-sectional studies is, naturally, preferable for evaluating cohort, age, and situation effects — as well as for analyzing "invariant change" or stability in the process of change. In practice, multiple cross sections of actual television viewing in representative samples of all ages at regular time intervals seem to give better prospects of diachronic analyses of such dynamic relationships, even if the analyses can be valid only for net effects at the aggregate level, as it is not possible to identify offsetting trends due to intraindividual change.

This argument can be demonstrated by examining cross-sectional data on the total amount of time spent viewing by different age groups. Figure 2, based on the repeated cross-sectional studies at APRD (Filipson & Rydin, 1989), shows the actual viewing of three broader age groups from 1972 to 1988 (note, however, that the time series is incomplete for 1972 to 1976). Children's viewing has, apart from fluctuations in different years, diminished during the last two decades. This decline is relatively greater among younger children than among older ones (including 12-year-olds). (From the teenage years on, the trend is indistinct.)

No similar decline over time seems to have been observed within the MPP. Could the reason be that the attitudinal component of the habits comes into play (i.e., in spite of decreased viewing, a given age may have the same attitude toward television in different years)? Could the reason be that the MPP is based on samples of young people in southern Sweden (i.e., perhaps children's television viewing has not diminished there, as in the rest of the country)? Or is the explanation to be sought in panel effects, panel mortality, or special opportunities for satellite television in the south of Sweden?

It seems as if the lack of observation of decreased television viewing over time among the MPP children can be explained much more easily: Children's television habits have been studied over too short a period. The children in grade 3 (9-10

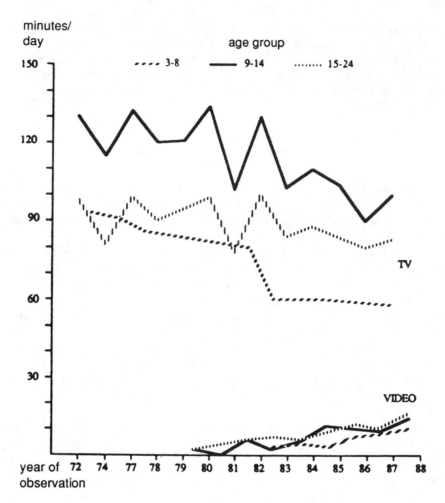

Figure 2. TV and video viewing (minutes) in an average day, by age group and year of observation.
SOURCE: Filipson and Rydin (1989). Reprinted by permission.

years of age) have participated in only one wave (1978/79) and the children in grade 5 (11-12 years of age) in only three waves (1976/77, 1978/79, and 1980/81). After that, only teenagers were included in the panels.

The combination of panel and cross-sectional studies is, according to Rosengren, also the best strategy for studying "invariant change." Of course, mere cross-sectional studies are not as appropriate for studying stability in causal processes and not at all appropriate for studying stability in intraindividual change. But other kinds of stability, for instance, level stability (the magnitude or quantity of a given phenomenon, at the individual and/or aggregate level, e.g., in the amount of television watched), does not appear to have been better elucidated by data in the MPP. As mentioned, the range of the decline in television viewing in the age span 10/11-15 seems to be overestimated in the MPP due to the attitudinal component of the questions. But, in addition, the exaggerated range of this decline seems to depend on the fact that an average is constructed in the MPP over panels and waves, although younger children are included only during a shorter and earlier period in the panels, at which time children's actual television viewing was more extensive. The result that the age-specific level stability between panels (i.e., the amount of television watched at a special age) is very high is thus overrated, as it, in fact, embodies cohort or period effects (or a decreasing age effect).

From the data summarized in Figure 2, a standard cohort table can be made with each age on the y axis and each period on the x axis (and the reverse) or a period by age regression matrix. Cohort effects are then observable as variations across diagonals, age effects as variations across rows, and period effects as variations across columns.

Yet rigorous statistical techniques would not be sufficient for evaluating, in particular, cohort and period effects on children's and young people's television viewing during the last two decades. In addition to such techniques, knowledge is needed on how media structure and society have changed. I shall give some examples of how such knowledge may lead to quite different conclusions about results of media use over time.

Societal and Industrial Influences
on Television Viewing

A closer examination of Figure 2 demonstrates that the decline in television viewing in the period 1972-1982 was most pronounced among 3- to 8-year-olds, while the decrease in viewing among 9- to 14-year-olds occurred mainly in the 1980s. This difference could indicate a cohort effect. A possible cause of such a cohort effect, if any, could be that adults, because of a lively public debate in the 1970s, became more aware of the negative side of television viewing and therefore became more restrictive regarding small children's viewing. (Only viewing of adult programming has diminished among 3- to 8-year-olds — their viewing of children's programs is as extensive as earlier; see Schyller, 1989a.) Furthermore, the 1970s saw many Swedish mothers entering the labor market, and an increasing number of children were enrolled in day-care institutions, where television viewing is relatively rare. Perhaps less time for children and parents together also brought about a choice not to fill that time with so much television.

Changes in industry structure when the second Swedish channel came on line in 1969, something that led to doubled viewing among children immediately afterward, could also be an explanation for the decline by positing a fading "charm of novelty." Further, the national television company has been the subject of two reorganizations since 1969, which may have contributed to smaller period effects. Moreover, the more distinct decline in viewing of national television among 9- to 14-year-olds during the 1980s might have been, at least in part, caused by the introduction of the VCR and satellite television.

The use of VCRs began to spread in Sweden around 1980. By 1990, two-thirds of all children and adolescents had access to videocassette viewing at home. They watch VCRs more than do adults. However, as shown by data from the MPP, too, VCR viewing has not to a high degree replaced television viewing, but has become a complement to it, although VCR viewing influences television viewing somewhat in the form of time shifting (a trend that is strengthened in areas with satellite television) (Filipson, 1989a, 1989b; Schyller, 1989a, 1989b).

Reception of satellite television started in Sweden on a trial basis in 1984 and was lawfully regulated in 1986. By 1990, one-fourth of all children and adolescents had access to satellite television at home. More than adults and toddlers, 9- to 14-year-olds and 15- to 24-year-olds use satellite television, and they watch more television as a whole than children of the same age without satellite television. Their use of satellite television is at the expense of national television (Filipson, 1989c).

Interpenetration of Cohort and Period Effects

Apart from the fact that cohort and period effects are difficult to separate, they are often not causally distinct. In particular, this may be true of children and young people who pass various developmental or maturational stages with new kinds of needs, leading, in our case, to an active adoption of new media and media contents. Of all events and historical forces, those that take place during childhood and adolescence, the most formative socialization period, impress a cohort. At the same time, children and young people are more susceptible to period effects, too. For example, families with children and youth continuously lead in purchases of new media apparatuses in Sweden. Period effects in the form of new media in the market, then, may in their turn be the origins of cohort effects. A Swedish example can be found in cinema. Movie attendance before the VCR was a pronounced youth activity. It no longer is now, as adolescents have annexed the VCR medium. Movie theaters are mainly occupied by 25- to 44-year-olds, who became used to moviegoing in their youth (Gahlin & Wigren, 1986).

Another example of how a period effect may result in a cohort effect could appear if children of today demand in the future more entertainment and music television — as in satellite programming — than national public service television offers and that today's adults find best. At the same time, young people's great interest in Anglo-American satellite television can be explained by a cohort effect based on the fact that younger persons have greater skills in English than older generations.

Recently, however, commercial Scandinavian and Swedish-language satellite channels started transmissions, and more interest in them is found among adults. A cohort effect may thus already be superseded by a new period effect. An important question, then, is this: How long must a cohort effect endure to be interesting? Generally, I suppose, it does not become really interesting until it extends into adulthood — in other words, until it embraces a "real" generation.

A third example of a period effect that may transform into a cohort effect is represented by listening to records and cassettes, which among children and adolescents has to a great extent replaced radio listening. This is the most dramatic change in Swedish children's media use during the last decades (von Feilitzen, 1989). Maybe a possible cohort effect will manifest itself among adults to come, as a greater amount of listening as a whole (radio plus recordings).

A more outright cohort effect appears to exist regarding book reading. Contrary to popular belief, book reading has increased somewhat in Sweden during the last decades, among children, youth, and adults as well. One of several probable explanations is a long-term rise in the education level in the country. The analogue is not noticed for various newspapers and periodicals. Children's reading of newspapers, weeklies, and comics declined in the 1970s and 1980s. Among adults, reading of newspapers is stable. So in the case of newspapers we might be talking about a transient child and youth phenomenon (von Feilitzen, 1988).

To sum up: A penetrating analysis of cohort, age, and period effects has to extend over a long time, in terms of both periods and ages (children as well as adults ought to be included). My opinion that better cohort studies must cover a span of 20 or more years is shared by Glenn (1977). Furthermore, comprehensive knowledge is required not only about the individual's psychological and social characteristics, but also about societal changes that take place during the course of the analysis. Finally, the analysis of cohort, age, and period effects within the field of mass communication should involve the interplay among all mass media. It is not only, as Rosengren emphasizes, within adolescence that a functional reorganization of media use occurs. The introduction of new media has functionally replaced and in other ways influenced established media and media use for all. The media that suffer are those that have the same sort of entertaining, informative, and social functions as the new ones, particularly if the established media have no extra advantages regarding form and availability. To put it another way: If two media have similar content, the individual will choose the one that has the best combination of pictures, sound, and text; that gives the best possibilities for his or her own control; and that he or she can best exploit in terms of time, place, and economy (von Feilitzen, 1988).

CONCLUDING REMARKS

Rosengren gives many more examples than I have commented upon to illustrate the question of "invariant change" — the extent to which our results and theories are valid over time and social space. His answer seems slightly pessimistic — instability and variance in the results of the MPP sometimes appear greater than expected.

I do not believe there is much reason for pessimism. For one thing, the MPP has hitherto focused on perhaps the most instable period of life, puberty and adolescence. Furthermore, continuity in change within the area of mass communication might best be sought at a *meso level.* It is not reasonable to expect stability in all details at a micro level, as random and other faults always play some role. Nor is it reasonable to expect structural invariance at the macro level over many nations and decades. The more general the theories (societal conflict/consensus, activity/passivity in the socialization process, and so on), the more stable they are, of course. But the more concrete the theories, the more they must be valid for only certain time periods and social spaces, as history does not repeat itself, as society changes more and more rapidly, and, in our case, as we live in a period of explosive communication technology. Media and communication are always part of larger societal structures and processes. Because the media primarily are apparatuses and the use of them functionally reorganizes itself when technology changes, the probability is also greater that results and theories on media *content* are more valid than results and theories on media *as such.* The medium is *not* the message.

REFERENCES

Filipson, L. (1989a). Kabel och satellit-tv (Cable and satellite television). In C. von Feilitzen, L. Filipson, I. Rydin, & I. Schyller (Eds.), *Barn och unga i medieåldern. Fakta i ord och siffror* [Children and young people in the media age: Facts in words and figures]. Stockholm: Rabén & Sjögren.

Filipson, L. (1989b). Radio, skivor/kassetter och musik [Radio, records/cassettes, and music]. In C. von Feilitzen, L. Filipson, I. Rydin, & I. Schyller (Eds.), *Barn och unga i medieåldern. Fakta i ord och siffror* [Children and young people in the media age: Facts in words and figures]. Stockholm: Rabén & Sjögren.

Filipson, L. (1989c). *Satellit-tv:s publik. Fublikstudie i svenska kabel-tv-omraden mars 1989, barn och ungdomar 3-18 ar* [The audience of satellite television, March 1989: Children and adolescents 3-18 years of age]. Stockholm: Swedish Broadcasting Corporation, Audience and Programme Research Department.

Filipson, L., & Rydin, I. (1989). *Ung med Tvaan, Ett med Bjorne* [Children's and adolescents' television viewing]. Stockholm: Swedish Broadcasting Corporation, Audience and Programme Research Department.

Gahlin, A., & Wigren, G. (1986). *Hur manga gick pa bio 1985-86?* [Cinema attendance 1985-86]. Stockholm: Swedish Broadcasting Corporation, Audience and Programme Research Department.

Glenn, N. D. (1977). *Cohort analysis.* Beverly Hills, CA: Sage.

Hoijer, B. (1972). Utbudet och publikmekanismerna [Output and audience mechanisms]. In Swedish Broadcasting Corporation, Audience and Programme Research Department, *Radio och TV moter publiken* [Radio and television meet the audience] (pp. 174-202). Stockholm: Sveriges Radio.

Lund, S., & Ulvaer, B. P. (1983). *Fjernsynssaing blant barn og voksne. De som ser mye og de som ser lite* [TV viewing among children and adults: Those who view much and those who view little]. Oslo: Universitet I Oslo, Institutt for Presseforskning.

Schyller, I. (1989a). Barn och ungdom tittar pa svensk TV [Children's and adolescents' viewing of television in Sweden]. In C. von Feilitzen, L. Filipson, I. Rydin, & I. Schyller (Eds.), *Barn och unga i medieåldern. Fakta, i ord och siffror* [Children and young people in the media age: Facts in words and figures]. Stockholm: Rabén & Sjögren.

Schyller, I. (1989b). Video och bio [VCR and cinema]. In C. von Feilitzen, L. Filipson, I. Rydin, & I. Schyller (Eds.), *Barn och unga i medieåldern. Fakta i ord och siffror* [Children and young people in the media age: Facts in words and figures]. Stockholm: Rabén & Sjögren.

von Feilitzen, C. (1988). *Why and where to? Trends in children's mass media use.* Stockholm: Stockholm University, Center for Mass Communication Research.

von Feilitzen, C. (1989). Mediernas kamp om fritiden [Media struggle for leisure]. In C. von Feilitzen, L. Filipson, I. Rydin, & I. Schyller (Eds.), *Barn och unga i medieåldern. Fakta, i ord och siffror* [Children and young people in the media age: Facts in words and figures] (pp. 109-124). Stockholm: Rabén & Sjögren.

Nothing Lasts Forever: Instability in Longitudinal Studies of Media and Society

JOHN P. MURRAY
Kansas State University

THE Swedish Media Panel Program (MPP) is an ambitious research project that promises to provide significant insights into the ways in which children and youth use media at various stages in their development. The major strength of this program is the incorporation of both cross-sectional and longitudinal approaches to the study of media use.

The central thesis of the Rosengren chapter is the suggestion that there is great stability in media use patterns. In assessing this issue, characterized as "stability in change," he notes four types of possible stability: *Level stability* relates to the magnitude or quantity of a phenomenon at the individual or aggregate level; *normative stability* is stability in an individual's ranks or differences; *ipsative stability* is the ordering of attributes of an individual over time; and *structural invariance* is the continuity of the structure of a phenomenon over time and experience. Rosengren feels that the MPP is ideally suited to providing insights on three of these four types of stability: level and normative stability and structural invariance. While he concedes that cross-sectional studies also are capable of addressing many of these issues, he notes that the MPP is an especially sensitive combination of cross-sectional and longitudinal approaches and provides more powerful analyses.

Perhaps this is the case. It is certainly true that the MPP provides a large body of data from several cohorts across an extended time period of about 15 years. But Rosengren's conclusions about "stability in change" seem unwarranted or, at least, too broad.

Correspondence and requests for reprints: John P. Murray, Department of Human Development and Family Studies, 303 Justin Hall, Kansas State University, Manhattan, KS 66506-1403.

Communication Yearbook 14, pp. 102-110

CHANGING TIMES, CHANGING RESULTS

I believe that the results of both the Swedish study and other cross-sectional and longitudinal studies support the conclusion that there may be stability within a given age/gender/class group, but that there is considerable instability across historical time and psychological developmental periods or socialization experiences. In short, the notion of "stability in change" is a relatively circumscribed phenomenon and the more interesting task is to describe the nature of change in the MPP and other longitudinal and cross-sectional studies.

We know, from studies in North America, Europe, and Australia, that there is one aspect of stability that is in agreement with the findings from the Swedish study, namely, the "structural invariance" of children's television viewing patterns. In reviewing a large number of cross-sectional studies, Susan Kippax and I have found a fairly stable pattern of children's television viewing across ages or developmental periods in various countries (Kippax & Murray, 1979; Murray, 1981). The general form of these viewing patterns is a rather rapid increase in viewing from infancy through preschool years, a slight plateau during middle school years, followed by a brief rise in early adolescence leading to a decline in television viewing in later adolescence. In Rosengren's report, his Figure 3 does not contradict this general pattern.

However, the important point in this "structural invariance" is the fact that there is no "level stability" in the viewing behavior of children across age, gender, class, socialization experiences, or country. In our reviews we found large differences in the magnitude of viewing from one country to the next (Murray & Kippax, 1979). The explanations for these differences may turn on variations in the nature of the broadcasting structures in differing countries. For example, we found that viewing time was lower in countries with fewer broadcast channels and shorter daily broadcast schedules. Ironically, these characteristics — fewer channels and shorter times — often coincided with a publicly supported or government-operated broadcasting system that also provided more programming tailored to the needs of young viewers.

One explanation of this seeming contradiction is the fact that countries with longer broadcast days and more channels tend to be dominated by commercial broadcasting rather than publicly supported broadcasting systems. In a commercial broadcasting structure, there is little attention paid to specialized programming for children and youth. For example, in the United States there are no regularly scheduled, daily or weekly, specialized, age-specific programs for children and youth on the three major commercial broadcasting systems (ABC, CBS, NBC). In such broadcasting environments, children's television viewing tends to be focused on mass audience programming such as cartoons or comedy programs designed for an undifferentiated viewership of 2- to 12-year-olds. The interesting policy issue that findings such as these raise is the fact that broadcasting systems that cater to the needs of children through specially designed programming may encourage more learning and less viewing. Nevertheless, I have dwelt on this example of structural invariance and level *in*stability as a cautionary note on Rosengren's tendency to see too much stability in children's media environment.

Thus, while there is evidence for the structural invariance that Rosengren seeks in the viewing patterns of children and youth, there is more to this issue of stability and change that calls into question the central thesis of Rosengren's report. I believe that he does not deal adequately with some of the obvious sources of instability in longitudinal studies, namely, changes in technology and social experiences. For example, one of the sources of change that Rosengren does note in the MPP findings is the introduction of VCRs in Sweden. A second source of change (which is admittedly more difficult to identify and quantify) is the reported decline in punk music around 1980, which causes the odd decline in music listening noted in his Figure 4 during the 1980/81 wave. Given these obvious examples of major change that affect the findings in the MPP, it is curious that Rosengren has focused the discussion on stability rather than change.

What is most interesting about longitudinal studies is the ability to track changes in response to shifts in technology or socialization experiences. To give an example of the ways in which changes in social structure and technology can greatly alter the life experiences of children and youth, I draw your attention to Figure 1, which presents the results of some of our research on the introduction of television in the Australian Outback (Murray, 1980; Murray & Kippax, 1977, 1978, 1979). This figure presents the activity patterns of mothers, fathers, and children (ages 8 to 12) living in three towns with differing access to television: No-TV (no access), Low-TV (one year's experience with one channel), and High-TV (five years' experience with two channels). Although this is a cross-sectional study, it can be noted that there are great variations in the ways in which children and adults spend their time in these three communities. In particular, the use of alternative media (radio, reading, records, cinema, theater/concerts, and public events) was greatly reduced in the two television towns compared to the level of activity in the No-TV town. Moreover, this "instability" of activity patterns across the towns suggested that there might be some differential influences of television in relation to the *recency* of its introduction. In this instance, it is clear that the lowest levels of involvement in alternative media were evident in the Low-TV town, the one with the most recent experience with television. Of course, this part of the study was cross-sectional and the differential activity patterns are merely suggestive of some temporal fluctuations in relation to the availability of television. Would there be any way to tease out the influence of the novelty effect in the introduction of television? The answer is yes, because there were repetitions of the social changes occasioned by the introduction of television.

To track changes over time, we returned to these three towns two years later, when the former No-TV town had received television broadcasting (now called the New-TV town). On the basis of our initial findings (shown in the V-shaped curve of Figure 1), suggesting the greatest change had occurred in the town where television was new, we predicted that the greatest displacement of activities would take place in the No-TV/New-TV town. Figure 2 provides an illustration of the

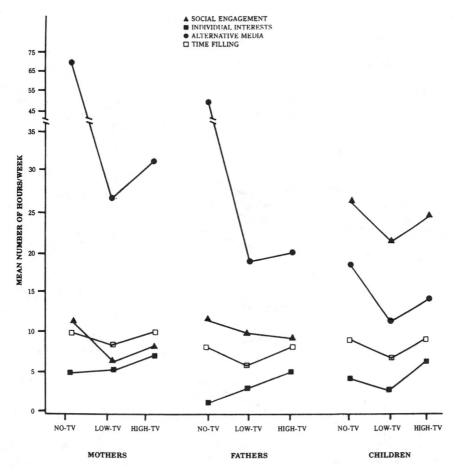

Figure 1. Parents' and children's activity patterns in three towns with differing television experience.

differential activity patterns of 8- to 12-year-old children in the three Outback towns before and after the introduction of television in the No-TV town. It is clear that there is a predictable shift in activities related to the use of alternative media and that the greatest effect was demonstrated among children for whom television was a novelty. Findings such as these highlight one of the issues (or problems) that Rosengren needs to address in the Swedish study, namely, the importance of accounting for shifts in technology or social conditions during the course of the longitudinal research.

Similar, and perhaps more important, issues arise when one deals with some of the subtle influences of changing technology or social conditions. The results of studies of the introduction of television in several Canadian communities by Williams (1986) illustrate that the availability of television can lead to changes in children's reading patterns and development of reading skills that greatly affect school performance and may change their life circumstances. So, too, Williams

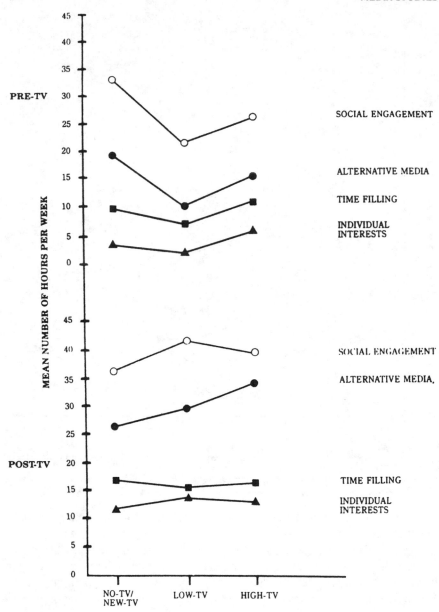

Figure 2. Children's activity patterns before and after the introduction of television.

demonstrates that the introduction of television can lead to changes in children's aggressive behavior. Returning to the Australian study, we have demonstrated some subtle and complex influences of variations in the nature of television programming available in the three Outback towns. Figure 3 is the plot of multidimensional scaling analyses of children's conceptions of crime and violence in the

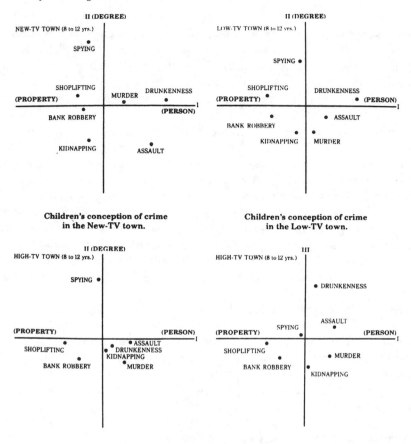

**Children's conception of crime
in the New-TV town.**

**Children's conception of crime
in the Low-TV town.**

**Children's conception of crime in the High-TV
town—dimensions I & II.**

**Children's conception of crime in the High-TV
town—dimensions I & III.**

Figure 3. Children's conceptions of crime in the study areas.

three communities following the introduction of television and its establishment in all three towns. Here, the issue is the effect of the varying nature of television programming available in the High-TV town, which received both public broadcasting and commercial broadcasting channels, versus the Low-TV and New-TV towns, which had access only to the public broadcasting channel.

What we see demonstrated in Figure 3 is the influence of variations in the symbolic communications environment of children being manifested in some measure of their "worldview" in relation to the issue of crime and violence. In this instance, we believe that we were tapping into the effects of differential television programming that played a role in shaping the social reality of these youngsters. The children in the New-TV and Low-TV towns had access only to the public, government-operated television channel (the Australian Broadcasting Corporation channel), which provided very few programs that could be classified as violent/crime/action-adventure. On the other hand, children in the High-TV town had seven years of viewing experience with both the public channel and a commercial channel. The commercial channel carried much more crime and violent action-adventure programming than the public channel, and the children in the High-TV town spent more time watching the commercial channel.

The results of the multidimensional scaling analyses on children's conceptions of seven crimes (shoplifting, drunkenness, bank robbery, spying, kidnapping, assault, and murder) show a much more differentiated pattern in the views of children in the High-TV town than those held by their cohorts in the New-TV or Low-TV towns. In general, children in the towns with access to public television provide a straightforward, two-dimensional conception of crime based upon the dimensions of person or property versus degree of seriousness. Children in the High-TV town, with access to more crime and violence on television, see the two dimensions of person-property and degree of seriousness, but they overlay a third dimension that is vaguely suggestive of a notion of crimes against social structure or the social order. These would be crimes not solely against persons or property but against governments and organizations (e.g., the confluence of spying and kidnapping in dimension III).

Here we have a subtle shift in the worldview of children living in the Australian Outback who are unlikely to witness, in their small towns of 2,000 or 3,000 population, major instances of terrorism or international intrigue. And yet, the symbolic environment afforded by the differing structures of television and the local and national history of broadcasting may greatly alter their experiences and expectations. Of course, we do not know to what extent these communication influences are reflected in diverse aspects of children's behavior. But we do know that any longitudinal study of media and society must be alert to the subtle influences operating in various waves and cohorts.

ON CONCLUSIONS AND CONSEQUENCES

The results of the MPP are encouraging because this is a project with a large sample of children and adolescents who have been followed (at least in some subsamples) for almost 15 years. However, the focus on stability in this most recent report misses, in my view, the most important likely consequence of this study: the explication of change in media use and the consequences of these changes.

The importance of longitudinal studies is obvious to communication scholars, but there are very few such studies because of equally obvious problems concerning commitment of time and money. The studies that have been completed, such as that by Williams (1986) in Canada and the work of Eron and his colleagues in the United States, Finland, and Australia (Eron, 1982; Huesman & Eron, 1986; Huesman, Eron, Lefkowitz, & Walder, 1984), have provided important insights into the diverse effects of television. These recent longitudinal studies have taken their place with earlier cross-sectional and quasi-longitudinal studies in Australia (Murray & Kippax, 1979), England (Belson, 1959; Himmelweit, Oppenheim, &

Vince, 1958), and the United States and Canada (Schramm, Lyle, & Parker, 1961) to help scholars track the changing influence of one of the most influential forms of mass media, television. In addition, there are some emerging findings from studies in the United States (e.g., Huston, Wright, Rice, Kerkman, & St. Peters, 1987) that will help us to track the changing media environment of children and adolescents occasioned by the diffusion of VCRs and cable.

The Swedish MPP has the potential to provide detailed analyses of the subtle and shifting effects of changing media environments on the ever-changing social reality of children and youth. This is a very important role for the MPP because policymakers and scholars throughout the world are increasingly mindful of the need for more, and more sensitive, longitudinal data on which to base recommendations for public policy. For example, in the United States, the American Psychological Association has undertaken a review of the impact of television on American society that will have direct relevance for policies and regulations being considered by legislators (Huston et al., 1990). To ensure that these policies are attuned to the needs of the society, we must have the fine-grained analyses that can come only from large-scale longitudinal studies such as the Swedish MPP. I look forward to further reports from Rosengren and his colleagues that will provide the micro- and macroanalyses that scholars may use to understand the complex relations of media and society.

REFERENCES

Belson, W. A. (1959). *Television and the family.* London: British Broadcasting Corporation.

Eron, L. D. (1982). Parent child interaction, television violence and aggression of children. *American Psychologist, 21*, 197-211.

Himmelweit, H. T., Oppenheim, A. N., & Vince, P. (1958). *Television and the child: An empirical study of the effects of television on the young.* London: Oxford University Press.

Huesman, L. R., & Eron, L. D. (Eds.). (1986). *Television and the aggressive child: A cross-national comparison.* Hillsdale, NJ: Lawrence Erlbaum.

Huesman, L. R., Eron, L. D., Lefkowitz, M. M., & Walder, L. O. (1984). Stability of aggression over time and generations. *Developmental Psychology, 20*(6), 1120-1134.

Huston, A. C., Donnerstein, E., Fairchild, H., Feshbach, N., Katz, P., Murray, J. P., Rubinstein, E. A., Wilcox, B., & Zuckerman, D. (1990). *Television and society: Report of the American Psychological Association Task Force on Television and Society.* Washington, DC: American Psychological Association.

Huston, A. C., Wright, J. C., Rice, M. L., Kerkman, D., & St. Peters, M. (1987, April). *The development of television viewing patterns in early childhood: A longitudinal investigation.* Paper presented at the meeting of the Society for Research in Child Development, Baltimore.

Kippax, S., & Murray, J. P. (1979). *Small screen, big business.* Sydney: Angus & Robertson.

Murray, J. P. (1980). *Television and youth: 25 years of research and controversy.* Boys Town, NE: Boys Town Center.

Murray, J. P. (1981). Children and the structures of television in industrialized nations. *Television & Children, 4*(1), 33-45.

Murray, J. P., & Kippax, S. (1977). Television diffusion and social behaviour in three communities: A field experiment. *Australian Journal of Psychology, 29*(1), 31-43.

Murray, J. P., & Kippax, S. (1978). Children's social behavior in three towns with differing television experience. *Journal of Communication, 28*(1), 19-29.

Murray, J. P., & Kippax, S. (1979). From the early window to the late night show: International trends in the study of television's impact on children and adults. In L. Berkowitz (Ed.), *Advances in experimental social psychology* (Vol. 12, pp. 253-320). New York: Academic Press.

Schramm, W., Lyle, J., & Parker, R. (1961). *Television in the lives of our children.* Stanford, CA: Stanford University Press.

Williams, T. M. (1986). *The impact of television: A natural experiment.* New York: Academic Press.

3 Media Performance Assessment in the Public Interest: Principles and Methods

DENIS McQUAIL
University of Amsterdam

This chapter offers a characterization and an overview of a particular tradition of media research that has been concerned with the assessment of the quality of mass media "performance" according to a number of normative standards relating to different conceptions and perceptions of the "public interest." Typical features of the research, which has often been related to considerations of media policy and is broadly in line with "social responsibility" media theory, include a positivistic approach, a preference for objective (generally quantitative) methods, and a focus on media content as the main object of research. A general framework for assessing media performance is constructed in which the main normative criteria deployed are those of independence, diversity, objectivity, solidarity, and cultural quality. These concepts are discussed and alternative possibilities for operationalizing them in empirical research are proposed and evaluated. Aside from reviewing a research tradition, the aim of this chapter is to help solve problems of applying normative ideas in objective assessment procedures. A second, no less important, aim is to contribute to clarity of thought about some normative concepts that are commonly evoked in respect to key roles the mass media play in the public sphere of society.

MEDIA PERFORMANCE AND PUBLIC INTEREST: ORIGINS AND CONTEXT

The expression *performance assessment* in discussions of mass media has wide currency, but no single or precise meaning. It can, for instance, refer to any of the following: the self-assessment by the media industry in achieving its economic, product, or audience goals; evaluation of working of public policies for mass media (e.g., in respect to monopoly or cultural standards); critical evaluation of many possible aspects or cases of the work of media; or evaluation of the success of campaigns to inform, persuade, mobilize, sell, and so on. None of these, by

AUTHOR'S NOTE: This chapter is the foundation for the forthcoming book, *Media Performance*, to be published by Sage Publications, 1991.

Correspondence and requests for reprints: Denis McQuail, Studierichting Communicatiewetenschap, Universiteit van Amsterdam, Oude Hoogstraat 24, 1012 CE Amsterdam, The Netherlands.

Communication Yearbook 14, pp. 111-145

itself, quite captures what is central to this review, although each does imply a systematic evaluation of what the media are doing according to some independent criteria of achievement.

The type of media performance assessment (MPA) discussed here can best be understood by reference to a particular tradition of applied media research concerning the working of the mass media in modern democracies, a tradition that has significant origins in the Commission on Freedom of the Press (Hutchins, 1947). This commission sought to evaluate the American press of the time and to establish a framework of standards of performance quality appropriate to a "socially responsible" press. Although the commission itself engaged in very little empirical research, the idea of social responsibility and the principles it enunciated have guided much subsequent work. There have also been commissions of inquiry into the functioning of the mass media in several other countries that have combined a similar task of public assessment with programs of empirical research, for instance, in Britain (Royal Commission on the Press, 1947, 1977), Sweden (Gustaffsson & Hadenius, 1976), Canada (Davy, 1970; Kent, 1981), and the Netherlands (McQuail & van Cuilenburg, 1983).

The main "problems" of the press that initially provoked this kind of response from society, in the form of inquiry and research, concerned especially the possible consequences of press concentration (for diversity and political balance) and the need to ensure an informed electorate in a democracy. Inevitably, wider questions have been picked up, especially to do with accusations of "sensationalism," with claims of minorities for access, and with questions of cultural and moral values in media content.

In these matters, scrutiny has also been extended to broadcast media in many countries. The broadcast media were also much more regulated and more legitimately subject to public evaluation and accountability. The priorities of public concern were also somewhat different, with more attention given to protection of the social order, protection of the young, fairness in political matters, and the interests and claims of various minorities.

The character and scope of what is at issue can also be clarified by reference to the work of Lemert (1989), who outlines a similar approach. He suggests that we can distinguish four main schools of media criticism: Marxist, cultural/critical studies, social responsibility, and empiricist. His own chosen purpose is to show "how social science techniques can be used to evaluate and criticize the performance of present and future news media" (p. 11). This is one of the aims of the current work, and "media performance assessment" might be described as a hybrid of the social responsibility and empiricist schools of criticism. This review tries to forge such a "union" by linking a set of normative principles with a set of research procedures, with the intention of illuminating both.

This is the background that has shaped the school of social theory and research under discussion and given it several distinctive "biases" of its own in respect to problem definitions and choice of research methods. In particular, there have been biases toward the cognitive (news and information) and the political, although, in relation to television, questions of culture and morality have been just as prominent. The potential relevance of research to public policy-making (regulation of, or intervention in, media systems) has put a premium on research evidence that seems "hard" enough to stand up in political or legal debate and that is also "communicable" to a lay audience — members of the public, politicians, and media practitioners. These requirements lean in the direction of what some would term "scientism," others simply empiricism. With this in mind, we can specify the principal features of the media performance research enterprise.

CHARACTERISTICS OF THE
PERFORMANCE RESEARCH ENTERPRISE

First of all, the chief beneficiary of the media activities to be assessed and of the research carried out will be the public, community, or society (however variously these can be conceptualized), rather than the media organization, individual media "consumers," or clients of the media (advertisers, campaigners, and the like). The researcher will consequently be external to the media under scrutiny. The focus here is on what the media do, as seen primarily from a "public interest" perspective (or that of the "public good" or "general welfare," to use expressions with less of an economic connotation), a point of view that aims to consider the welfare of the society as a whole and in the longer term, rather than particular and immediate interests. The research described might also contribute to the "public good" in more than one way, for instance, by assisting the formation or evaluation of public policy, by directly stimulating better media provision, or by contributing to an informed public opinion about media in a democracy.

We do not have to presume any single specific version of what constitutes the "public good." We need only accept that there are potential benefits (or deficits) from the working of media, for community or society, over and above the immediate satisfaction of individuals or private organizations. Even among those outside the media claiming to speak on behalf of the public good there are likely to be several divergent perspectives and points of view, with different criteria and different standards of evidence. Despite much dispute and spilling of ink over the concept of "public interest," the weight of opinion seems to be that it remains a useful concept in public life (Downs, 1962) and one from which we can never entirely escape (Held, 1970).

Second, the methods of media performance assessment research are systematic and objective, according to normal canons of the social sciences, often similar to those used by the media for their own self-evaluation. This criterion differentiates MPA from much qualitative evaluation, moralistic judgment, or routine review and criticism. It also implies the need for standards and measures that can be reliably applied in inquiry and deliver results that are dependable and carry wide credibility. Assessment will typically relate to general (average) performance over time and not to particular cases or incidents.

Third, the main focus of the research will be on *positive* aspects of what the media do, rather than negative ones, thus on what the media claim to be doing in the interest of their public, or what "society" expects the media to be doing, rather than on failings or unintended side effects. This is consistent with the idea that media are widely expected to deliver some benefits to society, beyond private interest, a basic presumption of the whole research tradition. It also largely excludes from consideration here much "assessment" of media that focuses on (unintentional) damage to individuals or society by portrayals of violence, crime, deviance, and so on.

Fourth, most MPA research has, in practice, been concerned more with the media *product* and service offered than with effects or audience reach, or with the structure of the media. The one *indispensable* component of research design is some attention to content (the most direct evidence of what the media actually do), and the most commonly used method has been that of content analysis. Performance assessment is, nevertheless, not synonymous with content analysis. It is usually necessary as well to take some account of media structures (which may govern actual performance) and also often necessary to have other (noncontent) data for purposes of comparison, or for understanding the context.

The most useful other kinds of research evidence are derived from the producers of media content (by way of survey or observation) or from the media audience, which can provide one obvious kind of evaluation. Several commissions of inquiry (notably the British and Canadian examples cited above) have combined research into press content, readers, and journalists within a single program.

Research in the tradition of performance assessment has encountered three main kinds of difficulty. One is the divergence of perspective noted above. Another relates to the need to establish specific criteria of performance that are relevant to the chosen "public interest" perspective. A third is to find operational indicators of the chosen criteria that can yield systematic, dependable, and communicable evidence and that might be introduced into the public debate. Each problem is dealt with in this review, although the crucial issue remains—that of bridging the gap between normative (thus subjective) standards and objective research. We can deal with this issue only by accepting limitations of time, space, and scope of the discussion; therefore, I will discuss only media of some capitalist, democratic societies during the last three or four decades, and will deploy some of the main normative criteria that have been applied to the media in these times and places.

A summary working definition of *media performance assessment* can be formulated at this point as follows: the assessment of what mass media do, according to alternative "public interest" criteria and divergent perspectives, by way of objective and systematic methods of analysis independently applied to their general level of performance, taking account of other relevant evidence.

A particular feature of the approach adopted in this review is an emphasis on the interplay between normative criteria and empirical operationalization. The very attempt to convert a norm or standard into an empirical measure of performance can illuminate the meaning of social-theoretical principles. This attempt obliges the theorist to say precisely what counts as evidence of conforming to a particular normative principle should consist of. We may reasonably have some doubts about the validity as well as the usefulness of a principle that cannot be exemplified in practice or experience. At the very least, such a principle is likely to be vague and unlikely to stand up to the rough world of media policy debate. A corollary of this line of reasoning is the view that close attention to problems of operationalization is itself a useful theoretical activity as well as an essential part of the empirical research process.

A GENERALIZED STRATEGY
FOR PERFORMANCE RESEARCH

While research procedures in the tradition described have varied considerably, there is something like a common logic to inquiry that typically takes the following sequence:

- diagnosis of an aspect of media performance as "problematic" according to a chosen perspective and in respect to one or more normative expectations
- specification of a criterion of adequate performance in respect to a given aspect of content or provision
- specification of relevant media and levels at which criteria of performance are to be applied
- choosing or designing appropriate indicators of the criteria that can be systematically applied to content or service provided
- actual systematic application of measures in a formulated research design
- interpretation of findings and conclusions concerning level of performance, or extent of the problem as originally diagnosed

In practice, many aspects of a research design will be determined by the chosen level or focus of application and by the extent to which the problem can be dealt with in terms of media content (in relation to some external standard). The question of level of inquiry, while fundamental, is also a relatively simple one to deal with, and the answer is usually given or implied in the initial problem formulation. We can choose to assess (an aspect of) media at any of the following levels: all media in the whole society (the "macro" level); a particular media sector (the "meso" level), for instance that of the daily newspaper, the periodical, network television, or the local press; and a single media channel (the "micro" level), such as a newspaper or a TV channel or station. The *focus of research* refers to the kind of

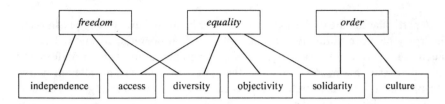

Figure 1. Main normative principles of media performance.

content or media "function" that is at issue, or to a particular case chosen for study (e.g., an election campaign public demonstration, terrorist outrage).

More complex problems are posed by decisions about the kinds of evidence that might be required in addition to content data. These can include data about the structure of the media system, especially where concentration or monopoly is at issue; evidence of the internal working of a media organization; and data about audience behavior or response. Finally, one must keep in mind the need to apply standards and measures that are *appropriate* to the media sector or "function" under study. Expectations of performance in both informational and cultural matters have to be established with due regard for the chosen intention of media provision, the kind of audience envisaged, and the *context* of normal reception.

THE MAIN NORMATIVE PRINCIPLES DEPLOYED
IN MEDIA PERFORMANCE ASSESSMENT

The basic principles that have been most frequently invoked in debates about media performance are few in number, even if rich in meaning, and usually in need of much elucidation. They often have deep roots in history and in social and political thought relating to essential matters of social order, individual freedom, the rights of minorities, justice, and equality. This essential background cannot be reviewed here, nor can all the linkages and nuances of the main concepts be discussed. Instead, we need to go directly to the concepts themselves as they have appeared in the discussion of media and society in the period of research under review. Even so, we must acknowledge the primacy of three familiar and potent principles of political philosophy that have enjoyed currency and status since the age of Enlightenment: freedom, equality, and solidarity (which may be represented here by the broader term *order*) (see McQuail, 1986a). The guiding normative principles of the performance of Western media systems are inextricably related to these three concepts, somewhat as shown in Figure 1.

Freedom is the principle with the longest history and widest reference in the debate, but it is also the one most difficult to assess in performance, by any objective test. It is less a criterion than a *condition* of several kinds of valued performance. It is thus more an attribute of structure or context than of content, showing itself, for instance, in the number and variety of independent channels. A good deal of research on media freedom has, consequently, focused on the presence or absence of regulations or constraints affecting the independence of media organizations or mass communicators. A complication, however, is that freedom may not lead to any predictable given outcome in *performance* terms. In the nature of the concept, freedom is simply permissive and can lead to any individual outcome, ranging from extreme deviance to total (albeit voluntary) adherence to established power.

Under conditions of freedom, however, we would expect there to be more *diversity*, thus a range of options for any "receiver" and also "access" to a range of channels for expression. While freedom may have an equalizing tendency, in some circumstances equality may be inconsistent with unlimited individual freedom (e.g., the freedom to own large sections of the media). Unbridled use of freedom can also be in conflict with expectations of order and certain forms of culture (especially those favored by social elites).

The general principle of *equality* has to be translated into other terms more directly recognizable in media performance. The most commonly used terms are *access, diversity*, and, to an extent, *objectivity*. Equality can be taken to mean any or all of the following: an equal or fair access to channels of communication; an equal treatment of (or lack of discrimination among) groups or sectors in society in the media attention they receive; a universal provision for the audience, or equal chance of reception for all; a dedication to reducing social inequality. The connection with objectivity indicated in Figure 1 is secured by reference to component notions of balance and impartiality in reporting opposed points of view (see below). The link to solidarity relates to the notion of citizenship and equality within microsocial groupings.

The general concept of *order/solidarity* refers to matters of social cohesion and integration — the normative and cultural integrity of a society or community. The reference is a dual one — to informal processes of social control and to the collective social identity and consciousness of a society or component part. These are complex matters that direct our attention to what are labeled *solidarity* and *culture* in Figure 1.

The solidarity principle, in turn, has two aspects. It relates to conformity, or lack of conformity, to established moral, ethical, or legal standards. This is the "view from above," as it were, the dimension of control. There is another aspect, more genuinely "solidaristic," which refers to the self-identity and sense of belonging to subgroups, as well as to community and society. Culture covers a wide range, but it has two basic aspects — one relating to "way of life," another to cultural artifacts (including media "texts"). All these matters are dealt with more extensively below.

ALTERNATIVE PERSPECTIVES
ON PRINCIPLES OF ASSESSMENT

Media performance research requires the investigator to make normative choices and to allocate priorities as between alternative criteria and alternative measures or indicators of performance. As I have pointed out, there is no one simple version of the "general good" and no escape from making value judgments. The outline of the main principles just provided maps out a terrain and offers some dimensions for evaluative judgment. Research can be guided by greater or lesser concern for freedom, or equality, or order. The harder choices may come later, when one has to choose among different indicators of agreed-upon principles, embodying different evaluative standards. For instance, on the matter of freedom, there is a choice to be made among the freedom of the proprietor, of the journalist, of the "voice" in society, and of the public (e.g., freedom to hear a diversity of voices).

In the context of possible policy-making for media, the main source of variation is likely to be whether one looks at the media from *outside*, with a view to regulation or possible intervention "in the public interest," or from *inside*, from the point of view of the media themselves. While performance assessment, as defined here, is mainly carried out according to the "external" view, it is important not to disregard the view from within, especially when the positive goals of performance improvement associated with MPA may coincide with media professional goals.

There are choices, or important differences of emphasis, within each of the two perspectives named. In the case of the "outside" (regulatory) perspective, we can posit a dimension of interventionism, ranging from the strongly interventionist — favoring institutional engineering in the interest of more equal access, diversity, and the like — to the "conservative" view that would favor only the minimum regulation necessary to preserve public order or morals. At midpoint, a "liberal" perspective would tend to emphasize the need for regulation in order to ensure reasonable operating conditions for the media in general.

From within the media, a similar dimension is likely to distinguish a "social participant" view, favoring greater social responsiveness and accountability, from a purely "business" perspective, leaving all to the market. In between, various pragmatic, media professional views are likely to accept the need for some form of self-control and the relevance of some kinds of assessment research directed at the improvement of current practice.

Apart from this general differentiation of emphasis (and also of acceptability of MPA research), there are a number of specific complaints or claims that fall under one or other of the basic principles mentioned: denial of access or unfair representation, cultural or moral lapses on the part of the media, claims of political bias, demands for certain kinds of cultural or informational provision, and so on.

The complex network of interrelated principles that has been briefly indicated can be regarded as having shaped the framework of media assessment research as it has developed over 40 years or more. It is from this framework that the main principles and guidelines for research have been derived, since it has largely set the terms of debate over media performance, from the point of view of the public interest and possible policies for media. The concepts that have been turned into measures of performance have also been named and described. The principal ones are dealt with in turn in the sections that follow. One main purpose will be to show

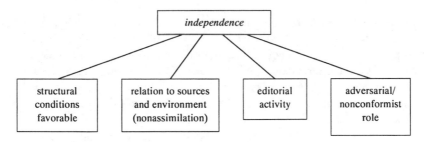

Figure 2. Guide to indicators of media independence.

how these quite abstract concepts have been, or can be, converted into practical tools for assessment of media. Another equally important aim is to shed more light on the meaning of these evaluative concepts.

FREEDOM: PRINCIPLES OF PERFORMANCE AND ASSESSMENT STRATEGIES

The empirical assessment of press freedom has been limited by several problematic features, some already noted. Freedom is essentially permissive and limits on freedom are restrictive. The results of either are as likely to show in omission as in commission. The fact that freedom is a structural condition means that, up to a point, it can be "read" off of, or predicted from, the institutional arrangements. It is apparent, for instance, that nearly everywhere, broadcast news is formally less free than newspaper news, and this shows in the greater caution and neutrality of the former on a range of sensitive issues.

In some countries there are also authoritarian situations where the question of freedom can be assessed largely by reference to rules and regulations alone or by recording instances of exceptional media bravery in defying authority. However, in many countries where freedom is a guaranteed condition, authorities also, on occasion, use their power to intervene in the media for some "reason of state" or "public interest," or engage in various forms of open or hidden censorship. In the nature of these cases, conventional systematic research cannot contribute very much to exposing these conditions, practices, and incidents.

Even so, there are some consistent expectations from free media that can guide assessment. Where there is freedom, there should, in general, be more of a tendency to criticize those in power, to give positive attention to those without power, or to deal with matters that might offend the powerful, whether as governments or as clients and advertisers. Where there is freedom we can also expect to find differentiation of, and independence from, sources. Media operating freely are also likely to be active, vocal, campaigning, and engaged with their own audiences. The general nature of expectations is presented in Figure 2.

Until the 1960s, or thereabouts, inquiry into press freedom generally focused on structural conditions, involving two main kinds of research. First, there were measures of the degree of media concentration in terms of numbers of independent newspaper titles in a circulation area, measures of the size and range of large media conglomerates, and measures of cross-media ownership (e.g., press and broadcasting in the same hands) (Borstel, 1956; Nixon, 1960; Nixon & Hahn, 1971; Nixon & Jones, 1956). Second, there have been international comparisons of press or media systems designed to index the number and kind of government controls on the operation of the press (Farace & Donohew, 1965; more recently, Weaver, Buddenbaum, & Fair, 1985). Both kinds of inquiry were characteristically American, geared to U.S. experience, or reflecting First Amendment principles of no government intervention.

Adequate measures of the structural conditions of media concentration are certainly essential for a type of performance research concerning the issue of monopoly (e.g., Picard, McCombs, Winter, & Lacy, 1988). Some effects of monopoly on content are, in principle, testable. For instance, it can be postulated that a monopoly situation of a newspaper in a circulation area will lead to a narrower range of views being available, less coverage in general, some bias toward interests of groups favored by the proprietors or by a local elite, or lower quality through absence of competition. Alternative, more "positive," predictions are also possible. An economically secure monopoly might be more independent of advertisers, more able to use profits for better service, more inclined, because of the monopoly position, to offer a wider range of views or greater objectivity than a more partisan paper in a competitive situation. Effects postulated from chain ownership are also mixed and follow similar lines. The main strategies for research on performance as reflected in content have been to look at a paper, or papers, before and after changes in the degree of competition (e.g., Lacy, 1987; McCombs 1987; Rarick & Hartman, 1966), or to compare competitive with monopoly newspapers (Bigman, 1948; Borstel, 1956; Nixon & Jones, 1956) or different papers possessed by a single chain (Wagenburg & Soderlund, 1975), or to compare the papers in one chain with those in another. The comparative method is nearly always employed, since there is no absolute measure of independence.

In such comparisons, the measures of quality of performance used have generally concerned one or more of the following: the direction of political endorsements (as between established parties), the range of issues dealt with editorially, and the volume and variety of content, with particular reference to locally relevant, or self-originated, content. Most of the studies of the effects of monopoly situations and chain ownership and reviews of such studies (e.g., Baer, Geller, Grundfest, & Possner, 1974; Fletcher, 1981; Stempel, 1973) have, in fact, found little conclusive evidence to support the predictions of the critics of monopoly and concentration.

The question of measuring independence in performance has been approached in ways other than by reference to concentration and its possible effects. As suggested above, media that use their freedom ought to be known by their works. One general heading for indicators of use of freedom is "editorial vitality," which refers to qualities associated with independence and activity on the part of a medium. Bogart (1979), basing his suggestions on a survey of editors of U.S. daily newspapers, offers the following set of empirical criteria of editorial quality (this version is adapted from Fletcher, 1981):

(1) a high ratio of staff to wire copy (indicating editorial vigor and individuality)

(2) a large newshole (indicating commitment to news content, as well as financial success)

(3) a high ratio of news interpretation and backgrounds to spot news (indicating a successful adjustment to the television age)

(4) a large number of letters to the editor (indicating capacity to engage the reader)

(5) wide diversity of political columnists (indicating a willingness to provide a general forum for political debate as a substitute for competition)

While these are not all equal or direct measures of freedom as such, they could all be regarded as outcomes of an independent editorial policy, rather than one restricted by group policy, government, or economic shortage.

In the same vein, additional measures have been suggested and applied in press assessment. For instance, Lemert, in several publications, has applied measures of the degree of "mobilizing information," which he defines as "any information which allows people to act on the attitudes they already have" (see Lemert, 1989; Lemert & Ashman, 1983; Lemert & Cook, 1982; Lemert, Mitzman, Siether, Hackett, & Cook, 1977). For instance, content that gives times, dates, places, and names in relation to matters of controversy or in editorial comments is more "vigorous" than vague commentary. The concept of "active editorial policy" as an index of use of freedom can also be derived from a normative perspective on the journalistic role, according to which it should be participant and advocative (Janowitz, 1975: Johnstone, 1972: Weaver & Wilhoit, 1986).

There are further definitions and operationalizations to be found, for instance, in the index of journalistic "activity" employed by Clarke and Evans (1980), which involves measuring the frequency of interviewing candidates, talking with campaign managers, contacting supporters' groups, and using libraries and other sources.

Another measure relevant to freedom that has been developed deals with *conflict* in various forms. Thus Thrift (1973), in his study of the effect of chain ownership on content, measured "editorial vigor" in terms of four indicators: the degree of attention to local topics (see also Kariel & Rosenvall, 1981), the use of *argumentative* forms in editorial comment, the location of issues in a *controversial* context, and the degree of mobilizing information, as defined by Lemert et al. (1977). Donohue, Olien, and Tichenor (1985) report research that relates "conflict reporting" to other factors, including ownership. They define local conflict in the news as "space devoted to reporting about manifestly differing positions or statements about a public issue from at least two persons, factions or interest groups in the community" (see also Cony, 1953; Riffe & Shaw, 1982).

This particular approach to indexing freedom derives mainly from the tradition of conceiving the press as having a watchdog or adversarial role in society, and therefore as likely to voice, or give access to, criticism of authority (Rivers & Nyham, 1973). The incidence of "investigative" reporting can also provide a viable index of performance of the critical function in society. There are, however, problems in identifying what might count in this category. It is important to differentiate between "hard" and "soft" targets of investigative reporting. The former are those with power and resources to fight back. Stories critical of the powerful are more resource consuming and risky even if the will is present to report them. Special notice should also be taken of investigations that do not have obvious returns in the way of audience appeal or public reward (for instance, unpopular causes or unsensational victims).

A related line of approach associates the actual use of media freedom with a generally nonconformist performance. The implicit theory is that freedom involves a distancing from established power and authority and a sympathy with those with less established power in society. This also has some connection with the view that media should not become too dependent on particular institutional sources, or even "assimilated," in Gieber and Johnson's (1961) terms. Measures of independence from sources are not easy to apply directly, but Chittick (1970), Sigal (1974), and others since (Berkowitz, 1987; Brown, Bybee, Wearden, & Straughan, 1987; Miller, 1978; Molotch & Lester, 1974) have classified quoted or documented sources in news according to their position in the institutional and power hierarchy.

For instance, Sigal found 81% of sources to be "officials" and, in general, twice as many sources were classified as "routine" as were called "enterprise." Analysis of foreign news usually offers opportunities for recording the closeness of reports to official (especially foreign ministry or military) sources and to lines of national foreign policy (e.g., Adams, 1982; Becker, 1977; Larson, 1984). This is open to several explanations, but deviation from official policy is likely to indicate editorial independence.

Related to this approach is the research on treatment of minority groups, also discussed below. The degree and quality of attention paid to more nonconformist groups in society has been measured by comparison with the treatment of established groups (e.g., Shoemaker, 1984). This is, indirectly, a measure of media "conformity," and one would expect a free medium to be less conformist. The attempt to measure conformity goes back a long way (Bigman, 1948; Breed, 1958), but has not been much developed. Several other possibilities remain as lines of investigation into freedom in performance. One concerns freedom from pressure by advertisers, although this has yielded very few results from systematic content analysis.

Another, more fruitful, line of investigation has been into the undue reliance by news media on official sources and public relations (e.g. Baerns, 1987; Sigal, 1974; Turk, 1986). Such research is, inevitably, laborious, since it generally requires comparing reports over a large span of time or topics with an even more voluminous set of possible source material in a form that is rarely very accessible. The links of dependency or symbiosis with sources are very hard to track down and demonstrate.

These observations underline the fragility of any link that can be established between empirical indicators of content and the complex concept of freedom or independence. We are reminded of the importance of other kinds of evidence on this point, especially reports by observers (e.g., Gans, 1979), judgments of those working within the media about the actual autonomy they enjoy (e.g., Bowers, 1967; Meyer, 1987; Weaver & Wilhoit, 1986), the views of media audiences, and the degree to which they regard their chosen media to be acting independently (e.g., Einsiedel & Winter 1983; Immerwahr & Doble, 1969).

The attempt to operationalize freedom in press performance has directed our attention to a number of tasks or functions widely attributed to media in modern societies — especially those that have to do with critical, adversarial, watchdog, and investigative activities. There is obvious difficulty in objectively distinguishing appearances show from the reality. The exercise of freedom that really counts often brings no reward — often the reverse. The consideration of possible measures of use of freedom is reminiscent of a somewhat hoary but seemingly still valid view that "a cantankerous press, an obstinate press, a ubiquitous press must be suffered by those in authority to preserve the even greater values of freedom of expression and the right of people to know" (Judge Gurfein, *United States v. New York Times Co.*).

A very large territory has also been omitted in this discussion, which deals only with a limited sphere of media activity — that of conventional news reporting. Left out of account, largely because it is still unexplored territory in research terms, is the possible exercise of freedom (or lack thereof) in broadcasting by directors, producers, editors, and decision makers in the spheres of drama, docudrama, talk shows, and even comedy and entertainment programming where controversial matters may be involved. The principles by which we recognize the use of freedom are likely to be similar, although the methods have to be different and are largely undeveloped and untried. What we know about this territory, which is not as well protected by the norms of the media institution, is largely derived from anecdote and case lore, rather than systematic inquiry.

DIVERSITY: PRINCIPLES AND
ASSESSMENT RESEARCH STRATEGIES

The main appeal of diversity lies in the underlying promise of choice and of change. At the level of a whole society, media diversity means that there will be a number of independent media from which to choose (thus a relation with freedom). *Diversity in media* refers to real choice in several respects: choice of different kinds of media (press, radio, TV), of alternative channels; of function or type of content (information, entertainment, culture); of direction, principle, and belief; of geographical relevance (local, regional, national); and of language, ethnic, or cultural identity.

An idea usually central to diversity is that media should, in some way, *reflect* or express the same diversity that exists in the society, and in more or less the same proportion (McQuail & van Cuilenburg, 1983). However, there are two sub-principles of diversity that are in some tension with each other. Proportionate representation, or reflection of social reality, is not the only possibility. There is an alternative principle of open or equal diversity (closely related to the idea of equality), which stresses the value of giving the same degree of access to all "voices," streams, or types of media content that are recognized as having a legitimate claim. In practice, this is not fully realizable, but it can be approached as an ideal or standard and it is a genuine alternative to proportional reflection. An example of open and equal diversity is the allocation in some countries of equal television air time to the contending parties in elections which occurs in several countries.

Arguments in favor of this version of diversity include the view that the reflective principle may keep small "voices" at a permanent disadvantage and thus inhibit change (minorities always remain so). Proportional allocation of access may also not provide sufficient media time or space for communication needs to be met with a minimum level of adequacy. Thus the reflective type of diversity goes with stability and continuity, while open access goes more with social change.

Another distinction of principle that has consequences for research is between an "internal" and an "external" type of diversity. The first is appropriate at the (micro) level of a single channel or newspaper, for instance, and refers to the offering of a full range of relevant differences by the *same* medium — varied media functions, varied points of view, alternative versions of the same events, and so on. This is now the common model or standard, for national radio or television channels especially, but also for newspapers, which try to serve large, undifferentiated publics in an impartial way. It is a model often thought appropriate under conditions of monopoly (e.g., the "one-paper city" or the typical national public service television channel) and also more appropriate to a situation (now very common) in which most people read only one newspaper.

The notion of internal diversity also tends to be most compatible with the professional journalistic tendency toward objectivity (Weaver & Wilhoit, 1986) and with a more secular, pluralistic, and less ideologically divided form of society than was common in the past. The alternative "external" diversity model is more applicable at the macro or meso level — relating to a media system or sector. It indicates a range of alternative media that, although internally homogeneous, are very different from each other in function, editorial stand, and so on. In this situation, the system as a whole is diverse, but the media experience of any one typical audience member is homogeneous. The model is illustrated by the generally fading situation of a strongly party-aligned press in a multiparty democracy, or by the division of broadcasting access between political and religious streams, as in the Netherlands (Wieten, 1979).

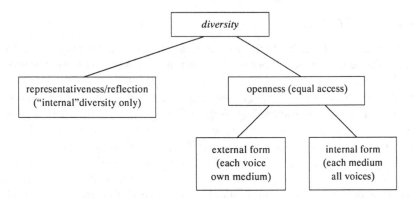

Figure 3. Component criteria for diversity assessment.

In order to deploy any of these types of diversity criteria in assessment research, a judgment has still to be made about the most relevant differentiating variables according to which media should be assessed. Is it to be politics, religion, class, language, cultural taste, or some other dimension? Normally, this choice will be influenced by what happens to be most significant in a given society and its media system.

It is difficult, if not impossible, to assess media diversity, as outlined, without reference to "extramedia data" (i.e., other evidence about the society). This evidence will probably consist of the relevant distributions of the chosen variables, for comparison, in the society itself. The main elements in diversity research are shown in Figure 3. An additional consideration is the extent to which media channels are actually available to, or reach, audiences. While large-scale, general media usually achieve this, the many separate channels of the "external" type of media system may well have little effective reach, thus failing in practice to add much to diversity. This calls for attention to "audience diversity."

The main strategies for investigating media diversity are relatively simple. Differentiation can be assessed by mutual comparison of all sets of chosen content examples or by comparing any media content to some extramedia standard of variation (e.g., a population norm). A typical strategy is to categorize content according to criteria that can also be applied to external "reality" such as the distribution of political allegiance or opinion. The more the media content distribution conforms to the external (societal) distribution, the more "positive" the result according to the standard of "reflective" diversity. The more content is *equally* distributed between the main significant "voices" in society, the more positive the result in term of "openness" or "equal access." In the following paragraphs, the main fields of application of the diversity concept are considered separately.

Politics

In the case of politics, the basic (extramedia) standard of diversity is usually derived from the distribution of political support in the country. The classification of media content according to political direction can be carried out in several different ways. News content can be assessed in terms of its reference to one or other party or politician or according to its political source. Content can also be classified according to issues or topics, with a view to establishing the "political agenda" (Hofstetter, 1976; Klein & Maccoby, 1954). Different media may offer different agendas, which can be compared to party agendas (Chaffee & Wilson, 1977; Graber, 1976; Kraus & Davis, 1976). Editorials can be classified according to their direction or tendency in ideological terms or simply in terms of their endorsement of party or candidate (Geis, 1987). The political diversity of a media sector (e.g., that of the daily newspaper) can be assessed in terms of the number of titles or the overall balance of circulation, classified by political leaning or endorsement. Detailed analysis of editorial content on key issues can produce sophisticated indicators of left or right leaning of a given media channel.

Minorities

Any media system claiming to be diverse should give access to a wide range of minorities. *Access* can refer to direct entry to channels on independent terms or simply to appearance as a referent in media content. The question most often raised is whether minority groups, movements, and ideas are "visible" in content proportionally to their incidence in the society. This would be to apply a criterion of "reflective" diversity. In general, the more reference to such groups or movements, the higher the degree of diversity. In this connection, consideration has been given to ethnic, language, or cultural minorities (e.g., Halloran, 1976), but there is also a case for treating women as a minority for these purposes, given the subordinate position of women as represented in most media (e.g. Franzwa, 1974; Gallagher, 1981; Seggar & Wheeler, 1973; Tuchman et al., 1978).

A wide range of minority, fringe, or even deviant groups can be considered (Fedler, 1973; Shoemaker, 1984), and the appropriate standard of diversity will depend on the nature of the group. For instance, the claim of women to representative treatment is the same as the claim to "equal" access. Montgomery (1989) describes the efforts of many minority groups and causes to secure more and more favorable treatment in U.S. network television entertainment. In some countries, the representation of regional cultures, or interests, in national-level media may also be at issue.

Audience Choice

Diversity can be interpreted more narrowly, simply as the range of real choice offered to the audience as a set of consumers. This question has been raised mainly in the context of assessing the possible effects of media concentration or in situations where diversity is defined purely in market terms. There are a good many examples of research into the effects of concentration (e.g., Picard et al., 1988), and other research has been directed from time to time at assessing the range of choice offered by U.S. networks, when these held an effective monopoly of national television (e.g., Dominick & Pearce, 1976). More recently, the potential effects of increased commercialism on the diversity of television offerings have received attention (e.g. Blumler, Brynin, & Nossiter, 1986). Other research has looked at the duplication of news offerings by supposedly competing news media (Donohue & Glasser, 1978; Glasgow Media Group, 1976; Lemert, 1974; Luttberg, 1983; McQuail, 1977).

The question of diversity in the sense of variety and choice has been controversial in Europe because of increasing press monopoly and in the United States for the additional reason that Federal Communications Commission regulations used to require stations to offer choices to viewers and listeners (Owen, 1979). The proliferation of new cable channels has given new impetus to the demand for measures of degree of choice in television or radio offerings. Aside from simply treating quantity of offerings as diversity, the main methods employed have been as follows: Content is categorized into an agreed-upon set of categories and measures of variety are calculated, estimating degree of choice (number of different content categories) offered by a service over a period of time or the degree of choice available to a hypothetical viewer/listener at a point in time (e.g., Litman, 1979). The outcomes of such measures are heavily reliant on the category system chosen and cannot easily allow for other differences in quality of what is offered.

Reflecting Social Reality

A remaining large area of inquiry concerns balance, or representation of the external social reality as variously measured in mass media of all kinds, fiction as well as nonfiction. The extent to which media reflect the social reality is a question of diversity as well as of objectivity, insofar as we expect a balanced or representative picture — a media diversity roughly equivalent to the visible diversity of social life.

Again, there is no limit to the possibilities, but several questions have recurred in research. One concerns the representation in news of the geographic diversity of the real world. Several studies have compared relative attention to other countries in foreign news with the actual distribution of geographical space or population, showing a high degree of concentration on certain regions and countries, and thus a low diversity of coverage (e.g., Gerbner & Marvanyi, 1977; Womack, 1981). In particular, small and/or poor countries are largely invisible or presented in a distorted manner in the news attention of larger, richer countries (Larson, 1984; Mowlana, 1985).

The social world has also been shown to be represented unfaithfully in media (especially fiction) content. Relatively missing or lacking in prominence are the old, the poor, routine occupations, and everyday experience (Cassata & Skill,

1983; Greenberg, 1980). The wider the gap between media representation and the actual lifeworld of the audience, the more distorting effects on the construction of social meaning can be posited and the less well the audience is served in some of its needs, especially those that concern coping with real experience.

Audience Diversity

There are two main issues that might be investigated with respect to audience diversity. First, there is the question of audience composition, where two alternative diversity standards are available, one of internal, the other of external diversity, already described with reference to media content. As applied to audiences, the internal variant refers to those that are heterogeneous in composition, usually large and usually attracted to media sources that offer a wide range of content and "balanced" points of view. The alternative case is one where a potentially large audience is fragmented into relatively self-contained and homogeneous minority audiences, each somewhat different from the others.

The second main issue concerns diversity of reception (in terms of both selection and interpretation) on the part of an audience. We know that messages as received often differ from messages as sent, and that this may mean either a widening or a narrowing of the diversity at the point of reception. Often the "bias" in selection by audiences tends to accentuate a bias that may also be built into the content. For instance, relative lack of attention to certain kinds of international news in content as offered may be followed by differential audience avoidance of the same kinds of news. However, diversity of audience *interpretation* may also restore variety that seems missing in content as sent (e.g., Liebes & Katz, 1986). Methods of research for establishing diversity of reception are still at an early stage of development.

OBJECTIVITY:
PRINCIPLES AND RESEARCH STRATEGIES

The relation of "objectivity" to the three fundamental values (in Figure 1) is not obvious at first sight, partly because of the dual meaning of objectivity (see Figure 4) — as "truth" and as "impartiality." The range of application of the objectivity criterion applies primarily to the informational function and to content alone and thus is narrower than either freedom or diversity. Even so, its importance to the media is hard to exaggerate, and it has acquired a central place in the practice of media assessment research.

There is, also, an important connection with fundamental values. First, without freedom, media objectivity is not likely to be possible. Second, the media claim to free operation (ready access to information and right to publish) is strengthened or protected by the practice of objectivity. Third, without objectivity, there would be less freedom (e.g., for unpopular or minority voices) to be heard in an undistorted

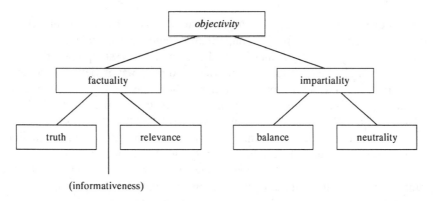

Figure 4. Component criteria of objectivity.

way. The practice of objectivity also involves diversity in recognizing alternative points of view, and vice versa. Objectivity can support equality by allowing no distinction according to the power of advocates or sources, judging only according to relevance.

Apart from these links, objectivity has been a frequent criterion of assessment just because it is so important both to journalists and to audiences. It underpins the *credibility* of media sources and thus serves the needs of the audience for reliable information. Most modern news media set a lot of store by their claim to objectivity in its several meanings. Policies for broadcasting in many countries impose, by various means, a requirement of objectivity on their public broadcasting systems, sometimes as a condition of their independence.

It is not easy to define objectivity, but one version of its various components has been set out by Westerstahl (1983) in the context of research into the degree of objectivity shown by the Swedish broadcasting system. This version (Figure 4) recognizes that objectivity has to deal with values as well as with facts, and that facts also have evaluative implications.

In this scheme, *factuality* refers, first of all, to a form of reporting that deals in events and statements that can be checked against sources and are presented free from comment or at least clearly separated from any comment. Factuality involves several other "truth criteria": completeness of an account, accuracy, and an intention not to mislead or suppress what is relevant (good faith). The second main aspect of factuality is *relevance.* This is more difficult both to define and to achieve in an objective way. It relates to the process of *selection* rather than to the form of presentation, and requires that selection take place according to clear and coherent principles of what is significant for the intended receiver and/or the society (Nordenstreng, 1974). In general, what affects most people most immediately and most strongly is likely to be considered most relevant.

According to Westerstahl's scheme, impartiality presupposes a "neutral attitude" and has to be achieved through a combination of balance (equal or proportional time/space/emphasis) between opposing interpretations, points of view, or versions of events and neutrality in presentation. Under conditions of external diversity, as described above, the impartiality component of objectivity can be waived, although the component of factuality cannot. The assumption is that there will be alternative media to tell the story from another point of view. For instance, a strongly partisan paper in a partisan system is not expected to present the reader with all points of view, although the reader still expects reliable information.

The scheme in Figure 4 has been given an extra element, that of *informativeness*, that is important to the fuller meaning of objectivity. The reference is to qualities of informational content that are likely to improve the chances of actually getting information across: being noticed, understood, remembered, and so on. This is the pragmatic side of information, which is often undervalued or neglected in assessment, but is essential to the fuller notion of performance.

The field of objectivity research that has been mapped out can now be dealt with according to the four main elements indicated: truth, relevance, balance, and neutrality (of presentation). In general, according to Rosengren (1981), the former two relate to more cognitive aspects of objectivity; the latter two, to more evaluative direction. He also characterizes truth and neutrality more as pertaining to form and presentation, while relevance and balance are closely linked to processes of selection.

Truth Aspects of Objectivity

The main task for performance assessment is to identify, in the eventual media product, the signs of those strategies pursued by journalists (we are essentially in the territory of journalism) for gaining credibility (Gaziano, 1983). Four main criteria have been deployed in research on this aspect of information quality: amount of information provided, completeness of accounts, accuracy, and factualness.

Quantity of Information

The simplest measure to apply records whether or not information is offered on a given topic or an event and the quantity of information presented. This has been carried out by counts of space, time, or words and is usually expressed as a percentage of available "newshole" (Bush, 1960). Despite its simplicity it is a powerful tool, especially when coupled with a relevant category system of possible topics and with possibilities for comparison with other media sources or with a version of external "reality" (Blackman & Hornstein, 1977; Golding & Elliott, 1979, McQuail, 1977).

Completeness or Fullness of Account

For assessment on this point, an external criterion is indispensable, though rarely available in an adequate form. There are atypical cases where one can define a total universe of relevant information — for instance, the verbatim record of a meeting or the text of an address. Political campaign situations may also provide a universe of relevant content for practical purposes (Danielson & Adams, 1961). In principle, in such cases, the universe is provided by the *sources* (e.g., the political parties). An alternative strategy is to find some other "media" source or archive of main facts, or one can take the reporting by a set of media as constituting the relevant universe for practical purposes and for assessing relative completeness of a given account (McQuail, 1977). Most real *events* are too complex and ambiguous for completeness of reports even to be conceivable. It is also difficult to determine how much, or what proportion, can be considered "enough" information.

Accuracy

A good deal of attention has been paid in the literature on journalism to the question of measuring accuracy (see Stone et al., 1987). Three main strategies have been employed. One is to check reports against any available record of the factual aspects of what is reported. Such external records will vary a good deal in quality, from official statistics to partisan and subjective versions of events. Complete accuracy checks are impossible, but content analysis can provide an accuracy index, and other media sources may be used for identifying inaccuracies.

A second strategy is to check back with sources referred to for their assessment of accuracy of reports (Ryan & Owen, 1977; Tankard & Ryan, 1974). Sources are not likely to be neutral judges of reports, and such checking is also partial and time-consuming, but the method does allow the relative significance of errors to be assessed, since this varies a good deal and content analysis alone is likely to find only the more trivial inaccuracies. The third strategy is to appeal to audience members for their estimates of accuracy (e.g., Kocher & Shaw, 1981). Examining headlines for their accuracy in relation to the stories that follow (e.g., Marquez, 1980) offers an additional line of research, and the same possibility is offered by captions to photos or by verbal comment on television visuals.

Factualness

This term refers to several aspects of the form of media information. The most general requirement of "factualness" is that facts are clearly separated from comment or opinion. Facts are to be recognized by some formal properties, especially their reference to some "real" event and their being, in principle, "checkable." An additional aspect relates to what might be called information "density" (Asp, 1981): the relative number of items of information per time/space unit. A reverse measure would be that of "redundancy," which can also be formally measured (Taylor, 1953).

Relevance Aspects of Objectivity

The best, and perhaps only, judge of relevance is often thought to be the intended receiver, according to a definition of relevance in terms of what the audience finds useful or interesting. There is, nevertheless, an alternative view that some kinds of information are objectively more significant than others (Hemanus, 1976; Nordenstreng, 1974). A third view, often heard from professional journalists, is that relevance is a special quality of which they are the best judges by virtue of their experience and developed intuition. The first version of relevance leaves the audience to decide. The second version requires either some theory (e.g., Marxism) or some authority to make a value judgment, or some other choice of perspective to be adopted. The third relies on the interpretive skills of journalists, which can be variable. All three versions of relevance refer to a principle of *selection*, of what is to be offered or given prominence.

In any case, the common notion in each version translates relevance into *significance* or *pertinence* — the question of what matters and what is to the point. In the absence of any fixed criterion or ultimate authority, a number of attributes of content can serve as indicators of relevance, as long as we take into account the purpose of the information and the intended audience. Relevance is always relative.

Some situations lend themselves to quite sensible kinds of relevance research, provided that we make certain assumptions. For instance, in election campaigns, policy and issue content is more relevant to political choice than procedural or human interest news (Graber, 1976). Measures of "sensationalism" (e.g., Dominick, Wurtzel, & Lometti, 1975; Tannenbaum & Lynch, 1960) have been developed to deal with the obverse of what is relevant. In general, measures of relevance imply a distancing from the "superficial," "personal," and "human interest" aspects of content. In so doing, however, they may leave out the possible effects of such "nonrelevant" content in gaining attention, which is a necessary condition of communication effect ("informativeness").

Relevance can also refer to the degree to which people are affected or touched by a report or an event. The more people affected in some way, the more relevance. This implies that we can assess the relevance of information by reference to the factors of time, proximity, scale, and intensity. The sooner, the closer to home, the more people affected, and the greater intensity of effect, the more relevance (see Galtung & Ruge, 1965).

Informativeness (A Note)

This note relates to the entry appended to the Westerstahl (1983) scheme (Figure 4) on the dual assumption that information quality ultimately has to meet the test of informing people and that the degree of success in conveying information is also a relevant measure of performance. There has been much research into content factors that might relate to informative potential, especially various measures of "readability" and verbal difficulty (e.g., Flesch, 1982). As an extension of this tradition, there have also been inquiries into the comparative information capacity of different channels, with attention to other factors besides difficulty level that could help communication, such as the concreteness, personalization, and emotional appeal of the chosen message and presentation forms (e.g., Trenaman, 1967).

Finally, there has been an upsurge of interest in the empirical measurement in natural settings of the degree to which television news leads to comprehension and recall of news reports (Robinson & Levy, 1986). This research is often designed to yield lessons for the improvement of news formats. The results are often consistent with the view noted above that "irrelevant" aspects of content may well be productive in the informational task and not simply distracting.

Balance Aspects of Objectivity

The approach to assessing balance and neutrality, the two remaining sub-concepts of neutrality entered on Figure 4, will vary according to the kind of news or informational text we are dealing with. News texts can have evaluative bias or tendencies of different kinds and for different reasons (Hackett, 1984). Three main kinds of bias in news can be identified (McQuail, 1986b): (a) partisan reporting from a declared political or value position; (b) "unwitting" bias, where a consistent tendency occurs unintentionally, for instance, through ethnocentricity or reliance on limited sources, or deployment of conventional news values or frames of interpretation; and (c) manipulated news, designed to appear objective, but having a tendentious purpose.

The objectivity requirements of balance (which may also be known by the cognate terms of *impartiality, fairness,* or *evenhandedness*) and of impartiality can be assessed in different ways. A first requirement will be identical to that already mentioned: a clear separation of fact from comment, specifically, a clear identification of value judgments and of their source (whose judgments they are), which might be the writer/presenter or, more likely, one or more of the protagonists in an event account. The analyst will, in any case, have to attempt to make the separation, if it is not made in the text itself.

Apart from this, two main strategies of analysis are available. First, the space/time of any text can be allocated to the doings or sayings of the main parties or protagonists on the assumption that a balanced news report will give attention to reference persons or events either in equal degree, in a way proportional to their involvement in the event (the principle of representation), or according to their significance in the whole (the principle of relevance).

A second strategy, based on the assumption that even objective, balanced news will report some factual matters that carry evaluative implications and associations, is to assess the overall balance that is struck between the main referents/actors in terms of their *association* with "positive" or "negative" events or things (Westerstahl, 1983). Balance here is equated with evenhandedness of direction.

A few examples may clarify the strategies and the choices to be made between them. Research on political (campaign) communication often looks at the balance of content devoted to competing parties or candidates as a measure of media objectivity (e.g., Clarke & Evans, 1980; Danielson & Adams, 1961; Graber, 1976; Hofstetter, 1976; McCombs, 1967). In another field of institutionalized conflict, that of industrial relations, there is an expectation that parties to disputes (e.g., management and workers) should get equal chances to state their cases (Glasgow Media Group, 1976; McQuail, 1977). Allocation of content to the relevant "sides" in these cases has usually proved feasible. There are circumstances, however, where equal representation or representative treatment cannot be expected and where the notion of balance may be inappropriate — for instance, in matters of serious crime, violation of human rights, or terrorism (Paletz et al., 1982).

Research into balance, in terms of evaluative direction or of association with negative or positive aspects of events, is also well represented in the research literature. Various social out-groups have been shown to be associated systematically in news reporting with "bad news" for the majority. For instance, strikers have been associated with misery for the general public (Glasgow Media Group, 1976, 1980), welfare claimants with fecklessness (Golding & Middleton, 1982), immigrants with conflict and social problems (because of nonacceptance by the "host" society; Hartman & Husband, 1974; van Dijk, 1987), youth with disorder (Cohen, 1972), and various minority groups with bad news for society (Fedler, 1973; Shoemaker, 1984).

There are several alternative research methods for such work, but use is often made of the concept of "image" (as in Sreberny-Mohammadi, 1984), referring to constellations of (often negative or stereotypical) features that tend to characterize some object of reference. A very sensitive and theoretically grounded research method for analyzing the evaluative direction of verbal texts is "evaluative assertion analysis" (see Holsti, 1969; van Cuilenburg, de Ridder, & Kleinijenhuis, 1986), developed some time ago by Osgood, Tannenbaum, and Suci (1957). This method can help establish the built-in evaluation of particular referents that appear in texts and also the evaluative structure of complete texts.

Neutrality of Presentation

The last sector of the objectivity field to be dealt with concerns the *manner* of presentation, which can affect the impression created on a reader, listener, or viewer, independent of substance. This also often reflects, or indexes, the conscious or unwitting bias of the source, communicator, or medium. There are many different ways in which presentation can embody an evaluative tendency, whether intentionally or not. Diverse examples are to be found in the complaints of those who feel they been portrayed in an unfavorable or unflattering light.

At the simplest level, it is usually quite easy to identify and tabulate emotive and "colored" or value-laden words and expressions, and to find their directional relation to the referents of interest in news texts (Geis, 1987). This may be especially relevant to the analysis of headlines, where emotive words often occur.

The use of words that influence meaning has parallels in visual and aural presentations, where choices of camera angles, photographs, music, graphics, and backgrounds can all be used, or are open to interpretation, as devices for giving direction or bias to informative texts and messages (see, for instance, Glasgow

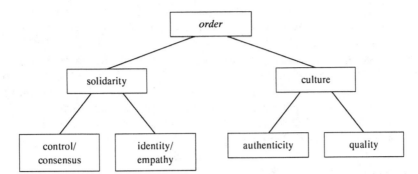

Figure 5. Component criteria of order.

Media Group, 1980, 1985; Kepplinger, 1983). The makeup of newspaper pages, the placing and juxtaposition of items (including photographs and different stories), which are open to analysis, can all contribute to evaluative effects.

Evaluative direction is given to messages not only by the specifics of language or presentation, but also by the location of an account within a particular context or framework in which the "reader" is led toward a particular interpretation that is never made clear. News "items" are typically, even necessarily, placed in "frames of relevance" — wider contexts and formats that are assumed to be widely understood (Altheide, 1985). These frameworks usually allocate positive and negative values, employ certain kinds of discourse, identify heroes and villains, or activate latent sympathies (see Geis, 1987; van Dijk, 1987).

ORDER (SOLIDARITY AND CULTURE): PRINCIPLES AND ASSESSMENT STRATEGIES

The two entries (solidarity and culture) under the general term *order* in Figure 1 are closely related (see below). Solidarity has two main aspects: control and conformity from the point of view of established authority, and its more genuinely solidaristic, or "we," function, as if *on behalf of* component or subordinate groups in society. In the former meaning, solidarity is in tension with freedom, although in the second sense, freedom and solidarity may be close together.

The distinction is not easy to sustain because of the intimate connection between the two. Any "social order" implies processes of binding together that involve both social control and voluntary attachment (thus solidarity) and also the sharing of meanings and definitions, as well as ways of life and actual experience (thus culture). Culture expresses and promotes solidarity and solidarity generates forms of culture.

Solidarity also involves the social control and hegemonic tendencies that have been attributed to mass media, especially in critical theory. The alternative meaning of solidarity — the view from the subgroup or from "below" — is more likely to relate to subcultural and minority identity, attachment to local community and local culture.

Media assessment with respect to culture opens up diverse possible lines of procedure, since the concept is the most general of all those so far introduced. *Culture* here refers to any organized set of symbolic forms, but different cultural spheres have to be identified and given an empirical location. The three main alternatives for identification are (a) by way of a group or set of people (identified by gender, locality, class, language, and so on), (b) by a set of activities (work, home, sport, politics), or (c) by way of particular forms and artifacts (books, films, performances, genres, designs).

In practice, the main concerns of media assessment in cultural matters have been related either to people (especially the representation of subcultures and the relation of media content to the local place and local cultural identity) or to matters of quality of forms and artifacts (types of culture). The main issues for performance assessment are thus also presented in Figure 5, under the two headings *authenticity*, referring to the question of genuine representation of the culture of a group, and *quality*, referring either to aesthetic (form) or to moral (content) aspects of culture.

Solidarity (Types of Order)

This discussion seeks to identify several varieties of solidarity, each related to the concept of social cohesion and each relevant to research on mass media. An essential background question is that of *whose order* we are talking about, the recurrent matter of perspective necessary for evaluating media performance. The distinctions that follow (types of order) each imply an answer to this question.

Order as Control

From the perspective of a hypothetical established authority, the main questions that have arisen for media assessment concern the representation of various kinds of disorder, on the assumption that this may lead to an effect of disorder in society. Most attention has thus been given to individual crime, aggression, and violence as portrayed in media, especially in fictional content. But other kinds of deviance may attract a similar kind of attention, for instance, social unrest, rioting, or even institutional political or economic corruption. There is little evidence of much concern with the last two of these, but there has been sporadic attention to rioting and unrest, as in the United States in the late 1960s (Paletz & Dunn, 1969) or Britain at the start of the 1980s. If one extends this category or "order" concerns to the question of the media portrayal of terrorism, international or national, then a considerable literature can be unearthed (Schmid & de Graaf, 1982).

Research in this field of inquiry tends to concentrate on news and information content, but, in fact, social unrest and terrorism are also major themes of fiction (Schlesinger, Murdock, & Elliott, 1983). Research has dealt with the possible effects of such themes, the degree of sensational attention paid to them, the interpretive framework in which such reports are placed, and the question of whether such acts are justified. From the point of view of authorities, "good" media performance consists of cooperation with authorities and silence or bad publicity for the "other side."

The field of inquiry into crime, violence, and aggression is too extensive even to begin to summarize (but see Comstock, Chaffee, Katzman, McCombs, & Roberts, 1978). It is enough to say that there is no shortage of methods for assessing the amount and kind of media portrayals of crime, violence, and similar forms of deviance. A good example is provided by the "cultural indicators" research of Gerbner and associates (e.g., Gerbner & Gross, 1976), which has provided a continuing index of the representation of violence on U.S. television since the mid-1970s. More recently, attention has been paid to pornography and sexual aggression as a special form of content (e.g., McCormack, 1980; Zillmann & Bryant, 1982). In this field, quantitative content evidence is often supplemented by qualitative assessment on matters such as the relative attractiveness, rewards, and realism of portrayals of individual disorderly acts.

Order as Consensus

The degree to which media express or, alternatively, undermine a supposed broad consensus in society on fundamental political or social values has been empirically examined from the perspective of both supporters and critics of the existing social order. A surprising amount of assessment research can be placed within this framework, and methods and strategies are generally much the same as those already discussed in relation to diversity, freedom, and objectivity. Supporting a consensus can also often take the form of delegitimating or stigmatizing marginal groups in the society.

Order as Identity

The other side of the coin of social control and consensus maintenance by mass media is the possibility for expression and recognition of either dominant or minority values and identity. For the mainstream of civil society, the notion of citizenship is relevant here as a form of attachment that presumes equality of rights and of conditions of "information and cultural welfare." There is some evidence that values and beliefs expressed in media content can be regarded by citizens as helping to forge and support national culture and identity (e.g., Katz, Gurevitch, & Haas, 1973, in relation Israel). Critics of the dominant consensus imply or state a demand for alternative media to help sustain alternative identities.

This aspect of media performance can also be studied at levels below that of the national culture, for instance that of region or locality. A key theme of research into local or community media has been the degree to which they give expression to the values and interests of their local publics (e.g., Cox & Morgan, 1973; Edelstein

& Larsen, 1960; Jackson, 1971; Janowitz, 1952; Kariel & Rosenvall, 1981, 1983; Stamm, 1985).

Solidarity also refers to the link between media and a wide variety of minority or special interest groups. Research here is largely coextensive with research into the external diversity of media: the degree of separate access for ethnic, language, or other subcultural minorities. Some of these minorities will consist of dissenting and oppositional elements within society. The relevant strategies and methods for solidarity research are inevitably diverse, but the essential component will be some measure of the degree to which a medium speaks on behalf of, and represents, the values and interests of its own special public.

Order as Empathy

The term *empathy* itself is unfamiliar in discussions of media assessment, although a corresponding idea can be recognized in research findings about the perceived "functions" or gratifications of mass media for their audiences (Rosengren, Palmgreen, & Wenner, 1985). In that context it appears, for example, as a reference to the contribution of "reality" content to achieving insight into the experiences of others, especially those in widely different social circumstances. We can easily recognize a type of media content that sets out to give sympathetic attention to problems experienced by individuals or groups. To an extent, it is the "prosocial" equivalent of media labeling and stigmatizing of out-groups. Typical examples of such media provisions would include attention to natural disasters and to victims of hunger, accidents, illness, terrorism, war, oppression, and torture. Indicators of media empathy would be based on the amount and kind of positive (and sympathetic) attention given to many different categories of "victims." Sometimes individuals in the same categories as are elsewhere stigmatized can appear as objects of empathy (e.g., victims of AIDS, convicted prisoners, immigrants).

Within the framework of empathy we may also locate the more systematic, long-term attention to major human problems of a global kind, including those of war and peace (e.g., Varis, 1986), world poverty and development, and attention to the natural environment. In general, established methods of content analysis can readily be applied to this set of questions about media performance, although the indicators of empathy have not yet been developed and tested.

Culture

The field of inquiry summarily mapped in Figure 5 involves attention to two main problems of media performance: the extent to which what is produced and offered genuinely reflects the culture (in its many aspects) of the society, region, group, or community for whom it is destined, and the intrinsic qualities of what is offered, as judged according to a potentially wide range of aesthetic or moral criteria.

Cultural Authenticity and Integrity

Several aspects of the first problem have already been dealt with, especially in connection with access and diversity, but the principles and typical lines of research can be exemplified by reference to international communication issues. In discussions of such international issues, the question of integrity and authenticity of media content has taken a central place, especially as defined within the framework of the "cultural imperialism" thesis (Boyd-Barrett, 1977; Mattelart, 1984; McPhail, 1981; Mowlana, 1985; Schiller, 1969; Tunstall, 1977).

At this level, the main questions concern (and equivalent questions can be formulated at other levels) the survival of local, indigenous cultures and languages and attention in content to locally relevant contexts and problems, models, and so on. The main principle at stake is whether media offer materials for a healthy, autonomous, and relevant cultural development, based on existing traditions and current experience. The problem has grown in scale and scope along with the internationalization of television distribution and trends toward a one-way cultural flow of media content from North to South.

It is sometimes identified in Europe (also in Latin America and Canada) in terms of either an increased "Americanization" or "Anglo-Americanization" that threatens the vitality of local cultural production or the autonomy and viability of separate national and language cultures in Europe. In this context, assessment research has been primarily concerned with measuring the degree to which the national or home culture is represented in output. The process of "transnationalization" of media has been looked at in several of its forms—content, consumption, and effects.

Cultural content can also be assessed according to its relation to the experience and background of intended or probable audiences. A premium would be placed on "realism" and relevance to normal experience.

Cultural "Quality"

Two main aspects of cultural provision have usually been chosen for emphasis—one relating to what might be called *aesthetic* quality, the other to *moral* quality (although the two are not easy to separate). There are, of course, innumerable possibilities for evaluative assessment, depending on perspective, standard, and the matter of whose cultural values are to be deployed. In the nature of MPA, it is established values that have most often been applied.

Attention to quality in terms of aesthetic or artistic standards has, not surprisingly, languished in the hands of social scientists for lack of objective criteria and rules for operationalization and also because of the loss of the old certainties about what counts as "good" in culture. Aside from the position of cultural relativism, there is a powerful school of thought in relation to culture generally and the popular arts in particular that supports the view that such matters have to be left to the receivers—the actual decoders, "readers," or deconstructors of texts (Fiske, 1987).

Nevertheless, some of the "old" questions about cultural quality have been resurrected at a time of deregulation and policy-making for new media, and when public debate about the cultural quality and effects of media provision is lively. Here I can report only a few of the possible strategies for research in this difficult terrain. Two main lines seem to have been followed. One has taken the presumed consensus of the cultural-artistic establishment as a source of criteria and sought to identify "cultural quality" of performance, artists, and so on in media offerings in terms of such traditional and, inevitably, elitist standards. The main alternative has been to look at media content in terms of devices and features that might index "superficiality," "triviality," "sensationalism," and in general the subordination of art (truth, beauty, integrity) to commerce (mass-market success). The "indicators" consist of such content elements as exaggerated emotionalism and conflict of characters, melodrama, and dominance of (especially visual) attention-gaining devices.

There is also the possibility of treating the degree of "commercialism" of content and service as an index of cultural quality in its own right, as it were. This would commonly be regarded as a negative quality, because of the links between commerce and manipulative intention and the potential conflict with the integrity (truth quality) of the message. Indicators of commercialism of a media service can be found in the amount and obtrusiveness of advertising, the reliance on sponsors, the practice of "merchandising," and displaying brand-name consumer items in content.

An implicit assumption of many approaches to evaluation is that positive cultural quality is likely to be associated with appeal to a small minority, some mental effort, and probably some education or acquired "cultural capital" necessary for reception and enjoyment. The cultural content so identified is likely to consist either of traditional "high" culture or of novel and experimental forms that are not readily accessible to the uninitiated or untrained. Evidently, much remains to be done to establish and apply indicators that are not rooted in hierarchical and, in the end, elitist versions of aesthetic quality.

There are some less conventional and little-used possibilities for research that are less elitist and easier to apply. Thus diversity itself can be treated as a cultural as well as a social value and measured in terms of the range and differentiation of offerings, according to indicators of genre, taste, theme, and the like, or the intended audience ("taste culture" or minority group). An index of novelty, recency, or originality can also be considered at the level of channel or service, reflecting the degree of repetition and seriality and the recency of items. Unconventionality, controversialness, and even outright unpopularity might also be regarded as relevant indicators of an innovative cultural program policy.

Finally, quality may be indexed in terms of economic cost of production (for audiovisual media, at least). While there is no necessary correlation between cost and quality, certain kinds of cultural quality can be had only at great expense (original drama, for instance). Within the media industry itself, high cost would certainly be thought a necessary condition of quality in professional production terms and in terms of audience appeal.

Elitist values usually dominate when the question of moral quality of media content is examined, although they do not necessarily have to. Many different social or cultural values can be indexed by various forms of content analysis — for instance, values to do with personal relations, family, gender, private morality, consumption and life-style, beliefs, education, and tolerance (or prejudice). It is for the researcher to choose whether to emphasize conventional morality (e.g., incidence of nudity or explicit sex) or to pay more attention to alternative moral questions (e.g., to do with gender exploitation, militarism, consumerism). Methods for empirical value analysis of texts do exist, although they may not be fully adequate to the task.

CONCLUSION

The tradition of research which has been described may seem to stem from a time which is slipping away — one characterized by fear of either big business or big government, by limitations of access to channels, by ideological conflicts, closed national frontiers, and dominance by the print media. A contrary perception of our own time is that there is more supply and choice of media options than we are able to cope with, reduced fears of total or mass society, less dependence on centralized media, more pragmatism than ideology, rather open media frontiers. In addition, it is not the print media, oriented to information and opinion, which dominate, but television, oriented to image, entertainment, and mood.

In relation to matters of culture and morality, there is a good deal more uncertainty than in the past. The problems of "old media" situations are, thus, not the same as those of the present, and the relevant norms and strategies of enquiry may also be different. There is something in this view, however overdrawn the degree of discontinuity and however dependent, it is an altered perspective rather than an altered reality. There are still threats from concentration, often in new, more international forms, and still extensive needs for an ever-growing supply of high quality information (according to much the same standards). The demands laid on citizens in democratic societies for making informed choices are greater rather than less in a more complex and interdependent world, and information equality seems as remote as ever. There is little sign of a reduction in racism or in other kinds of discrimination, and the social conflicts referred to in the above discussion are by no means resolved.

The lesson to be drawn is not that this kind of research is obsolete or that the framework of normative principles has changed very much. What is called for is a change of priorities and new strategies and methods. Three main kinds of adaptation seem called for. First, the complexities of media structures and the interrelations between media, often across national frontiers, require new frameworks and means of analysis. Second, research will have to focus more on what reaches people and what they do with it rather than, as in the past, on what is sent from channels. Third, the methods for handling questions of evolving new forms of "culture" (drama, entertainment, etc.), especially in nonprint forms, need to be developed and redeployed within a more adequate framework of evaluative principles. There is reason to believe that fundamental methodological work is now being done, although the development of relevant frameworks of principles seems to lag.

Although the frontiers can be pushed forward to some degree, there will be limits to what can be achieved by the kind of quantified evidence which still carries weight in discussions of media policy, and, ideally, one would hope for an increased receptivity for other kinds of evaluative discourse than that characterized in the research tradition described here, however useful it is likely to remain. Finally, it can be suggested that, far from being outdated, the kind of research reviewed, which provides *information* on which to base judgments, will have a significant place in a form of society to which information is central. The decreasing possibility for effective control and regulation of a legal kind increases the need for control carried out by means of informed judgment and debate.

REFERENCES

Adams, W. C. (Ed.). (1982). *Television coverage of international affairs.* Norwood, NJ: Ablex.

Altheide, D. (1985). *Media power.* Beverly Hills, CA: Sage.

Asp, K. (1981). Mass media as molders of opinion and suppliers of information. In C. Wilhoit & C. Whitney (Eds.), *Mass communication review yearbook* (Vol. 2, pp. 332-354). Beverly Hills, CA: Sage.

Baer, W. S., Geller, H., Grundfest, J. A., & Possner, J. B. (1974). *Concentration of mass media ownership: Assessing the state of current knowledge.* Santa Monica, CA: RAND Corporation.

Baerns, B. (1987). Journalism versus public relations in the FRG. In D. L. Paletz (Ed.), *Political communication research.* Norwood, NJ: Ablex.

Becker, L. B. (1977). Foreign policy and press performance. *Journalism Quarterly, 54,* 364-366.

Berkowitz, D. (1987). TV news sources and news channels: A study in agenda building. *Journalism Quarterly, 64,* 508-513.

Bigman, S. K. (1948). Rivals in conformity: A study of two competing dailies. *Journalism Quarterly, 25,* 127-131.

Blackman, J. A., & Hornstein, H. A. (1977). Newscasters and the social actuary. *Public Opinion Quarterly, 41,* 295-313.

Blumler, J. G., Brynin, M., & Nossiter, T. (1986). Broadcasting finance and programme quality. *European Journal of Communication, 1*(3), 343-364.

Bogart L. (1979). Editorial ideals, editorial illusions. *Journal of Communication, 29,* 11-21.

Borstel, G. H. (1956). Ownership, competition and comment in twenty small dailies. *Journalism Quarterly, 33,* 220-222.

Bowers, D. R. (1967). A report on activity by publishers in directing newsroom decisions. *Journalism Quarterly, 44,* 43-52.

Boyd-Barrett, O. (1977). Media imperialism: Towards an international framework for the analysis of media systems. In J. Curran, M. Gurevitch, & J. Wollacott (Eds.), *Mass communication and society* (pp. 116-134). London: Arnold.

Breed, W. (1958). Mass communication and socio-cultural integration. *Social Forces, 53,* 326-35.

Brown, J. D., Bybee, C. R., Wearden, S. T., & Straughan, D. M. (1987). Invisible power: Newspaper news sources and the limits of diversity. *Journalism Quarterly, 64,* 45-54.

Bush, C. R. (1960). Content and mise en valeur: Attention as effect. *Journalism Quarterly, 37*, 435-437.

Cassata, M., & Skill, T. (Eds.). (1983). *Life on daytime television*. Norwood, NJ: Ablex.

Chaffee, S. H., & Wilson, D. G. (1977). Media rich, media poor: Two studies of diversity in agenda-building. *Journalism Quarterly, 54*, 466-474.

Chittick, W. O. (1970). *State department, press and pressure groups*. New York: John Wiley.

Clarke, P., & Evans, S. H. (1980). All in a day's work: Reporters covering congressional campaigns. *Journal of Communication, 30*, 112-121.

Cohen, S. (1972). *Folk devils and moral panics*. London: McGibbon & Kee.

Comstock, G., Chaffee, S., Katzman, N., McCombs, M., & Roberts, D. (Eds.). (1978). *Television and human behavior*. New York: Columbia University Press.

Cony, E. R. (1953). Conflict-cooperation content of five US dailies. *Journalism Quarterly, 30*, 15-22.

Cox, H., & Morgan, D. (1973). *City politics and the press*. Cambridge: Cambridge University Press.

Danielson, W., & Adams, J. B. (1961). Completeness of coverage of the 1960 campaign. *Journalism Quarterly, 38*, 441-452.

Davy, K. D. (1970). *The uncertain mirror* (Report, Vol. 1, of Special Senate Committee on Mass Media). Ottawa: Canadian Government Publishing Centre.

Dominick, J., & Pearce, M. C. (1976). Trends in network prime-time programming 1953-1974. *Journal of Communication, 26*(1), 70-80.

Dominick, J. R., Wurtzel, A., & Lometti, G. (1975). TV journalism vs. show business: A content analysis of Eyewitness News. *Journalism Quarterly, 52*, 213-218.

Donohue, T. R., & Glasser, T. L., (1978). Homogenization of content in Connecticut newspapers. *Journalism Quarterly, 55*, 592-596.

Donohue, T. R., Olien, C. N., & Tichenor, P. J. (1985). Reporting conflict by pluralism, newspaper type and ownership. *Journalism Quarterly, 62*, 489-499, 507.

Downs, A. (1962). The public interest: Its meaning in a democracy. *Social Research, 29*(1), 1-36.

Edelstein, A., & Larsen, O. (1960). The weekly press, contribution to a sense of urban community. *Journalism Quarterly, 37*, 489-498.

Einsiedel, E. F., & Winter, J. P. (1983). Public attitudes on media ownership: Demographic and attitudinal correlates. *Journalism Quarterly, 60*, 87-92.

Farace, V., & Donohew, L. (1965). Mass communication in national social systems. *Journalism Quarterly, 42*, 253-261.

Fedler, F. (1973). The mass media and minority groups: A study of adequacy of access. *Journalism Quarterly, 50*, 109-117.

Fiske, J. (1987). *Television culture*. London: Methuen.

Flesch, R. (1982). *The art of readable writing*. New York: Collier.

Fletcher, F. (1981). *The newspaper and public affairs* (Research Study 7). Ottawa: Royal Commission on Newspapers.

Franzwa, H. H. (1974). Working women in fact and fiction. *Journal of Communication, 24*, 104-109.

Gallagher, M. (1981). *Unequal opportunities: The case of women and the mass media*. Paris: UNESCO.

Galtung, J., & Ruge, M. (1965). The structure of foreign news. *Journal of Peace Research, 1*, 64-90.

Gars, H. (1979). *Deciding what's news*. New York: Free Press.

Gaziano, C. (1983). The knowledge gap: An analytic review of media effects. *Communication Review, 10*(4), 447-486.

Geis, M. L. (1987). *The language of politics*. New York: Springer-Verlag.

Gerbner, G., & Gross, L. (1976). Living with television: The violence profile. *Journal of Communication, 26*(2), 173-199.

Gerbner, G., & Marvanyi, G. (1977). The many worlds of the world's press. *Journal of Communication, 27*(1), 52-66.

Gieber, W., & Johnson, W. (1961). The city hall beat: A study of reporter and source roles. *Journalism Quarterly, 38*, 289-297.

Glasgow Media Group. (1976). *Bad news*. London: Routledge & Kegan Paul.

Glasgow Media Group. (1980). *More bad news*. London: Routledge & Kegan Paul.

Glasgow Media Group. (1985). *War and peace news.* London: Routledge & Kegan Paul.
Golding, P., & Elliott, P. (1979). *Making the news.* London: Longman.
Golding, P., & Middleton, S. (1982). *Images of welfare.* Oxford: Basil Blackwell.
Graber, D. (1976). Press and TV as opinion resource in presidential campaigns. *Public Opinion Quarterly, 40,* 283-303.
Greenberg, B. S. (1980). *Life on television.* Norwood, NJ: Ablex.
Gustaffsson, K. E., & Hadenius, S. (1976). *Swedish media policy.* Stockholm
Hackett, R. A. (1984). Decline of a paradigm? Bias and objectivity in news media studies. *Critical Studies in Mass Communication, 1,* 229-259.
Halloran, J. (Ed.). (1976). *Race as news.* Paris: UNESCO.
Hartman, P., & Husband, C. (1974). *Racism and mass media.* London: Davis Poynter.
Held, V. (1970). *The public interest and individual interests.* New York: Basic Books.
Hemanus, P. (1976). What is news? Objectivity in news transmission. *Journal of Communication, 26,* 102-107.
Hofstetter, R. (1976). *Bias in the news.* Columbus: Ohio State University Press.
Holsti, O. (1969). *Content analysis for the social sciences and humanities.* Reading, MA: Addison-Wesley.
Hutchins, R. (1947). *A free and responsible press.* Chicago: University of Chicago Press.
Immerwahr, J., & Doble, J. (1969). Public attitudes towards freedom of the press. *Public Opinion Quarterly, 46*(2), 174-194.
Jackson, I. (1971). *The provincial press and the community.* Manchester: Manchester University Press.
Janowitz, M. (1952). *The community press in an urban setting.* Glencoe, IL: Free Press.
Ianowitz, M. (1975). Professional models in journalism: The gatekeeper and the advocate. *Journalism Quarterly, 52*(4), 618-626.
Johnstone, J. W. L. (1972). Professional values of American journalists. *Public Opinion Quarterly, 36,* 522-540.
Kariel, H. G., & Rosenvall, L. A. (1981). Analysing news origins of Canadian daily newspapers. *Journalism Quarterly, 58,* 254-259.
Kariel, H. G., & Rosenvall, L. A. (1983). Cultural affinity displayed in Canadian daily newspapers. *Journalism Quarterly, 60,* 431-436.
Katz, E., Gurevitch, M., & Haas, H. (1973). On the use of mass media for important things. *American Sociological Review, 28,* 164-181.
Kent, T. (1981). *Royal Commission on Newspapers report.* Ottawa: Canadian Government Publishing Centre.
Kepplinger, H. M. (1983). Visual biases in television campaign coverage. In E. Wartella, C. Whitney, & S. Windahl (Eds.), *Mass communication review yearbook* (Vol. 4, pp. 391-405). Beverly Hills, CA: Sage.
Klein, M. W., & Maccoby, N. (1954). Newspaper objectivity in the 1952 campaign. *Journalism Quarterly, 31,* 285-296.
Kocher, D., & Shaw, E. F. (1981). Newspaper inaccuracies and reader perception of bias. *Journalism Quarterly, 58,* 471-474.
Kraus, S., & Davis, D. (1976). *The effects of mass communication on political behavior.* University Park: Pennsylvania State University Press.
Lacy, S. (1987). The effects of intra-city competition on daily newspaper content. *Journalism Quarterly, 64,* 281-290.
Larson, J. F. (1984). *Television's window on the world: International affairs coverage of the U.S. networks.* Norwood, NJ: Ablex.
Lemert, J. B. (1974). Content duplication by the networks in competing evening newscasts. *Journalism Quarterly, 51,* 238-244.
Lemert, J. B. (1989). *Criticizing the media.* Newbury Park, CA: Sage.
Lemert, J. B., & Ashman, M. G. (1983). Extent of mobilizing information in opinion and news magazines. *Journalism Quarterly, 60,* 657-662.

Lemert, J. B., & Cook, R. H. (1982). Mobilizing information in broadcast editorial and free speech messages. *Journal of Broadcasting, 26*, 493-496.

Lemert, J. B., Mitzman, B. N., Siether, M. A., Hackett, R., & Cook, R. H. (1977). Journalists and mobilizing information. *Journalism Quarterly, 54*, 721-726.

Liebes, T., & Katz, E. (1986). Patterns of involvement in TV fiction. *European Journal of Communication, 1*(2), 151-172.

Litman, B. (1979). The television networks, competition and program diversity. *Journal of Broadcasting, 23*, 393-409.

Luttberg, N. R. (1983). News consensus: Do U.S. newspapers mirror society's happenings? *Journalism Quarterly, 60*, 484-488, 578.

Marquez, F. T. (1980). How accurate are the headlines? *Journal of Communication, 30*(3), 30-36.

Mattelart, A. (1984). *International image markets.* London: Comedia.

McCombs, M. (1967). Editorial endorsements: A study of influence. *Journalism Quarterly, 44*, 545-548.

McCombs, M. (1987). Effect of monopoly in Cleveland on diversity of newspaper content. *Journalism Quarterly, 64*, 740-744, 792.

McCormack, T. (1980). Feminism, censorship and sado-masochistic pornography. In T. McCormack (Ed.), *Studies in communication* (pp. 37-61). Greenwich, CT: JAI.

McPhail, T. (1981). *Electronic colonialism.* Beverly Hills, CA: Sage.

McQuail, D. (1977). *Analysis of newspaper content* (Royal Commission on the Press, Research Study 4). London: HMSO.

McQuail, D. (1986a). Is media theory adequate to the challenge of the new communication technologies? In M. Ferguson (Ed.), *New communication technologies and the public interest.* London: Sage.

McQuail, D. (1986b). From bias to objectivity and back: Concepts of news performance and a pluralistic alternative. In T. McCormack (Ed.), *Studies in communication* (pp. 1-36). Greenwich, CT: JAI.

McQuail, D., & van Cuilenburg, J. J. (1983). Diversity as a media policy goal. *Gazette, 31*(3), 145-162.

Meyer, P. (1987). *Ethical journalism.* New York: Longman.

Miller, S. H. (1978). Reporters and congressmen: Living in symbiosis. *Journalism Monographs, 53.*

Molotch, M., & Lester, M. J. (1974). News as purposive behavior. *American Sociological Review, 39*, 101-112.

Montgomery, K. (1989). *Target: Prime time.* New York: Oxford University Press.

Mowlana, H. (1985). *International flow of information: A global report and analysis* (Reports and Papers on Mass Communications No. 99). Paris: UNESCO.

Nixon, R. B. (1960). Factors relating to freedom in national press systems. *Journalism Quarterly, 37*, 13-28.

Nixon, R. B., & Hahn, T. (1971). Concentration of press ownership: A comparison of 32 countries. *Journalism Quarterly, 48*, 5-16.

Nixon, R. B., & Jones, R. L. (1956). The content of non-competitive vs. competitive newspapers. *Journalism Quarterly, 33*, 299-314.

Nordenstreng, K. (1974). *Informational mass communication.* Helsinki: Tammi.

Osgood, C. E., Tannenbaum, P., & Suci, G. (1957). *The measurement of meaning.* Urbana: University of Illinois Press.

Owen, B. M. (1979). Regulating diversity: The case of radio formats. *Journal of Broadcasting, 21*(3), 305-319.

Paletz, D. L., & Dunn, M. (1969). Press coverage of civil disorders. *Public Opinion Quarterly, 3*, 328-345.

Paletz, D. L., et al. (1982). The IRA, the Red Brigade and the ALN in the *New York Times. Journal of Communication, 32*(2), 162-171.

Picard, R. G., McCombs, M., Winter, J. P., & Lacy, S. (1988). *Press concentration and monopoly.* Norwood, NJ: Ablex.

Rarick, G., & Hartman, B. (1966). The effect of competition on one daily newspaper's content. *Journalism Quarterly, 43*, 459-463.

Riffe, D., & Shaw, E. F. (1982). Conflict and consensus: Coverage of 3rd world in two U.S. newspapers. *Journalism Quarterly, 59*, 616-626.

Rivers, W. L., & Nyham, M. J. (1973). *Aspen notebook on government and the media.* New York: Praeger.

Robinson, J., & Levy, M. (1986). *The main source.* Beverly Hills, CA: Sage.

Rosengren, K. E. (1981). Bias in news: Methods and concepts. In C. G. Wilhoit & H. de Bock (Eds.). *Mass communication review yearbook* (Vol. 1). Beverly Hills, CA: Sage.

Rosengren, K. E., Palmgreen, P., & Wenner, L. (Eds.). (1985). *Media gratification research: Current perspectives.* Beverly Hills, CA: Sage.

Royal Commission on the Press. (1947). [Report] (Cmd. 7700). London: HMSO.

Royal Commission on the Press. (1977). [Report] (Cmd. 6810). London: HMSO.

Ryan, M., & Owen, D. (1977). An accuracy survey of metropolitan newspaper coverage of social issues. *Journalism Quarterly, 54*, 27-32.

Schiller, H. (1969). *Mass media and American empire.* New York: Augustus M. Kelly.

Schlesinger, P., Murdock, G., & Elliott, P. (1983). *Televising terrorism.* London: Comedia.

Schmid, A. P., & de Graaf, J. (1982). *Violence as communication.* Beverly Hills, CA: Sage.

Seggar, T., & Wheeler, P. (1973). The world of work: Ethnic and sex representation in TV drama. *Journal of Broadcasting, 17*, 201-214.

Shoemaker, P. J. (1984). Media treatment of deviant political groups. *Journalism Quarterly, 61*, 66-75.

Sigal, L. V. (1974). *Reporters and officials.* Lexington, MA: D. C. Heath.

Sreberny-Mohammadi, A. (1984). The "World of News" study. *Journal of Communication, 34*(1), 121-134.

Stamm, K. R. (1985). *Newspaper use and community ties: Towards a dynamic theory.* Norwood, NJ: Ablex.

Stempel, G. H. (1973). Effects on performance of a cross-media monopoly. *Journalism Monographs, 29.*

Stone, G., et al. (1987). Local TV news and the good-bad dyad. *Journalism Quarterly, 64*, 37-44.

Tankard, J. W., & Ryan, M. (1974). News source perceptions of accuracy in science coverage. *Journalism Quarterly, 51*, 219-225.

Tannenbaum, P. H., & Lynch, M. D. (1960). Sensationalism: The concept and its measurement. *Journalism Quarterly, 37*, 383-391.

Taylor, W. L. (1953). Cloze procedure: A new tool for measuring readability. *Journalism Quarterly, 30*, 415-433.

Thrift, R. R. (1973). How chain ownership affects editorial vigor of a newspaper. *Journalism Quarterly, 50*, 321-331.

Trenaman, J. S. (1967). *Communication and comprehension.* London: Hutchinson.

Tuchman, G., et al. (1978) *Hearth and home: Images of women in mass media.* New York: Oxford University Press.

Turk, J. van S. (1986). Public relations' influence on the news. *Newspaper Research Journal, 7*(4), 15-28.

Tunstall, J. (1977). *The media are American.* London: Constable.

van Cuilenburg, J. J., de Ridder, J. & Kleinijenhuis, J. (1986). A theory of evaluative discourse. *European Journal of Communication, 1*(1), 65-96.

van Dijk, T. A. (1987). *News analysis.* Hillsdale, NJ: Lawrence Erlbaum.

Varis, T. (1984). The international flow of TV programmes. *Journal of Communication, 34*(1), 143-152.

Varis, T. (Ed.). (1986). *Peace and communication.* San Jose, Costa Rica: Editorial Universidad para la paz.

Wagenburg, R. M., & Soderlund, W. C. (1975). The influence of chain ownership on editorial comment in Canada. *Journalism Quarterly, 53*, 93-98.

Weaver, D., Buddenbaum, J. M., & Fair, J. E. (1985). Press freedom, media and development: A study of 34 nations. *Journal of Communications, 35*(2), 104-117.

Weaver, D., & Wilhoit, G. C. (1986). *The American journalist.* Bloomington: University of Indiana Press.

Westerstahl, J. (1983). Objective news reporting. *Communication Research, 10*, 403-424.

Wieten, J. (1979). Media pluralism. *Media, Culture and Society, 1*, 166-180.

Womack, B. (1981). Attention maps of 10 major newspapers. *Journalism Quarterly, 58*, 260-265.

Zillmann, D., & Bryant, J. (1982). Pornography, sexual callousness and the trivialization of rape. *Journal of Communication, 32*(4), 10-21.

Atlas Shrugged: Assessing the Media Performance Assessment Domain

DOUGLAS BIRKHEAD
University of Utah

D
ENIS McQuail is a skillful surveyor of mass communication theory. In the preceding chapter he has outlined a strategy of critical inquiry and mapped out a research terrain to represent it. The approach is described as a union of the social responsibility and empirical schools of media criticism. The merger is said to link normative principles with the research procedures of the social sciences. The work is careful and exacting, and many researchers can benefit from this thoughtful demarcation of the field.

But the precision of the effort also raises a problem. McQuail's focus is so tight as to invite distortion, or at least misunderstanding, of the critical enterprise. So much is "unlinked" in forging the union of norms and empirical methods as to call into question how participation, observation, and expression combine to fashion critical judgment. What McQuail describes as a process of critical inquiry of media performance will strike many readers as not actually "doing" criticism at all, or only a desensitized and detached version of it. I want to deal with this issue of how criticism is constructed in my commentary. I also want to consider McQuail's work as a strategy for displaying a record of critical inquiry, and to discuss how such a discourse is best represented.

I hope to avoid two dangers in my review. First, I will hold to the notion of "criticism" rather than the more removed idea of "assessment" in approaching the task of judging the media. I will touch upon politics, and also speak of ideology, morality, and history. Clearly, I take to the topic in ways that McQuail does not. I am open to the charge that I change the subject; I hope this is not the case. I intend for us to end up talking about the same things. I believe the difference in our views is not so much a matter of what we choose to look at as how we choose to look.

Correspondence and requests for reprints: Douglas Birkhead, Department of Communication, University of Utah, Salt Lake City, UT 84112.

Communication Yearbook 14, pp. 148-154

Second, my engagement with McQuail's text is undertaken with considerable respect for its contribution to media studies. My comments themselves would be distorted or misunderstood if taken as a venture to disallow the work under discussion. In a sense I want to explore why I am both inspired and troubled by what McQuail writes.

I want to begin by suggesting that the ambiguity I feel toward McQuail's approach to media evaluation is a reasonable response. Indeed, I think it is anticipated by McQuail himself. If some of us who consider ourselves media critics question whether McQuail is really offering a method of media criticism, or is somewhat misleading in presenting a truncated version of one, it should be noted he is prepared for this reception. McQuail does not wish to be seen *trying* to do criticism, at least not groping through the full murkiness of that complex activity. McQuail is nowhere more meticulous in his essay than in qualifying what his approach is *not*. If we have other expectations, he is ready to say that is not his fault. He knows we are out here in our various guises of critical disposition; he simply chooses to write around us.

McQuail adopts a form of high empiricism, claims an identity with social responsibility, then stakes off his territory from Marxist and cultural studies. The media are seen as having beneficiaries and positive functions in society rather than victims, social failings, or unintended side effects. He describes the procedures of media performance assessment (MPA) as systematic and objective, differentiating the approach "from much qualitative evaluation, moralistic judgment, or routine review and criticism" (p. 113). The delimitation of media performance is primarily a reduction to content, "the most direct evidence of what the media actually do" (p. 114), with only a comparative or contextual interest in institutional practices or other forms of social interaction or impact. McQuail wants it understood he is talking about media evaluation in a very disciplined way.

What he is up to is plain enough: to devise a scientific strategy of investigation that involves "standards and measures that can be reliably applied in inquiry and deliver results that are dependable and carry wide credibility" (p. 113-114). McQuail does not directly disparage the aspects of media evaluation his approach leaves out of consideration, or researchers who try to grapple with them. He does not even claim that media content itself necessarily contains interpretive significance. Its principal value is utility. Content is classifiable and measurable. Its appeal is methodological. That is the intended appeal of MPA as a whole, especially when fitted out with McQuail's contribution, an analytical framework of media principles.

CRITICAL ESTRANGEMENT

To media critics beyond the pale, there is quite an adjustment in orientation being called for here. Consider, for example, the missionary distance suggested by the following definition: "Criticism is hellfire, death and destruction, war and revolution, and all the fun there is in rockets and gas bombs and smoke-screens and camouflage, butchery and a danse macabre of ghosts, of murdered kings and princes gone mad withal, that's what criticism is" (Carnevali, 1985, p. 39). McQuail understandably wants to avoid association with such effusion. I don't insist he try to close the gap. What I'm saying about my own estrangement, however, is that I consider both examples of evaluation to be extreme. My sense of ambiguity about McQuail's approach comes from a position somewhere in the middle. I believe my response is reasonable, in other words, because I think it is ordinary. Any reader might reasonably expect to feel somewhat disjointed by McQuail's restrictive approach to media evaluation in the near-name of criticism, even if the practicality of the approach is beyond question.

McQuail invokes a manner of seeing media evaluation as logical, objective, precise, productive, positive, policy friendly. No reasonable observer can escape this effect altogether, and I take it as an effect of agreement. McQuail succeeds, one might say, to the degree he holds our attention in a particular way. But his approach also strikes the typical observer, I would argue, as unstable. What seems so understandably controlled in one manner of thinking becomes grossly confining in another. Necessary demarcations of focus turn into the serious omission of essential features. What is external in one view becomes internal in the other. Logical lines take on ideological shadings. A trim landscape is transposed into a field of play.

The reason, I believe, is that McQuail's approach wavers in and out of contact with common understanding of what critical activity entails as everyday human perception, reaction, and judgment. To manage variables, we are asked to circumvent our own critical capacities. We are not called upon to be either outraged or outrageous. We are to treat the rich, interpretive possibilities of critical response and moral judgment with suspicion. Ultimately we are to believe there is a "right" criticism, a transcendent spot to stare at, if only we hold the appropriate gaze.

CRITICAL POWER

I want to turn, however, to the power of McQuail's arguments. I think his essay contains two compelling points. The first involves his theory of method. McQuail claims his approach operationalizes the main normative criteria that have been applied to the media in conventional, democratic-capitalist societies. Thus, it can be argued, while his focus is highly exclusionary, it converges on extremely important and fundamental variables of assessment. Second, McQuail maintains that his MPA perspective is not an arbitrary construct, but an actual tradition of media study, and therefore is supported by a significant record of research that continues to develop and expand. In effect, McQuail assigns his approach roles both in the theory and in the history of the discipline.

Briefly, MPA contends that normative principles of media performance can be determined, specified in the form of criteria for media content, and measured in a formulated research design. McQuail surveys several decades of research to define and substantiate the approach. He identifies three foundational principles "that have enjoyed currency and status since the age of Enlightenment" (p. 116): freedom, equality, and order. He develops a pattern of relationships among these values and what he considers the guiding normative principles of Western media systems: independence, access, diversity, objectivity, solidarity, and culture. Each media principle, in turn, is divided into normative components. The result of the effort is a hierarchical order of assessment criteria that approximates levels of generality. Undergirding the framework are assumptions about the accountability of the media in terms of the "public interest" and the requirements of democratic society, the tenets of social responsibility theory (Siebert, Peterson, & Schramm, 1956). McQuail uses the schema to organize a large number of research studies, from political campaigns to cultural imperialism.

The work is extremely valuable as an overview of a significant body of research and contains many useful suggestions of relationship and integration. One difficulty with the "tightness" of the research strategy McQuail concedes: Not all the principles discussed are transcribed easily into content categories. "Freedom" is an example. Some of the research McQuail cites stands outside a strict interpretation of MPA procedures. His observation of a "common logic" to inquiry in much media evaluation research is no doubt accurate. But he perhaps construes the logic too narrowly as embedded in the rationale of content analysis rather than in a broader empirical perspective. Most of the researchers surveyed find themselves in common company, but some may chafe at the notion of content as an "indispensable component" to measure. There also is a fundamental drawback in the logic of performance-as-content: Much evaluation of the media, as in everyday life, concerns how something is accomplished, not just the merits of the accomplishment itself. Pulitzer prizes do not justify all-white newsrooms, for instance.

My comments to this point, however, romance the dangers I introduced at the beginning. There are numerous aspects of media evaluation that could be discussed in a strategy of critical inquiry. They simply are not the concerns of this one. In a way, I have discussed restrictions no differently than McQuail's own conscientious qualifications about his approach. "We can deal with this issue only by accepting limitations of time, space, and scope" (p. 114), he advises, and describes performance as only one form of calling the media to account. McQuail has attempted an exercise in formalist theory, probing the analytical relationships among concepts that differ in their abstractness and complexity. He has achieved such a structural theory. He has not attempted to discriminate among values in terms of ideological importance for making specific critical arguments. We will not learn whether diversity is more important than objectivity as a normative criterion for the media, for example. Nor are we guided in determining which studies are actually worth reading for critical insight (each fills a framework "space" and therefore performs a theoretical function regardless of particular acumen). But these are not purposes of the theory, nor perhaps even possibilities of formalist theorizing, which strives for logical and definitional order.

CRITICAL DISCOURSE

McQuail maintains that his framework of normative principles is drawn from a long-standing debate on the role of the media in society. The framework is hardly removed from criticism as an activity, McQuail could rightfully insist. It is a structure *of* critical discourse, what critics and other observers have been talking about, and basing their arguments and judgments on. While recognizing there is no consensus on standards of media performance, he contends the debate has proceeded with logically formal and relatively consistent interpretations of what the norms mean. Moreover, the meanings of the norms are inextricably related in patterned ways. Objectivity, for example, is subsumed in the meaning of equality. The values of culture are more conceptually related to the principle of order than to equality or freedom. A number of researchers have been interested in applying norms from this debate as measurable performance standards. Since the researchers have been dealing with a "given" set of values linked in analytical ways, their studies can be mapped as a distinct research field. That field reflects some sense of self-awareness as a bounded community of scholars, chartered in method and interest, and now "charted" in theory as a unified and legitimate site of scholarship.

MPA assumes a stance of political and normative neutrality. It purports to operationalize social responsibility press theory, which is taken as a generally shared public philosophy of the media across democratic societies. MPA researchers present themselves as drawing upon the public's own norms, values and expectations. Performance assessment is seen as a form of the democratic political system's own accountability process. MPA seeks to identify and represent the public interest, avoiding sharp ideological divides. The approach underplays any distinction between the professional ideals of media practitioners themselves and the principles of their mainstream media watchdogs. The MPA community claims to be largely external to the media, although it does not deny itself a role in policy-making or media consulting.

MPA is a remarkable illustration of doing "normal" social science in the manner described by Kuhn (1970) for the hard sciences. The paradigm encompasses method, theory, and value. A tradition of research is structured as a progressive movement toward empirical and logical discovery. Advances are measured in the refinement of tools and in the differentiation of concepts into more precise distinctions. Interpretations are said to mirror social reality itself, the press ethic of the Western world.

Even more striking is the degree to which MPA assumes a judgmental role toward the media in a manner similar to the investigative stance of journalists themselves. Glasser and Ettema (1989) describe how investigative reporters objectify society's own standards in assessing social and political performance. Journalists also claim a "sphere of consensus" on "enduring values" in which to work. Moral claims are transposed into empirical claims to document breaches in the moral order. The press as watchdog in the public interest "seeks to be both a detached observer of fact and a 'custodian of conscience,' " working on the tangent of objectivity and adversarialism (Glasser & Ettema, 1989, p. 1). Journalists engage the moral order primarily as agents of legitimacy. However, because the value consensus on which reporters rely is more tenuous than the press contends, journalists do make some contribution to moral change. Glasser and Ettema suggest investigative reporters help to articulate standards that are rarely self-evident and apply them to specific situations. Where many standards might apply, reporters focus and select among them. To this process of influence and gradual moral refinement, Glasser and Ettema add an "ironic complication": Because journalists are so intent on maintaining the appearance of objective detachment and avoiding even a vocabulary of ethics, they subvert critical discussion as an open mode of discourse in society (pp. 17-18). When investigative news stories do not summon moral outrage, "journalism needs only to fall silent" (p. 18).

McQuail largely duplicates this strategy of critical investigation exercised by a segment of the press itself. He assumes a stable and consistent moral order that can be operationalized into performance standards for the media. His task of forging a union "by linking a set of normative principles with a set of research procedures" (p. 112) echoes what Glasser and Ettema (1989) characterize as the "objectification" of moral standards by the press, "the special contribution of investigative journalists in the ongoing cultural process by which morality is not only reinforced but also defined and refined through application to new and ever-changing conditions" (p. 3).

Both McQuail and investigative journalism claim only to borrow and apply the norms that society has developed. The difference is McQuail's insistence on his high empiricism. But here, surely, his exclusive methodology, including his dismissal of "much qualitative evaluation, moralistic judgment, [and] routine review and criticism" (p. 113) arises to haunt his approach. His theory claims to define a moral order for the media drawn from a long tradition of critical debate in society, yet his method rejects much of this debate as lacking rigor, clarity, and authority. McQuail discredits the epistemological base of his own normative landscape.

CRITICAL METAPHOR

Faultfinding on another's research ground can be taken, of course, as the inevitable reaction of anyone who does not belong on the premises in the first place. McQuail rightfully can point to a significant and valuable body of research from the MPA perspective. He has some analytical justification for seeing a common logic in it, and describing the research in terms of interrelated normative concepts shaping a kind of terraced field of study. He may indeed take satisfaction in finding, exploring, and making intimate a "place" of research, to be comfortably lived in, or even visited.

But as a final observation I want to address a remaining reservation that even more familiarity with the approach probably would not allay. This misgiving does not concern the proper placement of a research tradition—what lies within or outside the terrain, how the boundaries are marked, where the appropriate divisions are to be made. The problem is the metaphor of territory—place, site, location, field, map, boundary, space — altogether. MPA is preoccupied with dimensions into which its topical matters don't quite seem to fit. The question is how best to go about depicting a record of critical inquiry, how discourse and dialogue are to be recorded for others to comprehend and contribute to.

McQuail chooses, for commendable analytical reasons, the imagery of space. I believe the better metaphor is time. Ultimately the preference may be only one of sensibility. I construe inquiry as a conversation, as Michael Oakeshott (1962) teaches, a way of speaking-in-community with give and take on many levels of seriousness and with some pose taking, but devoted to both truth and human solidarity. Despite McQuail's premium on "research evidence that seems 'hard' enough to stand up in political or legal debate and that is also 'communicable' to a lay audience" (p. 113), I do not hear a particularly social voice in the enterprise. I sense instead the discursive mannerisms of expertise and authority.

Shotter (1984) reminds us of our linguistic biases in terms of "space-talk" and "time-talk." It is the tenor of our Enlightenment heritage, to which McQuail makes reference, to search for fixed and timeless things. What is static can be disassembled and studied in parts. The lesson from the Enlightenment for comprehending the world is to divide difficulties into as many parts as possible and to reconstruct them into a system, "supposing the parts to have order among themselves which accounts for the events observed" (Shotter, 1984 pp. 35-36). Beginning with spatial relationships, reality can be tackled like a series of mathematical problems, with geometry being translated into algebra and higher mathematics, and observers stepping out of the picture altogether, presenting "a world only of third persons" (p. 35).

This mapping offers a marvelous atlas of the physical world, vitally important for getting ourselves about. But it does not display, without some distortion, the social world, with its events and products of social and moral interaction. Humans are temporal "things," inextricably beings-in-time whose ideas and values, and even procedures and standards of logic, are relative to history. All we know about ourselves is contingent upon the moments knowledge is created, expressed, and reinterpreted in discourse. Norms such as McQuail describes exist in how they are collectively recalled and presented for application. They are most wisely applied with the full realization that we participate in their meaning with every act of judgment. That's what criticism is.

REFERENCES

Carnevali, E. (1985, January 6). Noted with pleasure. *New York Times Book Review*, p. 90.
Glasser, T. L., & Ettema, J. S. (1989). Investigative journalism and the moral order. *Critical Studies in Mass Communication, 6*, 1-20.
Kuhn, T. S. (1970). *The structure of scientific revolutions.* Chicago: University of Chicago Press.
Oakeshott, M. (1962). *Rationalism in politics and other essays.* London: Methuen.
Shotter, J. (1984). *Social accountability and selfhood.* Oxford: Basil Blackwell.
Siebert, F. S., Peterson, T., & Schramm, W. (1956). *Four theories of the press.* Urbana: University of Illinois Press.

Into the Twilight Zone

JAN SERVAES
Catholic University of Nijmegen

Who governs and controls the media? Whose interests do they serve? What resources do they use? What is the nature of their products? What needs are being met and what are not met? These are just some of the general questions that should be central within any program of communication research. . . . In short, we need the knowledge that only research can provide before we can develop adequate communication policies. Ideally, such policies should be based on "total" knowledge (i.e., on the operation of the media in the wider social-economic-political setting), and on "public" needs rather than on "partial" knowledge and "private" needs as is so often the case at present. (proposal for an International Program of Communication Research, Paris, 1971)

T
he above quotation aptly summarizes the research design and philosophical tradition to which Professor Denis McQuail adheres. In his chapter, McQuail has been able to grasp the complexity of what he terms media performance assessment (MPA) as not only a theoretical but an applied discipline, which involves policy research. Majchrzak (1984) divides the overall policy research field into four disciplines on the basis of its focus and applicability (see Table 1). Within this typology McQuail focuses particularly on the third and fourth types as the two elements that are crucial to the theoretical underpinnings of his approach: attention to basic social problems (Type 3) and concern for the application and "relevance" of research recommendations (Type 4).

I have great sympathy for his attempt to link together a set of normative (thus subjective) principles with a set of systemic and "objective" research standards, and with his plea for a change of priorities and new strategies and methods (Servaes, 1989c). The main thrust of my commentary will be toward extending that discourse at two levels: the "macro" level (all media in the whole society) and the "meso" level (by way of the process of news production). Specifically, I will take a critical, interpretive approach that, in contrast to McQuail's more traditionally social scientific one, emphasizes issues of power and "cultural identity" as significant in the assessment of media performance.

Correspondence and requests for reprints: Jan Servaes, Institute for Mass Communication, Catholic University of Nijmegen, P.O. Box 9108, 6500HK Nijmegen, The Netherlands.

Communication Yearbook 14, pp. 155-162

TABLE 1
A Typology of Policy Research

Applicability	Focus	
	Technical	Fundamental
Low	(1) analysis of policy	(3) analysis of fundamental policy research
High	(2) technical research	(4) policy and planning research

PERSPECTIVE TAKING

McQuail argues that MPA, in practice as in theory, ought to be based on "hard" evidence, provided and supported by "objective" social scientific research. The traditional positivist approach implicitly starts from the assumptions that all knowledge is based on an observable reality and that social phenomena can be studied on the basis of methodologies and techniques adopted from the natural sciences. However, as Anthony Giddens (1976), among others, has pointed out, the social sciences differ from the natural sciences in at least four respects: (a) Contrary to the natural sciences, the social sciences are in a subject-to-subject relationship where normative and power relationships hold; (b) they deal with a preinterpreted world in which the meanings developed by the active subjects form part of the production of that world; (c) the construction of a theory of society therefore necessitates a double hermeneutics; and (d) the logical status of generalizations in the social sciences differs from natural scientific generalizations. The social sciences, therefore, are hermeneutic and nomological in nature, and need to be approached from a critical perspective.

Contrary to traditional approaches of power factors, which I consider static and top-down oriented, I argue in favor of a more dynamic and multiple approach to power relationships. This implies a more dialectic and multicentered perception of power factors that also takes counterpower or empowerment into account.

In general, one can, in relation to the topic of power and interests, distinguish among three problem areas: the mutual dependence between the macro level of the society or the system and the micro level of social actions; the positions and the opportunities of the subjects; and the relationship of domination, dependence, and subordination of power and interest contrapositions. These problem areas are central in the present-day social scientific and social psychological discussions and have yielded a variety of disciplines and interpretations.

In communication sciences, we usually refer to Siebert, Peterson, and Schramm (1956) for an interpretation of these issues of power and interests. These authors start from the assumption that "the press always takes on the coloration of the social and political structures within which it operates. Especially it reflects the system of social control whereby the relations of individuals and institutions are adjusted" (pp. 1-2). Referring to special political science models, they discern four normative press theories: authoritarian, Soviet-communist, liberal, and social responsibility.

These normative media theories have come under severe scrutiny. The work of John Merrill (1974) and his colleagues (e.g., Gordon & Merrill, 1987; Merrill & Lowenstein, 1979) deserves to be mentioned explicitly in this context. Their thesis is that, on the one hand, Siebert et al.'s classic models are based on an overly restricted (Western) description of concepts such as freedom and democracy that allows little or no generalization, and that, on the other hand, reality often does not comply with the principles defined in philosophical terms.

Therefore, Merrill proposes a double but integrated distinction with both economic and philosophical bases. However, the thesis mentioned above, which was Siebert et al.'s starting point, was never questioned. Merrill and Lowenstein (1979), like Siebert et al., think that

> media systems are, of course, closely related to the kinds of governments in which they operate; they are, in essence, reflective and supportive of the governmental philosophy. . . . When viewed in this way it is possible to say that all press systems are enslaved — tied to their respective governmental philosophies and forced to operate within certain national ideological parameters. (p. 153)

Next he brings in a distinction on both the economic (*social* would have been a better term) and the philosophical base. In terms of economics, Merrill discerns three forms of dominant ownership structures: (a) private media (ownership by individuals or nongovernment corporations, supported primarily by advertising or subscriptions), (b) media owned by different parties (ownership by competitive political parties, subsidized by party or party members), and (c) media owned by the government (owned by government or dominant government party, subsidized primarily by government funds or government-collected license fees).

This economic basis could be expanded threefold. First of all, not only the "ownership structures" but also the direct and indirect control mechanisms and structures could be taken into account. Second, ownership and control structures can be of a local, national, international, or transnational nature. And, third, the splitting up into private, public, and mixed sectors, on the one hand, and a distinction between control and/or property structures within the production versus distribution sector, on the other hand, seem to allow a more useful classification.

In addition, I would like to introduce a third dimension that seems to me of major importance to the above discussion — that is, a more cultural-anthropological dimension. Culture is not only the visible, nonnatural environment of individual and organized subjects, but is also and primarily their normative context. In the patterning of their social existence, people continually make principally unconscious choices that are directed by the applicable intracultural values and options. The social reality can then be seen as a reality constituted and cultivated on the basis of particular values, a reality in which the value system and the social system are completely interwoven and imbued with the activity of each other. Cultures derive an "identity" from the fact that a common worldview and ethos are active in the network of institutions or apparatuses of which they consist. In other words, in the study of concrete cases, one must be attentive to the following aspects: (a) the characteristics and dimensions of the cultural reference framework (i.e., the worldview, the ethos, and their symbolic representations), (b) the interaction and interrelation with the environment of power and interest, and (c) the "ideological apparatuses" by which the cultural reference framework is produced and through which it is at the same time disseminated.

These factors are illustrated extensively in Servaes (1989a, 1989b), where I describe how communication principles have been regarded in distinct cultural settings. I also emphasize the importance of an interrelated examination of three dimensions (philosophical, political economic, and cultural) in a societal context based on power relationships. Such an interrelated examination leads to at least four conclusions of a general nature.

First, in one nation one can have different ownership and control structures on the one hand, and several philosophies with regard to the functioning of the media on the other.

Second, the above distinction can be expanded toward individual media structures. The press in a certain country can, for instance, be in private hands but still operate from a "free press theory" base, while the broadcasting system is run by the government and uses and/or propagates more social-centralistic or social-liberal ideas.

Third, this approach also provides a more appropriate methodology for analyzing normative views on communication at the distinct local, regional, national, and international levels of a given community. And, finally, as power relationships are looked at in a multidirected and dialectic fashion, this approach does not limit itself to a top-down perspective only. This implies also that so-called participatory or user-oriented modes of communication can be explained and analyzed from this perspective.

ECONOMIC, POLITICAL, AND CULTURAL INFLUENCES AND THE PRODUCTION OF NEWS

Over the last three decades, an alternative form of journalism has emerged to challenge traditional ways of reporting human experience. These "new" journalists, rather than ordering their stories according to the conventionally accepted "who, what, where, when, why, and how" framework, use devices and formats common to literary writing. Rather than attempting to remove themselves from the stories they are reporting, these new journalists seem to participate. New journalism as a method of reporting has created much controversy, and, in general, has gained little acceptance in the everyday writing of the news. How, then, to account for the differences and the emergence of an alternative form of journalism? How is it that two groups of writers who call themselves journalists can offer such differing interpretations of human experience?

Are misrepresentations the result of the structure and culture in which news (or media content in general) is produced (and therefore of an unintended nature), or more intentionally aimed to distort and sometimes falsify reality? In my opinion, the production of news is influenced generally by the political, economic, and cultural system as well as by the actual situation in which the production, transmission, and consumption of information take place.

This implies, first, that news may never be considered as only a series of facts or a window through which one looks at the external world: "Rather it is a cultural product and the accounts and description of the world which it gives are produced from within a specific interpretive framework" (Glasgow Media Group, 1980, p. 3). Second, news is an organizational product, generated by routine occupational practices in an institutional setting with specific performance demands as well as limits of time and resources. These organizational and institutional factors also shape the structure in which news is being produced. Third, news is manufactured by journalists who, often unconsciously, select and interpret a number of facts, based on an unclear vision on society. Hence Golding and Middleton (1982) correctly state that "we should never forget that news production, like all other social activities, involves real people doing real jobs about which they are able to reflect and over whose content they have considerable autonomy" (p. 112).

Therefore, I perceive news as the result of combined action based on institutionally determined and collectively made choices under the current economic, political, and cultural interest constellations.

NEWS AND THE CREATION OF CULTURAL MYTH

News production has a lot in common with other social practices that are carried out on a routine basis in a formalized institutional context. It is at this point that the concept of professionalization comes into play. On the one hand, journalists and media workers in general use a specific paradigm of reality to cover events in the world; on the other hand, professionalism also provides news makers with a set of "implicit" practices of production. In other words, professionalism offers journalists "a legitimate (and legitimating) way of seeing the world as well as practical frameworks which stipulate how to assemble stories to report on perceived happenings" (Dahlgren, 1984, p. 6). In addition, professionalism not only gives a handhold to news makers, it also contributes to the general perceptions about news for the public at large.

Therefore, in my opinion, the news production process contributes to the societal ideation process, that is, the manner in which not only the rational or cognitive, but also the irrational or intuitive elements of knowledge, ideas, and information are passed on. In this case, ideation is to be seen not only as a distribution of specific facts or events but rather as a generalized angle of vision on social reality with strong affective and subjective components.

According to Roland Barthes, "A myth has a double function: it points out and it notifies, it makes us understand something and it imposes it on us." Joseph Campbell (1988) adds, "A dream is a personal myth; a myth is the public dream of a society" (p. 10). Myths are generally expressed through the narrative form of storytelling. Myths are human phenomena (creations of the human mind and spirit); at the same time, they are cultural phenomena (they effectively organize the way we, as a group, view portions of our world). Therefore, White (1985) argues:

> National cultures are structured around myths which explain the origins of the particular national grouping, their specific national identities and their concepts of national destiny. Such national mythologies seek a grounding in broader cosmic myths, and thus gain a sacred, timeless character. Myths function more at the unintentional, symbol level, defining that which a national society is trying to become. Mythological functions are likely to be especially strong at times of national crisis, rapid change or external threat. (pp. 19-20)

In my opinion, the invasion of Grenada in 1983 was such a period, wherein myths were strongly emphasized. In a comparative research project on its coverage in the Western European, U.S., Canadian, and Caribbean press, we studied it from this perspective (see Servaes & Drijvers, 1986).

Every society seems to cultivate the "myth" of an "enemy": Us versus Them, Good versus Bad. The image of an external enemy seems to be used to create internal harmony. Let me illustrate this by providing a number of examples given by American scholars. First, Robertson (1980) writes:

> Most Americans agree that the United States is among the most powerful nations on earth. They would also agree that that power ought to be "good for something." They believe America has a mission and that its destiny is not simply to be rich and powerful and big, but to be so for some God-given purpose. . . . Most would and do argue about what the mission ought to be, or about what America's destiny really is, but few would disagree that America is uniquely effective in the world. Americans may be beginning to doubt the effectiveness of American power for the good, but they show little sign of giving up the belief — whether the "good" is defined as assuring a supply of petroleum, destroying oppressive dictatorships, preventing pollution, bringing "all power to the people" at home and abroad, solving the energy crisis, creating world government, or colonizing the moon. (p. 25)

Levin (1987), in his historical analysis of the talk radio phenomenon, reaches the conclusion that

> the majorities of [American] people believe that capitalism is a precondition for the maintenance and protection of basic freedoms and rights. Americans do not believe

that such rights are possible in socialist or communist societies. Free enterprise is the core American idea. Free politics depends on its existence. The right to organize politically provides some with the hope that political remedies exist. (p. 68)

And what about examples in the area of news production? Parenti (1986), for instance, argues with regard to the relationship between the U.S. media coverage and foreign policies that "objectivity means reporting U.S. overseas involvements from the perspective of the multinational corporations, the Pentagon, the White House, and the State Department, and rarely questioning the legitimacy of military intervention (although allowing critical remarks about its effectiveness)" (p. 51).

Starting from the assumption that there is a basic coherence and logic to the domain of the mythic that runs "parallel" to the informative dimensions of news, I would like to argue that the subliminal mode of ideation is operating under circumstances that are of a discursive ("content"), technical ("medium"), and contextual or societal nature.

The views on news production and media performance I have articulated in this commentary exceed the traditional research approaches on news production in general and content analysis in particular. This kind of research mainly deals with "transmission problems." That is, more traditional studies tend to focus on questions concerning the "selection" (How does news selection happen on the basis of a mass of events?), the "translation" (How do events become news?), the "control" (How are journalists checked?), the "choice," (How objective, comprehensive, or newsworthy is the news?), and the "effect" (How much or what does the public understand of the news?).

Addressing the questions mentioned above certainly is useful if one wishes to study the "rationalistic" issues of news. However, as I have argued, the impact of news may well lie behind this rationalistic dimension and may be of a more subjective, ideological, or mythical nature. Researching these nonrationalistic dimensions requires an interdisciplinary focus (see Jensen, 1987; Marcus & Fischer, 1986). However, one of the major problems is "how to combine a variety of methodologies in the same research design so that these mutually reinforce and complement each other" (White, 1985, p. 23). That, in my opinion, can be accomplished only by combining normally separately used research methodologies, that is, quantitative and qualitative analyses.

In Servaes and Drijvers (1986) we therefore conclude that the mythic domains of news production perform four basic operations on a regular basis: (a) They establish and concretize the social order as part of our cognition; (b) they legitimate and celebrate the basic and dominant structures, functions, and leadership of the social order; (c) they serve to explain and interpret what transpires that is of relevance for the social order; and (d) for the public, the mythic domain integrates and implicates, evoking identification and loyalty to the social order.

REFERENCES

Campbell, J. (1988). *The power of myths.* Garden City, NY: Doubleday.

Dahlgren, P. (1984). *Beyond information: TV news as a cultural discourse.* Stockholm: School of Journalism.

Giddens, A. (1976). *New rules of sociological method.* London: Hutchinson.

Glasgow Media Group. (1980). *More bad news.* London: Routledge & Kegan Paul.

Golding, P., & Middleton, S. (1982). *Images of welfare: Press and public attitudes to poverty.* Oxford: Martin Robertson.

Gordon, D., & Merrill, J. (1987, May). *Power—the key to freedom: A four-tiered social model.* Paper presented at the annual meeting of the International Communication Association, Montreal.

Jensen, K. (1987). Qualitative audience research: Toward an integrative approach to reception. *Critical Studies in Mass Communication, 4*(1).

Levin, M. (1987). *Talk radio and the American dream.* Toronto: Lexington.

Majchrzak, A. (1984). *Methods for policy research.* London: Sage.

Marcus, G., & Fischer, M. (1986). *Anthropology as cultural critique: An experimental moment in the human sciences.* Chicago: University of Chicago Press.

Merrill, J. (1974). *The imperative of freedom: A philosophy of journalistic autonomy.* New York: Hastings.

Merrill, J., & Lowenstein, R. L. (1979). *Media, messages and men: New perspectives in communication.* New York: Longman.

Parenti, M. (1986). *Inventing reality: The politics of the mass media.* New York: St. Martin's.

Robertson, J. (1980). *American myth, American reality.* New York: Hill & Wang.

Servaes, J. (1989a). Beyond the four theories of the press. *Communicatio Socialis Yearbook: Journal of Christian Communication in the Third World, 7,* 38-45.

Servaes, J. (1989b). Cultural identity and modes of communication. In J. Anderson (Ed.), *Communication yearbook 12* (pp. 383-416). Newbury Park, CA: Sage.

Servaes, J. (1989c). *One world, multiple cultures: Towards another paradigm on communication for development.* Louvain, Belgium: ACCO.

Servaes, J., & Drijvers, J. (1986). *Grenada: Een kruidnagel in de Europese pers. Onderzoek naar de berichtgeving over de invasie van Grenada in enkele Europese kwaliteitskranten.* Louvain, Belgium: CeCoWe.

Siebert, F., Peterson, T., & Schramm, W. (1956). *Four theories of the press.* Urbana: University of Illinois Press.

White, R. (1985, March). *The significance of recent developments in the field of mass communication.* Paper presented at Sommatie, Veldhoven.

4 A Media Industry Perspective

JEREMY TUNSTALL
City University

This chapter argues for an *industrial* perspective in media studies. Such a perspective was adopted by several founding fathers of media research. An industrial approach can draw upon relevant research traditions in several fields of social science; the insights of organizational studies are one example. Contemporary media are characterized by large, complex organizations. An occupational sociology perspective reveals that media organizations have characteristic occupational strata. In the middle are the "professionals" and technical/production work force, and at the bottom there is a layer of unskilled extras. At the top of media organizations are entrepreneurs, baronial executives, and celebrity performers. Media research has tended to leave these starry individuals to the popular press, but, in doing so, has ignored much that is important to, and characteristic of, the media industry. Comparative studies between national media industries can be instructive. This chapter reviews a number of recent British studies and points to the need for an agreed-upon conceptual framework suitable for comparative and other studies of the world media industry.

T HIS essay advocates a macroindustrial approach to media research that had its first call by Max Weber. Speaking in 1910, Weber called for research on the finances of the press and the dynamics of news agencies; he discussed advertising, ownership, and monopoly issues and was interested in comparative research on the popular press in the United States, Germany, and Britain (Hardt, 1979). The industrial perspective on the media was well represented in early American media research. First among these writings was Robert Park's *The Immigrant Press and Its Control* (1922), which looked at this continent-wide phenomenon in both micro and macro terms. Park showed how government policy and societal pressures in general, and advertising finance in particular, shaped the content of the immigrant press. Other exemplary works are those by Leo Rosten (1937, 1941) on Hollywood and on Washington correspondents. Rosten has shown that careful selection of a strategic research site can produce intimate interview material and can at the same time shed light on the national media industry. Also relevant is Theodore Adorno's (1941) work on the New York music industry, which remains the classic in that field. Adorno shows in some detail how the musical structure of popular songs reflects the commercial practices

Correspondence and requests for reprints: Jeremy Tunstall, Communications Policy Research Centre, City University, Northampton Square, London, ECIV OHB, England.

Communication Yearbook 14, pp. 163-186

of the music industry. Paul Lazarsfeld and Robert Merton used detailed survey data to focus on the New York media as a national industry.

Despite this promising start, the media industry perspective fell into some disrepair as the bottom-up emphasis of contemporary media research — an emphasis that has, perhaps, even been strengthened in recent decades by qualitative (semiology, structuralist, and other) approaches — became predominant. My suggestion is that more research — including audience and content studies — should adopt an *industry* perspective. To put this another way: Media scholars might do well to pay more research attention to the kinds of issues covered in the trade publications. Such attention, I believe, would lead to a recognition that (a) media organizations per se offer different characteristics of organizing in structure and hierarchy, (b) the industry is becoming globalized in ownership and product, and (c) national (and local) differences will continue to persist and will justify comparative research.

MEDIA INDUSTRY ORGANIZATIONS

In Weberian terms, media organizations seem to constitute a mixed case, containing a contrary mix of the rational/bureaucratic and the charismatic/creative. This mix can be seen easily in bureaucratic routines of production processes existing side by side with acceptance of the idiosyncratic demands of creativity. It can also be seen in egalitarian characteristics of media organizations existing in the presence of steep hierarchies of authority.

As to the latter, pointing in the nonbureaucratic, nonhierarchical direction is the tendency of media organizations to "bulge in the middle" (Tunstall, 1971). Both press and broadcast organizations employ a wide range of professional expertise, craft skill, and experience; many of these people are paid very similar amounts of money, while there are relatively few people earning substantially more and only a minority earning substantially less. Such a bulge in the middle emphasizes relationships of equality, collegiality, and persuasion. Due to uncertainties of organizational goal and product market, media organizations rely heavily on "internal selling" — people try to persuade their colleagues and immediate superiors (and inferiors) as to the merits of their intentions and preferences.

However, these collegial, persuasive, consensual, and near-equal relationships are not the whole story. Media organizations also have strong hierarchical elements. Media organizations often exhibit "baronial" power, the individual executive who — partly due to previous success — acquires an exceptional degree of autonomy and hierarchical authority.

The hierarchical principle is salient in media organizations in several ways. Power is typically vested in the hands of individual barons, not least for creative reasons. "One person in charge" recognizes the individual creativity canon — the director's movie, the TV producer's series, the editor's publication. However, paradoxically, this recognition of individual creativity, plus the need for quick decisions in the face of deadlines (or the high cost of a day's filming), gives the creative baron a high degree of dictatorial power. Since some of this power is also delegated downward, the result often is a hierarchy with clearly demarcated steps, departmental managers, and substantial differences in pay and conditions.

Media organizations tend to exhibit further characteristics and managerial devices that favor hierarchy and control, rather than colleagueship and autonomy. One such device is the audience ratings system, well analyzed by Beville (1985). Various versions of, and selections from, these ratings are known to everyone from the top managers to the general public. Especially in broadcasting organizations, the availability of ratings is a potent management device that preprograms the organizational response. There is often no need for senior management to request departmental managers to improve their ratings: The simple circulation and availability of the ratings figures within the organization will carry the same message and will also provide frequent updates about the ongoing competitive situation. Media organizations are unusual in being preprogrammed by research findings in so much detail and with such frequent updates.

Media organizations lend themselves to preprogramming in yet other hierarchical ways. Organizational goals can often be expressed in terms of a very simple but effective percentage formula. For example, most British and American daily newspapers operate on specific ratios of advertising pages to editorial pages. Both the total number of pages and the ad/editorial ratios differ sharply between heavy and light advertising days of the week. Senior management sets these ratios and, by, for example, reducing the weekday ratio of editorial to advertising pages, can significantly change the working conditions and prevailing goals of editors and journalists.

Yet another easily available means for radical transformation is provided by the internal fragmentation of many media organizations. For example, the separate publications in a large magazine group, or the separate sections within a large broadcasting organization, can be grouped and departmentalized in many different possible ways. Such organizations often undergo frequent regroupings, while individuals and units are also transferred between departments. Such changes again emphasize hierarchy in general and the ease with which senior management can impose on subordinate managers and producers new targets, new goals, and new working conditions.

Occupational Structures
Within National Media Industries

Despite the opportunities for fragmentation and control, there also exist continuing structures that are larger than any given organization. Occupational structure, for example, is one of the most obvious ways in which there is a single media industry wider than the separate single-medium sectors. "Journalists" work in many subareas of the media, while members of the Screen Actors' Guild have worked for decades in advertising commercials, television, and movies.

The media occupations exhibit strong elements of occupational community — the overlapping of work and nonwork relationships. The most celebrated media occupational community is located in Beverly Hills and surrounding suburbs. Another powerful occupational community is centered on the BBC Television Centre in west London. The suburban location, the intensity of the working experience, the peculiar working hours, and the generous supply of talented colleagues as potential friends (and rivals) means that BBC personnel may find most of their social life focusing on the BBC.

The media occupations also have in common the emphasis on skills of presentation and self-presentation. Actors are obviously a leading example, but most television producers, directors, and writers seem equally articulate and adept at selling themselves, their ideas, and their plans. Nor should print journalists be forgotten; their daily experience of telling stories turns all journalists into professionals of the anecdote and partly explains why they tend to make such congenial companions. And the list goes on — advertising agency personnel (across yet another wide range of expertise) are once again experts of self-presentation, talk, and wit. All of this charm, intelligence, wit, and communication skill is of course one reason academics find media folk hard to beat as enticing interview material. Only politicians can compete.

Nor is talk the sum of their communication skill. These are not only talking but writing occupations. Throughout media occupations the written word — pithy and pointed — remains crucial; not just the written press, but television continues to be a heavily scripted medium. So also are movies, advertising, and much of radio. Media people are people of the word — spoken and written. They tend to be the people who at school were good at writing and speaking up in class, but bad at math and science.

Nevertheless, the occupational charm, communication, community, and colleagueship are there partly as direct resistance to the opposite and powerful strains of hierarchy in the same occupations. Media occupations reflect the steep hierarchies of the media industry. The performance occupations — such as actors and musicians — have a smallish number of active stars, a substantial body of the regularly employed, and a majority of seldom employed, low-paid, part-timers (Wills & Cooper, 1988).

More generally, among the variety of media occupations and work one can — as in the Indian caste system — detect four major occupational layers. At the top are the entrepreneurs, the senior executives, and the star performers; these people typically command sizable sums of money, and they may control time slots (broadcast executives) or access to particular pages (departmental editors). Everyone at this top level has to combine "creative" with "business" concerns; creative requirements are balanced against budgets.

The second layer is made up of the professionals or those in "professionalizing" occupations. These are mainly people with such creative occupations as TV producers and writers, print journalists, and actors. These occupations typically have professional associations or unions (or, in Hollywood, guilds). As creative professionally oriented workers, those in this layer are concerned not just with pay but with creative "autonomy." These professionals may experience a fair degree of autonomy — although less so in the most mass-market-oriented work settings. Even mass-market-oriented professionals often experience autonomy because they have internalized (and hence regard as legitimate) the major goals and organizational styles of their employers.

Relatively unobtrusive controls over professional performance are, of course, not unknown in the world of the ancient professions. Laboratory tests of various kinds, analyses of tissue removed in hospital surgical operations, and cross-referrals between colleagues are some of the controls exercised on the performance of medical professionals. Lawyers operate in the public sphere, allowing easy occupational surveillance. In the media occupations the back output and current performance of the media organization itself are potent indicators of what is expected. I have already noted the internal significance of audience ratings; there are other sets of numbers that may have a similar function in other areas. Some journalists see "page traffic" research; British television producers, in addition to ratings and share numbers, also see a continuing "Appreciation Index."

A third layer of media occupations is made up of the "crafts." Leading examples of contemporary crafts are the skills to be found in television production. Some of the more "artistic" skills may be performed by women, but the more technical skills in television — in Los Angeles as in London — are mainly performed by men.

Male dominance was, of course, even more noticeable in the traditional printing skills of the press, which have been forced into retreat (or in some cases abolition) by new computer and electronic technology. An interesting study of highly skilled print workers in the London newspaper industry is *Brothers: Male Dominance and Technological Change* by Cockburn (1983). Like other studies of the London newspaper printers, this study predicted that the traditional craft power would not continue much longer — the study was published before the "Murdoch Revolution" arrived.

The fourth great layer of media occupations includes all those below the craft level — many of these jobs being carried out by women. This quite large area of media work has been studied very little — despite the fact that it is an expanding area.

Below these four major layers are the media equivalent of outcasts. This lowest level of media employment is typified by the extras of the film and TV world. But the other media occupations also have their extras — part-time and semiprofessional musicians, free-lance journalists and part-time correspondents, the voluntary staff at the community radio station.

These hierarchical layers of media occupations are continually in a state of flux. The emergence of a new piece of technology is often seen by participants as offering the possibility of upward movement. The late Philip Elliott and his colleague Geoff Matthews (1987) have analyzed the maneuvering that occurred in early BBC radio between different occupational groups seeking to claim expertise and control over those aspects of music that did not obviously belong to engineers.

Tom Burns's (1977) study of the BBC of the early television years provides an especially perceptive analysis of the increasing strength of the *lighting* skill in television.

While occupations, professional associations, and guilds are attempting to move upward and grab hold of any potential escalator effects of new technologies, it is the task of some members of the top layer to move things in the opposite direction and to search for potential downward-moving technologies.

At midcentury, newspaper unions, at least in metropolitan centers, were able to bid up the price of their printing services. And in the early decades of television a similar phenomenon occurred. In Los Angeles and New York, there was a strong element of both craft and professional media groupings demanding, and attaining, a significant share of television's financial success. There has been a similar escalation of earnings and industry costs in Britain and especially in the ITV system.

This earnings and cost escalation has led to the phenomenon of the million-dollar television series episode—a remarkable cost for what remains a quick-and-cheap style of production. London earnings and costs are substantially lower than those in Los Angeles and New York, but they have been subject to similar rapid escalation. This has led to the conventional industry wisdom that television costs tend to rise faster than inflation.

Radical cost-cutting efforts have hit some media occupations more severely than others. There are many opportunities here for revealing comparative research—not least because the broadcast and video employers appear determined to be still more industrially assertive in the 1990s than they were in the late 1980s.

THE INDUSTRIAL SHAPE OF PERSONAL POWER:
MEDIA TYCOONS, BARONS, AND STARS

Social scientists have several reasons for tending to avoid the enormous focus on individuals and personality in the media. After all, this is how the media cover the media, how fan magazines and commercial hucksterism focus on the world of entertainment. The personality approach fits better with the 30-second commercial than with the 30-footnote article. Academics may also sense an ideological account that lies behind a personality approach. As some of the recent attempts to combine academic analysis and gossip show, gossip has a tendency to triumph over analysis. The detached academic critic may become an unofficial spokesperson for the self-serving industry view in which articulate and sympathetic individuals struggle valiantly against the commercial odds, and manage to score some significant achievements.

Stephen Hess, in *The Ultimate Insiders* (1986), has successfully shown the interaction of two star systems—one in the media, the other in politics. Hess found that media coverage of the U.S. Senate focused overwhelmingly on a handful of senators; but much of this was based on a *political* criterion, namely, the chairman-ship of key committees (pp. 30-43).

Media individuals and celebrity personalities can be classified into three cate-gories: the tycoon-entrepreneur, the baronial executive, and the star performer. Some individuals belong to more than one such category. A common characteristic is that each type of individual can shift sizable financial resources and thus make projects happen. The term *bankable* was first used to describe those Hollywood stars whose involvement would ensure the financing of a movie. But in an era of financial deregulation, bankability is even more crucially a characteristic of the successful entrepreneur or baronial executive. Nowadays bankability allows baro-nial executives to become entrepreneurs; the "management buyout" fashion gives both banks and successful executives added potency. Financial and accountancy skills are central, and individuals who are believed to possess such skills can move remarkably quickly. Advertising agency developments of recent years are perhaps an extreme illustration of a more general trend.

Prominent media individuals have an equally prominent legal dimension. A hallmark of the media baron and the performance star alike is the special contract of employment (not for the star the standard house contract, carefully honed over the years by the employing company's lawyers). In the prominent media individual's personal support team, the lawyer has a secure place.

Of the tycoon-entrepreneurs it can safely be stated that while much has been written and said, much less is systematically known. However, information is available about the personal style of contemporary media tycoons. If the definition of *tycoon* involves owning, operating, and taking risks, then all media tycoons do those three things. They also tend to be takeover specialists; they build their possessions by buying struggling media companies and returning them to profit. Each individual tycoon has a certain management style and particular skills, and these are linked to the types of media property that he or she controls. Rupert Murdoch, for example, proclaims that his media empire encompasses four conti-nents, but his empire is composed of a smallish number of relatively large media businesses, enabling Murdoch to visit all of his properties at regular intervals. These personal visits and his hyperactive managerial style (of continually buying and selling media stakes) keep his employees alert and discourage the appearance of corporate fat.

Murdoch tends to focus on just one of his major locations, sometimes for much of a single year. After he acquired full control of Twentieth Century Fox and Metromedia (September 1985), his main attention switched back to London and the secret move of his newspapers to a new printing plant, which occurred in January 1986. Murdoch launched his Fox Network in October 1986. In 1987, Australia was Murdoch's major activity location — in a series of deals, culminating in November 1987, Murdoch got out of commercial TV and acquired control of 60% of the Australian daily press. In 1988 Murdoch seems to have concentrated on the United States, with the purchase of *TV Guide* and the rest of Triangle Publications.

Murdoch has tried to avoid the commercial mistakes that can result from newspaper owners becoming too interested in politics and prestige. Murdoch is willing to own prestige publications so long as they also make a profit. Overall, Murdoch has mainly bought loss-making or down-market media properties, partly because these usually are the ones available for purchase.

Murdoch's entrepreneurial style involves financing media acquisitions by heavy bank borrowing. This method in turn depends upon maintaining his financial track record. The heavy interest charges gear the whole operation to extracting maximum profits from Britain and Australia (in both of which locations major additional acquisitions are almost impossible); these profits then feed into the U.S. operation and additional acquisitions.

Baronial executives seem to have been prominent in the media for several, or even many, decades. The old Hollywood studio cartel system of the 1930s featured baronial power; studio executives' power stretched into distribution, exhibition, and production—but barons could also be toppled by entrepreneurs and bankers back East. An earlier type of baron was the "sovereign" newspaper editor, who was allowed to rule his editorial domain with a rod of iron.

Media organizations are strongly segregated into very different functions—creativity, production, sales, advertising, and so on. Presiding entrepreneurs have often chosen to focus on company finances and on exercising political influence. Meanwhile, they have relied on barons to look after particular segments of the business.

Two developments of recent decades have probably increased the potential for baronial power. One is the trend toward publicly quoted media companies. But second, in Britain (and elsewhere in Europe) the continuing growth of huge public service broadcasting organizations has led to the emergence of public service barons. In the BBC, the chief executive is the director-general; this is an exceptionally demanding post that can leave little time for detailed involvement in the running of particular channels. Two key barons in the BBC are the "controllers" of the two national television channels. Such a controller is a potent figure because he or she oversees the schedule of an entire national channel, and also determines what programming will get financed; the current budget for BBC1 is about $800 million, and the controller is normally a successful TV producer. At lower levels than this there are lesser barons in charge of sizable programming fiefdoms.

Other nonmedia influences feed into these media baronies. The whole of British broadcasting still retains a powerful aura of the civil service, the cultural public bureaucracy, the university (as well as the entertainment arcade) of the nation. There is a strong British civil service tradition of relying upon a small elite of administrators (with humanities educational backgrounds), and the idea of "Put a good chap in charge and let him get on with it" remains potent in British life. There may be another British tradition feeding into the baronial pattern; coming from the stage—and prevalent in the broad areas of drama and entertainment—is the tradition of the actor-manager.

Star performers are, of course, the most obvious examples of individual prominence in the media. The star system will presumably be forever associated with Hollywood. Since all the other film industries of the world are Hollywood influenced, it is difficult to separate out specifically Hollywood — as opposed to simply film industry — influences in the emergence of star systems elsewhere. Certainly the basic economies of scale and the focus on celebrity performers have occurred everywhere, including the Communist bloc and the Third World. The Indian film industry's star system includes the phenomenon of the million-rupee player and a variant on the Hollywood "gross player" — namely, the cash-in-advance player (Armes, 1987, p. 113).

We lack studies of the crossover of the American star system from movies to television fiction and comedy and then on to TV news, sport, weather, and beyond. We also lack cross-national comparative studies. But peculiarities of the U.S. system seem to have limited the possibilities for national stardom and million-dollar annual earnings to a relatively small elite. The annual number of nationally distributed movies does not allow for many star billings; TV series allow veto power to only one or two key roles per (successful) series, and the practice of running and repeating series across the year keeps the total number of series quite small. Even in the more chaotic music business, major new developments of the music video and MTV kind focus yet again on the repeated playlist concept — which still favors the dominance of a few current megastars.

In the British media there appears to be much less of a sharp break between megastars and ministars. Such requisites of megastardom as huge audience and salary numbers are not available in the domestic British market alone. On the other hand, British television, being much less dominated by across-the-year fictional series, is proportionately more dependent on other linking and audience-sustaining devices — including familiar crossover personalities. British prime-time television also focuses much less upon fiction. Its prime-time offerings feature more nonfiction formats, including chat shows and game shows as well as "current affairs" and minority interest magazine-feature programming. The need to provide anchors, interviewees, reporters, and contestants for this wide array of programming provides work for perhaps 200 star faces on British television. One indication of the British system's strong demand for middle-range celebrities, rather than megastars, is a pattern followed in recent years by a number of British women news anchors; having anchored news shows and thus acquired celebrity, these women have tended to move (rather than be pushed) into the role of free-lance anchor/personality, appearing on a range of nonnews shows.

Talent agents have played a part in these latter events in Britain. American talent agents moved from New York to colonize the movie industry in the interwar period. Later they represented the network news talent in New York. We need to know more about these talent agents for several reasons: They "package" not only movies but, increasingly it seems, the network and local TV news; they are clearly one of the key links between the business and creative wings of the media; and agents cross over between media as well as between nations.

TOWARD A GLOBAL MEDIA INDUSTRY

Previous to 1970, most of the international influences present in the media industry followed a pattern of one-way flow from the United States into the rest of the world. Perhaps the three greatest of these flows involved Hollywood exports, the international news agencies, and the international advertising agencies.

The 1970s, however, saw much more of a balancing flow as other players came into the market, and the 1980s saw a strengthening of these globalizing trends. The Japanese became entertainment and information exporters of their own, and Japanese dominance of the U.S. domestic equipment market has been extended from radios to television sets and video recorders. Western European penetration of the U.S. media market was substantially extended during the 1980s. Major sections of U.S. book publishing became foreign owned, as did recorded music companies and several consumer magazine companies. Leading Madison Avenue agencies (such as Ted Bates, J. Walter Thompson, and the Ogilvy Group) came under British ownership.

What seems to be emerging quite rapidly is an increasing degree of ownership integration among the media industries of the United States, Japan, Australia, Canada, Britain, West Germany, France, and Italy. This increasing integration of at least eight national media industries has numerous implications as well as causes.

National Laws Bring International Ownership

National antimonopoly rules interact internationally. This phenomenon has lain behind the wave of foreign purchases of U.S. media properties. Obviously the weakness of the dollar in the late 1980s contributed, but U.S. antitrust law and regulation played a larger part; antitrust law prohibits many possible intra-U.S. purchases. For example, the television networks have not been allowed to buy Hollywood production houses; with the most obviously interested U.S. companies thus being disqualified, the way has been left open to Australians, Europeans, and the Japanese.

Regulations against cross-media ownership within single U.S. cities have encouraged U.S. companies to diversify nationally. Buying across markets, they have tended to stick to newspapers and broadcast and cable television. The largest European media companies are also prevented by domestic antimonopoly restrictions from further domestic media expansion. Forced to look outside their domestic market, these European companies know that Europe-Europe mergers are difficult to consummate; hostile takeovers are largely unknown in Europe (except in Britain). Thus the domestic U.S. market has an almost irresistible attraction. When surveying the U.S. market, these European companies find that they cannot buy into television, which is closed to foreigners; newspaper and cable MSO purchases by Europeans are also largely unknown — these are the "cash-flow" targets of American companies. European takeover ambitions, consequently, move toward books, music, and film companies.

Deregulatory policies in general — and the deregulation or nonregulation of new technologies in particular — played a major role in 1980s moves toward a single, more global, media industry. For example, the deregulation of space led to an explosion of satellite-to-cable offerings. Cable growth and the emergence of new independent television stations caused problems for the television networks (Tunstall, 1986). In the mid-1980s all three U.S. networks changed ownership. Not the least important of the associated changes was that a spate of disposals of subsidiaries led to major purchases by foreign companies — the CBS music interests went to Sony, while RCA music went to Bertelsmann of West Germany.

Such takeovers also emphasized the possibility of the software and programming industry becoming a subordinate wing of the global electronics companies. The most remarkable case here was Sony, which in 1989 added Columbia Pictures to its CBS music interests. Sony has major hardware ambitions in such fields as high-definition television, and is obviously aiming for a version of hardware-software "lock-in." Such strategies had been pursued by American companies in the past, but General Electric's purchase of RCA (and NBC) seemed to offer fewer opportunities, not least because of NBC's network status, which ruled it out of program acquisition and syndication.

Deregulation has become an invisible U.S. export that, during the 1980s, had a big impact in Europe. In France and West Germany, the policy debates that led to the opening up of commercial television certainly used American deregulatory terminology and ideas (Dyson & Humphreys, 1988). But even deregulatory ideology has not been a simple one-way flow. In telecommunications, for example, the Thatcher administration was advocating telephone network competition in 1981, the year previous to the Reagan administration's (January 1982) decision to pursue the breakup of AT&T. Moreover, in terms of a radical break in commercial television, the key event was the decision of the Italian Constitutional Court to end the state broadcasting monopoly. This decision, which led to a version of commercial TV less regulated than anything yet seen in the United States, occurred in 1976.

The subsequent "Berlusconi phenomenon" (named for the Italian commercial television magnate) initially involved the importing of Hollywood television output on a scale not previously seen in Europe. But during the 1980s, Berlusconi's three national commercial channels increasingly used more Italian-made programming. Moreover, Berlusconi began to extend his empire into France, Germany, and Spain, thus helping to create the beginnings of a Europewide production industry.

An even more obvious example of the convergence of national media industries into global activity is the home video. This new technology has in practice largely been manufactured by Japanese companies. In the most populated nations of Western Europe, the VCR has been much more popular than cable. On their Japanese VCRs, however, Europeans tend to see either their own national time-shifted television programming or Hollywood films and series.

Hollywood: More Global,
More Powerful, and Less American

In the 1980s, while the New York television networks experienced a declining audience share, Hollywood — in its many guises — grew stronger. Hollywood became less dependent upon sales to the TV networks. Independent stations, cable, and the home video markets all expanded, and the theatrical film market remained fairly buoyant. The expansion of channels and competition abroad (and especially in Europe) allowed Hollywood to export more programming as well as to charge higher prices per hour.

During the 1980s, Hollywood ownership remained highly volatile. The previous *diversified conglomerate* pattern increasingly gave way to Hollywood companies becoming part of *integrated communications companies.* Three mergers illustrate this move. First, Rupert Murdoch's news company acquired Twentieth Century Fox (and later the Metromedia TV station group). Second, in 1989, the Time-Warner merger created a new domestic U.S. media colossus — with its own means of distribution via movie theaters, cable, satellite-to-cable (Home Box Office), audio (Warner), home video, and book stores — bigger than any network. In addition, the Time-Warner-Lorimar combination was, at the time of the merger, the biggest supplier of prime-time programming hours to the networks. A third crucial merger — also in 1989, as I have noted — added the Columbia Pictures production house to the Sony-CBS music combine.

These changes were in several respects a return to a much earlier Hollywood tradition. Here again was a truly dominant Hollywood, not only in the United States, but in the world. As in the early Hollywood, some of the ownership was foreign (or at least foreign born). Now, however, Hollywood's foreign owners originated not from Eastern Europe, but from Australia and Japan. Perhaps the key change was that the Hollywood pipeline into the global market no longer carried simply theatrical films. It now had multiple audio as well as multiple video formats suitable for multiple market "windows" and multiple "technologies."

Interaction of Global and
National Media Industry Factors

Media globalization made some important advances in the 1980s: Deregulatory and free-market policies led to increasing imports of programming, and a pattern of globalized ownership affected several of the "lesser" media industry segments. Hollywood itself incorporated most of these trends — "Hollywood" encompassed more media forms, and sold them through more windows, more widely across the world; but Hollywood itself came to be more globally owned — with significant elements of foreign control.

Nevertheless, national media industries remained strong, and by 1990 there was still very little sign of foreign ownership of the major media of newspapers and network television. These major media have retained not only their cash-flow strength, but also their political significance. The tendency of several nations to allow combined press-television ownership has strengthened forces that are often national and conservative in several senses. Language continues to be a highly conservative force; nationally made material remains extremely popular and even imported material has to conform to locally traditional translation patterns — broadly speaking, the weaker national markets stick to subtitling while the stronger national markets insist on dubbing.

What happens to national media industries in Europe in the 1990s will depend heavily on broader changes in the familiar trinity of business, technology, and politics. "National" turbulence, both above and below the level of the nation-state, seems likely to continue. It therefore is probably quite safe to predict the increasing strength of national media industries in at least some respects. International media forces will also almost certainly acquire increasing strength in certain respects and at the world level as well as at the level of Europe and other world regions.

NATIONAL MEDIA INDUSTRIES: COMPARATIVE PERSPECTIVES

In order to gain a full appreciation of the globalization of media, we need to look at media industries comparatively. Academic media researchers need a comparative focus to recognize that the media are increasingly following the standard commercial pattern of integration into a single industry and adopting "global" strategies. Unfortunately, the majority of media researchers stick to studying one media sector in one corner of one nation.

Most media literature is written for home audiences. Consequently, it is difficult to find a good brief description of, for example, what a U.S. television network does, or what constitutes a U.S. media "market" (a term unknown elsewhere), or how a typical U.S. daily newspaper is organized. For British media, the situation is even worse because there are few textbooks (in the U.S. sense) dealing with the media. Consequently, some otherwise quite media-sophisticated scholars seem to believe that Britain has Nielsen TV ratings, that British television is directly subsidized by the British government, and that there is a newspaper called the *London Times.* Nor is this solely a matter of U.S.-U.K. mutual ignorance. Within Europe each nation has its own highly distinctive system — Belgium for example is radically different from the Netherlands. Inevitably, with some 20 national systems in Western Europe alone, the average level of ignorance about neighboring nations is extremely high.

With what then should comparative national media studies be concerned? There are many possibilities, but my suggestion would be, if in doubt, to go for the most obviously large and public organizations, events, and issues. For example, the single year of 1985 saw takeover attempts launched at all three U.S. networks; ABC was merged with smaller Capital Cities, NBC (RCA) was merged in General Electric, and CBS was "put into play" by Ted Turner's junk bond bid. CBS later did have a change of ownership and thus all three networks were under new control. Also in 1985 Rupert Murdoch became the effective controller of the Metromedia station group and of Twentieth Century Fox; in addition, nearly one-third of all U.S. television stations changed hands in a two-year period. A fruitful comparison might be made between these U.S. events and what happened in France in the same period. During the mid-1980s France went from three to six national television networks and saw a major switch toward commercial owner-ship and advertising finance.

To offer just one further example of a comparative research project that could throw light on the media industry more widely: Financial journalism in both the United States and Europe has had a major expansion in recent years in that financial newspapers sell more copies, more newspapers now carry special finan-cial sections, and many new openings for financial programming have appeared in broadcast and cable television and radio. On the other hand, in Europe as in the United States, there are powerful strains toward monopoly in the provision of financial news. In the United States, Dow Jones is in a dominant position through the *Wall Street Journal* and the AP-Dow Jones service. This connection has a special significance in financial news. But there is a wider media industry signifi-cance in that the dominant AP news agency (with UPI now in a relatively subordinate position) should be linked to the *Wall Street Journal*, the serious newspaper with the largest nationally spread sale. In Britain, the situation differs only in detail. The Reuters news agency has recently been through a period of extraordinary growth and profitability—due mainly to its dominant position in Europe in the provision of electronic financial data and currency dealing facilities (see Reuters, 1986/1987). The *Financial Times* is in a dominant position in the financial press and its parent company now also owns the leading financial daily in France, *Les Echos*. A comparative study of these two situations would tell us much not only about financial news but about the media industry.

U.S. and British Television Networks:
The Difficulties of an "Easy" Comparison

There are, of course, good reasons comparative studies do not abound. While access and travel costs are obvious, the central difficulty would appear to be the basis for comparison. Consider, for example, the problems in what might seem to be an easy comparison between the United States and the United Kingdom.

An American network consists most obviously of some 200 local stations that are owned by other companies; it has key "owned and operated" stations; the network runs a transmission operation; it operates and promotes a schedule of programming; it commissions programming from production houses; the network itself produces the flagship network news and related programming; it sells advertising spaces and inserts commercials into its scheduled transmissions; the network also undertakes various self-regulatory activities and political relationships.

Most academic studies consider in detail only one or two of these eight network activities, although there are some honorable exceptions (e.g., Besen, Krattenmaker, Metzger, & Woodbury, 1984). In view of the paucity of good academic research on the U.S. networks, it is hardly surprising that even fewer comparative network studies have been undertaken. One recent comparative study of the U.S. and British networks is thus of special interest. The study was conducted for the Peacock Committee (Peacock, 1986), which was set up by the Thatcher government to investigate BBC finances in general and in particular the possibility of the BBC carrying advertising. This Thatcher-appointed and predominantly free-market committee somewhat reluctantly reported against advertising on the BBC as an immediate possibility; a key problem was that in an otherwise unchanged four-channel national system the main casualties would have been ITV and Channel Four, not BBC1 and BBC2. The loss of advertising to the BBC and the price fall due to competition would — it was feared — have bankrupted some of the smaller, but high-cost, regional ITV companies.

However, one additional reason for the Peacock Committee's reluctant thumbs-down on immediate BBC advertising was a report that the committee commissioned. *Research on the Range and Quality of Broadcasting Services* (1986) is not a title designed for best-seller status. The authors are Jay Blumler (of Leeds University and the University of Maryland), Tom Nossiter (London School of Economics), and Malcolm Brynin (Leeds University). The purpose of the research was to consider the likely impact of advertising finance on the range and quality of programming. A total of 200 senior executives and producers were interviewed in London, New York, and Los Angeles.

Blumler et al. (1986, pp. 108-110) argue that advertising contributes to five pervasive features of U.S. network television:

(1) Competition for advertising not only intensifies audience-maximization pressures, but also universalizes such pressures across all programming, day and night.

(2) The system confers upon advertisers a "near-proprietary right" to have their interests served by television.

(3) The detailed involvement of advertising interests is highly institutionalized, allowing advertising considerations to enter detailed programming decisions.

(4) The intimate connection between particular programming and specific categories of advertising creates a powerful logic of audience maximization, which places proposals for nonformula programming at a severe disadvantage. Executives representing the audience numbers logic can and do "interfere in virtually all aspects of production."

(5) Advertising finance "pours a tremendous amount of money into television"; it also results in up to five commercial "pods" accompanying 22 minutes of network news.

The Blumler et al. study includes further criticism about the lack of range of American network programming: At any given time of the day the viewer's choice of programming is severely limited. Even within a particular programming category, there is a strong tendency toward a single formula. The advertising-based U.S. system requires a quick and "immediate appeal" that tends to rule out any complexity of meaning; competition tends to focus on surface effects, settings, and quick excitement; there is a dilution of "identifiable place or social character"; creative risk-taking is avoided; public issues, if addressed at all, receive formula treatment; criteria of balance and neutrality (and consultation with pressure groups) are applied in inappropriate cases, notably in fictional programming.

The Blumler et al. account of the four British national television channels is distinctly more favorable — although the authors see commercial trends toward audience maximization, formula programming, advertising intrusion, and bland uniformity as slowly undermining British standards of "public service broadcasting." Documentaries are no longer scheduled in mid prime time; British current affairs/news comment programs now have smaller audiences and budgets and can do less original filming in distant locations. The cost of original drama has risen faster than costs in general and faster than review in particular. Nevertheless, Blumler et al. believe that the general ethos of the British system still provides a wider choice and is more truly focused on serving the audience than is an American system that gives advertising and its representatives a veto over all aspects of programming.

Blumler et al. clearly regard British drama programming as superior to the Hollywood output. Britain makes a full range of television drama, from soap operas to series, serials, docudramas, short series, and "single plays" (the nearest U.K. equivalent to U.S. made-for-television movies). It is the single plays and (noncostume) short series, by celebrated writers, that carry the most prestige in fictional television in Britain.

The flavor of this drama output is well conveyed in *The Largest Theatre in the World* by Sutton (1982), who was boss of BBC Television Drama Group — in charge of the BBC's entire fictional output. The title is revealing — Sutton continually refers to television fiction as "drama," "plays," and "theatre." His book describes the BBC's drama production, an output much larger than that of any single Hollywood studio; the proximity of the BBC drama effort to the London West End stage; the heavy stress placed on *writing* in British television drama, including the use of celebrated theater playwrights such as Harold Pinter; and the emergence of specialized television writers who in some cases are more honored than the star actors who perform their works.

"Good of its kind" has always been the goal of British television output over a range of programming types that is too varied to lead to easy categorization. As Buckingham (1987) shows in *Public Secrets: Eastenders and Its Audience* an attempt is made — even in a superpopular twice-weekly soap opera — to deliver high-quality acting of the predominantly low-life characters, to deal centrally with difficult social issues such as race and intrafamily violence, and to lead, rather than to follow, public opinion. *Eastenders,* which quickly came to top the British ratings, was unusual in being the subject of some preliminary audience research. But Buckingham's account nevertheless still indicates that the process of commissioning this major early prime-time twice-weekly series was carried out with — at least by Hollywood standards — a minimum of negotiation and argument. This comes about because the tradition of "producer autonomy" goes alongside a tradition of quick decisions. A new BBC project has to go past only two or three meetings and two or three key executives in order to acquire a budget and a time slot in the schedule. Perhaps a final quotation from Tom Nossiter is appropriate here. He indicates the British style of broadcasting organization decision making:

> In contrast to the American system where the "Darwinnowing" process takes place through a long chain of schedulers, executives, producers and analysts, all applying a single evolutionary criterion for survival — fitness for the highest ratings — the BBC system is simple, short but multi-dimensional. (Blumler et al., 1986, p. 46)

Blumler et al.'s comparison, then, strongly favors the four British national channels against the three U.S. networks. This comparison also illustrates the very great difficulty of using the comparative approach in order to throw light on a particular media system or television network structure. This comparison was addressing a British policy question: What does aggressive competition for advertising revenue do to a national network system? Starting from the British networks, it then looked at the three U.S. networks; in doing so it ignored the independent stations, PBS, and cable, which obviously greatly add to the available programming choices.

Of the many available possibilities, I want to consider one additional critique of Blumler et al.'s report. This critique would see their comparison as not only ideologically elitist, but also as unrealistic and sentimental about the British system. Surely Blumler et al. are ignoring the point that Britain's television production system is no less "industrialized" than that of the United States. My response must be that Britain certainly has a television production "industry," but it is nevertheless a different type of industry.

In Britain there is almost no syndication market and no gold-mine reward for daily stripping of lengthy series reruns; there is not even the U.S. system of a 23-week "season." By comparison with the United States, Britain largely operates a "miniseries" system. Many shows run for six, eight, or thirteen episodes and then stop. The same show may reappear (perhaps in a changed format) a year later for another miniseries run. This short series approach is followed partly because *writers* are honored, and it is believed that writers should not be forced to write more episodes than they want to. (The inevitable Hollywood response of "Hire some more writers" does not obtain in London.) Actors also do not want to be tied up in a very long television series with annually only four months or so free (as in Hollywood); leading British actors typically want to work on the London stage and in films as well. In this way television and stage borrow and shape each other's stars.

The difference between the British and American degrees of "industrialization" is also illustrated by the soap opera. In the United States there is a demand for daily soaps and the industry generates a supply. In Britain even the cheaper kinds of soap have usually not been daily; the long-running British soaps (like *Coronation*

Street) have mostly run for either two or three (25-minute) episodes per week. In the late 1980s imported Australian five-day-a-week soaps (such as *Neighbours*) became extremely popular—indicating a strong U.K. demand. But the British industry has been reluctant to supply this demand. A major reason for this reluctance is that producers, directors, writers, actors, and talent trade unions all believe that *daily* soap production debases artistic standards and requires unacceptable working conditions.

The industrial climate of American network television results partly from the more intense competition for ratings, including several very similar programs involved in head-to-head competition in a single time slot. But the industrial climate is also powerfully shaped by the fact that the networks do not own the shows; the networks—it could be argued—compensate for their frustrated desire to own the shows by aggressively commanding and demanding detailed involvement in scripts, casting, and other programming details. In industrial terms, the networks contract out the work, but require the contracted producers to follow highly detailed specifications.

The British industrial climate is substantially different. In particular, the BBC (which has largely set the style of production) makes the bulk of its own programming. In the BBC, the departmental executive probably feels much freer than his or her Hollywood equivalent. By virtue of holding that particular job, a BBC programming executive normally controls certain relevant time slots in the network schedule as well as the funding with which to fill the slots. Left largely alone by the people above, the executive can ignore advertising completely and only has to achieve a reasonable audience rating, not needing to kill the opposition in order to protect access to a syndication gold mine.

The ITV system is different from that of the BBC, but ITV producers are largely insulated from specific advertising pressures and ITV companies have usually been able to hang onto their time slots in the annual schedule for long spans of years.

Perhaps an oddity of the British system is that the most "industrial" production conditions obtain in some of the more serious types of output. Channel Four has a remit to make "minority" programming; but production is contracted out and again—as in the United States—is more tightly monitored and controlled. In some respects the news output is the most industrialized and an obvious major exception to the standard miniseries approach.

Comparative Hypothesis: Competition for a Single
Revenue Source Results in Imitative Uniformity

As seen from Europe, American network television overall appears to insult the audience's taste. On the other hand, European, and especially British, visitors see a sharp contrast between American newspapers and television. Seen from abroad, American television appears to aim at the bottom half of the population (in terms of education and income level), while American newspapers aim at the top half. The typical American daily newspaper does, of course, have a more up-market audience profile than does the typical television network affiliate station. In Britain, the broad comparison is reversed. It is the television output overall that is somewhat more serious, "elitist," or up-market than the audience. But the British national daily press—or the tabloid part of it that accounts for about 82% of national daily sales—is much more entertainment oriented than is British television. Foreign visitors react with astonishment to British tabloid newspapers. Nearly two-thirds of some of these publications is "look at" material—pictures, massive headlines, cartoons, and display advertising; the focus is on melodrama and entertainment—crime, sex, money, entertainment stars, sports, and royal family gossip. Most of the familiar "junk-food" criticisms of American television are equally commonly made of the British tabloid press.

Why then do American network television and British popular newspapers both insult public taste, while British television and American daily newspapers seem somewhat to flatter public taste? There must be many complexities and difficulties in such a broad comparison, but much of the contrast derives (I believe) from the different sources of revenue.

"Down-market," uniform, "junk-food" American network television and British tabloid newspapers have in common a dependence on a single dominant source of revenue for which there is fierce competition. American network television engages in imitative competition because of its dependence on mass-market national *consumer advertising*. The British tabloid press engages in imitative competition because of its dependence on mass-market *sales* revenue, a point unfamiliar to most Americans. American newspapers operate from an advertising revenue base (something Rupert Murdoch took some years to accept fully). British tabloid dailies, of course, carry advertising—but it is not so profitable as it at first appears. Rupert Murdoch's London tabloid daily the *Sun* in 1988-1989 was charging £26,000 (about $40,000) per page. However, most of this revenue was spent in producing 4.2 million daily copies of the page. Most of the tabloid advertising revenue is, in fact, taken up by producing and printing just the advertising pages. British tabloids are, therefore, not advertising revenue based, but sales revenue based. For these tabloids circulation figures have the same dominating influence as ratings and share numbers in U.S. network television.

But while Britain's six national daily tabloids are engaged in a circulation-and-sensationalism competition, Britain's five national daily broadsheet papers are quite different. They charge much higher advertising rates. The *Financial Times*, for example, charges about 16 times per page more than the *Sun* per thousand circulation. The five up-market dailies (with 18% of national daily sales) actually have three major sources of income—sales, classified advertising, and display advertising—like most U.S. newspapers. This much broader revenue base leads to a much broader range of subjects receiving editorial coverage.

In the United States it is nearly the entire daily newspaper press that has these three sources of revenue. American newspapers also typically face only limited head-to-head competition; the result is publications that are variously described as "serious," "responsible," "elitist," and "monopolistic."

Competition for a particular source of revenue has not yet existed in British television. Two BBC channels are license-fee financed (the traditional pattern across Western Europe); ITV and Channel Four have been advertising financed, but under a complex set of arrangements that have avoided direct competition for advertising. The Conservative government's 1989-1990 legislation was designed to introduce direct advertising competition by creating a new advertising-financed Channel Five for 1993.

The basic hypothesis made apparent in this comparative analysis is that competition for a single source of revenue drives programming toward imitative uniformity. Some other consequences also appear to follow; in particular, competitive dependence on a single revenue source tends to maximize the power of the powerful. Groups or individuals capable of affecting the single revenue stream acquire an element of veto control. For example, interest groups that could withdraw advertising or a segment of the audience are, de facto, allowed to veto particular themes and approaches. In addition, individual star actors may acquire veto power, especially if a series is dependent on a star who can then threaten to terminate a successful television series before it accumulates enough episodes to strike syndication gold. Given that situation, the actor's agent can "negotiate up" (in Hollywood parlance). Here actor power mops up available revenue; this increases costs, thus reinforcing the competitive drive to maximize audience numbers and to stick with a winning formula.

A good part of the power of this hypothesis comes from its ability to migrate across media and economic ecologies. I have argued here, for example, that U.S. television behaves much the same as U.K. tabloid newspapers, though they are obviously different media in different economic ecologies. The hypothesis, in turn, is dependent upon and is the reward for comparative analysis.

AN INDUSTRY FOCUS: PROBLEMS IN RESEARCH

Access

Media industry research strategies, as proposed here, imply focusing research attention on areas and issues that are already of interest to senior management, national policymakers, the national media, and stock market analysts. One positive advantage of the interests of such people is that they generate speeches, reports, publications, and research reports of various kinds. A possible difficulty may be that research access becomes less easy to obtain.

There is also the opposite problem — that those who do obtain research access at fairly elevated media industry levels may become a little too friendly toward their subject matter. Paul Lazarsfeld was clearly on excessively friendly terms with CBS. *The Politics of Broadcast Regulation* became a standard text from its first edition in 1973, but it did present a rather favorable pluralist/functionalist view of this segment of Washington politics; thus the fact that its senior author, Erwin

Krasnow, was at the time of its third edition (Krasnow, Longley, & Terry, 1982) general counsel to the National Association of Broadcasters could be taken as an example of overintimacy. Also vulnerable to the same criticism is *Inside Prime Time* (Gitlin, 1985), which, while more highly readable, fails in key respects adequately to update *The Hollywood TV Producer* (Cantor, 1971).

In this context an exemplary study is *Books: The Culture and Commerce of Publishing,* by Coser, Kadushin, and Powell (1982). These authors and their research assistants clearly obtained excellent access to the New York publishing industry; despite an intimate "inside" account, they also managed to maintain a strong element of critical detachment.

Another who has demonstrated an admirable balance of intimacy and detachment is the British sociologist Simon Frith. *Music for Pleasure,* Frith's (1988) book of "essays in the sociology of pop," reprints some articles from academic journals as well as other pieces that originally appeared in newspapers and music publications.

Content, Audience, and Media Industry

Much research on both media content and media audiences in the past has ignored the industrial context. Much (but not all) of this research suffers from snapshot and fragmented perspectives. Semiology, like quantified context analysis, typically concentrates on a detailed analytical "reading" of a limited number of "texts." These approaches often ignore (or take for granted) the perspectives of both the originating industry and the receiving consumer; both industry and consumer tend to see media content much more as a continuing stream. From the viewpoint of industry the content of the media is "product"; particular programs and titles are "brands."

Some semiologists are willing to write full-length books about the contents of a very few films. This may be rather like analyzing the supermarket by a detailed inspection of one loaf of bread and one can of beans. Such an analysis would miss the essential point that most supermarket sales are of repeat-purchase products. Consumers typically buy loaves of bread and cans of beans by the hundreds each year; similarly, consumers typically consume hundreds of daily newspapers and many hundreds of hours of television per year.

The research of Robert Park, Leo Rosten, and Theodore Adorno generally has made clear that media content conforms to industrially defined formats. For example, to understand why American popular songs were so similar-but-slightly-different, Adorno considered several aspects of the national media — including Hollywood, commercial radio, and song plugging.

While in recent years semiology was influencing content research, a more qualitative approach to audience research was focusing upon the ways in which families and other real-life groups consume the media (e.g., Morley, 1980). This particular research trend is a fruitful one for the development of a more realistic media industry perspective.

A worrying problem in this connection is that only the media industry itself is fully equipped (and financed) to conduct research on the necessary industrial scale. Academics have difficulty in obtaining funds for a single national sample survey or a single content study; as works like *Cableviewing* by Carrie Heeter and Bradley Greenberg (1988) indicate, new technologies will further increase the complexity of audience research.

It follows from this circumstance that reanalysis of industry research will potentially be rewarding. Some of the work of the Newspaper Advertising Bureau in New York is of considerable interest; and some of it—for example, on non-readership of daily newspapers by young adults and members of ethnic minorities—can be used for purposes other than those intended by the newspaper publishers who fund the research.

In *Television and Its Audience,* Barwise and Ehrenberg (1988) show what can be done in the comparative reanalysis of the major American and British television ratings services. One crucial point is that these authors do not see the audience only in terms of the usual demographic or personality characteristics. The continuing nature of the ratings services allows these authors to discover much about the overlap of audiences and hence about overall patterns in the audience's preferences for programming. Barwise and Ehrenberg both teach at the London Business School and have marketing backgrounds. Their negative findings are among their most interesting; the network television audience (in both the United Kingdom and the United States) is only very weakly segmented by social class or other obvious variables. Nearly all viewers spread their viewing across a range of programming categories; most audience members exhibit only semiloyal behavior even to their favorite programs. Very few network programs attract audiences with distinctive profiles. The authors seem reluctant to characterize their conception of the audience directly; but this is a study that indicates the advantages of both industry data and a more industrial conception of audiences and content.

CONCLUSIONS

This chapter has argued for a comparative *industrial* perspective in mass communications research. Those who adopt this perspective will be part of a convergence of commercial, policy, and academic concerns. For example, much current policy debate, in many different national settings, focuses on the industrial relationship between television transmission networks and the production of programming. Policy decisions, which set or relax legal constraints of this kind, have enormous commercial consequences. Such issues are of equally great academic interest.

One of my suggestions has been that, when looking across the various media industries, we should distinguish between the more financially stable "cash-flow" media (such as conventional television and daily newspapers) and the more volatile "one-off" media (for example, movie theaters and recorded music). Such a distinction leads to a focus upon strategies adopted by the one-off media to achieve a somewhat more secure cash flow. It also points to the importance of media products marketed through a sequence of windows. Not least, this perspective suggests that studies of the advertising business, and advertising-oriented business strategies, should be central. Just as financial concerns can never be far from the minds of such senior "creators" as TV executive producers or newspaper executives, so also academic researchers need to think finance.

In order to pursue meaningful comparative studies, we need a workable conceptual framework. At the very least, we must avoid the assumption that such obvious terms as *TV network* retain their meanings across national boundaries. One approach may be to acknowledge that there are several main types of networks — for instance, those that do or do not own local stations/outlets. Similarly, there are a few main types of *TV series* (such as the miniseries and the long continuing series), and there are perhaps three main variables in television *soap* drama: time of day, episodes per week, and high/low budget.

Another dimension essential for even the most simplistic cross-national comparison is some distinction of a national versus local kind. My tentative suggestion would be for two levels above the national. One "international" level involves culturally and linguistically similar nations (e.g., United States-Canada, France-Belgium, Mexico-Venezuela). A second international level is the global or semiglobal. Similarly, my suggestion is for three levels below the national. These might be "regional" (e.g., Quebec, France-Belgium, Scotland, an Indian state), "local" (a city and local area, such as the U.S. media "market"), and "community" (small town, rural area, single suburb). Without some such set of distinctions, international discussion — even on apparently simple topics such as local radio or daily newspaper — becomes a frustrating babel.

My suggestions also include a comparative focus on the pattern of hierarchy, power, and division of labor in the mass communications industries. At the top level this includes looking at two phenomena that tend to make academics nervous: One is companies, the other is individuals. We need to consider media tycoons and performance stars, as well as look at the major media companies that attract stock market analysis.

Finally, in adopting a comparative approach, we need to ask in what respects a single global media industry is developing, as well as in what respects the national and subnational levels remain strong or are becoming stronger. One promising hypothesis may be that it is the "one-off" media that already exhibit strong global tendencies at the company level — the recorded music "Big Five," the "international" advertising agencies (all based in New York, London, and Tokyo), and Hollywood global domination of theatrical movies. In the "cash-flow" fields, however, national control remains strong, not least because most national governments around the world are reluctant to allow TV stations and channels or national newspapers to be foreign owned.

Nor should we ignore the connection between global and local levels. The Soviet Union is only one of many nations in which millions of citizens seem to reject national media offerings, while preferring a mix of regional/local and international output.

REFERENCES

Adorno, T. (1941). On popular music. *Studies in Philosophy and Social Sciences, 9*(1).

Armes, R. (1987). *Third World film making and the west.* Berkeley: University of California Press.

Barwise, P., & Ehrenberg, A. (1988). *Television and its audience.* London: Sage.

Besen, S. M., Krattenmaker, T. G., Metzger, A. R., & Woodbury, J. (1984). *Misregulating television: Network dominance and the FCC.* Chicago: University of Chicago Press.

Beville, H. M. (1985). *Audience ratings: Radio, television, cable.* Hillsdale, NJ: Lawrence Erlbaum.

Blumler, J. G., Nossiter, T. J., & Brynin, M. (1986). *Research on the range and quality of broadcasting services.* London: HMSO, for the Peacock Committee on Financing the BBC.

Brown, A. (1986). *Commercial media in Australia.* Saint Lucia: University of Queensland Press.

Buckingham, D. (1987). *Public secrets: Eastenders and its audience.* London: British Film Institute.

Burns, T. (1977). *The BBC: Public institution and private world.* London: Macmillan.

Cantor, M. G. (1971). *The Hollywood TV producer.* New York: Basic Books.

Cockburn, C. (1983). *Brothers: Male dominance and technological change.* London: Pluto.

Coser, L. A., Kadushin, C., & Powell, W. W. (1982). *Books: The culture and commerce of publishing.* New York: Basic Books.

Dyson, K., & Humphreys, P. (1988). *Broadcasting and new media policies in Western Europe.* London: Routledge & Kegan Paul.

Elliott, P., & Matthews, G. (1987). Broadcasting culture: Innovation, accommodation and routinization in the early BBC. In J. Curran, A. Smith, & P. Wingate (Eds.), *Impacts and influences: Essays on media power in the twentieth century* (pp. 235-258). London: Methuen.

Frith, S. (1988). *Music for pleasure: Essays in the sociology of pop.* Cambridge: Polity.

Gitlin, T. (1985). *Inside prime time.* New York: Pantheon.

Hardt, H. (1979). *Social theories of the press.* Beverly Hills, CA: Sage.

Heeter, C., & Greenberg, B. S. (1988). *Cableviewing.* Norwood, NJ: Ablex.

Hess, S. (1986). *The ultimate insiders: U.S. senators in the national media.* Washington, DC: Brookings Institution.

Krasnow, E. G., Longley, D., & Terry, H. A. (1982). *The politics of broadcast regulation* (3rd ed.). New York: Saint Martin's.

Morley, D. (1980). *The "Nationwide" audience: Structure and decoding.* London: British Film Institute.

Lazarsfeld, P. F. (1973). *The politics of broadcast regulation.*

Park, R. E. (1922). *The immigrant press and its control.* New York: Harper.

Peacock, A. (1986). *Report of the Committee on Financing the BBC.* London: HMSO.

Reuters. (1986/1987). *Reuters holdings PLC: Annual report.* London: Author.

Rosten, L. C. (1937). *The Washington correspondents.* New York: Harcourt, Brace.

Rosten, L. C. (1941). *Hollywood: The movie colony, the movie makers.* New York: Harcourt, Brace.

Sutton, S. (1982). *The largest theatre in the world: Thirty years of television drama.* London: BBC.

Tunstall, J. (1971). *Journalists at work.* Beverly Hills, CA: Sage.

Tunstall, J. (1986). *Communications deregulation: The unleashing of America's communications industry.* Oxford: Basil Blackwell.

Wills, G., & Cooper, C. L. (1988). *Pressure sensitive: Popular musicians under stress.* London: Sage.

Organizational Media Theory

J A M E S A . D A N O W S K I
University of Illinois at Chicago

All large organizations are "media organizations" because they must use media to manage meanings for organizational symbols held by members of the internal and external environment. This commentary discusses a theory of organizational media, presenting results from two studies of the 100 largest U.S. corporations and from seven studies of 199 Chicago organizations. The theory accounts for why organizations use space- and time-shift media, and what relationships these media have to the status of communication management, to shared meaning for organizational symbols, to the abstractness and orgocentrism of meanings, to cultural convergence after merger/acquisition, to organizational time perceptions, and to financial valuation in the marketplace. Although it is assumed that an adequate theory should explain all kinds of organizations' media use, some observers wish to isolate the media industry for study. Accordingly, the theory is used to generate a set of 20 hypotheses about organizational changes in the media industry.

I F we consider theorizing about media and organizations, as Tunstall has, perhaps our starting assumption is that our theory should explain how *all* organizations manage and use media, and how they affect those media. It would be ideal if our theory could explain how organizations like television networks operate with respect to media, as well as how any other kinds of organizations do, from soup canners to nuts manufacturers. Accordingly, this commentary is a step in that direction. At the end of this treatment, I shall return to the observations of the media industry Tunstall has made. I will evaluate these observations in the context of my theoretical orientation.

ORGANIZATIONS AS MEDIATION SYSTEMS

I define *media* broadly. They include electronic transmission technologies, such as video, telephone, and computer; they also include nonelectronic technologies, such as print, photos, and graphics (see Gumpert & Cathcart, 1986, for typologies

Correspondence and requests for reprints: James A. Danowski, Department of Communication and Theatre, University of Illinois at Chicago, IL 60680.

Communication Yearbook 14, pp. 187-207

of media). Organizations use these media for both internal and external communication. I conceptualize "mediation" as *fundamentally* an organizational-level activity. The creation and maintenance of the means of information gathering, message creation, packaging, and dissemination all require organized social agreements. These are about task differentiation, integration, standards for workmanship or performance, and technical standards for the interfacing of hardware and software used (Anderson & Meyer, 1988). *Signification* is defined in the semiotic tradition as the creation of signs, which stand for something else, such as icons and symbols. Systems of signs include manifest message content, as well as message form and packaging and relationships among messages in a medium and across media.

An organization is usually made up of more than one cohesive group, typically three or more. There is a naming, labeling, and identification of the organization. Organizational identity specialists design and implement visual and spatial significations that identify the organization. These include such visuals as logos, letterhead, exterior signs, and decor. At the same time, public relations practitioners manage semantic features of organizational signification texts for internal and external publics. These activities, and other mediated communication, constitute managed, mediated signification systems. Because we observe organizations to place varying importance on mediated signification, we assume it is worth theorizing about.

If we take a systems view, we assume that theories of mediation apply to social systems, as well as to their subsystems. By studying organizations as social systems (Katz & Khan, 1978), we have more numerous and more varied elements to sample than if we studied whole societies. There are hundreds of thousands of organizations, but only a few hundred societies.

In the following section, the overarching question is, Why and how do organizations seek control over content and its distribution through media? I approach this question through examining what patterns there are across the ways organizations organize communication management functions, their uses of media for internal and external communication, and the meanings that internal and external social actors hold. I also question whether there are differences across media in their signification effects on meanings, based on how these media shift time and space.

MEANING MARKETS

Organizations seek control over the meanings that interacting individuals interpret about these organizations. Individuals form and change their valuations through communication with other people. As these valuation exchange processes are more organized, they become formal markets. Differences in people's valuations drive the buying and selling of shares of ownership in organizations. In a fundamental sense, these stock markets are "meaning markets." Individuals set an economic value through their interpretations of the meaning of an organization's signification. The organization signifies X, individuals interpret the meanings of X, and can trade on differences in their meanings. The greater the differences in meaning, the higher the volume of trading. People generally appear to move their money where their meaning is.

Stock, in this sense, is defined as a share of the organization's signification production potential. This potential is connected with the corporation's message-making, distribution, and meaning-management prospects. Buyers of an organization's stock expect that in the future the organization will manage the means of its signification sufficiently to influence individuals' valuations positively.

Finance scholars take a compatible view of markets and information. The "efficient market" hypothesis (Fama, Fisher, Jensen, & Roll, 1969), for example, suggests that a stock's price reflects all available information about a firm. Price changes are an indicator of new information having been available (Arbel & Jaggi, 1982; Davies & Caves, 1978; Niederhoffer, 1971; Pearce & Roley, 1985).

Based on the assumptions of the efficient market hypothesis, we have an excellent and easily obtained measure of a publicly owned organization's valuation by its economic environment — its stock price. This is the average price for all transactions across buyers and sellers at a particular time. So, stock price is a measure of the collective marketplace valuation of a corporation. This operationalization of value is reliable, precise, reproducible, available at low cost, and valid for many world organizations.

While not all organizations are publicly owned and traded in organized financial markets, the theory in its broader expression can account for valuation of other organizations. Whether an organization's stock is traded, we assume that organizations seek to control the economic resources necessary to reach their other goals. This assumption holds regardless of whether the organization is privately or publicly held, profit or nonprofit, a socialist state agency or an entrepreneurial venture in a free-market society. Nevertheless, how one measures economic resources will vary by culture and by local organizational factors.

Yet, overall, we assume that an organization seeks to optimize its resource control to achieve its other goals. How publics value the organization has an effect on its ability to obtain resources (whether from government funding, private donations, sales, or whatever), its management of these resources, and their expenditure. These effects may be expressed through a variety of forces: political control via legislation or regulation, individual voting behavior, social control through community activism about organizations' social responsibilities, inter-organizational resource dependencies, and market forces. Combinations of these and like forces have an impact on organizational resource control.

VARIATIONS IN ORGANIZATIONS'
LOCUS OF MEANING CONTROL

Local Space Control

Being an organization requires management of social meanings about it by internal and external actors. People regulate meanings most effectively, although often not most efficiently, through face-to-face interaction. (The evidence for interpersonal influence is too extensive to cite here.) Driven by its need to manage organization-related meanings, if the organization is small enough to control interpersonal communication networks directly, it will first attempt this control. It will focus on regulating who can talk with whom about what topics, when, and for what purposes. But as organizations become somewhat larger they cannot as easily control interpersonal interaction. So they shift their control focus from interpersonal networks to local physical space.

Control of space has powerful *direct* effects on interpersonal communication. Proximity — how close people are to one another — is a strong predictor of who talks with whom (Monge & Kirste, 1980). Space control also indirectly affects meanings. Individuals with more interlocking personal networks (whose contact persons also communicate directly with one another) have more restricted spatial locations for their social contacts (Danowski, 1986). Conversely, individuals with more radial networks (whose contact persons do not interact with one another) talk with people over a wider geographic area. Regions with less migration and less mobility have more interlocking personal networks. These interlocking networks make more use of present-tense verbs (Danowski, 1987). As individuals focus on the space to which they are immediately bound, their awareness is bound to the present situation.

Although local control may be effective, it is often not efficient. Movement control requires intensive local surveillance, enforcement, and costs. This is true whether control is maintained through automated physical access systems or through rules restricting movement within or across borders and enforced by security forces. Organizations must monitor information boundaries intensively to limit the introduction of competing social frameworks. In short, because monolithic local control of space is costly, it has limited long-run optimality for the control of meaning.

Size of the social system, in number of individual members, is another factor that limits local control. As systems become larger beyond some relatively small level, interpersonally managed meanings quickly reach a control ceiling and become unmanageable. There are several likely reasons. Individual communicators have limits on information processing (Miller, 1956), and there are "span of control" limits on direct interpersonal management that constrain interpersonal influence. Also, in larger organizations there are longer interpersonal network paths, so there is more distortion of the original message due to information leveling, sharpening, and assimilation (Allport & Postman, 1947). These informa-tion-processing limits move the system to create *mediated* signification systems. The organization trades off less direct control of meaning for wider distribution of signification. Although the amount of meaning control per message is lower with mediation, the net effect is more meaning control across the entire large system. This greater control occurs because higher volumes of messages are distributed to more individuals.

Mediation Factors

Organizations' size directly relates to their ability to obtain, transform, and distribute resources. Because this ability is economically rewarded and because organizations seek economic resources to reach their goals, they seek to become larger. Yet, size-related factors constrain their ability to control signification directly so that the local units maintain collective identification with the system. Thus signification management is increasingly important.

Based on this reasoning, I have hypothesized that as organizations are larger, communication management departments have higher status. This is represented by two things: reporting level in the hierarchy and budget. Status is associated with how close to the top of the organization a unit reports. Status also comes from having more resources, defined in terms of the amount budgeted for communica-tion relative to the number of communication employees, a variable that we can think of as "relative capitalization."

Supportive evidence comes from research that found that across a sample of 35 organizations, public relations practitioners who reported higher in the organiza-tion had higher usage of and preference for mediated communication, and a lower preference for face-to-face interaction (Danowski, 1986). Another study of 33 organizations that I am currently completing found that larger organizations had communication departments reporting closer to the top, and had larger communi-cation budgets per communication worker (Status study).[1]

Besides size limits, other factors appear to increase the importance of mediation. One such factor is environmental uncertainty. Organizations seek to reduce their environmental uncertainty to maintain stability in their internal structures (Katz & Kahn, 1978; Thompson, 1967). As uncertainty increases, long-range planning is less effective because competitive time frames become shorter. To get around this planning problem, organizations segment into a set of smaller "strategic business units" (SBUs; Rothschild, 1980). This diversification enables faster planning and shorter time horizons in each of the units.

Diversification also affects the needs for signification. As there are more diverse units with more varied domains of meaning and time horizons, the need to coordinate meanings increases, because diversification strengthens local semantic associations to the immediate strategic business unit, while it weakens the associ-ations to the overall corporate entity. As there are more separate SBUs, the meanings people attach to the overall corporate symbols become more fragile and fragmented. Under these conditions, organizational size is already beyond the threshold for effective local space control, so increased diversification moves organizations to more signification production. Maintaining sufficient identification of its publics with it requires more mediated meaning management for publics, including employees, investors, customers, and regulatory bodies. Conversely, as organizations reduce diversification and become more internally integrated, the importance of mediation decreases. Interpersonal communication then has increased value for meaning management and for the basic work of the organization.

With increased market competition driving diversification, the organization requires better competitive intelligence, in information richness and timeliness. Public relations, advertising, and market research firms, among others, gather such information about the environment and provide it to organizations. At the same time, organizations must more clearly differentiate their products or services from those of competitors. As customers identify unique benefits, they are less price sensitive in choosing products. The main way in which organizations attempt to position product features and benefits in customers' minds is through media, using public relations product promotion, coupled with advertising.

Intensified Investor Relations Needs

In surveying institutional investors about their information needs and processing, I have found that more diversified organizations are harder for investors and analysts to understand. They report needing more information as diversification increases. They also want more breakdowns of information by product lines or segments. As the organization becomes more diversified, analysts and investors desire more interpretation from the organization about the meanings of the financial data. At the same time, the audiences or constituencies of the organization become increasingly diverse. Variance increases in their information content needs, and in their preferred communication channels. The organization, therefore, needs to use more diverse channels for distributing this information to them. Thus more diversified organizations depend more on their signification for their financial health. Less diversified, more monolithic organizations depend less on their signification. Analysts tie their prices more to economic performance, and more conservatively interpret the stock price-to-earnings ratio (Rockart, 1979).

A study of the *Fortune* 100 corporations (Danowski, Barnett, & Friedland, 1986) found support for the hypothesis that as organizations were more diversified, they were more central in interorganizational networks defined according to shared public relations firms. Being more central means that there are fewer intermediate nodes between them and other nodes, on average (Freeman, 1979). Greater centrality gives them more control over information flowing in the network. So we assume that as mediated signification needs increase, organizations move toward positions of greater information control in interorganizational networks. Here signification control for external publics is more effective.

Empirically, we also found that more centralized organizations had significantly more media coverage in the *Wall Street Journal* (Danowski et al., 1986). In a follow-up study, we found that greater centrality was associated with higher daily stock price volatility (Danowski, Barnett, & Friedland, 1987). This finding is consistent with the efficient markets assumption that stock prices reflect the net valuation of all available information about a company.

ORGANIZATIONAL MEDIA RICHNESS, SPACE, AND TIME BINDING

To this point I have treated mediation as a simple, undifferentiated construct. Are some media more effective for the management of meaning? "Media richness" research (Trevino, Lengel, & Daft, 1988) conceptualizes this construct as the extent to which media reduce the equivocality—the diversity or ambiguity—of potential meanings (Weick, 1979) at the individual level. Organizational members are thought to choose media based on their ability to transport information that reduces equivocality.

In contrast, I conceptualize media richness at the organizational level. An organization must maintain sufficient ambiguity and abstractness of identity signification for different subunits and individuals to project their own meanings onto them and identify with the organization. Large-scale organization requires both equivocality creation ("strategic ambiguity"; Eisenberg, 1984, 1986) and equivocality reduction. Media are usually better at creating equivocality, while unmediated interpersonal communication is usually better at reducing it. (Exceptions would include situations of strong conflict driven by other forces, such as territorial or political struggles.) So, as I shift to the organizational level, I take the opposite view, compared with Daft and others, as to which media are richer. Richer organizational media create *more* equivocality about organizational symbols.

I conceptualize the equivocality of organizational signification in terms of the semantic networks associated with them. Consider words as nodes in a network. They are linked to other words through their co-use by people. As two words move closer to each other across people's meanings for signification, the stronger the link is between the word pair. By mapping the word-pair cooccurrence networks across large numbers of people, and by doing network analysis on these data, we can quantify qualitative meanings using a semantic network model (Danowski, 1982, 1988a, 1988b, 1988c; Danowski & Martin, 1979). Less equivocal signification has a simpler semantic network. It has fewer nodes discriminated, less differentiation of nodes into subgroups, and more integration of subgroups.

Space Shifting

Just as organizations require more mediation as they get larger, I propose that they use different kinds of media as they move up the mediation scale. Consider that different media loosen space and time binding in different magnitudes. The most concrete loosening is of space only, which occurs with synchronous media. These require individuals still to be communicating at the same time, even though they are in different places. Examples are normal telephone communication and audio or video teleconferencing. Such space-shifting communication technologies enable more distance transcendence. They trade off synchronous telecommunication for transportation (Nilles, Carlson, Gray, & Hanneman, 1977). These trends call into question physical propinquity as a primary predictor of organizational communication network activity (Monge & Kirste, 1980). Korzenny (1978) has suggested the variable of "electronic propinquity" when people use communication technologies.

In large organizations, space-shifting media appear generally best at fostering the perception of shared meaning for system-level signification. In the Merger study (see note 1), we found across 56 organizations that greater use of video and video teleconferencing was associated with perceptions of more shared meanings for organizational logos and slogans within and across the top, middle, and lower levels in the organizational hierarchy. This finding is consistent with a point discussed earlier: For creating uniformity of meaning, space-shifting media are the next best thing to direct control of interpersonal communication and of local space.

Yet, there may be a rival explanation. Space-shifting media may foster an illusion of shared meanings. Organizational video and its commercial companion, broadcast television, normally do not focus much on showing a diversity of meanings for signification. Usually only during crisis recovery, as the system tries to restabilize by interpreting the meaning and significance of the crisis, do these media make individual meanings the message content (Danowski & Edison-Swift, 1985; Schramm, 1971). So, in normal time, individuals usually see only their own meanings as the link between social time and social space. This link becomes the basis for their reflexive projection of their own meanings onto other people. Moreover, video presents visual images that people take as real. They think everyone else sees the same thing they see. This would result in an illusion of shared meaning, or false consensus.

Time Shifting

Time shifting is a decontextualizing of a higher order than space shifting. Consider eight ways in which time links with the communication process (Danowski, 1988a):

(1) *time distancing between message encoding and decoding*, which ranges from large distances to zero distance, when the encoders and decoders are synchronously communicating

(2) *time marking in the framing of the message*, such as by putting date and/or time codes on message headers, as occurs for newspapers, electronic mail, FAX, and data bases

(3) *tensing of content*, the extent to which the text orients to the past, present, and future

(4) *time awareness* of the decoders

(5) *time unitizing,* the size of the social/organizational system time interval used for management

(6) *time linearity versus periodicity,* whether the system views time as cyclical or moving only forward

(7) *time coding channel and message access by social units,* the former making it possible to tell who got messages at what times, the latter enabling tracing of message diffusion networks

(8) *over-time repetition* of messages

These eight social time variables are not independent. Media that are asynchronous, having a time distance between message encoding and decoding of greater than zero, share other time attributes. Examples of asynchronous organizational media include data base information systems, electronic mail, voice mail, and traditional print information such as memos, newsletters, newspapers, and reports. Examples of synchronous communication are telephone, audio and video teleconferencing, and face-to-face interaction. Between the extremes of space- and time-shifted media are normal video and traditional audiovisual media.

Overall, asynchronous media externalize time from the communication process. They "freeze" time for the framing of the message. These media fix time in the message format. As this is the case, time more freely varies in the content. These messages can address the past and the future to a greater extent than those in which time framing of the message varies. In addition, time awareness of decoders during the communication activity increases with greater time marking of messages. With these time-shift media there is also a lower present-action orientation. This fosters more abstractness in their message content. Time is further externalized from the communication experience through the monitoring of people's access times to the medium and to the message. This makes visible the trace of message movement through the system (Danowksi, 1988b).

Conversely, as communication becomes more synchronous, such as with the telephone or teleconferencing, there is less framing of messages by time marking. Without this explicit time framing, the communication process becomes more important relative to the content, compared to freeze-frame media. Accordingly, as content is more present tensed, communicators become less time aware, and are more subjectively immersed in a process. The informal expression for this is "spacing out." In this high process orientation, message style or packaging is increasingly important over content. There is also an action inversion. Action in the content is increasingly important, while active processing of participants declines. People who take a more passive posture in processing information need to be stimulated more by message form or packaging to be aroused to action (Grunig, 1982). They are unlike those people already activated, who place more attention on content. Slicker form is likely to lead active processors to discount its value more. If it looks too good to them, then they think it must be watered down, less useful information, or self-serving propaganda.

Time-Shifting Media Decontextualized

As time-shift media free participants from the needs to share space and time for communication, they most fully decontextualize the communication processes. As this occurs, people depend less on physical contexts for the framing of their signification and meanings. They depend more on the sharing of increasingly abstract conceptual frames and symbol/referent systems. This reduces the need for the analyst to contextualize the communication activity in physical space and time. Rather, he or she must account more for the signification and meaning networks of communicators. It is interesting to consider that contemporary attention to organizational culture (Nadler & Tushman, 1986) roughly parallels the implementation of new media in organizations (Rice & Associates, 1984). These computer-based media appear to intensify the focus on the management of meanings.

Media and Organizational Time Perception

Shifting time requires externalizing it from the communication experiences of participants. This fosters a more linear perception of time, rather than of seasons and natural cycles. Linearity of organizational time perception is necessary for coordination of different social times within subunits. We hypothesized that high space-shift organizations have more cyclical social time. In contrast, high use of time-shifting media should be linked to linear perceptions of time and to a longer time horizon. The Organizational Time study (see note 1), with a sample of 34 organizations, revealed that cyclical time perception was positively associated with video use and with audio teleconferencing use. Also, audio media use correlated with the perception that the organization operated according to its own natural rhythms. Overall, these findings support the proposition that space shifting is associated with periodic organizational oscillation.

The study also found support for the hypothesis that greater use of time-shift media is associated with more linear perceptions of time and with longer time horizons. This time orientation was significantly and positively correlated with use of FAX, data bases (vendor supplied and in-house), electronic mail, computer conferencing, computer bulletin boards, employee newspapers, photos, and slides. Based on biological research in neural networks (Choi & Huberman, 1983; Grondin, Porod, Loeffler, & Ferry, 1983; Guevara, Glass, Mackey, & Shrier, 1983; Holden, Winlow, & Hayden, 1982), we hypothesize that in time-shift organizations, rather than time actually being fully linear, time-varying processes are more likely to have the form of deterministic chaos. These are nonstationary waves, rather than the periodic waves generated by synchronous space-shift media systems. There is no regular beat to the wave as there is in a periodic cyclic system, so people see the nonstationary wave as going up somewhat linearly. But, as what goes up comes down, this downward track is again perceived as a somewhat linear decline, until the track heads upward again. This is time shifting of the wave. It is another way to see the effects of time-shift media.

TABLE 1
Media Time-Structure Correlates

Time-Shifting Media	*Space-Shifting Media*
Decontextualized	Contextualized
Content important	Process important
Packaging aesthetics less valued	Packaging style highly valued
Future and past tensed	Present tensed
Linear time perception	Cyclical time perception
Longer time horizon	Shorter time horizon
Analytically oriented content	Action-oriented content
Abstract content	Concrete content
Relational content	Orgocentric content
Active decoding	Passive decoding
Formal environment	Informal environment
Stable system functions	Volatile system functions
Static visuals	Motion visuals
Textual coding	Oral coding
Communicators autonomous	Communicators interdependent
Status task based	Status socioemotionally based
Acceptance of dominance	Conflict over domination
Openness to boundary spanning	Boundary guarding
Radial network structure	Interlocking networks

We also hypothesize for future testing that organizations with more use of time-shifting media unitize social/organizational time in smaller intervals. These range downward, from years, quarters, months, weeks, days, hours, minutes, to seconds. Time-shifting media make information production and distribution more efficient and accountable. They lower or remove the social time float in interpersonal actions. For some people, "it's in the mail . . ." has an elastic social time width, perhaps stretching for days into the future. In contrast, FAX, for example, has a much narrower social time window. This limits social time float to hours or minutes instead of days. So, with increasing time-shifting media use, people may experience more social time compression. Table 1 lists some summary distinctions among synchronous and asynchronous media in terms of form, content, and participants.

Time Shifting and Network Route Dependency

Social time information is route dependent. The more that social time is shifted, the more the mediation system is network dependent for its message distribution. This means that messages are less likely to be broadcast uniformly to people and more likely to be distributed differentially through limited social networks.

Space-shift media spew messages in a spatially uniform way, creating a more socially entropic (equal) distribution of information. In contrast to this omnidirectional broadcasting, time-shift media control the routing of information among social elements. Messages activate only some relatively small proportion of possible paths in the social matrix as they beam through it. This socially negentropic (unequal) distribution fosters formation of information elites.

Our time- and space-shift distinction connects with the sociological literature on "structural equivalence" (Burt, 1982). From this perspective, people need not directly communicate for structural effects to be evident, because they share common characteristics of social positions. Hence this is called a positional model. An alternative model is the cohesion model. It is based on direct relationships, through communication among the social actors. These distinctions line up with our discussion of differences in the social implications of space- and time-shift media. The sharing of media content in the space-shift media system defines a positional or spatial relationship based on time correlation of receivers with respect to messages. In other words, they all get the same message at the same time as they are scattered or shifted over a wide space. In contrast, time-shift media foster cohesion among communicants. This cohesion is based on spatial correlation among receivers, rather than time correlation, which instead is widely varied because of asynchronicity. The shared space relationship is one of propinquity defined by message flow as people or other social units pass messages to one another. In short, time-shift media foster greater value for interpersonal relationships, with more diversification and inequality across them. Although messages may be distributed with the aid of technology, people send these messages on a more point-to-point basis from one person to another, rather than broadcasting messages to a large collectivity.

Messages that are broadcast, rather than routed through specific interpersonal networks, have less interpersonal-relational quality. Compared to network-routed signification, people appear less likely to talk about the meanings of broadcasted signification. Their relationships are weaker, less binding, and less personal. These relations are based merely on sharing common exposure to messages (communication equivalence), rather than on sharing contacts with people along the path of routed, time-shifted information (communication cohesion). Accordingly, space-shift media foster more uniform, but simpler, meanings for signification. Time-shift media foster more abstract and complex meanings, and these are more unequally distributed across the social system. This inequality increases the basis for information exchange.

MEDIATION, POWER, AND SOCIAL STATUS

The externalizing of time from the communication experience and the explicit managing of this social time point to an important benefit of time-shifted media. They enable organizations to reestablish control over a special kind of space for interpersonal communication. But this space is not physical; the time-altered space is mediated social space. It is defined not by proximity of people in physical locations, but by proximity in terms of processing mediated, time-shifted information in common at different times.

In the time-shifted system, social status derives from how centrally positioned people are within the information flow network over time. In contrast, in the space-shifted system, social status is based more on individuals' positions within the physical space control system. Position within a territorial dominance hierarchy is important. Power is the control of physical space, signified in securing the corner office. It is different in the time-shifted environment. There, power is securing an earlier time window in information distribution networks. It is when you know who you know, not what space you control, that more often counts. Time-shifted systems define power in information-processing terms. Individuals are valued for getting and passing the right messages from and to the right people at the right time. If we conceptualize information as coded energy waves, then individuals in the time-shift system obtain power based on their absorption, transformation, and radiation of valued waves to others at optimal social times. Accordingly, information-processing skills and network position are the basis for an information meritocracy in time-shift systems.

COMMUNICATION MANAGEMENT
STRUCTURE AND MEDIA

To summarize globally, organizations derive power by establishing and maintaining mediation that fractures the rhythmic cohesion of space and time that people experience in simple face-to-face groups. With this disjuncture and fractionation of time and space, individuals are left with either control of space or control of time, but not both. I have argued that greater power comes to organizations that control social time, rather than social space. Consider that in environments without media, individuals have the most control over both space and time. In effect, they set their own social time within their space. Space-shift media systems take away some of the individual's control over local space. Information content is externalized from individuals and uniformly distributed through space. This allows individuals to internalize time as they experience their processing of these messages. The reverse occurs in time-shifted systems. Organizations externalize social time from individuals and control it rather than control space. They extract social energy and distribute it beyond the tactile bounds of unmediated social community. They establish information refineries and distribution networks with technological infrastructures. Content, however, is more under local individual control in terms of its selection, processing, storage, retrieval, and production.

Consider the hypothesis that organizations with more centralized communication structures find time-shifting media more useful. A centralized communication structure has a communication department linking with other departments that do not link much with one another. The communication department is radially, or centrally, positioned in the interdepartmental network. When communication departments are centrally positioned and other departments do not communicate much with one another, each of these departments has more autonomy. They are likely to develop increasingly different orientations. The departments become more internally cohesive and homogeneous in attitudes toward the work unit (Danowski, 1974, 1976a, 1976b, 1980). At the same time, the various departments become more heterogeneous relative to one another in their interdepartmental identification. More mediated communication is required to build and maintain identification with the organization.

The central communication department is positioned to manage and control signification efficiently. The other departments, more internally interlocking and using more synchronous communication, act in the present. The central communication department couples history and a vision of the future and links them to present action. Moreover, the time marking of message form in time-shift media enables central communication departments to be the organization's "timekeepers," its social time machine, the system clock. They maintain a more linear time, standardized, and marked. This linearization provides the carrier for the transport of time-shifted messages. In a study of 49 organizations, we found support for the hypothesis that centralization of communication management in organizations is associated with more time-shifted media use (Time-Shift Media; see note 1). These time-shifted media included newsletters and newspapers, photos and slides, and electronic mail, computer-based training, and data bases.

ORGANIZATIONAL STRUCTURE, MEDIATION, AND NETWORKS OF SHARED MEANINGS

I have argued that relationships among social units are more important in a network of routed, time-shifted information, and we have empirically found that organizations with more centralized communication departments use more time-shift media. So we hypothesized that organizations with more central communication departments have meanings for organizational identities that are less orgocentric. They are less focused on attributes of the organization itself, and more focused on other units in their environment and on their relationships with them. To test this hypothesis, we asked communication managers in two studies (Images I and II; see note 1) two open-ended questions: "What image does your organization try to project to external publics?" and "What images do other departments in the organization have of your department?" Responses were content coded for relational or orgocentric words. Results showed the expected higher relational orientation for more centralized interdepartmental networks. The organizations with less centralized, interlocking networks had more orgocentric semantic content.

We have reasoned that more central units, because they link with more diverse other units, need more abstract ways of representing themselves so that different units can understand them without their having to tailor a different message for each. Contemporary public relations principles suggest that creating different messages about the organization for different audiences is bad practice. It is better to "speak in one voice," consistently saying the same thing about the organization's orientation. Speaking in one voice to more diverse audiences requires more abstract messages. Given this reasoning, we tested the hypothesis that organizations with more centralized communication have more abstract semantic content in their organizational identity meanings. We found in a sample of 34 organizations (Images I; see note 1) that organizations with more centrally positioned communication departments had significantly more abstractness in their managers' descriptions of the organization's image.

IDENTITY MANAGEMENT AND
CULTURAL CONVERGENCE AFTER MERGERS

Major discontinuities in organizational structure, such as merger or acquisition, present challenges for organizations to manage meanings through signification control. Our theory of organizational mediation suggests that time-shift media are more effective than space-shift media in fostering cultural convergence. This is because time-shift media stimulate more interpersonal communication to reduce the equivocality that they create. This interpersonal communication increases the rate of cultural convergence.

To test this hypothesis, we identified 56 organizations (Merger; see note 1) that had been merged, had acquired other organizations, or had themselves been acquired. We measured speed of identity management changes after merger and acquisition, in terms of how quickly the organizations changed their exterior and interior signs bearing the organization name and/or logo. We also measured perceived cultural convergence, and media use. We found that the use of space-shift media was positively correlated with the speed with which organizations changed their exterior signs. Yet, neither of these variables was related to perceived cultural convergence. After controlling for length of time since merger/acquisition, only use of the time-shifted media of employee newspapers, newsletters, and photos were strong correlates of cultural convergence. Also associated with perceived convergence was having more centrally positioned communication departments.

ORGANIZATIONAL STRUCTURE
AND MEDIATION IN THE MARKETPLACE

At the beginning of this theoretical explication, I pointed to the valuation of shares in an organization's signification potential and meaning markets as a good way of thinking about how interacting individuals interpret organizations' messages and trade on differences in their valuation. Then, I proceeded to treat mainly intraorganizational processes. Here I return to consideration of the market-place of meanings to see whether there is any evidence for relationships among internal organizational communication structure, media used, meanings for organizational signification, and valuation in the marketplace.

Market Valuation and Mediation

Does the environment place more value on companies that time-shift signification more? In Danowski (1988c), I examined 14 organizations' communication correlates of stock prices. I defined a greater premium valuation, or overvaluation, to occur as the stock price for a company exceeded its objective measure of shareholder value. Shareholder value was indexed by its cash flow, discounted for the cost of debt and taxes (Rappaport, 1986). In contrast, as the stock price dropped below shareholder value, this was defined as an undervaluation of the organization.

I found the following communication variables associated with greater stock price premiums:

- more overall media use, in particular, FAX, computer bulletin boards, employee newspapers, computer-based training, and voice mail
- communication managers reporting higher in the organization
- less uniform perceived shared meanings for organizational symbols within the lowest levels and between the lowest and middle levels and the lowest and top levels
- greater importance placed on external news

These findings support the basic premise about management of meaning with which I began this treatment: Individuals in the environment of organizations value them based on their interpretations of the meanings of signification that the organization produces. Time-shifted signification is more equivocal than space-shifted signification, and subsequently enables individuals to reduce this equivocality through increased interpersonal communication. Time-shifted signification is differentially distributed through social networks, which leads to differences in the valuations of signification across people. These meaning differences create more volatile "meaning markets" in which individuals trade on differences in their valuations, buying and selling shares in the organization's signification production system. People pay premiums for the signification systems that, by shifting time, give them control of their local space. So, in a way, "time is money," giving the old adage a new theoretical interpretation.

IMPLICATIONS OF THE THEORY FOR
UNDERSTANDING MEDIA ORGANIZATIONS

We can now take Tunstall's industry observations and subject them to theoretical treatment. Such an effort can inform both the theory and the analysis of the media industry. Tunstall's commentary on the media industry is useful to such an application of the theory because there are some good structural alignments of Tunstall's observations with my theory. His focus on diversification/integration and organizational structures is consistent with the focus of my line of theory and research (Danowski, 1987, 1988a, 1988c; Danowski et al., 1986, 1987).

A central proposition Tunstall offers is that media organizations are evolving toward a "single, more global, media industry" (p. 173). This movement would occur as formerly separate media organizations merge and acquire one another. Tunstall points to media organizations as diversifying out, and acquiring other media organizations. Some may think this observation of both integration and diversification in the same industry a contradiction; it is not, however, if we carefully isolate levels of analysis.

Typically, we need to distinguish precisely our level of observation when theorizing. This is because as we move between levels—here, for example, between industry and organization levels—there is a structural inversion. The opposite structural pattern holds at adjacent levels. Cognitively integrated individuals are in diversified dyads; diversified dyads are in integrated groups; integrated groups are in diversified organizations; diversified organizations are in integrated industries; integrated industries are in diversified national economies; diversified national economies are in integrated international economies. So this structural inversion principle explains why Tunstall's observations about media organizations' diversification within the industry can also be seen as the integration of that industry at the next level of analysis upward.

Nevertheless, my theory is pitched at the organizational level, rather than at the industry level. So it is best to examine Tunstall's observations from the more micro level, the organization. At the level of the organization, the pattern within the media industry is one of increasingly diversified corporations. A company that formerly held only a film production company but then acquired a television distribution company, cable companies, and book and magazine publishers would be an increasingly diversified company. If that company left the various subsidiaries as relatively autonomous strategic business units, then my theory would predict that with the increased media organization diversification, the following changes would also occur:

- decreased use of space-shift media
- increased use of time-shift media
- decreased importance of face-to-face interpersonal communication (less internal personal "selling")
- decreased control of local space, including decreased physical consolidation of units in the same countries, regions, cities, or buildings
- decreased restrictions on facilities use and lowered security
- increased size of organizational units
- higher reporting level for organizational communication management
- power based increasingly on control of time-shift information and less on position

- increased centrality of the organizational communication management function (less interlocking relations with other organizational functions and operating in a more radial role, like the hub providing the only connection among spokes)
- increased expenditures for communication management, relative to the number of communication management employees
- increased abstractness of organizational symbols
- decreased orgocentrism and more relational symmetry with external publics
- increased importance placed on external news about the organization
- decreased perceived shared meaning for organizational symbols
- faster cultural convergence of acquired and merged units
- longer time horizons and smaller basic time interval units with higher social time compression
- decreased present-action focus and increased past and future focus
- more analytical orientation and more strategic planning
- more pseudolinear (deterministic chaos) and less cyclical time perceptions
- increased stock price premiums relative to cash flow

We see that Tunstall's material provides us with a useful means of applying our more general theory to his observations about the media industry, and generating a set of hypotheses about organizations in it. These hypotheses are empirically testable. We have operationalized nearly all the variables in our series of seven organizational media studies conducted over the past five years. If the hypotheses were supported for organizations within the media industry, as they have been across industries (including media), then this support would further my beginning premise: to theorize about media organizations in the same way one would theorize about any other organization. Most abstractly, we assume that all large organizations are media organizations. Mediation is the primary means for managing meanings for organizational symbols in large systems.

NOTE

1. This study is among seven conducted by my students and me. In each study a different sample of Chicago organizations was drawn. In the remainder of this chapter I will refer to different studies by their focal constructs. The criterion for selecting an organization for the samples was that it had a communication department with at least three members. Trained student interviewers conducted personal interviews with communication managers in each organization, using a structured questionnaire. Each study used the same core instrument but added other measures depending on the particular research questions. The core instrument included a battery of scaled items measuring the organization's degree of use of 27 organizational media. Meanings for organizational symbols were identified by asking respondents open-ended questions about what their organizations' logos and slogans meant to them. The verbatim answers were analyzed using automated semantic network analysis (Danowski, 1988b). Six 10-point scales were used to measure the perceived shared meaning for organizational symbols among top, middle, and lower levels in the organization, and across each pair of levels. The Images I study ($n = 3$) was the first of the series. It used the same core instrument components except for the media items. In their stead, we tested a set of such items that were improved for the remaining studies. The Images II study ($n = 33$) added the refined media-use questions. The Time-Shift Media study ($n = 53$) focused on communication management structure and media use. In the Merger study

(n = 56), items were added about the perceived cultural convergence of the merged organizational units. For the Organizational Time study (n = 34), which was concerned with perceptions of time in organizations, a set of twenty 5-point scales was added, asking respondents how much people in the organization talked about time in various ways, such as cyclical or linear, and about aspects of the future. Questions were also asked about interdepartmental communication networks, in which respondents estimated the frequency of communication between their departments and the three departments they communicated with most, as well as between each of the three pairs of such departments. In addition, the Status study used the same sample as the Image I study, and measured the reporting level of the communication department, the number of communication employees, and the annual budget for communication management. In the Financial Performance study, which used a subsample of 14 organizations from the Time-Shift Media study, variables were computed from data reported by Value Line and were added to the basic core set of variables on the organizations. I am grateful for the research assistance of the following graduate students, each of whom helped develop and execute at least one of the studies as part of her thesis research: Kathryn Kozlowski, Carolyn Delucca, Sue Bell, and Heather Kumerer.

REFERENCES

Allport, G., & Postman, L. (1947). *The psychology of rumor.* New York: Henry Holt.

Anderson, J. A., & Meyer, T. P. (1988). *Mediated communication: A social action perspective.* Newbury Park, CA: Sage.

Arbel, A., & Jaggi, B. (1982). Market information assimilation related to extreme daily price jumps. *Financial Analysts Journal, 38*, 60-66.

Burt, R. S. (1982). *Toward a structural theory of action.* New York: Academic Press.

Choi, M. Y., & Huberman, B. A. (1983). Dynamic behavior of nonlinear networks. *Physics Review Abstracts, 28*, 1204-1206.

Danowski, J. A. (1974, April). *An information processing model of organizations: A focus on environmental uncertainty and communication network structuring.* Paper presented at the annual meeting of the International Communication Association, New Orleans.

Danowski, J. A. (1976a). Communication network analysis and social change: Group structure and family planning in two Korean villages. In G. Chu (Ed.), *Communication and group transformations for development* (pp. 277-306). Honolulu: East-West Center.

Danowski, J. A. (1976b, May). *Environmental uncertainty and communication network structure: A cross-cultural, cross-system test.* Paper presented at the annual meeting of the International Communication Association, Portland, OR.

Danowski, J. A. (1980). Group attitude-belief uniformity and connectivity of organizational communication networks for production, innovation, and maintenance content. *Human Communication Research, 6*, 299-308.

Danowski, J. A. (1982). A network-based content analysis methodology for computer-mediated communication: An illustration with a computer bulletin board. In M. Burgoon (Ed.), *Communication yearbook 6* (pp. 904-925). Beverly Hills, CA: Sage.

Danowski, J. A. (1986). Interpersonal network radiality and non-mass media use. In G. Gumpert & R. Cathcart (Eds.), *Intermedia* (3rd ed., pp. 168-175). New York: Oxford University Press.

Danowski, J. A. (1987, February). *Who-to-whom communication network structures and semantic activation networks.* Paper presented at the Seventh Annual Sunbelt Social Networks Conference, Clearwater Beach, FL.

Danowski, J. A. (1988a, May). *Media richness: Decontextualizing communication and changing the semantics of organizational symbols.* Paper presented at the annual meeting of the International Communication Association, New Orleans.

Danowski, J. A. (1988b). *Organizational infographics and automated auditing: Using computers to unobtrusively gather as well as analyze communication.* In G. Goldhaber & G. Barnett (Eds.), *Handbook of organizational communication* (pp. 335-384). Norwood, NJ: Ablex.

Danowski, J. A. (1988c, June). *Communication variables in investor relations.* Paper presented at the National Investor Relations Institute, Phoenix, AZ.

Danowski, J. A., Barnett, G. A., & Friedland, M. (1986). Interorganizational networks via shared public relations firms: Centrality, diversification, media coverage, and publics' images. In M. L. McLaughlin (Ed.), *Communication yearbook 10* (pp. 808-830). Beverly Hills, CA: Sage.

Danowski, J. A., Barnett, G. A, & Friedland, M. (1987, May). *A theory of media dependency: Interorganizational network position, media coverage, and daily stock price volatility.* Paper presented at the annual meeting of the International Communication Association.

Danowski, J. A., & Edison-Swift, P. (1985). Crisis effects on intra-organizational computer-based communication. *Communication Research, 12,* 251-270.

Danowski, J. A., & Martin, T. H. (1979). *Evaluating the health of information science: Research community and user contexts* (Report No. IST78-21130). Final report to the Division of Information Science of the National Science Foundation.

Davies, P. L., & Caves, M. (1978). Stock prices and the publication of second-hand information. *Journal of Business, 51,* 43-56.

Eisenberg, E. M. (1984). Ambiguity as strategy in organizational communication. *Communication Monographs, 51,* 227-242.

Eisenberg, E. M. (1986). Meaning and interpretation in organizations. *Quarterly Journal of Speech, 72,* 88-97.

Fama, E. F., Fisher, L., Jensen, M., & Roll, R. (1969). The adjustment of stock prices to new information. *International Economic Review, 10,* 1-21.

Freeman, L. C. (1979). Centrality in social networks: Conceptual clarification. *Social Networks, 1,* 215-239.

Grondin, R. O., Porod, W., Loeffler, C. M., & Ferry, D. K. (1983). Synchronous and asynchronous systems of threshold elements. *Biological Cybernetics, 49,* 1-7.

Grunig, J. E. (1982). The message-attitude-behavior relationship: Communication behaviors of organizations. *Communication Research, 9,* 163-200.

Guevara, M. R., Glass, L., Mackey, M. C., & Shrier, A. (1983). Chaos in neurobiology. *IEEE Transactions on Systems, Man, and Cybernetics, 13,* 790-798.

Gumpert, G., & Cathcart, R. (1986). Mediated interpersonal communication: Toward a new typology. *Quarterly Journal of Speech, 69,* 267-277.

Holden, A. V., Winlow, W., & Hayden, P. G. (1982). The induction of periodic and chaotic activity in a molluscan neurone. *Biological Cybernetics, 43,* 169-173.

Katz, D., & Kahn, R. (1978). *The social psychology of organizations.* New York: John Wiley.

Korzenny, F. (1978). A theory of electronic propinquity: Mediated communication in organizations. *Communication Research, 5,* 3-23.

Miller, G. A. (1956). The magic number seven plus or minus two: Some limits on our capacity for processing information. *Psychological Review, 63,* 81-97.

Monge, P. R., & Kirste, K. K. (1980). Measuring proximity in human organization. *Social Psychology Quarterly, 43*(1), 110-115.

Nadler, D. A., & Tushman, M. L. (1986). *Strategic organizational design.* Homewood, IL: Scott, Foresman.

Niederhoffer, V. (1971). The analysis of world events and stock prices. *Journal of Business, 44,* 193-219.

Nilles, J. M., Carlson, F. R., Jr., Gray, P., & Hanneman, G. J. (1977). *Telecommunication transportation tradeoffs.* Reading, MA: Addison-Wesley.

Pearce, D. K., & Roley, V. V. (1985). Stock prices and economic news. *Journal of Business, 58,* 49-67.

Rappaport, A. (1986). *Creating shareholder value: The new standard for business performance.* New York: Free Press.

Rice, R. E., & Associates (1984). *The new media: Communication, research, and technology.* Beverly Hills, CA: Sage.

Rockart, J. F. (1979). Chief executives define their own data needs. *Harvard Business Review, 57*(2), 81-92.

Rothschild, W. E. (1980). How to insure the continuous growth of strategic planning. *Journal of Business Strategy, 1*(1), 11-18

Schramm, W. (1971). Communication in crisis. In W. Schramm & D. F. Roberts (Eds.), *The process and effects of mass communication* (pp. 525-553). Urbana: University of Illinois Press.

Thompson, J. (1967). *Organizations in action.* New York: McGraw-Hill.

Trevino, L., Lengel, R., & Daft, R. (1988). Media symbolism, media richness and media choice in organizations: A symbolic interactionist perspective. *Communication Research, 14*(5), 553-575.

Weick, K. E. (1979). *The social psychology of organizing* (2nd ed.). Reading, MA: Addison-Wesley.

SECTION 2

PUBLIC OPINION AND PUBLIC INFLUENCE

5 Propaganda and American Ideological Critique

J. MICHAEL SPROULE
San Jose State University

Since 1900, different schools of thought have emerged in the United States concerning the implications of propaganda for the rational-democratic society. The conversation among progressive propaganda critics, communication practitioners, rationalists, communication scientists, conservative humanists, and political polemicists reveals the panorama of American experience with and interpretation of mass persuasion. Although selectively remembered today, this dialectic provides an ideological critique that is not only powerful, but historically grounded in the vicissitudes of American culture. When fully recovered, the long-standing American dialogue on propaganda supplies a useful alternate vocabulary to Marxism for analyzing the diffusion of ideology through such ostensibly neutral channels of public communication as news, entertainment, government agencies, religion, and education.

ONE recent symptom of the revival of critical media studies in the United States has been the reemergence of *propaganda* as a significant theoretical term for the study of social influence (Jowett, 1987; Sproule, 1987d). Renewed attention to American propaganda criticism is particularly useful as a theoretical counterpoint to contemporary Marxist studies. The post-Vietnam return of critical media inquiry in the United States brought to prominence a number of significant Marxist writers, including Antonio Gramsci (Femia, 1981), Stuart Hall (1982), Louis Althusser (1971), members of the Frankfurt school (Jay, 1973), and various exegetes of Marx himself (e.g., Parekh, 1982). Marxist criticism has invigorated American media studies through such key concepts as ideology, hegemony, ideological apparatuses, and state ideological mediation (Real, 1986).

But the "ideological turn" in modern criticism is not simply a Marxist turn, notwithstanding the work of Hall (1982) and others who treat the "rediscovery of

AUTHOR'S NOTE: Grateful acknowledgment for support of this research is due the National Endowment for the Humanities for awarding me a Fellowship (FB-21790-83), a Summer Stipend (F-21734-82), and a Travel to Collections Grant (FE-21009-87).

Correspondence and requests for reprints: J. Michael Sproule, Department of Communication Studies, San Jose State University, San Jose, CA 95192-0112.

Communication Yearbook 14, pp. 211-238

ideology" as chiefly a conversation among Marxist theorists and critics. Through a wide-ranging dialogue over propaganda, American writers have created a parallel body of theory and criticism. The historical conversation among progressive critics, media practitioners, rationalists, grand theorists, communication scientists, conservative counterprogressives, and political polemicists reveals how Americans have experienced and interpreted the rise and maturation of mass persuasion. This literature provides a rich alternate perspective to Western Marxism for understanding the paradoxes that inhere to creating a rational-democratic society in an age of mass media.

IDEOLOGICAL HEGEMONY?
PRACTITIONERS VERSUS MUCKRAKERS

The early colloquy between practitioners of public relations and the muckrakers set the first important context for Americans to confront the phenomenon of ideological hegemony. Nevertheless, this first American conversation about ideological apparatuses differed considerably from the typical Marxist approach to the problem. Marxist criticism treats the channels of modern communication as apparatuses for the ideological hegemony of a dominant class (e.g., Ewen, 1976). Marxists disagree about whether the phenomenon of class functions as a sole or partial explanation for ideological currents in society (compare Hall, 1982; Parekh, 1982), and Marxists debate whether the state plays a direct or indirect role in promoting ideological hegemony (compare Althusser, 1971; Hall, 1982). Nevertheless, the tendency of Marxist criticism is to treat class and state as central in the direction of ideological apparatuses. In contrast, the American dialectic between public relations practitioners and muckrakers focused little on the state. Of more concern to Americans was the implication for democratic social organization of the new marriage between private institutions and the emerging professions of mass communication.

By the early twentieth century, the American national government had embraced various progressive reforms, notably railroad regulation and antitrust action. The ability of dissidents to prompt government regulation of economic life alarmed business interests, with the result that business increasingly saw a need to bypass the state and speak directly to the public. In response to this crisis, Ivy Lee, a young reporter, became one of the first of the modern public relations practitioners. Lee convinced his clients that, in the new era of professionalized media organizations, American business could no longer rely on bribery and threats as avenues to good press coverage. Illustrative of the Lee approach was his success in persuading the Pennsylvania Railroad to abandon its efforts to block news coverage of railroad accidents. Lee established a new policy of assisting reporters with good facilities, a helpful attitude, and copious handouts (Hiebert, 1966).

As a spokesman for the incipient practitioner approach to propaganda, Lee (1925) denied that the public relations activities of powerful private institutions created any kind of ideological hegemony that upset the balance of forces in society. In Lee's view, business persuasion was more a logical and limited outgrowth of traditional American boosterism. According to Lee, the essential impact of public relations was to make business practices more attuned to public opinion, and therefore inherently more enlightened. Furthermore, by keeping to their own ethical codes, public relations practitioners deterred corrupt practices of persuasion. Lee emphasized that social truth was always elusive. In a world of intellectual relativism, Lee's remedy for problems of propaganda was to have editors and publishers demand to know the sources of the information and facts they printed.

The emerging practitioner approach to propaganda, typified by Ivy Lee, prompted critical comment from the American muckrakers. Muckraking writers developed an ideological critique of covert business persuasion from the traditional American perspective of competitive politics. Representative of the muckraker's discovery of propaganda as enemy to reform was Ray Stannard Baker's (1906) essay, "How Railroads Make Public Opinion." Baker reported about how a group of railroads hired a public relations firm to keep track of newspaper coverage of congressional debate over railroad regulation. The firm also visited newspaper editors and distributed self-serving articles, noting when they were printed as news. Avoiding direct bribery, the railroad campaign nevertheless put economic pressure on newspapers by encouraging local businesspersons to write letters or sign petitions against further regulation of railroads. Baker argued that special interest public relations of this kind created a tainted news that subverted the general public interest. Muckrakers and progressives were developing an American vocabulary to explain a problem that, in terms of Marxism, might be seen as the establishment of a business ideological hegemony through control of the apparatus of news.

Will Irwin's (1911/1969) series of articles for *Collier's* on the American newspaper gave the first comprehensive progressive treatment of American mass communication. Irwin reflected the typical progressive treatment of institutional ideology by describing news content as a reflection of the economic needs of newspapers. According to this interpretation, newspaper campaigns for reform were usually more a sensational device for circulation building than a product of journalistic conscience. Irwin further identified two ideological obstacles to the accuracy of news. Since "modern business demands mutual favors," newspapers inevitably avoided offending their major advertisers (Irwin, 1911/1969, p. 52). Second, since editors and publishers typically associated with the wealthy and powerful, they tended to assimilate upper-class views. Irwin reflected the reformist orientation of progressivism in his call for increased professionalism as the route to an honest journalism.

The collision of corporate propaganda and muckraking produced a ferment over ideological competition conducted through public relations, advertising, and newspapers. Muckrakers argued that the alliance of hired media agents and commercially organized channels of communication made it impossible for the unorganized public to regulate rationally the competition of institutions and interest groups. In contrast, the practitioner school treated institutional social influence as a normal outgrowth of traditional American boosterism and self-advancement. In neither case, however, did this debate presuppose that mass manipulation required the state to institute or arbitrate ideological hegemony. Further, while Marxists doubt the public's ability to function in an atmosphere of ideologically tainted communication, American progressives were more optimistic about the public. Progressives believed that their muckraking exposés of propaganda could provide an educational antidote that would keep ideological diffusion from incapacitating the public. Further, progressives such as Irwin were hopeful that their idea of ideologically objective journalism would increasingly gain sway (Schudson, 1978).

IDEOLOGICAL APPARATUSES:
THE PROGRESSIVE APPROACH

While progressive propaganda criticism did not begin with the state as the archetypal source of ideological manipulation, the Great War did show that the American government was capable of pursuing an ideological hegemony. However, unlike Marxists, progressive critics treated state propaganda in the Great War less as a central problem and more as a harbinger of how various private institutions and interest groups would compete after the war. Working from this perspective, American progressives developed a body of criticism focused on the array of social forces that competed for control of what Marxists would call the ideological apparatuses of civil society: education, news, religion, and entertainment.

Central to understanding the different treatment of ideological apparatuses by progressivism and Marxism is recognition of the popular audience that developed for the former body of ideological critique. By 1915, the idea of propaganda began to enter popular American parlance through exposés of the German propaganda campaign in America. With the outbreak of the Great War, agents of the imperial German government, and their cohorts in German-American and Irish-American communities, strove to cultivate neutralist sentiment in the United States. Pro-German propagandists sent out copious pamphlets and also encouraged American opinion leaders to express views and take actions favorable to the Central Powers (Viereck, 1930). While the British undertook a similar (and, ironically, more extensive) propaganda campaign, the Germans were less cautious than the British, allowing pro-Berlin propaganda operations to merge with espionage and sabotage (Irwin, 1937). This volatile brew of symbols and subversion proved disastrous for the German cause in the United States when the *New York World* published documents that exposed the whole German operation. In four consecutive days of front-page revelations, the *World* laid bare Germany's effort "to establish newspapers and news services, finance professional lecturers and moving picture shows, and to enlist the support of American citizens and publish books for the sole purpose of fomenting internal discord among the American people to the advantage of the German Empire" ("How Germany Has Worked," 1915, p. 2). The result was to make American supporters of Germany, such as George S. Viereck, editor of *The Fatherland*, appear to be little more than hirelings of Berlin. "The German propaganda" became a common catchphrase in discussions of the war.

Postwar disillusionment further established a wide popular audience for issues of propaganda. Exposé accounts showed that many tales of German war atrocities were exaggerated, mythical, or even faked by Allied propagandists (Ponsonby, 1928). The postwar period also saw the uncovering of Britain's secret wartime propaganda campaign in the United States (Viereck, 1930). In addition, famous war correspondents, such as Philip Gibbs (1920, 1921), apologized for their role in creating news propagandas that helped prolong the war by sanitizing for public consumption the horrible conditions on the Western Front. Finally, the 1920s brought a new view of America's own Committee on Public Information. Directed by such journalist progressives as Ray Baker and Will Irwin (who earlier had muckraked the communication industry), the CPI propagated a blend of Wilsonian idealism and anti-German muckraking. The committee used pamphlets, news handouts, magazine advertisements, films, speakers, posters, war expositions, and every other possible means to present the war as nothing less than a worldwide struggle of good versus evil (Mock & Larson, 1939; Vaughn, 1980). Under the impact of postwar exposés, the CPI came to be seen as a sly purveyor of propaganda.

The exposure of German propaganda, together with revisionist thinking on the propagandas of the Allies and the CPI, established a social and intellectual context for a wide-ranging debate in the United States over issues of propaganda. The existence of popular interest in propaganda meant that writers on mass persuasion usually avoided technical vocabulary and sought to activate certain widely shared assumptions about American democracy.

Fresh from their respective services with army psychological warfare and the CPI, progressives Walter Lippmann (1919a, 1919b, 1922) and Will Irwin (1919) articulated the renewed progressive critique of propaganda. Lippmann reflected on Allied censorship and propaganda, concluding that the chief problem of modern democracy was protecting the channels of public communication from propaganda. Without safeguards against propaganda, Lippmann (1919a) argued, public opinion was "exposed to every prejudice and to infinite exploitation" (p. 626). Writing of his days with the CPI, Irwin (1919) admitted that "we never told the whole truth—not by any manner of means. We told that part which served our national purpose" (p. 54). More troubling to Irwin was the clear evidence that propaganda continued to taint news coverage in the postwar period, notably in biased news accounts of the Versailles Treaty and the Russian Revolution.

Unlike Marxist critics, for whom the state is either central to ideological domination (Althusser, 1971; Femia, 1981) or crucial as a legitimater of hegemony (Hall, 1982), American propaganda critics of the 1920s treated the state propaganda of the CPI as but a precursor of assaults to come by interest groups on society's forums of communication. These prognostications proved correct. Advertising agencies, which donated their services to the CPI, now argued that they could do for business what they had done for the sale of war bonds (Lee, 1937/1973), and the 1920s saw a veritable explosion in business expenditures for advertising. The war years also stimulated the growth of public relations. Edward L. Bernays (1923, 1928) is representative of the wartime propaganda workers who realized that they could make a good living as consultants promoting the interests of business and industrial clients.

Not only did advertising and public relations grow during the 1920s, but the postwar period saw the rise of radio as a vital new channel of business boosterism. In addition, by 1928, radio addresses and short political pitches were becoming a significant component of electioneering (Craig, 1954). If radio was the new voice of key industrial and political persuaders, market research provided the eyes and ears of the communication industry. Market research firms provided helpful data to advertisers on the size and composition of radio audiences (Hurwitz, 1983). Likert's (1936) effort to measure the sales influence of radio programs typifies the marketing approach that transformed radio from a cultural vehicle into a channel of national commerce.

Propaganda analysts feared that the emerging communications industry threatened democracy by giving private institutions and interest groups a new ability to mold minds before the public could formulate and articulate its will. However, progressive critics of mass persuasion did not base their analysis on a Marxist vision of a class-oriented ideological hegemony engineered by the state. The rational democratic community described by the propaganda critics more often represented a hearkening back to the direct democracy of the old agricultural republic now endangered by the muckraker's nemesis of elite propaganda campaigns. Such a focus fit the traditional link in American culture between private go-getters and their cadres of boosters (Boorstin, 1973). Lacking such a term as *ideological state apparatuses*, progressives nevertheless focused on the efforts of interest groups to covertly co-op news, religion, entertainment, and education.

Reactivating the muckraker's old theme of ideologically tainted news, postwar progressive critics demonstrated that private interest groups were able to influence the reporting of newspapers. Heber Blankenhorn, a progressive journalist and Lippmann's immediate superior in army psychological warfare, provided an important early case study. Blankenhorn served as consultant to the Commission of Inquiry of the Interchurch World Movement, a group investigating the publicity campaign of the steel industry during the 1919 strike. The commission's report criticized steel industry leaders for their effort to characterize the strike falsely as nothing more than an outbreak of domestic bolshevism (Commission of Inquiry, 1920, 1921). Further illustrating the concern of progressives for ideological distortion in news, Walter Lippmann and Charles Merz (1920) wrote a still-remembered propaganda critique of inaccurate and biased reporting by the *New York Times*. According to Lippmann and Merz, the leadership of the *Times* wanted to "ward off bolshevism." This goal created "obstacles to the free pursuit of facts," and caused the Timesmen to accept as truthful any and all antibolshevik or pro-Czarist sources.

At about the same time that Blankenhorn and Lippmann were giving case study accounts of propaganda in the news, Upton Sinclair wrote his personal narrative, *The Brass Check* (1919), showing how domestic reformers usually were ignored or subjected to biased treatment by the press. Today's writers often characterize Sinclair's book as exaggerated and naive in its treatment of journalism and as sentimentally self-serving in its tone (e.g., Emery, 1972, p. 699). However, Sinclair's muckraking of the press profoundly influenced George Seldes, I. F. Stone, and other major journalists (Grenier, 1972; George Seldes, personal communication, May 12-13, 1984), encouraging them to confront and combat obstacles to professional journalism. Soon Seldes (1929) wrote his own critique of press practices, focusing on postwar censorship and propaganda in Europe. More controversial was Seldes's later classic, *Lords of the Press* (1938), in which he summarized the ideological constraints on news that resulted from the direct control of newspaper chains by opinionated owners.

In addition to laying bare ideologies in news, progressive propaganda critics showed that religion could be another wellspring for the ideological contamination of public opinion. H. L. Mencken published several critical pieces on the role of preachers and teachers in pandering to wartime manias (e.g., Hicks, 1927). The definitive account of the preachers' role in World War I came from the pen of sociologist Ray Abrams (1933). Abrams traced the move of religious leaders from pacifism to war, showing how preachers became self-ordained propagandists for wartime state ideology. Typical of Abrams's book was his treatment of Newell Dwight Hillis, a clergyman who specialized in parroting atrocity tales. Illustrating the frequently self-serving nature of wartime preaching, Abrams related how Hillis helped the American Bankers Association promote war bonds by writing, at their behest, a book on German atrocities. Postwar progressive critics discovered that propagandists still sought the stamp of religious legitimacy for their self-serving partisan ideologies. In its investigation of the 1919 steel strike, Heber Blankenhorn's Interchurch Commission (1921) found that many clergy simply reiterated the view of steel executives that the strike was the opening shot of the bolshevik revolution in America.

The rise of centrally produced radio programs and films caused progressive propaganda critics to explore whether entertainment was not becoming a third channel for covert diffusion of partisan ideologies. Larrabee (1920) observed a covert, cultural dimension of film propaganda that included making the rich seem more villainous than the poor, and associating crime with use of liquor. He found direct propaganda in a small percentage of films that took positions in favor of religious groups, relief campaigns, or political measures.

Not only did progressive critics fear the partisan manipulation of movies, they, like the Frankfurt school critics (Horkheimer & Adorno, 1944/1972), explored the general cultural implications of mass entertainment. Of particular concern was the influence of films on the minds of the more than 11 million children under age 14 who attended films weekly (Dale, 1935b, p. 73). Critics pointed out that children were exposed to films originally prepared for adults, in which crime, sex, and vulgarity were rampant. Moreover, argued Edgar Dale in one of the Payne Fund volumes, movies gave an unrealistic picture of modern life. Dale's (1935a) content analysis showed that leading film characters pursued overwhelmingly personal goals, with only 9% of their objectives being social in nature (p. 185). In a companion study, Herbert Blumer (1933/1970) explored the effects of movies on the young. Blumer found that movies exerted a powerful "emotional possession" on youngsters, as shown by the nature and content of their reported dreams.

In a fourth foray into propaganda as ideological diffusion, progressive propaganda critics turned to problems of partisan material in education. The progressive critique of educational propaganda paralleled, but was distinct from, the Marxist analysis of education as an ideological apparatus. One difference was that progressives did not regard the educational system as a passive target for reactionary propaganda. Progressives believed, instead, that they could transform the schools into ideologically sensitive bastions against propaganda in all spheres of life.

Progressives were active during the years between the world wars in exposing propaganda in education. Charles Beard (1919) wrote an early account of how a syllabus circulated by the New York City Department of Education contained disguised propaganda for universal peacetime military service. Two influential articles in H. L. Mencken's *American Mercury* showed how American college teachers had eagerly taken on the role of propagandist during the Great War (Angoff, 1927; Grattan, 1927). Teachers themselves explored problems of propaganda inherent in offers from outside groups of educational materials and prize contests (e.g., McAndrew, 1930). Investigations by the National Education Association (1929) and the American Association of University Professors (Seligman, 1930) showed that the National Electric Light Association, in particular, had been subsidizing textbook authors to write favorably about privately owned power plants.

Not only did progressive educators confront propaganda as an ideological interloper in the curriculum, they worked to make the schools into a forum against propaganda. In higher education, propaganda analysis became both an important theoretical postulate and a significant pedagogical concept (Lasswell, Casey, & Smith, 1935). Propaganda analysis took its place in a variety of academic fields, such as sociology (Lumley, 1929, 1933), political science (Childs, 1934; Odegard, 1928, 1930), psychology (Dodge, 1920; Doob, 1935), history (Bruntz, 1930; Hodder, 1922; Squires, 1935), journalism (Casey, 1939; Dale, 1941), English (Hayakawa, 1939; Jewett, 1940), speech (Graves, 1941; Johnson, 1939), and education (Biddle, 1932; Kilpatrick, 1939). Propaganda concepts soon moved from higher education to secondary school teaching (Ellis, 1937; Rosenthal, 1939; Talbot, 1944). Until America entered World War II, propaganda analysis stood as the dominant American perspective for analyzing social influence (Sproule, 1987a). The progressive view of propaganda became so widely diffused into general public consciousness that, during the 1930s, Americans viewed propaganda as the major cause of World War I (Gallup, 1972, vol. 1, p. 192).

The Institute for Propaganda Analysis, chartered in 1937, emerged as the culmination of the progressive antipropaganda movement. The institute received its initial support from a progressive philanthropist, Edward Filene, who worried that extremist groups at home and abroad were undermining the public's ability to decide issues rationally (Lee & Lee, 1979; Sproule, 1985). The institute's monthly bulletin, *Propaganda Analysis,* enjoyed a wide circulation among the nation's educators and opinion leaders, and the institute prepared and sold educational materials that were used by adult education groups and by an estimated million students yearly (Fine, 1941). The institute's program embodied the progressive philosophy that the modern public could function effectively once it understood how ideology came to bear on public communication.

The progressive propaganda critics emphasized private institutions and organizations as culprits in giving an ideological patina to news, religion, entertainment, and education. Yet, like the Marxist critics, progressives realized that the state might act to upset the balance of ideological forces in society. So propaganda critics combed government to find instances of antiprogressive propaganda. For instance, Wohlforth (1930) provided readers of the *New Republic* with an exposé of the War Department's citizenship courses given to 260,000 young men at high schools, colleges, and training camps. The army's program warned students of the dangers of pacifism, "mobocracy" (rule by the "masses"), and "socialistic" policies. Wohlforth argued that the army program purveyed an ideology of complacency toward the status quo, stuffing students "with the sawdust of reactionary platitudes, tin-whistle ideals and big business morality" (p. 258). The classic treatment of the propaganda alliance of business and government came in the work of Engelbrecht and Hanighen (1934) through their book, *Merchants of Death,* in which they argued that arms manufacturers used public relations techniques to promote war scares that helped spur higher levels of arm sales.

During the 1920s and 1930s, the progressive propaganda critics developed a wide-ranging program to combat the problem of partisan ideological diffusion through news, religion, entertainment, education, and government. In contrast to Marxist scholars, however, progressives were optimistic about the public's ability to withstand propaganda, especially since progressives believed they could turn the ideological apparatuses, particularly education, into weapons against the powerful propagandas.

THE RATIONALIST AND
PROFESSIONAL RESPONSES

With its wide popular audience, progressive critique became the dominant school of thought on propaganda during the years between the two world wars. Yet, the Great War laid a foundation for two competing perspectives on mass ideological diffusion. The first, a rationalist approach to propaganda, reassessed the cognitive competence of the public. The second, a renewed practitioner perspective, optimistically saw the new methods of propaganda as servants to postwar democracy.

Rationalism shared with progressive critique a similar social impetus in postwar disillusionment and revisionism. However, the rationalist response to propaganda embodied a distinctly different view of the failures of the war years. For most progressives, the major lesson of the Great War was that institutions could induce the public to a fury of excitement and hate by diffusing self-serving ideologies into the public mind. While pessimistic about society's persuaders, progressives nevertheless reflected traditional American optimism about the rationality of public opinion. Progressives had faith in the essential cognitive competence of the public, believing all that was necessary to combat propaganda was to inform the public about how modern institutions diffused their ideologies through news, religion, entertainment, education, and government.

In contrast to the emphasis of propaganda critics on institutional manipulation, rationalists took as their mission to dissect wartime evidences of human irrationality. The Great War's intense hatred, mania against all things German, and spy paranoia threatened the view of modern society as rational. Rationalists believed that the Great War demonstrated that the public needed education in how to think straight more than mere information about the apparatuses of propaganda. The rallying point of the rationalist school was John Dewey's (1903, 1910, 1916/1953) work to develop a method of rational analysis suitable for modern technical society. Dewey laid the foundations for a straight-thinking approach to propaganda that aimed to make readers and listeners more rational by focusing their attention on the logical requirements of scientific observation and inference.

The 1920s and 1930s saw an emerging view of the incompetent public, as psychologists, logicians, and educators developed a literature of straight thinking (Clarke, 1929; Glaser, 1941; E. D. Martin, 1920; Thouless, 1932). In contrast to propaganda analysis, which focused on the diffusion of self-serving ideology (Edwards, 1938), the pedagogies of straight thinking emphasized the assessment of the logical consistency and rationality of message texts. Typical exercises in straight thinking included relating premises to conclusions, testing assumptions, and restraining emotions that might act as barriers to rational decision making.

Communication practitioners, as well as proponents of straight thinking, challenged progressive assumptions about the social problem of propaganda. Under fire for pandering to public credulity, practitioners of public relations, advertising, radio, film, and polling felt impelled to respond to their critics. Ironically, the first postwar articulators of the practitioner perspective were those progressives who had taken wartime service as U.S. government propagandists. While the fighting raged, the CPI's work understandably was seen chiefly in terms of the practitioner's view that propaganda merely elaborated traditional American boosterism. After the war, George Creel, progressive journalist and CPI chairman, argued that the CPI program not only ignored hate material and atrocity stories (Creel, 1920/1972, p. 56), but that the CPI proved "propagandists do *not* have to lie" (Creel, 1941, p. 345). Charles Merriam (1919), director of CPI efforts in Italy, and later linchpin of the University of Chicago's Department of Political Science, similarly defended the honesty of U.S. propaganda. Also, Blankenhorn (1919) gave a practitioner view of army propaganda when he detailed how German morale crumbled in the face of army leaflets that both reprinted Woodrow Wilson's idealistic speeches and listed the relatively lavish food rations given to prisoners surrendering to the American army.

While Creel, Merriam, and Blankenhorn contributed a practitioner's view of wartime persuasions, the major spokesman of the postwar communication professionals was Edward L. Bernays, the public relations expert. Bernays, a pre-World War I theatrical press agent, had worked for CPI and was impressed with how the committee's worldwide campaign made Woodrow Wilson a hero even to Italian peasants (E. L. Bernays, personal communication, May 19, 1984). According to Bernays, propagandists understood that members of the public experienced diverse group loyalties. The role of the public relations counsel was to identify appeals that tapped the often conflicting stereotypes held by the public. Particularly important in public relations was the effort to "create news" (Bernays, 1923, p. 183), since news, not editorial opinion, was vital in channeling public opinion.

Bernays (1923) challenged the progressive critics who argued that covertly manufactured news marked a manipulative threat to democracy. On the contrary, Bernays argued, special pleading was the American way. The United States operated on the basis of open competition "organized by leadership and propaganda" instead of having decisions be made by "committees of wise men." To deplore the unseen organization of mass opinion would be "to ask for a society such as never was and never will be" (1928, pp. 9-18). Finally, like any other professional group, public relations counsels necessarily developed codes of ethical practice to function in a world of ambiguity and conflict. "Therefore, the public relations counsel must maintain an intense scrutiny of his actions, avoiding the propagation of unsocial or otherwise harmful movements or ideas" (1923, p. 215). Ethics was also good business, according to Bernays (1928), since manufacturers could not deceive consumers without losing public confidence. In articulating his view of a benign propaganda, Bernays drew on the traditional American go-getting spirit and optimism about self-promotion.

The progressive, rationalist, and practitioner approaches to propaganda represented the main lines of conversation in the interwar popular debate over mass ideological diffusion. Of the three, only progressive propaganda analysis roughly paralleled the Marxist interest in ideological hegemonies effected through social apparatuses. However, in their treatment of ideological diffusion, progressives focused less on the state and expressed optimism about using education as a counterweight to propaganda. In opposition to progressive critique, practitioners argued that persuasion was difficult to attain and described their power as merely facilitating existing lines of social competition. For their part, rationalists shifted the entire focus of the debate over propaganda from ideologies and apparatuses to the reasoning power of the consumer of propaganda.

NEW ACADEMIC APPROACHES TO PROPAGANDA

Progressive critique marked the dominant 1920s and 1930s school of thought on propaganda both in general society and in American higher education. However, for scholars who sought a deep understanding of the social phenomena of mass persuasion, propaganda analysis was not an entirely satisfactory body of literature. Writings in the propaganda analysis school contributed only a tepid level of theorizing and data collection for use in unraveling the rich cultural issues raised by propaganda. The result was a twofold reaction against propaganda analysis in higher education — first, by those who wanted to construct grand theories of symbolic interaction, and second, by those who wanted to apply new social science research methods to problems of mass communication.

The wellspring of 1930s grand theories of mass symbolic inducement was the Chicago school of social science, a literature that began around the turn of the century. Chicago school writers were progressives whose personal interests in constructing academic theories tended to outweigh their desire to spur practical reforms (Bulmer, 1984). While sympathetic to progressive reform, Chicago school writers chiefly labored to work out a grand theory of symbolic social influence (e.g., Mead, 1934). One of the first Chicago school writers to make a mark on problems of propaganda was Robert E. Park (1904/1972), who helped bring to the attention of Americans the work of European social scientists on mass society and mass culture. Park's work had the effect of helping to "Americanize" pessimistic European theories of the alienated and vulnerable mass audience (Bramson, 1961). Park's theory presented social influence as involving an alternation between excitable, suggestible crowds and rational, discursive publics. Charles H. Cooley, though not directly affiliated with Park's program, nevertheless was closely allied to the Chicago group and influenced them (Faris, 1967). Like Park, Cooley (1909) translated the idea of mass audience into the more optimistic progressive view of the public as subject to rational appeals and improvement through education. Park's disciple, Blumer (1939), elaborated on collective behavior as an American version of the mass society thesis, and later became a critic of the variable analysis approach of communication research (Blumer, 1969).

In addition to articulating theories of collective behavior, the Chicago group responded to the exigence of the Great War's powerful persuasions. Both Charles Merriam, Chicago political scientist (and wartime CPI director in Italy), and Harold Lasswell, Merriam's student, began to develop symbolic theories to account for contemporary communication phenomena. While Merriam and Lasswell were by no means disinterested in social reform, as shown by Merriam's work for the Hoover Research Committee (President's Research Committee on Social Trends, 1933), the work of the two was more oriented to refining academic social theory than to furthering specific progressive reforms (Lasswell, 1927; Merriam, 1934). For example, Lasswell's critical analysis of World War I propaganda seemed consistent with the general interests of progressive propaganda critics. Yet, Lasswell's approach to propaganda stemmed less from the muckraking tradition of realist progressivism and more from a larger theoretical program, influenced by Mead, of examining "the place occupied by the symbolic among the nonsymbolic events of war or peace" (Lasswell, 1927/1971, pp. x, xiii). Lasswell also became increasingly concerned about methodology in content analysis (Lasswell & Blumenstock, 1939).

Because of their theoretical depth, the symbolic theories of the Chicago school are important resources for understanding mass communication. For this reason, many reviewers today treat the Chicago school as *the* essential pre-World War II wellspring of American media theory (Bineham, 1988; Bramson, 1961; Czitrom, 1982; Hardt, 1989; Robinson, 1988). In the context of the 1920s and 1930s, however, the Chicago school actually exerted relatively little impact on the major interwar dialogue on propaganda (in society in general and in academe) that pitted progressive critics against rationalists and practitioners. Yet, the disproportionate retrospective impact of the Chicago school does point to the importance of theoretical depth in the longevity of social theories. The conceptual thinness of progressive critique caused Leonard Doob, a significant 1930s propaganda critic, to abandon propaganda analysis in favor of scientific communication research in the mode of the Yale attitude studies. Doob believed that propaganda analysis failed as a critical paradigm because it lacked the legitimating theoretical depth of Marxist criticism (L. W. Doob, personal communication, May 20-21, 1982).

One specific intellectual pressure on American social scientists further explains their search for alternatives to propaganda analysis. During the 1920s and 1930s, many social researchers believed that by turning to statistical, survey, and experimental methods of research they could construct a truly scientific understanding of modern society (Veysey, 1965). As a result, American scholars began to separate into competing humanist and social science camps. The widening chasm in purpose and method between humanist and scientific scholarship was not, at first, distinctly defined in the area of propaganda studies. The Social Science Research Council's bibliography on propaganda drew freely from both critical and quantitative sources (Lasswell et al., 1935). And the early courses in public opinion and propaganda marked a marriage of the critical analysis of society's persuaders with a statistical treatment of the vicissitudes of public attitude (Childs, 1934, pp. 4-6). Further, some of the first quantitative studies of message effects treated the problem of how to better induce resistance to propaganda (Biddle, 1932; Osborn, 1939). Finally, early attitude studies often explicitly posed the question of whether persuasive effects were socially desirable or not (Remmers, 1938; Thurstone, 1931).

Nevertheless, the 1920s saw the emergence of the entrepreneurial social scientist who merged an academician's interest in social research with a practitioner's knack for bringing cutting-edge knowledge to bear on practical problems of persuasion. In 1921, a group of 170 psychologists formed the Psychological Corporation to provide institutions with techniques of personnel testing, market research, and advertising testing (Cattell, 1923). The work of George Gallup is another example of how scientific communication researchers turned to practitioner issues. Gallup left academe to join the ranks of the independent practitioners who provided survey research for American business, broadcasting, and government (Gallup & Rae, 1940). The Princeton Radio Project, under the joint leadership of Paul Lazarsfeld, Hadley Cantril, and Frank Stanton, marked a similar linking of commercial interests and academic research (Cantril, 1940; Lazarsfeld, 1939, 1940; Lazarsfeld & Stanton, 1944). As commercial pollsters and market researchers began to make significant technical advances, academicians worked to bring the new methods more fully into the social science theory and curriculum (Cantril, 1967).

While distinct from progressive critique, the grand symbolic theory and scientific approaches reinforced the dominant progressive tendency to look away from state-dominated apparatuses as the main obstacle to attainment of the rational-democratic society. The symbolic theorists focused on problems of mass society, and the communication scientists looked to methodology for a route to certified knowledge about social influence.

PROPAGANDA AGAINST
THE DOMINANT MODE OF PRODUCTION?

The grand theory and communication research schools of thought on propaganda (both later critiqued by Mills, 1959) represented challenges to propaganda analysis from academicians of progressive inclination. However, the 1930s also saw two important challenges to progressive critique emerge from rightist opponents of progressivism, both in politics and in academe. The right-wing perspective on American propaganda raises an interesting issue in connection with the Marxist assumption that communication apparatuses purvey an ideology that supports the dominant mode of (capitalist) production. Rightist critics pointed to certain anticapitalist tendencies in progressivism that, along with other left-wing views, sometimes infiltrated education, journalism, and administrative agencies of government. Rightist counterprogressives were alert to expose and purge propaganda *against* the dominant capitalist mode of production. The two arms of the right-wing challenge to progressivism came from polemicists in politics and humanists in academe.

By the late 1930s, conservative politicians were alarmed by the success of progressivism in turning certain ideological apparatuses toward progressive purposes. The major critics of journalism (Irwin, Lippmann, Sinclair, Seldes) were already anticipating the American Newspaper Guild, an organization that helped give institutional clout to the muckraking, progressive spirit of journalists. Further, with the coming of the New Deal, progressives began to take service in government agencies, turning administration into a tool for progressivism. But progressives put particular store in the power of education to promote a rational-democratic society. Leaders of the progressive education movement encouraged teachers to prepare students for a society that would be based on social cooperation rather than economic competition (Cremin, 1961, pp. 257-264). The particular success of the Institute for Propaganda Analysis in securing a wide market for its antipropaganda materials offered more proof that progressive education could function as a major obstacle to ideological manipulation.

The successes of progressivism in journalism, government, and education prompted a reaction by rightist politicians and polemicists. The archetype of the polemical approach to propaganda was the infamous House Un-American Activities Committee. In 1938, HUAC came under the control of an anti-New Deal coalition led by Congressman Martin Dies of Texas. Under Dies, HUAC became more a forum for opponents of organized labor and the New Deal than a body for exposing extremist propaganda. The Dies Committee showed a particular fascination for dissecting such New Deal ideological apparatuses as the Federal Theater Project (U.S. House of Representatives, 1938, vol. 4, pp. 2729-2873). With an interest in purging the government of progressivism, Dies attacked FTP plays, a number of which did, in fact, give a stinging critique of American economic organization. Exhibiting his tendency to maximize any conceivable connection between New Deal progressivism and Soviet Marxism, Dies (1940) termed the plays "straight Communist propaganda" (p. 300). Taking the antiprogressive campaign into education, J. B. Matthews, Dies's chief investigator, labeled the Institute for Propaganda Analysis a left-wing subversive group ("Dies Scrutinizes," 1941).

At the same time that rightist opponents of the New Deal waged polemical warfare against progressivism in government and education, conservative humanists were expressing similar, though more reasoned, concerns about the New Deal's expansion of government persuasion. The 1930s saw an ironic intellectual role reversal in which progressives showed relative sympathy to state ideological mediation in contrast to conservatives, who enlisted for service in that tangent of propaganda analysis that exposed New Deal promotionalism (Hofstadter, 1955, pp. 233-234, 317). Conservative critics viewed propaganda by business groups as a noncontroversial private matter, whereas they believed that propaganda had no place in an ostensibly neutral public government. In contrast, progressives cheered Roosevelt for going directly to the people in order to bypass the rightist-controlled communication industry (M. Lerner, 1943).

In addition to criticizing the infiltration of progressive ideology in government, conservative humanists began, during the 1930s, to critique the successes that progressivism enjoyed in public education (Cremin, 1961). This line of attack intensified after World War II, reflecting the American assumption that opposing propagandas ever compete for control of the various forums of public communication. For instance, William F. Buckley, Jr. (1951) first gained national visibility through his charge that the Yale University faculty purveyed an agnostic, collectivist ideology.

Before 1940, progressive propaganda analysis amounted to the main line of American thought on the problem of ideological diffusion through the various apparatuses of cultural communication. Rounding out the American dialectic on propaganda were practitioners, rationalists, grand theorists, communication scientists, rightist polemicists, and conservative humanists. Given the diverse 1920s and 1930s literature of American ideological critique conducted under the rubric of propaganda, we have reason to inquire why histories of American media research typically feature only the contributions of the grand theorists and scientific researchers (e.g., Delia, 1987; Hardt, 1989). Particularly ironic is today's treatment of progressive propaganda analysis. This once-dominant school of media criticism is usually presented through the lens of a stereotyped and pejorative "magic bullet" formulation (DeFleur & Ball-Rokeach, 1982; Lowrey & DeFleur, 1983; Rogers, 1962/1983; Schramm, 1971; compare Sproule, 1987a, 1989). The loss of the rich inter-world war American dialectic on propaganda has done lasting damage to American ideological critique by obscuring important lines of experience, research, argument, and theorizing. To understand how America's earliest conversations on ideological critique were virtually extirpated, we need to look at the transformation in American propaganda theory and criticism that took place during World War II and the subsequent Cold War.

IDEOLOGICAL CONSENSUS?

During the war years, the suspension of the American dialectic on propaganda created an intellectual vacuum in which Marxist sources began to take the place of native American critical writings. The tendency to substitute Marxist analysis for progressive critique is clearly reflected in Lazarsfeld's (1941) celebrated juxtaposition of critical (i.e., Frankfurt school) and administrative research. Marxist critics (e.g., Gitlin, 1981; Hall, 1982) tend to accept the assertion of 1940s communication scientists that the only two programs of ideological critique against which American communication research competed were the grand theory of mass society and the Frankfurt school. To understand why a "critical paradigm" often has become a Marxist paradigm, we must look at the effect the war had on the American dialogue over propaganda.

From the point of view of propaganda studies, the major effect of Pearl Harbor was to set in motion a social climate conducive to the expansion of communication research, the scientific school of thought on modern propaganda. As a result, although 1930s communication research was not completely distinct from progressive propaganda analysis, the two paradigms were self-consciously separate 20 years later. By the 1950s, attitude studies emphasized ways to improve the success rate of persuaders, and "public opinion" came to mean a "non-ethical, largely quantitative" process (Albig, 1957, p. 21). The war years provided fertile soil for the expansion of three related approaches to quantitative investigation: content analysis, experimentation, and survey research. As each of these lines of research stretched to meet the needs of wartime Washington, American academicians moved away from a critical viewpoint on mass persuasion.

Lasswell's (1927/1971) masterpiece analysis of the propaganda symbols of the Great War exhibited a critical edge. However, Lasswell (1933) increasingly espoused the scientific approach to content analysis based on his acceptance of the practitioner's assumption that competition of propagandas rendered mass persuasion socially neutral. Belief in the cultural amorality of propaganda allowed Lasswell to eschew a critical scrutiny of messages in favor of studying "under what conditions do words affect power relationships?" (Lasswell & Leites, 1949, p. 18). Lasswell's quantitative propaganda studies offered the promise of extracting useful meanings from enemy communications during the war, and Lasswell developed a research program under U.S. government auspices. During the 1950s, content analysis came to be understood as a quantitative scientific method primarily oriented to "determination of the effects of communications" (Berelson, 1952, p. 15). In contrast to the progressive propaganda critics, who aimed to energize the general public, Lasswell (1951a) believed that he and his colleagues in policy science could contribute to democratic reform by acting as midwives for good policies implemented by and from society's top echelons.

A small, though important, aspect of wartime social research was the experimental program of the Army's Research Branch, directed by Carl I. Hovland. Hovland's Experimental Section provided useful studies that tested the effects on soldiers of various training and orientation films, including the army's "Why We Fight" series, designed to inculcate the official view of the causes and nature of the war (Hovland, Lumsdaine, & Sheffield, 1949). Not only did the army research aid in the diffusion of such individual techniques as the Program Analyzer, which correlated expressions of like and dislike by audiences to segments of program content, but the work of the army's Experimental Section served as the precursor of the much-heralded Yale attitude change studies of the 1950s (Hovland, 1957; Hovland, Janis, & Kelley, 1953; Janis & Hovland, 1959). Not that all social scientists favored adopting the army's research program as a model for the postwar social sciences. Humanistically oriented scholars, such as Robert S. Lynd (1949) and Alfred McClung Lee (1949), suggested that army-style social research was likely to produce a trend toward undemocratic social engineering. However, after the war, the Carnegie Corporation underwrote publication of a series summarizing the U.S. Army's research program (Hovland et al., 1949; Stouffer, Suchman, DeVinney, Star, & Williams, 1949), and these books became the "paradigm of the new social science" (D. Lerner, 1950, p. 220).

Survey methods amounted to an important third component of the emerging school called communication research. Early advances in survey techniques frequently came from outside of academe, under auspices of private research firms. Gallup and Archibald Crossley were two important practitioners who made early advances in applying polling to problems of market research, political advertising, and assessing broadcast audiences (Crossley, 1957; Hurwitz, 1983). During the late 1930s and early 1940s, such academicians as Princeton's Hadley Cantril became interested in bringing the newest survey methods into the purview of academic social scientists (Cantril, 1967). Important in the solidification of the communication research point of view was the confluence of commercial and academic survey researchers resulting from both the Princeton Radio Project and the Army Research Branch described previously. Princeton's Office of Radio Research emerged as a cooperative project of Princeton social science, the Rockefeller Foundation, and Frank Stanton's research department at the Columbia Broadcasting System. Later reincarnated as Columbia University's Bureau of Applied Social Research, the radio project produced many important studies of how media generate large audiences and influence them (Cantril, 1940, 1944; Lazarsfeld, 1939, 1940; Lazarsfeld & Stanton, 1944).

During the postwar period, survey researchers saw a potential for using their research methods to effect social reforms through administrative action. The result was a research program to combat anti-Semitism that brought together communication scientists (Flowerman, 1947; Lazarsfeld, 1947) and emigré critical scholars of the Frankfurt school (Adorno, Frenkel-Brunswick, Levinson, & Sanford, 1950; Lowenthal & Guterman, 1949/1970). Later, however, as the scientific mission of communication research became more entrenched, the idea of using survey and experimental methods for institutionally promoted ideological reform began to seem somewhat naive (N. Glazer, personal communication, May 14, 1984). Administrative research, with its premise of a society united against commonly perceived threats, increasingly lost its vestige of critical purpose.

Under the influence of the Lasswell, Princeton-Columbia, and U.S. Army research programs, communication research—the scientific approach to propaganda—became predominant in academic social science, displacing humanistic propaganda analysis. For leading American social scientists, critical analysis seemed unnecessary in an era when scientists helped enlightened administrators to solve national problems. Lazarsfeld, in particular, became a spokesperson for the view that media effects were the chief consideration in understanding propaganda and that the time for "impressionistic" critical studies of propaganda had passed (Lazarsfeld & Merton, 1943). Reinforcing this call for an emphasis on the process of managerial persuasion was the demonstration that survey research could unravel many of the mysteries of how people responded to campaign propaganda (Lazarsfeld, Berelson, & Gaudet, 1944/1968). When a committee of the Society for the Psychological Study of Social Issues prepared a reader on public opinion (Katz, Cartwright, Eldersveld, & Lee, 1954), the volume included materials on progressive propaganda critique only at the insistence of one committee member, Alfred Lee, former executive director of the Institute for Propaganda Analysis (A. M. Lee, personal communication, June 13, 1987).

Social conditions of the 1950s further acted to create a surface of disarming ideological consensus among students of mass persuasion. Provisions for tax-exempt status encouraged this development by mandating that research organizations not engage in activities construable as propaganda or lobbying. Also relevant was the U.S. government's mania for internal security, which resulted in both Lazarsfeld and Lasswell finding themselves under scrutiny by security personnel. Lazarsfeld's transgressions included having once attended a meeting sponsored by the American Writers Congress, an organization later cited as a communist front group (Lazarsfeld, 1954). Lasswell ran afoul of the security establishment in view of his possession of various communist propaganda leaflets — residue of his 1930s research on propaganda content (Lasswell, 1951b).

One result of the anticritical mood of the Cold War was a turn to a scientifically neutral approach to social controversy. Illustrative is the Klapper and Glock (1949/1954) study of how newspapers functioned as conduits for polemical charges by the House Un-American Activities Committee against Edward U. Condon, chief of the National Bureau of Standards. Arguing that members of the Bureau of Applied Social Research lacked competence to evaluate the actions of HUAC or the truth of its allegations, Klapper and Glock offered instead a statistical tabulation of whether attacks by HUAC led to favorable or unfavorable treatment of Condon in various newspapers.

The 1950s saw the scientific approach to propaganda become predominant in higher education. The neutral appellation of *communication* emerged as a sign that a "value-free" approach was replacing the old designator of *propaganda* originally introduced by the progressive critics. Subject entries in *Psychological Abstracts* for 1942 list 27 articles under the headings of "propaganda" or "propaganda analysis" and only 1 under "communication"; in 1948, the split was 18 and 16, respectively; in 1952, it was 14 and 42. While a few academicians still employed the term *propaganda* as a significant theoretical concept (e.g., Lee, 1952), the propaganda analysis paradigm was generally forgotten or was recast as a primitive precursor to communication research that erred by naively treating communication as a "magic bullet" (Sproule, 1987a, 1989). During the 1950s, sundry critical works on communication still received occasional attention (Innis, 1951; Packard, 1957; Gilbert Seldes, 1950/1970). But the new communication scientists worked from the perspective of researching ways to help persuaders better succeed in a climate where mass media interacted with personal contacts (Katz & Lazarsfeld, 1955; Rogers, 1962/1983). Critiques of quantitative communication research (Blumer, 1969; Mills, 1959) represented a distinct minority position in an era when scientifically oriented scholars seemed poised to provide definitive, certified knowledge about the social process of communication.

Not only did World War II and the Cold War encourage academicians to pursue administrative problems to the neglect of social criticism, but the wartime desire for consensus gave credence to the polemicists. The polemical approach to propaganda, first honed by HUAC in the 1930s, became a socially significant force during the 1940s and 1950s, with headlines generated by various House and Senate internal security committees. Notable were the HUAC hearings on communist infiltration of Hollywood as evidenced by allegedly favorable treatment of Russia in films produced during World War II (U.S. House of Representatives, 1947). Such propaganda critics as George Seldes found themselves before Joe McCarthy's government operations committee answering questions about their loyalty (G. Seldes, personal communication, 1984). The success of polemicists in characterizing social criticism as incipient disloyalty acted as a real damper to publication of critical propaganda studies. For instance, Alfred Lee's publisher was nervous about issuing his critical study of propaganda (Lee, 1952) due to the strident McCarthyism of the day (A. M. Lee, personal communication, 1987).

Polemical attacks on the progressive propaganda critics further nudged educators in the direction of rationalistic pedagogies of critical thinking that were politically neutral (Sproule, 1987b, 1987c). Before Pearl Harbor, straight thinking amounted to a relatively minor strain of thought in American pedagogy — and one often subsumed by propaganda analysis. However, by the early 1940s, the rationalist, textual approach to propaganda became dominant in the American school curriculum. Two political conditions of the early 1940s worked to make rationalism the more appealing educational response to problems of propaganda. First, the war with Germany and Japan caused progressives to turn from emphasis on the machinations of domestic elites to an urgent effort to promote national solidarity against fascism. Progressives feared that propaganda analysis might prevent Americans from rallying to the antifascist crusade (M. Lerner, 1941; Smith, 1941). At the same time, progressives began to feel uncomfortable about the quasi-isolationist ideology in propaganda analysis. For example, the Institute for Propaganda Analysis came under fire for treating the pre-Pearl Harbor communications of Britain and Germany as equally an effort to sway Americans with self-serving propaganda (Garber, 1942; Mumford, 1946).

In contrast to propaganda analysis, straight thinking carried less in the way of troublesome political ideology. The focus was on messages taken as ideal types rather than as embedded in social struggle. In its yearbook for teachers, the National Council for the Social Studies now recommended straight thinking, with a Deweyesque focus on the steps of rational analysis (Anderson, 1942). This turn to rationalism marked a change from the council's earlier endorsement of propaganda analysis (Ellis, 1937). During the post-1945 years, propaganda analysis was overshadowed by such works on critical thinking as that by Black (1952) and the mechanics of the Watson-Glaser test of critical thinking (which had originally been prepared in cooperation with the Institute for Propaganda Analysis). The legacy of textual rationalism continues to the present day. A survey by Nickerson, Perkins, and Smith (1985) shows that 1980s methods of critical thinking usually focus on textual analysis, avoiding wider issues of how powerful interest groups diffuse their ideological messages through the agencies and technologies of the communication industry.

Belief that 1940s and 1950s society was based on a relative consensus, together with increasing political attacks on social critics, led to an amnesia about America's pre-World War II conversation about propaganda. The result was to reinforce a tendency, begun by Lazarsfeld (1941), to associate ideological critique with Marxist theory. While some contemporary scholars have begun to mine the legacy of early propaganda scholarship (e.g., Jowett & O'Donnell, 1986), contemporary critics who reflect the progressive tradition do not ordinarily present their work as a continuation of an ongoing conversation begun by the muckrakers. Further, it is unlikely that most of today's propaganda critics view the diverse literatures of the pre-World War II American propaganda dialectic as relating to a common problem, with the result that its overall impact is lost. For instance, few mass media scholars would consider critical thinking, polemical propaganda analysis, or defenses by practitioners as providing vital insight into their field, notwithstanding the common historical roots of these literatures in the 1920s and 1930s search for the rational-democratic society.

THE RETURN OF IDEOLOGY
IN PROPAGANDA CRITIQUE

The upheavals of the 1960s again showed the need for and social value of criticizing powerful institutions. The earliest post-Vietnam propaganda studies were pursued by popular writers under such rubrics as "selling" (McGinniss, 1969) and "lying" (Wise, 1973). In reaching for a popular audience, post-Vietnam propaganda criticism sometimes took up polemical cudgels, as illustrated by the Vietnam-era teach-ins (H. H. Martin, 1966), Nader's attacks on misleading business practices (Ross, 1973), and Chomsky and Herman's (1979) thesis of a conservative effort to reestablish the interventionist Cold War ideology weakened by the Indochina debacle.

Just as World War I brought about an overlapping of popular and academic progressive critique, so too did post-Vietnam and post-Watergate attitudes draw forth a response from academicians. In the field of mass media, the result was to confound the dominant paradigm of communication research, with its value-free premises springing from a vision of ideological consensus (see Gerbner, 1983). Following the pattern of the 1930s, the new wave of critical propaganda studies began to take as its major point of departure the ideological construction and coloring of news (Bagdikian, 1983; Crouse, 1973; Gans, 1979; Gitlin, 1980). In addition, the new school of progressive propaganda critique has followed the 1930s pattern of paying attention to such ideological apparatuses as entertainment (Gitlin, 1985; MacDonald, 1985; Postman, 1985), education and marketing (Schiller, 1973), and opinion polling (Ginsberg, 1986). As was the case during the 1930s, the renewed school of progressive propaganda criticism includes a curricular response. Today's propaganda analysis increasingly brings issues of ideological diffusion into the mainstream rationalist literature of critical thinking (Hosterman, 1981; Kahane, 1971; Rank, 1974, 1982, 1984).

Given today's amnesia about 1930s propaganda analysis, it is surprising that post-Vietnam media critics, listed above, reflect progressive assumptions more than the Marxist vision and vocabulary. Yet, the great attention to Marxist critical theory during the 1980s (e.g., McKerrow, 1983; Real, 1986) suggests that American writers increasingly may turn to Marxist assumptions in developing a theory of ideological manipulation. Marxist theory represents an important repository for ideological critique, but today's students of mass media would do well to reexamine the powerful American dialectic on propaganda that dates back to the muckrakers. However, it is not enough for today's media critics to consider only progressivism's popular and academic literature on propaganda. If critics are to make solid judgments about the manipulation of the ideological apparatuses, they must also attend to the schools of thought that compete with progressive propaganda critique, for instance, works by and about practitioners (Ogilvy, 1987; Schudson, 1984). In addition, rightist polemical critics (Schlafly, 1964; Stormer, 1964) and conservative humanist critics (Dinsmore, 1969; Efron, 1971; Lefever, 1974) continue to give a truculent commentary on the ability of progressivism to win influence in education, media, and government. Important cultural critiques of progressive education as corrosive to social stability have come from Weaver (1953), Bennett (1984), and Bloom (1987).

Since 1900, progressives, practitioners, rationalists, grand theorists, communication scientists, right-wing polemicists, and counterprogressive humanists all have contributed to an American dialectic about propaganda. If Americans are to conceptualize and respond to the communication industry successfully, it will help if they understand the complex issues in terms applicable to American experience, history, social organization, and criticism. The idea that social influence proceeds by means of large economic classes employing stable ideological apparatuses is not consistent with fundamental American experience. More familiar to Americans is the idea of tactical propaganda battles waged between and among shifting alliances of organizations, factions, and leaders. The importance of competition in the arenas of propaganda is underscored by commentators who fault the Frankfurt school for giving undue weight to forces that attempt to stabilize society (e.g., Held, 1980, pp. 399-400).

Some 90 years of competition among schools of thought on propaganda shows that the United States has not yet fully come to grips with the social role of its media of communication. The unresolved dilemmas that mass communication poses for a democratic society are embodied in today's debates over advertising on children's television, religious broadcasting, the market-driven "dumbing down" and social blandness of textbooks, violence on television, and the social role of news. The historical dialogue in the United States over matters of propaganda can stimulate the dialectical imagination of American critics as they confront these and other issues of the media age.

REFERENCES

Abrams, R. H. (1933). *Preachers present arms.* New York: Round Table.

Adorno, T. W., Frenkel-Brunswick, E., Levinson, D. J., & Sanford, R. N. (1950). *The authoritarian personality.* New York: Harper Brothers.

Albig, W. (1957). Two decades of opinion study: 1936-1956. *Public Opinion Quarterly, 21,* 14-22.

Althusser, L. (1971). *Lenin and philosophy and other essays.* New York: Monthly Review Press.

Anderson, H. R. (Ed.). (1942). *Teaching critical thinking in the social studies.* Washington, DC: National Council for the Social Studies.

Angoff, C. (1927). The higher learning goes to war. *American Mercury, 11,* 177-191.

Bagdikian, B. H. (1983). *The media monopoly.* Boston: Beacon.

Baker, R. S. (1906). How railroads make public opinion. *McClure's Magazine, 26,* 535-549.

Beard, C. A. (1919). Propaganda in the schools. *Dial, 66,* 598-599.

Bennett, W. H. (1984). To reclaim a legacy. *Chronicle of Higher Education, 29*(14), 1, 6-21.

Berelson, B. (1952). *Content analysis in communication research.* Glencoe, IL: Free Press.

Bernays, E. L. (1923). *Crystallizing public opinion.* New York: Boni & Liveright.

Bernays, E. L. (1928). *Propaganda.* New York: Liveright.

Biddle, W. W. (1932). *Propaganda and education.* New York: Teachers College, Columbia University.

Bineham, J. L. (1988). A historical account of the hypodermic model in mass communication. *Communication Monographs, 55,* 230-246.

Black, M. (1952). *Critical thinking* (2nd ed.). New York: Prentice-Hall.

Blankenhorn, H. (1919). *Adventures in propaganda.* Boston: Houghton Mifflin.

Bloom, A. (1987). *The closing of the American mind.* New York: Simon & Schuster.

Blumer, H. (1939). Collective behavior. In R. E. Park (Ed.), *An outline of the principles of sociology* (pp. 219-280). New York: Barnes & Noble.

Blumer, H. (1969). *Symbolic interactionism: Perspective and method.* Englewood Cliffs, NJ: Prentice-Hall.

Blumer, H. (1970). *Movies and conduct.* New York: Arno. (Original work published 1933)

Boorstin, D. (1973). *The Americans: The democratic experience.* New York: Random House.

Bramson, L. (1961). *The political context of sociology.* Princeton, NJ: Princeton University Press.

Bruntz, G. C. (1930). Propaganda as an instrument of war. *Current History, 32,* 743-747.

Buckley, W. F. (1951). *God and man at Yale.* Chicago: Regnery.

Bulmer, M. (1984). *The Chicago school of sociology.* Chicago: University of Chicago Press.

Cantril, H. (1940). *The invasion from Mars.* New York: Harper.

Cantril, H. (1944). *Gauging public opinion.* Princeton, NJ: Princeton University Press.

Cantril, H. (1967). *The human dimension.* Princeton, NJ: Princeton University Press.

Casey, R. D. (1939). The national publicity bureau and British party propaganda. *Public Opinion Quarterly, 3,* 623-634.

Cattell, J. M. (1923, November). The psychological corporation. *Annals of the American Academy of Political and Social Science, 110,* 165-171.

Childs, H. L. (1934). *A reference guide to the study of public opinion.* Princeton, NJ: Princeton University Press.

Chomsky, N., & Herman, E. S. (1979). *After the cataclysm.* Boston: South End.

Clarke, E. L. (1929). *The art of straight thinking.* New York: Appleton.

Commission of Inquiry of the Interchurch World Movement. (1920). *Public opinion and the steel strike.* New York: Harcourt, Brace.

Commission of Inquiry of the Interchurch World Movement. (1921). *Report on the steel strike of 1919.* New York: Harcourt, Brace.

Cooley, C. H. (1909). *Social organization.* New York: Charles Scribner's Sons.

Craig, H. N. (1954). *Distinctive features of radio-TV in the 1952 presidential campaign.* Unpublished master's thesis, State University of Iowa, Iowa City.

Creel, G. (1972). *How we advertised America.* New York: Arno. (Original work published 1920)

Creel, G. (1941). Propaganda and morale. *American Journal of Sociology, 47,* 340-351.

Cremin, L. A. (1961). *The transformation of the school.* New York: Knopf.

Crossley, A. M. (1957). Early days of public opinion research. *Public Opinion Quarterly, 21,* 159-164.

Crouse, T. (1973). *The boys on the bus: Riding with the campaign press corps.* New York: Ballantine.

Czitrom, D. J. (1982). *Media and the American mind from Morse to McLuhan.* Chapel Hill: University of North Carolina Press.

Dale, E. (1935a). *The content of motion pictures.* New York: Macmillan.

Dale, E. (1935b). *Children's attendance at motion pictures.* New York: Macmillan.

Dale, E. (1941). *How to read a newspaper.* Chicago: Scott, Foresman.

DeFleur, M. L., & Ball-Rokeach, S. (1982). *Theories of mass communication* (4th ed.). New York: Longman.

Delia, J. G. (1987). Communication research: A history. In C. R. Berger & S. H. Chaffee (Eds.), *Handbook of communication science* (pp. 20-98). Newbury Park, CA: Sage.

Dewey, J. (1903). *Studies in logical theory.* Chicago: University of Chicago Press.

Dewey, J. (1910). *How we think.* Boston: D. C. Heath.

Dewey, J. (1953). *Essays in experimental logic.* New York: Dover. (Original work published 1916)

Dies, M. (1940). *The Trojan horse in America.* New York: Dodd, Mead.

Dies scrutinizes propaganda study. (1941, February 23). *New York Times,* pp. 1, 21.

Dinsmore, H. H. (1969). *All the news that fits.* New Rochelle, NY: Arlington House.

Dodge, R. (1920). The psychology of propaganda. *Religious Education, 15,* 241-252.

Doob, L. W. (1935). *Propaganda: Its psychology and technique.* New York: Henry Holt.

Edwards, V. (1938). *Group leader's guide to propaganda analysis.* New York: Institute for Propaganda Analysis.

Efron, E. (1971). *The news twisters.* Los Angeles: Nash.

Ellis, E. (Ed.). (1937). *Education against propaganda.* Washington, DC: National Council for the Social Studies.

Emery, E. (1972). *The press in America* (3rd ed.). Englewood Cliffs, NJ: Prentice-Hall.

Engelbrecht, H. C., & Hanighen, F. C. (1934). *Merchants of death: A study of the international armament industry.* New York: Dodd, Mead.

Ewen, S. (1976). *Captains of consciousness.* New York: McGraw-Hill.

Faris, R. E. L. (1967). *Chicago sociology, 1920-1932.* Chicago: University of Chicago Press.

Femia, J. V. (1981). *Gramsci's political thought.* Oxford: Clarendon.

Fine, B. (1941, February 21). Propaganda study instills skepticism in 1,000,000 pupils. *New York Times,* pp. 1, 14.

Flowerman, S. H. (1947). Mass propaganda in the war against bigotry. *Journal of Abnormal and Social Psychology, 42,* 429-439.

Gallup, G. (Ed.). (1972). *The Gallup poll: Public opinion, 1935-1971* (Vols. 1-3). New York: Random House.

Gallup, G., & Rae, S. (1940). *The pulse of democracy.* New York: Simon & Schuster.

Gans, H. J. (1979). *Deciding what's news.* New York: Vintage.

Garber, W. (1942). Propaganda analysis—to what ends? *American Journal of Sociology, 48,* 240-245.

Gerbner, G. (Ed.). (1983). Ferment in the field [Special issue]. *Journal of Communication, 33*(3).

Gibbs, P. (1920). *Now it can be told.* New York: Harper.

Gibbs, P. (1921). *More that must be told.* New York: Harper.

Ginsberg, B. (1986). *The captive public.* New York: Basic.

Gitlin, T. (1980). *The whole world is watching: Mass media in the making and unmaking of the new left.* Berkeley: University of California Press.

Gitlin, T. (1981). Media sociology: The dominant paradigm. In G. C. Wilhoit & H. DeBock (Eds.), *Mass communication review yearbook* (Vol. 2, pp. 73-121). Beverly Hills, CA: Sage.

Gitlin, T. (1985). *Inside prime time.* New York: Pantheon.

Glaser, E. M. (1941). *An experiment in the development of critical thinking.* New York: Teachers College, Columbia University.

Grattan, C. H. (1927). The historians cut loose. *American Mercury, 11,* 414-430.

Graves, H. F. (1941). Public speaking in propaganda. *Quarterly Journal of Speech, 27,* 29-38.

Grenier, J. (1972). Upton Sinclair and the press: *The brass check* reconsidered. *Journalism Quarterly, 49,* 427-436.

Hall, S. (1982). The rediscovery of "ideology": Return of the repressed in media studies. In M. Gurevitch, T. Bennett, J. Curran, & J. Woollacott (Eds.), *Culture, society and the media* (pp. 56-90). London: Methuen.

Hardt, H. (1989). The return of the "critical" and the challenge of radical dissent: Critical theory, cultural studies, and American mass communication research. In J. A. Anderson (Ed.), *Communication yearbook 12* (pp. 558-600). Newbury Park, CA: Sage.

Hayakawa, S. I. (1939). General semantics and propaganda. *Public Opinion Quarterly, 3* 197-208.

Held, D. (1980). *Introduction to critical theory.* Berkeley: University of California Press.

Hicks, G. (1927). The parsons and the war. *American Mercury, 10*, 129-142.

Hiebert, R. E. (1966). *Courtier to the crowd: The story of Ivy Lee and the development of public relations.* Ames: Iowa State University Press.

Hodder, F. H. (1922). Propaganda as a source of American history. *Mississippi Valley Historical Review, 9*, 1-18.

Hofstadter, R. (1955). *The age of reform.* New York: Vintage.

Horkheimer, M., & Adorno, T. W. (1972). *Dialectic of enlightenment.* New York: Continuum. (Original work published 1944)

Hosterman, C. A. (1981). Teaching propaganda. *Communication Education, 30*, 156-162.

Hovland, C. I. (1957). *The order of presentation in persuasion.* New Haven, CT: Yale University Press.

Hovland, C. I., Janis, I. L., & Kelley, H. H. (1953). *Communication and persuasion.* New Haven, CT: Yale University Press.

Hovland, C. I., Lumsdaine, A. A., & Sheffield, F. D. (1949). *Experiments on mass communication.* Princeton, NJ: Princeton University Press.

How Germany has worked in U.S. to shape opinion, block the Allies and get munitions for herself, told in secret agents' letters. (1915, August 15). *New York World*, pp. 1-3.

Hurwitz, D. L. (1983). *Broadcast ratings.* Unpublished doctoral dissertation, University of Illinois, Urbana-Champaign.

Innis, H. A. (1951). *The bias of communication.* Toronto: University of Toronto Press.

Irwin, W. H. (1919, December). An age of lies. *Sunset, 43*, 23-25, 54, 56.

Irwin, W. H. (c. 1937). *Let's not be suckers again.* Typescript, Box 1, Irwin Papers, Hoover Institution Archives.

Irwin, W. H. (1969). *The American newspaper.* Ames: Iowa State University Press. (Original work published 1911)

Janis, I. L., & Hovland, C. I. (1959). *Personality and persuasibility.* New Haven, CT: Yale University Press.

Jay, M. (1973). *The dialectical imagination.* Boston: Little, Brown.

Jewett, A. (1940). Detecting and analyzing propaganda. *English Journal, 29*, 105-115.

Johnson, A. (1939). Propaganda analysis and public speaking. *Southern Speech Bulletin, 4*(3), 12-15.

Jowett, G. S. (1987). Propaganda and communication: The re-emergence of a research tradition. *Journal of Communication, 37*(1), 97-114.

Jowett, G. S., & O'Donnell, V. (1986). *Propaganda and persuasion.* Newbury Park, CA: Sage.

Kahane, H. (1971). *Logic and contemporary rhetoric.* Belmont, CA: Wadsworth.

Katz, D., Cartwright, D., Eldersveld, S, & Lee, A. M. (Eds.). (1954). *Public opinion and propaganda.* New York: Dryden.

Katz, E., & Lazarsfeld, P. F. (1955). *Personal influence.* New York: Free Press.

Kilpatrick, W. H. (1939). Propaganda, democracy, and education. *School and Society, 49*, 405-409.

Klapper, J. T., & Glock, C. Y. (1954). Trial by newspaper. In D. Katz, D. Cartwright, S. Eldersveld, & A. M. Lee (Eds.), *Public opinion and propaganda* (pp. 16-21). New York: Dryden. (Original work published 1949)

Larrabee, H. A. (1920). The formation of public opinion through motion pictures. *Religious Education, 15*, 144-154.

Lasswell, H. D. (1927). The theory of political propaganda. *American Political Science Review, 21*, 627-631.

Lasswell, H. D. (1933). Propaganda. *Encyclopaedia of the Social Sciences, 12*, 521-528.

Lasswell, H. D. (1951a). The policy orientation. In D. Lerner & H. D. Lasswell (Eds.), *The policy sciences: Recent developments in scope and method* (pp. 3-15). Stanford, CA: Stanford University Press.

Lasswell, H. D. (1951b, October 23). [Affidavit]. Army-Navy-Air Force personnel security board file, Lasswell Papers, Manuscripts and Archives Division, Yale University Library.

Lasswell, H. D. (1971). *Propaganda technique in World War I.* Cambridge: MIT Press. (Original work published 1927)

Lasswell, H. D., & Blumenstock, D. (1939). *World revolutionary propaganda.* New York: Knopf.

Lasswell, H. D., Casey, R. D., & Smith, B. L. (Eds.). (1935). *Propaganda and promotional activities: An annotated bibliography.* Minneapolis: University of Minnesota Press.
Lasswell, H. D., & Leites, N. (1949). *Language of politics.* Cambridge: MIT Press.
Lazarsfeld, P. F. (1939). Radio research and applied psychology. *Journal of Applied Psychology, 23,* 1-7.
Lazarsfeld, P. F. (Ed.). (1940). Progress in radio research [Special issue]. *Journal of Applied Psychology, 24,* 661-859.
Lazarsfeld, P. F. (1941). Remarks on administrative and critical research. *Studies in Philosophy and Social Sciences, 9,* 2-16.
Lazarsfeld, P. F. (1947). Some remarks on the role of mass media in so-called tolerance propaganda. *Journal of Social Issues, 3*(3), 17-25.
Lazarsfeld, P. F. (c. 1954). [Memorandum]. File 002/8, Series 1, Box 2, Lazarsfeld Papers, Rare Book and Manuscript Library, Columbia University.
Lazarsfeld, P. F., Berelson, B., & Gaudet, B. (1968). *The people's choice* (3rd ed.). New York: Columbia University Press. (Original work published 1944)
Lazarsfeld, P. F., & Merton, R. K. (1943). Studies in radio and film propaganda. *Transactions of the New York Academy of Sciences, 6,* 58-79.
Lazarsfeld, P. F., & Stanton, F. N. (1944). *Radio research: 1942-1943.* New York: Duell, Sloan & Pearce.
Lee, A. M. (1949, September). Review of *The American soldier* (2 vols.). *Annals of the American Academy of Political and Social Science, 265,* 173-175.
Lee, A. M. (1952). *How to understand propaganda.* New York: Rinehart.
Lee, A. M. (1973). *The daily newspaper in America: Evolution of a social instrument.* New York: Octagon. (Original work published 1937)
Lee, E. B., & Lee, A. M. (1979). The fine art of propaganda analysis—then and now. *Etc., 36,* 117-127.
Lee, I. L. (1925). *Publicity.* New York: Industries.
Lefever, E. W. (1974). *TV and national defense.* Boston, VA: Institute for American Strategy.
Lerner, D. (1950). The *American soldier* and the public. In R. K. Merton & P. F. Lazarsfeld (Eds.), *Continuities in social research* (pp. 212-247). Glencoe, IL: Free Press.
Lerner, M. (1941). *Ideas for the ice age.* New York: Viking.
Lerner, M. (1943). *It is later than you think* (2nd ed.). New York: Viking.
Likert, R. (1936). A method for measuring the sales influence of a radio program. *Journal of Applied Psychology, 20,* 175-182.
Lippmann, W. (1919a). The basic problem of democracy, I. *Atlantic Monthly, 124,* 616-627.
Lippmann, W. (1919b). Liberty and the news. *Atlantic Monthly, 124,* 779-787.
Lippmann, W. (1922). *Public opinion.* New York: Macmillan.
Lippmann, W., & Merz, C. (1920, August 4). A test of the news. *New Republic, 23*(Suppl.), 1-42.
Lowenthal, L., & Guterman, N. (1970). *Prophets of deceit* (2nd ed.). Palo Alto, CA: Pacific. (Original work published 1949)
Lowery, S., & DeFleur, M. L. (1983). *Milestones in mass communication research.* New York: Longman.
Lumley, F. E. (1929). The nature of propaganda. *Sociology and Social Research, 13,* 315-324.
Lumley, F. E. (1933). *The propaganda menace.* New York: Century.
Lynd, R. S. (1949). The science of inhuman relations [Review of *The American soldier*, Vols. 1-2, and *Experiments on mass communication*]. *New Republic, 121*(9), 22-25.
MacDonald, J. F. (1985). *Television and the red menace.* New York: Praeger.
Martin, E. D. (1920). *The behavior of crowds.* New York: Harper & Row.
Martin, H. H. (1966). The rhetoric of academic protest. *Central States Speech Journal, 17,* 244-250.
McAndrew, W. (1930, July 19). French wine-growers and American school children. *School and Society, 32,* 96-97.
McGinniss, J. (1969). *The selling of the president 1968.* New York: Trident.
McKerrow, R. E. (1983). Marxism and a rhetorical conception of ideology. *Quarterly Journal of Speech, 69,* 192-205.

Mead, G. H. (1934). *Mind, self and society.* Chicago: University of Chicago Press.

Merriam, C. E. (1919). American publicity in Italy. *American Political Science Review, 13,* 541-555.

Merriam, C. E. (1934). *Political power: Its composition and incidence.* New York: Whittlesey.

Mills, C. W. (1959). *The sociological imagination.* New York: Oxford University Press.

Mock, J. R., & Larson, C. (1939). *Words that won the war.* Princeton, NJ: Princeton University Press.

Mumford, L. (1946). *Values for survival.* New York: Harcourt, Brace.

National Education Association. (1929). *Report of the committee on propaganda in the schools.* Washington, DC: Author.

Nickerson, R. S., Perkins, D. N., & Smith, E. E. (1985). *The teaching of thinking.* Hillsdale, NJ: Lawrence Erlbaum.

Odegard, P. (1928). *Pressure politics: The story of the Anti-Saloon League.* New York: Columbia University Press.

Odegard, P. (1930). *The American public mind.* New York: Columbia University Press.

Ogilvy, D. O. (1987). *Confessions of an advertising man.* London: Pan.

Osborn, W. W. (1939). An experiment in teaching resistance to propaganda. *Journal of Experimental Education, 8,* 1-17.

Packard, V. (1957). *The hidden persuaders.* New York: McKay.

Parekh, B. (1982). *Marx's theory of ideology.* Baltimore: Johns Hopkins University Press.

Park, R. E. (1972). *The crowd and the public and other essays.* Chicago: University of Chicago Press. (Original work published 1904)

Ponsonby, A. (1928). *Falsehood in war-time.* New York: E. P. Dutton.

Postman, N. (1985). *Amusing ourselves to death: Public discourse in the age of show business.* New York: Viking.

President's Research Committee on Social Trends. (1933). *Recent social trends in the United States* (Vols. 1-3). New York: McGraw-Hill.

Rank, H. (Ed.). (1974). *Language and public policy.* Urbana, IL: National Council of Teachers of English.

Rank, H. (1982). *The pitch.* Park Forest, IL: Counter-Propaganda Press.

Rank, H. (1984). *The pep talk.* Park Forest, IL: Counter-Propaganda Press.

Real, M. R. (1986). Demythologizing media: Recent writings in critical and institutional theory. *Critical Studies in Mass Communication, 3,* 459-486.

Remmers, H. H. (1938). Propaganda in the schools: Do the effects last? *Public Opinion Quarterly, 2,* 197-210.

Robinson, G. J. (1988). "Here be dragons": Problems in charting the U.S. history of communication studies. *Communication, 10,* 97-119.

Rogers, E. M. (1983). *Diffusion of innovations* (3rd ed.). New York: Free Press. (Original work published 1962)

Rosenthal, B. (1939). Teaching the recognition of propaganda in the social studies classroom. *Social Studies, 30,* 268-272.

Ross, D. K. (1973). *A public citizen's action manual.* New York: Grossman.

Schiller, H. I. (1973). *The mind managers.* Boston: Beacon.

Schlafly, P. (1964). *A choice not an echo.* Alton, IL: Pere Marquette.

Schramm, W. (1971). The nature of communication between humans. In W. Schramm & D. R. Roberts (Eds.), *The process and effects of mass communication* (pp. 3-53). Urbana: University of Illinois Press.

Schudson, M. (1978). *Discovering the news.* New York: Basic Books.

Schudson, M. (1984). *Advertising, the uneasy persuasion.* New York: Basic Books.

Seldes, George (1929). *You can't print that!* Garden City, NY: Garden City.

Seldes, George (1938). *Lords of the press.* New York: Julian Messner.

Seldes, Gilbert (1970). *The great audience.* Westport, CT: Greenwood. (Original work published 1950)

Seligman, E. R. A. (1930). Propaganda by public utility corporations. *Bulletin of the American Association of University Professors, 16,* 349-368.

Sinclair, U. (1919). *The brass check: A study of American journalism.* Pasadena, CA: Author.

Smith, B. L. (1941). Propaganda analysis and the science of democracy. *Public Opinion Quarterly, 5,* 250-259.

Sproule, J. M. (1985). Clyde Miller: Twentieth century pioneer of free speech. *Free Speech Yearbook, 24,* 27-37.

Sproule, J. M. (1987a). Propaganda studies in American social science: The rise and fall of the critical paradigm. *Quarterly Journal of Speech, 73,* 60-78.

Sproule, J. M. (1987b). Whose ethics in the classroom? An historical survey. *Communication Education, 36,* 317-326.

Sproule, J. M. (1987c). Ideology and critical thinking: The historical connection. *Journal of the American Forensic Association, 24,* 4-15.

Sproule, J. M. (1987d). Review of *Propaganda and communication,* by G. S. Jowett and V. O'Donnell. *Quarterly Journal of Speech, 73,* 517-520.

Sproule, J. M. (1989). Progressive propaganda critics and the magic bullet myth. *Critical Studies in Mass Communication, 6,* 225-246.

Squires, J. D. (1935). *British propaganda at home and in the United States from 1914 to 1917.* Cambridge, MA: Harvard University Press.

Stormer, J. A. (1964). *None dare call it treason.* Florissant, MO: Liberty Bell.

Stouffer, S. A., Suchman, E. A., DeVinney, L. C., Star, S. A., & Williams, R. M. (1949). *The American soldier* (Vols. 1-2). Princeton, NJ: Princeton University Press.

Talbot, S. W. (1944). Propaganda analysis in high school. *Sociology and Social Research, 28,* 290-295.

Thouless, R. H. (1932). *Straight and crooked thinking.* New York: Simon & Schuster.

Thurstone, L. L. (1931). Influence of motion pictures on children's attitudes. *Journal of Social Psychology, 2,* 291-305.

U.S. House of Representatives. (1938). *Investigation of un-American propaganda activities in the United States* (Vols. 1-17). Washington, DC: Government Printing Office.

U.S. House of Representatives. (1947). *Hearings regarding communist infiltration of the motion picture industry.* Washington, DC: Government Printing Office.

Vaughn, S. L. (1980). *Holding fast the inner lines.* Chapel Hill: University of North Carolina Press.

Veysey, L. R. (1965). *The emergence of the American university.* Chicago: University of Chicago Press.

Viereck, G. S. (1930). *Spreading germs of hate.* New York: Liveright.

Weaver, R. M. (1953). *The ethics of rhetoric.* Chicago: Regnery.

Wise, D. (1973). *The politics of lying.* New York: Vintage.

Wohlforth, R. (1930). Catch 'em young—learn 'em rough. *New Republic, 64,* 257-258.

Propaganda Critique:
The Forgotten History of
American Communication Studies

GARTH S. JOWETT
University of Houston

ICHAEL Sproule's articulate reminder of the significance of propaganda studies as an important part of our intellectual heritage in the twentieth century could not have come at a more opportune moment. A close reading of this essay and the other important perspectives that he has provided us in the last two years opens up an important new debate about the past, present, and future of the field of communication studies in the United States (Sproule, 1989). In the last decade, we have witnessed a bewildering shift in the dominant methodologies (paradigms) of communication studies in American universities. Where only a decade ago there was almost complete domination by a largely statistically based empiricism, in the decade of the 1980s new, humanistically based methodologies emerged to provide a serious challenge to this hegemony. Whether they be called "critical inquiry," "cultural studies," or the host of other names under which these new modes of analysis go, they have already had an observable impact on the literature of the field, and are the subject of intense debate at academic conferences. The proponents of the "critical" approach, as well as some of its detractors, feel that it is only a matter of time before critical studies achieves an equal status with the statistically based empiricism. In fact, critical studies' strongest supporters have as their stated aim the displacement of so-called objective empirical research from its lofty perch by a more socially and politically aware hybrid combination of empiricism and critical research (Grossberg, 1987).

In the wake of this intense "ferment in the field" (Gerbner, 1983), there has been a renewed search for the intellectual wellsprings of communication research. But tracing this elusive history has proven to be much more than merely an intellectual exercise, for the task has become both complex and contentious. What started out

Correspondence and requests for reprints: Garth S. Jowett, Department of Communication, University of Houston, Houston, TX 77204-3786.

Communication Yearbook 14, pp. 239-248

as a means of examining "how we got to where we are" has, in fact, turned out to be an ongoing reassessment and reevaluation of the various "explanations" of the history of mass communication research in twentieth-century scholarship. It now appears that there are several "histories" of the subject, depending on which particular current ideological position is read back into the past. Not even the "events" that would constitute such a history are agreed upon, as diffuse schools of thought and specific lines of inquiry vie for inclusion in the basic narrative. We are currently witnessing the gradual reconstitution of a more accurate, more inclusive history of the field. As a specific example, there is now an attempt to redress the harm done by those post-World War II scholars who devised the mythology of the "magic bullet theories" as a means of collectively describing the prevailing notions of mass media influence in the period before 1939 (Delia, 1987; Sproule, 1989). It has now been quite clearly established that postwar mass communications research gathered much of its own empiricist strength by deliberately juxtaposing itself to the straw man of the magic bullet or direct influence theories of previous decades. One unfortunate result of this selective interpretation of history was to relegate all previous (nonempirical) communications research into some sort of subjective limbo reserved for social or political commentary, rather than to see it as a serious early form of cultural analysis.

The relatively sudden emergence of the mass media as a major factor in the shaping of both society and its culture in the period between 1890 and 1930 caught many people off guard. In particular, the widespread practice of propaganda during World War I demonstrated that in the hands of skillful practitioners these new media, commanding as they did audiences of millions, could become powerful instruments for molding public opinion. While the role of the war as a factor in the history of mass communications research has sometimes been misinterpreted (especially when used to justify the existence of the magic bullet theory as the means by which contemporary scholars explained the success of propaganda efforts), it was nonetheless a watershed in making the social critics, as well as the general public, aware of the inherent power these media forms were capable of exerting. In response to these emerging social and cultural forces, a variety of critiques were developed in the first 40 years of this century, most of which were forgotten or ignored after they were swept away in the rise to prominence of empirical research after 1939. It was this vacuum, created by the banishing of these culturally based evaluations of the role and function of mass media within the unique American societal context, that a new generation of scholars would attempt to fill by using a variety of Marxist-based theoretical perspectives, many of which are wholly inappropriate for the task within the context of U.S. society.

Michael Sproule has made a major contribution to this ongoing debate by his reconstitution of a largely ignored, but very important, intellectual perspective, which he calls "progressive propaganda critique." He makes a strong case for considering this approach as one of the dominant cultural critiques of mass communication in the period before 1939, and one that once played a significant role in shaping public attitudes toward the media. There was a range of progressive propaganda critiques, encompassing as they did examinations of the potential power of the emerging media to influence news, entertainment, education, politics, and religion. By carefully examining the nature of these critiques and responses, Sproule is clearly able to demonstrate that the work of these early propaganda analysts, and their important role in the history of mass communications research, has been unjustly relegated to the fringes of communication research and critical theory.

Explicit in Sproule's work has been the underscoring of the fundamental and profound differences between European-based Marxist critiques of media and culture and the indigenous progressive propaganda critiques. The Marxist theories take as their central theme the relationship between the state and ideological control through a variety of agencies, including the mass media. In classical Marxist theoretical terms, the media are seen as a means of production (of ideas) that conforms to the capitalist industrial system, including ownership by a monopolistic capitalist class, that is also nationally or internationally organized to serve the interests of that class. Thus the media disseminate the ideas and worldviews of this ruling class, while at the same time preventing the creation of alternative ideas that could lead to the formation of new consciousness and eventually organized opposition. This notion of the media as a "tool of capitalism," with some variation, is the philosophical underpinning for all Marxist theories of media and culture. While the terrain of debate on Marxist philosophy had shifted considerably by the 1970s, especially in the work of Althusser and Gramsci, Sproule notes that "the tendency of Marxist criticism is to treat class and state as central in the direction of ideological apparatuses" (p. 212).

The American progressives in their propaganda critiques paid very little attention to the role of the state or its agencies. They focused firmly on the implications that the new media of information and entertainment had for the continued success of the American democratic system. Their prime concern was whether or not the democratic process could be subverted by the misuse of the inherent power of the media. Because their experience with the persuasive capabilities of these new media was relatively limited, the progressives were reticent about granting free rein to such an unknown quantity, choosing instead to be more cautious in their interpretation of the First Amendment, especially as it applied to the entertainment function of the media. Not only was there a long history of the social control of entertainment to act as a precedent, but the power to educate through the guise of entertainment had been widely understood for centuries (Jowett, Reath, & Schouten, 1976).

PROGRESSIVE PROPAGANDA CRITIQUE IN ACTION:
THE MOTION PICTURE AS A CASE STUDY

Nowhere was this caution about the inherent powers of the new media more obvious than in the progressives' attitudes and actions toward the introduction of the motion picture. The movies had no sooner been exhibited in their penny-arcade form in 1894 than they were subjected to censorship and legal restraint. The first recorded court case involving a movie was *People v. Doris* in 1897 (Randall, 1968). Almost from their first appearance, movies were subjected to the intense scrutiny of social workers, teachers, and members of the clergy, as well as those interested in the welfare of children or the general moral state of the public. These were the "progressives," that group historian Robert Wiebe (1967) notes would "form the bulwark of those men and women who dedicated themselves to replacing the decaying system of the nineteenth century" (p. 129). It is ironic that while their training and urban orientation provided them with the insight to recognize that the old ways and old values could no longer meet the demands of the emerging urbanized society, they forged their urban ideals in the crucible of the traditional rural-based value system. While the progressives were concerned about the development of viable urban bureaucracies, they also indicated a concern for the individual that tended to resonate those Protestant values found in villages and small towns. For this reason, anything that suggested a potential threat to the democratic ideals that had become an integral part of the American experience was of concern.

The progressives also placed a great deal of faith in "science" and the use of rational scientific reasoning as a means of solving society's problems. In particular, the emerging social sciences of psychology and sociology were lauded because they offered a greater understanding of the behavior of humankind both individually and as a collectivity, while the study of economics and political science would assist in the formation of an orderly and systematic infrastructure for society. Educational theory also became more scientific in approach, and this resulted in a major reorientation of the American school system toward a pragmatic form of "learning by doing," which adapted the subject matter to the everyday world and the needs of the child. The school was now perceived as never before as a lever of social change, and the educator as a social reformer (Cremin, 1964). Because of the difficulty in legislating against the introduction of technology, the school also became the ideal place to give instruction on how to cope with significant cultural changes that resulted from such innovations. As Sproule indicates throughout his essay, the school was seen by the progressives as an important site for combating the problems associated with the potential threat of media propaganda, and the centrality of education and the school within the progressives' ideology helped to shape subsequent attitudes toward the movies. Once it became obvious that these seemingly innocuous diversions could inform as well as entertain, educators took a vital interest in the issue of "the evils of the movies." By 1910, the motion picture proved itself to be a potent competitor to the formal instruction of the classroom, and many a teacher was heard to complain about the unfair nature of the competition (Jowett, 1976, pp. 91-94).

Why all this fuss about the motion picture? Surely there were other more pressing issues in society, and certainly there were more obvious vices that deserved the attention of the reformers and social workers. In fact, a great deal of attention was devoted to child labor, prostitution, public health, and housing conditions, but the time and amount of energy devoted to examining the movies appears to be anomalous in comparison. Sproule's contention that the progressives were afraid that "the emerging communications industry threatened democracy by giving private institutions and interest groups a new ability to mold minds before the public could formulate and articulate its will" helps to provide an answer (p. 216). The movies, because of their enormous popularity (especially for young audiences) and immediate public visibility, were potent symbols of the increasing loss of control being experienced by the progressives over the socialization of the population in general and the child in particular. As a form of communication, the motion picture established direct contact with its audience, at least a third of which was under the age of 16, thereby circumventing the traditional socializing role of the home, church, and school in imparting information. Alarmed reports filtering back about children learning crime and sex techniques directly from the movies confirmed the fears that film and other outside agencies were threatening to replace these bastions of the democratic system. At the very least, they represented an uncontrolled force that could disrupt and subvert the flow of information so necessary in a democratic society.

By 1915 it was obvious that the motion picture was not a passing fad, so to minimize any harmful impact while it was still being evaluated (and potentially co-opted for more "positive" purposes), it had to be neutralized. This move resulted in a philosophical split in progressive ranks concerning the merits of legalized censorship versus industry self-regulation, but the conservative progressive element eventually triumphed and the end result was the infamous Supreme Court decision, *Mutual Film Corporation v. Industrial Commission of Ohio* (Jowett, 1989). In this case, involving the refusal of the Mutual company to submit films for approval prior to exhibition in the state of Ohio, the Supreme Court unanimously ruled that motion pictures could be legally censored. The Court refused to consider the defendant's claims that motion pictures should be considered under the protection of the First Amendment. Why was this so? The answer lies in Justice McKenna's description of motion pictures, for despite their educational and entertainment value, motion pictures were to be treated differently because

> they may be used for evil, and against that possibility the statute was enacted. Their power of amusement and, it may be, education, the audiences they assemble, not of women alone or men alone, but together, not of adults only, but of children, make them more insidious in corruption by a pretense of worthy purpose or if they should degenerate from worthy purpose. . . . We would have to shut our eyes to the facts of the world to regard the precaution unreasonable or the legislation to effect it a mere wanton interference with personal liberty. (*Mutual*, 1915, p. 242)

In trying to gauge what was on the minds of the justices as they considered what to do with this new information medium, there was little doubt that they were unwilling to leave the general public unprotected from what they saw as a powerful, unregulated social force. It is here that a clear articulation of the progressive propaganda critique is seen. Also, the court recognized that the movies were different from the other mass media, especially because of their wide popular appeal. The implications of this popularity clearly disturbed them. The telling phrase was Justice McKenna's declaration that

> it cannot be put out of view that the exhibition of moving pictures is a business pure and simple, originated and conducted for profit, like other spectacles, not to be regarded, nor intended to be regarded by the Ohio constitution, we think, as part of the press of the country or as organs of public opinion. They are mere representations of events, of ideas and sentiments published and known, vivid, useful and entertaining no doubt, but, as we have said, capable of evil, having power for it, the greater because of the attractiveness and manner of exhibition. (*Mutual*, 1915, p. 244)

Thus the movies were capable of disseminating ideas, but the fear of the court was that they *could* be used for "evil" purposes by those seeking merely to make a profit, and that this danger was only increased by the enormous inherent attraction the medium held for the public, especially those classes that were more susceptible to outside influences, and therefore needed to be protected.

What the 1915 *Mutual* decision symbolizes is the fear that many progressives, and others in the community representing more traditional concerns for morality, felt about the increasing role of the mass media as potential sources of "uncontrolled" social and cultural information. John Collier (1915), the secretary of the National Board of Censorship, a group set up to provide self-regulatory advice to the film industry, was one of the few individuals astute enough to realize what the motion picture really symbolized for the reformers. He pointed out:

> It is clear that the court was swayed by what it believed about public opinion and public necessity; that its grounds for decision were psychological, not primarily legal, and were the consequences of its lack of first-hand experience with motion pictures. (p. 516)

It should be made clear that the philosophies of the progressive propaganda critics did not necessarily encourage the imposition of legal censorship of the media. However, in this particular case, the enormous inherent appeal of the movies for all segments of the population had literally caught them off guard, and the *Mutual* decision was a necessarily harsh and quick remedy while the realities of "movie influence" were examined more objectively. Unfortunately, such objective and scientific evaluations were never really undertaken, and the more zealous reformers seized upon the legality of censorship to impose their will and values on the motion picture industry for more than 50 years.

The Supreme Court can be faulted for this decision on several legal issues (Jowett, 1989), but the end result was that between 1915 and 1952 the motion picture was subjected to a range of legalized prior censorship, the only time in the history of this country that such wide sanctions were imposed on one mass medium. In 1952 the courts began a series of decisions that gradually removed all the legal reasons for film censorship by the late 1960s. Today only the vague threat of "obscenity" remains as grounds for censorship, and then only after the actual exhibition of the film.

PROGRESSIVE PROPAGANDA CRITIQUE
AND THE AMERICAN CULTURAL CONTEXT

The most provocative aspect of Sproule's essay lies in his suggestion that by reviving the tradition represented by the progressive propaganda critics we could develop a more historically valid conceptualization of the role of the media in American society. He points out that "the idea that social influence proceeds by means of large economic classes employing stable ideological apparatuses is not consistent with fundamental American experience" (p. 232). He has every right to be concerned about the somewhat uncritical way in which American scholars have turned to Marxist theories instead of seeking explanations that are more in keeping with the unique aspects of American society and culture. Sometimes, when attempts are made to apply Marxist-based theories to American situations, there is an instinctive reaction that these simply do not pertain to the American ideological experience. The key Marxist questions surrounding the concepts of hegemony and ideology that have dominated European thought often seem to have a forced quality within the American context. Sometimes the basic structure of the society is so fundamentally different as to render such applications impossible. (I am thinking in particular of the difficulties in trying to apply the much-vaunted work of David Morley, 1980, on television and the British family to the American family structure, with its multi-television set households and myriad channels. Clearly any discussion of the "empowerment" surrounding television viewing in this case must take these fundamental differences into account. Unfortunately, this accounting has seldom been the case.) One is also forced to ask whether much of the tortuous prose associated with critical theory is not the result of trying to make these theories "fit" into spaces they are clearly not designed for.

What Sproule's work does is to point out the importance of understanding the ideological implications of media practices and audience reactions within the indigenous sociocultural context. It is for this reason that not only the study of the history of the mass media and mass media research is so necessary, but also the intensive historical examination of the range of public reactions to the media. It is, after all, these articulated reactions that ultimately gave shape to the discourse about the role and function of the media in our society. It was these reactions, rather than objective scientific measurement, that provided the platform for the construction of the regulatory infrastructure that governs our media practices. Also, from the point of view of intellectual history, the examination and evaluation of these reactions will provide ample evidence to substantiate the philosophical differences between European concerns for the media and those found in the United States.

As an example, when European scholars examined the nature of mass society as an ongoing response to the overthrow of the "natural order" stemming from as far back as the French Revolution, they were concerned with the emergence of "the masses" into positions of political and cultural power (Bramson, 1961; Brantlinger, 1983). In the United States, where, following the revolution, the masses had always been recognized as a fundamental part of the structure of society, this concern was not a major intellectual preoccupation. While many American scholars (Macdonald, 1965) have attacked the "mass" culture that has emerged from the interaction between egalitarian society and the extensive media system, this discourse has almost never been framed within class terms — until very recently, that is. American scholars, following the tradition of the muckrakers and progressive propaganda critics, were more concerned about the institutional control and manipulation of information, and the ultimate effects that this had on the freedom and quality of choice for the individual American within this mass culture. Dwight Macdonald (1965), in his famous essay "Masscult and Midcult," made the point that "it is precisely because I do believe in the potentialities of ordinary people that I criticize Masscult" (p. 11).

The American intellectual approach to the emergence of the mass media was clearly less concerned with issues surrounding the ideological implications of the hegemonic control by a ruling elite. A systematic examination of the responses to the new media within the American context shows that there were far more advocates than opponents. It is, however, possible to identify three universal concerns stemming from both groups. The first centered on the effects of the new media on existing institutions, such as the school, the church, politics, and other activities such as reading and other recreational forms; the second was the question of changing values; and last, overshadowing everything else, was the concern for children. As Robert Davis (1976) notes in his extensive examination of rhetorical responses to media innovations:

> Both advocates and attackers argued from the influence of media on children. Their arguments were developed in the context of entertainment, education, morality, social values, and religion, and the judgements of the media were made on grounds of their influence on children in these particular areas. (p. 710)

This was a quite different agenda from that suggested by the various Marxist critiques, although, with some manipulation, one could show parallel concerns.

America was a vast country with a difficult mission, an almost impossible attempt to create a single nation while at the same time preserving certain regional identities. After the Civil War, the new media were to play a major role in helping to create this national identity, but in so doing they set in motion a whole series of new concerns. Eventually the motion picture was the first of the major mass media to underscore the problem of the centralized production but localized consumption of media content. Movies were made in the exotic locale of Hollywood, but consumed in every city and village in the country, where it was impossible to have each individual film conform to variations in local values and mores. This disjuncture was one of the prime reasons the issue of social control of the movies received so much attention. In fact, all of the national media, especially the movies and later radio, were breaking down the geographic isolation that had protected these local practices. In their examination of Middletown (Muncie, Indiana) in the mid-1920s, Lynd and Lynd (1929) noted that "at no point is one brought up more sharply against the impossibility of studying Middletown as a self-contained, self-starting community than when one watches these space-binding leisure-time inventions imported from without — automobile, motion picture, and radio — reshaping the city." These were the prime concerns of the indigenous American media critiques, and they are fundamentally different from the focus on ideology that dominates Marxist-based theories.

In conclusion, the strength of Michael Sproule's argument lies in his careful articulation of the extent of the progressive propaganda critique. I know of no other body of work that has brought together such a wide range of sources to demonstrate the extent of the concern over the potential propaganda dangers inherent in the new media. Sproule's call for a renewal of interest in this critique as a means of establishing a uniquely American perspective on the role of the media strikes an immediately resonant chord. As Walt Whitman wrote in 1871, "Our fundamental want today in the United States, is of a class and the clear idea of a class, of native authors, literatures, far different, far higher in grade than any yet known, sacerdotal, modern, fit to cope with our occasions, lands, permeating the whole mass of American mentality, taste, belief, breathing into it a new life" (quoted in Macdonald, 1965, p. 72). In this essay and in his other work Sproule has thrown down the gauntlet; it remains to be seen if American critical and cultural theorists are willing to accept the challenge of creating a theoretical framework based firmly within the American historical experience.

REFERENCES

Bramson, L. (1961). *The political context of sociology.* Princeton, NJ: Princeton University Press.

Brantlinger, P. (1983). *Bread and circuses: Theories of mass culture and social decay.* Ithaca, NY: Cornell University Press.

Collier, J. (1915, September 14). The learned judges and the films. *Survey.*

Cremin, L. (1964). *The transformation of the school.* New York: Random House.

Davis, R. E. (1976). *Response to innovation: A study of popular argument about new mass media.* New York: Arno.

Del:a, J. G. (1987). Communication research: A history. In C. R. Berger & S. H. Chaffee (Eds.), *Handbook of communication science* (pp. 20-98). Newbury Park, CA: Sage.

Gerbner, G. (Ed.). (1983). Ferment in the field [Special issue]. *Journal of Communication, 33*(3).

Grossberg, L. (1987). Critical theory and the politics of empirical research. *Mass Communication Research Yearbook, 3,* 86-106.

Jowett, G. S. (1976). *Film: The democratic art.* Boston: Little, Brown.

Jowett, G. S. (1989). "A capacity for evil": The 1915 Supreme Court *Mutual* decision. *Historical Journal of Film, Radio and Television, 9*(1), 59-78.

Jowett, G. S., Reath, P., & Schouten, M. (1976). *The history of social control of the media* (Report of the Royal Commission on Violence in the Communications Industry, 4). Toronto: Queen's Printer.

Lynd, R. S., & Lynd, H. M. (1929). *Middletown.* New York: Harcourt, Brace & World.

Macdonald, D. (1965). *Against the American grain: Essays on the effects of mass culture.* New York: Random House.

Morley, D. (1980). *The "Nationwide" audience.* London: British Film Institute.

Mutual Film Corporation v. Industrial Commission of Ohio (1915). 236 U.S. 230 U.S. Supreme Court.

Randall, R. S. (1968). *Censorship of the movies.* Ann Arbor: University of Michigan Press.

Sproule, M. (1989). Progressive propaganda critics and the magic bullet myth. *Critical Studies in Mass Communication, 6*(3), 225-246.

Wiebe, R. H. (1967). *The search for order.* New York: Hill & Wang.

Critical Rhetoric
and Propaganda Studies

R A Y M I E E. M c K E R R O W
University of Maine

MICHAEL Sproule provides an important descriptive analysis of antipropaganda studies in relation to American ideology. In responding to his essay, I am not in disagreement with the historical linkages drawn between progressive responses to propaganda in the early twentieth century and their reappearance under different guises in contemporary media criticism. Sproule's observation that "today's students of mass media would do well to reexamine the powerful American dialectic on propaganda" (p. 231) is supported with clear argument and solid documentation. His claim that such reexamination provides a "theoretical counterpoint to contemporary Marxist studies" (p. 211), however, deserves further discussion. The aims of these orientations are so markedly different as to belong to separate realms. While the surface manifestations regarding the unmasking of ideology — whether at the level of the state or of the society — appear similar and thus may seem to be "parallel" analyses, their underlying assumptions are radically at odds with one another. In responding to Sproule's excellent analysis, I shall set forth some of the key assumptions underlying what has elsewhere been termed a "critical rhetoric" (McKerrow, 1989). By contrasting these assumptions with those undergirding a "progressive criticism," the aims and limitations of both will be more clearly articulated.

In a recent essay, I reviewed two dominant forms of critique and offered eight principles that would, if implemented, orient the critic toward the practice of a critical rhetoric (McKerrow, 1989). The goal of that study was to engage rhetoric in a reappraisal of its original impulses as a "transformative practice rather than as a method" of inquiry (p. 91). Instead of seeking a conception of rhetoric that apologizes for its inability to meet Platonic standards of universal truth, a critical rhetoric seeks to reestablish the rhetorical tradition in terms that reflect its theoretical contributions. Thus a critical rhetoric perceives language as material and

Correspondence and requests for reprints: Raymie E. McKerrow, Department of Speech Communication, University of Maine, Orono, ME 04469.

Communication Yearbook 14, pp. 249-255

reclaims knowledge as doxastic rather than epistemic and as particular or nominalist rather than universal. The perspective calls for the critic to assume the role of "inventor" in the analysis of diverse texts that address the public (in a reversal of the "old criticism's" perspective on "public address"; Sproule, 1988). Ultimately,

> a critical rhetoric seeks to unmask or demystify the discourse of power. The aim is to understand the integration of power/knowledge in society — what possibilities for change the integration invites or inhibits and what intervention strategies might be considered appropriate to effect social change. (McKerrow, 1989, p. 91)

CRITICISM/CRITIQUE

The initial fundamental distinction that undergirds a critical rhetoric differentiates *criticism* and *critique*. Benhabib (1986) provides a useful point of departure:

> While criticism . . . stands outside the object it criticizes, asserting norms against facts, and the dictates of reason against the unreasonableness of the world, critique refuses to stand outside its object and instead juxtaposes the immanent, normative self-understanding of its object to the material actuality of this object. (p. 33)

Ideological criticism, as conducted under the rubric of antipropaganda studies, privileges standards of judgment that are not themselves subject to review. The commitment to a "rational democracy" is of paramount importance (a commitment shared by propagandists and critics alike). In contrast, the task of a critical rhetoric is to engage in a constantly recursive critique in which "the criteria it presupposes in its inquiry are not different from the ones by which the object or phenomenon judges itself" (Benhabib, 1986, p. 33).

As a criteriological mode of inquiry, criticism entails an implicit commitment to Platonic ideals of universal truth. Critique, on the other hand, abstains from universalist appeals to unchanging standards of judgment. The telos of criticism thus lies in the perpetuation of the ideals of a "rational democracy," and the measurement of "reality" as it falls short of those ideals. The telos of critique has two potential objects. In terms of a critique of domination, of state or institutional hegemony, the telos is that of emancipation. In terms of a critique of freedom, the telos is that of a never-ending self-reflexivity that does not privilege one form of "rationality" apart from others. As is clear from Sproule's analysis, the kind of "critique" of ideology practiced by propaganda critics is limited to criticism — it in no way achieves the status of an *ideologie-kritik*. This is not to say that both do not participate in "demystification" of the discourse of power, but it is to say that they do so with different ends in view, and with different rationales underlying their respective pursuits. Criticism operates from an acceptance of the tenets of rational democracy, while critique offers the possibility of challenging those tenets. This leads us to a second fundamental distinction: that between permanence and change.

PERMANENCE/CHANGE

Consistent with its Platonic leanings, criticism yields an evaluation that ultimately serves the interests of the dominant ideology. Whether mild or severe, polite or caustic, criticism of the kind practiced by the propaganda critics of the early twentieth century was not interested in altering the social order. The goal of those critics, laudable as it may be, was to preserve democracy by ferreting out those who would seek to undermine its most basic strengths. Thus there is an assumed "fixedness" about the social order that is under siege by propagandists; remediation requires (through an optimistic faith in the people's judgment) open discussion and debate.

Critique, on the other hand, does not privilege rational democracy, or the present social order, above other possible organizational matrices that might be put into place. In Laclau and Mouffe's (1985) formulation, the emphasis on change is clear: "Society" is not a fixed entity, but instead is perceived as an incompletely known "field of differences," any one of which may assume hegemonic status at a given time (p. 111). To preserve some semblance of order, those "fixations" present — the accepted modes of social practice at a given time — are "partial fixations" (p. 112). From this perspective, there is nothing sacrosanct about "rational democracy," nor is the definition of that concept immune to change. At the moment, its articulation has come to dominate the field of discourse. At any given moment, the possibility of change presents itself under the terms of a self-reflexive critique — either the concept can be redefined to suggest a different social order under newly accepted tenets, or a new concept can take the field in its place (e.g., Laclau & Mouffe's sense of "radical democracy").

Criticism and permanence, as reviewed thus far, fit the purposes of "ideological critique" as practiced by the progressives in their attack on propaganda. Underlying the practice is a commitment to the values of democracy, and a blindness to the role of their own "propagandizing" on behalf of those values. Progressive critics, regardless of the purity of their motives, or the rightness of their cause, were equally guilty of masking some values in giving priority to others. What the language or vocabulary of progressivism did not do then, and cannot provide now, is a self-reflexive review of its own assumptions. Just as the Committee on Public Information articulated a "good/evil" dichotomy in promoting the American war effort, so their critics painted a similar black/white picture of the "crimes against humanity" occasioned by deception and covert persuasion. Critique and change, on the other hand, offer a different set of assumptions from which one might challenge the present order. Self-reflexiveness and the possibility of challenge offer openings not present in the "alternative" perspective. A focus on the agent and agency involved in protecting permanence or creating the rationale for change offers a further clarification of the distinctions between a "progressive" and a Marxist analysis.

AGENT/AGENCY

The analysis of propaganda by the progressive critics offers evidence of both an "old criticism" and an emergent "managerial rhetoric" (Sproule, 1988). On the one hand, the analysis presumed a commitment to the assumptions of "old criticism" insofar as it recognized the power of images tied to specific persons or a persona (as in the case of J. D. Rockefeller's transformation from "reviled symbol" to "grandfatherly folk figure"; Sproule, 1988, p. 469). On the other hand, the analysis reflected the growing awareness of impersonal "managers" who would create public opinion before the public even knew it had one. Interest groups and, to a lesser extent, government agencies were perceived as capable of preempting the public's ability to make independent decisions on issues of national importance.

Depending on the strain of Marxism that is utilized, the same orientation toward agent or agency can be found. In its classic sense, Marxist theory precludes the role of an active agent (though it is arguable whether Marx himself intended such a conclusion). If the role of the economy, as dictated by the forces of production, is perceived as overdetermining all else, there is no substantive role an agent can play, even in bringing about a change in the forces of production, without revolution. As Giddens (1979) notes, in reference to Althusser's structuralist critique:

> It is not a coincidence that the forms of social theory that have made little or no conceptual space for agents' understanding of themselves, and of their social contexts, have tended greatly to exaggerate the impact of dominant symbol systems or ideologies upon those in subordinate classes. (p. 72)

This view gives rise to Sproule's contrast between the optimism of the progressives and the negativism of Marxists: The public either has and can take a role in its own behalf or is unlikely to do so as a result of being subjected to a dominant force. In contrast, a theorist such as Therborn (1980) promotes the role of agents in creating social change: Through a simultaneous process of "subjection and qualification," human beings are

> subjected to a particular order that allows or favours certain drives and capacities . . . [and are] qualified to take up and perform . . . the repertoire of roles given in the society into which they are born, including the role of possible agents of social change. (p. 17)

Whether critiqued as part of "managerial rhetoric" or part of a "critical rhetoric," discourse analysis requires a theory that allows for the action of an agent. The focus may well be on hegemony within institutional or political themes, but there needs to be a sense in which "subjects" can articulate their desires. Otherwise, we are left with a determinism that precludes intervention. In such a closed system rhetoric has no value.

As a further differentiation, the "confusion" within Marxist studies cited by Sproule deserves a further look. In his view:

> Marxists disagree about whether the phenomenon of class functions as a sole or partial explanation for ideological currents in society . . . , and Marxists debate whether the state plays a direct or indirect role in promoting ideological hegemony. . . . Nevertheless, the tendency of Marxist criticism is to treat class and state as central in the direction of ideological apparatuses. (p. 212)

The distinctions alluded to can best be discussed by contrasting indeterminacy with overdetermination.

INDETERMINACY/OVERDETERMINATION

As Laclau and Mouffe (1985) suggest, "There is nothing inevitable or natural in the different struggles against power, and it is necessary to explain in each case the reasons for their emergence and the different modulations they may adopt" (p. 152). In the absence of a fixed system of social relations governing acceptable or unacceptable uses of power and in the absence of any "determined" sequence of events, indeterminacy reigns supreme. Sproule's contrast between progressive and Marxist "critiques" downplays the importance of this distinction. While overdetermination dominates the Marxist philosophy of *some* theorists, it by no means dominates all, and is arguably a minority position within contemporary Marxist scholarship. The determination of struggle on the basis of economic relations, the reduction of struggle to the difference between class and state, and the preoccupation with the "state" as the only locus of power are themes that run through some Marxist critique (e.g., Althusser), but are not the only bases from which to launch a critical project. The argument that both state and class, as "entities," must articulate their positions in terms of the public has assumed a prominent role in Laclau's (1977) and Therborn's (1980) interpretations. Thus the people or the public assumes the central role, with state and class as interactants. While Sproule is correct with respect to his comments on the nature of Marxist discourse on hegemony, his review presents a narrower portrait of the terrain than a wider-angle lens would capture.

Instead of concentrating on "state power" as the locus of hegemony, some Marxist critics articulate a broader conception of domination. Laclau and Mouffe (1985), for example, discuss the concept in terms of liberal and conservative political perspectives, and note that changing definitions of "liberal" legitimate different "rights" accorded to the public:

> From the traditional definition of Locke—"liberty is to be free from restraint and violence from others"—we had passed with John Stuart Mill to the acceptance of "political" liberty and democratic participation as an important component of liberty.

> More recently, in social-democratic discourse, liberty has come to mean the "capacity"
> to make certain choices and to keep open a series of real alternatives. It is thus that
> poverty, lack of education, and great disparities in the conditions of life are today
> considered offenses against liberty. (pp. 171-172)

What is "hegemonic" in this context is the dominance of a particular perspective
on liberty — a perspective that legitimates state control or particular social relations
as being in the interests of the people. Implicit in this review of changing definitions is the indeterminacy principle: There is no absolute or fixed sense in which
liberty is to be defined, nor is there any privileged position given to the concept
such that it cannot be altered in the future.

PROGRESSIVISM/MARXISM
AS THEORETICAL COUNTERPOINTS

This brief review of elemental differences brings us back to a central claim in
Sproule's analysis. I agree with his observation that progressive critics in the early
twentieth century provide a rich resource for understanding the social and political
debates of that era. More important, without calling direct attention to the issue,
Sproule unmasks the interaction of power and knowledge that affected the "progress" toward value-free or neutral discussions of issues within academe: "Polemical attacks on the progressive propaganda critics further nudged educators in the
direction of rationalistic pedagogies of critical thinking that were politically
neutral" (p. 230). One does not *require* the language of Marxist studies (e.g.,
ideological apparatuses) to understand the pressure placed on academe to engage
in criticism rather than critique.

At several points in the essay, Sproule notes that the progressive critics did not
choose to avail themselves of a critical vocabulary that would place their observations in a Marxist critique. Some of the reasons this did not occur as a natural
inclination should be clear. They "did not base their analysis on a Marxist vision
of a class-oriented ideological hegemony engineered by the state" (p. 216) because
to do so would commit them to an enterprise that goes much further than their own
analyses, and subjects their own assumptions to examination. As Sproule goes on
to note, their analysis was grounded in the "direct democracy of the old agricultural
republic" (p. 216). The resolve was not that of social change beyond the tenets of
a safe and secure set of assumptions. Marxist analysis would be antithetical to this
perspective. Thus the mere lack of a term such as *ideological apparatuses* did not
deter them — they would not have been in a position to employ such a term had it
been in vogue within Marxist critique at the time they were writing.

The second rationale for avoiding Marxist language is alluded to by Sproule in
noting the activities of "rightist politicians and polemicists" (p. 225). The political
environment shifted dramatically from the end of World War I to the beginning of
the Korean War. Infatuation with left-leaning thinkers, in vogue during the 1920s

and 1930s, became a sign of anti-Americanism in the aftermath of World War II. Other research paradigms (symbolic interactionism) and coping strategies (straight thinking) could be pursued without fear of reprisal by rightist ideologues. Arising from a commitment to an Aristotelian rationalism and a Platonic idealism, an emphasis on textual analysis has its advantages. Capable of being perceived as politically neutral, it functions as a means to elevate an otherwise "soft" or "mushy" analysis to the rigor of the natural sciences (avoiding political troubles is only one motivation underlying the "sciencizing" of social research).

The recent turn to Marxist language in the analysis of ideological discourse is prompted by more than the desire to understand the manipulative efforts of a hegemonic class or institutional grouping (p. 231). First, as noted above, a Marxist critique exists in order to suggest potential interventionist strategies. It is openly teleological, while holding its own goals open to future critique. Second, the "overdetermination" thesis, which would reduce analysis to the causal forces of modes of production or the hegemony of a dominant class, has lost its hold. One can develop a critique that focuses on "influence" rather than "causality" (McKerrow, 1989). Third, other subjects have come to the fore in the analysis of an "indeterminate" set of social relations. The interaction of power and knowledge, irrespective of its source, is a central focus of contemporary study. Thus the kind of Marxist analysis that Sproule alludes to as the "theoretical counterpart" of progressive criticism is only one variant, and a more limited one at that.

Thus, although the study of the progressive and rationalist critics is worthy in its own right, it is not a substitute for Marxist analyses, as it does not ask the same questions. A "parallel" attention to the role of institutions, as in the case of both progressive and Marxist analyses, does not presume that the studies reach identical conclusions, or that their rationales are congruent. While it may function as a theoretical counterpoint to a critical rhetoric or other Marxist analysis, the progressive criticism of American ideology will fall short of the demands of a critique of the discourse of power.

REFERENCES

Benhabib, S. (1986). *Norm, critique, and utopia: A study of the foundations of critical theory.* New York: Columbia University Press.

Giddens, A. (1979). *Central problems in social theory.* Berkeley: University of California Press.

Laclau, E. (1977). *Politics and ideology in Marxist theory.* London: New Left.

Laclau, E., & Mouffe, C. (1985). *Hegemony and socialist strategy: Towards a radical democratic politics* (W. Moore & P. Cammack, Trans.). London: Verso.

McKerrow, R. E. (1989). Critical rhetoric: Theory and praxis. *Communication Monographs, 56,* 91-111.

Sproule, J. M. (1988). The new managerial rhetoric and the old criticism. *Quarterly Journal of Speech, 74,* 468-486.

Therborn, G. (1980). *The ideology of power and the power of ideology.* London: New Left.

6 The Theory of Public Opinion: The Concept of the Spiral of Silence

ELISABETH NOELLE-NEUMANN
Institut für Demoskopie Allensbach

This chapter describes the spiral of silence, a theory first introduced in 1972 and published as a book in 1980. It argues that public opinion did not appear first in the eighteenth century, but has existed in all human societies for thousands of years as a force exerted on governments and individuals, creating and maintaining the consensus necessary for society's functioning. The word *public* in the concept of "public opinion" is to be interpreted in the sense of "public eye," "visible to all," and thus as social control. *Opinion* refers to publicly visible and audible expressions of opinion as well as public behavior regarding value-laden issues. Its power derives from our social nature, from the willingness of society to threaten isolation in reaction to forbidden opinions and behaviors, and from the individual's fear of isolation. This fear causes individuals to register continually any changes in society's approval by means of a "quasi-statistical sense," and to voice agreement upon increase in approval and to remain silent upon decrease, thus contributing to further decline in the popularity of the originally held opinion. The pressure of public opinion is a source of constant conflict for governments in weighing measures in order to win public support. Individuals also experience ongoing conflict between their individual inclinations and convictions and the social demands to conform. This chapter discusses the consequences of public opinion for the classical theory of democracy and for an understanding of mass media effects. The chapter also provides hypotheses and methods for testing them, and presents the example of public opinion concerning nuclear energy.

I N the mid-1930s, expectations for the fledgling science of public opinion were at a high after the method of representative population surveys had proved itself with predictions for the U.S. presidential election of 1936. Just a few months later, the first issue of the newly founded journal *Public Opinion Quarterly* appeared, with Allport's march, "Toward a Science of Public Opinion" (1937). In 1957, Hyman's essay "Toward a Theory of Public Opinion" was still confident, if naively so. By 1970, impatience was beginning to be felt. At the 25th Annual Conference of the American Association for Public Opinion Research,

Correspondence and requests for reprints: Elisabeth Noelle-Neumann, Institut für Demoskopie Allensbach, 7753 Allensbach, Federal Republic of Germany.

Communication Yearbook 14, pp. 256-287

Brewster Smith (1970) lamented that research has "not yet faced the problem of how opinions of individuals articulate to produce social and political consequences. The problem of articulation implied in any conception of public opinion as a social fact is primary agenda for political science and for sociology" (p. 454). And Sydney Verba (1970) maintained:

> Much political public opinion research is irrelevant for the development of macro-political theory dealing with the relationship between mass attitudes and behavior and significant political outcomes. The main reason for this irrelevancy is the focus in most public opinion research on the individual citizen as a unit of analysis. (p. 455)

Basically, both speakers demanded an answer to the same question: How does the sum of individual opinions as determined by public opinion research translate into the awesome political power known as *public opinion*? Almost 2,500 years before, Aristotle had written in his *Politics* (1313/1986) that the power of the people's collective opinion enabled a king to rule and that, should a king lose the support of public opinion, he would be a king no more.

It is not only governments that are subject to the pressure of public opinion. Every individual, every member of society, is subject to the pressure of public opinion. John Locke wrote in the late seventeenth century that there is not 1 in 10,000 who remains untouched when public opinion turns against him (Locke, 1894, 1:479). To quote James Madison (1788/1961), one of the U.S. Constitution's founding fathers: "If it be true that all governments rest on opinion, it is no less true that the strength of opinion in each individual, and its practical influence on his conduct, depend much on the number he supposes to have entertained the same opinion. The reason of man, like man himself, is timid and cautious, when left alone; and acquires firmness and confidence, in proportion to the number with which it is associated" (p. 340). Thus it has been known since antiquity that public opinion exerts pressure on the government as well as on every individual in society. But how this pressure develops and functions is a subject that social research has yet to deal with successfully.

Progress toward these explanations has been made more difficult by the narrow application of the term *public opinion* to the processes of government (see Childs, 1965; Wilson, 1933). The previously acquired knowledge that public opinion burdens every single member of society — as John Locke and James Madison so movingly describe, and as Tocqueville (1856/1955, p. 752) shows by portraying public opinion as a yoke to which every individual must submit — appears to have been lost.

It is the proposition of the present essay that we will make no progress toward a theory of public opinion if we do not adopt a completely different concept of public opinion. Public opinion must be defined as a force, and we must try to understand where this force is derived from and what effects it can have on society.[1] My own understanding of public opinion and the theory I have of it began with survey results for which I could not find an explanation.

THE PUZZLE OF
THE 1965 ELECTION IN GERMANY

In the fall of 1965, as head of the Allensbach survey research institute, I was working on election research about the upcoming German federal election. In the course of my research, I came upon a surprising finding: For a period of six months, the two major parties had been locked in a neck-and-neck race, with essentially no change in the number who intended to vote for them. At the same time, however, there was a dramatic change in expectations as to who would win the election. In midwinter, when the first estimates were recorded, expectations were about even for both parties, but six months later, about two months before the election, they favored the Christian Democrats four to one (Noelle-Neumann, 1984, chap. 1). This increase in expectations of a Christian Democratic victory proved politically significant. Shortly before the election, the neck-and-neck race between the parties was resolved in the direction suggested by the expectations of who was going to win: In the last two weeks preceding the election, the Christian Democrats gained almost 4% of the vote and the Social Democrats lost approximately 5%. The Christian Democrats emerged as the victors in the national election of 1965 with a 9% lead.[2]

If there was such a difference in the trends measured, as we observed during the eight months before the election of 1965, the two questions — about individual voting intentions and about expectations as to who would win — must have measured very different things. Rather than being another way of estimating voting intentions, the question "Who is going to win the election?" was a way of measuring the perceptibility of voting intentions. Given this puzzle, the following hypothesis began to emerge: If there was a difference in the public show of voting intentions between the two camps, this difference was bound to result in overestimating the more publicly visible camp and underestimating the less visible one. These estimates — in turn, according to the hypothesis — set a dynamic process in motion: The visibility of one side encouraged its other supporters to make a public commitment, thus increasing the impression of numerical superiority. Conversely, supporters of the side with less public visibility were discouraged by being underestimated. They were increasingly reduced to silence, causing their other supporters to conceal their convictions, to the point where this camp began to lose its public presence.[3]

THE CONCEPT OF THE SPIRAL OF SILENCE

The puzzle of 1965 and its explanations gradually emerged as the concept of the spiral of silence. The theory assumes that in the social collective, cohesion must be constantly ensured by a sufficient level of agreement on values and goals, and that this agreement is termed *public opinion.* In addition to being sought on current political issues, agreement also manifests itself in many external modes of behav-

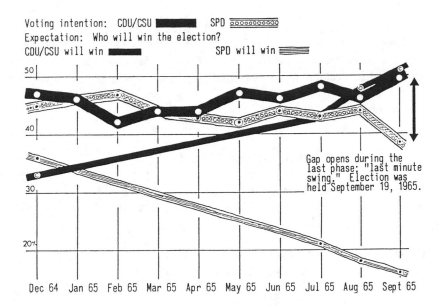

Figure 1. The election year puzzle of 1965. Voting intentions remained almost unchanged for many months, indicating a neck-and-neck race between the CDU/CSU and the SPD. At the same time, however, the notion that the CDU/CSU was going to win spread among voters. How did that come about? In the end we found a bandwagon effect in the direction of the expected winner of the election. SOURCE: Allensbach Archives, IfD Surveys 1095, 1097, 1098, 2000, 2001, 2002, 2003, 2004, 2005, 2006.

ior, such as expectations regarding customs or fashion. Individuals who deviate from the consensus are threatened with isolation and ostracism. For their own part, individuals have a fear of isolation (which is generally unconscious and probably genetically based). This fear induces them constantly to check accepted opinions and modes of behavior and the potential and direction of change. The theory ascribes a quasi-statistical sense of individuals making such assessments. The results of these assessments influence people's behavior, specifically their willingness to speak out. If people believe that their opinions are shared in a consensus of public opinion, they have the confidence to speak out — whether in public or in private — displaying their convictions with buttons and bumper stickers, for instance, but also through the clothes they wear and other publicly visible symbols. When people feel they are in the minority, they become cautious and silent, thus further reinforcing the impression in public of their side's weakness, until the apparently weaker side disappears completely except for a small hard core that clings to values from the past, or until the opinion becomes taboo.

For this development in the process of public opinion, I introduced the term *spiral of silence* in 1973 (Noelle-Neumann, 1973, p. 43).[4] It should be kept in mind that this theory was developed to explain an empirically observed phenomenon that had occurred in an election year and that other theories must be measured by their ability or inability to explain a shift in public opinion when victory expectations increase for one party from 33% to 51%, and decrease for the other party from 36% to 16%, while the voting intentions of the population remain practically unchanged (Noelle-Neumann, 1974a, p. 321). An event such as this, recorded in 1965, can definitely be caused only by extremely strong forces. Thus it may be presumed that we are dealing with a phenomenon that can be subjected to systematic empirical observation and analysis.

ASSUMPTIONS OF THE THEORY TO BE TESTED

Testing the theory is complicated because it is initially based on four separate assumptions and then upon a fifth that deals with the interrelationships among the previous four (Noelle-Neumann, 1989b, pp. 299ff.):

(1) Society threatens deviant individuals with isolation.

(2) Individuals experience fear of isolation continuously.

(3) This fear of isolation causes individuals to try to assess the climate of opinion at all times.

(4) The results of this estimate affect behavior in public, especially the open expression or concealment of opinions.

(5) This assumption connects the above four. Taken together, they are considered responsible for the formation, defense, and alteration of public opinion.

Any test of the theory must deal with each of the four assumptions individually, and should then progress to case studies, analyzing the interrelationship posited by the fifth assumption via the process of public opinion.

Testing the Threat of Isolation

The theory considers the cohesion of society to be based on the threat of isolation against individuals who deviate from common values, and it considers the strength of common convictions — referred to as public opinion — to result from the social nature of human beings, who fear isolation. The threat of isolation and fear of isolation are basic elements of the theory. It is therefore not surprising that these concepts have provoked considerable criticism. Are individual members of society really threatened with isolation? Do they really fear isolation, and does fear of isolation inform their actions? Could this be the motive for conformity, or are there much better explanations based on human rationality? Imitation may be viewed as social learning, for example, in order to adopt what has proved itself; or does striving for success, recognition, or reward represent the desire to be on the winner's side, the bandwagon effect?

The doubts expressed about the assumptions of the threat of isolation and the fear of isolation are understandable. These assumptions are not in keeping with the theory of rational democracy; they are not in keeping with our cherished ideal of the autonomous individual, or with the high value assigned to liberalism and tolerance. The keywords *threat of isolation* and *fear of isolation* are not listed in the various encyclopedias of sociology, social psychology, and political science. Strong empirical evidence is required to demonstrate convincingly that the threat of isolation and the fear of isolation play a focal role in the process of public opinion.

Such evidence cannot be provided by direct polling, although this has been tried. In some surveys, respondents have been asked openly, "Do you fear isolation? Very much — somewhat — not at all?" The threat of isolation and fear of isolation are seen as socially undesirable modes of behavior and reaction, and people remain largely unconscious of them. Therefore — as Durkheim clearly states in his *Rules of the Sociological Method*, published in 1895 — when a subject under investigation cannot be tackled directly, indicators must be found; that is, symptoms that are not identical with the subject, but that enable us to draw conclusions on the subject.

As part of my election research in the 1970s, I already used such an indicator for the threat of isolation, by including a question about the tires of a car being slashed that displays a sticker for a political party (Noelle-Neumann, 1984, pp. 52ff.), as well as another question about a driver who is a stranger in a city and is refused information by a pedestrian. "I should mention that the driver is wearing a political badge on his jacket. What do you think: which party did this badge support?" is the way the test question ends (Noelle-Neumann, 1984, pp. 55ff.) A question was also included about which party's posters were most often defaced or ripped up, as an indicator of public threat of isolation against the supporters of this party.

But I also experienced failures. Several tests, which might be termed sociometric, did not work out properly. Respondents were shown pictures of settings with a group of people and a person who stood or sat at a distance from the group, as if excluded. But these scenes, rather than being interpreted as a threat of isolation, were thought to be leadership situations, with the isolated person representing a superior (Noelle-Neumann, 1984, pp. 50ff.).

I found the threat of isolation described in many different fields, including anthropology, where it was included in Margaret Mead's (1937) description of public opinion processes among primitive peoples (Noelle-Neumann, 1984, p. 102ff.); and in Haviland's (1977) findings on gossip, which he chose as a subject of scientific research among the Zinacanteco tribe; and, quite generally, in the legal history of the pillory, which has appeared in many variations in different societies. But I had been searching for a very simple test of the threat of isolation, and this I did not find until I examined the literature on group dynamics.

One of the objectives of group dynamics — which began to be developed in the 1930s as a special field of social psychology — was to study what gives groups cohesion: What ensures their continuity? What happens when individual group members violate the rules and thereby threaten to destroy the group?

In the experiments of group dynamics research, a three-stage process was recorded: In the first stage, the group tries by persuasion and friendliness to regain the member who is violating the rules. If this does not succeed, the deviating member is threatened, in the second stage, with exclusion from the group. The third stage, when all has been to no avail, marks the end. This is expressed by researchers in group dynamics as "the group redefines its boundaries," which means the group expels the deviating member (Cartwright & Zander, 1968, p. 145). This is highly reminiscent of the words used by Edward Ross (1969) in his book on social control, where he describes how society enforces conformity of a recalcitrant individual until the "dead member drops from the social body" (p. 92; see also Noelle-Neumann, 1984, p. 95). I was interested in the methods for threatening individuals, and found many clues in the conformity experiments carried out in France and Norway by Stanley Milgram (1961), who resourcefully employed acoustic threat signals: whistling, booing, and derisive laughter.

These clues finally led me to design a threat test for use in representative population surveys in the Federal Republic of Germany as well as in Great Britain. The text of the question in the first survey ran as follows:

> I would like to tell you about an incident which recently took place in a large public meeting on nuclear energy. There were two main speakers: One spoke in favor of nuclear energy and the other opposed it. One of the speakers was booed by the audience. Which one do you think was booed: The speaker supporting nuclear energy or the speaker opposing it?

A majority of 72% of German respondents were of the opinion that the speaker in favor of nuclear energy had been booed; 11% assumed that the opponent of nuclear energy had been booed. Less than one-fifth of the population remained undecided (Allensbach Archives, 1989). In Great Britain, the supporter of nuclear energy was also clearly associated with a hostile climate of opinion, but to a lesser degree (see Table 1). This indicates that the existence of a threat of isolation was known to the respondents in both Germany and Great Britain, and they also believed they knew how strong each side was in terms of the climate of opinion; only one out of six was undecided.

The same test can serve to measure the strength of the threat of isolation attached to other issues. The more clear-cut the majority and the minority are in the climate of opinion, the more it may be assumed that this will influence the willingness to speak out or keep silent in public.

It is doubtful, however, whether the test questions, as presented to respondents in the Federal Republic of Germany and Great Britain, would be acceptable in other cultures that are characterized by more reticence in social intercourse. Even though the pressure to conform, as expressed by public opinion, seems to have existed at all times and in all cultures — for instance, in China, where two characters next to each other have represented *public* and *opinion* since the fourth century (Kim, 1989) — the questions must be phrased so as to be universally applicable if the spiral of silence is to be tested as a universal theory. In Japan, for example, the following version was developed for testing the threat of isolation:

TABLE 1
Testing the Threat of Isolation in the Federal Republic of Germany and England:
Population 16 and Over

Nuclear Energy
Question: "I would like to tell you about an incident which took place recently at a large public meeting on nuclear energy. There were two main speakers: One spoke in favor of nuclear energy and the other opposed it. One of the speakers was booed by the audience. Which one do you think was booed: the speaker supporting nuclear energy or the speaker opposing it?"

	February 1989 *Federal Republic* *of Germany* *(%)*	*March 1989* *Great Britain* *(%)*
Supporter of nuclear energy	72	62
Opponent of nuclear energy	11	25
Undecided	17	13
Total	100	100

SOURCE: Germany: Institut für Demoskopie Allensbach, IfD Survey 5016, question 38; 2,213 respondents. Great Britain: Social Surveys (Gallup Poll) Limited, approximately 1,000 respondents.

There was a debate about nuclear energy at a neighborhood meeting. One person present spoke out in favor of nuclear energy, while another spoke out against it. One of the two later heard that there had been gossip behind his back condemning him. What do you think: which of the two was condemned behind his back?

This version of the test utilizes the fact that in all societies rumor acts as a tool of the threat of isolation.

Testing Fear of Isolation

Obtaining empirical evidence for the fear of isolation must be approached in a similar manner as for the threat of isolation. Even those who have been critical of the theory of the spiral of silence although recognizing the existence of fear of isolation as a motivating force in human acts have demanded that the fear of isolation should be more clearly measurable (Glynn & McLeod, 1985, pp. 47ff., 60).

In initial publications on the theory, I referred to Asch's (1951, 1952) famous length-of-line experiment from the early 1950s as proof that fear of isolation exists. But these laboratory experiments were rejected by the critics for a number of reasons. It was argued that the unsuspecting test person — who had to choose which one of three lines of varying length was just as long as a standard line — had really only agreed with the obviously mistaken judgment of the ten others, who knew the purpose of the experiment, because he did not trust his own judgment, and not because of fear of isolation. Moreover, further experiments by Asch had shown that

TABLE 2

Cross-Cultural Comparison of Embarrassing Situations:
West Germany, Spain, and South Korea

Question: "These cards describe some situations people might find themselves in at one time or another. Could you please distribute the cards onto this sheet according to whether you would find the situation embarrassing or not? Please simply put aside the cards with situations you have no opinion on."

Would Find Embarassing	*Federal Republic of Germany* 1983 (%)	*Spain* 1984 (%)	*South Korea* 1986 (%)
Somebody slaps you in public.	79	83	92
You are unjustly accused of being a shoplifter by an employee in a store.	78	89	88
In a department store you accidentally knock over a valuable crystal glass which falls down and breaks.	78	84	92
While at a restaurant, you spill soup on your pants.	70	73	74
You are at the cash register in the supermarket with a cartful of groceries when you discover you don't have any money along.	69	65	84
You are at the theater and have a cold but you don't have a handkerchief along.	63	66	41
You are attending a concert with a friend. Your friend falls asleep and begins snoring.	63	59	63
In a group you're standing with, someone is being discussed who is listening all the while and then joins the group.	56	51	64
Someone makes fun of you in front of others.	56	68	76
In the middle of a busy street you suddenly slip and fall down flat on your face.	56	76	75
In the train, you open the door of the bathroom and someone is sitting there who has forgotten to lock the door.	55	71	88
You address someone by the wrong name.	52	37	65
You are over at a friend's house when you happen to enter a room where someone is undressing.	50	73	94
You meet an old friend whom you're excited about saying hello to, but he walks out without so much as a glance in your direction.	49	46	64
You meet an old friend whose name you can't think of.	45	41	66

Would Find Embarassing	*Federal Republic of Germany* 1983 (%)	*Spain* 1984 (%)	*South Korea* 1986 (%)
You feel sweaty after doing some work but you have to go shopping before you can wash up.	44	44	22
You are planning to spend a vacation with friends. When you arrive at your destination you discover that what is involved is a nudist beach.	43	59	–
You are in a train and the ticket collector comes but you can't find your ticket.	–	–	92
You tell a joke to friends and no one laughs.	40	41	46
The plumber comes and your apartment is messy.	36	43	36
Because you did your laundry too late, it's still hanging on the line to dry at Easter [Korea: on New Year's Day].	33	17	28
You have to make an important telephone call that takes a bit longer than usual from a public phone booth. There are two or three people in line behind you.	31	39	69
You are approached by a television reporter with his TV camera on.	28	39	74
By chance you succeed in saving a small child from drowning. As a result, a reporter absolutely insists on taking your picture for the local paper.	27	37	62
You run out of butter or margarine at the weekend and have to go to the neighbors to borrow some.	27	27	40
You notice around noon that your shoes haven't been cleaned.	26	25	11
In a hotel room you can hear what is going on in the room next door through the thin walls.	24	33	35
You run into someone on the street and don't know whether you should greet him.	23	37	48
In a train compartment that is half empty, one of the other travelers suddenly begins talking to himself.	15	31	23
You dial the wrong number while phoning.	12	16	26
You are addressed by the wrong name.	12	18	28
Total	1343	1498	1766
n	2009	1499	342

SOURCES: West Germany: Allensbach Archives, IfD Survey 4031, August 1983, population 16 and over. Spain: DATA, S.A., June 1984, population 15 and over. South Korea: Tokinoya, September 1986, population 20 and over.
NOTE: A dash indicates the question was not asked.

when one or two persons named the right lines, this was enough to keep most test persons from making the wrong choice. It was argued that the fear of isolation could not be particularly strong if just a few other persons were enough to make the test person stand up for his own judgment (Salmon/Kline, 1985, p. 8). This elimination of the fear of isolation in the artificial seclusion of the laboratory — without an actual threat of isolation, without moral or aesthetic convictions being involved, and without being in public — certainly did not prove that the fear of isolation would be weak under realistic conditions. Just as in the case of the threat of isolation, however, the need was evident for a simple, reality-oriented test that could be included in normal interviews in population surveys.

First, using the controversy on smoking in the presence of nonsmokers as an example, I developed the "threat test" (Noelle-Neumann, 1984, pp. 42ff.). During the interview smokers were shown a sketch that depicted one person saying furiously: "It seems to me that smokers are terribly inconsiderate. They force others to inhale their health-endangering smoke." Respondents were asked to phrase responses to this. The results showed that, in this situation, in the presence of nonsmokers, many smokers were clearly less willing to speak out in public for smoking.

Embarrassment as an Expression of Fear of Isolation

It was the study of Erving Goffman's works that did the most to prove the existence of fear of isolation and operationalize it in survey research. Goffman used neither the phrase *fear of isolation* nor the term *public opinion*. He set out to investigate how the behavior of individuals changes depending on whether they are on their own or with others. The focus of his research was the social nature of humans. Here, he went one step further than researchers in group dynamics, who limited themselves to the study of human groups — primary groups or reference groups. Goffman shed light on an area that had been a blind spot in science up to then: the public from the point of view of social psychology. The laconic title of one of his publications, *Behavior in Public Places* (1963), introduced the consciousness of being in public as a subject of scientific research.

In Darwin's *The Expression of the Emotions in Man and Animals*, published in 1873, he discusses human reactions that occur when individuals are in the presence of others, but hardly ever when they are on their own. Feelings of embarrassment are a clear indication of humans' social nature, which is manifested, according to Darwin, in many visible physical reactions, including blushing or turning pale; sweating; stuttering; making nervous gestures; speaking in a tight, cracked, or abnormally high or low voice; grinning unnaturally; and looking away (about which Darwin comments that people try to avoid noticing that they are being observed by others by reducing eye contact; p. 330).

Darwin distinguishes between two sides of human nature, one oriented outward and the other directed inward: When individuals orient themselves outward, they conform to their social nature; this is confirmed by objective signs, such as blushing, which is not found in animals. Darwin makes distinctions among feelings of guilt, shame, and embarrassment: A person may be deeply ashamed of a minor lie without blushing, but will blush as soon as he or she believes that the lie has been detected. Shyness, Darwin states, leads to blushing. But shyness is merely a sensitivity to what *others* may think of one, a sensitivity due to humans' social nature.

Goffman (1956) pursued Darwin's observations further, setting up a program for future research. This was to include situations individuals feel to be embarrassing, and types of persons whose sensitivity to embarrassment is especially highly developed (p. 270). Goffman assumed that embarrassment was caused by the disclosure of incompetence, clumsiness, or having infringed upon the law. He thought that embarrassment was a form of mild punishment, forcing people to live within certain confines, at least in public.

However, in his research on the fear of isolation and its role in the process of public opinion, Michael Hallemann from the University of Mainz arrived at results that indicate embarrassment is also an expression of fear of isolation. Hallemann (1986, 1989), in cooperation with the Institut für Demoskopie Allensbach, conducted a two-step study of embarrassing situations. In a first step, a sentence-completion test was included in a normal representative survey with 2,000 interviews. The respondents were presented with a drawing—the men with a sheet showing men and the women with a sheet showing women. One person is saying to the other, "Can you imagine what happened to me yesterday—it was so embarrassing: I . . . ." The interviewer asks: "Here are two people talking. Unfortunately, the man/woman got interrupted in mid-sentence. But what do you think he or she wanted to tell, what could have happened to him or her?"

In a second step, Hallemann used the replies to this question from about 2,000 respondents to design 30 situations. During the subsequent Allensbach survey, these situations, written on separate cards, were presented to respondents with the following question: "These cards describe some situations people might find themselves in at one time or another. Could you please distribute the cards onto this sheet according to whether you would find the situation embarrassing or not?" (Allensbach Archives, IfD Survey 4031, August 1983).

The various embarrassing situations are listed in Table 2, along with the findings from the Federal Republic of Germany, Spain, and Korea. A few years later, the series of questions was replicated (Allensbach Archives, IfD Survey 5021, June 1989). There appears to be hardly any change in what people find embarrassing. The results of the replication were almost identical to those of the first survey. Until this test, we had assumed that embarrassment largely depended on cultural traditions and would vary greatly from country to country. While these differences do exist, there is much that is held in common.

In all three countries, a situation where someone has saved a child from drowning and is to be photographed for the local paper is felt to be embarrassing by a sizable proportion of the population: 27% in West Germany, 37% in Spain, and 62% in South Korea. This demonstrates that embarrassment not only involves violations of proper behavior, as Goffman assumed, but that many individuals also are embarrassed by attracting attention, by finding that others are looking at them in public—even if it is laudable behavior that accounts for this.

There is also remarkable agreement among the three countries with regard to the situation, "You tell a joke to friends and no one laughs." This was felt to be embarrassing by approximately 40% of respondents, which may be explained in part by the dual role of laughter, which has been described by the French medievalist Jacques Le Goff (1989). Le Goff explains that Hebrew and Greek had two different words for sociable laughter, which creates bonding, and for derisive laughter, which sets someone apart, but that this distinction was lost in Latin. It could be that the refusal to laugh when someone tells a joke signifies a rejection of solidarity, and that this rejection is then interpreted as isolation.

Hallemann came closer to the objective of measuring the fear of isolation than anyone else had. Depending on the number of situations that the respondent considered embarrassing, a score was calculated, rating the sensitivity of the respondent's social nature as very exceptional, exceptional, average, limited, or very limited, with the fear of isolation correspondingly rated. Using controversial topics with a potential to isolate the individual, he investigated the tendency of persons with high and low scores on sense of embarrassment to speak up or keep silent, and found that individuals with a stronger sense of embarrassment also had a stronger tendency to remain silent in conversations about controversial topics. Hallemann then examined whether there might be a general connection between the high score for embarrassment and keeping silent; but the results showed that individuals with a strong sense of embarrassment were just as willing as the average to join in conversations about noncontroversial topics. I will come back to this point when discussing how to test the fourth assumption, the influence of the climate of opinion on the willingness to speak out in public.

Testing the Quasi-Statistical Sense

The theory of the spiral of silence states—as its third assumption—that fear of isolation causes people to try to assess the climate of opinion. To describe this phenomenon, the term *quasi-statistical sense* has been coined: People, the proposition runs, have the ability to estimate how strong opposing sides are in the public debate.

As indirect evidence for the third assumption, I have referred previously to the observation that in an interview the large majority of respondents do not hesitate to answer questions such as, "What do most people think about this?" which indicates that they had already arrived at an idea before the interview (Noelle-Neumann, 1984, p. 10, Table 1). Not only in Germany but also in Great Britain (Gallup Political Index, 1987, 1988) and the United States (Donsbach & Stevenson, 1984), it has been shown that the majority of the population is quite prepared to make estimates when asked about the relative strength of the different camps.

TABLE 3
Attitudes Toward Abortion: The Trend

Question: "Here are two people talking about abortion during the first few months of pregnancy. Which of these two comes closest to saying what you think too?"

[Presentation of an illustration with the following remarks:

"Any abortion means killing unborn life. That's why it shouldn't be allowed on principle. It should only be permitted when the life of the pregnant woman is endangered."

"I don't agree. Every woman has the right to decide whether she wants to have a child or not. On principle, she should therefore be free to have an abortion or not."]

	April 1972[a] (%)	July 1983 (%)	January 1988 (%)
For; right to abortion	59	44	33
Against; generally no right to abortion	25	39	49
Undecided; no opinion	16	17	18
Total	100	100	100

SOURCE: Allensbach Archives, IfD Surveys 2081, 4030, 4099 I + II
NOTE: a. The text of the original in question 1972 was as follows: "It has been proposed that abortion should be permissible during the first three months of pregnancy. What do you think — are you for or against allowing abortion during the first three months?"

The fact that such a high proportion of the population assesses the relative strength of different sides contradicts the assumption that the participants in the process of public opinion mainly constitute "attention publics" or interest groups, characterized by interests and knowledge (e.g. Davison, 1989; Lang & Lang, 1981). As soon as a subject of public debate acquires a moral dimension — Davison (1989) speaks of "moral fervor" — and is thus linked to a threat of isolation, it will be taken up by public opinion, penetrating the very walls (Ihering, 1883, p. 180) and "the farthest removes of the Alps" (Müller, 1777/1819, p. 41), as eighteenth- and nineteenth-century authors put it.

One of the criticisms raised in the scientific discussion was that most individuals would not base their assessments on what they observed, but would transfer their attitudes — a "looking-glass perception" (Taylor, 1982) — to the assessments of how most people think. Moreover, the assessments of the climate of opinion were said to be wrong often.

Tests have confirmed the looking-glass perception, yet it has also been established that the collective perception of the *increases* and *decreases* in the strength of a given camp functions correctly, independent of a person's convictions. The example shown in Tables 3 and 4, covering the period from 1972 to 1988, shows the trend of opinion on abortion as well as the assessments of the climate of opinion made by supporters and by opponents of more liberal abortion laws. Another

TABLE 4
Assessment of the Climate of Opinion Correctly Mirrors
the Actual Trend in Attitudes

Question: "What do you think: are most people in Germany for or against allowing abortion [every other interview used 'termination of pregnancy'] on principle during the first three months?"

	April 1972[a] (%)	July 1983 (%)	January 1988 (%)
Total Population			
most are in favor of the right to abortion	45	28	34
most are opposed	18	36	38
half and half, undecided	37	36	38
Total	100	100	100
Persons in favor of the right to abortion			
most are in favor of the right to abortion	61	45	39
most are opposed	13	21	24
half and half, undecided	26	34	37
Total	100	100	100
Persons opposed to a general right to abortion			
most are in favor of the right to abortion	23	17	16
most are opposed	34	52	50
half and half, undecided	43	31	34
Total	100	100	100

SOURCE: Allensbach Archives, IfD Surveys 2081, 4030, 4099 I + II.

NOTE: a. The text of the original question in 1972 was as follows: "Quite apart from your own opinion: do you think most people in Germany are for or against allowing abortion in the first three months?"

example, concerning opinion on the death penalty, has already been presented during the first stage of the ongoing critical discussion, and has shown that the change in the climate of opinion is correctly perceived, independent of personal positions (Noelle-Neumann, 1985, pp. 73ff.).

Assessments of the climate of opinion are often distorted, a situation that has been referred to since the late 1920s as "pluralistic ignorance" (Fields & Schuman, 1976; Katz, 1981; O'Gorman & Garry, 1976; Taylor, 1982). This generally agrees with the theory of the spiral of silence, which posits that the assessment of the climate of opinion derives from two sources: immediate observation by individuals in their own spheres of life and indirect observation through the eyes of the mass media. If a certain point of view predominates in the mass media, this will result in an overestimate of this point of view. This does not invalidate the assumption, however, that individuals constantly try to use their quasi-statistical sense to assess how strong each side is.

Testing the Assumption That the Climate of Opinion Influences Speaking Out and Keeping Silent

The result of this assessment — according to the fourth assumption — strongly influences the individual's behavior in public as regards stating or concealing opinions, speaking out or keeping silent. The strength of one camp's signals, or the weakness of the other's, is the driving force setting the spiral in motion. To test this, I first used in election research a question about the willingness to state one's convictions in public, for instance, by displaying campaign buttons or bumper stickers (Noelle-Neumann, 1980, p. 158). Speaking out or keeping silent at the grass roots was also approached the other way — that is, from the point of view of the person addressed: "Has anyone approached you recently as to how you should vote?" If yes: "And for which party?" (Noelle-Neumann, 1986, p. 81).

Most frequently, the willingness to speak out on controversial issues has been measured in survey research by questions such as the following: "Assuming you are on a five-hour train ride and someone in your compartment starts talking very *favorably* about [in every other interview: *very unfavorably* about] the . . . party. Would you like to talk to this person, or would you prefer not to?" But once the theory had crossed some borders, there were complaints that the test would not work in other countries, since a five-hour train trip was far too unusual a situation for respondents to imagine. A substitute was therefore developed: "Assuming you are on a five-hour bus trip, and the bus makes a rest stop and everyone gets out for a long break. In a group of passengers, someone starts talking about whether we should support . . . or not. Would you like to talk to this person, to get to know his or her point of view better, or would you prefer not to?" (Allensbach Archives, IfD Survey 4093/II, Question 71A).

The German-American research team of Donsbach and Stevenson (1984, 1986) designed a question in which a television reporter asks people on the street for an interview on a controversial topic. The disadvantage here is that the public dimension is especially large. Television, after all, constitutes the largest public dimension today. Hallemann found that the fear of isolation increases with the size of the public; this means that, for a test question such as this, there is an especially large group of persons who refuse to speak out on principle, independent of whether they sense that the climate of opinion favors them or not. The results of this kind of question are thus less meaningful.

One of the criticisms put forward was that speaking out or keeping silent, or displaying one's convictions by means of badges, bumper stickers, and ribbons, was dictated by personal disposition and inclination. However, as I have already pointed out in previous publications, it is not a question of an alternative between personal dispositions and reactions to the threat of isolation; the various circum-stantial factors act together and they may weaken or strengthen each other, but not negate each other's influence (Noelle-Neumann, 1984, pp. 29ff.). Research on embarrassment has confirmed that human beings have different levels of sensitiv-ity to the threat of isolation. At the same time, it has shown clearly that more sensitive individuals are not less willing to stand up for their views in general, but only where controversial issues involving a threat of isolation are concerned (see pp. 25ff.).

CASE STUDY OF A PROCESS
OF PUBLIC OPINION: NUCLEAR ENERGY

In conclusion, the interplay of the four modes of behavior in the process of public opinion are to be described using the example of nuclear energy. In this case an important prerequisite has been fulfilled: A media content analysis is available covering the period from 1965 to 1986 for seven of the most influential print media in West Germany, four national papers and three weekly magazines (Kepplinger, 1989). In the context of analyzing processes of public opinion, *influential* always refers to media that tend to be cited by other media.

For the second half of the 1970s, the content analysis shows a strong overall increase in articles on the subject of nuclear energy and, at the same time, a change from a positive to a negative assessment of nuclear energy (Figure 2). It was not until the mid-1970s that Allensbach surveys began to measure the attitudes of the population on nuclear energy plants and the assessment of the climate of opinion about nuclear energy plants, at a time when reporting on the subject had already increased in the media and the tenor of this reporting was already negative. But a relative majority of the population supported nuclear energy until 1984. In con-trast, the assessment of the climate of opinion, of how most people think about nuclear energy, was already negative when measurements were first conducted in 1977 and became increasingly negative beginning in 1979. It is appropriate to use the term *pluralistic ignorance* here (see Tables 5 and 6).

In the long run, much of the population adjusts its attitudes to the tenor of the media and to the climate of opinion as assessed (see Figure 3). Until the spring of 1981, assessments of how the climate of opinion on nuclear energy would develop *in the future* were predominantly positive. Beginning in fall 1981, the supporters of nuclear energy plants increasingly took up a defensive position. There is almost no one anymore who anticipates an increase in support for nuclear energy plants (see Table 7).

The fierceness of the debate about nuclear energy is shown by the willingness of supporters to speak up, which, until 1981, surpassed the willingness of oppo-nents of nuclear energy to speak up. It was not until 1987 that the supporters of nuclear energy began to lag behind the opponents with regard to their willingness to speak up (see Table 8). When the new question was designed in 1989 to test the

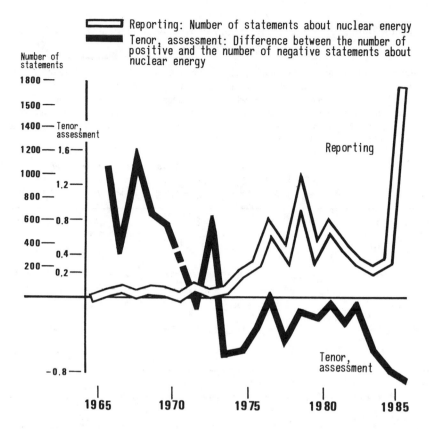

Figure 2. Content analysis: how seven influential print media treated the topic of nuclear energy between 1965 and 1986.
SOURCE: Kepplinger (1988, p. 665).

threat of isolation, the results showed that supporters of nuclear energy faced a strong threat of isolation.

This example is instructive, showing the part played by different elements in the process of public opinion in chronological terms. The tenor of the media, or a change in the tenor of the media, precedes a change in assessing the climate of opinion. A change in assessing the climate of opinion precedes a change in one's own attitudes. Behavior — the willingness to speak up — adjusts to the assessment of the climate of opinion, but also, conversely, influences assessments of the climate of opinion, in a process of interaction that creates a spiral.

Nonetheless, the process of public opinion does not appear to have concluded. Supporters of nuclear energy, who found themselves in the minority in 1988 — at 25%, compared with 47% for the opponents (Table 5) — demonstrate a striking willingness to speak up in view of the pressure from the climate of opinion they are subject to (Table 8); they have not given in to the spiral of silence. This resistance could be described as a "hard-core" situation.

TABLE 5
Attitude in the Federal Republic of Germany Toward Nuclear Energy Plants,
1977 to 1988: Population 16 and Over

Question: "On balance, how much would you say you favor or oppose the continued use of nuclear
energy in the Federal Republic? Could you tell me according to this illustration with the black and
white boxes? This is the way you do it: The white box at the top means 'very much in favor' and the
black box at the bottom means 'very much opposed.' So the more you are in favor of nuclear energy,
the higher up the white box you will choose, and the more you are opposed to it, the lower down the
black box will be that you select. What do you think?"

	Sept. 1977 (%)	March 1979 (%)	May 1979 (%)	Sept. 1979 (%)	March 1981 (%)	Oct. 1981 (%)	June 1984 (%)	July 1986 (%)	Feb. 1988 (%)
In favor of nuclear energy plants (+ 2 to + 5)	45	49	46	42	49	34	44	32	25
Opposed (−2 to −5)	23	20	36	27	22	30	23	41	47
Undecided	32	31	28	31	29	36	33	27	28
Total	100	100	100	100	100	100	100	100	100
n	2002	960	947	2032	1035	1983	2079	2175	2100

SOURCE: Allensbach Archives, IfD Surveys 3047, 3065, 3070, 3073, 3094, 4001, 4045, 4075, 5000.
NOTE: a. As measured by the Stapel Scale, + 5 = "very much in favor of nuclear energy plants" to −5 = "very much
opposed."

The concept of the hard core (Noelle-Neumann, 1974b, p. 48) has been subject
to a great deal of misinterpretation. Rather than comprising persons with especially
stable attitudes (e.g., persons who always vote for the same party), as has sometimes been assumed (Glynn & McLeod, 1985, p. 54), it consists of a minority who
have been overpowered and relegated to a completely defensive position in public
as regards its convictions. The behavior of this minority in public is hardly
susceptible to the threat of isolation or ruled by fear of isolation anymore. The
hard-core minority is, in fact, often especially willing to speak out. Depending on
the topic in question, the minority may be a sect that "drops from the social body"
or an avant-garde, setting the process of public opinion in motion anew and
deciding it in an opposite sense.

MEDIA, PUBLIC OPINION,
AND THE SPIRAL OF SILENCE

This essay on the theory of public opinion and the concept of the spiral of silence
focuses on a systematic presentation of the assumptions made by the theory and of
the instruments to test these assumptions. A systematic presentation is required

TABLE 6

Assessing the Climate of Opinion on Nuclear Energy Plants in
the Federal Republic of Germany: Population 16 and Over

Question: "Aside from your own opinion for the moment, do you think most people in the Federal
Republic are in favor of or opposed to nuclear energy plants?"

	Sept. 1977 (%)	March 1979 (%)	May 1979 (%)	Sept. 1979 (%)	March 1981 (%)	Oct. 1981 (%)	June 1984 (%)	July 1986 (%)	Feb. 1988 (%)
In favor of nuclear energy plants	24	24	21	21	28	17	14	14	13
Opposed to nuclear energy plants	32	32	36	32	24	36	38	44	49
Fifty-fifty, impossible to say	44	44	43	47	48	47	48	42	38
Total	100	100	100	100	100	100	100	100	100
n	2002	1950	947	2021	1035	1983	2079	2175	2100

SOURCE: Allensbach Archives, IfD Surveys 3047, 3065, 3070, 3073, 3094, 4001, 4045, 4075, 5000.

because the initial essay (Noelle-Neumann, 1974a; see also Noelle-Neumann, 1989a) was a very much abridged presentation. The concept was thus prone to oversimplification in the scholarly discussion (Donsbach, 1987; Donsbach & Stevenson, 1984, 1986).

In general, the model was interpreted as consisting merely of two independent variables and one dependent variable. The two independent variables were (a) majority and minority opinion on a given topic as perceived at the time of the survey, and (b) expectations as to which opinions will increase in the near future and which will decrease. The dependent variable was interpreted to be the willingness to speak out or the tendency to keep silent resulting from fear of isolation. The resulting dynamics make the side that is willing to speak out appear stronger, while the side that tends to keep silent seems weaker than it is and thus becomes progressively weaker.

It is obvious that this abridged model lacks certain dimensions: the element of publicness, which is essential to the process of public opinion, and the condition that the process takes place only in morally loaded debates (the threat of isolation does not apply to topics that do not have a moral or aesthetic component). The early and late stages of the spiral, with the avant-garde and the hard core, were omitted, as was, most important, the influence of the mass media.

Some researchers who tested the spiral of silence suggested that the media be excluded to begin with, in order to simplify the tests (Glynn & McLeod, 1985, p. 44). But in this case, the theses of the spiral of silence would be refuted on all

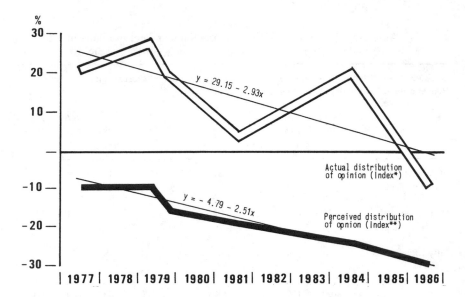

Figure 3. Pluralistic ignorance about attitudes toward nuclear energy. Actual and perceived distribution of opinion on nuclear energy.

SOURCE: Mathes (1989); survey data are taken from the Allensbach Archives, IfD Surveys 3047, 3065, 3070, 4001, 4045, 4075.

*Index actual ratio: supporters minus opponents of nuclear energy.

**Index perceived ratio: percentage of those who considered the supporters in the majority minus the percentage of those who considered the opponents in the majority.

the issues where there is a large gap between the tenor of the media and popular opinion. I have never found a spiral of silence that goes against the tenor of the media, for the willingness to speak out depends in part upon sensing that there is support and legitimation from the media.

In a review of all the tests of the spiral of silence that have come to his attention, Donsbach (1987, pp. 336ff.) states that they have often disregarded important conditions of the theory, for example, failing to take into account the position of the mass media and the tenor of the media, which, as a result, acts as an intervening variable. As soon as there is a gap between the tenor of the media and the majority opinion of the population, the well-known "silent majority" results (which, contrary to Smith, 1970, may not be an "invention" of President Nixon). Rather than refuting the theory of the spiral of silence, the "silent majority" shows how strongly the mass media must be seen to influence the process of public opinion. The tenor of the media generates a threat of isolation. The tenor of the media is essential to an assessment of the climate of opinion, and the media enable people to express themselves by providing words and arguments to articulate the views of the side they support. It is not until a topic has attained high priority in the media that pressure builds up that, in turn, generates a threat of isolation and fear of isolation.[5]

TABLE 7

Expectations in the Federal Republic of Germany About How the Climate of Opinion on Nuclear Energy Plants Will Develop in the Future: Population 16 and Over

Question: "How do you think things will develop — will more people or less people be in favor of nuclear energy a year from now in West Germany?"

	Sept. 1977 (%)	*March 1979* (%)	*May 1979* (%)	*Sept. 1979* (%)	*March 1981* (%)	*Oct. 1981* (%)	*June 1984* (%)	*July 1986* (%)	*Feb. 1988* (%)
More people will be in favor of nuclear energy	37	43	38	38	37	23	14	9	4
Less people will be in favor of nuclear energy	20	17	25	18	18	25	24	49	58
Nothing will change	21	21	16	25	24	29	42	27	25
Undecided, don't know	22	19	21	19	21	23	20	15	13
Total	100	100	100	100	100	100	100	100	100
n	2002	1950	947	2032	1035	1983	2079	2175	2100

SOURCE: Allensbach Archives, IfD Surveys 3047, 3065, 3070, 3073, 3094, 4001, 4045, 4075, 5000.

At least six kinds of information are required in the analysis of public opinion; it may be stated that the following information from surveys and media content analyses is required to analyze a process of public opinion and to make forecasts about future trends:

(1) the locus of majority opinion

(2) assessment of the climate of opinion (What do most people think?)

(3) future expectations of success (Which side will win? Which side will lose?)

(4) willingness to stand up for one's convictions (willingness to speak out) in public

(5) extent to which the topic has an emotional and moral component

(6) intensity and tenor of the discussion of the topic in the agenda-setting media (media that are cited by other media and heeded by politicians)

If this information can be compiled on a given topic, good forecasts can be provided about the development of public opinion. These forecasts extend far beyond traditional analyses using survey data, which are strictly based on the distribution of opinion in the population according to surveys of individuals.

TABLE 8

Willingness to Speak Out in the Federal Republic of Germany on the
Debate About Nuclear Energy Plants: Population 16 and Over

Question: "Assume you are on a five-hour train ride and someone in your compartment starts talking
very *favorably* about nuclear energy plants [in every other interview: very *unfavorably* about nuclear
energy plants]. Would you like to talk to this person?"

	Sept. 1977 (%)	*May* 1979 (%)	*March* 1981 (%)	*Oct.* 1981 (%)	*June* 1984 (%)	*July* 1986 (%)	*July* 1987 (%)	*Feb.* 1988 (%)
Supporters of nuclear energy								
would like to talk	56	61	60	56	45	47	39	45
would prefer not to	37	33	32	36	44	44	46	45
no opinion	7	6	8	8	11	9	15	10
Total	100	100	100	100	100	100	100	100
n	912	427	509	657	873	693	208	519
Opponents of nuclear energy								
would like to talk	51	64	52	48	45	49	47	52
would prefer not to	42	32	36	41	43	37	42	35
no opinion	7	4	12	11	12	14	11	13
Total	100	100	100	100	100	100	100	100
n	454	248	225	624	524	906	472	994

SOURCE: Allensbach Archives, IfD Surveys 3047, 3070, 3094, 4001, 4045, 4075, 4092/II, 5000.

SODALITY AND THE SPIRAL OF SILENCE

In the abridged version of the theory published in the *Journal of Communication*, the fact that the entire process of the formation of public opinion is based on human *social* nature was not emphasized enough. Rousseau (1750-55/1964) provides a matchless description of this social nature: "Man, as a social being, is always oriented outward; he first achieves the basic feeling of life through the perception of what others think of him" (p. 193). We might also speak of "social self," which is the focus of George H. Mead's (1934) theory: The "social self" is always worried about what "significant others" think.

The theory of the spiral of silence is based on assumptions about humans' social nature that are more far reaching than previous assumptions had been, however. Rather than limiting itself to "significant others" or reference groups, the theory focuses on people's great sensitivity to the impression they make in *public*. This public is Edmund Burke's (1791/1975) "public eye" and "public ear" (p. 66). Public in the sense of "for all to see, for all to hear." The public as an anonymous tribunal, as an authority that judges each individual. The social psychological dimension of the public as a medium in which public opinion can create the fear of isolation and issue the threat of isolation demands more attention than it was accorded in the initial accounts.

Because it was not made clear that the theory was based on social nature and the public eye, James Beninger (1987) came to the conclusion that the spiral of silence was a model "of atomized individuals at the mercy of centralized media" (p. 551). In fact, it is based on the very ability John Locke had already described, of arriving at a common assessment or prejudice and threatening the person who does not go along with the consensus. Rather than feeling atomized, the individual feels embedded in solidarity, with its needs and sensitivity.

THE TRANSFORMATION OF
INDIVIDUAL OPINIONS INTO PUBLIC OPINION

It is now that Verba's claim concerning the cause of failure in public opinion theory can be refined. Verba (1970), as noted earlier, held that public opinion theory had not developed because it "usually focuses on the individual as a unit of analysis" (p. 455). But this claim was not quite correct. It is not the fact that the individual has been the unit of analysis that has kept a theory from being developed, but the fact that the social nature of the individual has been neglected.

Questions in opinion research are oriented toward the individual's opinion, behavior, and knowledge: "Are *you* in favor of . . .?" "Are *you* interested in . . .?" "Are *you* concerned about . . .?" "Do *you* prefer . . .?" And so on. Questions about the climate of opinion would take the following form: "How do most people think?" "What is on the increase . . . ?" "What is IN, OUT?" "What might you have a falling out over with even the best of friends?" "Who is jeered?" "Who is snubbed?" Such questions, which are oriented toward observing the social setting, and thus toward the individual's social nature, have not been included systematically in analyses of opinion research, especially not in election research.

It is not that human social nature has been completely neglected in social research. In his famous essay, "Toward a Science of Public Opinion," Floyd H. Allport (1937) describes shoveling snow on the sidewalk as an expression of public opinion (p. 18), but no conclusions have been drawn from this in opinion research. Thus the vital question of how the mighty structure known as public opinion develops from the sum of individual opinions, which opinion research expresses in percentages, has not been answered — public opinion, which induces fear and trembling in governments, forcing them to take political action and "producing social and political consequences" (Smith, 1970), and which forces the individual to at least keep quiet if he or she does not share that public opinion (Bryce, 1888-1889).

As far as we know, it is constant interactions among people, due to their social nature, that account for the transformation of the sum of individual opinions into public opinion. The threat of isolation, the fear of isolation, the continual observation of the climate of opinion, and the assessment of the relative strength or weakness of different sides determine whether people will speak out or keep silent.

All these processes of public opinion that involve great effort — determining topics of public debate, defending public opinion, changing public opinion, the upheaval of values, right up to and including playful variations of fashion — ensure society's integration and ability to act.

THE GENERAL PUBLIC AND
THE ELITE IN PUBLIC OPINION

Harwood Childs (1965) has compiled some 50 definitions of public opinion. Aside from the bizarre cases in which the tool is confused with the subject to be measured, all of these definitions can be grouped in two categories. First are definitions that regard public opinion as a consensus based on a majority of the population and requiring some process of cohesion. Second are definitions that consider public opinion to be the opinion of the elite members of society.

Childs reads as if one definition were to be chosen over the other, either the concept of general consensus or the concept of the elite. But this is not the case. We will not make any progress with a theory of public opinion if we are unable to determine the effectiveness of the elite in the process of public opinion. No one would seriously question the major influence the elite exerts on the process of public opinion and the lead it takes in the formation of public opinion. But we must abandon the notion that took hold increasingly in the nineteenth and twentieth centuries of the elite — responsible, well-informed persons, who are capable of making assessments and whose views would be heeded by governments (Speier, 1950) — as the primary agents of public opinion.

According to everything we have learned so far from the theory of public opinion, the only members of the elite who will influence the process of public opinion are those who have access to the public and take recourse to this when it comes to essential issues in the process of public opinion. There is no need to abandon ideas about the role of an informed public, the role of a concerned public (Wilson, 1933), the role of interest groups, and the role of the public as bystander (Lang & Lang, 1981). We must simply keep in mind that while they represent influences on public opinion, they do not constitute the pressure and social control of public opinion itself.

WHAT MAKES SOCIETY POSSIBLE?

Everyone is subject to this pressure and control, even those who do not vote and even those who are not interested. While I was concluding my work on this chapter, a colleague, Hans Zetterberg, called my attention to the myth of Protagoras, as described by Plato. According to this myth, talents were divided up among the people according to Zeus's instructions, with each person being given a different talent—for example, a craftsman's gift, or a musician's gift, or the gift of healing. Finally, Hermes was to distribute political gifts, the sense of justice and the sense of shame. Hermes asked, should I distribute these gifts just as I did the others, or should I distribute them to everyone? "To everyone," said Zeus, "everyone is to share in them; for cities could not arise if only a few shared in these gifts, as they do in the others" (see Hubbard & Karnofsky, 1982).

The informing idea of this myth is expressed in Protagoras's question: "Does there not have to be something which all citizens share in if there is to be a nation at all?" It is odd that group dynamics focuses so on the question of what gives groups cohesion, but does not address the question of how cohesion is guaranteed in the nation. The theory of the spiral of silence has often been accused of lacking rationality. It is true that this analysis of the process of public opinion can provide no guarantee that the better view will prevail. But a process of public opinion that is based on the threat of isolation and the fear of isolation should not be called irrational, for it is obvious how much society stands to gain from its cohesion and integration.

CONCLUSION

The conclusions to be drawn from the theory of the spiral of silence apply first of all to survey research itself, which gave rise to the theory and enabled it to be tested empirically. In addition to the repertoire of questions relating to the individual situation—facts, behavior, opinions, motives—there is a new type of question relating to the individual's social nature: the individual's observations about the threat of isolation and fear of isolation; quasi-statistical assessments of the past, the present, and the future; agenda-setting and the climate of opinion; and the individual's behavior in the public eye.

Conclusions for scholarly work in a broad sense consist of the application and testing of the theory:

- In political science (e.g., the theory of democracy), this application might result in a new assessment of how the pressure of public opinion is taken into account by the political leadership. The theory promises to yield the most extensive results when applied to election research (Noelle-Neumann, 1990). An area that has not yet been affected, the role of public opinion in totalitarian systems, as has been dramatically witnessed, might be opened up to analysis by this theory.[6]

- In social psychology, the theory may well apply to the study of tolerance and aggression toward minorities and foreigners, the theory of opinion leaders, and research on stereotypes.
- In sociology, it would appear useful in the analysis of societies when examining the degree of consensus or integration, and in situations where integration is endangered, by crises.
- In history, an application may be found in the study of how great rulers have dealt with public opinion (Noelle-Neumann, 1989b, pp. 270ff.) or in the analysis of revolutions.
- In communication studies, it would be particularly useful when studying the effect of the mass media (Noelle-Neumann, 1989c) and propaganda in addition to rhetoric and analyses of literature (Noelle-Neumann, 1989b, pp. 266-322).
- In law, It would be helpful in studying the relationship between public opinion and the law (Exner, 1990).
- Finally, in theology and philosophy, its application might be in moral philosophy, where actions arising from humans' social nature are subject to a new assessment.

In addition, several of the social science theories developed in this century will need to be linked with the theory of public opinion. These might include reference group theory, the theory of rational choice or collective action, theories of group dynamics and conformity, or the theory of symbolic interaction. All of this opens up new perspectives on future work.

The most important consequence of the theory may be, however, its potential for creating an understanding of our dual nature, subject to the polarity between individuality and social nature.

APPENDIX

An overview of definitions of the elements of public opinion used in the theory of the spiral of silence may serve as an aid to comparing traditional concepts of public opinion according to Wilson (1933) and Childs (1965) with this presentation:

- *Public:* This is the public eye, the public as an authority that passes judgment and that is feared equally by governments and by individual members of society.
- *Opinions:* These are attitudes and modes of behavior in areas that are value-laden.
- *Formation of public opinion:* Different views in value-laden areas lead to consensus seeking with the aid of the social psychological threat of isolation and exploitation of people's fear of isolation, until one view wins out and becomes dominant.
- *Agents of public opinion:* These include all the members of society at a certain time in a certain place (Plato explicitly includes children).
- *Integration function:* In traditional twentieth-century interpretations of public opinion (for example, in Wilson, 1933) the emphasis is on the idea of participation. In the concept of the spiral of silence, public opinion serves to integrate society.
- *Public opinion:* This is interpreted as a process that takes place continuously in public, that is based on humans' social nature, and that ensures the formation and maintenance

of consensus in value-laden areas. It is the goal of this discussion to arrive at a conception of public opinion that emphasizes and elucidates the power of public opinion. In operational terms, the definition has not changed since the theory was first published: Public opinion is an opinion in value-laden areas that can be voiced in public without fear of sanctions and upon which actions can be based in public.

NOTES

1. That a completely new approach would be required to understand the concept of public opinion and to base a theory upon became evident to me while I was researching the literature for my inaugural lecture at the University of Mainz. The topic I had chosen was "Public Opinion and Social Control." It was not until decades later that I learned that the renowned dean of Harvard Law School, Roscoe Pound (1930), had held a lecture with the same title. His concern at the time was that legislators should not pass laws that ran counter to widely held opinions, since they would not be obeyed. By *social control* he meant legislation and the law. He applied the term in a far more restricted sense than Edward Ross (1901/1969), who had chosen this term — first coined, as far as we know, by Herbert Spencer (1879/1966, p. 118) — as the title of his book published in 1901. Ross explicitly included public opinion among the forces of social control. He described the social nature of man as vividly as John Locke had 300 years earlier. Whether he was inspired by Locke is a matter of conjecture, as he does not quote him. But, like Locke, he is stirred by the knowledge of the great sensitivity and vulnerability of human social nature: "It is not so much the dread of what an angry public may do that disarms the modern American, as it is sheer inability to stand unmoved in the rush of totally hostile comment, to endure a life perpetually at variance with the conscience and feeling of those about him" (p. 105).

It seems incomprehensible that the connection between the pressure of public opinion and the social nature of man should have been forgotten in the twentieth century. My research into the literature showed that the connection was known from the sixteenth to the nineteenth century, and I was even able to trace this knowledge and the term (see Cicero, 1980, p. 344).

2. It did not occur to me that this episode might provide the key to understanding the phenomenon of public opinion. Seven years later, a personal experience, which I have described elsewhere (Noelle-Neumann, 1988), provided me with an explanation, which was tested in the German federal election of 1972 and then formulated as the hypothesis of the spiral of silence.

3. This explanation accounted for the divergent responses regarding voting intentions and antici-pated election results. It did not, however, clarify why one side — in 1965 the Christian Democrats — raised its level of public visibility so much that the other side was put on the defensive, after both had started out on equal footing at the beginning of the year. One possible explanation is the publicity showered on the then CDU/DSU chancellor, Ludwig Erhard, when he accompanied the queen of England on her triumphal procession during her first visit to Germany after World War II in the summer of 1965. But this will always remain at the level of speculation after the passing of so many years.

4. With the precision of a botanist describing a plant, Tocqueville (1856/1955) uses the example of believing Christians to delineate the process of such a spiral of silence in his book on the downfall of the monarchy and the French Revolution: "Those who retained their belief in the doctrines of the church became afraid of being alone in their allegiance and, dreading isolation more than error, professed to share the sentiments of the majority. So what was in reality the opinion of only a part . . . of the nation came to be regarded as the will of all and for this reason seemed irresistible, even to those who have given it this false appearance" (p. 155).

5. The influence of the mass media is not the only decisive factor in the process of public opinion, however. When there is a gap between the tenor of the media and the majority opinion of the population, the results are often a superficial consensus that is unstable, full of contradictions, and susceptible to rapid change if real developments should disprove expectations.

6. Politics has been much quicker than academic research to apply the theory of the spiral of silence. Conradt (1978, pp. 40ff.) describes in his report on the German federal election of 1976 that three years following the initial publication of the theory, election campaign strategists used the findings from the theory to fight a spiral of silence.

REFERENCES

Allport, F. H. (1937). Toward a science of public opinion. *Public Opinion Quarterly, 1*, 7-23.

Aristotle. (1986). *Politik* (O. Gigon, Trans.). Munich: Deutscher Taschenbuch Verlag.

Asch, S. E. (1951). Effects of group pressure upon the modification and distortion of judgments. In H. Guetzkow (Ed.), *Groups, leadership, and men: Research in human relations* (pp. 177-190). New York: Russell & Russell.

Asch, S. E. (1952). Group forces in the modification and distortion of judgments. In S. E. Asch (Ed.), *Social psychology.* Englewood Cliffs, NJ: Prentice-Hall.

Back, K. W. (1988). Metaphors for public opinion in literature. *Public Opinion Quarterly, 52*, 278-288.

Beninger, J. R. (1987). Toward an old new paradigm: The half-century flirtation with mass society. *Public Opinion Quarterly, 51*, 46-66.

Beyle, H. C. (1931). *Identification and analysis of attribute-cluster-blocs.* Chicago: University of Chicago Press.

Bryce, J. (1888-1889). *The American commonwealth* (Vols. 1-2). London: Macmillan.

Burke, E. (1975). An appeal from the new to the old Whigs. In E. Burke, *The works* (Vol. 4, pp. 61-215). New York: Georg Olms. (Original work published 1791)

Cartwright, D., & Zander, A. (Eds.). (1968). *Group dynamics: Research and theory* (3rd ed.). New York: Harper & Row.

Childs, H. L. (1965). *Public opinion: Nature, formation, and role.* New York: van Nostrand.

Cicero (1980). *Atticus-briefe* (H. Kasten, Trans.). Munich: Artemis.

Conradt, D. P. (1978). The 1976 campaign and election: An overview. In K. H. Cerny (Ed.), *Germany at the polls: The bundestag election of 1976* (pp. 29-56). Washington, DC: American Enterprise Institute for Public Policy Research.

Darwin, C. (1873). *The expression of the emotions in man and animals.* London: Murray.

Davison, W. P. (1989, August). *The future of public opinion in liberal democratic societies.* Paper presented at the Fourth International Conference of Professors World Peace Academy, London.

Donsbach, W. (1987). Die Theorie der Schweigespirale [The theory of the spiral of silence]. In M. Schenk (Ed.), *Medienwirkungsforschung* [Media effects research] (pp. 324-343). Tubingen: J. C. B. Mohr.

Donsbach, W., & Stevenson, R. L. (1984, May). *Challenges, problems and empirical evidences of the theory of the spiral of silence.* Paper presented at the annual meeting of the International Communication Association, San Francisco.

Donsbach, W., & Stevenson, R. L. (1986). Herausforderungen, Probleme und empirische Evidenzen der Theorie der Schweigespirale [Challenges, problems and empirical evidences of the theory of the spiral of silence]. *Publizistik, 31*, 7-34.

Exner, B. (1990). *Öffentliche Meinung und Recht* [Public opinion and the law]. Mainz: Johannes Gutenberg University.

Fields, J. M., & Schuman, H. (1976). Public beliefs about the beliefs of the public. *Public Opinion Quarterly, 40*, 427-448.

Gallup Political Index. (1987, July). No. 323. London: Social Surveys Ltd.

Gallup Political Index. (1988, August). No. 336. London: Social Surveys Ltd.

Glynn, C. J., & McLeod, J. M. (1985). Implications of the spiral of silence theory for communication and public opinion research. In K. R. Sanders, L. L. Kaid, & D. Nimmo (Eds.), *Political communication yearbook* (pp. 43-65). Carbondale: Southern Illinois University Press.

Goffman, E. (1956). Embarrassment and social organization. *American Journal of Sociology, 62,* 264-271.

Goffman, E. (1963). *Behavior in public places: Notes on the social organization of gatherings.* New York: Free Press.

Hallemann, M. (1986). Peinlichkeit and öffentliche Meinung [Embarrassment and public opinion]. *Publizistik, 31,* 249-261.

Hallemann, M. (1989). *Peinlichkeit: Ein Ansatz sur Operationalisierung von Isolationsfurch im sozialpsychologischen Konzept öffentlicher Meinung* [Embarrassment: An approach to operationalization of the fear of isolation in the social-psychological concept of public opinion]. Unpublished doctoral dissertation, Johannes Gutenberg University, Mainz, West Germany.

Haviland, J. B. (1977). *Gossip, reputation and knowledge in Zinacantan.* Chicago: University of Chicago Press.

Hubbard, B. A. F., & Karnofsky, E. S. (1982). *Plato's Protagoras: A Socratic commentary.* London: Trinity.

Hyman, H. H. (1957). Toward a theory of public opinion. *Public Opinion Quarterly, 21,* 54-60.

Ihering, R. von (1883). *Der Sweck im Recht* [The purpose of law]. Leipzig: Breitkopf & Hartel.

Katz, E. (1981). Publicity and pluralistic ignorance: Notes on the 'spiral of silence.' In H. Baier, H. M. Kepplinger, & K. Reumann (Eds.), *Öffentliche Meinung and sozialer Wandel* [Public opinion and social change]. Opladen: Westdeutscher Verlag.

Kepplinger, H. M. (1988). Die Kernenergie in der Presse: Eine Analyse zum Einflu subjektiver Faktoren auf die Konstruktion von Realitat. *Kölner Zeitschrift für Soziologie und Sozialpsychologie, 40,* 659-683.

Kepplinger, H. M. (1989). *Künstliche Horizonte. Folgen, Darstellung und Akzeptanz von Technik in der Bundesrepublik Deutschland* [Artifical horizons: Consequences, presentation and acceptance of technology in the Federal Republic of Germany]. Frankfurt: Campus Verlag.

Kim, S. C. (1989). *Begriffe der Öffentlichen Meinung und ihre Funktion als soziale Kontrolle im ostasiatischen Verstandis* [Concepts of public opinion and their function as social control in an East Asian context]. Unpublished doctoral dissertation, Johannes Gutenberg University, Mainz, West Germany.

Lang, K., & Lang, G. E. (1981). The public as bystander: Its political influence. In H. Baier, H. M. Kepplinger, & K. Ruemann (Eds.), *Öffentliche Meinung und sozialer Wandel* [Public opinion and social change] (pp. 39-49). Opladen: Westdeutscher Verlag.

Le Goff, J. (1989, May 3). Kann denn Lachen Sünde sein? Die mittelalterliche Geschichte einer sozialen Verhaltensweise [Can laughter be a sin? The medieval history of a form of social behavior]. *Frankfurter Allgemeine Zeitung, 102,* N3.

Locke, J. (1894). *An essay concerning human understanding* (A. C. Fraser, Ed.). Oxford: Clarendon.

Machiavelli, N. (1950). *The prince and the discourses* (L. Ricci, E. R. P. Vincent, & C. Detmold, Trans.). New York: Random House.

Madison, J. (1961). The Federalist No. 49. In J. E. Cooke (Ed.), *The Federalist* (pp. 338-347). Middletown, CT: Wesleyan University Press. (Original work published 1788)

Mathes, S. (1989). *Sozial-optische Täuschung durch Massenmedien: Die Einschätzung des Meinungsklimas im Konflikt um die Kernenergie durch Personen mit viel und wenig Fernsehnutzung.* Unpublished master's thesis, University of Mainz, West Germany.

Mead, G. H. (1934). *Mind, self and society: From the standpoint of a social behaviorist.* Chicago: University of Chicago Press.

Mead, M. (1937). Public opinion mechanisms among primitive peoples. *Public Opinion Quarterly, 1,* 5-16.

Milgram, S. (1961). Nationality and conformity. *Scientific American, 205,* 45-51.

Müller, J. von. (1819). Zuschrift an alle Eidgenossen [Letter to all Swiss citizens]. In J. G. Müller (Ed.), *Samtliche Werke* [Complete works] (pp. 24-50). Tubingen: J. G. Cotta'sche Buchhandlung. (Original work published 1777)

Mutz, D. C. (1989). The influence of perceptions of media influence: Third person effects and the public expression of opinions. *International Journal of Public Opinion Research, 1,* 3-23.

Noelle-Neumann, E. (1973). Kumulation, Konsonanz und Öffentlichkeitseffekt: Ein Neuer Ansatz sur Analyse der Wirkung der Massenmedien [Cumulation, consonance and the effect of publicness: A new approach to the analysis of the effect of the mass media]. *Publizistik, 18*, 26-55.

Noelle-Neumann, E. (1974a). Die Schwiegenspirale. Uber die Entstehung der öffentlichen Meinung [The spiral of silence: On the origins of public opinion]. In E. Forsthoff & R. Horstel (Eds.), *Standorte im Zeitstrom* [Positions in the flow of time] (pp. 299-330). Frankfurt/Main: Athenaum.

Noelle-Neumann, E. (1974b). The spiral of silence: A theory of public opinion. *Journal of Communication, 24*, 43-51.

Noelle-Neumann, E. (1980). Kampf un die Öffentliche Meinung: Eine vergleichende sozialpsychologische Analyse der Bundestagwahlen 1972 und 1976 [The struggle for public opinion: A comparative social-psychological analysis of the 1972 and 1976 Bundestag elections]. In E. Noelle-Neumann (Ed.), Wahlentscheidung in der Fernsehdemokratie [Voting decisions in the television democracy] (pp. 144-190). Freiburg, Wurzburg: Ploetz.

Noelle-Neumann, E. (1984). *The spiral of silence: Public opinion —our social skin.* Chicago: University of Chicago Press.

Noelle-Neumann, E. (1985). The spiral of silence: A response. In K. R. Sanders, L. L. Kaid, & D. Nimmo (Eds.), *Political communication yearbook* (pp. 66-94). Carbondale: Southern Illinois University Press.

Noelle-Neumann, E. (1986, November). *Election research and the climate of opinion.* Paper presented at the Seminar on Opinion Polls, Strasbourg, France.

Noelle-Neumann, E. (1988). Toward a theory of public opinion. In H. J. O'Gorman (Ed.), *Surveying social life: Papers in honor of Herbert Hyman* (pp. 289-300). Middletown, CT: Wesleyan University Press.

Noelle-Neumann, E. (1989a). La Spirale du Silence: Une theorie de l'opinion publique [The spiral of silence: A theory of public opinion]. In *Le Nouvel Espace Public: Hermes Cognition Communication Politique* (pp. 181-189). Paris: Editions du Centre National de la Recherche Scientifique.

Noelle-Neumann, E. (1989b). *Öffentliche Meinung. Die Entdeckung der Schweige Spirale* [Public opinion: The discovery of the spiral of silence]. Vienna: Ullstein.

Noelle-Neumann, E. (1989c). Die Theorie der Schweigespirale als Instrument der Medienwirkungsforschung [The theory of the spiral of silence as a tool of media effects research]. *Kölner Zeitschrift für Soziologie und Sozialpsychologie, 30*, 418-440.

Noelle-Neumann, E. (1990). Meinungsklima als neue Dimension der Wahlforschung [The climate of opinion as a new dimension of election research]. In M. Kaase & H. D. Klingemann (Eds.), *Wahlen und Wähler. Analysen aus Anla der Bundestagswahl 1987* [Voters and voting day: Analyses on the occasion of the federal election 1987] (pp. 481-530). Opladen: Westdeutscher Verlag.

O'Gorman, H. J., & Garry, S. L. (1976). Pluralistic ignorance: A replication and extension. *Public Opinion Quarterly, 40*, 449-458.

Pound, R. (1930). Public opinion and social control. *Proceedings of the national conference of social work* (pp. 607-623). Chicago: University of Chicago Press.

Ross, E. A. (1969). *Social control: A survey of the foundations of order.* Cleveland, OH: Press of Case Western Reserve University. (Original work published 1901)

Rousseau, J. J. (1953). The social contract. In F. Watkins (Ed.), *Political writings.* London: Nelson. (Original work published 1762)

Rousseau, J. J. (1964). *The first and second discourses* (R. Masters & J. Masters, Trans.). New York: St. Martin's. (Original work published 1750-55)

Salisbury, J. of. (1963). *The statesman's book of John of Salisbury* (J. Dickinson, Trans.). New York: Russell & Russell. (Original work published 1927)

Salmon, C. T., & Kline, F. G. (1985). The spiral of silence ten years later: An examination and evaluation. In K. R. Sanders, L. L. Kaid, & D. Nimmo (Eds.), *Political communication yearbook* (pp. 3-30). Carbondale: Southern Illinois University Press.

Smith, B. W. (1970). Some psychological perspectives on the theory of public opinion. *Public Opinion Quarterly, 34*, 454-455.

Speier, H. (1950). Historical development of public opinion. *American Journal of Sociology, 55,* 376-388.

Spencer, H. (1966). *The works of Herbert Spencer* (Vol. 9). Osnabruck: Otto Zeller. (Original work published 1892)

Taylor, D. G. (1982). Pluralistic ignorance and the spiral of silence: A formal analysis. *Public Opinion Quarterly, 46,* 311-335.

Thucydides. (1981). *Geschichte des Peleponnesischen Krieges.* Munich: Deutscher Taschenbuch Verlag.

Tocqueville, A. de. (1948). *Democracy in America* (H. Reeve, Trans.). New York: Knopf. (Original work published 1835-1840)

Tocqueville, A. de. (1955). *The old regime and the French revolution* (S. Gilbert, Trans.). Garden City, NY: Doubleday. (Original work published 1856)

Verba, S. (1970). The impact of the public on policy. *Public Opinion Quarterly, 34,* 455.

Warner, L. (1939). The reliability of public opinion surveys. *Public Opinion Quarterly, 3,* 376-390.

Wilson, F. G. (1933). Concepts of public opinion. *American Political Science Review, 27,* 371-391.

Reflections on the "Spiral of Silence"

MIHALY CSIKSZENTMIHALYI
University of Chicago

O NE of the fundamental aspects of the human condition, according to Hannah Arendt (1958), is *plurality*, that is, the unavoidable fact that each man and woman is in some important respect unique, different from everyone else, yet cannot exist in solitude, but only in close cooperation and dialectic contrast with one another. This need to establish contact and consensus despite deep differences in perspectives and interests is what makes us political animals. One of the implications of this state of affairs is that human behavior cannot be fully understood except from a systems perspective, that is, from a viewpoint that takes into account the mutual effects of interactions among individuals, institutions, and the symbol systems they inherit and create.

The work of Elisabeth Noelle-Neumann is a good example of such a systemic viewpoint, even though she never explicitly claims it to be so. But most of the basic questions raised in her writing deal with problems inherent in the condition of human plurality. Her central theoretical questions — namely, where does public opinion come from, how is it shaped, and how does it affect behavior — are important because men and women potentially hold innumerable different opinions about everything, yet in order to act effectively they must reach a common view about important issues.

Of these important issues on which consensus must be reached, the one that interests Noelle-Neumann most — and is certainly one of the most fundamental — concerns the formation of political opinion. In an electoral democracy but indeed even in the most tyrannical forms of government (as the fate of the various Eastern European dictators who were recently deposed has shown), the right to lead and to decide must eventually rest on the agreement of a significant segment of the population.

Correspondence and requests for reprints: Mihaly Csikszentmihalyi, Department of Psychology, University of Chicago, 5848 South University Avenue, Chicago, IL 60637.

Communication Yearbook 14, pp. 288-297

In ancient times, it was held that *vox populi* was *vox Dei*. About a hundred years ago, Emile Durkheim (1893/1964) subtly reversed the equation by claiming, in effect, that the *vox Dei* was nothing but the *vox populi* — in other words, that what various cultures hold to be divine injunctions were the beliefs of the community expressed in symbolic forms made compelling by emotional and aesthetic elaborations.

It is one thing to recognize the awesome power of public opinion, whether expressed in religious beliefs, political action, or consumer choices; many thinkers, from Aristotle to James Madison, have done so, and Noelle-Neumann has elegantly summarized their insights. But it is much more difficult to describe, with the tools of the social sciences, the dynamics of how this opinion is formed and what its consequences are. It is to this difficult task that Noelle-Neumann has devoted her energies in the past few decades.

I will not try to summarize Noelle-Neumann's current position, which is based on her reflections on the results of her extensive empirical studies, and interpreted in the light of her extensive readings in philosophy, history, and the literature of communication and public opinion research. Her chapter in this volume clearly outlines the trajectory of her thought, and it would be both presumptuous and redundant to replicate what she has written. Instead, I would like to examine those points in her argument that in terms of my understanding are most interesting, or controversial, or theoretically generative. This analysis might cast a different light on some of the issues, a light that might illuminate some of the more obscure and complex passages in this arduous theoretical journey.

Why is public opinion so powerful? One of the central issues confronted by Noelle-Neumann is the "awesome power" of public opinion. Unless we understand how basic this power is, she claims, we are bound to dangerously underestimate its sway in human affairs. The way I interpret her argument, the power of public opinion has two main sources. One is a distal one, operating in evolutionary, historical time on entire communities and social systems. The second is a proximal cause, operating at the level of individual feelings and beliefs.

SOCIETAL LEVEL OF ANALYSIS

The distal cause for the existence of public opinion is speculative, but grounded in sound reason. Stated in terms of a "group selection" model of cultural evolution, those communities that fail to form a consensus concerning common action will not be able to function as well as communities that do, and hence with time the former will gradually be supplanted by the latter. It would follow, then, that successful social systems must have ways to institutionalize consensus, including the formation of a more or less stable, more or less binding, climate of opinion.

In Noelle-Neumann's work, this societal level of explanation for the power of public opinion — which she calls the "integrative function" — is often implicit, but rarely examined directly. As a result, some potentially important questions risk being neglected. One of these is, Are there *qualitative* differences in the way societies arrive at a consensus among differing views? I suspect Noelle-Neumann would answer this question with an emphatic yes, but in her effort to make the spiral of silence a concept with universal applicability, she might have assumed too much similarity among societies, with the result that we might lose sight of some important differences.

The anthropological record suggests the existence of a wide spectrum of ways in which cultures have resolved the problem of integration. While all of these solutions are based on some common climate of opinion, in some societies, conformity is enforced through an almost paranoid fear of one's peers, including one's closest relatives (e.g., Dobuans, Nigerians), while in others a great latitude is allowed for individual differentiation, and consensus seems to emerge spontaneously and without coercion from the sharing of different viewpoints (e.g., Navajos, Kalahari bushmen). One would expect, for example, that in societies held together by what Durkheim called "mechanical solidarity," characterized by outward rules and coercion, the role of public opinion would be very different from societies in which "organic solidarity" prevails.

Or, to use another model, in her analysis of political behavior, Hannah Arendt (1958) distinguishes social systems on the basis of how much room they give to the "public sphere." Her ideal-type community is the Greek *polis*, where the public sphere had the widest latitude. The Greek citizen had the right to argue his opinion freely against that of all his compatriots in the agora and could persist in his minority opinion without fear of ostracism, even though the majority carried the day. The power of public opinion, in her view, would be greatest in societies where the public sphere is weak or absent; that is, where individuals have no recognized opportunity to debate their peers, or where they are afraid to do so for fear of ostracism or retribution. Arendt believed that the public sphere, which reached its peak in Greece 2,000 years ago, has since been losing ground everywhere to mass conformity. Whether she is right or not, however, the point is that the force of public opinion varies depending on the economic, political, and cultural institutions of social systems. It is never entirely powerless, and never completely sovereign; between these two extremes its dominion holds a broad sway. One of the consequences of this fact for Noelle-Neumann's theory of public opinion is to suggest a number of questions that future scholarship will have to address, dealing with the relationship of public opinion to the other institutions of society.

Values and Public Opinion

In her definition of what public opinion is, Noelle-Neumann states that it "is a process that takes place continuously in public . . . and that ensures the formation and maintenance of consensus *in value-laden areas*" (pp. 258; emphasis added). If we assume, as it seems perfectly justified to assume on the basis of historical and anthropological evidence, that societies vary a great deal in terms of how "value-laden" they are, then it follows that the importance of public opinion should vary as a function of how important values are to the integration of society. Pitrim Sorokin (1962), for instance, has claimed that "ideational" societies such as existed in Europe in the Middle Ages rely heavily on common values, whereas "sensate" societies like Rome in the second century or the contemporary United States are held together more by contracts and compromise than by values. If this is true, then public opinion must be less dominant in these latter societies.

But even if values were equally important in ensuring solidarity in every social system, it seems clear that values apply to different institutions with differing strengths from one society to another. Party politics in the United States is not as value-laden as it is generally in Europe, and therefore the formation of public opinion in politics must be less relevant in the United States than in Germany or France. On the other hand, business transactions are based more heavily on ethical values such as fairness and reciprocity in the United States, and hence presumably a shared climate of opinion relating to entrepreneurial behavior is more important here than in most other places.

In other words, if the function of public opinion is to achieve a consensus on values, it becomes extremely important to know which areas are laden with values, and which are not. A comparative study of public opinion that does not take account of this fact would be doomed from the start, because comparing, for example, opinions about religion in Northern Ireland and Denmark would be like comparing apples with oranges, since the strength of the link between values and religion in the two societies is so different.

The Agents of Public Opinion

While it makes sense to claim, as Noelle-Neumann does, that all members of society, children included, are agents of public opinion, it also seems sensible to recognize the differences that exist among societies in terms of what sanctions various types of agents are permitted to impose in order to achieve consensus.

The Navajo achieve unanimity by sitting in council until everyone agrees on a common action or a shared interpretation of reality. The Chinese communists use public confessions and shaming by professional agents of conformity to enforce consensus. Certainly it should make a great difference to the quality of public opinion which of these two processes is being used.

A recent event may illustrate my point: In a greeting card I received this past Christmas from a cousin living in Budapest, he notes how incredibly strange it is for him to speak his mind freely to strangers after 42 years. "For the first time in my adult life," he writes, "I am not afraid to say in public what I feel." When the agents of conformity have the enforcement powers that the secret police have in communist countries, the scope of public opinion is very different from what it is in societies where citizens have about equal rights to influence consensus.

Of course, throughout history inequality in influencing public opinion has been much more the rule than the exception. When one reads the painstaking accounts of the fourteenth-century trials of the Inquisition in southern France reported by

Le Roy Ladurie (1979), one realizes what incredible efforts the agents of the church invested in preserving consensus on matters of religious belief and practice. In every epoch, those who held power in any of its forms — economic, religious, political, or social — also tried to mold public opinion in their favor. And, as they have had greater resources than the average person, presumably their ability to do so has been proportionally greater.

But what makes public opinion such an exciting phenomenon is its relative independence from other forms of power. No matter how many resources the privileged agents of public opinion bring into the arena, they are usually unable to dominate the climate of opinion completely. In Western Europe, for instance, after World War II a curious split developed between those who held economic and political power and those who had a greater-than-average influence in affecting public opinion. In some countries, like Germany and Italy, a large part of the press and many universities became for several decades conscious tools of left-wing politics, at odds with the establishment. To a large extent, public opinion was formed by forces that were in opposition to the status quo. It is too early to say what the long-term effects of these efforts to mold the climate of opinion will be, although they seem to have failed. At the other extreme has been the failure of political bodies with economic and coercionary powers to maintain their desired status quo: The effects of the state propaganda in Eastern Europe in the past 12 months have shown themselves to have been utterly ineffectual. For almost half a century, the Soviet-supported governments in East Germany, Poland, Czechoslovakia, Romania, and Bulgaria had imposed a rigid ideological consensus through every public medium of communication. Yet now we know how shallow such indoctrination has been. Apparently, when people share common experiences, they can form a consensus about values even without the opportunity to voice their opinions in public.

Such recent historical examples suggest that public opinion may be more impervious to manipulation by its privileged agents than Noelle-Neumann's model allows for. In the short run, the media, the educational institutions, the established churches can help create a climate of opinion that serves the purposes of those who control them. But, in the long run, consensus seems to be based on experience, and efforts to interpret reality that are clearly deceptive will be exposed and will end in failure.

Two Kinds of Public Opinion?

Reflection on Noelle-Neumann's definition of public opinion in light of recent historical events raises the question as to whether it is useful to distinguish between at least two ways in which public opinion may be formed. Borrowing from the field of motivational psychology, we may call the first process *extrinsic* and the second *intrinsic*.

The extrinsic process of public opinion formation exists when conscious agents of communication try to impose a certain set of beliefs or attitudes on the population at large. This process might get participants involved in public debate, as at kolkhoz meetings in the Soviet Union, at Chinese commune meetings, or in Western marketing campaigns where prospective consumers' views are solicited. Despite their public nature, however, these processes of opinion formation are consciously manipulative.

Intrinsic opinion emerges out of more spontaneous, organic reactions, either to open debates or to concrete experiences. The ideal situation is symbolized by the *polis*, where competing ideas were evaluated and the most deserving ones were adopted on their merit. A less ideal but alternative way is that of the multiparty system, where different platforms are tailored to appeal to different goals and strivings of the electorate. In repressive systems, intrinsic opinion is more likely to be based on private reflections nurtured in solitude, or shared only in the most intimate circle of friends. However, given the opportunity, these privately arrived at opinions may explode into the open, suggesting that a consensus had been building for years in the society as a whole. How else can one explain what happened in East Berlin, Prague, or Bucharest last year?

Opinion formed extrinsically can be quite effective as a form of consensus. Billions of Chinese have been repeating the slogans handed down by the party for almost half a century, keeping the system intact. If my cousin in Budapest had died in 1988, he would have never known what it felt like to speak his mind freely. For long periods of time, people are willing to act as if they believe the opinions they are forced to express—and an outside "objective" observer could not tell the difference. But the fragility of a consensus held together by extrinsic means is revealed when the agents of public opinion are no longer able to enforce the party line. At that point, the sum of individual reflections on a common experience wells forth as a new force, and sometimes a set of values and beliefs diametrically opposed to the ones that have been prevalent carries the day.

THE INDIVIDUAL LEVEL OF ANALYSIS

Noelle-Neumann justly argues that without a certain amount of consensus, expressed in public opinion, it would be difficult for a community to survive. But community needs must be somehow transformed into personal motives if they are to be effective. The proximal roots of public opinion formation must be found at the level of individual psychology. It is at this level that Noelle-Neumann's contribution to our understanding of public opinion is perhaps the most powerful.

Noelle-Neumann suggests that fear of isolation and a sense of shame are the ways that evolution has found to instill in us a willingness to cooperate with our fellow beings. Just as the painful pangs of hunger warn us that we must eat if we wish to survive, the pain of ostracism keeps us seeking acceptance from our peers, so that the community, and we in it, can survive. The Greek word *idiot* meant a person whose idiosyncrasy separated him or her from the community, a person whose beliefs and actions could not be predicted. Such a person could not survive alone, and a society of idiots would also perish.

There is no question that Noelle-Neumann has identified a very important fact, a phenomenon that should be at the center of the social sciences, yet one that is very often completely ignored by many sociologists, psychologists, anthropologists, and political scientists. Although Salomon Asch (1952) and Stanley Milgram (1974) in psychology, and Erving Goffman (1974) in sociology, among others, have shown how sensitive our actions are to what we think others think of us, the importance of this relationship has yet to be absorbed by the respective disciplines.

In my own research, I have been repeatedly struck by how dependent people's feelings and thoughts are on the social environment in which they find themselves. Most people feel despondent and lonely when alone, and almost everyone's moods improve dramatically in the company of others — regardless of whether these are friends, acquaintances, or strangers (Csikszentmihalyi & Csikszentmihalyi, 1988; Csikszentmihalyi & Larson, 1984; Kubey & Csikszentmihalyi, 1990). There is no question that we are programmed to seek out the company of our conspecifics, and to find pleasure in their acceptance. Conversely, there is ample evidence that isolation and solitude are painful, and that people in general will go to great lengths to avoid them. So far, I would agree entirely with Noelle-Neumann's analysis to the effect that the fear of isolation is what gives power to public opinion.

On the other hand, here too, as I did earlier in terms of the social functions of public opinion, I would like to explore the meaning we might find in the differences from what appears to be the general rule. I am not sure, for instance, that Plato was right when he reported that Zeus gave all mortals equal doses of a sense of shame. In fact, the story of Protagoras quotes Zeus as saying, "for cities could not arise if only a few shared in these gifts." Perhaps the reason so many cities never arise, or that so many decline after having risen, is that the sense of shame (or, more broadly, the sense of mutual dependence on the good opinion of others) is in fact lacking in many people.

In other words, we cannot accept as a given that all people are equally sensitive to social rewards, and therefore to social influences. Even though fear of isolation is certainly one of the most universal and one of the strongest facts of human psychology, there are certainly important individual differences in this trait. And in this case — as in so many instances concerning human psychology — the exceptions may turn out to be more instructive than the general norm.

In the social conformity studies conducted by Asch and by Milgram, there was always a small but constant percentage of subjects who refused to go along with the experimentally induced social pressures. Who were these people? Because the research was focused on conformity, little attention was paid to those subjects who represented disconfirming evidence in the experiments. Yet could we not learn much by understanding why some persons are relatively immune to the pressure of public opinion when this conflicts with their own convictions? Why do some people appear to fear isolation less than others and are able to tolerate solitude? Are these individuals idiots without a sense of shame, or are they persons with superior self-confidence who are relatively independent of social approval? Probably both kinds of people are represented in the small minority that is resistant to social pressures.

In work not reported in the present chapter, Noelle-Neumann herself has begun to explore some of the individual differences that bear on these issues. Using a short questionnaire, she has been able to differentiate respondents along a continuum of what she calls *Personalitatstercke*, or personality strength (PS). People who are high on PS are self-confident, extroverted, involved. They participate more socially, take on positions of responsibility, and are asked by others to express their opinions on a variety of topics. Although educated, high-status, middle-aged men tend to have higher scores on PS, this trait is to a large extent independent of age, sex, and social status characteristics, and its effects actually are most marked among respondents of lower class statuses. Personality strength appears to be an individual trait that makes a person more likely to be an opinion leader than simply a consumer of other people's opinions.

Throughout most of its history, humanity has recognized that certain individuals have above-average abilities to influence others. This gift of power has been conceptualized in rather similar ways across many different cultures. Typical is the Polynesian belief that mana, the spiritual force that permeates the universe, is concentrated more strongly in a few persons, who then become recognized as the natural leaders of the community.

The belief in the importance of such personal powers has declined in the last few millennia, as the importance of impersonal powers accessible to anyone has increased. Today any person, no matter how weak and ineffective, can be awesome, provided he or she has access to the power mediated by money, a title, or technology. Any idiot with a gun, or with inherited money, will appear more powerful than the wisest Polynesian islander who has neither. Yet, despite the fact that personal power is now eclipsed by the power of artifacts, it is still true that, other things being equal, we pay more attention to people who possess certain traits, and we are more likely to be influenced by them.

Who are these people, and what are these traits? Knowing more about this question will add a great deal to our understanding of how public opinion works. Noelle-Neumann has shown us the way to get an answer.

THE SPIRAL OF SILENCE

All the pieces of Noelle-Neumann's theoretical model fit together in the dynamic process of opinion formation she has called the "spiral of silence." In its present form, this process is described by four assumptions that claim that each person, in order to avoid becoming isolated, keeps trying to assess what other people think so that his or her public behavior will not stand out and be a cause of ostracism. Change enters this model as follows: When a given segment of society, through its agents, succeeds in making it appear that opinion is swinging in a certain direction, then the silent majority, who has no alternatives to propose, tends to accept the apparent "consensus," believing it to be what everyone believes.

This view of how public opinion is formed, maintained, and changed is a convincing and satisfying one. The reflections developed thus far suggest, however, some three points where further clarification will be useful.

(1) If we take, for instance, the first assumption Noelle-Neumann advances — "Society threatens deviant individuals with isolation" (p. 260) — we immediately need to consider several conditions, such as the following: (a) Societies differ greatly as to what they define as deviant, as to which deviant behaviors involve values, and so on. (b) Societies differ in terms of how much they tolerate, or actually encourage, deviance. Certain social institutions (e.g., the agora) may develop to resolve divergent opinions, thereby decreasing the likelihood deviance will arise. (c) Societal threats against deviance involve not only isolation, but also a great variety of material sanctions. The threat of ending up in a concentration camp, or of losing one's job, can be a more powerful deterrent to deviance than the fear of isolation.

(2) The second assumption ("Individuals experience fear of isolation continually") is probably correct, although there are likely to be large individual differences in such fear, a fact that may or may not be important to take into account.

(3) The third and fourth assumptions are that "the fear of isolation causes individuals to try to assess the climate of opinion at all times," and "the results of this estimate affect behavior in public, especially the open expression or concealment of opinions." With these assumptions also, I would wish to take into account the following conditions: (a) Individuals differ in terms of how much they fear isolation, and hence in terms of how sensitive they are to the climate of opinion. (b) Some persons will be apt to comply with their estimate of what public opinion is, others will be immune to it, and still others might actively oppose it. Social statuses and individual traits — such as personality strength — mediate the effects of the fear of isolation. (c) Compliance with public opinion can be either extrinsic or intrinsic. If it is extrinsic, consensus will not be maintained unless other forms of sanction against deviance are used.

CONCLUSIONS

The points raised above may or may not help advance the applicability of the theory of the spiral of silence to the analysis of empirical data. I agree completely with Noelle-Neumann's effort to make her theory as economical and succinct as possible. Clearly in its present form it works well in accounting for the ups and downs of the West German electoral behavior between 1965 and the present. It also helps explain other changes in opinion concerning such issues as abortion and nuclear energy (but, in this latter case, I would also have liked to know how objective events, such as the Three Mile Island near-disaster and the Chernobyl disaster, influenced these changes).

But is the theory in its present form universally applicable? It is one of the paradoxes of science that the more universal a law tries to be, the more initial conditions it must take into account. If we wish to know the temperature of boiling water at sea level, there is only one condition we have to know: heat. But to know it anywhere on earth, one must also take elevation and atmospheric pressure into account. It is possible that to make the spiral of silence explain changes in the climate of opinion in different cultures, relating to different values, some additional conditions will have to be considered. I am especially curious to know how the theory would explain such apparent transformations in the climate of opinion as have taken place recently in Eastern Europe. Of course, no theory in the social sciences that I know of could have predicted — or even explained post hoc — such events. Nevertheless, I hope that the spiral of silence will be able to help us interpret what happens as we move through history, because of the various candidates for a theory of public opinion it is certainly the most original, comprehensive, and useful.

REFERENCES

Arendt, H. (1958). *The human condition.* Chicago: University of Chicago Press.

Asch, S. (1952). Group forces in the modification and distortion of judgments. In S. Asch (Ed.), *Social psychology* (pp. 450-473). Englewood Cliffs, NJ: Prentice-Hall.

Csikszentmihalyi, M., & Csikszentmihalyi, I. (Eds.). (1988). *Optimal experience: Studies of flow in consciousness.* New York: Cambridge University Press.

Csikszentmihalyi, M., & Larson, R. (1984). *Being adolescent: Conflict and growth in the teenage years.* New York: Basic Books.

Durkheim, E. (1964). *The division of labor in society.* New York: Free Press. (Original work published 1893)

Goffman, E. (1974). *Strategic interactions.* Philadelphia: University of Pennsylvania Press.

Kubey, R., & Csikszentmihalyi, M. (1990). *Television and the quality of life.* Hillsdale, NJ: Lawrence Erlbaum.

Le Roy Ladurie, L. (1979). *Montaillou.* New York: Vintage.

Milgram, S. (1974). *Obedience to authority.* New York: Harper & Row.

Sorokin, P. (1962). *Social and cultural dynamics.* New York: Bedminster.

Silent Majorities
and Loud Minorities

SERGE MOSCOVICI
Ecole des Haute Etudes en Sciences Sociales

T HE spiral of silence — what a powerful metaphor! It strikes us by a kind
of intuitive truth and also by the heuristic image it suggests. People
usually consider public opinion as a trademark of democracy, a stock
exchange of ideas resulting from thousands of debates and dialogues in which
numerous individuals participate. We could easily apply to it what Tocqueville
(1957) wrote about liberty: "At all times what so strongly attached the hearts of
some men to it are its very charms, its own spell independent of its benefits; it is
the pleasure of being able to speak, act and breathe without any constraint under
the sole government of God and the laws" (p. 26).

Indeed, is public opinion possible where there is no liberty? In the same spirit,
Tarde (1910), who coined the notion in social psychology, strongly affirmed the
connection between public opinion on one hand and the liveliness of speech — the
variety of public exchanges and talk in society at large — on the other. It was
obvious for him that progress and changes in opinion spell the progress and
intensity of conversation in public places. On the contrary, silence, what he called
"universal mutism," was the sign of stagnation and even absence of public opinion.
He thus joined a trend of Western thought for which, as Pascal wrote, "silence is
the greatest of prosecutions; never did the saints keep silent."

Now Professor Noelle-Neumann reverses this vision of things by making
silence the incentive of public opinion, the determinant of its evolution in a certain
direction. Not those who speak but those who do not make consensus possible and
set the pace of public opinion. The paradox is attenuated when you bring her theory
in connection with a viewpoint widely supported in political science. It states that,
in order to function well, a democracy depends not on the participation but on the
ignorance and indifference of a large number of voters. These, limiting the
influence and expression of some layers of society, ensure the stability and

Correspondence and requests for reprints: Serge Moscovici, Ecole des Haute Etudes en Sciences
Sociales, Laboratoire de Psychologie Sociale, 44 Rue de la Tour, 75116 Paris, France.

Communication Yearbook 14, pp. 298-308

cohesion of political life. Like the spiral of silence, the spiral of apathy thus allows the ruling elites to rule legitimately. As brief as these introductory remarks are, they might still be sufficient to explain the hold this idea has upon us and conjure up a set of notions that are at the basis of the theory and give it a wide scope.

A NOTION IN CRISIS

When I first read Noelle-Neumann's (1980) book, a number of things about the nature of public opinion became clear to me. Straightforward, synthetic conceptions like hers are too scarce not to please, especially when they put a new perspective on facts previously taken for granted. Her chapter in this volume presents novel aspects, answers some criticisms, and achieves a level of precision that we missed earlier. I do not intend to comment on the whole, nor do I pretend to remain neutral, since, in the course of my scientific career, I have sought other solutions to the problems she raises.

Above all, the crisis of the concept of public opinion lies at the heart of this chapter. She describes the crisis in the right terms: Two outcomes are possible — either give up the concern with the concept and substitute another for it or try to solve the difficulties so as to keep what is essential. I, for one, am sure that the concept of public opinion belongs to the past. It corresponds to a time marked by the birth of public space in the last century (Habermas, 1987), of representative democracy, and of the written press — in short, the birth of the Enlightenment in the classic sense, trying to give a reasonable expression to the diversity of individual interests and beliefs, while providing for their participation in common action (see Allport, 1937; Stoetzel, 1943).

Yet the blossoming of social movements, the emergence of means of communication, and the formation of great bureaucracies and mass organizations with the ideologies capable of mobilizing them have changed our societies from top to bottom. If you want to elucidate social reality and collective action, you have to take into account the meanings human groups share from inside as the condition of their living together. Understanding the relationships between people and groups through their system of meanings becomes part and parcel of social reality, its essential part in fact. This is because such meanings help people to experience society as more than a commodity, something actually made by themselves.

The more generally the system is shared, the greater part it plays in people's siding for or against something, in communication and behavior. So, when assessing opinions and attitudes, people do not start from scratch; they necessarily draw from the rich corpus of notions, symbols, and images underlying their reflections and binding them to others. These permanently created and shared systems that impart meaning to our reality and action I have named *social representations*. They offer a possibility of going down to the root of opinions and attitudes, grasping, in Verba's (1970) words, "the relationship between mass attitudes and behavior and significant outcomes" from both cognitive and practical viewpoints. A long time ago, I proposed that the concept of social representation replaces those of opinion and attitude (Moscovici, 1963). The latter lead to procedures that force us to treat "society as if society were only an aggregation of disparate individuals" (Blumer, 1948, p. 545), and they appear too static and limited to account for contemporary reality. And despite some reservations that were to be expected, the reasons we advanced in this direction appeared plausible and in keeping with the evolution of societal psychology (Farr, 1990; Jaspar & Fraser, 1984; McGuire, 1986).

These preliminaries may not account for the peculiar situation of the concept of public opinion in science, but they suffice for our immediate purpose. They lead to a provisional conclusion, the consequences of which will presently appear more clearly. When a research worker examines fluctuations in response to a survey about nuclear energy, for example, he or she can deduce from them that they reflect the degree to which some people advocate it while others abstain from censuring it. Is this just a change in trend, an increase of the pros and a decrease of the cons or vice versa, or is it also something else? Might it be the index of change affecting the social representations people have of nuclear energy, how they learn about it, conceive their relation to their environment, and consider their daily life in general? In the course of the process of change, some symbols and images are dropped because fewer and fewer people use them, while others are created and then diffused. In parallel, a new language replaces the old one and determines the meaning of the words in everyone's mouth or in the media. Consequently, what is also registered through the fluctuations of pros and cons in the survey is often the change of the modes of thinking, feeling, speaking — in short, the representations of society at large. People become more or less favorably disposed to nuclear energy — to revert to the example — but the meaning of nuclear energy is no longer the same. It is unavoidable that this complicated situation becomes a source of confusion. Especially, it gives birth to the idea that the manifest opinion and attitudes of social reality are independent of the shared background of beliefs, mental representations, and values. In this case, the symptom is mistaken for the phenomenon.

MAJORITIES AND MINORITIES

In order to solve the crisis that preoccupies her, Noelle-Neumann thinks that a more thorough theory of the formation of public opinion ought to be proposed, without, however, interfering with the concept itself and the place it holds in the social sciences. She contends that the social analogy between control and conformity could serve as a scaffolding for building a conception of public opinion as a force binding the "social individuals" — the phrase is hers — to society at large. In order to define the inner nature of this force, she associates the social phenomenon of deviance with the individual action of silence. As in the laboratory experiments (Schachter, 1951), the deviant is talked to but does not reply. This is an important step in her analysis, and interesting for several reasons.

First, the very association could be taken as symptomatic of the necessity for an individual's action to serve as a unit in research work on public opinion, which many deny. Then the analogy indicates that a single principle can be found and isolated to explain a number of apparently complex and unstable facts. By the way, notice the function of the sociological analysis in this context. It does not serve to identify some social institution (government, media, or the like) that would be privileged to exert influence or control. Rather, we can surmise that the pressure toward consensus resulting in opinion common to all originates in any member of society.

In this sense, I endorse the steps and propositions included in Noelle-Neumann's chapter. So I shall abstain from discussing her interpretation in detail, chiefly because her arguments are convincing. My agreement, however, is given within limits, insofar as my own work in this area questions the bias toward conformity in the human sciences and has resulted in a theory of social influence (Moscovici, 1976) different from that which inspires those classic works. In that effort, I have endeavored to explain the innovation phenomenon: why opinions and attitudes can be changed by a deviant minority, not why they are preserved and diffused by a majority, to show that both minorities and majorities exert reciprocal influences. Thus silence can influence as well as speech, though not in the same way. This conclusion brings us to envisage conformity in a different light.

Owing to this fact, my comments on Noelle-Neumann's chapter may appear colored by a viewpoint very remote from hers about what represents our common interest. So as to diminish this divergence, I shall neither treat the inner structure of the spiral of silence theory nor examine whether it fits the data well. My main concern in what follows will be its generality and the conditions in which it can be taken as valid. To this end, I shall carefully analyze only its basic premise so as to specify its consequences.

QUASI-STATISTICS

Noelle-Neumann defines public opinion as the result of a consensus proper to maintain social cohesion. What enables us to discover the direction of this consensus is that fact that people have a "quasi-statistical" sense. Individuals are supposed to be capable of discovering what they have in common and anticipating the tendency that dominates among them. Discovering it influences their disposition to speak out or keep silent as they side with the majority or minority. Here is a capital passage of the chapter on this point:

> When people feel they are in the minority, they become cautious and silent, thus further reinforcing the impression in public of their side's weakness, until the apparently weaker side disappears completely except for a small hard core that clings to values from the past, or until the opinion becomes taboo. (p. 259)

The popular idea that "the rich get richer and the poor get poorer" appears as a psychic postulate: Majorities get more and more in the majority and minorities dwindle out of sight. No wonder the theory explains the flux of public opinion and the reflux of individual, let alone deviant, opinion. But can it be accepted without serious reservations? My first remark is self-evident. If you observe most democratic countries in the last decades, you can see that public opinion is generally divided on most issues and the differences between majorities and minorities are very small. To be sure, in France, Germany, or Italy there is a government of such and such a tendency, but which party has really won or lost an election has often become a matter of interpretation. Is the majority in the United States Republican or Democrat? For that matter, the surveys made before the elections have been mistaken more than once about the differences between the votes each party would get. It follows that the "quasi-statistical sense" by which people anticipate who the consensus will favor ought to be very subtle, subtler in any case than that of the measuring instruments of specialized agencies.

At least one study has suggested that our common statistical sense, if it does exist, is not subtle at all (Higgins & Barg, 1987). Rather, it would tend to make us overlook the base rate of a population, overrate the importance of unique cases, and build up illusory correlations. Here lies the dilemma. In a sense, Noelle-Neumann has good reasons to contend that people anticipate which way the wind of opinion will blow and try to let themselves be carried by it. On the other hand, social psychology prevents us from thinking that they achieve it through a "quasi-statistical" flair reflected in the surveys. In the present state of our knowledge, the manner in which people foresee coming events and the directions they will take remains a riddle. And it would be premature to lean upon our knowledge to solve an even greater riddle, the influence that the quasi-statistical knowledge people possess exerts on their behavior.

However, let us suppose for a moment that this sense exists and people are capable of anticipating the trend of opinion. Assuredly, Noelle-Neumann's chapter has a theoretical character and I will not burden it with particular considerations. Nevertheless, one is important. For a party to contend that opinion is favorable to it and show itself assured of being in the majority can entail two unwanted, even dangerous, consequences. On one hand, the fact demobilizes its supporters, who, sure to carry the day, express their preferences less and less to adversaries or the indifferent. Thinking that the public agrees with them encourages party members to keep silent. On the other hand, in order to prevent the majority from getting too strong or the minority too weak, part of the opinion goes to rescue the underdog and speak in its favor, thereby restoring a certain amount of fairness, for, if there is no merit in helping the victor, there is a great deal of it in succoring the one who risks being defeated. *Causa victrix diss placuit sed victa Catoni.*

Whatever the reality of the phenomenon and its causes, we observe that the relation between the anticipation of being in the majority or minority and speaking or remaining silent is neither exclusive nor univocal. There are thresholds above which a behavior can turn into its reverse, the majority getting silent and the minority loud, or the reverse. Small inversions of this kind have large effects. We can often watch a mere 1-2% shift in the votes change victory into defeat. These particular considerations are not new, but they ought to be better understood. If they were, then we would understand better why the majority seldom reaches unanimity and the minority seldom dwindles to the point of disappearing altogether.

THE FEAR OF ISOLATION

Let us now view the premise from the affective side. Three out of the five hypotheses of Noelle-Neumann's theory conjure up the threat and fear of isolation. Both emotions make public opinion appear as a veil hiding private opinions, just as mass psychology hides and absorbs individual psychology (Moscovici, 1985). No need to demonstrate that the members of the group expressing a viewpoint opposite to the one the majority agrees upon are isolated and excommunicated by legal measures, political institutions, and deep-rooted customs. A scholarly survey of the charges brought against subversive thought would show them to have outlawed just the works and social movements that have shaped our culture. Simultaneously, the men who fell victims to the threat, from Socrates to Christ, from Luther to Freud and Marx, to name just a few, are precisely those held up as examples to generations trained in obedience and submission to authority. The main drift of the threat is clear enough, pointing to the supreme arrogance of believing that one individual alone can face his or her fellow citizens' opinions, people's religions, and ancestors' traditions. Asking the questions one should not ask, breaking the connivance owing to which some things can be said and others forbidden, are seen as a sign of childish pride and narcissism persisting in adult life. As Nietzsche put it: "To be an exception passes for a guilty deed." He is echoed by Ibsen in his *Enemy of the People*, when the title hero is warned by a friend: "The particular must at all costs be subordinate to the general or, better, to the authorities."

Obviously, insubordination or deviance can be perceived as aggression breaking the consensus. Hence the reaction of ostracism, which is to sanction or prevent this risk. Beyond its social and psychic reasons, some would ascribe it a genetic basis. Masters (1984) writes:

> The phenomenon of ostracism is a class of customs and practices that involves exclusion from normal social interaction with all (or virtually all) of a group's other members. Ostracism can therefore be defined as a rupture of the prior pattern of social integration. . . . Indeed it seems reasonable to hypothesize that some form of ostracism may well be universal in human societies. (p. 877)

No matter how you look at it, this side of the theory seems unquestionable. In support of her theory, Noelle-Neumann uses the fear of embarrassment as an index of the fear of ostracism. The findings accumulated in her cross-cultural studies are impressive and convincing. No doubt you may think that when a person behaves in an unexpected manner publicly, utters a discordant or odd opinion, he or she feels immediately judged by others. Disturbing the routine of things, making oneself conspicuous, disturbs the person per se. Here silence restores the order of things, ensures the return to the familiar, on the condition that the cost of self-love is not too great. In any case, this premise of the theory is not subject to discussion and requires no further evidence. Its consequences can be admitted easily: The consensus of public opinion is made possible by the reflux of those who, fearing ostracism, draw back from collective dialogue and abstain from uttering aloud a conviction whose decline they anticipate. They thus yield to the rising flux of those who, feeling less and less isolated, propagate in numerous ways (badges, posters, conversations) a conviction that is on the rise. Though this hypothesis has to be limited to the approximative facts demonstrating it (like every hypothesis, for that matter), it is the dynamic center of the new theory of public opinion. It sinks a wedge into the ideas according to which this opinion represents the distribution of the choices made by individuals following, in Ibsen's words, their "own path."

DISSENT

Curiously enough, the chapter includes the account of a series of surveys on the reactions to nuclear energy plants, which obliges us to consider the theory from a different angle — I would even say, to question its generality in the area assigned to it. In fact, we see that mass media and opinion surveys register like fine barometers the evolution of an atmosphere that is more and more hostile to nuclear energy plants. How to explain it, if not by introducing the factor that, however omnipresent, is so seldom mentioned? I mean social movements, active minorities that have been leading a vast, sometimes violent campaign of civil disobedience against the official policies and dominant views of society. Numerous books have been written on the subject, and I need not go back over it. When thinking over many recent events, including dissident movements in Eastern Europe, you may think it is true that the individual, as a rule, is afraid of being isolated, blamed by friends, excommunicated by coreligionaries — in short, afraid of everything resembling ostracism. This suffices to discourage any inconsiderate gesture or thought. But is not there more to it? We can suppose that such an individual complies for lack of genuine persuasion, a profound involvement in belief. One who is deeply convinced and sticks to a belief can overcome the fear of the isolation that publicly adopting a definite position might entail. In other words, not only other people's reactions but also one's own strength determines speaking out or not.

Good sense and the observation of individuals who opposed nuclear energy plants from the start inspire my remarks about why they have overcome the fear of expressing what seems to them the truth and disregarded the potential insults, disparagements, and excommunications of the majority — all the more quixotically as they try to break isolation itself and convert their opponents into supporters. We deal here with dissidents who turn into the members of an active minority desirous to spread their opinions or beliefs. As I have explained elsewhere, we have distinguished deviance from dissidence, the anomie of a subgroup defining itself with regard to the majority from the antinomy of a subgroup opposing its own goals and values to those of the majority (Moscovici, 1976). The former keeps silent to escape censure, while the latter is all the louder as it wants to make itself known and the truth manifest, whatever the consequences.

As Carlyle (1842) has noted: "Every new opinion, as its starting, is precisely *a minority of one.* . . . On the whole, a thing will propagate itself as it can" (p. 95). Not as it can: A thing follows regular social and psychic processes. We have been studying ideas for about 20 years (Moscovici, 1988; Mugny, 1980), and have been able to show that an idea propagates itself on the condition that it is consistent and influences a number of people without their realizing it. The hidden impact of minorities accounts for the apparently sudden evolutions and veerings on public opinion and also for the pluralistic ignorance alluded to by Noelle-Neumann. Indeed, many people find out one day that they have new beliefs or behaviors, having been converted from within (Maass & Clark, 1983), without realizing that the same thing has happened to their children, relatives, or neighbors. Hence we may wonder whether the threat of ostracism can be considered as an independent factor, the mainspring of public opinion. All the more, as overcoming the fear of isolation does not seem to require heroic motivations, as stated by Havel, the former dissident and now president of the Czech republic:

> They were not highly motivated members of the opposition with political ambitions, nor were they former politicians expelled from the power structures. They had been given every opportunity to adapt to the status quo, to accept the principles of living within a lie and thus to enjoy life undisturbed by the authorities. Yet they decided on a different course. (Havel et al., 1985, p. 46)

It thus appears that, according to whether we deal with a silent majority or an active minority, the threat of ostracism can induce quite opposite behavior. As Noelle-Neumann remarks, "The hard-core minority is, in fact, often especially willing to speak out" (p. 274). Thus she points to the horizon beyond of her own theory.

Let me here open a parenthesis. Dissident individuals and movements are the carriers of a social representation that underlies their conviction or mode of life in the most various fields, such as trying to change people's reactions toward their environment, everyday democracy, military service, or scientific and technological progress. Transfers from one area of opinion to another can be foreseen, owing to the representation that has been diffused by the so-called new social movements, and to proceedings that are very similar. Kepplinger and Hachenberg (1980) aptly show that not the "hesitant silence of those who refused military service" but "the provocative activity of their defenders" started the publicizing process, and add that "the activity of a claiming minority inside and outside the press has influenced the opinions in the population for a long time to come." And they clearly distinguish between "an initial phase with the active involvement as the cause of change and a phase of conflict, caused by the passive fear of isolation" (p. 519).

Much could be added to these remarks, yet I shall close the parenthesis I opened to show that sometimes, to understand reality better, we have to take into account first and foremost the representations shared by the members of the group. The parenthesis gave us the opportunity to observe that we can no longer limit ourselves to a social psychology of conformity to the majority, as soon as we have asked the question, What are the sources of change in public opinion? The spiral of silence theory appears in this chapter too much tilted in that direction. Taken together, Noelle-Neumann's remarks and empirical data make us realize the fact, as if she wanted to bring into relief the excesses that the reader is more liable to commit than the author. She reminds us how fast these evolutions are in a time when change is not only frequent but, in addition, a value. Furthermore, we share a culture that considers the existence of dissensus as normal as the search for consensus. In other words, the emergence of active minorities obeying a single impulse in the midst of a more or less amorphous majority has become an essential factor of life in common. Speaking of "hard cores," "sects," and "young people," Noelle-Neumann does not seem to do justice to their importance, when we see how many significant fractions of each social class are involved in them.

As a matter of fact, the social and psychic makeup of these groups that stand apart ought to be scrutinized more closely and taken into consideration if we want to explain the ups and downs of public opinion. It is not enough to mention them; one has to bring them into account as much as the mass media, if not more, in order to grasp how a new trend of beliefs, of representations, breaks into society, or why an existing trend is subject to such a strong reversal in so few years, as the trend about nuclear energy plants. As Park remarks: "It is in the mind of the marginal man — where the changes and fusions of culture are going on — that we can best study the process of civilization and progress" (cited in Coser, 1971, p. 366). Even more, people have agreed for a long time that particular attention must be given to these marginals, so as to ensure a spirit of dialogue and liberty. In a famous essay, John Stuart Mill (1859) declares:

> If either of two opinions has a better claim than the other, not merely to be tolerated, but to be encouraged and countenanced, it is the one which happens at the particular time and place to be in minority. That is the opinion which, for the time being, represents the neglected interests, the side of human well-being which is in danger of obtaining less than its share. (p. 186)

Examining things from this angle — that of the necessary expression of minorities in public opinion — Noelle-Neumann's analyses are hesitant about the meaning to be given to the data presented. With a slight change in the terms, one could come to a conception of the flux and reflux of those opinions that aims now at conformity, now at innovation. To achieve this it would be enough to give greater attention to the social psychology peculiar to active minorities as well as to that of the majorities ready to comply. The former are too much disregarded and the latter are given too much weight with regard to what happens in reality. This is a basic counterposition to the point of view that has now become classic. Let us recognize that this chapter refers to it and that facts are treated in it that, to a certain extent, might upset the presuppositions of the spiral of silence theory.

CONCLUSION

Unfortunately, I am not conversant with all the literature dedicated to the theory. I suppose that imperative reasons have compelled the author to close her chapter with the myth of Protagoras. According to it, the gods made society possible by distributing among humans the sense of justice and the sense of shame that enabled them to live together. No doubt persons had also been given a common representation of what shame and justice are, so that they could recognize shameful or unjust deeds, and distinguish them from deeds that, however similar, have no moral significance. In short, they had been given a religion, the religion of their city. Logically, the spiral of silence depends on the sense of shame we experience when we think, behave, or speak in a manner that does not conform to the rules — a sense kept awake by other people's blame. This feeling would ensure the cohesion and integration of society by giving a rational meaning to the threat and fear of isolation. But, in the latter half of the century, we have learned that cohesion and integration are not a good per se. They can lead to the most dreadful evils, the self-destruction of societies (Moscovici, 1988). This is why, in their wisdom, the gods of the Greek philosopher have added the sense of justice that obliges us to disobey and speak out, to do our duty, even if we incur the risk of being ostracized. Plato, who wrote the dialogue about the myth, also wrote of the man who, alone in front of his fellow citizens accusing him of serious offenses, defended justice. In this myth, public opinion joins the sense of shame to the sense of justice, for lack of which the citizen's obedience would be everything and his virtue nothing.

It is difficult to assess the worth of comments in general. These have a limited scope with regard to the possible fields of application. Above all, they aim at starting a dialogue, seeking to displace the prevailing viewpoint by orienting it toward the phenomena of evolution and innovation that hold too modest a place in our social sciences. These are not a discovery; they are a truth and ought to penetrate better into the theories that, like Noelle-Neumann's, have the power to explain one of the most essential aspects of life in common.

REFERENCES

Allport, F. H. (1937). Towards a science of public opinion. *Public Opinion Quarterly, 1*, 7-23.
Blumer, H. (1948). The mass, the public and public opinion. In A. M. Lee (Ed.), *New outline of the principles of sociology* (pp. 85-93). New York: Rinehart.

Carlyle, T. (1842). *On heroes, hero-worship and the heroic in history.* London: Chapman & Hall.

Coser, L. (1971). *Masters of sociological thought.* New York: Harcourt Brace Jovanovich.

Farr, R. M. (1990). Waxing and waning of interest in societal psychology: A historical perspective. In H. T. Himmelweit & G. Gaskell (Eds.), *Societal psychology* (pp. 46-65). Newbury Park, CA: Sage.

Habermas, J. (1987). *Théorie de l'agir communicationnel.* Paris: Fayard.

Havel, V., et al. (1985). *The power of the powerless.* Armonk, NY: M. E. Sharpe.

Higgins, T. E., & Barg, J. H. (1987). Social cognition and social perception. *Annual Review of Psychology, 38,* 369-425.

Jaspar, J. M. F., & Fraser, C. (1984). Attitudes and social representations. In R. M. Farr & S. Moscovici (Eds.), *Social representations* (pp. 101-124). Cambridge: Cambridge University Press.

Kepplinger, H. M., & Hachenberg, M. (1980). Die fordernde Minderheit. *Kölner Zeitschrift für Soziologie und Social-Psychologie, 32,* 508-534.

Maass, A., & Clark, R. D., III (1983). The hidden impact of minorities: Fourteen years of minority influence research. *Psychological Bulletin, 95,* 428-450.

Masters, R. D. (1984). Ostracism, voice and exit: The biology of social participation. *Social Science Information, 25,* 877-893.

McGuire, W. J. (1986). The vicissitudes of attitudes and similar representational constructs in twentieth century psychology. *European Journal of Social Psychology, 16,* 89-130.

Mill, J. S. (1859). *On liberty.* London: T. W. Parker.

Moscovici, S. (1963). Attitudes and opinions. *Annual Review of Psychology, 14,* 231-260.

Moscovici, S. (1976). *Social influence and social change.* London: Academic Press.

Moscovici, S. (1985). *The age of the crowd.* Cambridge: Cambridge University Press.

Moscovici, S. (1988). *La machine à faire des dieux.* Paris: Fayard.

Mugny, G. (1980). *The power of minorities.* London: Academic Press.

Noelle-Neumann, E. (1980). *Die Schweigespirale.* Munich: Riper.

Schachter, S. (1951). Deviation, rejection and communication. *Journal of Abnormal and Social Psychology, 46,* 190-207.

Stoetzel J. (1943). *Théorie des opinions.* Paris: P.U.F.

Tarde, G. (1910). *L'opinion et la foule.* Paris: Alcan.

Tocqueville, A. de. (1957). *L'ancien régime et la Révolution.* Paris: Gallimard.

Verba, S. (1970). The impact of the public on policy. *Public Opinion Quarterly, 34,* 455.

7 Setting the Media's Agenda: A Power Balance Perspective

STEPHEN D. REESE
University of Texas at Austin

This chapter reviews the burgeoning number of studies seeking to explain what sets the media's agenda, and integrates them within a power balance framework. The concept of power is used in a critical evaluation of the agenda-setting metaphor and its limitations when expanded to include influences on media content. The organizational perspective, taken by much "media sociology" research, has examined power relations within organizations. This approach restricts the power of journalists, who are viewed as constrained by bureaucratic structures. Alternatively, journalists may be viewed as agents of the organization's power in their dealings with other institutions. These power relations between the media and sources can be examined at individual, organizational, and institutional levels and are discussed in terms of interdependency and symbiosis. A media organization may manifest its power through its ability to define a reality through reporting and structuring of information, in spite of efforts by involved sources to dictate a different reality. Other indicators of both source and media power are specified, and the implications of different balances of media-source power are discussed. Treating power as a series of changing relationships helps avoid the tendency to regard media or sources as inherently and statically powerful. The powerful can manipulate the media, but under some conditions media assert their own power and agenda.

IN Roman mythology, the god Janus could look in two directions at once, thanks to his two faces. Appropriately, his name was given to the first month of the year, which stands between the new year and the old. Like Janus, the agenda of issues and events found in the news media assumes a similar forward- and backward-looking stance. This media agenda simultaneously projects forward a powerful structuring effect on audience perceptions, while itself indicating the powerful influences behind its creation.

The media have an indirect, yet powerful and pervasive, effect on public opinion by limiting and prioritizing public perceptions of important issues. By formally conceptualizing and testing this agenda-setting process, McCombs and Shaw (1972) set the research agenda for droves of communication researchers. In their comprehensive review of this research tradition and related policy agenda-setting

Correspondence and requests for reprints: Stephen D. Reese, Department of Journalism, College of Communication, University of Texas at Austin, TX 78712.

Communication Yearbook 14, pp. 309-340

studies, Rogers and Dearing (1988) conclude: (a) "The media influence the public agenda"; (b) "the media agenda seems to have direct, sometimes strong, influence upon the policy agenda"; and the media indirectly influence policy as well because (c) "the public agenda, once set by, or reflected by, the media agenda, influences the policy agenda" (pp. 579-580). By focusing on these influences, the agenda-setting approach implicitly adopts the pluralistic values of democratic theory, bringing public opinion to center stage. Assuming that public opinion directly affects public policy makes setting the public agenda an important media effect.

In recent years, communication researchers have begun to look backward as well, toward the origins of the media agenda. Perhaps, as McCombs suggests, having satisfied themselves that media content did have effects, communication scholars felt justified in turning their attention inward, toward the processes creating that content (M. McCombs, personal communication, 1988). Effects on opinion remain important, but in different respects. This shift away from the "public" is perhaps more attuned to an elite-centered view of political influence. The public does not keep up with politics or participate enough to assign it a direct role in the political process. Rather, policy alternatives originate with elites, who seek to manage the climate of opinion in their favor. Elites contend with each other, often through the media, for favorable opinion, as one of many scarce resources (e.g., Paletz & Entman, 1981, pp. 184-195). Focusing on agenda creation highlights these processes.

This chapter picks up where Rogers and Dearing (1988) left off, by reviewing the burgeoning number of studies seeking to explain the media's agenda. These studies are diverse and are knitted together only loosely, if at all, by the agenda-setting metaphor. But then, one strength of the robust agenda concept is its ability to pull together previously unconnected lines of research. For now I use Rogers and Dearing's (1988) term, "media agenda-setting" (as distinct from public and policy agenda-setting), to refer to those studies using the media agenda as a dependent variable.[1] Media agenda-setting includes all of the influences affecting media content.

PURPOSE OF THIS STUDY

Power Perspective

In reviewing media agenda-setting, this chapter focuses on power relations as an organizing theme for a diverse set of research studies. Power is central to social analysis, whether openly examined or not. Studies can be compared based on where they look for the exertion of power. A Marxist scholar, for example, typically views the most significant power as ultimately lying in society's economic formations. Studies of individual journalists imply that they have significant power in creating the news product. Organizational analysis, on the other hand, assumes that individuals are constrained in their power by structures beyond their immediate control. Similarly, we can consider some organizations more powerful than others. Setting the media agenda is itself an exercise in power, as many competing factions strive to get on the agenda and do so in ways favorable to their interests. By recognizing this fact, we can clarify the power relationships within and across social formations that result in the agenda displayed in the media.

Diversity of Studies

The diversity of media agenda-setting studies complicates finding any single theoretical approach. Indeed, Swanson (1988) notes that the very meaning of *agenda* is different at each level of analysis, and that "each level of agenda-setting is likely best understood by theoretical conceptions that are specific to that level" (p. 614). This heterogeneous research ranges across many different levels of analysis and research traditions, unlike the more homogeneous agenda-setting studies. The major agenda-setting variables — the media agenda and some measure of public opinion, with various audience characteristics serving as intervening factors — have been used similarly across many studies. The underlying process is psychological and straightforward. The media manipulate the salience of agenda items, by paying more or less attention to them, thus cuing audience members to their importance in a process mediated by each individual's need for orientation.

When we look for the media agenda's antecedents, however, we are open to the whole wide range of cultural, institutional, and organizational forces, which leads to an equally wide range of theoretical and methodological perspectives. Thus, unlike the public agenda-setting studies, carried out largely by communication scholars, media agenda-setting has received attention from many scholars from as many social science disciplines, bringing their own economic, political, sociological, psychological, and anthropological perspectives. In addition, media agenda studies lead naturally to normative and ideological questions. Taking the media agenda as problematic and not as a given encourages difficult and power-oriented questions: Whose values are reflected? Whose are suppressed? What values should be on the agenda? Not surprisingly, many media agenda-setting studies have an explicit ideological stance or make prescriptions toward improving media content or revealing its underlying biases.

News Versus Entertainment

Although many studies have examined both news and entertainment content (e.g., Ettema, Whitney, & Wackman, 1987), this chapter focuses on the news agenda. I recognize, of course, that the lines between news and entertainment have become blurred. Many movies are factually based, out of "today's headlines," while news itself, television news in particular, always has been infused with entertainment-style techniques and values. But agenda-setting is at heart a theory of political influence, and this influence is exerted most directly through the news media, channels that still differ in important ways from entertainment. Both news and entertainment content represent a cultural mapping of sorts, and both are the products of similar organizational logic (e.g., Hirsch, 1977). The fact remains, however, that unlike news, entertainment fare is largely an artistic creation and determined entirely within the media (Elliot, 1972). News producers do not have complete control over the issues and events that form the raw material for their product and depend on powerful, self-interested external sources for that material. This chapter will consider how these sources influence content by dictating and responding to organizational routines.

Social Science Approach Versus Focus on Text

Many scholars from both humanistic and Marxist traditions have focused on the meaning of news media content as a text with embedded cultural and ideological meanings. Examples include rhetorical (Burke, 1945), semiotic (Eco, 1976), and cultural analyses (e.g., Gitlin, 1980). Because I examine those processes acting on the media agenda, I follow the traditional social science approach, which may be considered "more attuned to how symbols are produced than to what they mean and more attuned to industrial and organizational context than to the text itself" (Ettema et al., 1987, p. 749). Finally, while providing a general review of media agenda-setting, I draw many of my examples from the broadcast media — a result of my own scholarly interest, plus the fact that the broadcast industry seems to be undergoing the most rapid change in more obvious ways.

THE MEDIA AGENDA

The Agenda Metaphor and Definitions

There has been no shortage of studies examining the media agenda (taken broadly as news content) as a subject in itself. The "agenda" metaphor makes easy intuitive sense, but is flexible in the definitions that can be applied. A few have predominated in the literature, however. Rogers and Dearing (1988) define the media agenda as a "list of issues and events that are viewed at a point in time ranked in a hierarchy of importance" (p. 565). Shaw (1977) views events as discrete happenings, limited by space and time, as opposed to issues that consist of cumulative news coverage of a series of related events subsumed under some larger category. Funkhouser (1973) makes a similar distinction between issues based on "newsworthy" events (Vietnam, crime, student unrest, urban riots) and others (race relations, inflation, drugs/narcotics, ecology) (p. 534). Practically speaking, it is often hard to differentiate between the two. Many news stories combine both types of information: An event serves as a news "peg" that justifies examining the larger issue, or many separate events may be combined as evidence of a larger issue.

Media Consonance

Comparing agendas across media shows important regularities. Indeed, the degree of similarities in coverage has been one factor leading scholars to examine the powerful organizational and institutional forces behind this standardization. As befits the value placed on diversity, the terms applied to this similarity have somewhat pejorative connotations: *consonance, conformity, duplication, homogeneity, standardization, "three-in-one news,"* and *uniformity*. Several studies have examined print media similarities (Bigman, 1948; Donohue & Glasser, 1978; Gieber, 1956; Riffe & Shaw, 1982), particularly as influenced by the wire services (Cutlip, 1954; Gold & Simmons, 1965; Snider, 1967; Stempel, 1962). Newspapers appear to agree less on selection of specific stories (Stempel, 1959). The three television networks are the most functionally equivalent media and, predictably, the most similar (Altheide, 1982; Buckalew, 1969; Capo, 1983; Dominick, 1981; Foote & Steele, 1986; Fowler & Showalter, 1974; Graber, 1971; Hester, 1978; Lemert, 1974; Meeske & Javaheri, 1982; Riffe, Ellis, Rogers, Van Ommeren, & Woodman, 1986; Weaver, Porter, & Evans, 1984).

Cross-media comparisons also find agreement on the relative categorical, or topical, proportions of news (Lasorsa & Wanta, 1988; McCombs & Shaw, 1972; Stempel & Windhauser, 1984). Stempel (1985) found a similar pattern in the news "mix" across major media, but, again, much less agreement on specific stories, except among the three networks. Story similarity may be greater during campaign periods, as Patterson (1980, p. 764) found was the case for 1976 presidential campaign coverage by television, newspapers, and newsmagazines.

Studies like these have examined cross sections of media content, and have found them similar in agenda priorities. Another way to look at media similarities, however, is over time, as the media "converge" on big stories. Intermedia similarities may be the greatest for these big, high-profile, national stories. In this process, the media discover issues and respond to each other in a cycle of peaking coverage, before largely dismissing issues. In 1986, for example, the major national media — elite press, networks, and newsmagazines — discovered the cocaine issue. The media followed each other in a crescendo of coverage, peaking in the summer months (Danielian & Reese, 1988; Reese & Danielian, 1988).

In recent years, media convergence on the big stories seems to have grown: African famine, AIDS, Mideast terrorism (the TWA hijacking and various hostage dramas), and the farm crisis. There is empirical support for this hunch: Merriam and Makower (1988) report that early in the 1980s

> only one or two stories a year commanded 10 percent or more of all national coverage in any two-week period. By 1985, there were 14 such stories. In 1986, there were 23, from the space shuttle and Chernobyl disasters to tax reform and the federal budget deficit. (p. 43)

Have our problems grown so severely in just a few short years, or have the media converged on selected issues with more vigor? More attention is needed as to how the media converge, not only with increasing quantity of topical information, but also in their angles, slants, and selections of sources.

Sources and Channels

The analysis of news sources takes an important step beyond a strictly "topical" description of content, by identifying "whose" agenda is being promoted. This approach assumes that source selection largely determines how stories are framed, and the tone they will take, whether quoted directly or not. The reliance of news reports on official sources has been well documented. Gans (1979), for example, found that already-prominent people, the "knowns," over half of whom are government officials, dominate network and newsmagazine news, with "unknowns" making up only a fifth of the coverage. Sigal (1973) drew a similar conclusion from his analysis of the *New York Times* and the *Washington Post*: American and foreign government officials accounted for three-fourths of all news sources. The same pattern held true for these papers in 1979 and 1980 (Brown, Bybee, Wearden, & Straughan, 1987). Furthermore, information from these sources is gathered primarily through institutionalized, routine channels, such as press conferences, press releases, and official briefings. Few stories are gathered through reporter enterprise and initiative (Sigal, 1973).[2]

Content Versus Objective Conditions

Standardization of media content and volatile convergence on big stories leads us to question how related news is to real events. Political theory has the same problem media scholars have had in explaining how "a previously dormant issue can be transformed into a highly salient political controversy at a specific point when the basis of the grievance has existed for some time; for example the pollution problem" (Cobb & Elder, 1972, p. 9). This phenomenon sets the stage for agenda-setting hypothesis itself. In testing it, three things must be demonstrated: (a) The media and public agenda correlate, (b) the media agenda preceded the public agenda in time, and (c) alternative explanations that both respond to third factors, such as objective conditions, have been ruled out. The third condition must also be satisfied to justify examining what "sets" the media's agenda. If the media simply reflect objective conditions, little room is left for organizational and other factors. This restriction has not been the case, however.

Funkhouser (1973) conducted one of the early studies comparing coverage with objective indicators. He found little correspondence between issue coverage and the underlying conditions, even those event-based issues: American involvement in Vietnam peaked in 1968, whereas news coverage peaked in 1966. Urban riot articles peaked in 1967, while the number of civil disturbances peaked in 1968. (Note the key assumption that underlying statistical indicators picked by Funkhouser are good indications of reality.) In the cocaine issue mentioned above, there was no objective evidence of a drug epidemic at the time of the coverage, as Kerr (1986) notes: "In recent weeks, as the intense attention to drugs has faded, some have asked if the reaction to drugs was appropriate, and how it is that the press and Congress sometimes suddenly discover and then dismiss a major national problem" (p. 1).

Many studies have compared news coverage with quasi-objective baselines, finding that they do not correspond closely. Violent crimes against people are covered at a rate disproportional to property or nonviolent crimes (Ammons, Dimmick, & Pilotta, 1982; Antunes & Hurley, 1977; Fedler & Jordan, 1982; Roshier, 1981). News overrepresents geographic regions: namely, the two coasts (Dominick, 1977; Graber, 1988). Similarly, in international news, developed countries receive disproportionately high coverage relative to their populations (Larson, 1983). In addition, Adams (1986) found that the severity of foreign natural disasters accounts for less than a tenth of the variation in the attention they are given by the U.S. television networks.[3]

Events and objective reality (such that we can know it) provide a start in predicting the media agenda. If an earthquake destroyed Los Angeles, Californians would think it real enough and the media would no doubt cover it. Events are not nearly enough, however, to help us understand media agenda-setting. Events may be grist for the media mill, but they are events as seen through the eyes of powerful sources and other bureaucratic organizations. Indeed, Molotch and Lester (1974) argue that events themselves are occurrences that sources promote into the news. Perhaps the question of whether media respond to objective reality is moot, given the necessarily subjective way reality is filtered before reaching the press and audience.

A POWER PERSPECTIVE
ON CREATING THE NEWS AGENDA

The standardization of the media agenda, reliance on a few key sources, and convergence on big issues in ways predicted poorly by objective conditions all suggest important power roles being played out behind the scenes. Although many studies have explored influences on the media agenda, few have carried the agenda paradigm over intact from the traditional agenda-setting public opinion studies. That is, few studies identify a specific agenda of issue priorities originating with influential news sources that set, in turn, the media agenda. Exceptions would include Turk's (1986) study of the Public Information Office's public relations efforts in two Louisiana state agencies. She showed that newspapers using those agencies' information featured an agenda of issues that reflected the issue agenda and priorities contained in the information efforts by the agencies. In addition, the reanalyses of White's (1950) gatekeeper study by McCombs and Shaw (1977) and Hirsch (1977) and Whitney and Becker's (1982) experimental test resemble the traditional agenda-setting model, in showing that the agenda established by the wire service influenced the newspaper editor. The remainder of this chapter takes a broader view of influences on the media agenda, considering any forces acting on news media content, including what does not get into the news media, what does, and how it is presented. These influences may be viewed as coming from within or without the news organization. I will review these two major perspectives with emphasis on the role of power in each.

Power as a Relationship

Before proceeding further, a working definition of *power* is needed. The word is used often in everyday conversation to refer to such traits as strength, clout, and influence. Social analysts use it too, but often without an adequate theory of power to go with it. For example, media are said to be powerful to the extent that they can produce powerful effects in an audience. Powerful media produce powerful effects. But who is actually producing these effects? Often, the media just pass along what they are given by other power centers. Can the media be said to be powerful if they simply serve as a conduit for the power of others? If the president makes a speech, and the media carry it, and the speech has the desired effect, can the media be said to have produced the effect? By not tracing the chain of power far enough, we fail to come to grips with the origins of power. Clearly, the power of the media is a function of their relations with other power centers. How can this relationship be conceptualized?

Both coercive and exchange relations of power may be found in media-society relationships.[4] A newspaper may expose a corrupt politician, in spite of efforts to suppress the story. Or the politician may have enough resources to sue the paper and effectively shut it down. More frequently, the politician uses the media and vice versa in a mutually agreeable manner. In either case, both seek to further their own interests. These are the kinds of relations that will be of particular interest here. More often than not, the relationship between media and society can be described as symbiotic. It is precisely because it is symbiotic that it often does not appear that either party is exerting power over the other.

Many measures can be used to signify power relations. Domhoff (1970), for example, looks for the accretions and correlates of power in his study of social elite classes: Who wins? Who governs? Who has the most of what society has to offer? In exchange relationships, Parenti (1978) notes that those with the most to gain are the least powerful. Thus we should look for what resources each party commands. How dependent is one on the other, and for what? Who has more at stake in the relationship? These questions suggest several indicators of power that can be applied to the media source relationship below.

The Media Agenda and Values

Critical studies of influences on news content generally judge media performance by some value-based standard related to power. They differ according to how political power is thought to be exercised in society. The dominant democratic pluralist model of society values diversity: The more media voices, the better. This pluralistic model of media performance is found in many policy discussions as well. The Federal Communications Commission, for example, chose to deregulate much of broadcasting during the Reagan administration, reasoning that the number of media outlets made it possible for market forces to ensure diversity. Power is viewed as distributed across many competing interests. These interests act as "veto groups" as they vie with one another to create a more or less stable political equilibrium. Even the elites are viewed as sufficiently divided as to make unlikely any undue concentration of power (e.g., Rose, 1967). As McQuail (1986) states, the relevant question in media research using a pluralistic model is "whether media offer opportunities for politically diverse audiences and/or audience interests to flourish" (p. 143). Studies based on a pluralistic model of society often do not examine power explicitly. They accept the power relations in society as a given, for power is not considered problematic if the many diverse "veto group" power centers carry on a self-maintaining and balanced political process.

A more critical, radical view of media focuses on top-down control of the media agenda. Power is viewed as much more concentrated, whether in elites or proper-tied classes, and the media agenda is seen as both expressing and furthering the power of these interests. Critical scholars focus on showing how the restriction of voices furthers class dominance, making power a central concern. This is particularly so because individuals are viewed as unable to compete effectively against major power centers in society, which use their power to manipulate people in ways contrary to their natural interests. Institutions are not accepted as a given, but rather examined in terms of their implications for existing power structures (e.g., Parenti, 1978, 1986).

The theory of hegemony, as proposed by Gramsci (1927/1971), has been a strong theme running through critical analyses of media. *Hegemony* refers to the means by which the ruling order maintains its dominance, and to the systematic engineering of mass consent. Media institutions serve a hegemonic function by continually producing a cohesive ideology, a set of commonsensical values and norms, that serves to reproduce and legitimate the social structure (see also Gitlin, 1980, pp. 252-282). Hegemonic values in news are said to be particularly effective in permeating "common sense," because they are placed there not by coercion, but indirectly, through the interconnections between the media and other power centers. Hegemony may be considered the way ruling elites legitimate their power into authority. Assuming that the media serve a hegemonic function, however, does not in itself explain through what mechanisms this happens. Neither does it explain the variations in hegemonic control—subversive elements do creep in. If hegemony were completely effective, nothing could alter the status quo. A closer examination of the variations in power between the news media and society helps color in some of the underlying processes that contribute to or erode hegemonic control.

Problems with the Agenda Metaphor

The agenda metaphor itself has implications for how power is conceptualized. One problem with metaphors, of course, is that by highlighting one model of reality, they make it difficult to view a phenomenon in any other way. The agenda metaphor is confined, by definition, to manifest news coverage. This restriction is appropriate for a theory that predicts effects of media coverage, but it becomes problematic when we consider the media agenda itself as the dependent variable. By confining ourselves to those issues that made the agenda, we exclude all those that perhaps should have been there but were not. In addition, as Schattschneider (1960) argues, groups "go public" when they want to enlarge the field of play to increase their power position. We expect issues to emerge when there are internal disagreements among elites — the many other things on which elites agree remain beneath the surface of media attention.

In the related agenda-building tradition in political science, issues are usually defined around contention (e.g., Cobb & Elder, 1972). Issues arise when competing interests vie for distribution of scarce resources. This model does not deal effectively, however, with the problem of nonissues, that is, when contention is not overt and obvious. In critiquing the news agenda metaphor, we can borrow some of the same criticisms made about policy agendas. First, issues and events are clearly not independent "items." As Rogers and Dearing (1988) note, it is important to recognize that one item influences others. Devoting more attention to one item leaves less room for others. Indeed, as community power theorists tell us, by promoting one agenda item, civic activists may drive other issues away (see Crenson, 1971, p. 165). Bachrach and Baratz (1962), for example, criticize pluralists who focus only on overt decisions by governing boards. They suggest examining how the scope of the process is narrowed to only those issues of innocuous nature to A. Just because issues make the agenda (media or otherwise) does not necessarily mean they are the key issues — this ignores the restrictive face of power (their "second face").

Molotch and Lester (1974) make a similar point: By taking decisional "events" pluralists have guaranteed diversity by focusing only on those issues on which elites disagree. Lukes (1974) goes a step further by arguing that traditional community power studies also overlook those nonarticulated conflicts of power that are prevented from even coming up (his third dimension of power). Lukes argues that the most effective power prevents conflict from arising in the first place. The media agenda, too, is confined by definition to those issues that were allowed into the public policy forum, and fails to cover the range of actual and incipient conflicts in society. To understand the range of forces acting on the agenda, we must also come to grips with those items not allowed on the agenda, or those not even defined as potential issues.

Perspective of This Chapter

I assume that the mainstream media do represent the interests of the powerful in society and operate in concert with them. Many critical scholars, such as Parenti (1986), Herman (1986), and Domhoff (1967, 1970, 1979), view the mass media as little more than accessories for the ruling elites. The media are not, however, simply a conduit for the status quo, but represent a power center in their own right. A complete analysis needs to consider how media interact with other powerful agencies in society, to account for the complexity, tensions, and variations in a mediated society. The connections between elite centers and mainstream media are not always obvious. The task of this chapter is to point out and explicate some of these connections that underlie power relationships, and discuss their implications for media agenda-setting.

POWER WITHIN ORGANIZATIONS

The Organizational Approach

Among the most prominent strands of media sociology research has been the organizational, a perspective that views media as complex organizations with their own goals and routines shaping the news product. Taken broadly, this includes all levels of media production, from individual journalists to the larger media industry. Power is clearly defined in an organizational setting. When journalists become members of organizations, they submit themselves to the power of the organization, a form of legitimate power often characterized as authority. In exchange for having a job, the worker conforms to the requirements of the organization (as citizens submit to the authority of the government — most readily when its power is considered legitimate). This approach helps balance the early individual-level analyses, characterized by the original "gatekeeper" study by White (1950). His analysis of "Mr. Gates" focused on an editor's subjective reasons for picking stories for the paper. The large number of autobiographies by journalists is one indication that they certainly would like to believe the romantic image of the crusading reporter. If the early studies gave the individual journalist too much power in determining the news product, the organizational approach has severely limited that power by enclosing journalists within concentric rings of constraining routines and organizational and institutional pressures.

Our understanding of the news-making process has been advanced considerably by research that ties together these different levels of mass media decision making. Three in particular have provided an excellent explication and review of studies at different levels: Hirsch (1977), Dimmick and Coit (1982), and Ettema et al. (1987). I will not attempt to repeat their reviews here, but I will point out their similarities. Although they differ somewhat in labeling, all three reviews conceptualize media decision making as a hierarchy, such that decisions made at one level constrain those made at lower levels. Organizations are viewed as rational, goal-directed entities that structure themselves internally and within industries to maximize their goals. The individual/occupational, intraorganizational, and interorganizational levels may be considered to progress from a closed-system framework, in which the organization is taken as the surrounding environment of system activity, to an open-system perspective, which emphasizes larger units of analysis and activities at organizational boundaries, and explains change through external causes (Hirsch, 1977, p. 18).

Individual/occupational level. According to Hirsch (1977), the occupational level "focuses on occupational roles, careers, and the interaction of mass media organizations with the individuals fulfilling them" (p. 17), exemplified by White's "gatekeeping" study. These studies attempt to explain variations in news content by variations in the individual, such as ideological slant (Lichter, Lichter, & Rothman, 1986), values (Johnstone, Slawski, & Bowman, 1973; Weaver & Wilhoit, 1986), and perceptions of the audience (Pool & Schulman, 1959).[5]

Intraorganizational level. The second level considers the structure of the organization as a whole and how it adapts to its environment. Studies at this level recognize that organizations exert social control on their members and proceed to ask questions concerning "who exercises power and for what reasons" (Hirsch, 1977, p. 26). Journalistic norms and bureaucratic routines of news work are seen as rational ways in which the organization copes with uncertainty. Sigal (1973) and Gans (1979) have produced excellent analyses of the internal workings of the *New York Times* and the *Washington Post* and CBS, NBC, *Time*, and *Newsweek*, respectively. The differences between the individual and intraorganizational perspectives is shown by Bantz, McCorkle, and Baade (1980), who argue that a local television news organization conforms to a "factory" model. The division of labor produces a "product" efficiently, but the process is at odds with a craft tradition, which values worker autonomy and control.

Interorganizational/institutional/industrial level. This level "examines relationships between organizations or professions and the larger societal environment in which they operate" (Hirsch, 1977, p. 17). Studies at this level explain how organizations are affected by other influential media and wire services, as well as by their political and legal environments. The latter focuses mostly on overt influence by the FCC, antitrust law, and the like. Issues of cross-ownership of media and competition are also pertinent here. Industrial analysis examines organizations as but one part of a more complex interrelated industry system. Turow (1985), for example, examines how organizations within media industries depend on one another for scarce resources. One organization may be said to exert power over another by influencing the other's agenda, as elite newspapers often do for television. Conversely, television may be said to have had a powerful influence on the shape of *USA Today*, designed to appeal to TV viewers with its bright colors and brief news items. The wire services have power when they exert a standardizing influence on news content in what Turow (1985) calls their "linking pin" roles.

Problems with Organizational Analysis

The organizational perspective necessarily focuses attention inward, toward the organization, its structure, and goal-seeking processes. Obviously, however, these activities do not take place in a vacuum. By focusing on the organization, we place it at the center of analysis and consider other organizations only as providers of "resources" that the media organization needs to carry on its affairs. The media organization has power over people within it and also over other organizations. But, in turn, media organizations have power exerted over them. The organizational perspective restricts the power of journalists, who are viewed as constrained by the power of the bureaucratic structure they work in. Alternatively, journalists may be viewed as agents of the organization's power in their dealings with those outside the organization. The organization empowers the journalist. A network correspondent, for example, stands a greater chance of speaking with the president than would the average citizen. These power relations external to the organization take place at the boundaries of the organization, at each of the three levels discussed above, but tend to be obscured by an organizational emphasis.

According to Hirsch (1977), power relations among organizations fall under the interorganizational level, where "open-systems" analysis is most often found. Here, however, we most often find studies of relations among organizations from a single industry. Turow (1985), for example, borrows from industrial sociology in applying a resource dependency model to the mass media industry. He identifies several different organizations within media industries (producers, investors, patrons, creators, unions, distributors) that have power roles in that they control scarce resources needed by others. This "industrial" model, applicable to both news and entertainment, conforms to Hirsch's (1977, p. 13) call to deemphasize the "uniqueness" of news relative to entertainment, arguing that the organizational similarities outweigh the differences. It fails to deal effectively, however, with the most important interorganizational power relation for news organizations — between the media organization and news sources. In Turow's "industry-centric" model, sources are considered just another "resource" necessary for the organization to reach its goals. These resources are not provided by disinterested parties, however, but rather by powerful political and economic forces with their own value-based messages to promote. The resulting content is a direct result of the relative power that these external sources are able to exert.

Organizational analysis naturally impels attention to the center of organizations, but this has the effect of giving low priority to the media source relationship, a key interaction at the "boundaries." In addition, Hirsch (1977) observes correctly that studies at the individual/occupational level theoretically deal with people at all levels of the organization, but, practically speaking, concentrate most often on the most available subjects, front-line journalists. This selection has the effect of ignoring important interactions at other levels, such as between those more elite media decision makers (editors, news directors, and so on) who interact with other powerful elites outside the organization. (Gans, 1979, for example, notes that top newsmagazine editors are expected to circulate with other movers and shakers to get ideas about important issues.) Paradoxically, editors exert significant power over reporters, but studies of them as individuals are still considered part of the occupational (individual) level of analysis. Yet, they act as agents of the power of the organization in their interactions with groups outside their own organization. Consequently, these top-level media workers are often overlooked in organizational studies.

Another drawback of the organizational perspective is shared with functional analysis. Functional and organizational analysts observe enduring structures and patterns of behavior within organizations. From these they work backward, inferring that they are functional for the organization in fulfilling its goals. For a variety of reasons, observed structures may not be functional (e.g., Stinchcombe, 1968). Similarly, not all routines are in the best interests of the news organization, which depends on an audience accepting its product. Accepting public relations video releases may be functional for a television station in that the station gets news content efficiently (conveniently and free), but it may not be functional for the station's long-term credibility.

In his critique of the gatekeeper/organizational paradigm, Herman (1986) observes that it offers "little in the way of dynamics that would show how the media . . . are manipulated (or co-operate) in mobilization by others" (p. 174). Most studies that do examine power relations between news organizations and nonnews industry forces are restricted to the wielding of overt power. For example, Warner (1968) stresses the importance of the Federal Communications Commission as a major concern of network executives. Lowry (1971) found that Spiro Agnew's direct attack on the networks affected their coverage. By concentrating on what behaviors and structures are functional for the organization, we often overlook the fact that these same bureaucratic routines and journalistic views are also highly functional for external news sources. Routines of news work provide levers that power centers on the outside can grasp to influence news content. In the 1988 presidential campaign, Joan Didion (1988) observed how political journalists reported clearly "set-up" campaign events as though they were not: Because reporters like covering campaigns — such assignments lead to prestige and advancement, and get reporters out on the road — they "are willing, in exchange for 'access,' to transmit the images their sources wish transmitted. They are even willing, in exchange for certain colorful details around which a 'reconstruction' can be built, . . . to present these images not as a story the campaign wants told but as fact" (p. 21).

Candidates can use the journalistic reward system as leverage to get what they want in the press. A focus on power outside the organization prompts the question: Are campaign coverage routines equally functional for both news and political organizations, or have certain routines been exploited to the greater advantage of the source? In short, finding what makes organizations tick does not provide an adequate understanding of whose interests they serve. The news organization provides many access points for the expression and reception of power, as will be discussed below.

POWER ACROSS ORGANIZATIONAL BOUNDARIES

Defining Terms: Media and Sources

Media are often conceived of as a monolithic structure, although obviously they consist of many individual organizations, ranging widely in resources and, consequently, power. In the discussion below, I refer to media as separate organizations, or classes of organizations (e.g., national, local), when a relationship is referred to. The news media interact with many organizations, including the political system, public interest watchdog groups, and advertisers. No single adequate term exists to refer to these various other power centers that media deal with. As Blumler and Gurevitch (1986) note, the word *source* is ambiguous and has been applied both to organizations and groups and to individuals representing them. I use the term to refer to those many other entities with whom media enter into power relationships, which, in turn, specifically affect content. I will discuss power relations between media organizations to the extent that they increase or undermine an organization's power relative to other sources.

Power as Dependency

Dimmick and Coit (1982) contrast the hierarchical power exercised within organizations to that exercised across organizations where no clear hierarchy exists. This latter form of power is more subtle, perhaps, but no less important to our understanding of the news process. Looking horizontally across boundaries requires viewing media workers as empowered by their organization in their dealings with others and, in turn, having power exerted on them from those outside their organization. This power is most often a function of interdependencies. This notion is related to the dependency theory of DeFleur and Ball-Rokeach (1989) and the resource dependency perspective outlined by Turow (1985). Both consider media and other social systems as needing each other for vital resources. Dependency exists to the extent that the satisfaction of one party's goals is contingent on resources controlled by another (DeFleur & Ball-Rokeach, 1989). Interdependency means that one party is not completely powerful over the other, although the relationship may be asymmetrical. A media organization, for example, may seek out other sources, with varying degrees of difficulty, while sources may seek other channels for their views. This power can be observed by looking at the ways resources are shared in attaining mutual goals.

Media Power

The media can be thought to have power in two interrelated ways: in relation to sources, and in relation to other media. By being powerful among media, an organization also ensures a more solid power position with sources. Media power can be thought to vary to the extent that an organization has unique resources desired by sources. Under this definition, the power of media, elite media in particular, has certainly grown over the last several decades. As society grows in complexity, a few central elite media may be considered vital for providing a central forum for reporting and coordinating elite opinion (see Lasorsa & Reese, 1989; Weiss, 1974). This high profile and the influence the elite media have over other media mean they have tremendous resources to bestow on or withdraw from sources. Small low-power sources (primary candidates, small corporations, low-level functionaries in government) can benefit enormously if the *New York Times*, for example, chooses to bestow favorable coverage. One significant way a media organization may manifest its power is in its ability to define one reality through reporting and structuring of information, in spite of efforts by involved sources to dictate a different reality. In the case of the "Pentagon Papers," the *New York Times* may be said to have had power because it was able to dictate its reality in spite of government efforts to prevent it. More often, perhaps, sources are able to dictate the reality. Former presidential spokesman Larry Speakes encouraged favorable coverage of President Reagan by thinking like a television producer, providing photo opportunities with dramatic visuals, while restricting other possible coverage opportunities. Did he have power over the network correspondents? Yes, to the extent that correspondents were obliged to cover a reality dictated by the president. (Note that often TV reporters would try to undermine this power by commenting on the public relations techniques used to manipulate them, but they covered them nevertheless. See Levy, 1981, for an analysis of this phenomenon.)

Media organizations also vary in power relative to one another, with the more powerful helping define reality for others. But this dependency runs both ways. Ownership of one organization by another is an obvious case of intermedia dependency. Additionally, however, weaker media depend on the more powerful media for guidance, confirmation of news judgment, and the news itself, through, for example, wire and other syndicated services. One media organization's power to dictate a reality, however, is contingent on whether other organizations will accept it. More powerful media depend on less powerful ones for financial (e.g., syndication fees), and moral support (many papers did not follow the *Washington Post*'s lead on Watergate). Wire services are considered powerful, but they are nevertheless dependent on their clients. UPI, in trying to trim its budget, announced recently that it would focus on fewer stories, but stories having a good chance of being used by clients. It plans to develop a publishability/broadcastability quotient, to determine the level of acceptability of a particular story ("Supply-Side Thinking," 1988).

We generally think of national media as more powerful than local media. Local media have a smaller audience resource (circulation) and are more directly dependent on their own communities for economic support. Editors and producers are intertwined with community economic interests, while national media revolve around national power centers rather than any single community. (Power disparities are particularly apparent when a president is interviewed by a local television news anchor, or when a *60 Minutes* camera crew is sent to do an exposé in a small community.)

Source Power

The power of sources is somewhat easier to conceptualize. We are accustomed to thinking of people and groups as in or out of the "power structure." Officials have the weight of authority behind them, while others develop other resources of value to media, such as specialized expertise (think-tank experts, academicians, and the like). In recent years, scholars have become more sensitive to the power of sources over the media agenda, rejecting the naive notion of the media agenda as a town meeting. Elite sources, in particular, wield much more power over the media agenda than do individuals and public interest groups. Paletz and Entman (1981) argue that the agenda originates with elites and eventually filters down to the public. Rogers and Dearing (1988, p. 578) found no significant effect of the public's agenda on the media's agenda, which is far more responsive to the policy agenda (they note that congressional action on a 1966 auto safety law caused a jump in the *New York Times* coverage of traffic safety, although auto fatalities had been rising for several years). In spite of this assumption of policy elites' power, little research has examined the impact of the policy agenda on the media agenda (Rogers & Dearing, 1988, p. 583).

A Typology

These variations in both media and source power may be more easily seen in a typology that combines levels of media and source power. The resulting intersections of these two power dimensions offer suggestive ways of considering source/media relations, as well as helping classify typical studies.

High-power source/high-power media. When powerful media encounter powerful sources, the result is often a symbiotic relationship, characterized by close mutual operation, serving explicit and direct benefits for each party not possible if they did not work closely. Both need the other, and take steps to ensure that the relationship will be mutually beneficial. Parenti (1978) characterizes these mutually advantageous relations as "collusive" and contrasts them with "competitive" relations, which feature "asymmetric" exchange and "antagonistic rather than symbiotic" association (p. 20). He notes that collusive, or symbiotic, relations are frequently a response to or an anticipation of competitive ones. The purpose of collusive relations may be to forestall emergence of competing interests. Of course, symbiotic relations also arise in lower-power settings, but the stakes are higher otherwise, and so are the corresponding incentives to work out mutually agreeable terms.

When two equal powers collide, however, a competitive or adversarial relationship may also result. When presidential candidate George Bush was interviewed by Dan Rather on *CBS News*, a well-prepared and prominent source met an equally well-prepared and determined reporter. The result was an aggressive exchange. (However, each recognized that he would be needing the other, in more symbiotic terms, during the remainder of the campaign. Ultimately, there is an adversarial challenging of sources, but within a context of shared, symbiotically important values.)

Few studies explicitly conceptualize coequal media and sources. Some do, however, openly examine the interplay between the two (e.g., Miller, 1978), but more studies are needed on media elite and source interaction at the top levels. Linsky, Moore, O'Donnell, and Whitman's (1986) examination of media impact on policy may fit here. Largely nonideological analyses like Linsky et al.'s adopt an inside-the-beltway case study approach to the media as simply one elite balancing another. Media are assumed to be largely autonomous and powerful. However, the important role played by media in that study's cases (e.g., Agnew's resignation, the neutron bomb, Love Canal) consisted primarily of connecting elites together, exposing what one elite was doing, or forcing the media to come to grips with public and elite reaction.

High-power source/low-power media. When a powerful source encounters a less powerful media organization, the result is often co-optation and manipulation. By purchasing their own satellite time, for example, presidential candidates are able to offer local television reporters the chance to interview them. The candidate receives free air media coverage, with tame questioning from often underprepared local journalists (who nevertheless accept the exchange to gain credibility by being seen talking with a national figure). Similarly, President Reagan would on occasion meet privately with journalists from smaller papers around the country, bypassing the more difficult Washington press corps. Sources constantly attempt to place media in a low-power position by denying access, claiming media bias, threatening reprisals, and a variety of other ways. Structurally, the radical perspectives predict this relationship, with the media having little independent power compared with sources from the economic and political elite.

Low-power source/high-power media. When a powerful media organization covers a less powerful source, a number of situations result. The media may marginalize a weak source, as the *New York Times* and CBS did the student radicals in the 1960s (Gitlin, 1980). A national medium, like *USA Today*, may choose to provide innocuous life-style reports of average citizens. Ethical abuses may also be found in this context. Powerful media may intrude into the privacy of (low-power) individuals or damage their reputations, leaving the citizens with little recourse. (When CBS tackled General Westmoreland, it encountered a more powerful adversary, who nevertheless still failed to get satisfaction.) The organizational approach (e.g., Altheide, 1976; Epstein, 1973) tends toward this view by perspective, while the more popular accounts of the press predict it by reputation (e.g., Halberstam, 1979).

Finally, the low-power source/low-power media category is the most difficult to find examples for, and contains the desiderata of study. The best example may be the alternative press — relatively low-power media using mostly low-power sources to do relatively inconsequential stories.

Levels of Analysis and Power Implications

These shifting power relationships can also be viewed across the same general levels of analysis discussed earlier. At each level, resources controlled by media and sources that they bring to their interaction vary, placing them in one of the four cells discussed above. Many indicators signify media power at each level. Reporter-source interactions are logically placed at the individual level, and structures joining organizations (such as syndicated video services) are at a higher level. At the larger social system level, studies may analyze individuals, but as indicators of larger relationships. Studies of interlocking directorates, for example, treat individual board members as proxies for the converging interests symbolized by their presence and are logically place at a larger institutional level of analysis.

Individual level. Few studies have focused explicitly on how individual sources deal with the press, other than highly specialized sources, as in Hess's (1984) analysis of Washington press officers. Journalists are the side of the individual power equation most often examined. If numbers are any measure of power, journalists have certainly increased their ranks, 61% by one account just during the 1970s, mostly in television and radio (Weaver & Wilhoit, 1986). Linsky (1986) notes that the Washington, D.C., press corp alone has tripled since World War II, to include 10,000 journalists and 3,000 media organizations. The growth of sources, however, has outstripped that of journalists in D.C. — the federal government information staff grew from 146 in FDR's first term to 3,000 in 1964, reaching 19,000 in 1976, a greater percentage rate growth than that of reporters.

Of these journalists, a handful have come under special scrutiny. Perhaps the most notorious critic of journalistic power was former Vice President Spiro Agnew (1969), who was among the first to focus serious attention on journalist power, noting the influence of a "small group of men, numbering perhaps no more than a dozen 'anchormen,' commentators and executive producers," adding that this group has a "free hand in selecting, presenting and interpreting the great issues of our nation." Others, particularly from the conservative side, have picked up this theme. Lichter et al. (1986) claim that a new media elite has risen to take its place among the others, freestanding and accountable to no one. (Their argument that media power has gotten out of whack appear to rest on the rise of high-profile and high-salaried network news personalities.)

Having asserted this "power," they find that the voting patterns and social views of journalists at the elite media differ from both the public at large and a sample of business leaders. Conservative critiques such as these (see also Corry, 1986; Rusher, 1988) have no theory of power as such, however. Media power is presumed (largely by asserting autonomy and arrogance), and the differences between journalists and society at large are said to make that all the more disturbing. The implication is that media should be less powerful and should not interfere with the natural workings of social institutions. The journalistic culture is perhaps more liberal than mainstream America — elite journalists are more liberal than journalists as a whole (Weaver & Wilhoit, 1986) — but this may be a functional power posture for reporters, for whom a slightly left-of-center posture may help counter the predominantly conservative institutions they cover. This may empower them by making them less co-optable, and, therefore, may well improve their ability to produce content that the public can accept. Content that conformed totally to the status quo institutional view might be perceived by the public to be lacking in credibility.

In addition to studies of individual reporters' characteristics (e.g., Johnstone et al., 1973; Weaver & Wilhoit, 1986), others have examined the ways reporters interact with sources, particularly at the local level. Journalists are either passively reliant or collaborative with sources (Chibnall, 1975; Davison, 1974, 1975; Drew, 1972; Dunn, 1969; Gieber, 1960). Others, like Miller's (1978) analysis of members of Congress and reporters, show that interactions are characterized by symbiosis more often than by adversariness. Hess (1981) found that even the elite Washington press corps lacks institutional memory and a willingness to use documents, forcing reporters to rely on elite sources and each other.

One way to gauge the power of individual journalists in these interactions is by the extent to which they possess personal powerful attributes. These include income and education, certainly. Special expertise is obviously valuable as well from a reporter power perspective. The expertise of specialists like Dr. Timothy Johnson, of ABC News, should allow them to produce a better story on a medical issue than a general assignment reporter could. Powerful individuals in American culture are more often than not older, White, professional, and male, although these are not inherently desirable traits. How do journalists match these attributes? Clearly the general education level of journalists has risen since the Hutchins (1947) Commission called for better-schooled reporters (but, then, the United States as a whole has become better educated since then). Of course, not everyone finds an increased status for journalists desirable. Moynihan (1975, p. 319) claims that in 20 years the upper reaches of journalists in Washington changed from a group typical of other working Americans to today's important social elite, a position he says makes them hostile to American society and government.[6]

Over the last 20 years, however, salaries paid to journalists have not kept pace with the national average (or certainly with those in the important power centers journalists cover — lawyers, Fortune 500 executives, and the like). Journalists are becoming younger: News workers older than 45 are dropping out in greater numbers, no longer able to accept the lower salaries (Weaver & Wilhoit, 1986, p. 38). They are also becoming more female: 60% of journalism and mass communication students are now women (Weaver & Wilhoit, 1986, pp. 38-39). Women have gained the most ground in broadcast news (particularly in what remains of radio news). These gains may indirectly represent changes in the profession's status. The "feminization" of news work does not necessarily cause a reduction in the power position of the profession. But the influx of women into news work, in addition to reflecting the legitimate removal of barriers, indicates that its economic status has declined relative to other jobs, causing males to seek higher-status careers. (These concerns apply mainly to the local level. The top positions in national journalism remain attractive to both men and women.)[7]

Another individual-level indicator of power is the revolving door between journalism and public relations. A revolving door is common in fields enjoying a close symbiotic relationship (witness retired generals becoming consultants to defense contractors). To the extent that journalists bring media expertise to public relations, they help manipulate their former colleagues. The power asymmetry is seen in journalists changing careers for public relations jobs far more often than the reverse. Former journalists, who know the game and the players, are valuable to sources, whether at the national or local level. President George Bush's speech writer, Peggy Noonan, used to be a writer for *CBS News*. Knowing the desirability of the 10-second sound bite, she exploited them in her writing for Bush. *New York Times* diplomatic correspondent (now editor) Leslie Gelb worked for the State Department. Former NBC correspondent Bernard Kalb later worked as a State Department press spokesman. Even the patron saint of broadcast journalism, Edward R. Murrow, ended his career as head of the U.S. Information Agency.

Intraorganizational level. At the intraorganizational level, our attention is drawn to how an organization's (or class of organizations') structure and routines make it more or less susceptible to source power. We may expect that sources may strive to satisfy certain organizational goals to avoid being disadvantaged by others. Collusive relations often supplant competitive ones. Some organizational studies are more explicit than others in recognizing the power implications of organizational structure. Fishman (1980), for example, finds that the dependence of local reporters on the rhythms of local bureaucracies leads them to legitimate the existing political system by disseminating "bureaucratic idealizations of the world and by filtering out troublesome perceptions of events" (p. 154). These "phase structures," according to Fishman, make journalists susceptible to the view of the world suitable to the bureaucracies themselves. Others, like Gans (1979), recognize that sources do the leading on many stories, but do not explore the power implications of this process. Gandy (1982) offers the parsimonious notion of information "subsidy" to describe how source organizations exert power over the news. He suggests that many activities carried out by public relations practitioners influence the media agenda by partially or wholly underwriting the cost of the information for the news organization. From this economic model it follows that the views of the economically powerful will have a better chance of being placed in the media.[8]

Organizational structure effects on power can be seen most clearly, perhaps, when comparing newspapers with television, which appears to lend itself more to manipulation than do the print media. Many books have critiqued the shortcomings of television news (e.g., Altheide, 1976; Epstein, 1973). Compared to newspapers, broadcast journalism has several features that sources often exploit: the need for exciting visuals, desire to go "live," quicker deadlines, smaller staffs, more rapid turnover, and time constraints.

One way that organizations rationalize the news-gathering process is by treating news as a commodity that can be packaged, marketed, purchased, predicted, and controlled. Perhaps this tendency is only more obvious for television news (e.g., Bantz et al., 1980) ("Give me 20 seconds on the governor"). Satellite technology makes it easier than ever for local stations to purchase news in packaged form. These packages range from automotive tips to political interviews. An ad in *Broadcasting* magazine for the Newsfeed Network, for example, features a news director saying, "They [Newsfeed] have a Washington Bureau to go after top national stories and they'll even get me a 'react' from my Congressman!" To be cost-effective and marketable, packages like these have to be acceptable to many local stations, with the inevitable pull toward the safe story (i.e., not discomfiting to powerful sources).

Public relations firms are among those exploiting commoditized news. KGTV-TV in San Diego was among 23 stations airing a two-minute video story, looking like a locally produced news report, on problems with generic drugs. Unknown to the audience, a brand-name drug manufacturer, Key Pharmaceuticals, paid for the report, which gave it favorable mention. The Food and Drug Administration later labeled the report misleading (Hinds, 1987). Similarly, in early 1985, viewers of the Cable News Network saw an exclusive interview with Morocco's King Hassan II conducted by Meryl Comer (a former news anchor at WTTG-TV in Washington, D.C., which also aired the story). Viewers were not told that the story was an electronic press release, produced by a leading Washington public relations firm, Gray and Co. Nor were they told that Comer, also a regular on two U.S. Chamber of Commerce-produced business programs, worked for Gray (Battiata, 1985). The professional newslike appearance of these free features makes them appealing to stations, but they create serious ethical and power questions because control over content is turned over to self-interested sources.

Organization requirements demand new technologies, and these technologies in turn alter the organization and its power relations with others. Satellite technology, in particular, has seriously altered the power equation between networks and affiliates and between TV news and sources. Local stations can now send their reporters to high-profile national events, like political conventions, in greater numbers than ever before, and beam back their stories. Government figures can project messages to local stations via satellite, bypassing network reporters altogether. Satellite feeds to local stations paid for by political candidates maximize their control over the message. Stations in remote areas (read low power) may justify using these feeds as a means of getting access to candidates.

Interorganizational/institutional/industrial level. This last category takes in a broad range of studies, including relations among organizations and between those organizations and the larger elite and capitalistic formations in society. Institutional analyses of media concentrate on linking them to other power centers in society. Pluralist analyses have focused on issues such as monopoly versus competitive ownership in markets, cross and group ownership, and the resulting effects on diversity (Picard & Winter, 1985). These comparative analyses, like those conducted by McCombs (1987, 1988), have found little evidence that competition improves diversity. These studies do not typically link media to other power centers, and concentrate primarily on broad surface features of news, such as proportions of news devoted to various topics. Radical scholars assume that, competitive or not, media organizations are linked to other power centers in ways that further the status quo. From both Marxist and elite perspectives, the media are not seen as having much power independent of these other power centers. In either case, media are seen as instruments, inextricably tied to and used to further the interests of the powerful.

Murdock and Golding (1979) argue that a proper analysis of news production needs to focus on the economic context, as well as the class base, of control. Capitalism is said to have a generalized, abstracting drive to reduce everything to the equivalence of exchange value (Garnham, 1979, p. 133). This commodification of culture has important implications for power. Capital in the culture industry seeks out the most lucrative markets, with the most resources going to lucrative nonnews information gathering. Dan Schiller (1986) is one who finds that in the changing structure of the news commodity, the trend is toward ever more sophisticated means of data gathering for large corporations, and ever less effective information transmission to the masses.

Garnham (1979, p. 145) notes that the present stage of industrialization of culture is characterized by a sharpening struggle to increase productivity. Many recent developments in the United States highlight this trend, including several recent high-profile buyouts of media firms by nonmedia corporations (e.g., CBS, NBC). Media firms become just another profit center, and conform more closely to the corporate culture of parent firms. The well-publicized layoffs at the network level and the erosion of the lines between the business and news departments in many newspapers and TV stations are also examples. Laying off employees and closing bureaus are the most obvious signs of power loss. Less apparent is that by integrating themselves into the larger corporate structure, media companies lose their independent power in dealings with other power centers in that same structure.

Earlier in this century, publishers like William Randolph Hearst, Norman Chandler, and Henry Luce personified media power (e.g., Halberstam, 1979). Now this individual Luce-style power has been rationalized and corporatized to the point where, although media still have power, it is less personal and idiosyncratic, less buffered from the bottom line, more impersonal and sensitive to the requirements of capital markets, which favor short-term, high-yield performance. These new corporate values lead to new power relations, but nevertheless remain consistent with ruling elite interests. Now, media are more tied to abstracted elite interests, more subtle in the absence of more overt publisher biases. Ultimately, a political economy approach leads us to expect that economically based media decisions will tend to favor those with economic power.

The other major radical approach to media power is termed by Mosco and Herman (1981) the instrumental approach, as opposed to the Marxist, structural view. These theorists follow the lead of C. Wright Mills in tracing the pervasive control exerted by the ruling class, or "power elite," on the social structure. In *The Power Elite*, Mills (1956) proposes that the convergent interests of business, economic, and military elites form an apex at the top of the social structure. Class cohesion, assisted by connections and exchange of personnel between these sectors, strengthens and maintains this power elite. These interconnections are found by scrutinizing the ways members of the ruling class come in contact with one another (prep schools, clubs, boards of directors) and influence policy (stockholding, policy groups, funding of institutes and think tanks, political action committees). Elite analysts like Domhoff (1967, 1970, 1979) typically do not give the media as much independent power. According to Domhoff, media have a complex role in the opinion-shaping networks, and are merely one dissemination point among many for elite influence. At any rate, media are viewed as organically inseparable from elites, and thus as far from autonomous. Obviously, conflicts among elites are played out through the press, but they are far more instrumental for elites than they are antagonistic or adversarial to their interests.

Although this form of analysis has been applied less often to the media elite, many interconnections between media and other institutions present evidence of convergent interests and coordination. It indicates that, at best, the relationship is symbiotic. Dreier (1982), for example, examined the interlocks between media boards of directors and others, finding that the most prominent elite media companies (publishers of the *New York Times, Wall Street Journal,* and *Washington Post*) were the most strongly interconnected with other power centers (elite universities, Fortune 500 corporations, and so on). This position of elite media firms in the inner circle of the capitalist structure leads them, according to Dreier, to adopt a corporate, liberal philosophy. These media may adopt an adversarial tone on occasion (e.g., in the cases of the "Pentagon Papers" and Watergate), but only as a corrective, nonparochial action, in the best long-term interests of preserving the capitalist system.

A similar approach could be taken with other media representatives. Top media leaders circulate with other elites. Elite reporters spend time at top think tanks (Hedrick Smith wrote *The Power Game,* 1988, while at the conservative American Enterprise Institute). Midcareer fellowships, like the Niemans at Harvard, allow top journalists to spend time at major universities, rubbing elbows with elites and absorbing elite values. Top journalists, politicians, business leaders, and academicians often appear on panels together, usually without conflict. These are all avenues for the media elite to circulate with other elites, developing firsthand contacts, personal bonds, and shared values. It may not necessarily happen, but the general pattern suggests a symbiotic relationship. Journalists retain their own power base, but within a context of shared, symbiotic values.

Interorganizational level: intermedia power. Although relations between media and source organizations could be conceptualized, my major concern at this level is between media organizations. To the extent that one media organization has influence over others, it has proportionally greater power in relation to sources. As discussed earlier, by placing a story in the *New York Times,* a source can amplify the message manyfold when it is picked up by other media. Media sociologists have known for a long time that news workers follow other media for help in guiding their own selections. Breed (1980) describes it as dendritic influence: "The influence goes 'down' from larger papers to smaller ones, as if the editor of the smaller paper is employing, in absentia, the editors of the larger paper to 'make up' his page for him" (p. 195). Timothy Crouse (1972) observed this "intermedia agenda-setting" process occurring interpersonally among political reporters covering the 1972 presidential campaign. Clearly the elite papers, with the *New York Times* being perhaps the final arbiter (Gans, 1979, p. 181), help set the agenda for the smaller ones.

Most attention has been focused on political pack journalism. Campaigns are highly structured, ritualized, and covered in groups, and the change in the "story" is often ambiguous from one day to the next, leading journalists to rely on each other for help with interpretation. Other nonbeat-based issues show this phenomenon as well, however. For the cocaine issue, referred to earlier, the *New York Times* was able to establish the drug issue early in 1986, followed by the newsmagazines and networks (Reese & Danielian, 1988). Why do news organizations duplicate one another's coverage? As Hess (1981) notes, papers like to have the prestige of having a reporter at the center of events. Nevertheless, they often receive multiple versions of the same event, creating competition among reporters, yet pressures to conform with the common shared wisdom remain. As Sigal (1973) notes, "The consensible nature of news may even impede the breaking of stories that lack corroboration from opinion-leading newspapers. Once they do break, however, big stories will tend to remain in the news as first one news organization and then another uncovers additional information or a new interpretation" (p. 40).

Powerful sources can easily manipulate the pack, most visibly when reporters are herded about by campaign managers. Journalists may not like the system, but they do not want to chance missing a story expected by the editor back home. Candidates may use a divide-and-conquer ploy, by speaking with a few influential journalists at a time in a symbiotically helpful interview. These influentials will report the exclusive or pass a pool report back to the others. Either way, the rest follow their lead. Conversely, the pack may be empowered by its numbers. When the press is in a feeding frenzy, even powerful sources are obliged to respond to the press's agenda. Usually, sources are at the greatest disadvantage against a pack on the scent when factual material will be their undoing — Witness the Watergate case, the Iran-Contra scandal, Dan Quayle's military record, and John Tower's history of drinking. The press in full pursuit can be a powerful information-gathering tool. It is often only a matter of time before someone digs up enough additional material to keep the story in play. Also, the press may have converged on a story, like the drug issue, to such a great extent that even powerful political leaders are obliged to take some action, before their public opinion support base is threatened. Mainstream journalists do not duplicate each other entirely, of course. Particularly in recent years, the greater number of reporters covering campaigns generates pressure for papers to try to outhustle the others, as reporters try to make names for themselves (the *Miami Herald* and the Gary Hart affair, for example). The relationships among news organizations may be symbiotic insofar as they help one another in cross-validating their work. There is safety in numbers. Media are competitive to the extent that they can outdo one another in reporting some new fact or wrinkle, or in doing it faster than the others (the scoop). In this sense, many different organizations can produce content within a common consensual status quo framework, differentiating themselves from each other in minor ways. Even though there are more media outlets now than ever before (see Compaine, 1985), intermedia agenda-setting may reduce the diversity that would otherwise be expected. Strong centripetal forces act to standardize ever more diverse media. Following the lead of others lowers the cost by reducing risk. We may think of the national elite press as establishing an agenda to which other media add detail and color. The proliferation of political talk shows, news commentary programs, and other news channels adds to the total content, but often serves more to amplify this agenda than to change it in any structural way. Little research has examined this important issue of intermedia agenda-setting.

THE POWER BALANCE PERSPECTIVE

This chapter has attempted to frame and review a large and diverse body of literature. Because setting the media agenda encompasses so many different theoretical and methodological perspectives, a power framework helps organize these many studies and focuses attention on the key centers of influence, the resources at their command, and the linkages among them. More often than not, the traditional democratic pluralist model has obscured these phenomena by assuming the prevailing power relations as a given, rather than treating them as an object of study. By acknowledging the fact of power, we can address the means by which it is exercised in media-society relationships.

I have sketched a fairly crude picture of media and sources here, making few distinctions among different types of media and their agendas. Clearly the media agenda is not monolithic and varies from one medium to another, although here I have been more interested in similarities than in differences. More attention is needed to the different news media, including the specialized, prestige, and popular presses, and their relationships with one another and their sources. What is the influence of one medium over another? How do they differ in their relationships with sources, with what consequences for content? What are the changing roles of national and local media? Power balances are changing, for example, as local television news carries more national coverage, a traditional function of network news. New communication technologies are also changing the power equation, as they fundamentally alter the ways news is distributed.

By thinking about power relationships, I have directed attention to the interfaces between news and source organizations, giving importance to the ecosystem formed by these two intersecting systems. Whether media or sources have the greater power and where the desirable balance lies depends on one's perspective and theory of society. The performance of the press is often apt to disappoint all sides equally. Conservatives complain that the media are constantly at odds with our social institutions and national values. Clearly, the media adopt, or at least profess, an adversarial posture in many of their dealings with the power structure, although radical theorists would argue that media are still firmly within the establishment status quo camp. The media may be liberal but not radical in the sense that they do not question basic societal structure and values. I would argue that some independent nonsymbiotic power of media is necessary for them to carry out an aggressive adversarial surveillance function in society and report a picture of reality acceptable to an audience. To the extent that media do have power, it appears to be eroding in significant ways. By conceptualizing diverse indicators, like organizational structure and technological developments, in power terms, we can begin to grasp the implications of such changes for the ultimate power equation. By thinking about power as a series of changing relationships, we also avoid the tendency to think of one institution as inherently and statically powerful. Instead of asserting that media are manipulated by the powerful, we can begin to examine those conditions under which media are able to assert their own power and agenda, independent of other power centers, perhaps to the advantage of the less powerful.

NOTES

1. No single descriptive term has been accepted for this area of research. Closest, perhaps, is *media sociology*, which Davison, Boylan, and Yu (1982) note "seeks to explain why the content of mass communications is as it is" (p. 77). To avoid undue confusion, *media agenda-setting* is used for now, although, like all metaphors, it distorts while clarifying the phenomena to be described. *Agenda-setting* implies a mechanistic, one-directional, linear influence process that tends to place the media in a passive receiver mode. This paradigm may be less applicable to those phenomenological studies treating media as active constructors of reality (e.g., Molotch & Lester, 1974), or to those viewing media as inseparable appendages of the power elite.

2. Sources also have an important message based on how reporters use them in the internal construction of stories. *CBS News* correspondent Bob Faw reported a story on April 25, 1988, on candidate Michael Dukakis's presumed lack of foreign policy experience. Richard Nixon and Henry Kissinger were used as sources critical of Dukakis. Holding these men up as judges of foreign policy expertise makes a subtle statement about the standards against which Dukakis was to be judged. Although both are conservative Republicans, they were presented as "above the fray," and able to represent the foreign policy establishment, even though both presumably supported George Bush.

3. In the counting tradition of media content analysis, quantity is assumed to be an indicator of issue visibility and attention. This assumption is consistent with the agenda-setting paradigm, in which issues are ranked based on amounts of coverage. Because of the limited newshole, devoting more coverage to one issue leaves less room for others, thereby cuing the public to the issues' relative importance. Of course, by emphasizing quantity, content research often overlooks other qualitative, more fine-grained features.

4. Many definitions emphasize the coercive side of power. Max Weber (1958, p. 180) has defined power as realizing one's will in a communal action, even against the resistance of others. Dahl (1961) has a similar definition: A has power over B to the extent that A can get B to do something that B would not otherwise do. Parenti (1978, p. 20) emphasizes that, while some power relations are competitive, zero-sum games (one wins, one loses), many take the form of an exchange. These exchanges do not require that A coerce B, but rather focus attention on whose *interests* are best served by the relationship. B may have little choice in the exchange if A commands unique resources.

5. Even the prototypical individual-level study acknowledged that organizational pressures entered partially into Mr. Gates's decisions: The editor said he preferred stories slanted to conform to his paper's editorial policy (White, 1950, p. 390), and White (p. 389) questioned whether his Mr. Gates could refuse to play up stories if his competition was doing likewise.

6. It is unclear how membership in a social elite group makes journalists hostile to American values. On the contrary, it should link journalists even more strongly to the power elite. Shared elite schooling provides important links between top journalists and other members of the power structure. A recent survey of 20 top young business journalists, for example, found that all but 5 had attended Ivy League schools (the others were not much less prestigious: Duke, Northwestern, New York University, Trinity, and Williams) ("Meet Tomorrow's Editors," 1988). Journalism school graduates are more likely to populate the ranks below the apex of the profession.

7. Perhaps the argument can better be put thus: In a patriarchal society, the female work force has traditionally been ghettoized in low-status, low-wage occupations (waitress, clerk, data entry operator). Even when women perform work comparable to that performed by men they are often paid less. Conceiving gender as an indicator of power logically leads to the conclusion that advances by women into an occupation represent a pyrrhic victory, to the extent that males have allowed it by gravitating to more advantageous positions. The changing role of women in the mass media is an important but complicated subject that deserves more attention than I am able to give it here.

8. Of course, news organizations do not always acquiesce to being manipulated by sources. In the 1988 campaign, for example, a "Doonesbury" cartoon by Garry Trudeau pictured a Bush campaign "handler" calling a network television producer, telling him what the campaign story for that day was going to be, the "sound bite," and the photo opportunity. Furthermore, he said the network had no choice but to cover the event. Perhaps this unflattering portrait stung ABC, because shortly afterward came the second presidential debate, at which ABC News made a decision not to interview influential campaign representatives, "spin doctors," whose job it was to put a favorable cast on the candidate's performance. In addition, *Nightline*, with Ted Koppel, offered a forum for the two candidates to debate. Furthermore, the time was to be offered to one candidate if the other did not show up, thus preventing one candidate from vetoing coverage of the other.

REFERENCES

Adams, W. (1986). Whose lives count? *Journal of Communication, 36,* 113-122.

Agnew, S. (1969). Speech on television news bias. In W. Hammel (Ed.), *The popular arts in America* (pp. 195-204). New York: Harcourt Brace Jovanovich.

Altheide, D. (1976). *Creating reality: How TV news distorts events.* Beverly Hills, CA: Sage.

Altheide, D. (1982). Three-in-one news: Network coverage of Iran. *Journalism Quarterly, 59,* 482-486.

Ammons, L., Dimmick, J., & Pilotta, J. (1982). Crime news reporting in a black weekly. *Journalism Quarterly, 59,* 310-313.

Antunes, G., & Hurley, P. (1977). The representation of criminal events in Houston's two daily newspapers. *Journalism Quarterly, 54,* 756-760.

Bachrach, P., & Baratz, M. (1962). Two faces of power. *American Political Science Review, 56,* 948-970.

Bantz, C., McCorkle, S., & Baade, R. (1980). The news factory. *Communication Research, 7,* 45-68.

Battiata, M. (1985, March 27). Public relations or "news": Gray & Co. blurs the boundaries. *Washington Post.*

Bigman, S. K. (1948). Rivals in conformity: A study of two competing dailies. *Journalism Quarterly, 25,* 127-131.

Blumler, J., & Gurevitch, M. (1986). Journalists' orientations to political institutions: The case of parliamentary broadcasting. In P. Golding, G. Murdock, & P. Schlesinger (Eds.), *Communicating politics: Mass communications and the political process* (pp. 67-92). New York: Holmes & Meier.

Breed, W. (1980). *The newspaperman, news and society.* New York: Arno.

Brown, J., Bybee, C., Wearden, S., & Straughan, D. (1987). Invisible power: Newspaper news sources and the limits of diversity. *Journalism Quarterly, 64,* 45-54.

Buckalew, J. K. (1969). News elements and selection by television news editors. *Journal of Broadcasting, 14,* 47-54.

Burke, K. (1945). *A grammar of motives.* New York: Prentice-Hall.

Capo, J. A. (1983). Network Watergate coverage patterns in late 1972 and early 1973. *Journalism Quarterly, 56,* 595-602.

Chibnall, S. (1975). The crime reporter: A study in the production of commercial knowledge. *Sociology, 9,* 49-66.

Cobb, R., & Elder, C. (1972). *Participation in American politics: The dynamics of agenda-building.* Baltimore: Johns Hopkins University Press.

Compaine, B. (1985). The expanding base of media competition. *Journal of Communication, 35,* 81-96.

Corry, J. (1986). *TV news and the dominant culture* (Media & Society Monograph). Washington, DC: Media Institute.

Crenson, M. (1971). *The un-politics of air pollution: A study of non-decision making in the cities.* Baltimore: Johns Hopkins University Press.

Crouse, T. (1972). *The boys on the bus: Riding with the campaign press corps.* New York: Random House.

Cutlip, S. (1954). Content and Flow of AP News from Trunk to TTS to Reader. *Journalism Quarterly, 31,* 434-446.

Dahl, R. (1961). *Who governs?* New Haven, CT: Yale University Press.

Danielian, L., & Reese, S. (1988). A closer look at intermedia influences on agenda setting: The cocaine issue of 1986. In P. Shoemaker (Ed.), *Communication campaigns about drugs: Government, media and the public* (pp. 47-66). Hillsdale, NJ: Lawrence Erlbaum.

Davison, W. P. (1974). News media and international negotiation. *Public Opinion Quarterly, 33,* 174-191.

Davison, W. P. (1975). Diplomatic reporting: Rules of the game. *Journal of Communication, 25,* 138-146.

Davison, W. P., Boylan, J., & Yu, T. C. (1982). *Mass media systems and effects.* New York: Holt, Rinehart & Winston.

DeFleur, M., & Ball-Rokeach, S. (1989). *Theories of mass communication* (5th ed.). New York: Longman.

Didion, J. (1988, October 27). Insider baseball. *New York Review of Books,* pp. 19-31.

Dimmick, J., & Coit, P. (1982). Levels of analysis in mass media decision making. *Communication Research, 9,* 3-32.

Domhoff, G. W. (1967). *Who rules America now?* Englewood Cliffs, NJ: Prentice-Hall.

Domhoff, G. W. (1970). *The higher circles: Governing class in America.* New York: Random House.

Domhoff, G. W. (1979). *The powers that be: Processes of ruling class domination in America.* Englewood Cliffs, NJ: Prentice-Hall.

Dominick, J. (1977). Geographic bias in network TV news. *Journal of Communication, 27,* 94-99

Dominick, J. R. (1981). Business coverage in network newscasts. *Journalism Quarterly, 58,* 179-185.

Donohue, T. R., & Glasser, T. L. (1978). Homogeneity in coverage of Connecticut newspapers. *Journalism Quarterly, 55,* 592-596.

Dreier, P. (1982). The position of the press in the U.S. power structure. *Social Problems, 29,* 298-310.

Drew, D. (1972). Roles and decisions of three television beat reporters. *Journal of Broadcasting, 16,* 165-173.

Dunn, D. (1969). *Public officials and the press.* Reading, MA: Addison-Wesley.

Eco, U. (1976). *A theory of semiotics.* Bloomington: Indiana University Press.

Elliot, P. (1972). *The making of a television series.* London: Constable.

Epstein, E. J. (1973). *News from nowhere.* New York: Random House.

Ettema, J., Whitney, D. C., & Wackman, D. (1987). Professional mass communicators. In D. G. Berger & S. Chaffee (Eds.), *Handbook of communication science* (pp. 747-780). Newbury Park, CA: Sage.

Fedler, F., & Jordan, D. (1982). How emphasis on people affects coverage of crime. *Journalism Quarterly, 59,* 474-478.

Fishman, M. (1980). *Manufacturing the news.* Austin: University of Texas Press.

Foote, J., & Steele, M. E. (1986). Degree of conformity in lead stories in early evening network TV newscasts. *Journalism Quarterly, 63,* 19-23.

Fowler, J. S., & Showalter, S. W. (1974). Evening network news selection: A confirmation of news judgment. *Journalism Quarterly, 51*, 712-715.

Funkhouser, G. R. (1973). Trends in media coverage of the issues of the '60s. *Journalism Quarterly, 50*, 533-538.

Gandy, O. (1982). *Beyond agenda-setting: Information subsidies and public policy.* Norwood, NJ: Ablex.

Gans, H. (1979). *Deciding what's news.* New York: Random House.

Garnham, N. (1979). Contribution to a political economy of mass communication. *Media, Culture and Society, 1*, 123-146.

Gieber, W. (1956). Across the desk: A study of 16 telegraph editors. *Journalism Quarterly, 43*, 423-432.

Gieber, W. (1960). Two communicators of the news: A study of the roles of sources and reporters. *Social Forces, 39*, 76-83.

Gitlin, T. (1980). *The whole world is watching: The role of the media in the making and unmaking of the New Left.* Berkeley: University of California Press.

Gold, D., & Simmons, J. L. (1965). News selection patterns among Iowa dailies. *Public Opinion Quarterly, 29*, 425-430.

Graber, D. (1971). Press coverage patterns of campaign news: The 1968 presidential race. *Journalism Quarterly, 48*, 502-512.

Graber, D. (1988, May). *Flashlight coverage: State news on national broadcasts.* Paper presented at the annual meeting of the International Communication Association, New Orleans.

Gramsci, A. (1971). *Selections from the prison notebooks of Antonio Gramsci* (Q. Hoare & G. Smith, Eds. & Trans.). New York: International. (Original work published 1927)

Halberstam, D. (1979). *The powers that be.* New York: Knopf.

Herman, E. (1986). Gatekeeper versus propaganda models: A critical American perspective. In P. Golding, G. Murdock, & P. Schlesinger (Eds.), *Communicating politics: Mass communications and the political process* (pp. 171-196). New York: Holmes & Meier.

Hess, S. (1981). *The Washington reporters.* Washington, DC: Brookings Institution.

Hess, S. (1984). *The government/press connection: Press officers and their offices.* Washington, DC: Brookings Institution.

Hester, A. (1978). Five years of foreign news in U.S. television evening newscasts. *Gazette, 24*, 88-95.

Hinds, M. (1987, April 21). TV news gets a subtle sales pitch as the press release goes electronic. *New York Times.*

Hirsch, P. (1977). Occupational, organizational and institutional models in mass media research: Toward an integrated framework. In P. M. Hirsch, P. V. Miller, & F. G. Kline (Eds.), *Strategies for communication research* (pp. 13-40). Beverly Hills, CA: Sage.

Hutchins, R. M. (1947). *Commission on freedom of the press: Toward a free and responsible press.* Chicago: University of Chicago Press.

Johnstone, J., Slawski, E., & Bowman, W. (1973). *The news people: A sociological portrait of American journalists and their work.* Urbana: University of Illinois Press.

Kerr, P. (1986, November 17). Anatomy of an issue: Drugs, the evidence, the reaction. *New York Times,* p. 1.

Larson, J. (1983). *Television's window on the world.* Norwood, NJ: Ablex.

Lasorsa, D., & Reese, S. (1989, May). *News sources in the national media: A comparison of coverage of the stock market crash.* Paper presented at the annual meeting of the International Communication Association, San Francisco.

Lasorsa, D., & Wanta, W. (1988, May). *The effects of personal, interpersonal, and media experience on issue salience.* Paper presented at the annual meeting of the International Communication Association, New Orleans.

Lemert, J. B. (1974). Content duplication by the networks in competing evening newscasts. *Journalism Quarterly, 51*, 238-244.

Levy, M. (1981). Disdaining the news. *Journal of Communication, 31*, 24-31.

Lichter, S. R., Lichter, L., & Rothman, S. (1986). *The media elite: America's new powerbrokers.* Bethesda, MD: Adler & Adler.

Linsky, M. (1986). *Impact: How the press affects federal policy making.* New York: W. W. Norton.

Linsky, M., Moore, J., O'Donnell, W., & Whitman, D. (1986). *How the press affects federal policy making: Six case studies.* New York: W. W. Norton.

Lowry, D. (1971). Agnew and the network TV news: A before-after content analysis. *Journalism Quarterly, 48,* 205-210.

Lukes, S. (1974). *Power: A radical view.* London: Macmillan.

McCombs, M. (1987). Effect of monopoly in Cleveland on diversity of newspaper content. *Journalism Quarterly, 64,* 740-745.

McCombs, M. (1988). Concentration, monopoly and content. In R. Picard, J. Winter, M. McCombs, & S. Lacy (Eds.), *Press concentration and monopoly: New perspectives on newspaper ownership and operations* (pp. 129-138). Norwood, NJ: Ablex.

McCombs, M., & Shaw, D. (1972). The agenda-setting function of the mass media. *Public Opinion Quarterly, 36,* 176-187.

McCombs, M., & Shaw, D. (1977). Structuring the unseen environment. *Journal of Communication, 27,* 18-22.

McQuail, D. (1986). Diversity in political communication: Its sources, forms and future. In P. Golding, G. Murdock, & P. Schlesinger (Eds.), *Communicating politics: Mass communications and the political process* (pp. 133-149). New York: Holmes & Meier.

Meeske, M. D., & Javaheri, M. H. (1982). Network television coverage of the Iranian hostage crisis. *Journalism Quarterly, 59,* 641-645.

Meet tomorrow's editors today. (1988). *TJFR: The Journalist & Financial Reporting, 2*(13), 1, 6-9

Merriam, J., & Makower, J. (1988). *Trend watching; How the media create trends and how to be the first to uncover them.* New York: Amacom/Tilden.

Miller, S. (1978). Reporters and congressmen: Living in symbiosis. *Journalism Monograph, 53.*

Mills, C. W. (1956). *The power elite.* New York: Oxford University Press.

Molotch, H., & Lester, M. (1974). News as purposive behavior: On the strategic use of routine events, accidents and scandals. *American Sociological Review, 39,* 101-112.

Mosco, V., & Herman, A. (1981). Radical social theory and the communication revolution. In E. McAnany, J. Schnitman, & N. Janus (Eds.), *Communication and social structure* (pp. 58-84). New York: Praeger.

Moynihan, D. P. (1975). *Coping: On the practice of government.* New York: Random House.

Murdock, G., & Golding, P. (1979). Capitalism, communication and class relations. In J. Curran, M. Gurevitch, & J. Woollacott (Eds.), *Mass communication and society* (pp. 12-43). Beverly Hills, CA: Sage.

Paletz, D., & Entman, R. (1981). *Media, power, politics.* New York: Free Press.

Parenti, M. (1978). *Power and the powerless.* New York: St. Martin's.

Parenti, M. (1986). *Inventing reality: The politics of the mass media.* New York: St. Martin's.

Patterson, T. (1980). *The mass media election.* New York: Praeger.

Picard, R., & Winter, J. (1985). *Press concentration and monopoly: A bibliography.* New York: Association for Education in Journalism and Mass Communication, Mass Communications and Society Division.

Pool, I., & Schulman, I. (1959). Newsmen's fantasies, audiences and newswriting. *Public Opinion Quarterly, 23,* 145-158.

Reese, S., & Danielian, L. (1988). Intermedia influence and the drug issue: Converging on cocaine. In P. Shoemaker (Ed.), *Communication campaigns about drugs: Government, media and the public* (pp. 29-46). Hillsdale, NJ: Lawrence Erlbaum.

Riffe, D., Ellis, B., Rogers, M. K., Van Ommeren, R. L., & Woodman, K. A. (1986). Gatekeeping and the network news mix. *Journalism Quarterly, 63,* 315-321.

Riffe, D., & Shaw, E. F. (1982). Conflict and consonance: Coverage of Third World in two U.S. papers. *Journalism Quarterly, 59,* 484-488.

Rogers, E., & Dearing, J. (1988). Agenda-setting research: Where has it been, where is it going? In J. Anderson (Ed.), *Communication yearbook 11* (pp. 555-593). Newbury Park, CA: Sage.

Rose, A. (1967). *The power structure.* New York: Oxford University Press.

Roshier, B. (1981). The selection of crime news by the press. In S. Cohen & J. Young (Eds.), *The manufacture of news: Deviance, social problems and the mass media* (pp. 40-51). Beverly Hills, CA: Sage.

Rusher, W. (1988). *The coming battle for the media: Curbing the power of the media elite.* New York: William Morrow.

Schattschneider, E. E. (1960). *The semi-sovereign people: A realist's view of democracy in America.* New York: Holt, Rinehart & Winston.

Schiller, D. (1986). Transformations of news in the U.S. information market. In P. Golding, G. Murdock, & P. Schlesinger (Eds.), *Communicating politics: Mass communications and the political process* (pp. 19-36). New York: Holmes & Meier.

Shaw, D. (1977). The press agenda in a community setting. In D. Shaw & M. McCombs (Eds.), *The emergence of American public issues: The agenda-setting function of the press* (pp. 33-51). St. Paul, MN: West.

Sigal, L. V. (1973). *Reporters and officials.* Lexington, MA: D. C. Heath.

Smith, H. (1988). *The power game: How Washington works.* New York: Random House.

Snider, P. (1967). Mr. Gates revisited: A 1966 version of the 1949 case study. *Journalism Quarterly, 44,* 419-427.

Stempel, G. (1959). Uniformity of wire content in six Michigan dailies. *Journalism Quarterly, 36,* 45-48.

Stempel, G. (1962). Content patterns of small and metropolitan dailies. *Journalism Quarterly, 62,* 88-91.

Stempel, G. (1985). Gatekeeping: The mix of topics and selection of stories. *Journalism Quarterly, 62,* 791-796, 815.

Stempel, G. H., & Windhauser, J. W. (1984). The prestige press revisited: Coverage of the 1980 presidential campaign. *Journalism Quarterly, 61,* 49-55.

Stinchcombe, A. (1968). *Constructing social theories.* New York: Harcourt, Brace & World.

Supply-side thinking (beat AP) to be replaced by demand-side thinking. (1988, April 4). *Broadcasting,* p. 128.

Swanson, D. (1988). Feeling the elephant: Some observations on agenda-setting research (commentary on Rogers and Dearing). In J. Anderson (Ed.), *Communication yearbook 11* (pp. 603-619). Newbury Park, CA: Sage.

Turk, J. (1986, December). Information subsidies and media content. *Journalism Monographs, 100.*

Turow, J. (1985). *Media industries: The production of news and entertainment.* New York: Longman.

Warner, M. (1968). TV coverage of international affairs. *TV Quarterly, 7,* 60-75.

Weaver, D., & Wilhoit, G. C. (1986). *The American journalist; A portrait of U.S. newspeople and their work.* Bloomington: Indiana University Press.

Weaver, J. B., Porter, C. J., & Evans, M. E. (1984). Patterns of foreign news coverage on U.S. network TV: A 10-year analysis. *Journalism Quarterly, 61,* 356-363.

Weber, M. (1958). Class, status, party. In H. Gerth & C. W. Mills (Eds.), *From Max Weber: Essays in sociology* (pp. 180-195). New York: Oxford.

Weiss, C. (1974). What America's leaders read. *Public Opinion Quarterly, 38,* 1-22.

White, D. M. (1950). The gatekeeper: A case study in the selection of news. *Journalism Quarterly, 27,* 383-396.

Whitney, D. C., & Becker, L. (1982). "Keeping the gates" for gatekeepers: The effects of wire news. *Journalism Quarterly, 59,* 60-65.

Reflecting on Metaphors

LEE B. BECKER
The Ohio State University

T HE Reese essay, we are told quite straightforwardly, is intended to "pick up where Rogers and Dearing (1988) left off." The goal is to "knit together" a "burgeoning number of studies seeking to explain the media's agenda" (p. 310). As such, Reese argues, this literature can be viewed as coming under what is called "the agenda-setting metaphor."

In point of fact, Rogers and Dearing seem to have invited Reese or someone to take up this task by noting its importance and, at the same time, excluding it from their own essay. As a consequence, my comments in response to Reese are also to some extent in response to Rogers and Dearing. Basically, I wish to question the value of this continued extension of what both Reese and Rogers and Dearing, as well as others, refer to as the agenda-setting "metaphor."

In focusing on this extension of the agenda-setting metaphor I am ignoring much of what the Reese essay is about. I will not deal, for example, with the concept of power that really is at the heart of the essay. I will deal only indirectly with the level-of-analysis distinctions made. What I will discuss is the *rationale* for the review, which raises these important issues of power and level of analysis.

This decision to focus on the "metaphor" reflects my own concerns with the literature on what is termed *agenda-setting*. I have argued elsewhere that the existent work has been hampered by imprecision in terms of concepts and the rationale behind the theoretical linkages fundamental to the hypotheses offered (Becker, 1982). To some extent, these comments are an expansion of that argument in the specific context of the Reese essay.

THE METAPHOR

A metaphor, of course, is not meant as literal truth, but rather as a means of illustrating via reference to something similar. If we call agenda-setting a

Correspondence and requests for reprints: Lee B. Becker, School of Journalism, The Ohio State University, Columbus, OH 43210.

Communication Yearbook 14, pp. 341-346

metaphor, I suppose, we are saying that the term *agenda* is only a figure of speech. What *is* meant by the term *agenda*, however, has been problematic from the start. In an early article, my colleagues and I distinguished between three conceptually distinct meanings of the term for individual recipients of media messages (McLeod, Becker, & Byrnes, 1974). We spoke of perceptions of salience (that is, the view that an issue was important in some context, such as in an election campaign or to the "general public"), an individual salience rating (that is, the belief than an issue was important to the individual personally for something like a vote decision), and salience in terms of topic of interpersonal discussion. In Rogers and Dearing's more general view, we must distinguish among *mass media* agendas, *public* agendas, and *policy* agendas.

An *agenda*, Rogers and Dearing (1988) say, is defined "as issues or events that are viewed at a point in time as ranked in a hierarchy of importance" (p. 556). A mass media agenda, then, is a ranking of issues in the content of the mass media. The public agenda is a ranking of issues in public opinion. The policy agenda is the ranking of issues by political elites.

Most of the literature on agenda-setting has concerned itself with the public agenda, or the ranking of the issues in public opinion. Yet virtually nothing has been done to link the effect at the individual level (which I still prefer to call *issue salience*) conceptually to the effect at the societal level of mass opinion. To put it another way, we lack an adequate way to aggregate the findings conceptually. While in the knowledge gap literature (Olien, Donohue, & Tichenor, 1983) we can easily see how individual information acquisition can create a knowledge gap, we do not have such an understanding of how individual issue ratings come together to form a public agenda.

A simple aggregation of the nomination of individual items for the agenda shows that many, often a majority, nominate something other than the dominant issue. Yet this aggregation is the most common operationalization of the concept of *public* agenda. The picture would be clearer, of course, if we could show that individuals come to their different views of issue salience as a result of exposure to media with different agendas. The aggregate agenda, then, might be seen as the cumulative effect of competing forces of agenda building.

Such a view is not possible in part because analyses have rarely taken this perspective and in part because media content is most often quite similar. There simply is no justification in the present discourse on the topic for arguing how many individuals would follow the media lead and how many others would come to their own salience ratings.

To a considerable extent, this conceptual difficulty is intricately tied to other theoretical problems. As Swanson (1988) notes, the theoretical rationale for linking media content with public opinion has been poorly developed. Often it is simply not present at all.

THE CREATION OF MEDIA CONTENT

Reese, of course, is not overly concerned with the public agenda. His prime interest is the *mass media agenda*, or the way in which the news media rank the components of their content. Specifically, Reese is arguing that the agenda-setting metaphor suggests we look anew at another literature — namely, the literature on the creation of media content — to understand how mass media agendas are created. The reexamination should borrow conceptually (or metaphorically) from the literature linking media agendas with public agendas and, to a lesser extent, that linking both media and public agendas to policy agendas. This new area of inquiry is to be labeled *media agenda-setting*, or the study of the setting of the agenda of the media.

I do not argue that the existing literature linking media content to audience importance ratings relative to components of that content has provided new insights. The experimental work of Iyengar and Kinder on priming is particularly impressive (see, for example, Iyengar & Kinder, 1987). The gain from extension of this metaphor, however, must offset the loss for this strategy to be worthwhile. The gain would be in terms of new insights, new and appropriate concepts, and new theoretical justifications.

In my view, the value of this metaphor for a reexamination of the literature on the creation of media content turns on some important assumptions that are worthy of close examination. Specifically, it seems to me, the distinction between an event and an issue, made both by Rogers and Dearing and by Reese, merits particularly close scrutiny. The differences between events and issues suggest much about the role of media personnel and media institutions in creating the mass media agenda.

THE ISSUE/EVENT DISTINCTION

Drawing on earlier research, Reese defines an event as a discrete happening. An issue, in contrast, involves a series of events, often separated by space and time, having something that links them together. I would prefer to see an issue defined as something in dispute, that is, something about which it is possible to articulate more than one point or view. The definition offered by Reese and others seems overly simplistic. That problem, however, really is not a critical point here.

Reese, in fact, argues that it is often hard to make the distinction between an event and an issue in actual practice. Yet I find it important to make the distinction, for it is a distinction between a passive and an active medium. For this reason, the explanations of media behavior might well be quite different in the two cases. I would expect the media to cover events — some of which are created merely to attract that coverage, some of which come about for quite independent reasons — in rather easily predicted ways. In fact, I would suggest that most of the literature on news creation (see, e.g., reviews by Ettema, Whitney, & Wackman, 1987; Tuchman, 1988) focuses on the coverage of events.

The coverage of issues, on the other hand, does not seem to me to be so well addressed by the current literature. Yet only if it can be shown that the media play such an active, as opposed to a passive, role in creation of a public agenda can one truly justify the reexamination Reese is calling for. Otherwise, the current concepts and theoretical perspectives do quite nicely.

This is not to dismiss a media effect brought about through the routines of passive news coverage. I consider it an important media effect if it can be shown that the media, through their various routines, produce something that causes change in the attitudes of audience members, in their perceptions, in the information they have, or in their behaviors. That effect takes on added importance, however, and justifies Reese's reexamination, only if it can be shown that the media played some active role in issue identification. For the media to play what I have termed an active role, they would have to do something other than simply serve as a conduit. I would want to be able to show, in Reese's terms, that the media exercised power.

LOOKING FOR MEDIA ACTIVITY

Reese has made unit-of-analysis distinctions that, to some extent, reflect the perspective I am taking. News creation can be studied as the product of interorganizational constraints, intraorganizational pressures, and individual activities. I am essentially arguing that the active role I am seeking for the media most likely would come from analyses on the intraorganizational and individual levels. I would want to see that the media made decisions on issue coverage to meet intraorganizational needs or goals or as a simple reflection of individual behaviors. If the metaphor of the agenda is worth pursuing, we should see some evidence of sensitivity to it on the part of the media players.

Now, why might media organizations seek to organize issues in such a way as to create a public agenda and, possibly, thereby a policy agenda? One can speculate that this could be to protect the commercial environment within which the organization operates, to maximize profits, to satisfy advertiser needs, or to reflect owner interests. These dictates, however, are probably better at explaining very general orientations rather than individual decisions made on a day-to-day basis. In other words, they might well be better at explaining why the civil rights issue was not covered by the media until skilled leaders created events that demanded coverage than why famine in Africa or political unrest in Central America moves on or off the news pages or newscasts. It is hard to see how some issues, such as crime or drugs or unemployment, might be affected *in the short run* by these general dictates. Yet these are the kinds of issues that do vary in terms of levels of media coverage.

A distinct analytic strategy is to focus on individuals operating within the media environment to explain decisions on issue selection. Two distinguishable sub-strategies, not mutually exclusive, present themselves. First, one can study the characteristics of the individuals as predictors of such selection; second, one can study the characteristics of the environments within which the individuals work. The former strategy is a bit more conducive to the study of issue selection, and the latter suggests, once again, a certain passivity. In addition, the origins of these constraints would best be studied at the organizational, rather than individual, level of analysis.

What is it about the individual journalist that might suggest an interest in generating an issue agenda? Is an issue agenda something an individual journalist is likely to be aware of? One might turn to such variables as the education of the journalist (Becker, Fruit, & Caudill, 1987), the professional orientation of the journalist (McLeod & Hawley, 1964), or the role the journalist seeks to play in covering news (Johnstone, Slawski, & Bowman, 1973) to answer these questions. Yet it is hard to see how these variables would predict or explain selection of *specific* issues for a news agenda. In the end, it seems unlikely that journalists very often go about their work with the intent of creating a ranking of issues on the part of their readers and viewers.

SUMMARY

I am arguing that the case for reexamining the literature on media content creation within the context of the existing literature on agenda-setting can be justified only if it produces new insights for that literature or if that literature provides new insights for the ongoing work on agenda-setting. These insights might be in the form of new concepts or new theoretical rationales for linking concepts. In a general sense, the agenda-setting literature does suggest the importance of looking at media content as a product. But it does not offer any convincing case for new concepts. The existing work has not done a good job of explicating or validating the concept of issue or issue agenda. The idea of a "conscious" agenda created by the media does not seem particularly promising.

If the agenda-setting metaphor were dropped entirely from the literature reviewed by Reese, little would be lost. The literature of media content creation is adequately "capitalized" conceptually. The addition of poorly defined concepts from another analytic framework would seem to add little.

The case against the use of this terminology, on the other hand, is quite convincing. The conceptual imprecision and ambiguity of theoretical rationale already plaguing the work on agenda-setting is unlikely to be aided by expansion. What is needed instead is more attention to the narrow picture. The general picture will emerge at a later time.

The term *agenda-setting* carries with it a notion of media power. Historically, as Rogers and Dearing note, it is rooted in the period of a reexamination of media effects. To carry the term over to the literature of news creation suggests a power that at present cannot be documented. In fact, it seems unlikely to be justified.

It is better, it seems to me, to stick with the old terminology and add a new sensitivity to media selection, rather than a new set of concepts with unwanted baggage. The existing research on agenda-setting does suggest the importance of media content. Understanding all components of that content, including the selection of certain issues over others, will be valuable. At the same time, the term *agenda-setting* will be made larger by being restricted to cover less.

REFERENCES

Becker, L. B. (1982). The mass media and citizen assessment of issue importance: A reflection on agenda-setting research. In D. C. Whitney, E. Wartella, & S. Windahl (Eds.), *Mass communication review yearbook* (Vol. 3, pp. 521-536). Beverly Hills, CA: Sage.

Becker, L. B., Fruit, J. W., & Caudill, S. L. (1987). *The training and hiring of journalists.* Norwood, NJ: Ablex.

Ettema, J., Whitney, D. C., & Wackman, D. (1987). Professional mass communicators. In D. G. Berger & S. Chaffee (Eds.), *Handbook of communication science* (pp. 747-780). Newbury Park, CA: Sage.

Iyengar, S., & Kinder, D. R. (1987). *News that matters: Agenda-setting and priming in a television age.* Chicago: University of Chicago Press.

Johnstone, J., Slawski, E., & Bowman, W. (1973). *The news people: A sociological portrait of American journalists and their work.* Urbana: University of Illinois Press.

McLeod, J. M., Becker, L. B., & Byrnes, J. E. (1974). Another look at the agenda setting function of the press. *Communication Research, 1*, 131-166.

McLeod, J. M., & Hawley, S. E. (1964). Professionalization among newsmen. *Journalism Quarterly, 41*, 529-539.

Olien, C. N., Donohue, G. A., & Tichenor, P. J. (1983). Structure, communication and social power: Evolution of the knowledge gap hypothesis. In E. Wartella, D. C. Whitney, & S. Windahl (Eds.), *Mass communication review yearbook* (Vol. 4, pp. 455-461). Beverly Hills, CA: Sage.

Rogers, E. M., & Dearing, J. W. (1988). Agenda-setting research: Where has it been, where is it going? In J. Anderson (Ed.), *Communication yearbook 11* (pp. 555-593). Newbury Park, CA: Sage.

Swanson, D. L. (1988). Feeling the elephant: Some observations on agenda-setting research (commentary on Rogers and Dearing). In J. Anderson (Ed.), *Communication yearbook 11* (pp. 603-619). Newbury Park, CA: Sage.

Tuchman, G. (1988). Mass media institutions. In N. Smelser (Ed.), *Handbook of sociology* (pp. 601-626). Newbury Park, CA: Sage.

Agenda-Setting:
Power and Contingency

D. CHARLES WHITNEY
University of Illinois at Urbana-Champaign

I would like to do two things in this essay. First, I would like to comment critically on Reese's formulation of media agenda-setting. Second, while I agree with Reese that power, much as he has elaborated it, is an advance in studying media agenda-setting, I would like to explore a notion of contingency that I think is likewise fundamentally necessary in our understanding of media agenda-setting, and agenda-setting more broadly.

Reese has ably directed our attention at some very disparate strains of research related to the notion of who sets the media agenda and how. And as he ably shows, a concern with the construct of power must inform such study.

MEDIA AGENDA-SETTING AS AGENDA-SETTING:
THREE PROBLEMS

Before we can get there, however, a few comments are in order to locate Reese's work within the larger body of agenda-setting study. As he notes, the studies he reviews in large part do not derive from any explicit test of agenda-setting hypotheses:

These studies are diverse and are knitted together only loosely, if at all, by the agenda-setting metaphor. But then, one strength of the robust agenda concept is its ability to pull together previously unconnected lines of research. (p. 310)

Let us begin, as Reese does, by granting that *public* agenda-setting has been sufficiently well validated to allow us to turn to questions of *media* agenda-setting. In so doing, let us also stipulate that, compatible with Reese's argument, the larger

Correspondence and requests for reprints: D. Charles Whitney, Institute of Communications Research, 505 East Armory Avenue, 222B, University of Illinois, Champaign, IL 61820.

agenda-setting framework (see Rogers & Dearing, 1988) requires us to keep *policy* agenda-setting in mind as well. Thus in any discussion of agenda-setting, the public, media, and policy arenas must to some degree be all before us at once. In other words, we are concerned with the influence of each of these on the others. As others, most notably Swanson (1988), have commented, however, even the basic *concept* of agenda-setting — what it means to have the agenda *set* — means significantly different things in each arena. Thus for public agenda-setting to occur, the salience of an issue must be increased. For media agenda-setting to occur, that issue must be reported, and presumably the amount and prominence of reporting are the indicators of the degree to which the media agenda has been set. And by extension (Rogers & Dearing, 1988, pp. 576-577), policy agenda-setting is marked by the appearance, and prominence, of the issue in the public policy arena. Even if we restrict our focus primarily to the question of media agenda-setting, these requirements raise a number of problems, three of which — the notions of an issue, the public, and agenda interrelatedness — will be commented upon here.

ISSUES, PUBLICS, AND AGENDAS

In many respects, these problems can probably most clearly be seen by reference to an analogous development in another earlier stream of media research, that of the two-step flow of communication influence. Robinson (1976) has reformulated the original hypothesis, that "ideas often flow from the media to opinion leaders, and from them to less attentive segments of the population" (Lazarsfeld, Berelson, & Gaudet, 1948). The reformulation introduces the following important elements.

Content. Ideas is too simple. Opinion leaders glean *information* from the news media, but pass along *influence* to followers. One cannot, in other words, make any assumptions about, or ignore, content as an important dimension.

Opinion leadership. In 1955, Katz and Lazarsfeld noted that opinion leadership was *specialized* by topic, not a general characteristic of individuals. Robinson also shows that patterns of interaction and influence would suggest at least two classes of opinion leaders, those who lead but do not follow, and those who do both (opinion sharers); moreover, since opinion leadership involves interpersonal discussion, dialogue is implied, and even "pure" opinion leaders hear something from presumed followers.

Number of steps. There is no guarantee of two steps. Logically, there could be two, but there could also be more, from, say, the media to one opinion leader-sharer to another, and then to a less attentive auditor. Clearly, there are sometimes fewer: Where one is a "nondiscussant," the only possible source of influence (see Reese's discussion of dependency) can be from the mass media. And equally possible is the no-step nonflow, when the message is ignored.[1]

Let us see how these resemble problems for media agenda-setting.

Issue/Content

First is the problem of what we mean by an issue. Much of the conceptual fuzziness in agenda-setting writ large, as both Rogers and Dearing (1988) and Swanson (1988) have noted, is that an "issue" may at once be a topic, a controversy, or a discrete event[2] (see also Lang & Lang, 1983). For public agenda-setting, the priming hypothesis (Iyengar & Kinder, 1987) extends the realm to saliences of evaluations on issues to policymakers' performance. When we turn our focus to media agenda-setting, "issue," in addition to being topic, controversy, or event, and paralleling priming in some respects, may also be taken to mean *what gets said about* the topic or issue within the media (much of the literature Reese surveys is directed, as he notes, here rather than toward how much coverage is given to the topic/issue/event). When we focus on policy agenda-setting, the real question of interest may center far less on *whether* an issue, topic, or controversy is on the public agenda than on *what policy choices or options* are advanced. While for some issues, topics, or events the options may be simple (either Nixon is removed from office or not, whether Bush or Dukakis is elected), more often (what we do about AIDS, drugs, environmental pollution, taxation) they are not. Moreover, from the vantage of media effects on the policy agenda, present evidence suggests that media power is restricted to speeding up the emergence of agenda items, to moving items already on the agenda higher up it, or to moving items higher in the policy hierarchy from, for example, "specialized" units such as congressional committee staff to the Senate (Ettema et al., in press; Linsky, 1986; Strodthoff, Hawkins, & Schoenfeld, 1985). In other words, there is little evidence of *substantive* policy influence of, in short, specific policy formulations initiated by the news media.[3] The argument here, then, is that the relatively content-free assertions of the basic agenda-setting model do not map well onto the terrain of the media sociology literature that Reese surveys.

The Public

The second problem that shifting from the original — that is, public — agenda-setting formulation to media agenda-setting introduces is the nettlesome problem of the "public." In public agenda-setting, the public is the dependent variable; agenda-setting is indexed by changes in public salience measured at either the individual or the aggregate level. Moreover, most public agenda-setting studies have concluded that the public exerts relatively little influence on the media agenda. In media agenda-setting, however, we have several questions to ask about the public, most notably, What is it? Is it the anonymous, aggregate audience? If so, does it, or even could it, have an impact on mass communicators? And if so, how? Mass communicator sociology is at best unsettled on the matter; the usual formulation (Darnton, 1975; Gans, 1980) is that the audience exerts virtually no influence on making news, though others suggest journalists' audience notions

TABLE 1
The Three Main Levels of the Agenda-Setting Process,
by Level of Specialization/Specificity

Level	Media	Public	Policy
general or mass	mass, general interest	aggregate or mass public	general policymakers (e.g., president, Congress)
specialized, topic-specific	specialized	"focal publics," interest groups, individuals	specialists (e.g., regulatory agencies, departments, committees)

may influence news decision making (Pool & Shulman, 1959; Tichenor, Donohue, & Olien, 1967). If the public is something other than the aggregate, anonymous audience, then what? Does it also comprise all nongovernment or nonpolicy and nonmedia persons and groups? Where is the dividing line between policy and public, and between elites and nonelites? Are interest groups part of the public? How does our conception of sources of news and our ideas of the initiation of policy options fit here?

Reese notes that most views of political influence begin with elites, "who seek to manage the climate of opinion in their favor. . . . Focusing on agenda creation highlights these processes" (p. 310). A media agenda-setting model worthy of the name would be one that can adequately account for how social issues originate and come to influence public policy, and Reese's chapter is a good beginning here. From a media agenda-setting vantage point, some of our most interesting questions should deal with the variability of media treatment of potential and actual sources from each of the other domains. (See Reese's fourfold high/low media and source power typology. The parallel with the two-step flow analogy suggested above is the obvious one, that the "audiences" for communicated messages are interrelated, sometimes in nonobvious ways.)

Intermedia Agenda-Setting: Interaction Across Levels

Here, our analogy to the two-step flow model deals with both the transformation of content and the number and nature of steps in the process across levels of specialization (see Table 1). The third problem, highlighted by Table 1, deals with the nature of interaction among all elements in the table.[4] The usual formulation of the agenda-setting process (e.g., Rogers & Dearing, 1988) ignores the lower level, and most agenda-setting studies measure variables only at the upper level; in doing so, they imperil the finding of answers to significant questions about how all three agendas get set, and particularly how issues and policy options originate.

With relatively little research here, we are free to speculate a bit. Under routine circumstances, especially for slow-onset issues (Rogers & Dearing, 1988, p. 566), communication flows are probably densest *within* levels, either general or specialized: High-salience issues are played out at the general level, and communication about low-salience issues may be quite heavy across elements within a specialized domain while going virtually unnoted at the mass or general level.

We tend to forget that most public policy is formulated outside the public eye, that virtually all interest groups and interpersonal discussions operate there, and even that much "mass" communication is specialized. (Few of the 8,000-10,000 magazines published in the United States are aimed at general audiences, and only a fraction of the 50,000-60,000 book titles issued annually are aimed at mass audiences.) Most communication within a topic-specific domain is "insider," conforming to goals, values, and information shared only within that domain (see Carey, 1969, regarding "speech communities" and a general discussion). Intermedia agenda-setting implies interaction among media agendas, including movement from specialized to general media. What's interesting, of course, is how, and under what sets of circumstances, issues and policy options cross a salience threshold, and *how* they may be transformed when and if they do. Why—and how—did Francis Fukuyama's argument for the "end of history" cross from the insider *National Interest* to national political discourse? Was the appropriation true to the original argument, and how was it appropriated, and for what uses? What's happened to Fukuyama?

Gandy (1982) has noted that "information subsidies" have much to do with such transfers, and Turow (1984, 1985) has commented extensively on "linking-pin organizations" and their roles in effecting them (see also Reese, p. 321). More to the point, Turow (1985) also has argued that the enormous needs for information and novelty of the mass media furnish critical, even fringe, groups an opportunity to be heard, with their "oppositional" messages, but others argue that such transfers demand alteration of the content. Gitlin (1980), for example, argues that for the New Left, mainstream media omitted serious treatment of its goals and emphasized its combative tactics; Ettema et al. (in press) suggest that a journalistic "logic of particularism" steered media away from serious treatment of issues in the case examined, leading the story to be "recycled and rethematized until any coherent sense of 'the story' was lost."

Finally, while there has been a considerable amount of research on media relations with sources, and research has generally shown, as Reese notes, that high-status or high-power sources are treated respectfully by media, both interpersonally and in the press, while low-power sources are not (see also Fishman, 1980; Paletz, Reichert, & McIntyre, 1971). But missing from the literature is much in the way of treatment of how, and under what circumstances, sources may cross these levels (however, see Goldenberg, 1975). Nonetheless, the questions are interesting: When and how do journalists decide that sources "represent" a position that is of general, rather than specialized, interest? What do sources, either by altering their strategies and tactics or by altering their messages, do to facilitate this?

MEDIA AGENDA-SETTING AND CONTINGENCY

Three media agenda-setting studies that have appeared since Reese drafted his chapter illustrate a wider problem with agenda-setting that needs some elaboration. First, in an elaborate multiple regression study of Gallup "most important problem" data, "real-world" indicators of issues, and network television news lead stories, Demers, Craff, Choi, and Pessin (1989) found, for five issues, very little in the way of public agenda-setting evidence; at the same time, however, they *did* find, post hoc, *media* agenda-setting effects by the public, as indexed by prior Gallup data, for four of these issues. The authors note:

> Although these findings are not central to the major hypotheses tested in this study, they do underscore the importance of viewing media systems as reflecting — not just influencing — the basic values and structures of the larger social system. The key question for research in this area is, Who sets the media's agenda? (p. 810)

Second, in a study of TV and newspaper news coverage prior to and following four recent presidents' state of the union messages and issues covered in the addresses themselves, Wanta, Stevenson, Turk, and McCombs (1989) found that Nixon in one such address influenced subsequent coverage more than his address was influenced by prior coverage, while Carter's agenda in the address was more influenced by prior coverage than the address influenced subsequent coverage. Two Reagan messages (1982 and 1985) showed different patterns: In the former, Reagan appeared to be responding more to a television agenda but shaping the subsequent newspaper agenda, while in the latter, Reagan's agenda correlated more strongly with prespeech than with postspeech coverage, a pattern similar to that of the Carter 1987 address. The authors suggest a number of potential third variables that might have influenced the failure to find a pattern of media influence on the policy agenda, or vice versa.

Finally, in a wide-ranging study of media, public, and policy agenda-setting on the issue of international child abductions, Ettema et al. (in press) found virtually no general public agenda-setting effects of a *60 Minutes* segment on the issue; however, two concrete items related to *mis*information in the broadcast did show effects consistent with public agenda-setting. *Media* agenda-setting in the study is subtle and intricate: The story originates in a specialized medium, the New York-based *Norway Times*; its appearance on *60 Minutes* is "subsidized" by the Chicago-based Better Government Association; and the story then radiates out into other national media, where, as noted above, what "the story" or "the issues" are "have self-deconstructed before our very eyes" (Ettema et al., in press). Public and media agenda-setting show patterns of media-source cooperation made familiar by other studies from the Northwestern group (Cook et al., 1983; Molotch, Protess, & Gordon, 1987; Protess et al., 1987).

In sum, the three studies found no general pattern of either public or media agenda-setting. This is no novel finding; prior reviewers (e.g., Rogers & Dearing,

1988; Swanson, 1988) have also noted that the agenda-setting literature is pock-marked with glaring inconsistencies and null findings. Like them, we should not jettison the agenda-setting baby and keep the empirical bathwater. The more optimistic approach is to suggest why and how a range of contingent conditions inflects the effect, and what these conditions are.

The Ettema et al. study is especially interesting for present purposes, for it argues, as does Reese, that the interrelations among media, public, and policy must be understood through conceptions of power (for Ettema et al., "politics as game"). Moreover, the authors wish to question the "robustness" of the agenda metaphor, in ways compatible with notions of contingency, to which we next turn, requiring rather extensive quotation from their conclusions. According to Ettema et al. (in press): An understanding of agenda-setting through a metaphor of "politics as game,"

> alas, diminishes the agenda-researcher's hope for powerfully predictive generaliza-tions about public opinion and public policy. Understanding is never beyond hope, of course, but the conceptual language in which it is expressed will be drawn less from the predictable cause and effect than the vocabulary of infinitely malleable strategy and tactics. "This more ecological view of the media-policy process loses the advan-tage of neat research designs characteristic of the effects studies and substitutes the less exact methods of ethnography and history," argue Molotch and colleagues (1987: 46). "We give up testing the proposition that, *as a general rule*, media reports cause or do not cause opinion or policy consequences." But if research on agenda-setting at the institutional level of analysis must, to some extent, always be an exercise in ethnographic complexity and historical singularity, that research can still yield rich and rewarding accounts of policy games. A policy game yet to be played may be no more predictable than, say, a World Series game yet to be played, but we can still account for how games have gone and, what's more, appreciate The Game itself: the process of governance in the media age. That is something real enough and important enough to matter.

Several aspects of this paragraph deserve comment. The argument, rephrased, is that understanding agenda-setting at the institutional level (this is equally true at the organizational level) will not be characterized by predictability, by cause and effect, but rather by a set of *contingent relations*. We are forced to turn to the, by implication, inferior methods of the interpretive social sciences, and our goals, since prediction has been wrested from us, are "accounting" — that is, description and taxonomy — and "appreciation."

Ettema and his colleagues are wholly correct in how we will understand media (and policy) agenda-setting. The *problem* is that they are too modest about what we can learn and about how "scientific" we will be in the process.

Agenda-Setting and Contingency

None of the three recent agenda-setting studies discussed above offers any definitive evidence of "progress" in demonstrating the agenda-setting effect. Now, as then, it can be argued that none of these studies demonstrates its nonexistence, either, and so the contrary argument — that, at some level, agenda-setting "exists" — is devoutly to be preferred.[5] So, where do we go now? What does a contingency-based view imply?

If the mere existence of an agenda-setting effect is a cornerstone, then a failure to find presumed and intended effects leads us in two directions. First is toward better measurement (see Rogers & Dearing, 1988). More to the point, it leads us to taxonomy, to the cataloguing of the contingent conditions under which, and at what levels, the effect should or should not manifest itself, and virtually every agenda-setting study that *finds* equivocal results suggests post hoc contingencies, which furnish the basis of an inventory. As Reese notes, as have others before him, the "levels of analysis" question is an exceedingly important one. The nub of the present argument, like that of Ettema et al.'s (in press) and not far from Reese's if we are to understand "power" at any level above the individual, is that research must proceed ethnographically and historically. At the same time, we need not concede that this necessarily implies they proceed less exactly.

A colleague in another department tells the story of an unusually arrogant doctoral advisee who routinely terrorized fellow graduate students (and some faculty members). No one had heard, for some time, how his dissertation was going. One day, the colleague asked. "Ah! Well!," was the reply. "All the important work is done. The only thing I have left is writing it down." [6]

The categories into which we array our contingencies are at best still dimly understood. In some cases, we have dim theoretical notions that underlie how we characterize these conditions; in other cases, we operate without even awareness of these. Some of the important work is done: We have a basic metaphor, one that works. We have the beginnings of an inventory of contingencies, of suggestions for mechanisms for when the metaphor does not. There remains, however, a lot to be written down.

NOTES

1. Here, the wider social context of the two-step flow hypothesis bears a resemblance to Reese's problem with fitting power to media agenda-setting: In the former, there is no "flow" if the message is neither transmitted nor received; in the latter, we cannot speak of agenda-setting for things left off the agenda.

2. As if events were discrete; Fishman (1980), *inter alia*, notes that the journalist's idea about what constitutes an event is itself largely socially constructed.

3. Readers may be able to think of individual cases in which some individual or organization in the news media actually initiated a public policy option. A usual one from the lore of journalism, Walter Lippmann's having originated the idea of dismantling obsolete U.S. missile bases in Turkey in exchange for the removal of Soviet missiles from Cuba as a face-saving means for Khruschev to end the 1962 Cuban missile crisis, has been discounted by Allison (1971), who documents that the option had previously been discussed by President Kennedy and his advisers.

4. The following discussion owes a great debt to Strodthoff et al. (1985) and to Ettema et al. (in press).

5. I take the "consilience" of other writers, and experimental demonstrations (e.g., Iyengar & Kinder, 1987) most particularly, as evidence that there really is such a thing as agenda-setting. I would likewise argue that it, like the reformulated step-flow model, falls into the category of most other prominent hypotheses of communication effects we have worked with over the years: ones that would be by some considerable margin more interesting if they were always disconfirmed than when they are occasionally confirmed. For me, this is so since both the step-flow model and "agenda-setting," stripped to their essentials, basically say that intersubjective communication has taken place.

6. My thanks to Cary Nelson.

REFERENCES

Allison, D. (1971). *Essence of decision: Explaining the Cuban missile crisis.* Boston: Little, Brown.

Carey, J. (1969). The communications revolution and the professional communicator. In P. Halmos (Ed.), *The sociology of mass media communicators* (Sociological Review Monograph 13, pp. 23-38). Keele, Great Britain: University of Keele.

Cook, F. L., Tyler, T., Goetz, E., Gordon, M., Protess, D., Leff, D., & Molotch, H. (1983). Media and agenda-setting: Effects on the public, interest group leaders, policy makers, and policy. *Public Opinion Quarterly, 47,* 16-35.

Darnton, R. (1975). Writing news and telling stories. *Daedalus, 104,* 175-194.

Demers, D., Craff, D., Choi, Y.-H., & Pessin, B. (1989). Issue obtrusiveness and the agenda-setting effects of national network news. *Communication Research, 16,* 793-812.

Ettema, J., Protess, D., Leff, D., Miller, P., Doppelt, J., & Cook, F.L. (in press). Agenda-setting as politics: A case study of the press-public-policy connection. *Communication.*

Fishman, M. (1980). *Manufacturing the news.* Austin: University of Texas.

Gandy, O. (1982). *Beyond agenda-setting: Information subsidies and public policy.* Norwood, NJ: Ablex.

Gans, H. (1980). *Deciding what's news.* New York: Pantheon.

Gitlin, T. (1980). *The whole world is watching: The role of the media in the making and unmaking of the New Left.* Berkeley: University of California Press.

Goldenberg, E. (1975). *Making the papers.* Lexington, MA: D. C. Heath.

Gould, S. J. (1989). *Wonderful life: The Burgess Shale and the nature of history.* New York: Norton.

Iyengar, S., & Kinder, D. (1987). *News that matters: Agenda setting and priming in a television age.* Chicago: University of Chicago Press.

Katz, E., & Lazarsfeld, P. F. (1955). *Personal influence.* Glencoe, IL: Free Press.

Lang, G., & Lang, K. (1983). *The battle for public opinion: The president, the press and the polls during Watergate.* New York: Columbia University Press.

Lazarsfeld, P., Berelson, B., & Gaudet, H. (1948). *The people's choice.* New York: Columbia University Press.

Linsky, M. (1986). *Impact: How the press affects federal policy making.* New York: Norton.

Molotch, H., Protess, D., & Gordon, M. (1987). The media-policy connection: Ecologies of news. In D. Paletz (Ed.), *Political communication research* (pp. 26-48). Norwood, NJ: Ablex.

Paletz, D., Reichert, P., & McIntyre, B. (1971). How the media support local government authority. *Public Opinion Quarterly, 35,* 80-92.

Pool, I., & Shulman, I. (1959). Newsmen's fantasies, audiences, and newswriting. *Public Opinion Quarterly, 23,* 145-158.

Protess, D., Cook, F. L., Curtin, T., Gordon, M., Leff, D., McCombs, M., & Miller, P. V. (1987). The impact of investigative reporting on public opinion and policymaking: Targeting toxic waste. *Public Opinion Quarterly, 51,* 166-185.

Robinson, J. (1976). Interpersonal influence in election campaigns: Two step-flow hypotheses. *Public Opinion Quarterly, 40,* 304-319.

Rogers, E., & Dearing, J. (1988). Agenda-setting research: Where has it been, where is it going? In J. Anderson (Ed.), *Communication yearbook 11* (pp. 555-594). Newbury Park, CA: Sage.

Strodthoff, G., Hawkins, R., & Schoenfeld, C. (1985). Media roles in a social movement: A model of ideology diffusion. *Journal of Communication, 35*(2), 134-153.

Swanson, D. (1988). Feeling the elephant: Some observations on agenda-setting research (commentary on Rogers and Dearing). In J. Anderson (Ed.), *Communication yearbook 11* (pp. 603-619). Newbury Park, CA: Sage.

Tichenor, P., Donohue, G., & Olien, C. (1967). Predicting a source's success in placing news in the media. *Journalism Quarterly, 44*, 32-42.

Turow, J. (1984). *Media industries.* White Plains, NY: Longman.

Turow, J.(1985). Cultural argumentation through the mass media: A framework for organizational research. *Communication, 8*, 139-164.

Wanta, W., Stevenson, M. A., Turk, J., & McCombs, M. (1989). How presidents' state of the union talk influenced news media agendas. *Journalism Quarterly, 66*, 537-541.

SECTION 3

INTERPERSONAL INFLUENCE: CONFRONTATION AND ARGUMENTATION

8 The Episodic Nature of Social Confrontation

SARA E. NEWELL
West Chester University

RANDALL K. STUTMAN
Temple University

In this chapter we report a research program focusing upon one aspect or form of confrontation that we call *social confrontation*. The domain of social confrontation consists of situations in which an individual perceives that another person has violated a rule or norm for appropriate conduct. The major thrust of the research program is to describe the patterns of interaction that emerge as one individual confronts the other and the other responds. Guided by the interactional view (Watzlawick, Beavin, & Jackson, 1967), we approach such conversations as negotiated enactments through which participants not only exchange turns but also mutually construct the purpose of their interaction. A description is offered of social confrontation as a particular kind of communication episode. The enactment of confrontation is described in terms of initiation, development, and closure of the episode. In addition, a social cognition perspective is adopted as we explore factors that influence initiation of the confrontation process. We report research on perceived facilitators and constraints on the decision to confront as well as a measure of confrontativeness that taps salient beliefs about self and confrontation that may predispose individuals to approach or avoid confrontation. Finally, we examine the goals of confronters and how individuals rehearse in order to maximize goal accomplishment.

I N conflict situations, social actors frequently employ confrontative tactics to resolve their differences (Sternberg & Dobson, 1987). This preference may be due, in part, to the general effectiveness of confrontation as a mode of conflict resolution. Numerous studies have demonstrated that confrontation is highly effective in resolving conflict (Burke, 1970). More specifically, confrontation is known to facilitate integrative outcomes (Pruitt & Lewis, 1975; Schultz & Pruitt, 1978), to promote higher performance in organizations (Lawrence & Lorsch, 1967), and to correlate with task effectiveness (Jones & White, 1985). In bargaining situations, a confrontative orientation sometimes results in greater gains for both parties (Lewis & Pruitt, 1971).

Correspondence and requests for reprints: Sara E. Newell, Department of Speech Communication and Theatre, West Chester University, West Chester, PA 19383.

Communication Yearbook 14, pp. 359-392

The potency of confrontation makes it a highly desirable activity. For example, in organizational settings subordinates prefer managers who adopt a confrontational style as opposed to a nonconfrontational one (Wheeless & Reichel, 1988). Apparently, subordinates find assertive managers more rewarding than those who avoid communication during conflict. Other research proposes that managers also prefer the use of confrontation (Lawrence & Lorsch, 1967). Not surprisingly, marital couples also rely heavily on the use of confrontation to resolve differences (Fitzpatrick, 1988).

Despite the impressive record of confrontation, we possess scanty knowledge concerning the attributes of this activity. An examination of the conflict literature suggests that confrontation is any collaborative process between parties in a conflict. Yet even this general description is not clear. Researchers offer a wide array of definitions in an attempt to classify confrontation. Consider the diversity of several of these descriptions: (a) communication behaviors that attempt to integrate the needs of both parties (Putnam & Wilson, 1982); (b) expression of one's position in order to find a solution of mutual benefit (Filley, House, & Kerr, 1976); (c) discussion during a conflict (Sternberg & Dobson, 1987); (d) collaborative strategies (Thomas, 1976); and (e) a problem-solving mode (Blake & Mouton, 1964; Harnett, Cummings, & Hamner, 1973). The only consistent theme throughout these definitions is that confrontation is a communication process in which problems are brought out into the open so that the parties can negotiate and maintain social order.

Because of an inherent interest in this process, we embarked on a research program that was designed, as Sherlock Holmes once said, "to shed light on that which is so dark." Of primary concern was to examine the nature of confrontation descriptively, as well as to explore the antecedents of this activity. This chapter attempts to describe the results of this research as well as to explicate the implications of viewing confrontation as a communication process negotiated by social actors. In order to place our work on confrontation within the body of existing literature relevant to confrontation, we will first briefly summarize major approaches to the study of confrontation. Then we will describe our particular approach to the definition and study of confrontation.

REVIEW OF THE LITERATURE

Although *confrontation* appears frequently as a descriptive term in titles of scholarly articles across the disciplines, little research exists that directly addresses the nature of confrontation. The three arenas in which it has received specific attention are the study of social movements, the development of therapy techniques, and research on conflict management. As we will show, the researcher's definition of confrontation depends upon the particular kind of situation in which the behavior is located.

Not surprisingly, the study of social movements in the turbulent 1960s fostered a focus upon the "radical and revolutionary" (Scott & Smith, 1969) aspects of confrontation. According to this view, after other means of communication have been exhausted, confrontation serves as a tactic that draws attention to a social movement through public displays of opposition to, and rejection of, an institution (Andrews, 1969; Bailey, 1969; Burgess, 1970). Cathcart (1978) describes such a rhetoric of confrontation as ritualized conflict that "dramatizes the symbolic separation of the individual from the existing order" (p. 236). Thus, in the context of social upheaval, confrontative behaviors are inflammatory, revolutionary, and divisive, challenging the legitimacy of the social order.

In a quite different context, the psychology literature is filled with discussions of confrontation in therapy. However, the term *confrontation* is loosely used to describe everything from a particular style of the therapist, as in Gestalt therapy (Perls, Hefferline, & Goodman, 1969), to an activity that the therapist orchestrates among people in group therapy (e.g., Cima, 1985), to an outcome of therapy when the client finally confronts self. Confrontation, then, stands not as the particular subject of study but as a technique to be used or an outcome to be pursued.

One study, however, does describe the process of confrontation whereby the therapist uses a question-and-answer sequence to elicit contradictory statements from a client, finally confronting the client with a rhetorical question about the now apparent contradiction (Bleiberg & Churchill, 1975). Bleiberg and Churchill argue that this process may occur in ordinary conversation, so it has implications beyond the realm of therapy.

In the more general situation of conflict management, confrontation has been ambiguously described as a style or strategy. Blake and Mouton (1964) label as confrontative the style of directly confronting problems, bringing them on the floor for discussion. They conceptualize this behavior as demonstrating high concern for both self and other. The popularity of the Blake and Mouton scheme of conflict styles has led to a number of studies that examine the effectiveness of the different styles, including confrontation. Typically, in research on conflict styles, confrontation takes form in contrast to nonconfrontative, avoidance behaviors, including accommodation, or behaviors that attempt to move directly to a solution, such as forcing or compromising. The research that reports confrontation as the preferred style for managing conflict (Burke, 1970; Lawrence & Lorsch, 1967; London & Howat, 1978; Renwick, 1975) operationalizes confrontation as problem-solving behavior that addresses conflict directly, seeking causes and solutions. With this rather open-ended definition, it is not surprising that research has found confrontation to be a very beneficial approach to conflict management.

In each of these contexts, confrontation serves a function related to conflict. In the context of social movements, confrontation serves as the open expression of conflict, signaling the beginning of explicit oppositional interaction. It serves, symbolically, as a call to arms. In the context of therapy, confrontation is viewed as a necessary step to insight and change; it is both the means and culmination of a process used to uncover conflict and contradiction within the individual. In the more general arena of conflict management, confrontation behavior serves to initiate and follow through on problem solving; it brings a problem out into the open, where arguments can be presented and solutions negotiated. Common themes are apparent in these variations. Confrontation is primarily an action that reveals contradiction or opposition. Moreover, confrontation may be a necessary component of problem definition and resolution. These variations also suggest that confrontation may be best understood not as a single act but as part of a process related to conflict and negotiation.

Clearly, confrontation may be studied as an interactional phenomenon. In the context of social movements, confrontation is part of a process of social change. How the confrontation proceeds and whether or not social change is accomplished depend upon the interaction between the confronting movement and the confronted social institution. In the context of therapy, Bleiberg and Churchill (1975) go so far as to argue that successful confrontation by the therapist depends upon the cooperation of the patient in providing appropriate responses. Finally, in the context of conflict management, the characterization of confrontation as a style or strategy assumes a pattern of behaviors as well as an expectation that it will elicit responses from the other party that facilitate problem solving.

Recent work on interaction in problematic situations, including the study of complaints, accounts sequences, and repair moves, provides further insight into the kinds of interaction sequences — from initiation to response to resolution — that are relevant to confronting and discussing problems. We will briefly elucidate each of these lines of work. Stokes and Hewitt (1976) describe problematic situations as ones in which "interaction is disrupted, identities are threatened [and] people have intentions that run counter to others' wishes" (p. 842). They argue that problematic situations disrupt the social order, requiring interaction to realign conduct and culture. Confronting another may produce such a problematic situation. Thus an individual may carefully weigh the decision to confront. In research on consumer complaints, Day and Landon (1977) identify variations in states of dissatisfaction and how they affect the decision to complain. A key element appears to be the perception of the legitimacy of the complaint. Simple dissatisfaction with a product is often not enough to lead to complaining.

The bulk of research on problematic situations investigates how an individual will respond to being reproached (Blumstein et al., 1974; Cody & McLaughlin, 1985a; Goffman, 1971; Hewitt & Hall, 1973; Hewitt & Stokes, 1975; McLaughlin, Cody, & O'Hair, 1983; McLaughlin, Cody, & Rosenstein, 1983; Schonbach, 1980; Scott & Lyman, 1968). The basic response is an account, often in the form of an excuse or a justification (Scott & Lyman, 1968), but may also include a concession, a refusal (Schonbach, 1980), or an apology (Edmondson, 1981; Fraser 1981). The pattern of reproach-account forms the core for the "account sequence" of offense, reproach, account, and evaluation of the account (McLaughlin, Cody, & O'Hair, 1983; McLaughlin, Cody, & Rosenstein, 1983). The research on accounts particularly addresses the ways in which individuals strive to protect their self-image in light of problematic or threatening behavior.

Finally, research investigates how a problem becomes defined between interactants in terms of the substantive issues before them, as well as posing how interactants attempt to repair or resolve the problematic situation. In examining consumer complaints, Resnik and Harmon (1984) report efforts by the consumer to establish the legitimacy of the complaint. If the consumer representative fails to accept the legitimacy of the complaint, then the consumer may turn to compliance-gaining tactics or drop the complaint. Along a similar line, in the investigation of roommate complaints, Philipsen (1981) poses a "complaint episode." According to this model, the response to a complaint may focus upon the legitimacy of the complaint, accounting for the behavior, or future behavior. These two studies suggest that interactants strive to find a way to remedy or resolve the situation.

Following this line of reasoning, Morris and Hopper (1980) argue that interactants often cooperate to repair the problematic situation. This repair may require the reconsideration of the rules or expectations of the relationship. In doing so, the interactants may modify and thus remediate existing rules or legislate new ones to guide future action. In describing this process, Morris (1985) poses a remedial episode that describes the development of the interaction in terms of the substantive issues between the participants in their effort to define and resolve the problem. Significantly, this model marks a conceptual shift from a focus on face to a focus on the substantive issues involved when one individual reproaches another for his or her conduct.

Several conclusions can be drawn from the work on problematic situations that offer insight to the confrontation process. First, confrontation occurs in response to a number of situational elements and may reflect a conscious decision by an individual to confront. Second, confronting can be face threatening, leading to efforts to restore face. Third, how confrontation develops depends upon the substantive issues between the participants. Fourth, a pivotal issue is the legitimacy of the basis for complaint. Fifth, interaction tends to move toward a discussion of how the problem may be resolved.

From this review we can conclude that no single definition of confrontation will serve to cover the wide range of circumstances in which confrontation may be constituted and investigated. Instead, the researcher must strive to identify clearly the boundaries and conditions that delimit a particular definition and study of confrontation. The area of conflict management appears ripe for thoroughly specifying the kinds of situations in which confrontation occurs and for offering a more precise definition and understanding of the activity.

In the sections that follow, we will offer a particular definition of confrontation that we call *social confrontation*. This label is used to indicate that we are not attempting to define the universe of behavior that might be called confrontation, but rather are specifying particular boundaries and conditions for defining one form or aspect of confrontation. The definition of social confrontation will be elaborated through a description of the research process that produced it.

In this chapter, we report a research program focusing upon confrontation. Our primary emphasis and interest is in studying the interactional performance of confrontation in order to delineate confrontation from other kinds of communication activities and to describe variations in initiation, development, and closure. This line of research has the potential to provide pragmatic advice concerning communication strategies for the successful management of confrontation as well as to contribute to the growing body of literature on the negotiation and patterning of interaction. Although the crux of our interest is the performance of confrontation, we are irresistibly led to a supplementary interest in the factors that influence the occurrence of confrontation. Due to the potential consequences of confrontation for good or evil, the ability to predict or control the initiation of confrontation has led us to explore the issues surrounding commencement.

In reporting the research program, we begin by clarifying the domain of social confrontation and reciting the assumptions underlying the descriptive research. We then explore the performance of the episode by introducing descriptive claims supported by numerous examples from the data pool. Finally, we report on several studies from a cognitive perspective that address the supplementary concern for conditions that influence an individual to engage in confrontation.

THE DOMAIN OF SOCIAL CONFRONTATION

Our interest in confrontation began with a relatively simple question: What are situational variables that facilitate or constrain the decision to confront? In the process of asking research participants this question, we also asked them to describe recent instances in which they had confronted someone (Newell & Stutman, 1982). We vaguely defined *confrontation* for them as disagreeing with another's opinions or behaviors. Their written responses clearly demonstrated two features central to the definition of confrontation. First, social actors conceive of confrontation as a conversational activity, not a single act. The typical description provided a brief background on the situation, a description of the interaction that occurred when the participant confronted the other individual, and usually a statement concerning how the problem was resolved. Second, disagreement over behaviors differs from disagreement over ideas. In disagreement over behaviors, the conversations reflected a problem-solving orientation, with a movement toward resolution. For example, the following is a typical recollection of confrontation over behavior provided by one research participant:

> I confronted my brother for driving my car without my permission. He ran all the gas out of the car and brought it back dirty after I had just washed it. I was pretty hostile towards him and we got in a heated discussion about why he thought he had as much right to drive it because I hadn't paid my parents for the car yet. It was resolved by him conforming to wash it and fill the tank with gas, and we decided that since he would only be home for two more months that he could drive it when he wanted, but he had to let me know when and where he was going.

In contrast, the conversations over ideas were relatively static, with the interactants taking turns explaining their positions until there was no more to say. One research participant reported:

> I discuss (really argue) with my wife about the welfare system of this country, and the government's role in it. They usually begin when we hear about "Reaganomics" on the news or wherever. We both have different views and reasons for those views. The only thing we agree on is there is a problem with the way it is run now. We don't usually get mad at each other when we talk about this subject but we do get a bit frustrated because we each think we are right and are not willing to give an inch. So we usually air our views and try to convince the other we are right and when we can't, and we both know we can't, we just drop the subject — we just accept each other's point of view as their own.

Subsequent research, analyzing interaction generated through role-playing, reinforced these observations.

At this juncture we chose to pursue confrontation as residing in disagreement over behaviors and to treat disagreement over ideas as a separate phenomenon. In addition, examination of the interaction produced through role-playing contributed another characteristic of disagreement over behaviors. Behavior becomes problematic (disagreeable) when it is perceived to violate a social norm or a relational rule.

A definition of *confrontation* began to take shape that focused on an interaction sequence between a confronter and a confrontee in which the confronter questions, accuses, or reproaches the confrontee in some manner for behavior that violates a social norm or a relational rule (Newell & Stutman, 1983). Certainly this definition of confrontation as interaction concerning a perceived rule violation is bounded by the kind of situation in which the confrontation behavior is located. The set of confrontation-relevant situations that we typically rely upon in our research stem primarily from that first sample of open descriptions of recent confrontations, as well as from interviews with social actors seeking examples of situations that are relevant to a college student's day-to-day life. This set of situations includes the following:

(1) Your best friend doesn't seem to have time for you any more.
(2) A neighbor plays music very loudly late at night.
(3) Your roommate borrows your clothes without asking.
(4) You suspect your romantic partner has been seeing someone else.
(5) At the movies, the person behind you is talking in a loud tone of voice.
(6) You see someone in class cheating on an exam.
(7) A teacher gives you a grade on an assignment that you don't think is fair.
(8) At work your boss asks you to do something that you don't think is part of your job.
(9) Someone cuts in front of you in a line.
(10) An individual is smoking in a nonsmoking area.

These situations have in common the occurrence of behavior that may be viewed by the confronter as norm or rule violating, as well as typically placing the confronter in the role of an "injured party." A limited amount of data has also been generated concerning altruistic confrontation, in which an individual confronts out of concern for harm being done to the confrontee or to a third party.

We can now identify the boundaries and conditions that delimit our definition and study of confrontation. The domain of social confrontation consists of situations in which a confronter perceives behavior as norm or rule violating, is most often the "injured" party, and confronts the violator about this aberrant behavior. Social confrontation, then, is the interaction produced by the confronter and confrontee defining this situation. As the early stages of our research led us to view confrontation not as a single act, or as style of behavior, but as a type of interaction, we turned to the interactional view for guidance.

AN ADAPTATION OF THE INTERACTIONAL VIEW

The interactional view of communication owes allegiance to the work of Gregory Bateson and his associates (Watzlawick et al., 1967). With their holistic concern for systemic understanding of patterns, mutual influence, adaptation, and evolution, they have inspired a wide range of scholarly activity (see, for example, Wilder & Weakland, 1981). Although there is no consensus on precisely what the interactional view is, a body of work has emerged that suggests certain commonalities.

The interactional view is less a set of assumptions and more a framework that each user shapes and adapts (Fisher, 1981). Our work on social confrontation represents one adaptation. At times, our work has not been so much guided by the interactional view as answered by it. As in any symbiotic relationship, each component informs the other: The interactional view provides shape and insight to the study of social confrontation, and the study of social confrontation adds form and insight to the interactional view.

The key to the interactional view lies in its mandate to focus upon the patterns that emerge from the relationship between behaviors (Watzlawick et al., 1967). The question becomes how to observe the patterns. One approach focuses particularly on the sequential relationship between behaviors (or turns of talk), so that each turn is viewed both as a consequence of the prior turn and as an antecedent to the subsequent turn (Fisher, 1970; Fisher, Drecksel, & Werbel, 1979; Rogers & Farace, 1975). We choose to take a more macroscopic view. Beginning with a sample of completed interactions serving a common function (in this case, confrontation over perceived rule violation), we seek to identify the characteristics that the interactions share and that may serve to distinguish this type of interaction from other types of interaction. At the same time, we strive to describe how the interactions can vary from one another yet still maintain similar constitutive elements.

We assume that conversations serve a function for the participants, and, further, that participants enact and reveal their purpose in the pattern of interaction. As Fisher (1985) explains:

> No particular action is important, of course, until it meets the *summun bonum* principle of placing that action in reference with some connected and interpretable pattern that leads to some final end or purpose. Purposiveness is thus knowable only in the pattern or sequence of behaviors — that is, the interaction. (p. 513)

Certainly not all conversations lend themselves to this kind of analysis. Interactants vary in their cooperation and coordination, and, as a result, conversations vary in their coherence. In conversation, patterns emerge through the mutual influence of the interactants. Interactants pursue goals and strive to make one another's behaviors meaningful. In so doing, conversational coherence may be accomplished through cooperative interaction (Grice, 1975; Hopper, 1983). Coherence requires more than talking on the same topic; coherence requires producing a conversation that coalesces functionally (Jackson, Jacobs, & Rossi, 1987; Jacobs & Jackson, 1983; Jacobs, Jackson, & Hall, 1988).

The function of a conversation emerges from the interaction; therefore, the function is identifiable only retrospectively (Fisher, 1985). Bateson (1972) alludes to this peculiar quality of conversations in his metalogues with his daughter. To his daughter's inquiry, "What do you mean by a conversation having an outline? Has this conversation an outline?" he replies: "Oh, surely, yes. But we cannot see it yet because the conversation isn't finished. You cannot ever see it while you're in the middle of it" (p. 32). What a conversation is about and its purpose are open to continuous implicit or explicit negotiation between the participants. Only after it is complete can one accurately assess what has occurred.

However, we might also expect that members of the same culture would approach similar communication tasks in similar manners. Bateson (1972) suggests that the coherence of a conversation may be influenced by the substance of the conversation:

> Well, the ideas that we play with bring in a sort of rules. There are rules about how ideas will stand up and support each other. And if they are wrongly put together the whole building falls down. (p. 18)

The logical relationships between ideas, and between problems and solutions, suggest that functionally equivalent interactions might display common characteristic elements.

The concept of a communication *episode* may be used to denote interactions that possess characteristic elements of functional coherence. Harre and Secord (1972) define an episode as "any sequence of happenings in which human beings engage which has some principle of unity. Episodes have a beginning and end that can usually be identified" (p. 10). Episodes are recognizable by the general purpose of interaction; function is the unity principle (Newell & Stutman, 1987). Obviously, not all interactions lend themselves to episodic analysis; interaction may be fragmented, disjointed, incomplete, or functionally idiosyncratic.

Communication episodes are most easily defined as fitting within the confines of a conversation. Within the confines of a conversation we find it advantageous to draw the boundaries of an episode as large as is reasonable. So, for example, while we can identify an account sequence (failure event, reproach, account, and evaluation), we believe this sequence is often more meaningful within the larger context of the general conversational activity. If the conversational activity is social confrontation, then the account sequence is one segment of the episode.

This structure is significant because episodes provide a context for studying strategies and tactics of communication messages. Communication strategies and tactics, such as compliance gaining and accounts, take on different meaning and use depending upon the episode within which they are embedded. Further, because episodes are serial, strategies evolve over time. Although the particular topic may change, the kind of episode will recur as its function demands. How an episode is accomplished will have an effect on the patterning of future episodes and on the relationship of its interactants.

This view dictates that behavioral patterns are evolutionary; therefore, temporal relationships are critical in understanding the functional unity of an episode. Essentially, in studying patterns one examines change over time. Because change can occur both within an interaction and between interactions, the patterns that emerge with regularity suggest that this interaction reifies the ongoing relationship of the communicators. In this sense, reality is believed to be relationally constructed by the participants through the behaviors they perform (Berger & Luckmann, 1966).

To summarize, the interactional view leads us to approach conversations as negotiated enactments through which participants not only exchange turns but also mutually construct the purpose of their interaction. Conversational coherence emerges as interactants successfully coordinate their actions with one another to produce interaction that displays functional unity. The description of a particular type of episode then not only facilitates the study of how communication is used in the social construction of reality, but also leads to insight into how functional coherence is produced. Our adaptation of the interactive view leads us to study the accomplished episodes, focusing upon their patterns of development. This approach produces a description of the constitutive characteristics of interaction that define a particular type of episode, as well as identifying the significant ways in which the interaction varies.

ENACTMENT OF THE
SOCIAL CONFRONTATION EPISODE

The primary purpose of our research program has been to identify the characteristic markers of the social confrontation episode (Newell & Stutman, 1983,

1988), as well as to describe major variations in patterns of enactment (Newell, 1984; Newell & Adams, 1985; Newell & Stutman, 1989/1990). In this descriptive research, we have relied upon the analysis of transcripts of social confrontation interactions. These data have been generated primarily through role-playing exercises and supplemented with recalled interactions and naturally occurring confrontations. Currently, the data pool consists of 170 role-plays, 33 naturally occurring interactions, and 100 recalled interaction sequences.[1]

The analysis of the confrontation transcripts followed the methodology of grounded theory (Glaser, 1978; Glaser & Strauss, 1967). Initial stages of exploratory, descriptive research require the researchers to immerse themselves in the data. In our case that meant reading and rereading the transcripts. We compared and contrasted the different interactions, looking for what they had in common, as well as the major ways in which they varied. During this stage, we took notes on emerging conceptual devices for organizing and describing patterns. We worked somewhat independently at this time, later comparing and contrasting our conceptual schemes and arguing for various interpretations. According to the principles of grounded theory, once a conceptual scheme emerges, researchers must continue to test their interpretations against new data. This method of constant comparison stresses the importance of modifying conceptual schemes to fit the data. Part of this process includes analytic induction (Denzin, 1978), whereby researchers seek negative cases that test the adequacy of conceptual devices. The final test of the adequacy and validity of knowledge claims within grounded theory is intersubjectivity. The test occurs on at least two levels. Research collaborators must first come to agreement among themselves as to their interpretation of the data. Second, researchers have an obligation to document their claims amply with examples from the data. At this point, the reader must judge the reasonableness of our interpretations. Glaser and Strauss (1967) call this the "joint responsibility" for establishing the credibility for research.

Our analysis of the data has led us to several conclusions regarding how actors enact the social confrontation episode. Fittingly, we can best introduce these conclusions with an example from the data pool that typifies the social confrontation episode through its focus upon a problem of rule or norm violation and what might be done to redress this problem.

An Example of Social Confrontation

The conversation presented in Table 1 is the result of two participants role-playing the situation of one roommate confronting another over borrowing her clothes. Each turn of the conversation is numbered. The letters K and T indicate who is speaking, Kris (assigned the confronter role) or Tracy (assigned the confrontee role).

The confrontation unfolds as follows: The problem area is broached in turn 7 through a relatively nonevaluative observation. Turns 8-10 concern the specific problem of who gets to wear the shirt that day, but no general rule or expectation is referred to until turn 11. Here Kris makes clear that Tracy has violated an

TABLE 1
Example of Social Confrontation

1	K	Mornin' Tracy
2	T	Mornin' Kris
3	K	You're up awfully early. What's the occasion?
4	T	Oh, I've got some stuff to do at the library before class so I thought I'd go get a good early start and get that work done.
5	K	Well, you'll definitely be the first one at the library.
6	T	Yah, I know, wonderful, huh?
7	K	Oh, you're wearing my shirt.
8	T	Oh, yah, I just, I didn't have anything else to wear so I just pulled it out. I figured you wouldn't mind.
9	K	Well usually I wouldn't but that's — I really wanted to wear that shirt today.
10	T	Oh you did?? Well here I'll, here I'll take it off. I can wear something else.
11	K	Okay, but, I mean, while we're on the subject, I, you know it seems like you've been doing this a lot lately like borrowing my shirts. Usually that doesn't bother me but you've just been borrowing, been borrowing them a lot and really not asking.
12	T	Well I thought as long as we were roommates we'd do these things, I mean you've been borrowing a lot of my stuff too — my soap and my shampoo and stuff. I mean, and you've been borrowing some of my clothes too and, I mean that's just what you do when you're roommates.
13	K	Well, yah, well when you're roommates, but I usually ask you, you, you haven't been asking me.
14	T	Well, O.K., well I'm sorry I didn't realize. With the other roommates I've had and stuff we always just kind of borrowed, it was just kinda the thing. But I'll ask you from now on. Sorry about that.
15	K	Okay, I mean I didn't mean to be a pain but you know I've got four sisters and we uh always used to work out a system where we'd just ask before we borrowed.
16	T	Oh that, that's true, I just have never had to deal with that but, but that's fine we'll do that. Sorry about that.
17	K	Okay, great.

expectation or rule by borrowing clothes without asking. In turn 12, Tracy provides her understanding of the rule — that roommates simply borrow things from one another. In turn 13, Kris partially confirms this understanding but points to a condition of the expectation — you ask before borrowing. The major issue of this confrontation concerns what may legitimately be expected. As defined by the interactants, the problem arose because they did not share the expectation of asking before borrowing. In essence, then, Kris's expectation is constructed as an illegitimate one (Tracy couldn't be expected to follow a rule she did not know about or share). In turns 13 and 14, Kris and Tracy come to the agreement that asking before borrowing is a reasonable condition to expect in the future. In turns 15-17, the episode is brought to a close through apology and the offer of statements of commitment to the agreement.

As we see in this example, interactants jointly produce social confrontation. In other words, a confrontation is a conversational achievement. The conversation moves from initiation toward resolution, with the particular development based upon what is at issue between the interactants concerning the apparent rule violation. The episode is emergent; only in retrospect does line 7 become hearable as the initiation of confrontation. The episode itself, its function and meaning, is constructed by the participants through their behaviors. The function of social confrontation may be generally described as working through disagreement over behaviors and thus negotiating expectations for future conduct. Thus social confrontation episodes serve to clarify rules or expectations, to establish and maintain the legitimacy of rules, to punish rule infringement, to maintain social order, and to negotiate relationships.

Quite clearly, the episode moves from initiation toward resolution. Although the development of this and other episodes depends upon what is at issue concerning the rule and the perceived rule violation, the potential outcome is a more lucid understanding of what is to be expected in the future concerning the problematic behavior.

In order to capture the developmental aspect of communication episodes, the social confrontation episode can be roughly divided into three segments: initiation, development, and closure (Newell, 1984). These segments are significant because of the work that is necessary in each phase for the accomplishment of the episode and the achievement of the goals of the participants. The initiation phase is necessary to establish the purpose of the episode. It is a time for interactants to negotiate the activity they are performing. The developmental phase is important in defining the nature of the problem and what would serve as a resolution. The closure phase provides an opportunity to reach agreement and to make a commitment to a solution of the problem, as well as to do relational repair work. Each of these phases will be discussed below to demonstrate both the function of the phase and variations in performance.

Initiation

The initiation phase serves to identify or define the episode to be enacted. First, we will examine the various ways in which a confronter may choose to initiate the episode, then we will explore the problematic nature of initiation.

Goffman (1974) argues for the significance of the initiating act of an episode, comparing it to the beginning bracket of a mathematical equation:

> It is reasonable to assume that the beginning bracket not only will establish an episode but also will establish a slot for signals which will inform and define what sort of transformation is to be made of the materials within the episode. (pp. 255-256)

While the initiation act does not necessarily *determine* the outcome of the interaction, it does serve to frame the episode in a manner the participants may find difficult to escape.

Initiating acts of the social confrontation episode vary along two dimensions: focus and explicitness. The focus of the initiation act may be upon either the problematic behavior of the other or the confronter's own emotional response to the problematic behavior. The initiating act may also vary in the explicitness of message content and purpose. These variations may be captured within five tactics of initiation. The first three tactics reflect initiating acts that focus upon the behavior, representing three levels of explicitness. The last two tactics describe initiating acts that focus on the confronter's emotional response, representing two levels of explicitness.

The confronter may choose to initiate confrontation by *hinting*. Hinting makes use of an indirect speech act in which an individual means something more than what is being said (Searle, 1979). For example, a young woman noticing her roommate once again wearing one of her blouses without asking may simply comment, "Nice blouse." Initiation by indirect speech act requires a good deal of interpretive ability on the part of the confrontee to realize that he or she has been reproached. In addition, indirect speech acts give the confrontee an opportunity to act as if a reproach has not occurred. In a moderately direct manner, the confronter may *seek confirmation* that a particular behavior has taken place. For example, a young woman may confirm her suspicion that her roommate has borrowed her clothes once again by asking, "Are those my jeans you have on?" Or a suspicious young man might ask his romantic partner, "Have you been seeing someone else?" As with indirect speech acts, blame or reproach is not clear, but identification of potentially problematic behavior is implied by the question. Finally, a confronter can initiate confrontation directly, by *blaming or accusing* the confrontee of breaking a rule. For example, the roommate might say, "I can't believe you've borrowed my clothes again without asking me."

Instead of referring to the behavior of the confrontee, the confronter may instead make reference to his or her own emotional state. Reference to emotional state may also vary in degree of explicitness, from an indirect *emotional display* to a direct *emotional statement*. A confronter may nonverbally demonstrate an emotional state by acting "out of sorts" in a manner to prompt the confrontee to initiate the episode by asking if anything is wrong. Conversely, a confronter may directly state how she or he feels; for example, "My feelings are really hurt today." Emotional statements can, of course, vary in the degree to which they directly place blame on the confrontee.

A relic of viewing confrontation as something one person does to another is the predisposition to view the social confrontation episode as initiated when this confronting act occurs. Yet no single act or move is sufficient to initiate the episode under any condition (Newell & Stutman, 1989/1990). For example, consider a confrontation between roommates over a violation of a cooperative rule, such as warning another that the supply of household shampoo has been exhausted. A common initiation might sound like, "When I took a shower this morning, the shampoo bottle was empty." Given our knowledge of the perceived rule violation, it is difficult to imagine an actor interpreting this act as anything other than a complaint. With such an interpretation, a confrontation would surely unfold. Yet, there is no reason the receiver could not see this utterance as seeking sympathy and respond with "That burns me up, too," or as an excuse and respond with "No wonder your hair looks greasy." Only when the interpreter determines the speaker's intent as a reproach will the interaction become a confrontation. Quite obviously, however, the interpreter can strategically or naively misconstrue this act and place the burden back upon the confronter to reinitiate or to revoke the decision to confront. Hence the interaction between the confronter and confrontee ultimately defines whether this will be a social confrontation episode or something else. Thus we have come to view the initiation of social confrontation as problematic and negotiated.

The confronter often broaches the social confrontation-relevant topic in an indirect manner that requires the confrontee to interpret the implied complaint about rule-deviant behavior. The confrontee may be either unwilling or unable to draw this inference about the speaker's intent. Returning to the example in Table 1, we see a progression of statements made by the confronter as the confrontee's responses fail to recognize the problem as rule related. The confronter broaches the topic in turn 7 with the indirect observation, "Oh, you're wearing my shirt." The confrontee appears to suspect that something might be wrong, as she responds with an account: "Oh, yah, I just, I didn't have anything else to wear so I just pulled it out. I figured you wouldn't mind." The confronter now makes a direct statement of displeasure but is still not stating the general problem: "Well usually I wouldn't but that's—I really wanted to wear that shirt today." The confrontee responds with a remedy to the immediate problem, but there is still no sense that the problem is larger than this particular shirt on this particular day. Finally, in turn 11, the confronter explicitly states the general problem: "Okay, but, I mean, while we're on the subject, I, you know it seems like you've been doing this a lot lately like borrowing my shirts. Usually that doesn't bother me but you've just been borrowing, been borrowing them a lot and really not asking." The confrontee responds with her interpretation of expectations about borrowing between roommates, cooperating at this point in the enactment of a social confrontation episode.

In general, most initiating acts of social confrontation can be classified as complaints, as they express, directly or indirectly, dissatisfaction with the confrontee's behavior. If we view the initiating act of the confronter as an implied complaint about the confrontee's behavior intending to initiate discussion concerning the relevant rule or expectation, then the question becomes: What sort of response from the confrontee will satisfy the confronter's intent? Conversation analysts have suggested that a complaint is the first part of an adjacency pair. Sacks, Schegloff, and Jefferson (1974) describe complaints as being followed by either denial or rejection. Others propose that complaints are likely to elicit disagreement, justification, or apologies (Coulthard, 1977; Doelger, 1984;

Edmondson, 1981; Turner, 1970). Precisely because of this variety of possible responses to complaints, the definition of complaining has proven problematic for conversational analysts (Edmondson, 1981).

We contend that the successful initiation of a social confrontation episode is not determined by particular qualities or conditions of the complaint; rather, it emerges from interaction between speaker and receiver that effectively negotiates what is being enacted. To identify the episode initiated by a complaint, a minimum sequence of three moves must be examined. In responding to a complaint, the receiver may choose either to conform with the perceived intent of the complaint or to attempt to transform the communication episode. The complainer may then accept the receiver's interpretation of intent or reject the interpretation and try again to define the episode. Many instances of attempted confrontation may go awry as confronters abandon their intent in the face of a lack of cooperation by the confrontee in recognizing the confrontation.

Development

How the confrontation develops depends upon the way in which the interactants orient themselves to the problem raised by the apparent rule violation and to each other. Thus the development of the interaction may be described both substantively and relationally. On a substantive level, the problem becomes defined according to what is at issue between the interactants (Newell & Stutman, 1988). On a relational level, the interactants often develop a way of dealing with each other that defines their relationship for that encounter.

Content and relationship remain inexorably intertwined. Perhaps the major shared component is power. For example, a priori power relationships may be played out or challenged in the kind of episode enacted and the definition of what is at issue. Further, how interactants orient toward one another may represent strategic means of gaining control of the content of the episode and its development. But before we can more fully explore the implications of the connection between content and relationship, major patterns of how each develops within the confrontation episode must be described.

In initiating confrontation, the confronter has in essence made a claim about the other person's behavior that suggests both that the confrontee did perform behavior Y and, further, that behavior Y constitutes a violation of relational rules or social norms. Both of these points are arguable. Of course, the confrontee may challenge the legitimacy of the rule. An argument over the legitimacy of the confronter's expectations, then, may be the major substantive focus of the interaction. If the confrontee eventually grants legitimacy, then the focus may shift to the performance of the behavior.

Alternately, the confrontee may move the discussion to a higher level of abstraction by arguing that this was a "special" situation and invoke a superseding rule for such extenuating circumstances. If the confronter accepts this justification for behavior, then the episode may quickly end. On the other hand, the confronter may find this claim controversial and the episode is spent arguing this point.

Of course, the confrontee may implicitly grant the legitimacy of the confronter's expectations and focus upon the performance of the behavior in question. The confrontee may deny performing the behavior. Then the episode may be largely spent by the two parties presenting evidence for their contrasting positions and challenging each other's evidence.

In some instances, the confrontee may find it untenable to deny performing the behavior in question but instead chooses to deny that the behavior constitutes a violation of the rule. How the rule is to be defined and applied becomes the focus of controversy.

In other cases, the confrontee implicitly accepts the legitimacy of the confronter's expectations and acknowledges performing rule-deviant behavior, but denies responsibility for this action. In this instance, the confrontee offers an excuse, arguing anything — that the behavior was an accident, that others forced the confrontee to perform the behavior, or the like. Naturally, the confronter may find any excuse unacceptable and argument over the excuse given may ensue.

Finally, the confrontation may proceed without controversy. The confrontee admits wrongdoing and accepts responsibility for his or her behavior. The interaction may end very quickly or may focus upon how to remedy the situation.

The response of the "accused" to the confrontation serves as a bid for the line of development the episode will take. The confronter then evaluates the confrontee's response. The confronter's evaluation may either "hold" the interactants to a particular issue or allow them to move toward resolution. Of course, the development of any particular confrontation may not always proceed along such logical lines. The confrontee may try a number of different defenses, abandoning one when it proves unsuccessful and moving to another. For example, the confrontee may originally choose to deny performing the behavior, but when faced with incontrovertible evidence may shift to challenging the legitimacy of the confronter's expectation. Also, as has already been noted, the confrontee may not cooperate in the development of the episode. For example, the confrontee may respond with a counterconfrontation. Under these circumstances, the argument may become very confused, as multiple issues and problems are on the floor simultaneously.

In addition to defining the problem substantively, the interactants orient themselves toward one another and thus define the nature of their relationship for the episode. Identifying the ways in which the relationship may be defined is a much more difficult task than identifying the substantive issues. The researcher must examine interactions looking for how the interactants behave toward one another, and, of course, the variations are infinite. The characterization at this point in the research program is on a rather gross level and requires further refinement of methods to capture the nuances of implicit relationship definition, especially as they relate to confrontation. Below we propose characterizations of three different relational orientations enacted in social confrontation that are loosely based upon an exploratory study by Newell (1984). These characterizations rely upon a preponderance of elements occurring in the interaction that support the interpretation; not all interactions fit neatly into the categories. We will describe the ways in which interactants orient toward one another in terms of the messages they employ. For the sake of convenience, we describe these behavioral patterns as roles. Note that the labeling of a role reflects the researchers' interpretation of messages and not intentional selection of roles by social actors. As the following description will demonstrate, these patterns are enacted by the interactants, emerge throughout the conversation, and are implicitly negotiated by how each responds to the other.

Two variations fit within the general characterization of transgressor and victim. In one variation, the confronter's behavior essentially casts self as victim and the confrontee as transgressor. The confronter's behavior may be described as guilt inducing. The confrontee cooperates in this casting by playing the guilty and remorseful party. The confronter keeps the interaction focused upon the past failure event and exploits the situation by continually recounting how costly or hurtful the confrontee's behavior has been. The confrontee may try a number of different alternatives to move the conversation along, including empathy, remorse, statements of concern for the relationship, and attempts to discuss what they should do now. But the confronter rejects these transitions, returning to the damage done and pulling the conversation back to the failure event.

For example, in one case a jealous young man not only continues to return to how hurt he has been but also rubs it in by claiming additional harm. He tells his girlfriend that her behavior has made him do something he had promised her he would not do again:

R: And you haven't been home. And two of them times I called ya — my roommates saw ya one night, at the movie, with this Mike dude. Which made me just want to go do something drastic. So I did.
E: You did?
R: I went and got drunk.
E: Oh no.

Even after the girl encourages her boyfriend not to give up on them and to keep talking about the problem, he continues to return to the failure event. She suggests:

E: Well [sigh] I don't know where to go from here. How about let's skip the movie, do you want to go back to my house and I'll cook dinner. You can help me if you want. And then we'll watch TV and talk about it. Do you want to do that, or not really?
R: What if Mike comes over?
E: Mike's not going to come over.

In this version of victim-transgressor, the confronter effectively maintains control of the interaction, essentially blocking all attempts at repair by the confrontee. The confrontee cooperates by accepting these messages and behaving as the transgressor.

In another version of the victim-transgressor relationship, the confronter and confrontee exchange roles. In this case, the confrontee maintains innocence and plays victim to the confronter's transgression of false accusation. For the roles to be complete, the confrontee must play up the degree to which he or she has been wronged by this false accusation, and the confronter must display some degree of remorse or guilt for the false accusation. For example, an encounter between a dating couple began when the boyfriend dropped by the girlfriend's apartment to find out what was wrong, as she had been avoiding him. To his inquiry she takes the stance of victim:

> Oh, I don't know what to tell you. I've just heard some really shitty things that were really upsetting to me that to be honest with you made me sit home the last few days and cry. . . . Kris, I know from a very reliable source, not even just from a reliable source. I know it's factual. You had a date with someone else and that's so shitty because you informed me that you wanted us just to date, to be dating each other. All of a sudden I heard that you had a date with someone else. That sucks. It makes me look like a fool.

Kris, however, does not cooperate and play the transgressor. Instead, he challenges her role of victim:

> I could tell you *right now* that I think it's really *sick* that you have been sitting here for three days *brooding* over the fact that you were, you were *crying* over something that you didn't even know for sure happened, and now you are coming to me and if I didn't drag it out of you, you would still be carrying on. A year could pass, we could totally drift away from each other and you would have let all that happen on the premise that something maybe happened, instead of coming to me and asking me if it happened!

Kris has now reversed the roles of confronter and confrontee as well as victim-transgressor. The interaction continues as Kris challenges Tracy's "proof." As he uncovers how flimsy her evidence is he gets even more angry: "Well this sucks that I'm sitting here having to answer for something that was put into like an accusatory kind of thing that I didn't even do anything wrong." Tracy tries to deny the transgressor role: "Kris, let me remind you, if the situation were reversed you would do the same exact thing." But Kris persists in his casting:

> I would not. I would immediately confront you and I wouldn't confront you as a "Why did you do something." I would ask you straight up, "Did you go out with somebody else? Please tell me that you did or didn't."

Ultimately, this pair is left with two problems to resolve: How to prevent future misunderstandings and how to confront each other appropriately.

In other enactments, the confrontee and confronter may orient toward one another along lines of power. The power relationship may be based upon formal or informal roles between the parties. In instances of clear superior-subordinate relationships and acceptance of this relationship by the interactants, the confrontation may be quickly put to an end by the superior's either refusing to cooperate in the confrontation episode (Newell & Stutman, 1989/1990) or demanding a remedy from the subordinate. In other cases, the relative status of the individuals may not be so clear or may go unchallenged, and the participants may orient toward one another as objects to be moved. Typically, in this sort of enactment, one or both parties use a variety of compliance-gaining tactics in order to get what they want. While compliance-gaining tactics may occur in a variety of enactments, in this variation a preponderance of the interaction revolves around compliance-gaining moves. For example, a waiter attempts to get the restaurant manager to comply with the "rule" that his job description does not include busing tables:

> Well you know I can't afford just to bus tables. I make most — you know my wages — I haven't gotten a raise in six months and I make most of my money from tips. I can't afford it. I can't do it tonight.

The manager counters with a veiled threat to get the waiter to comply with the superseding rule that all must help to keep the restaurant going: "Steve, do you like your job?" The two parry back and forth, exhausting a variety of compliance-gaining tactics upon one another until a compromise is reached.

Finally, the interactants may orient toward one another as partners facing a common problem on which they must cooperate to resolve successfully. This type of enactment follows the description of collaboration (Blake & Mouton, 1964) in which each interactant behaves in a way that expresses high concern for both self and other. The exchange typically includes self-disclosure of feelings and accounts for actions that facilitate mutual understanding. The interaction provided in Table 1 may be described as collaborative.

These three variations of orientation toward one another are not mutually exclusive. Power is obviously a dominant theme in how individuals orient toward one another. One could view each of these patterns as simply representing different ways of enacting power. Successfully playing the victim, as either confronter or confrontee, is a way to gain control of the episode as surely as acting with the force of a superior position. In other cases, the interactants may struggle for power or collaborate.

Returning to the substantive issues that define the episode, we can see how content and relationship combine in the development of the social confrontation episode. Certain relational orientations appear to correspond to certain substantive issues. The role of confronter as victim is facilitated by the willingness of the confrontee to play transgressor by admitting guilt and appearing willing to accept responsibility. Conversely, the role of confrontee as victim often takes the form of denying performance of the behavior in question, casting the confronter as transgressor for even suspecting such a thing. Certainly, power relations will often go along with issues of legitimacy. If the confronter is of superior status, then the basis for confrontation may go unchallenged and the confrontee may be eager to do whatever is necessary to remedy the situation. On the other hand, a power struggle may frequently surround who gets to say what is legitimate. If interactants disagree upon what the rule is or should be, then each may strive to make the other comply with his or her wishes. Finally, the collaborative relationship could be enacted irrespective of issue.

Closing

Interaction in the social confrontation episode may be viewed as moving toward resolution. However, the term *resolution* must be used with caution. Its use does not imply that all interactants try to solve the problem before them, or that a "solution" agreed upon by the interactants will actually be implemented. What it does imply is that when faced with a problematic situation (Stokes & Hewitt, 1976), interactants typically seek to smooth over the breach or to restore order. The problem to be resolved in the closing of the conversation may be the conversation itself. The movement toward resolution signifies a recognition by the participants that there is a problem, and to close the conversation they need to either make at least minimal surface movements to resolve it or note their inability to do so. In fact, an offer of a remedy or an agreement not to break the rule again may be merely an attempt by the confrontee to close the conversation and get out of the uncomfortable situation. In addition, some confrontations get no farther than accusation and counterchallenge before one or both interactants walk away. We would describe this last case as episodically incomplete.[2]

The type of resolution the interactants construct depends upon how they have defined the problem. We will present five varieties based upon the descriptive work of Morris and Hopper (1980) and Newell and Stutman (1988). These resolutions are not mutually exclusive, and many constructions lend themselves to multiple resolutions.

When the problem is enacted as behavior that has caused harm to one of the interactants, resolution may take the form of a *remedy*, either offered or taken, to make up for the harm. The confrontee may offer remedies in the form of apologies and expressions of remorse or by offering compensation. Conversely, the confronter may extract remedies from the confrontee. These remedies may include psychological or physical abuse of the confronter. The very act of confronting may provide a remedy for the confronter by providing a forum for venting frustration or serving as punishment of the confrontee.

If the nature of the confronter's expectations has been a focal point in defining the problem, then resolutions may directly address what the rule should be for the future. *Legislation* occurs when the interaction constructs the problem as the failure of the interactants previously to work out a shared understanding of a rule for behavior. The interactants may then agree upon what the rule should be. Along the same lines, *remediation* addresses the problem of expectations needing to be further refined, and, in a sense, amended in order to respond to emerging situational contingencies. In other constructions of the problem, the failure is one of performance not living up to expectations rather than a failure to share a view of what should be. The outcome here is *reaffirmation* and realignment with the agreed-upon rule for behavior. Finally, the problem may remain ineffable. The participants cannot construct a mutual definition of the problem that renders it addressable; therefore, the episode ends with *no resolution.*

The various forms of resolution differ in their implications for future conduct. Remedies make no clear statements about what the confrontee will do in the future, but, because of their punishing nature, may serve to exert a force that constrains the confrontee's behavior. On the other hand, legislation, remediation, and reaffirmation all provide guidelines for conduct in the foreseeable future. A failure to reach a resolution suggests that the problem may be likely to recur. However, we cannot safely make any predictions as to what force "resolutions" will have in actual future conduct. A confrontee may acquiesce to the wishes of the confronter simply to get out of the conversation. A problem seemingly unresolved may never recur, as the confrontee secretly agrees with the confronter and resisted simply to save face. But we can expect that the resolutions will reappear in discussions of repeated performances of the deviant behavior. Repetition may move the confronter to extract a strong remedy or punishment. Or repetition in the face of past promises to respect the rule could provoke statements of distrust and disillusionment and may make future confrontations more difficult to resolve. Ultimately, we need to study the sequence of confrontation episodes within a relationship to see how one episode affects the next.

Closing is also a time to reorient toward one another. This reorientation may be a commitment to the resolution, suggesting solidarity, or statements of commitment to one another or the relationship that attempt to repair relational bonds. To illustrate variations in closing, two examples are provided.

The first example of a closing illustrates remediation with commitment and bonding. This episode began with a waiter confronting the restaurant manager for asking him to wash dishes. As we enter the conversation, the manager has just finished offering an explanation and proposed a plan for making sure employees share equally in helping out when things get busy. This proposal acts as remediation to the superseding rule that employees should be willing to do whatever is necessary when the restaurant is busy. The manager then asks for commitment from the waiter: "Now is that going to agree with you?" The waiter responds by offering commitment to the long-term proposal:

> That should be fine. It just took me by surprise and like I said, I didn't mind doing 'em — But all of a sudden this was in front of me. And like I know you might have slipped — But to me it sounds fine. Just so that I'll know you know that next time something happens that I'm asked, I'll walk back and do it.

The manager also takes responsibility for the situation and apologizes to the waiter: "And I guess it was kind of neglect on my part and I'm really sorry." Finally, the manager expresses appreciation to the waiter for agreeing to help out and for being a valuable employee, reaffirming her commitment to the relationship: "Okay, well *really* thanks a lot for coming in and you're doing a great job. We're really glad that we hired you."

Our second example of a closing also concerns a waiter confronting a manager over being asked to do something that is not part of his job description, busing tables. This closing combines a remedy with commitment. The waiter offers a remedy for that evening only:

> Okay, well — I'll do it [bus tables] for half the time, if you'll get somebody else to do it for the other half of my shift. I'm not going to do it my whole shift though.

The manager commits to the proposed remedy, "Hey, that's good then, I could go for that," and continues to refine the proposal to please the waiter: "You want the first half or the last half?" After his response she reiterates: "Okay, we'll go with that then." They end with appreciation expressed by the waiter, "Thanks for the compromise," and minimization by the manager, "No problem."

Essentially, confrontation brings a problem onto the conversational floor, where it can be discussed. The act of confronting others provides actors with the opportunity to account for their actions, challenge the basis for the confrontation, and so on. Social confrontation is a communication episode that may be initiated by one person confronting another over a perceived rule violation. The resulting interaction constitutes a struggle between actors to define and resolve the problem. As a result, the episode provides a forum for negotiating or maintaining social order.

SOCIAL COGNITION AND CONFRONTATION

One of the goals of our research program is to provide pragmatic guidelines for managing confrontation. We have found the interactional view very fruitful in describing what social confrontation is and how it is performed. The answers to what and how provide a basis for strategic choices by social actors. The advice implied by this description includes various ways to initiate or block initiation of the episode, choices about how to define the problem, and ways to orient toward the other person that may influence the direction and tone of the interaction, as well as a range of possibilities for closing the episode or resolving the problem. But management of the episode involves not only affecting its definition and development, but also influencing its occurrence. In some situations confrontation may be viewed as beneficial, and something to be encouraged. For example, managers may want to encourage employees to confront one another over inadequate job performance so that the manager is not the only enforcer of work standards. In other situations, confrontation may be viewed as disruptive and undesirable. For example, college presidents in the turbulent 1960s and early 1970s may have wished to be able to control or at least predict the occurrence of confrontation. In order to address these concerns we must consider why individuals confront. This shift requires a change in perspective. At this point we are no longer focusing upon interaction, but rather upon social cognitions. In the next section we briefly explain this perspective and report research that addresses the question of why individuals do or do not confront.

FACTORS INFLUENCING INITIATION

Exploring how individuals perceive situations and make choices to confront or not to confront presupposes a social cognition perspective. The basic assumption is that through experience individuals form beliefs about self, situations, and communication behavior that in turn influence perception, choices, and behavior (Fiske & Linville, 1980; O'Keefe, 1988; Schank & Abelson, 1977). These sche- mata or cognitive frames allow actors to distinguish one situation from another and to reduce uncertainty about the appropriate behavior in a given encounter. Research has demonstrated that actors use situational knowledge strategically, as a framework for evaluating others and as a guideline for behaving (Cody & McLaughlin, 1985b). Further, we assume that, although individuals may have idiosyncratic beliefs, members of a discursive community are likely to develop beliefs in similar categories that render their beliefs and actions comparable. Therefore, the beliefs and their influence may be generalizable among a segment of the population. For example, a growing body of research illustrates the impor- tance of situational perceptions for strategy and message selection (e.g., Mc- Laughlin, Cody, & Robey, 1980; Reardon, 1981; Sillars, 1980; Smith, 1984). The focus of this work has been to discern the global perceptions or mental categories leading to message use. These assumptions lead us to investigate the relevant beliefs and organization of information in the perception of confrontation-relevant situations.

Our investigation in this area has relied upon self-report and pencil-and-paper measures to identify beliefs and their relationship to the initiation of confrontation. In several studies, we have explored (a) how individuals organize information about confrontation-relevant situations, and how these perceptual elements vary between situations where they confront and situations where they choose not to confront; (b) the salient beliefs about self and confrontation that may predispose some individuals to rely upon confrontation consistently as the strategy of choice and others to avoid confrontation; and (c) the goals individuals strive to accomplish when confronting others and how they rehearse in order to maximize goal accom- plishment. Results in each of these areas will be presented briefly.

Facilitators and Constraints

Individuals do not always confront others over perceived rule violations. They may take other steps to address the problem or they may simply ignore the problem. To confront or not to confront may at times be a conscious choice made by an individual after careful assessment of the situation, whereas at other times it may be almost a reflex response to situational contingencies. In either case, behavior may be influenced by the internalization of past interactions and the cognitive frames individuals use to organize experience and to guide action (Schank & Abelson, 1977).

We have examined the perceived situational influences that impinge upon the action of confronting in a two-prong study (Newell & Stutman, 1989). In the first phase, 68 research participants were used as informants as to the characteristics of situations in which they would confront someone and the kinds of conditions under which they would feel constrained from confronting someone. They listed these conditions after first recalling recent instances in which they had and had not confronted someone. This task produced 194 statements of facilitating conditions and 196 of constraining conditions, which we reduced to 90 nonredundant statements. The qualitative analysis of these statements led us to identify seven elements that combine to facilitate or constrain the decision to confront. Each element may serve as either a facilitator or a constraint, depending upon the valence of relevant information. These seven elements form the individual's perceptual field of the situation. Their relative contributions to the choice to confront may vary from situation to situation.

First, an individual is influenced by the nature of the problem, its history, and its significance. In order to be moved to confront, an individual must perceive a *degree of urgency* about the problem that requires action. Certainly the degree of urgency will increase if there is something about this particular moment that exacerbates the problem either through an accumulation of grievances or because the behavior could cause serious harm. Second, the *nature of the relationship*, including varying degrees of intimacy and trust, and the balance of dominance and authority, may serve to facilitate or constrain the decision to confront. Third, the relationship between the two parties may influence the perceived *responsibility to confront.* Some relationships rest upon expectations of honesty and direct management of problems. In addition, some roles, such as parent or manager, carry with them the responsibility to confront subordinates over problematic behavior. Fourth, *impressions of the other* and how this individual is likely to respond are taken into consideration. Individuals may be perceived as approachable, defensive, open, hostile, and so forth. Not surprisingly, actors are less likely to confront others they perceive as combative or belligerent. Fifth, potential confronters assess not only the other individual, but also their own personal *resources.* To follow through on confrontation successfully requires time, energy, and information. Sixth, assessment of the *appropriateness of time and place* may lead to postponement until a better setting can be arranged. If other elements such as perceived urgency will allow, most individuals prefer to confront another in a neutral and private setting. Finally, the potential confronter weighs possible rewards and costs of confronting to assess perceived *outcomes.* Common rewards of confronting include the cessation of an annoying problem, an improved relationship, and a better understanding of each other. Conversely, costs include loss of face and increased hostility within the relationship.

Obviously, these seven elements are highly interrelated. For example, perceived urgency may be influenced by perceptions of the appropriateness of setting and role responsibility; urgency may, in turn, alter perceptions of personal resources or outcomes; and so forth. For the sake of theoretical clarity, the next task was to assess the regularity of these relationships and hence to explore the relative impact of these elements on the decision to confront.

In the second phase of the investigation, 297 research participants responded to 35 items reflecting the situational elements as they applied to two recent instances in which they had confronted someone and two instances in which they had chosen not to confront someone. An analysis of the close-ended responses reflecting the situational elements resulted in a more parsimonious explanation. Factor analysis of responses suggests that individuals select and organize information somewhat differently in the two conditions. Factors in the confront condition concern the relational context, perceived outcomes, perceived responsibility, and altruistic motivation. On the other hand, in the not confront condition, factors concern the nature of the problem, anticipated response from the other, potential negative consequences, and degree of self-interest. A total of 24 items discriminate between the two conditions and give insight into the circumstances under which an individual will be more likely to approach or avoid confrontation. The first 5 items from the discriminant analysis illustrate individuals' typical concerns when faced with rule- or norm-violating behavior:

(1) It is my responsibility to say something to the person.
(2) If I confront the person it will help me.
(3) I have the ability to influence the person.
(4) The problem could be handled better by someone else.
(5) I can no longer tolerate the behavior.

As a check on the completeness of the 35 items used to describe the situation, we included an open-ended question asking why the individual did or did not confront in each situation. While most answers were synonymous with included items, a few pointed to the significance of beliefs about self as a confronter and about the perceived utility of confrontation. This insight led to the development of a measure of confrontativeness (Stutman & Newell, 1988).

Confrontativeness

Based upon research participants' comments and the literature on beliefs, the perception of situations, and the selection of communication strategies (Fiske & Linville, 1980; Markus, 1977, 1983; O'Keefe, 1988; Schank & Abelson, 1977), we developed an instrument composed of 30 Likert-type items concerning the utility of confrontation and self-efficacy in performing confrontation. A 27-item measure of confrontativeness emerged after correlational item analysis of 210 participants' responses to the questionnaire.

Generally speaking, confrontativeness reflects a stable belief in the benefits of confronting others. The individual who views him- or herself as confrontative approaches problematic situations with the idea that confrontation is a strategic means of achieving one's goals. The highly confrontative person seizes the opportunity to confront others about their behaviors when those behaviors are viewed as unacceptable, problematic, nonproductive, or resulting in less favorable consequences. Conversely, the low confrontative person approaches the problem with the belief that confrontation is threatening, harmful, and uncomfortable. Therefore, the low confrontative hopes to avoid confrontation when possible.

The confrontativeness instrument provides a measure of an individual's predisposition to confront others based upon these relevant beliefs. A variety of checks on the reliability and validity of the instrument were made. Internal consistency was established using Cronbach's coefficient alpha (.88, $n = 210$). In order to establish both the uniqueness of the measure and the theoretical relationship with related concepts, we had 61 participants fill out both the confrontativeness measure and theoretically related measures. As predicted, significant ($p < .05$) but moderate correlations were found with argumentativeness, .36 (Infante & Rancer, 1982); assertiveness, .35 (Galassi, DeLo, Galassi, & Bastien, 1974); self-esteem, .31 (Bills, Vance, & McLean, 1951); communication apprehension, –.27 (McCroskey, 1970); and external locus of control, –.27 (Rotter, 1966). Further, predictive validity was established by administering the confrontativeness measure along with a measure containing 10 different scenarios that asked the participants how likely it would be that they would confront in each situation. Results confirmed our predictions. Individuals who scored on the high end (established using standard deviations from the mean) of the confrontativeness measure were significantly ($p < .05$) more likely to confront than were individuals who scored on the low end. The measure of confrontativeness served to explain 20% of the variance between the two groups (using eta squared). Therefore, we conclude that individuals who score on the high and low ends of the measure have predispositions to approach and avoid confrontations, respectively, across situations. On the other hand, mid-range scores reflect a tendency to be more strongly influenced by situational factors rather than a specific predisposition.

Confrontativeness may also be useful in understanding how dispositions influence the emergence of situations. Certainly our past communication experiences form a frame for viewing current situations. These experiences presumably culminate in a relatively stable set of salient beliefs about the performance of confrontation as measured by the confrontativeness instrument. We would expect the beliefs to influence behavior in a self-confirming manner (Markus, 1977, 1983). Recent research has suggested that the expression of a disposition creates a situation by eliciting particular kinds of responses (Thorne, 1987).

Together, the research on situational and dispositional factors clearly suggests that the decision to confront is goal driven. The exploration of goals in confrontation led to a study of rehearsal for confrontation.

Rehearsal for Confrontation

To establish what goals actors have when approaching confrontational episodes, we interviewed 75 subjects and asked them to recall recent confrontations and to describe their intentions and goals. Not surprisingly, we found that actors held multiple goals concerning the episodes. What we did not expect was that several of these goals stemmed from a preplanning stage in which the actors rehearsed their confrontation messages. These responses were followed up in questionnaires administered to 99 additional subjects (Stutman & Newell, 1990). The questionnaire consisted of open- and closed-ended questions concerning the goals in confrontation and the use of rehearsal to prepare to confront someone.

Once individuals have decided to confront someone (or perhaps while contemplating whether to follow through with the decision), they sometimes rehearse messages to maximize goal attainment. Interestingly, participant responses to the questionnaires suggest that rehearsal itself is driven by a concern for one or more performance goals. First, individuals desire to be argumentatively complete. That is to say, they desire to raise and air all of the pertinent arguments relevant to the rule violation. Second, individuals desire to maintain the position of the confronter rather than become the confrontee. From experience in social confrontation, actors know that the other can often turn the tables and become the confronter, accusing the original confronter of alternate or more serious violations. As a result, maintaining the role of the confronter throughout the episode is germane.

Generally, actors who do not report rehearsing for confrontation also do not report a concern for performance goals. This fact illustrates the difference between goals directed toward the outcome and goals directed toward the activity of confrontation. Although both groups share a concern for outcome or strategic goals, performance goals are held primarily by those who rehearse. Presumably, performance goals drive the need for rehearsal. In this sense, rehearsal demonstrates the purposiveness of interaction as well as the recognition of the effect of mutual influence. As one becomes confident of one's ability to manage the interactive process through rehearsal, strategic goals appear much more attainable.

For those individuals who do rehearse, this process generally takes one of three forms: (a) internalized, (b) externalized in private, and (c) externalized with a confederate. Internalized rehearsals consist of the individual imagining possible messages and responses of the other party. Privately externalized rehearsals occur when an individual practices his or her messages aloud, often in front of a mirror. Such rehearsals may include an internalized "filling in" for the other party in the conversation, or may even include speaking for the other party. Rehearsals with confederates utilize others to respond to the planned message to see how it is received and to practice responses to possible messages of the other party. In each of the forms, individuals engage in some type of message construction, although they sometimes rehearse only the opening lines of the episode. A primary reliance on any one form does not exist.

Despite individual differences in the structure of rehearsal, respondents consistently reported the same advantages of rehearsal. The most frequently cited benefit was an increase in ability to recall pertinent arguments. Recall was followed by benefits related to arousal. Subjects commonly reported that rehearsal enabled them to control their emotions and to remain rational in what they perceived as a highly volatile situation. As a result, rehearsal was thought to reduce anxiety and improve confidence. More than half of the respondents also claimed that rehearsal helped to produce more articulate speech, through word choice and thought organization. Finally, respondents also proposed that rehearsal enabled them to generate counterarguments they could not have crafted spontaneously.

In light of the research on rehearsal, the strategic goals of confrontation achieve greater clarity. Generally, individuals share five strategic goals as confronters. First, actors confront others as a means of influencing their behavior. The desired influence most commonly concerns a correction or cessation of a rule-violating behavior. Second, individuals confront others as a means of venting frustration. Individuals often allow dissatisfaction with another to build. Confrontation provides an outlet for this dissatisfaction and thus serves as a means for catharsis. Third, individuals view confrontation as a vehicle for the maintenance of a strong relationship. Through the establishment and clarification of relational or social rules, individuals reaffirm the value of the relationship. Through confrontation, individuals may manage how the other views the relationship and foster their own views. Fourth, individuals use confrontation as a means of retribution. By establishing a rule violation, individuals can seek restitution in forms ranging from apology to aggressive acts. For some actors, confrontation is the legitimating action that allows them to seek retribution without being seen as aberrant or cruel. Finally, individuals may use confrontation to gain enhanced understanding of the other person.

THEORETICAL AND PRACTICAL IMPLICATIONS

Our pursuit of confrontation has led us to rely upon two different perspectives, one focusing upon interaction and the other upon social cognition. Our allegiance is to the phenomenon of confrontation and striving to describe and explain it in all its richness and variety.

Throughout this chapter, we have attempted to make transparent the implications of social confrontation for understanding conflict. Conflict is typically defined as "at least two interdependent parties who perceive incompatible goals, scarce resources, and interference from the other party in achieving their goals" (Hocker & Wilmot, 1985, p. 23). Given the ubiquitous nature of conflict, the researcher or practitioner must narrow or focus the field of study in some manner.

Social confrontation represents one way in which to narrow the field of study. In addition, social confrontation brings into sharper focus how conflict enables actors to negotiate and maintain the social and relational order. Furthermore, both the tendency to confront (confrontativeness) and the manner in which the social confrontation episode is enacted relate to the literature on assertiveness and aggression. Research on social confrontation may provide insight into why some individuals are more aggressive or coercive and what patterns of interaction foster aggression. Now that a lucid picture of how actors perform confrontation exists, we can pursue questions related to the sequence of events, most notably, what actions lead to destructive and constructive patterns and outcomes.

A detailed understanding of the social confrontation episode also advances research and theory on communication episodes in general (Farrell & Frentz, 1979; Frentz, 1981; Frentz & Farrell, 1976; Newell, 1988; Newell & Stutman, 1987; Pearce, 1976; Pearce & Cronen, 1980). The research reported earlier illustrates the utility of the communication episode as a research construct for the holistic study of communication. As Fisher (1985) has noted, the interpretation of communicative actions can be found in the patterns of how those behaviors connect with one another. To discover the significance of those communicative patterns is to place them in context. Episodes provide that context. The social confrontation episode offers a vehicle for studying the use of accounts within the web of substantive issues and thus serves to bridge these two areas of research. Further, the episode construct illustrates how conversational coherence is accomplished by actors. Our intention is that this research will serve as a model for studying other communication episodes that have, to date, defied parsimonious explanation.

NOTES

1. Because of the difficulties inherent in gaining access to naturally occurring confrontations, we developed a role-playing method that involves assigning research participants to scenarios and roles that they find salient. Scenarios specify the relationship between the participants and the basic problem. The only instruction is that the injured party address the problem by confronting the other individual. For example, a typical scenario states: "Kelly and Kris have been dating steadily for about six months. Kelly suspects Kris has been secretly dating other people, and now decides to confront Kris." (See Newell & Stutman, 1988, for a thorough discussion of this method.) Participants then carry out the conversation between themselves as they normally would. These role-played interactions usually last from 5 to 15 minutes. While we have found this method to be very fruitful, there are unavoidable limitations. Especially lacking in role-playing are all of the history of ongoing relationships and, perhaps, the intensity of an actual confrontation. Therefore, the interaction produced through role-playing may be more orderly than naturally occurring interaction, where individuals are likely to counterconfront, bring up a laundry list of complaints, refuse to interact, or walk out in the middle of the conversation. Therefore, we have turned to collecting naturally occurring confrontations. Of course, the easiest to obtain require participants to recall, in as much detail as possible, the interaction in a recent confrontation. Here the problem lies in the likely bias of memory. To circumvent this problem, we have also collected a sample of naturally occurring confrontations that we have observed.

2. Describing an interaction as episodically incomplete does not imply that the actors have produced an imperfect performance. Rather, it reflects a theoretical position. "Communication episode" is a

theoretical concept for examining and describing interaction. As a theoretical stance, viewing interactions as episodically complete or incomplete raises questions for future research, including the following: Are incomplete episodes more likely to occur in public confrontations between strangers than in ongoing relationships? Do incomplete episodes more frequently lead to reoccurrences of confrontations than do complete episodes? What is the relationship between completion of episodes and satisfaction with communication or with the relationship? How do incompletions variously represent punishment, indecision, or intransigence?

REFERENCES

Andrews, J. R. (1969). Confrontation at Columbia: A case study in coercive rhetoric. *Quarterly Journal of Speech, 55,* 9-16.

Bailey, H. A. (1969). Confrontation as an extension of communication. In D. W. Parson & W. A. Linkugel (Eds.), *Militancy and anticommunication* (pp. 11-26). Lawrence, KS: House of Usher.

Bateson, G. (1972). *Steps to an ecology of mind.* New York: Ballantine.

Berger, P. L., & Luckmann, T. (1966). *The social construction of reality.* Garden City, NY: Doubleday.

Bills, R. E., Vance, E. L., & McLean, O. S. (1951). An index of adjustment and values. *Journal of Consulting Psychology, 15,* 257-261.

Blake, R. R., & Mouton, J. S. (1964). *The managerial grid.* Houston, TX: Gulf.

Bleiberg, S., & Churchill, L. (1975). Notes on confrontation in conversation. *Journal of Psycholinguistic Research, 4,* 273-278.

Blumstein, P. W., Carssow, K. G., Hall, J., Hawkins, B., Hoffman, R., Ishem, E., Mauerer, C. P., Spens, D., Taylor, J., & Zimmerman, D. L. (1974). The honoring of accounts. *American Sociological Review, 39,* 551-566.

Burgess, P. G. (1970). The rhetoric of moral conflict: Two critical dimensions. *Quarterly Journal of Speech, 56,* 120-130.

Burke, R. J. (1970). Methods of resolving superior-subordinate conflict: The constructive use of subordinate differences and disagreements. *Organizational Behavior and Human Performance, 5,* 393-411.

Cathcart, R. S. (1978). Movements: Confrontation as rhetorical form. *Southern Speech Communication Journal, 43,* 233-247.

Cima, R. L. (1985). Group conflict resolution: An overview of confrontative counseling. *Journal of Child Care, 2*(3), 1-15.

Cody, M. J., & McLaughlin, M. L. (1985a). Models for the sequential construction of accounting episodes: Situational and interactional constraints on message selection and evaluation. In R. L. Street, Jr., & J. N. Cappella (Eds.), *Sequence and pattern in communicative behavior* (pp. 50-69). Baltimore: Edward Arnold.

Cody, M. J., & McLaughlin, M. L. (1985b). The situation as a construct in interpersonal communication research. In M. Knapp & G. Miller (Eds.), *Handbook of interpersonal communication* (pp. 263-312). Beverly Hills, CA: Sage.

Coulthard, M. (1977). *An introduction to discourse analysis.* New York: Longman.

Day, R. L., & Landon, E. L. (1977). Toward a theory of consumer complaining behavior. In A. G. Woodside, J. N. Sheth, & P. D. Bennett (Eds.), *Consumer and industrial buying behavior* (pp. 425-437). New York: North-Holland.

Denzin, N. K. (1978). *The research act: A theoretical introduction to sociological methods.* New York: McGraw-Hill.

Doelger, J. (1984). *A descriptive analysis of complaints and their use in conversations.* Unpublished master's thesis, University of Nebraska, Lincoln.

Edmondson, W. J. (1981). On saying you're sorry. In F. Coulmas (Ed.), *Conversational routine* (pp. 273-288). New York: Mouton.

Farrell, T. B., & Frentz, T. S. (1979). Communication and meaning: A language-action synthesis. *Philosophy and Rhetoric, 12,* 215-255.

Filley, A. C., House, R. J., & Kerr, S. (1976). *Managerial process and organizational behavior.* Glenview, IL: Scott, Foresman.

Fisher, B. A. (1970). Decision emergence: Phases in group decision making. *Speech Monographs, 37,* 53-66.

Fisher, B. A. (1981). Implications of the "interactional view" for communication theory. In C. Wilder & J. H. Weakland (Eds.), *Rigor and imagination* (pp. 195-209). New York: Praeger.

Fisher, B. A. (1985). Pragmatics of meaning. In J. R. Cox, M. O. Sillars, & G. B. Walker (Eds.), *Argument and social practice: Proceedings of the Fourth SCA/AFA Conference on Argumentation* (pp. 511-522). Annandale, VA: Speech Communication Association.

Fisher, B. A., Drecksel, G. L., & Werbel, W. S. (1979). Social information processing analysis (SIPA): Coding ongoing human communication. *Small Group Behavior, 10,* 3-21.

Fiske, S. T., & Linville, P. W. (1980). What does the schema concept buy us? *Personality and Social Psychology Bulletin, 6,* 543-557.

Fitzpatrick, M. A. (1988). *Between husbands and wives: Communication in marriage.* Newbury Park, CA: Sage.

Fraser, B. (1981). On apologizing. In F. Coulmas (Ed.), *Conversational routine* (pp. 259-271). New York: Mouton.

Frentz, T. S. (1981). A generative approach to episodic structure. *Communication Quarterly, 29,* 12-20.

Frentz, T. S., & Farrell, T. B. (1976). Language-action: A paradigm for communication. *Quarterly Journal of Speech, 62,* 333-349.

Galassi, J. P., DeLo, J. S., Galassi, M. D., & Bastien, S. (1974). The college self-expression scale: A measure of assertiveness. *Behavior Therapy, 5,* 165-171.

Glaser, B. G. (1978). *Advances in the methodology of grounded theory: Theoretical sensitivity.* Mill Valley, CA: Sociology Press.

Glaser, B. G., & Strauss, A. L. (1967). *The discovery of grounded theory: Strategies for qualitative research.* New York: Aldine.

Goffman, E. (1971). *Relations in public.* New York: Harper & Row.

Goffman, E. (1974). *Frame analysis: An essay on the organization of experience.* New York: Harper & Row.

Grice, H. P. (1975). Logic and conversation. In P. Cole & J. L. Morgan (Eds.), *Syntax and semantics: Vol. 3. Speech acts* (pp. 41-58). New York: Academic Press.

Harnett, D. L., Cummings, L. L., & Hamner, W. C. (1973). Personality, bargaining style, and payoff in bilateral monopoly bargaining among European managers. *Sociometry, 36,* 325-345.

Harre, R., & Secord, P. F. (1972). *The explanation of social behavior.* Oxford: Basil Blackwell.

Hewitt, J. P., & Hall, P. M. (1973). Social problems, problematic situations and quasi-theories. *American Sociological Review, 38,* 367-374.

Hewitt, J. P., & Stokes, R. (1975). Disclaimers. *American Sociological Review, 40,* 1-11.

Hocker, J. L., & Wilmot, W. W. (1985). *Interpersonal conflict* (2nd ed.). Dubuque, IA: Wm. C. Brown.

Hopper, R. (1983). Interpretation as coherence production. In R. T. Craig & K. Tracy (Eds.), *Conversational coherence: Form, structure, and strategy* (pp. 81-98). Beverly Hills, CA: Sage.

Infante, D. A., & Rancer, A. S. (1982). A conceptualization and measure of argumentativeness. *Journal of Personality Assessment, 46,* 72-80.

Jackson, S., Jacobs, S., & Rossi, A. M. (1987). Conversational relevance: Three experiments in the pragmatic connectedness of conversation. In M. L. McLaughlin (Ed.), *Communication yearbook 10* (pp. 323-347). Newbury Park, CA: Sage.

Jacobs, S., & Jackson, S. (1983). Speech act structure in conversation: Rational aspects of pragmatic coherence. In R. T. Craig & K. Tracy (Eds.), *Conversational coherence: Form, structure, and strategy* (pp. 47-66). Beverly Hills, CA: Sage.

Jacobs, S., Jackson, S., & Hall, B. (1988). *Digressions in mediated discourse: Multiple goals and standing concerns.* Paper presented at the annual meeting of the Speech Communication Association, New Orleans.

Jones, R. E., & White, C. S. (1985). Relationships among personality, conflict resolution styles and task effectiveness. *Group and Organizational Studies, 10*, 152-167.

Lawrence, P. R., & Lorsch, J. W. (1967). *Organization and environment: Managing differentiation and integration.* Cambridge, MA: Harvard University, Division of Research, Graduate School of Business Administration.

Lewin, K. (1935). *A dynamic theory of personality* (D. K. Adams & K. E. Zener, Trans.). New York: McGraw-Hill.

Lewis, S. A., & Pruitt, D. G. (1971). Orientation, aspiration level and communication freedom in integrative bargaining. *Proceedings of the 79th Annual Convention of the American Psychological Association* (pp. 221-222). Washington, DC: American Psychological Association.

London, M., & Howat, G. (1978). The relationships between employee commitment and conflict resolution behavior. *Journal of Vocational Behavior, 13*, 1-14.

Markus, H. (1977). Self-schemata and processing information about self. *Journal of Personality and Social Psychology, 35*, 63-78.

Markus, H. (1983). Self-knowledge: An expanded view. *Journal of Personality, 51*, 543-565.

McCroskey, J. C. (1970). Measures of communication bound activity. *Journal of Personality, 51*, 543-565.

McLaughlin, M. L., Cody, M. J., & O'Hair, H. D. (1983). The management of failure events: Some contextual determinants of accounting behavior. *Human Communication Research, 9*, 208-224.

McLaughlin, M. L., Cody, M. J., & Robey, C. S. (1980). Situational influences on the selection of strategies to resist compliance-gaining attempts. *Human Communication Research, 7*, 14-36.

McLaughlin, M. L., Cody, M. J., & Rosenstein, N. E. (1983). Account sequences in conversations between strangers. *Communication Monographs, 50*, 102-125.

Morris, G. H. (1985). The remedial episode as a negotiation of rules. In R. L. Street, Jr., & J. N. Cappella (Eds.), *Sequence and pattern in communicative behavior* (pp. 70-84). Baltimore: Edward Arnold.

Morris, G. H., & Hopper, R. (1980). Remediation and legislation in everyday talk: How communicators achieve consensus. *Quarterly Journal of Speech, 66*, 266-274.

Newell, S. E. (1984). *Patterns of social confrontation.* Paper presented at the annual meeting of the Speech Communication Association, Chicago.

Newell, S. E. (1988). *The structure of communication episodes.* Paper presented at the annual meeting of the Western Speech Communication Association, San Diego, CA.

Newell, S. E., & Adams, K. L. (1985). Social confrontation in relationships of varying degrees of intimacy. In J. R. Cox, M. O. Sillars, & G. B. Walker (Eds.), *Argument and social practice: Proceedings of the Fourth SCA/AFA Conference on Argumentation* (pp. 634-647). Annandale, VA: Speech Communication Association.

Newell, S. E., & Stutman, R. K. (1982). *A qualitative approach to social confrontation: Identification of constraints and facilitators.* Paper presented at the annual meeting of the Speech Communication Association, Louisville, KY.

Newell, S. E., & Stutman, R. K. (1983). Interpersonal disagreement: The study of social confrontation. In D. Zarefsky, M. O. Sillars, & J. Rhodes (Eds.), *Argument in transition: Proceedings of the Third Conference on Argumentation* (pp. 725-739). Annandale, VA: Speech Communication Association.

Newell, S. E., & Stutman, R. K. (1987, May). *The study of communication episodes.* Paper presented at the annual meeting of the International Communication Association, Montreal.

Newell, S. E., & Stutman, R. K. (1988). A model of the social confrontation episode. *Communication Monographs, 55*, 266-285.

Newell, S. E., & Stutman, R. K. (1989, May). *Perceived situational factors in the decision to confront: Facilitators and constraints.* Paper presented at the annual meeting of the International Communication Association, San Francisco.

Newell, S. E., & Stutman, R. K. (1989/1990). Negotiating confrontation: The problematic nature of initiation and response. *Research on Language and Social Interaction, 23*, 139-162.

O'Keefe, B. J. (1988). The logic of message design: Individual differences in reasoning about communication. *Communication Monographs, 55*, 80-103.

Pearce, W. B. (1976). The coordinated management of meaning: A rules-based theory of interpersonal communication. In G. R. Miller (Ed.), *Explorations in interpersonal communication* (pp. 17-35). Beverly Hills, CA: Sage.

Pearce, W. B., & Cronen, V. E. (1980). *Communication, action and meaning.* New York: Praeger.

Perls, F. S., Hefferline, R. F., & Goodman, P. (1969). *Gestalt therapy.* New York: Julian.

Philipsen, G. (1981). Enthymematic discourse in conversational persuasion. *Communicator, 11*, 39-52.

Pruitt, D. J., & Lewis, S. A. (1975). Development of integrative solutions in bilateral negotiations. *Journal of Personality and Social Psychology, 33*, 621-633.

Putnam, L. L., & Wilson, C. E. (1982). Communicative strategies in organizational conflicts: Reliability and validity of a measurement scale. In M. Burgoon (Ed.), *Communication yearbook 6* (pp. 629-652). Beverly Hills, CA: Sage.

Reardon, K. K. (1981). *Persuasion: Theory and context.* Beverly Hills, CA: Sage.

Renwick, P. A. (1975). Perception and management of superior-subordinate conflict. *Organizational Behavior and Human Performance, 13*, 444-456.

Resnik, A. J., & Harmon, R. R. (1984). Consumer complaints and managerial response: A holistic approach. *Journal of Marketing, 47*, 86-97.

Rogers, L. E., & Farace R. V. (1975). Relational communication analysis: New measurement procedures. *Human Communication Research, 1*, 222-239.

Rotter, J. B. (1966). Generalized expectancies for internal and external control of reinforcement. *Psychological Monographs, 80*, 1-28.

Sacks, H., Schegloff, E., & Jefferson, G. (1974). A simplest systematics for the analysis of turn taking in conversations. *Language, 50*, 696-735.

Schank, R., & Abelson, R. (1977). *Scripts, plans, goals and understanding: An inquiry into human knowledge structures.* Hillsdale, NJ: Lawrence Erlbaum.

Schonbach, P. (1980). A category system for account phases. *European Journal of Social Psychology, 10*, 195-200.

Schultz, J. W., & Pruitt, D. G. (1978). The effects of mutual concern on joint welfare. *Journal of Experimental Social Psychology, 14*, 480-492.

Scott, M., & Lyman, S. (1968). Accounts. *American Sociological Review, 33*, 46-62.

Scott, R., & Smith, D. K. (1969). The rhetoric of confrontation. *Quarterly Journal of Speech, 55*, 1-8.

Searle, J. R. (1979). *Expression and meaning.* Cambridge: Cambridge University Press.

Sillars, A. L. (1980). The stranger and the spouse as target persons for compliance-gaining strategies: A subjective expected utility model. *Human Communication Research, 6*, 265-279.

Smith, M. J. (1984). Contingency rules theory, context, and compliance behaviors. *Human Communication Research, 10*, 489-512.

Sternberg, R. J., & Dobson, D. M. (1987). Resolving interpersonal conflicts: An analysis of stylistic consistency. *Journal of Personality and Social Psychology, 52*, 794-812.

Stokes, R., & Hewitt, J. P. (1976). Aligning actions. *American Sociological Review, 41*, 838-849.

Stutman, R. K., & Newell, S. E. (1988). *A measure of confrontativeness.* Paper presented at the annual meeting of the Speech Communication Association, New Orleans.

Stutman, R. K., & Newell, S. E. (1990). Rehearsing for confrontation. *Argumentation, 4*, 185-198.

Thomas, K. W. (1976). Conflict and conflict management. In M. Dunnette (Ed.), *Handbook of industrial and organizational psychology* (pp. 889-936). Chicago: Rand McNally.

Thorne, A. (1987). The press of personality: A study of conversations between introverts and extroverts. *Journal of Personality and Social Psychology, 53*, 718-726.

Turner, R. (1970). Words, utterances and activities. In J. Douglas (Ed.), *Understanding everyday life* (pp. 169-187). Chicago: Aldine.

Watzlawick, P., Beavin, J., & Jackson, D. D. (1967). *Pragmatics of human communication: A study of interactional patterns, pathologies, and paradoxes.* New York: Norton.

Wheeless, L. R., & Reichel, L. S. (1988, May). *A reinforcement model of the relationships of supervisors' general communication styles and conflict management styles to task attraction.* A paper presented at the annual meeting of the International Communication Association, New Orleans.

Wilder, C., & Weakland, J. H. (Eds.). (1981). *Rigor and imagination: Essays from the legacy of Gregory Bateson.* New York: Praeger.

Interpretive and Structural Claims About Confrontations

JOSEPH P. FOLGER
Temple University

C LAIMS about the meaning and structure of interaction are central to studies of face-to-face communication. A wide array of quantitative and qualitative interaction analysis methods can be classified by the claims they make about the structure and meaning of social interaction (Poole, Folger, & Hewes, 1987). Although these two characteristics are recognized as central concerns of interaction analysis, the relationship between them and the emphasis given to structural or interpretive claims in any given method is less clear and often controversial.

Recent methodological discussions of conversation analysis suggest, for example, that there is fundamental disagreement about the role that interpretive claims play in this method. Pomerantz (1989) contends that conversation analysts can offer studies that are aimed at sequence-focused analyses or interactants' world analyses. Sequence analyses provide a "strong sense of how a sequence is organized." Interactants' world analyses provide a "strong sense of how interactants relate to the on-going interaction" (p. 243). Pomerantz's position is that conversational analysts can give primary emphasis in their work to claims about structure or claims about culturally shared interpretations of the interactors.

In a response to Pomerantz, Jefferson (1989) tries to disabuse conversation analysts of the notion that interactants' world analyses are possible with the method. Her claim is that any attempt to access actors' interpretations is inconsistent with the fundamental purpose and method of conversation analysis. In Jefferson's view, the method enables researchers to characterize the features of conversational organization.

The opposing views on whether conversation analysis can lay claim to interactors' interpretations are not resolvable simply by recognizing the interdependence of structural and interpretive claims. In pointing to this interdependence,

Correspondence and requests for reprints: Joseph P. Folger, Department of Rhetoric and Communication, Temple University, Philadelphia, PA 19122.

Communication Yearbook 14, pp. 393-402

Jacobs (1987) notes that conversational "order consists of the ways in which the utterances make sense" (p. 436). Although any claims about order will inevitably be tied to some sense making by the analyst, the question of whether or not conversation analysis provides interpretive claims is still problematic.

The "sense" made of utterances depends on the status of the analysts' interpretive claims. There are several bases upon which sense or meaning can be attributed to messages (Folger, Hewes, & Poole, 1984; Poole & Folger, 1981). Messages can be meaningful (and thus structured) with respect to claims about the culturally shared interpretations of the messages. Or they can be meaningful with respect to the idiosyncratic interpretations of the interactors themselves. Recognizing that claims about structure are contingent upon meaning fails to clarify the actual interpretive work of the analyst.

Moreover, interaction analysis methods give emphasis or priority to either structural or interpretive objectives (Sigman, 1987). Some methods, like Jefferson's conception of conversation analysis, seek, as their primary objective, to characterize sequence, organization, or pattern in interaction. Other methods place primary emphasis on providing culturally shared or idiosyncratic interpretations that are at play in a given exchange. These latter methods often include observations about structure as an aid in constructing interpretations of the discourse, but their focus remains on reaching interpretive ends.

The point of this commentary is to illustrate how interaction analysis methods give priority to structural or interpretive objectives and to demonstrate how a shift in emphasis can yield different analyses of the same interaction phenomenon — in this case, the nature of confrontation. The aim is to provide contrasting views of how confrontation unfolds in discourse and to help clarify issues that prompt debates about the objectives of such methods as conversation analysis. Examining alternative methods can help clarify the evidence needed to support claims, establish the link between research objectives and research methods, and illustrate the possible influences or limitations on claims drawn from methods with structural or interpretive emphases.

STRUCTURAL AND INTERPRETIVE
STUDIES OF CONFRONTATION

The primary objective of Newell and Stutman's episodic analysis is to characterize the structure of social confrontation. This research identifies the markers of confrontation in discourse and describes possible patterns of enactment. The analysis of role-played, recalled, and naturally occurring confrontations provides a data base for claiming that confrontation has a three-part structure with possible variations in ways that this structure is enacted.

In order to arrive at these claims about the structure of confrontation, Newell and Stutman inevitably draw upon interpretive insights. Their immersion in the examples of confrontation consists essentially of interpretive work; it requires that they determine what speakers are doing in the exchanges and how the actions relate to some culturally shared sense of what confrontation is about in interpersonal life. It is in this sense that the interdependence of structural and interpretive claims is apparent. However, the interpretive work in the Newell and Stutman method is restricted. The interpretations are limited by the evidence used in analyzing the meaning of messages in the episodes. The interpretations are shaped by the amount of contextual information that is considered and used in the analysis. Little or no evidence is gathered about the background characteristics of each person in the examples, the history of the relationship between the interactors, or possible ironic, hesitant, or other vocal intonations of the speakers. Any of this information might influence the analysis. The interpretive work in Newell and Stutman's method occurs essentially at a culturally shared level, where the researchers interpret the discourse on the basis of their membership in the same language-using community as the interactors. The primary objective of the method is to characterize structural features of confrontation using this interpretive base.

In contrast to this approach, Labov and Fanshel (1977) offer a method that is aimed primarily at providing an interpretive analysis of 15 minutes of interaction between a psychiatric patient suffering from anorexia nervosa and her therapist. Although Labov and Fanshel's work is not focused on confrontation per se, the patient describes confrontations that have occurred recently in her life, and confrontations between the patient and therapist arise during the interview. These exchanges are analyzed in Labov and Fanshel's study of the interview segment.

Labov and Fanshel (1977) acknowledge that their method seeks primarily interpretive ends. In offering a rationale for their approach, they contrast their method with other analyses of therapeutic interviews. They note that none of the prior work concentrates "upon what is actually being said by the therapist and patient. . . . All of these investigators have minimized the 'meaning' of what is being said" (p. 21). They also contrast their approach with Sacks's method. Although they find the analysis of sequencing rules in conversation useful, they note that the "sequencing rules presuppose another set of relations, those between the words spoken and the actions being performed" (p. 25). Their concern lies primarily with the interpretive work of examining "actions and reactions that are dependent on the position of the speakers in the social networks of family, group, or therapeutic session" (p. 26).

Labov and Fanshel's research questions shape the interpretive methodology they develop. In broadest terms, their purpose is to understand what takes place in therapeutic interviews. They attempt to unveil implicit propositions, to determine why patients resist change, and to clarify how talk helps overcome resistance to change. Ultimately, they want to explain what students of therapy need to learn to do. These research objectives require the heavily interpretive methodology that Labov and Fanshel develop under the name *cross-sectional analysis*. This approach assumes that the broader context or forms of life of any interaction should be central to the analysis. They state:

> Though we are interested in microanalysis, we do not start with the small details of behavior. We recognize that their significance is often ambiguous in the abstract and can be defined only when the situation in which they are used is well known. (p. 27)

The cross-sectional method requires that the researcher analyze the definition of the situation, describe the fields of discourse that interactors employ (akin to identifying speech registers), study how speakers' paralinguistic cues shape interpretations, provide utterance expansions (all implicit messages that are understood by the speakers because of prior interactions or context), and analyze the higher-order pragmatic functions of the messages. This method is aimed at providing analyses of all idiosyncratic meanings that the interactors exchange in any given episode of interaction. In this approach, the researcher is not offering claims based upon culturally shared assumptions about the interpretations of messages. Rather, evidence is obtained that allows the researcher to analyze interpretations stemming from unique aspects of the relationship and interaction. A researcher is privy to these interpretations insofar as he or she obtains sufficient background information about the speakers and context. Labov and Fanshel's method makes researchers responsible to a broad base of information about the interactors, including, in this case, details of prior therapeutic sessions, medical histories, and interviews with the client or therapist.

LABOV AND FANSHEL'S
ANALYSIS OF CONFRONTATION

Labov and Fanshel parse the 15 minutes of interaction they analyze into five short episodes. In the first episode two issues arise that provide insights into the nature of interpersonal confrontation. For each example, I will briefly describe the nature of the issue as it arises in the interview, summarize Labov and Fanshel's analysis of the incident, and contrast their analysis with Newell and Stutman's view of confrontation.

Example 1

Early in the session, Rhoda, the patient, expresses concern about an action she has taken during the prior week. Specifically, Rhoda is uncertain about a request she made of her mother. Rhoda and her mother live together and share all household responsibilities. Rhoda is also in school and has, in the past, had problems managing the demands that school and home place on her time. Recently, Rhoda's mother went to visit and stay with Rhoda's sister. After several days, the household chores began to mount, and Rhoda called her mother to ask when she planned to return home.

In introducing the narrative to the therapist, Rhoda says, "I don't . . . know whether . . . I—I think I did—the right thing." This statement is viewed as confrontative in Labov and Fanshel's analysis. In the expansion of this utterance,

Labov and Fanshel suggest how Rhoda's comment indicates she is unsure about having followed a suggestion made by the therapist:

> I am not sure, but I claim that . . . I did what you say is right, or . . . what may actually be right, when . . . I asked my mother to help me by coming home after she had been away from home longer than she usually is, creating some small problems for me, and I tried to use the principle that I've learned from you here . . . that I should express my needs and emotions to relevant others, and see . . . if this principle worked. (p. 126; ellipses replace numerical references in the Labov and Fanshel system)

Labov and Fanshel suggest that in questioning her own behavior, Rhoda is posing a challenge to the therapist. Since Rhoda followed a principle discussed and recommended in therapy, if she doubts the behavior, she questions the therapist's competence. However, Rhoda's hesitancy in offering her doubts (conveyed primarily through vocal intonation) suggests that her challenge to the therapist is coupled with her own internal struggle, a struggle that is central to the therapy itself. Rhoda is in the process of testing and evaluating her own behaviors as they are reshaped in therapy. She is heavily involved in the work of therapy at this point in the session. She is struggling with her own resistance to changing the way she typically relates to others.

Labov and Fanshel suggest that the therapist's response acknowledges the complexity of Rhoda's challenge. The therapist offers only neutral or slightly positive reinforcement responses as Rhoda prefaces her narrative and as she recounts the call to her mother. The therapist responds to Rhoda's concerns only after Rhoda finishes the narrative and says again that she thinks she did the right thing. Labov and Fanshel describe the therapist's intonation as "exasperated" when she responds:

> Yes, I think you did, too. Well, so what's your question? You know you have a lot of guilt about it. You have a very full schedule.

The therapist's intonation and incredulous question respond to Rhoda's challenge. In a sense, the therapist defends herself against the challenge by being mildly indignant about and dismissive of Rhoda's concern. But at the same time, the delay in the therapist's response and the explanation offered to Rhoda for why she has difficulty accepting the efficacy of her own behavior suggests that the therapist is also taking into account the full complexity of Rhoda's message. The therapist's response allows the work of the session to proceed and actually helps Rhoda move through her own resistance.

Although the above summary is only a brief sketch of Labov and Fanshel's analysis of this exchange, it suggests a view of confrontation that differs somewhat from Newell and Stutman's. Labov and Fanshel identify Rhoda's opening comment as a challenge. They define *challenge* as any threat to the status of a listener. This definition fits within Newell and Stutman's initial conception of social confrontation (disagreement with another's opinions or behaviors) and it is consistent with an intuitive sense of what confrontation is about. However, the challenge Rhoda conveys to the therapist cannot be easily classified according to the distinction Newell and Stutman draw between confrontations over behavior and confrontations over ideas. In one sense, the confrontation is over an idea or principle, namely, that expressing one's needs to others is a sound basis for acting in the world. In another sense, the confrontation is over an implied recommendation or behavior of the therapist in a prior session. Both dimensions form the basis of the challenge to the therapist. Challenges, in the sense in which Labov and Fanshel define and exemplify them, are confrontative behaviors that may defy attempts to draw a sharp distinction between disagreements over ideas and behaviors.

Labov and Fanshel's analysis of this exchange also suggests that the enactment of confrontation can be heavily influenced by the definition of the situation in which the confrontation occurs. Although Newell and Stutman acknowledge this influence, their analysis may underplay its full impact. Labov and Fanshel's analysis clarifies significant situational influences on the development of this exchange. For example, although Rhoda's initial comment may be indirect, it would be a mistake to view it as a hint, as Newell and Stutman's analysis of initiation might suggest. The hesitancy and mitigation in Rhoda's comment reflect her internal struggle, a struggle that is clearly tied to the purposes of therapy. Similarly, the therapist's response reflects the complexity of the situation and is prompted mainly by the press of therapeutic objectives.

There is a real sense in which Rhoda's challenge hovers over the interaction, affecting the course of the exchange while not following the development that Newell and Stutman's analysis suggests. Pointing to the way in which confrontations are negotiated, Newell and Stutman note, "In responding to a complaint, the receiver may choose either to conform with the perceived intent of the complaint or to attempt to transform the communication episode" (p. 374). In contrast, Labov and Fanshel's analysis indicates that, at times, listeners do both simultaneously. The therapist acknowledges the complaint while allowing the confrontation to become part of the client's and therapist's work. The episode is transformed as the confrontation unfolds. This alternative response option for a confrontee emerges from Labov and Fanshel's analysis because their method captures how the definition of the situation influences the interpretation of an exchange.

Example 2

The second confrontation Labov and Fanshel analyze in the opening episode is one between Rhoda and her mother. Rhoda tells the therapist about the interaction that occurred when she asked her mother to return home. Rhoda recounts the dialogue in this exchange in much the same way that subjects recount their confrontations in Newell and Stutman's studies. Rhoda describes the dialogue as follows:

An-nd so — when I called her t'day. I said "Well, when do you plan t'come home?" So she said, "Oh, why?"

Although Rhoda confronts her mother about being away too long, there is a second confrontation in this exchange that Labov and Fanshel mark as crucial in understanding not only the relationship between Rhoda and her mother but Rhoda's own personal development. It is the concern raised about Rhoda's ability to accept normal, adult responsibilities. Labov and Fanshel document how this ostensible confrontation about Rhoda's ability to handle the household is intimately linked to a set of underlying propositions that are at the heart of concerns about Rhoda's mental health and the way in which her problems influence the relationship with her mother.

Labov and Fanshel describe how the mother's confrontation is embedded in a set of propositions that are at issue in their relationship and in therapy. These propositions can be displayed hierarchically as follows:

Rhoda needs her mother home, (because)
Rhoda's responsibilities are too heavy, (because)
Rhoda gets tired easily, (because)
Rhoda does not eat properly. (As a result)
Rhoda is not an adult member of the household.

What is at stake in this confrontation is an estimate of the severity of Rhoda's problem and how the mother views its significance in the family's day-to-day life.

Here again, the view of confrontation offered by Labov and Fanshel's analysis differs in important ways from Newell and Stutman's. What this confrontation is about and how it develops is not completely recognizable from a study of the culturally shared interpretations that are brought to bear by the Newell and Stutman approach. The structure of this confrontation is not identifiable solely from an analysis of the surface behavior being questioned. The idiosyncratic interpretations that are at play in this relationship affect the way the confrontation untolds.

The interpretations that Labov and Fanshel capture and use as a basis for their analysis suggest a different view of how, for instance, initiation can occur as a confrontation develops. A case can be made that the initiation of this confrontation occurs not when the mother asks "Oh, why?" but when Rhoda asks the mother when she plans to come home. Rhoda raises the issues related to her own competence and its link to the anorexia by asking her mother about her return. The mother's first response ("Oh, why?") carries confrontative overtones. It suggests that she does not accept the implication that she should return home. But the mother's question is, in an important sense, a prompt for Rhoda to continue raising the issue and for her to delve more deeply into the underlying propositions that are linked to Rhoda's concerns about the mother's absence. In other words, the mother's response acknowledges that Rhoda has raised an issue that questions Rhoda's own competence.

If Rhoda's comment is, itself, an initiating move in the episode, it justifies a reconsideration of some aspects of Newell and Stutman's analysis. It might, for example, justify a broader and more fluid conception of initiation, one that is based on identifying when key propositions that are central to the confrontation first get raised. Jacobs (1986) makes a similar move in recasting Bleiberg and Churchill's (1975) analysis of confrontation. This approach would provide a very different picture of the way confrontations develop. When a speaker "initiates" a confrontation that is ultimately directed toward him- or herself, the other interactor may take a far less assertive role as the confrontation unfolds. What it means to "cooperate" in the development of a confrontation episode can be quite different in this circumstance. The stages of development might unfold very differently if initiation is said to occur when the key propositions are first introduced in the interaction.

IMPLICATIONS

This brief comparative analysis offers some insight into the role that interpretive and structural claims play in discourse analysis. The status of Newell and Stutman's claims about discourse stands in sharp contrast to that of Labov and Fanshel's. Newell and Stutman's claims about the structure of confrontation rely on culturally shared interpretations. The work rests on strong empirical grounds because it offers no claims that require the type of evidence that Labov and Fanshel provide. It is important, however, that the interpretive basis of Newell and Stutman's work be fully recognized. The reliance on cultural interpretations and the overall emphasis on identifying structural properties need to be acknowledged explicitly as the basis for the method.

If the role that culturally shared interpretations play in offering structural claims is not recognized, disagreements like those between Pomerantz and Jefferson about conversation analysis will persist unnecessarily. Both Pomerantz and Jefferson follow a method that offers claims with the same status as those offered by Newell and Stutman. Conversation analysis requires interpretive claims that are based on culturally shared understandings. These interpretations allow the analyst to offer insights about structural properties of discourse. In calling for "interactants' world" analyses, Pomerantz seeks a fuller acknowledgment and explication of the underlying interpretive work required to characterize conversational structure. Jefferson's reluctance to allow for a shift in emphasis, a shift that would give prominence to the interpretive base of conversation analysis, may stem from a tendency to underplay the role that culturally shared interpretations hold in the method or from a fear of moving toward the demands that an analysis like

Labov and Fanshel's entails. Conversation analysts need not seek the same interpretive ends as Labov and Fanshel. They need not track the idiosyncratic interpretations that are indigenous to the interactors being studied. However, the interpretive work that is entailed in the method needs to be recognized and scrutinized. Analyses of the interactors' culturally shared world are an integral, but largely unacknowledged, part of conversation analysis.

The contrasting views of confrontation also point to the need for discourse analysts to consider links between their research objectives and methods. Labov and Fanshel's insights about the nature of confrontation do not stem solely from the unique characteristics of therapy. Rather, the interpretive objective of the research ultimately drives the analysis. The cross-sectional methodology could reveal similar points about the initiation of confrontation, the link between disagreements over ideas and behaviors, or the embeddedness of confrontations if it were applied, for example, to a confrontation between colleagues who have known each other for many years and are at odds personally and professionally. But these insights about confrontation would be found only if the research objective called for the kind of interpretive emphasis that Labov and Fanshel's method provides.

Given their objectives, Labov and Fanshel do not succeed if their research only tells us something about the structure of requests, challenges, and the like. They succeed if their structural insights ultimately enrich our understanding of some interpersonal process such as therapeutic interviews. The structural claims, though interesting in their own right, are secondary to the analysis of what happens between client and patient in the interview. Although Newell and Stutman's descriptive work need not focus on the way confrontations function in larger social contexts such as therapy or mediation, the utility of their structural analysis needs to be demonstrated. Newell and Stutman's descriptive work remains focused on the identification of structural properties of confrontation; it is not linked empirically to their later work on social cognition. Because alternative views of confrontation episodes are possible, the strength of their analysis must rest, in part, on why the structural claims matter. Without establishing the utility of the structural claims, we are not sure how Newell and Stutman's view of confrontations matters in interpersonal life.

Finally, the contrasting insights about confrontative exchanges suggest that attempts to draw rigid boundaries around a social phenomenon like confrontation may be elusive. Newell and Stutman's interpretive work would be strengthened by an active search for contrastive examples that suggest alternative ways in which confrontations develop (Jackson, 1986). Examination of such cases would not undermine the Newell and Stutman model, but would strengthen it by placing the model in a larger theoretical framework that clarifies definitional boundaries and suggests broader ways of thinking about confrontations across diverse contexts.

REFERENCES

Bleiberg, S., & Churchill, L. (1975). Notes on confrontation in conversation. *Journal of Psycholinguistic Research, 4,* 273-278.

Folger, J. P., Hewes, D., & Poole, M. S. (1984). Coding social interaction. In B. Dervin & M. J. Voight (Eds.), *Progress in communication sciences* (Vol. 4, pp. 115-161). Norwood, NJ: Ablex.

Jackson, S. (1986). Building a case for claims about discourse and structure. In D. G. Ellis & W. A. Donohue (Eds.), *Contemporary issues in language and discourse processes* (pp. 129-147). Hillsdale, NJ: Lawrence Erlbaum.

Jacobs, S. (1986). How to make an argument from example in discourse analysis. In D. G. Ellis & W. A. Donohue (Eds.), *Contemporary issues in language and discourse processes* (pp. 149-167). Hillsdale, NJ: Lawrence Erlbaum.

Jacobs, S. (1987). Evidence and inference in conversation analysis. In J. A. Anderson (Ed.), *Communication yearbook 11* (pp. 433-443). Newbury Park, CA: Sage.

Jefferson, G. (1989). [Letter to the editor regarding Anita Pomerantz's epilogue to special issue on sequential organization of conversational activities, Spring 1989]. *Western Journal of Speech Communication, 53,* 427-429.

Labov, W., & Fanshel, D. (1977). *Therapeutic discourse: Psychotherapy as conversation.* New York: Academic Press.

Pomerantz, A. (1989). Epilogue. *Western Journal of Speech Communication, 53,* 242-246.

Poole, M. S., & Folger, J. P. (1981). Modes of observation and the validation of interaction coding schemes. *Small Group Behavior, 12,* 477-493.

Poole, M. S., Folger, J. P., & Hewes, D. (1987). Analyzing interpersonal interaction. In M. E. Roloff & G. R. Miller (Eds.), *Interpersonal processes: New directions in communication research* (pp. 220-256). Newbury Park, CA: Sage.

Sigman, S. J. (1987). *A perspective on social communication.* Lexington, MA: Lexington.

Alignment Talk
and Social Confrontation

G. H. MORRIS
Texas Tech University

B ECAUSE social interaction frequently and expectably becomes problematic, communicators need some ways to "tune" social behavior to
meet their preferences. Sara Newell and Randall Stutman reveal a
grounded theory of one way this tuning occurs. Their focus upon social confrontation episodes is one of numerous inquiries into the nature of the structures
communicators use to align behavior with preferences for that behavior. In short,
it is a description of *alignment talk* between communicators (Morris & Hopper,
1987).

To me, and clearly to Newell and Stutman, this kind of inquiry is vitally
important and central to the concerns of the communication disciplines. The
practical value of a well-written theory of alignment talk would include its
potential for use in altering destructive patterns of interaction. As Newell and
Stutman write: "This line of research has the potential to provide pragmatic advice
concerning communication strategies for the successful management of confrontation as well as to contribute to the growing body of literature on the negotiation
and patterning of interaction" (p. 364). Although we seem very far away from
being able to use this literature to provide sound practical advice, this does provide
a strong justification for the inquiry, and for "getting it right."

As much as I would like it to be, the term *alignment talk* is not in general use as
a way to circumscribe this research domain. Instead, researchers have usually
framed their work more narrowly, as contributing to the study of problematic
situations (Hewitt & Hall, 1973), remedial interchanges (Goffman, 1971), aligning
actions (Stokes & Hewitt, 1976), accounting sequences (Cody & McLaughlin,
1985), remedial episodes (Morris, 1985), problematic events (Buttny, 1985), and
social confrontations. But a family resemblance can be seen in these circumstances, as they are all cases in which one party takes issue with what another party

Correspondence and requests for reprints: G. H. Morris, Department of Speech Communication, Texas
Tech University, Lubbock, TX 79409.

Communication Yearbook 14, pp. 403-413

does, and initiates a course of action aimed at getting that party to revise his or her conduct to meet preferences. They all feature a departure from "business as usual" to align conduct with preferences, which is followed by a return to nonproblematic social interaction (or at least that is the presumed aim of the alignment talk).

It might be charged that considering these disparate approaches as parts of the same general line of inquiry is not useful because it blurs important phenomenal distinctions. On the other hand, considering them in common can be beneficial if it generates presuppositional critique that eventually strengthens the individual approaches. This result would appear helpful at present, since the approaches comprise different stands on such issues as (a) what is problematic about the behavior that occasions alignment talk, (b) techniques by which communicators confront each other, (c) communicators' pursuit of given aims (e.g., blaming and accounting) over stretches of talk, and (d) explaining emergence of episodes and development toward different outcomes. Insofar as all these approaches have been cast as empirical examinations of actual social processes, confronting disparities between them seems well warranted.

In this commentary, I first highlight what I take to be key statements of Newell and Stutman's approach. Second, to provide a contrast, I detail one alternative approach, which is developed in my own work on alignment talk phases. Finally, I try to peer into the future of research into alignment talk in order to see how these alternative approaches will be transformed on the basis of the naturalistic inquiries that are currently under way.

SOCIAL CONFRONTATION EPISODES

Newell and Stutman's outlook on alignment talk, speaking very generally and loosely, is that one kind of alignment talk is a type of episode, something similar in kind to a dispute, a lesson, a family meal, a medical emergency, or a ceremony of some kind. Participants presumably create the episode as they interact, constructing it out of their attempts to make known what they are doing as well as their effort to achieve some particular, identifiable end. The social confrontation episode is one in which an injured party confronts the person whose behavior is injurious, after which the parties negotiate what it is appropriate to do, whether a violation has occurred, and what is to be done about it. Newell and Stutman's critical claim, then, is the existence of such a form of alignment talk. From this claim follows their discussion of the boundary conditions of this form of alignment talk, their association of social confrontation with a large field of research and theory, and their description of key activities within social confrontation episodes.

The episode type they identify, the social confrontation episode, is more encompassing than others that have been examined (e.g., remedial interchanges or accounting sequences), yet still possesses well-defined boundaries: "The domain of social confrontation consists of situations in which a confronter perceives behavior as norm or rule violating, is most often the 'injured' party, and confronts the violator about this aberrant behavior" (p. 366). This specification excludes cases in which more than two parties contest over behavior, in which confrontations pertain to matters other than rule violations, and in which one party confronts another about injuries being done to a third. It also does not pertain to cases in which two copresent parties find fault with nonpresent third parties.

Newell and Stutman's work clearly derives from several sources, but owes much of its form to studies of problematic situations:

> Several conclusions can be drawn from the work on problematic situations that offer insight to the confrontation process. First, confrontation occurs in response to a number of situational elements and may reflect a conscious decision by an individual to confront. Second, confronting can be face threatening, leading to efforts to restore face. Third, how confrontation develops depends upon the substantive issues between the participants. Fourth, a pivotal issue is the legitimacy of the basis for complaint. Fifth, interaction tends to move toward a discussion of how the problem may be resolved. (p. 363)

Two of these insights into the process of social confrontation—the notion of facework and the development of the interaction toward how the problem may be resolved—reflect what I take to be the usual approaches to problematic social interaction and provide useful comparisons. Both are approaches that Newell and Stutman acknowledge to be relevant to their own approach.

Aligning problematic social interaction has very often been treated as a matter of facework, following Goffman (1971), or as therapylike remedies for pathological communication patterns, following Bateson (1972). The Goffmanlike approach attends to how people ritually erase problems, such as by apologizing. People have merely to express that they did not mean to harm the other, that they are sorry, that they really do value the other after all, and so on. Parties collaborate in the deceit that, all other things being equal, they would consistently support and cherish each other, rather than commit any offensive deeds at all (Goffman, 1974).

The Batesonian solution is to view problems as inherent in and constituting destructive patterns of interaction, then to determine how members can detect and opt out of the pattern. An example is the pattern of transgression/victimization → reparation → transgression/victimization. In this case, solutions might include leaving the system, substituting nonviolent ways of expressing disapproval for violent ones that create victims, or finding a third party to victimize—anything but more of the same (Watzlawick, Weakland, & Fisch, 1974). The keys to this approach are the presence and detection of repetitive patterns in interaction and the achievement of therapeutic insight about the strategies for resolution.

Newell and Stutman's approach incorporates and transcends both of these. Their account acknowledges that facework might be evident in the construction of moves within the social confrontation episode, but diverts attention from strictly facework moves, such as apologies and rituals for terminating social confrontation episodes, toward the confrontation itself and the substantive issues it raises. In short, their approach concentrates on the substantive rather than the ritual elements of the process.

Newell and Stutman also move beyond typical statements of the "interactional view" reflected in the Batesonian approach when they stress means for resolving troubled social interaction, as opposed to problematic social interaction itself. In addition, they concentrate upon mundane problems and resolutions, in contrast to the major, consequential destructive patterns of interaction and therapeutic solutions common to the interactional view. They focus upon cases in which one party perceives another's behavior to violate a social norm or relational rule. A final choice that distinguishes them from the interactional view is their insistence that they are describing conversational activity:

> The interactional view leads us to approach conversations as negotiated enactments through which participants not only exchange turns but also mutually construct the purpose of their interaction. Conversational coherence emerges as interactants successfully coordinate their actions with one another to produce interaction that displays functional unity. The description of a particular type of episode then not only facilitates the study of how communication is used in the social construction of reality, but also leads to insight into how functional coherence is produced. (p. 368)

This is an attempt to tie episode-based description to the moment-by-moment emergence of talk in conversation. We will see later that this "conversational turn" is a critical maneuver for the subsequent development of their position.

In Newell and Stutman's account, there are several key activities within social confrontation episodes. At the forefront, of course, is the confrontation itself — a speech act of complaint, accusation, or reproach that presumably calls behavior into question on grounds of being a violation of rules. Other key activities include the negotiations of (a) the legitimacy of the complaint, (b) rules that pertain to the interaction in question, (c) compliance with or violation of these rules, and (d) ways to resolve the issues that separate the interactants' views of what is appropriate. Parenthetically, none of these has received much attention from researchers, even though all would appear central to the burgeoning literature on accounts (see Buttny, in press, for a review).

In sum, there are several distinctive aspects to Newell and Stutman's approach. They focus on *episodes* of social confrontation, rather than particular acts such as reproaches, accounts, or sequences of these. They focus on substantive rather than ritual issues in social confrontations. They characterize social confrontation as conversational in nature. They identify key interactional movements, including talk that functions to initiate the episode, establish the legitimacy of the complaint, or argue the supremacy of one rule over another. Finally, their account for episodic development is distinctive. They argue that action in social confrontation episodes is highly constrained by the substantive issues over which the parties dispute, rather than being fashioned by other contingencies (such as ritual concerns or sequential relations among forms of speech). The development of the episode toward resolution, in Newell and Stutman's account, centrally depends upon the invocation and resolution of substantive issues pertaining to the applicability of rules.

Overall, the social confrontation episode is a kind of dispute in which participants align their own and others' behavior to meet an emergent definition of appropriate conduct.

ALIGNMENT TALK PHASES

For some years I have sought to sketch an approach to alignment talk (Morris, 1985; Morris & Hopper, 1980, 1984, 1987). Like Newell and Stutman's, mine borrows from Bateson, insofar as I have pursued his cybernetic analogies to understand social interaction. Also like Newell and Stutman's, mine is founded on Goffman's outlook, in that it is an extrapolation of his ideas about the remedial interchange. I, too, seek to concentrate on substantive rather than ritual concerns, and seek to understand alignment talk as a means of developing and/or crystallizing rules. Like Newell and Stutman, I envision alignment talk as conversational in nature.

But these similarities in aims have not produced accounts of alignment talk that are all that similar. I consider there to be four key interactional moments of alignment talk, and they are somewhat different from the moments Newell and Stutman identify. Mine can be loosely considered as "phases" of the alignment process. They include (a) testing, (b) finding fault, (c) aligning, and (d) signing off. To appreciate these phases of alignment talk, it is necessary to view the locus of alignment talk not in the violation of a norm or relational rule, but rather in a divergence of one person's behavior from what another, the fault finder, would prefer. To assign the genesis of alignment talk to a violated rule is to reify the rule, and it is to fail to notice kinds of alignment talk that precede "confrontations" and follow remedies. Consider the following, for example.

Recently I was in conversation with the chief executive officer of a hospital. We heard some laughter coming from outside his office, following which he gradually broke off conversation with me, then beckoned for his executive assistant by name. She did not enter his office immediately, so he rose from his chair, poked his head out his door, and said to her, "Are you having some sort of party out here? Why wasn't I invited?" His "reproach" was met with stunned silence, then apologies.

My understanding of this event was, at the time, that his initial listening to the "party" while attempting to converse and his beckoning for his assistant were *tests* to see if the problem was severe enough (in this case, if it was a significant departure from what he thought his assistant was supposed to be doing) not to "let it pass." Since she did not reply, he determined that she was not properly at his beck and call, and so he moved to the phase of *finding fault*. His sarcastic "confrontation" resulted in the immediate cessation of the commotion, but there was no explicit discussion of any rule, or any grounds for the legitimacy or nonlegitimacy of the complaint, or discussion of whether or not the behavior was inappropriate under the circumstances. All his talk achieved was to show who was in control and to silence his employees. To dignify his talk as rule related would be stretching too far. The assistant, by means of her apology, acknowledged (unexplicated) fault. Then, by means of ceasing to "party" and also by apologizing, she *signed off*, signifying that she would act differently henceforth and bidding for the episode to be over. She might have taken the opportunity to *align*, such as by giving an account of the commotion or disputing the legitimacy of his complaint, but she declined.

From my present vantage point there are three things unsatisfying about the above analysis. I have not been able to specify the sequence more precisely than testing → finding fault → aligning → signing off, or to explain why some of the phases are often missing in a given case. Also, I am uneasy that the discussion of alignment talk phases rests on a recalled event, rather than on detailed analysis of a recording and transcript of the event. But when I have examined recordings of events like this, my attention is drawn to the particulars of how interactants achieve "moments" within alignment talk, and these little achievements often have little to do with overarching accomplishments such as Newell and Stutman's and my approaches describe. The moment-to-moment concerns of actual interactants seem to include all sorts of side issues, fun and games, maneuverings, facetiousness, and dirty pool that are not reflected in either approach.

Following is an example of alignment talk I have been examining for another project (Morris & White, 1990). I mention it here in order to display some of the foolishness that gets into transcripts but not into approaches to alignment talk. Excerpts of it are transcribed in the way of recent conversation analysis (see Atkinson & Heritage, 1984, for description of transcription notation). This conversation occurred in a telephone call between two friends:

```
13 Pam:    so what are you doin'
14 Glo:    U:hm. (.3) .hhhh nothin' I was j^uss-
15         >>I been tryin to call you<<for 'bout
16         the last fi:ve thousand da:ys what
17         happened
18         (0.2)
19 Pam:    I fell off the ear:th
20 Glo:    >>That's what I<<figured.
21         (1.0)
22 Pam:    I'm the sometimes disappearing friend
23         who abs- (0.3) unfortunately has to work
24         for a living
25 Glo:    .hh Ye:s but I mean like- (0.2) >>everybody
26         (i-) was try:in' to get a hold of you the
27         other<<night and they couldn't do it.
28 Pam:    I kn^ow Ih- okay one ni:ght. I
29         g(h)o by myself to the mall the
```

30	whole world falls apa(h)rt
31 Glo:	Are you s(h)erious it was s:*o*:
32	*f*unny.

Some of the particulars that strike me as interesting about this alignment talk are how the "confrontation" or "fault finding" is achieved (via exaggeration of an unhappy tale, plus an explanation request) —

14 Glo:	*U*:hm. (.3) .hhhh nothin' I was j^uss-
15	>>I been tryin to call you<< for 'bout
16	the last fi:ve thousand *da*:ys what
17	happened

— and pursued over several turns; how it is not explicit what the confronted party has done wrong, or how or why the confronter was injured by her friend; how the accused offers facetious accounts of her conduct —

19 Pam:	I fell off the ear:th

— and then takes refuge in her status as a working person —

22 Pam:	I'm the *sometimes* disappearing friend
23	who abs- (0.3) unfortunately has to w*o*rk
?4	for a living

— then admits where she was —

28 Pam:	I kn^ow Ih- okay *o*ne ni:ght. I
29	g(h)o by my*self* to the mall the
30	whole word falls apa(h)rt

— and how (several turns later) the discussion concludes with no resolution and no signing off, but rather with a well-orchestrated change to another topic. None of this dampens my enthusiasm for investigations of alignment talk. Instead, I am less and less inclined toward mapping "large structures" of alignment talk, and I become more and more enamored of the description of its intricacies and the delicacy with which it is performed.

COMING TRANSFORMATIONS

Most of the data I now pay attention to, and a considerable part (10% or so) of Newell and Stutman's corpus of data, consist of recordings and/or transcripts of actual interactions. Increasingly, we seek to ground our ideas in description of actual conversational activities. In all likelihood, our examinations of these

naturalistic data will have a strong influence over emerging descriptions of alignment talk. As a minimum, such analysis can flesh out descriptions of how people
confront one another, how other moments of the episode are achieved, and what
preferences can be discerned in how participants engage in social confrontation
episodes.

If I am correct that Newell and Stutman are embarked on a "conversational turn"
in their research, then it might be instructive to predict how the shape of the
phenomenon in which they are interested is going to be transformed in future
analysis. Among the most studied and well documented of microstructures of
conversation is that utilized to repair troubles in conversation (Jefferson, 1972;
Moerman, 1988). It is my belief that this research will become the prime model for
work in alignment of social interaction. In nearly two decades of work, Jefferson
has described in minute detail how conversational troubles are repaired. She notes
a preference for repairs that are self-initiated, as opposed to initiated by another.
She provides exacting description of how members indicate that something is
amiss (such as by a pause or word search), how they mark what is wrong (such as
by repeating the incorrect version with raised intonation), how they achieve repair
and show that this is what they are doing, and how they proceed. It turns out that
this is a ubiquitous social structure and is perhaps universal (Moerman, 1988). This
seemingly minute repair structure for conversational troubles, something to which
we ordinarily pay little attention, turns out to be a critical part of how people
understand each other. Many other moments of social life are furthered because
participants have access to and utilize such techniques of repair.

What I want to suggest is that investigations of alignment talk are more and more
going to take the form of research into repairs in conversation. The focus will be
upon how participants achieve particular "moments" within social confrontation
episodes or, generally, within alignment talk, and the payoff is going to be a harvest
of microstructures by use of which people assemble nonproblematic social interaction and increased knowledge of preferences participants display for how alignment talk is to be conducted.

Particular Achievements, Such as Finding Fault

To see that there is room for fine-grained analysis of particular achievements,
consider the following recollected social confrontation episode presented by Newell and Stutman:

> I confronted my brother for driving my car without my permission. He ran all the gas
> out of the car and brought it back dirty after I had just washed it. I was pretty hostile
> towards him and we got in a heated discussion about why he thought he had as much
> right to drive it because I hadn't paid my parents for the car yet. (p. 364)

If recordings of the event were available, they would reveal *how* the speaker
confronted his brother, how he expressed his hostility, and how the heated discus-

sion was generated and carried along. We would know if he had begun with a sad tale, then ascribed responsibility (Pomerantz, 1978), or explicitly formulated the problem with his brother's conduct, or made an accusation that singled his brother out as the culprit, or asked for an explanation, or given an advisory (Morris, 1988), or if he had perhaps reproached his brother by means of projected excuse (Cody & McLaughlin, 1985). All of these have been offered as techniques by which "confrontations" are performed, and it might be central to the development of theory about social confrontation to understand them better, and to attend to more of such microstructures.

The same suggestions apply to other moments within alignment talk, including how participants acknowledge or refuse to acknowledge that a complaint is legitimate, how they invoke a rule in the initiation of the episode or propose a superseding rule, and how they deny, accept responsibility, or exit the episode.

For example, an examination of the role-played transcript shown in Newell and Stutman's Table 1 reveals an interesting brand of maneuvering. After K says "you'll definitely be the first one at the library," T solicits K's agreement (facetiously, I think) that this would be wonderful. An expected next move would be to agree, or perhaps to sympathize with having to be at the library so early. But this does not happen. Instead, at turn 7, K remarks, "Oh, you're wearing my shirt." This "reproach" or noticing is extremely "exposed," since it occurs in a slot where approval has been explicitly requested. This rather oblique reference—"You are wearing my shirt"—somehow (mysteriously) suffices to elicit an account. In short, the alignment is other-initiated, not self-initiated, and it is "aggravated," not minimized. Is this an unusual datum, or is it characteristic of social confrontation episodes?

CONCLUSION

I have examined in this essay some forms of talk used to create alignment between people. Many of us are with Newell and Stutman in the conviction that there ought to be a nonviolent way for people to resolve differences successfully through talk. Discovering or inventing such a way ought to be a central preoccupation of those of us in the communication disciplines, and it is hoped that this discussion of alternative pictures of alignment talk might invite increased attention to actual and imaginable structures for repair of fractured social interaction.

It might be that a collection of structures is utilized in *interpersonal legislation.* This is the idea, presupposed in Newell and Stutman's research and in my own (Morris & Hopper, 1980), that if participants can create new rules for their relationships, they can or might subsequently treat each other differently. It would be useful to be able to talk fellow interactants into doing a repetitive and bothersome activity differently. It would be all the more valuable to do this persuasion through a negotiation of rules that creates alignment among the interactants about what to do, when, and why it matters. To be able to do it in a way that strengthens relationships would truly be magnificent. But the idea may rest on a faulty view of the genesis of interaction troubles.

Both Newell and Stutman and I seem to have presupposed that if people are having difficulty relating with one another, the problem is that they do not understand what each other wants. In other words, the interactants do not have consensus on the rules they presumably follow in creating and maintaining the little social system that is their relationship. Yet people often commit minor "misdeeds" even though they are fully aware that what they do is not what their fellow interactants prefer. Sometimes students, for example, seem to orient their behavior toward discovering just how much slack they can obtain before being reproached. The teacher's problem is not so much how to make sure students know what the teacher wants, but rather how to get them to comply with the agreements and understandings that have been made. This generalizes to other forms of relationships, including the intimate, in which the issue can become: How can I get my partner to do what he or she has promised?

Certainly the way to resolve this doubt is to explore alignment talk in naturalistic interaction. The instances examined in this essay, however, do not strongly evidence interpersonal legislation. They look more like contests of will, in which one party attempts to impose rules for the other's conduct. It would be useful to know what might have occurred to nudge the episodes toward interpersonal legislation. Perhaps it is something in the initial confrontation. Regardless, it appears to me that real moments of productive interpersonal legislation—of deliberate constitution of relationships—are rare. By contrast, variously stunted episodes, leading usually to remediation, if that far, or perhaps to crisis, are the rule. On empirical grounds, I doubt that interpersonal legislation is an oft-chosen course of action and suspect that what people actually do is more superstitious, capricious, and mean spirited.

A social system needs ways to rectify interactional problems. If the system is reasonably complex, a continuous stream of such problems arise. The system that possesses well-developed problem-solving machinery will tend to find occasions for putting it to use. If a system does not possess such machinery, social scientists will create it. So far as machinery for resolving interpersonal problems is concerned, contemporary middle-class Americans have a variety of techniques in use, and psychologists reliably produce new techniques that compete with lay techniques to some extent.

Future research will need to maintain a balance between deduction from grand theory, such as Goffman's and the interactional view of Bateson, and grounded theory developed through detailed (conversation) analysis of naturalistic social interaction. The general aim, I think, is to develop an account of how problems are remedied—how alignment is created—that is built from descriptive research that zeros in on structures evident in the organization of social interaction and conversation.

REFERENCES

Atkinson, J. M., & Heritage, J. (1984). *Structures of social action: Studies in conversation analysis.* Cambridge: Cambridge University Press.

Bateson, G. (1972). *Steps to an ecology of mind.* New York: Ballantine.

Buttny, R. (1985). Accounts as a reconstruction of an event's context. *Communication Monographs, 52,* 57-77.

Buttny, R. (in press). Accounts as remedial communication: A review of theory and research. In B. Dervin (Ed)., *Progress in the communication sciences.* Norwood, NJ: Ablex.

Cody, M. J., & McLaughlin, M. L. (1985). Models for the sequential construction of accounting episodes: Situational and interactional constraints on messages selection and evaluation. In R. L. Street, Jr., & J. N. Cappella (Eds.), *Sequence and pattern in communicative behaviour* (pp. 50-69). London: Edward Arnold.

Goffman, E. (1971). *Relations in public.* New York: Harper & Row.

Goffman, E. (1974). *Frame analysis.* New York: Harper & Row.

Hewitt, J., & Hall, P. (1973). Social problems, problematic situations and quasi-theories. *American Sociological Review, 38,* 367-374.

Jefferson. G. (1972). Side sequences. In D. Sudnow (Ed.), *Studies in social interaction* (pp. 294-338). New York: Free Press.

Moerman, M. (1988). *Talking culture: Ethnography and conversation analysis.* Philadelphia: University of Pennsylvania Press.

Morris, G. H. (1985). The remedial episode as a negotiation of rules. In R. L. Street, Jr., & J. N. Cappella (Eds.), *Sequence and pattern in communicative behaviour* (pp. 70-84). London: Edward Arnold.

Morris, G. H. (1988). Finding fault. *Journal of Language and Social Psychology, 7,* 1-25.

Morris, G. H., & Hopper, R. (1980). Remediation and legislation in everyday talk: How communicators achieve consensus. *Quarterly Journal of Speech, 66,* 266-274.

Morris, G. H., & Hopper, R. (1984). *Making problems, solving problems: A sketch of alignment talk phases.* Paper presented at the annual meeting of the Speech Communication Association, Chicago.

Morris, G. H., & Hopper, R. (1987). Symbolic action as alignment: A synthesis of rules approaches. *Research on Language and Social Interaction, 21,* 1-30.

Morris, G. H., & White, C. H. (1990). *Accounts in context.* Unpublished manuscript.

Pomerantz, A. (1978). Attributions of responsibility: Blamings. *Sociology, 12,* 266-274.

Stokes, R., & Hewitt, J. P. (1976). Aligning actions. *American Sociological Review, 41,* 838-849.

Watzlawick, P., Weakland, J., & Fisch, R. (1974). *Change.* New York: W. W. Norton.

9 Strategies of Reasoning in Spontaneous Discourse

MARY LOUISE WILLBRAND
RICHARD D. RIEKE
University of Utah

Oral reasoning in unplanned discourse is described by an inductively derived typology of types of reasons developed from data collected in a series of discourse studies. The basic core of reasons identified remained constant across ages, individual styles, situations, cultures, and populations. The frequency of types of reasons changes with each of these. One new type of reason was added with age, one with an academic situation, and one with culture.

BEFORE an inquiry can be taken seriously, the community of scholars must accept its object as truly open to question, and if there is one thing on which scholars typically pride themselves it is their ability to reason. It is our argument that the concept "reasoning," as applied to spontaneous spoken discourse, is an unusually foggy one that is in genuine need of inquiry per se.

AN APPROACH TO REASONING

In order to find out what reasoning or reason giving in discourse is, it is necessary to erase or at least set aside momentarily previous discussions of reasoning that are based on a priori assumptions that reasoning must be logically relevant, cognitively relevant, disagreement relevant, or planned. We will briefly present our arguments for setting these assumptions aside, and then set out our own perspective and present supporting research.

Logical Relevance

Because the influence of formal logic and its promise to provide a sure test of the validity of reasoning is so pervasive in modern society, reasoning is still often thought of in terms of its truth-preservation qualities as tested by formal logic

Correspondence and requests for reprints: Mary Louise Willbrand, Department of Communication Disorders, University of Utah, Salt Lake City, UT 84112.

Communication Yearbook 14, pp. 414-440

(Allwood, 1986). Even though various influential presentations have claimed that formal logic simply has no role to play in evaluating practical arguments (Perelman & Olbrechts-Tyteca, 1971; Toulmin, 1958, 1972), logic still pervades our thinking on the subject (Allwood, 1986; Jacobs, Allen, Jackson, & Petrel, 1985).

It is our position that the communicative act of people giving reasons should be examined without the preconceptions that come from our indoctrination in logic. It may be possible some time in the future to return to the question of truth maintenance and the role of formal logic. It may even be, as Allwood (1986) claims, that there is a natural inclination (possibly genetic) toward constructing spontaneous reasoning from the perspective of formal logic. It may be, as Hample (1986) claims, that arguments follow unconscious but formal rules. To obtain the data that may or may not support these speculations, we need an open-minded look at what people actually say in unplanned reasoned discourse.

Cognitive Relevance

Perhaps because of the inherent ambiguity of the English language, we use the term *reasoning* to talk about both the intrapersonal, cognitive process involved in thinking and the interpersonal, communicative process of offering reasoned discourse. But this is more than linguistic coincidence. Traditionally, we have spoken about whether the person gave the "real" reason behind a claim, suggesting that there should be a correlation between the mental process leading to the support of the claim and the social process of presenting and justifying it. Work in cognitive psychology and artificial intelligence still assumes this correlation and searches for ways to clarify it (Myers, Brown, & McGonigle, 1986).

While a close relationship between language and cognitive development has been assumed for years, cognition is often studied through nonverbal or problem-solving tasks. When discourse has been used, in work such as that by Piaget (1967; Piaget & Inhelder, 1969) or Kohlberg (Brown & Herrnstein, 1974; Modgil & Modgil, 1986), it has been used to describe stages of cognitive development, not stages of language development. If we are to have any hope of explaining the role of cognition in reasoning-oriented discourse, research must examine the observable social process of reasoned discourse before confounding the issue by looking at it in terms of inferences about cognitive activity. It will surely be possible and necessary someday to seek the intersections between cognitive research and reasoned discourse research. Such investigation may even prove ultimately that the language patterns in reasoning are isomorphic with cognitive activity, and both of them are adequately described by the principles of logic. We must begin, however, by building a storehouse of baseline data on the communicative act of reasoning.

Disagreement Relevance

Another way in which the concept of reasoning is befogged is its interaction with the process of disagreement. A potential outcome of our ambiguous language is the fact that the word *argument* can be used to designate the act or product of reasoned discourse or to refer to people's interacting in disagreement. O'Keefe (1977, 1982) is now regularly cited because he has supplied a way of distinguishing the two meanings: Argument$_1$ (arguments people make) and Argument$_2$ (arguments people have).

The thrust of research has been toward Argument$_2$, what people say in situations of disagreement (Benoit, 1981, 1983; Haslett, 1983; Jackson, Jacobs, Burrell, & Allen, 1986; Jacobs & Jackson, 1982; O'Keefe & Benoit, 1982; Trapp, 1983, 1986). We want to turn the focus toward reasons rather than disagreement.

Planned Reasoned Discourse

A long tradition of commentary has been generated around the critical analysis of planned reasoned discourse (Congalton, 1988; Cox & Willard, 1982). Little question remains that if people are carefully educated in various patterns of reasoning, and if they plan their messages carefully, they can construct discourse faithful to the reasoning pattern chosen (Jacobs et al., 1985).

Unplanned discourse is that lacking explicit forethought and organizational preparation (Ochs, 1979). Even an extemporaneous speech or debate is not unplanned; neither are hypothetical or reconstructed dialogues. Written reports of what one intended or thought was said, prepared after the fact, are not unplanned. To study unplanned discourse means that we must capture what is being said for the first time with no preparation or forethought of either content or structure.

PERSPECTIVE OF THE PRESENT STUDY

The purpose of our research is to investigate reasoning or reason giving as a discourse skill. The theoretical basis of this research is that discourse performance reflects communicative competence, and competence represents the abstract knowledge of the phenomenon under investigation, in this case, unplanned reason giving (Willbrand, 1982).

Having established reasoning-oriented discourse as an area in need of study, we faced the problem of how to proceed. It is easier to study a phenomenon if you already know what it is, and that probably explains, in part, why studies of reasoning tend to be directed by some preestablished concept such as disagreement or logic. For example, Piaget studied children's reasoned discourse, but he was looking for the emergence of Aristotelian syllogisms (Brainerd, 1978; Piaget, 1967; Piaget & Inhelder, 1969). Allwood (1986) studied spontaneous reasoning by adults, but he, too, examined the text for evidence of enthymemes and inserted implied assumptions in order to make them into complete syllogisms. Kohlberg (Brown & Herrnstein, 1974) has developed a major program to examine moral reasoning, but he focuses on the developmental levels evidenced only by moral arguments used in response to a moral dilemma. Although he used grounded theory to generate stages in the development of moral reasoning and continually adjusted his stages to respond to new data, he used a form of content analysis that considered only moral reason and grouped reasons according to preconceived categories of ethics drawn from philosophy (Modgil & Modgil, 1986).

If we accept the task of examining the full range of spontaneous reasoning without the guidance of any prior theory, how would we know reasoning when it occurred? Where would we go to find it? We could not simply record every utterance a person makes for a day or a week, for there would be no way to say which utterances were reasons. So there has to be some way to find utterances that people *intend* as reasons.

The most obvious place to find reasons that people openly declare to be reasons is in planned discourse. Another place to find reasons is in the presence of disagreement. But, again, we did not want to limit the study in such ways. We concluded that we had to begin with elicitation. We had to contrive situations that were as natural as possible but still set up a condition that called for reason giving.

What follows is a report of a series of studies conducted by our research group addressing reason giving in unplanned discourse across ages, populations, and situations. Each one will be discussed individually, but some general comments can be made that will reduce repetition.

Unplanned Reason Giving

To obtain unplanned reasoning, all participants were tape-recorded as they responded to a request for reasons on a subject for which they had received no prior warning. In each instance, the experimenters explicitly asked only for reasons, and said nothing throughout the period of response except to ask for more reasons or deny compliance. At no time did the experimenter supply reasons or give suggestions of any kind. We claim that the participants intended to supply reasons, and did so without coaching or preparation.

Coding the Verbatim Transcript

Tape recordings were transcribed with each utterance on a separate line. An utterance was defined as an uninterrupted word, phrase, or sentence followed by a pause or drop of inflection (as if for a period) or a rise of inflection (as in asking a question).

Transcripts were coded according to speech act analysis. Having freed ourselves of as many preconceptions as possible, we presumed that whatever people said in response to the request for reasons they intended as reasons. We further argue that the intent to give reasons is an illocutionary force (Willbrand, 1981).

According to speech act theory (Austin, 1962; Searle, 1969), the two parts of the speech act are the proposition and the illocutionary force. The factor that determines the illocutionary force is the speaker's intention. One illocutionary force is the intent of the speaker to reason. In these studies, the intent was specified by the design and affirmed by specific responses.[1] It was the propositions that were categorized.

Utterances were sorted into categories based upon commonalities among them. The categories were defined, refined, and, when necessary, revised. That process continues. The groupings were given labels designed to signify the commonality of the utterances as reason types. The taxonomy as it currently stands is presented in the appendix to this chapter. We consciously avoided using words drawn from logic and argumentation parlance. Every utterance was assigned a reason category, with the rare exception of comments that seemed to have strayed so far from coherence that no sense could be made of them. Even these were kept in the taxonomy under the label *other.*

The coding system has proved to be highly reliable. A coding manual, also constantly responsive to new data, has been written, with more detailed definitions and examples (including subcategories) than those given in the appendix. In each study, independent coders (different for each study) were trained in the use of the manual and then asked to code 10% of the utterances. The intercoder agreement was as follows: children = .96; adolescents = .98; adults = .92; mentally retarded = .95; autistic = .98; academic = .94.

The Situations

After several pilot studies, we concluded that the best way to get children to give spontaneous reasons was in a make-believe situation. Each child interacted with the experimenter, who played the role of a witch who constantly asked for reasons why she should free a baby animal being held hostage. While this situation was contrived, the children had no trouble understanding it. Another, unconstructed, form of elicitation was found in the schools, where children were asked to give reasons to explain events in stories they read during a Great Books discussion session.

In adult samples, subjects were asked to give reasons for the release of diplomatic hostages in Iran. Adolescent participants were asked to supply reasons for releasing fellow students, along with themselves, held hostage within the school. In each case, the experimenter role-played as one who controlled the hostages and who asked only for reasons to justify their release.

We argue that the hostage situations — children with a witch, adolescents and adults with a terrorist — are comparable. All situations were, in fact, imaginary. In another sense, however, they were quite real. All participants brought to the task well-established event knowledge (Nelson, 1986) or narrative rationality (Fisher, 1987). Children hear many stories of witches and their foul deeds. The press was filled with news of hostage situations much like those described to the adults and adolescents. The hostage situations all involve seeking compliance through reason giving to one who holds all power. Thus the situations were called "supplication." Our data collection is similar to Kohlberg's (1986), in which he used a variety of moral dilemmas in order to build a taxonomy of moral reasoning. The completely natural situation in the schools was a deliberately different situation.

The Participants

The studies reported here involved 1,985 participants. All were from various areas in Utah and Colorado, with the exception of French children, who were recorded in France. Children studied ranged in age from 3 to 9 years, the adolescents were 12 and 16 years old, and adults spanned ages 20 to 41. The adults included individuals who had been trained in intercollegiate debate as well as individuals who had no formal training in argumentation. And, finally, the participants included groups deemed to be developmentally both normal and disordered.

ANALYSIS AND RESULTS

Our description of discourse reasoning was guided by a series of questions: When and what types of reasons do people use? When do children use reasoning communication? Can developmental changes be noted? How do adults reason? How does their use of reason compare or contrast with that of children? Does their spontaneous reasoning show the effects of formal training in argumentation? Having found some differences between children and adults, we had to ask, How do adolescents reason, and when do they begin to adopt adult strategies? We sought to describe the pattern of reason-giving development from age 3 through adult. In addition, we placed our results alongside studies of compliance gaining and persuasion and described the relationship by asking, How does reasoning compare or contrast with the process of persuasion or compliance gaining?

Questions about our work have been raised concerning its focus primarily on one situation, which we have called supplication, and the fact that most of the reason giving was between a participant and a noninteracting experimenter. As to the latter, a series of failures and elicitation problems (Willbrand, 1987) suggested that this interaction was the most untainted experimental situation we could find. As to the former, we approached the question, How does a change in situation affect reason-giving performance? in one study involving children interacting with a peer group in a nonsupplication situation. We were anxious to see where and to what extent the typology derived from supplication situations accounted for this different situation.

Finally, we have begun to turn our attention toward reasoning by different sorts of people. We asked, Do people who have been diagnosed as having some type of brain dysfunction have different reasoning patterns? We report studies with the mentally retarded and the autistic. We also asked, Do people in other cultures have different reasoning patterns? We report on French children as a beginning step in answering this question.

Children's Reasons

The results of the first phase of our research into reason giving in children's supplicatory compliance gaining have been reported elsewhere (Willbrand &

TABLE 1
Mean Number of Reasons in Each Category by Age Groups

Category	3-Year-Olds	4-Year-Olds	5-Year-Olds	6-Year-Olds	7-Year-Olds	8-Year-Olds	Adults
Power authority	1.00	6.10	5.60	2.30	1.70	4.10	5.03
Own authority	7.60*	4.40	7.50*	.20	1.20	2.20	0.42
Bribes	0.00	0/10	0.70	3.10	0.50	2.80	0.39
Moral obligation	2.80	6.00	3.80	5.60	8.20	10.50*	6.87
Social pressure	1.10	6.00	2.30	1.90	2.00	1.90	9.23*
Listener benefit	0.00	0.00	0.00	0.00	0.00	0.00	10.55*
Alternative	0.00	-/40	0.60	0.80	1.00	0.70	1.21
Switch burden	0.10	2.90	4.20	1.40	1.70	2.80	9.47*
Closure attempt	0.10	0.60	0.10	0.10	0.10	0.10	0.76
Because	5.10*	1.40	2.60	0.20	0.60	0.10	0.00
Other	3.30*	1.90	0.70	0.50	1.20	0.00	1.08
Stall	3.50	2.70	2.90	3.50	2.90	1.80	4.40
Mean number of utterances	24.60	29.20	31.00	19.60	21.10	29.00	50.32*

*$p < .05$.

Rieke, 1986), so only a brief summary is needed here. Analysis of 60 children between 3 and 8 years of age generated a taxonomy of reasons given (see appendix for complete descriptions) and provided an initial answer to what types of reasons people use. The children used the following categories: power authority, own authority, bribes, moral obligation, social pressure, alternative, switch burden, closure attempt, because, stall, and other.

In terms of *when* children use reasoned discourse, children at 3 years (mean of 3 years, 5 months, noted herein as 3;5) do participate in reason-giving discourse. However, as a group they show less variety in reasons chosen (fewer categories) and significantly ($p < .05$) more because reasons and other, off-topic utterances (see Table 1). Predictably, reason giving begins to occur before 3 years of age. Some developmental changes were apparent. The repertoire of categories increased at 4 years and then remained constant. By 8 years the children used significantly more moral obligation reasons. However, the data were only partially age ordered, so a hierarchical clustering analysis was conducted (Baker & Derwing, 1982). This analysis revealed five groups of children who differed by reason strategy choice. While the entire age range of the children was represented in each group, the average age for each group demonstrated a sequential progressive age comparison (significant only at $p < .08$). Combining the results of the chronological age comparison and the hierarchical cluster analysis, moral obligation reasons were specified as most mature, whereas because (used alone) and other, off-topic comments were the least mature.

Another important outcome was that the hierarchical clustering analysis revealed that the category system constituted a discrete measure. The categories all yielded significant differences ($p < .05$).

Adults' Reasons

A group of 21 adult participants was asked to give reasons justifying the release of American hostages in Iran. Of the subjects, 10 were active members of a college intercollegiate debate team; 11 had no formal training in argumentation.

The first question addressed by this study was, What reasons do adults use in unplanned discourse? Table 1 displays the adults' reasons, along with the mean number of reasons used in each category by the other age groups studied. The overall results show that the adults use the same types of reasons that children use by 4 years of age, with two exceptions: Adults never use because alone, and they used one new category. This new category, important because it was new and the most frequently used reason by adults, was labeled "listener benefit." [2] These were reasons that justified compliance in terms of the interests or perspective of the person addressed. It included such utterances as these: "I don't think that you're going to accomplish the means that you intend to by taking us hostage." "This is not going to resolve your revolution." "This is not going to resolve your economic upheavals."

With listener benefit the most frequently given reason, other commonly used reasons (in order of frequency) were switch burden, social pressure, moral obligation, and power authority. Research in compliance gaining (Wheeless, Barraclough, & Stewart, 1983) predicted our categories of listener benefit, social pressure, and moral obligation. However, switch burden has never appeared in the literature, and power authority is not explicitly set out in extant typologies.

The next thing we searched for was whether people formally trained in debate would demonstrate that training in unplanned discourse. A one-way analysis of variance (ANOVA) revealed no significant ($p < .05$) differences between those trained in debate and those not so trained. Formal training is not as significant in differentiating people's spontaneous reasoning as we expected. We speculate that the effect of debate training will be manifest only in a planned interaction.

The adult data were subjected to a hierarchical clustering in order to search for systematic patterns or strategies in adult choice of reasons. Two groups emerged. Without losing sight of the substantial similarities, we observed these differences: Group 1 used significantly ($p < .05$) more switch burden and Group 2 used significantly more moral obligation. Each group had about the same number of debaters and nondebaters. Adult reasoning, then, can be defined by the repertoire of categories and subdivided by those who use a preponderance of either burden switching or moral reasons rather than by training in debate.

The adult and child data were compared in terms of mean number of reasons in each category plus mean number of utterances (see Table 1). A one-way ANOVA was used to test for differences in reason giving by age, and they were found in 8 of the 12 categories: own authority, moral obligation, social pressure, self-interest, switch burden, and mean number of utterances ($p < .05$). The Student-Newman-Kuels and Tukey multiple comparisons indicated that 3- and 5-year-olds used own authority significantly more than the other age levels; moral obligation was used significantly more by 8-year-olds. Because and other were used significantly more by 3-year-olds than any other age level. Adults used more utterances in general and significantly more listener benefit, switch burden, and social pressure reasons than any of the child age groups. Developmental changes seem clearly to influence reason giving.

Adolescents' Reasons

After studying the children and adults we concluded that we needed to consider adolescents to determine what changes occurred in those years. This study was conducted by Thomas (1988). The adolescent participants were ten 12-year-olds (mean 12;3) and ten 16-year-olds (mean 16;3).

The subjects provided data in an elicitation situation similar to that used with adults. However, the topic was changed in order to arrive at an age-appropriate situation. Participants were told that they must get a terrorist (the examiner) to release them from a school room where they were being held hostage. In this supplication the topic changed as well as the fact that here the participants were arguing for themselves and other victims.

The adolescent data are presented in Table 2. The first question was whether there was a difference in the performances of the two groups of adolescents. A 2 (age) by 9 (reason type) split-plot ANOVA (with repeated measures on the second factor) revealed no significant differences for age.

The next considerations were the types of reasons. There were no new types of reasons in this study. Own authority, power authority, and moral obligation were the most frequently used reasons listed in order of preference. Bribes, social pressure, alternative, stall, listener benefit, and switch burden were used infrequently. Closure attempt, because, and other were not used.

Among the categories used with high frequency, the preponderance of own authority was surprising. Adolescents' frequent use of own authority is comparable to the performances of the 3- and 5-year-old participants. The performances of the adolescents may reflect a return to immaturity or may indicate ego-centered adolescence (Garbarino, 1985; Lerner & Galambos, 1984). Another possible explanation is the effect of the situation. In the terrorist scene used with the adolescents, they were trying to free themselves as well as their fellow students. It seems reasonable to expect more own authority reasons when one is arguing for oneself.

Among the reasons adolescents used rarely, listener benefit becomes important. Listener benefit had appeared previously only in adults. Now it became apparent that it emerges, without necessarily being fully developed, during the adolescent

TABLE 2
Mean Number of Reasons in Each Category by 12-Year-Olds
and 16-Year-Olds and Adults

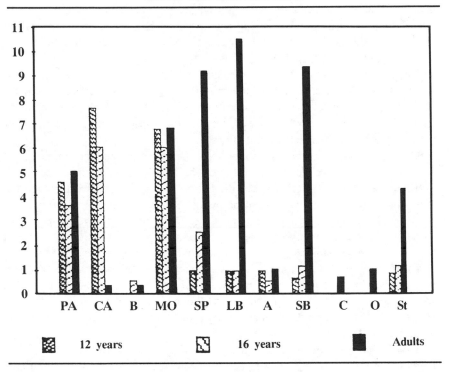

years. Flavell (1977) has stated that adolescents develop a sociocentric perspective that involves social systems role taking. Kohlberg's (1986) stages of moral development would lead us to expect those at a low level of development to concentrate on individualistic needs such as avoiding punishment, while higher levels focus on the social system or a social contract. Our adolescents used listener benefit in terms of the view of the individual, such as "You won't be in as much trouble if you let me go" (Kohlberg's Level I). Adult listener benefit reasons reflected the perspective of the social system, with propositions such as "This is not going to resolve your economic upheavals" (Kohlberg's Level II or III). Thus our research suggests that use of the social system perspective in spontaneous dialogue develops beyond 16 years.

In addition to listener benefit, major categories showing differences between adults and adolescents were social pressure and switch burden. Adolescents, like children, used these categories enough to indicate that they are in their repertoire, but there is a notable change in frequency in the adult years. No matter how you look at it, adolescents are quite different from adults.

Reasons in School Discussion Groups

As noted, one of our concerns was whether the taxonomy of reasoning strategies in the elicitation (supplication) situation was representative of reason giving in other situations. An already-existing school-connected Great Books discussion program provided a forum for studying reasons generated in spontaneous interaction among children (Bray, 1987).

Through the Junior Great Books program, children are given stories to read and a discussion group meets with a volunteer mother to discuss the stories. The mother is trained by school personnel to ask only "why" questions and to let the children respond freely. No child is required to respond, and responses are not corrected or praised. It is basically a peer discussion group.

This situation remained consistent with the supplication situations in important ways. Both situations called for the following: (a) unplanned discourse, (b) reason giving, (c) a trained adult elicitor who did not provide praise or correct any reason, and (d) normal children who could be matched in age to the initial group. The situation also changed in important ways: (a) The situation was real (not imaginary), (b) the discussion involved a peer group (not a power-supplicant dyad), and (c) academic discussion was the group's purpose (not achieving compliance).

The participants for the study were 8-9 years old and were selected so that their mean age corresponded to the mean age (8;5) of the 8-year-old group in the initial study. The discussion group contained 15 students. All students' utterances were transcribed, but 10 subjects were randomly selected in order to match the number of subjects to the initial study.

Table 3 shows the responses of the participants in this study and the original study. Several statistical methods were utilized. A t test showed no significant differences in the mean number of utterances used. The Spearman rank-order correlation was used to show if the categories used by both groups were ranked in the same positions. The results showed a high correlation between the groups: R^2 was .96, t was 2.07, with df = 18. Table 3 shows that the Mann-Whitney U Test showed a significant difference ($p < .05$ level) in only one category, moral obligation.

The moral reasons are particularly interesting. Both groups used the category more than any other, but in the academic discussion it was used significantly less than in supplication. The nature of a school setting or an intellectual discussion did not encourage greater use of moral reasons, in spite of finding incidental teaching increased types of moral reasons. The original category of moral obligation included subcategories of personal property, individual rights, group rights, species rights, sustaining life, and equity. In this study, another subcategory was added, courage/fear. While it is obvious that people might consider courage or fear an important value, we wondered why it suddenly appeared in this study and in no other. All of these responses occurred in the discussion of a story titled "The Monster Who Grew Small," which we subsequently read. In it, the words *fear,*

TABLE 3
Number of Responses of Children in Each Group

Category	Academic Argument	Supplication
Power authority	50	41
Own authority	36	22
Bribes	12	28
Moral obligation	68	105*
Social pressure	33	19
Alternative	0	7
Switch burden	0	28
Closure attempt	0	1
Because	0	1
Other	12	0
Stall	0	1
Listener benefit	4	0
Comparison/contrast	8	0

*$p < .05$.

courage, brave, and *coward* appear frequently. It became obvious that the responses were influenced by what the children had read. We reconsidered other stories and reasons, and this emphasis on courage was not apparent. It seems courage is a value that might be used only after some teaching or coaching. Courage or fear could have been a reason in any of the supplication situations, but it was not used by children, adolescents, or adults.

The academic discussion did result in two categories that had not been used by 8-year-olds. The first category was listener benefit. Listener benefit is primarily an adult category that we had seen emerging in adolescence. In this study, we found this reason used by the two eldest respondents, ages 8;11 and 9;2. Piaget and Inhelder (1969) used nonverbal tasks and concluded that children could not take the perspective of others until age 9 or 10. While social pressure, bribes, power authority, and moral obligation certainly seem to include perspective taking, only in listener benefit does the speaker clearly state the specific intent of considering the other person's position. It is now apparent that listener benefit can appear as early as 9, remains infrequently used through adolescence, and becomes a major form of adult argument.

A new category appeared here for the first time and was labeled "comparison." It was used by only one participant, although in different discussions. This seems to be a type of reason that appeared idiosyncratically. No other respondent used it.

There were five categories identified in the supplication study that were not used in the academic argument: alternative, switch burden, closure attempt, because, and stall. Of these categories, only alternative and switch burden appeared in substantial number in supplication.

Reasons by the Impaired

The reasoned discourse of the mentally retarded and autistic are considered in this section. Their reasons are compared with those of other participants.

Mentally Retarded

In the study of the language use of the mentally retarded, the most accepted pattern is to compare the performance of the mentally retarded to normals by matching the mental age (MA) of the retarded to the MA or chronological age (CA) of the normal population. Language development of the mentally retarded has been studied in this manner for years. By now it is established that the mentally retarded population displays developmental patterns that are qualitatively similar to normally developing children in syntax, semantics, and phonology. Likewise, studies have repeatedly demonstrated that mentally retarded children are deficient in various cognitive supports when compared to MA-matched normal children. Our knowledge of the language parameters of pragmatics and reasoning, however, is not so conclusive. These are relatively new areas of study.

Studies of speech acts used in spontaneous language of normal and retarded children in Brown's Stage I and Stage II reported little difference between normal and retarded children in intent or speech act categories (Coggins, Carpenter, & Owings, 1983; Owens & MacDonald, 1982). However, another study on normal preschoolers and mentally retarded children matched for language stage reported the normal children were more assertive, as evidenced by use of commands, demands, requests, and suggestions (Cimorell-Strong & Kreiling, 1981). That study also found that in normals, use of rejections, denials, and resistance increased across language stages, but in the retarded children, such negatives decreased.

While "reasoning" has been investigated in a few comparative studies, they have been nonverbal cognitive studies. One study used a verbal task (Kahn, 1976). In that study normal children and mildly and moderately retarded children with matched MAs of 7;3 to 7;6 were compared on their responses to questions about stories with moral dilemmas. Following Kohlberg's procedures, a moral maturity score was used. The conclusions were that the moderately retarded functioned at lower levels of moral maturity than the mildly retarded or normal.

Friedman, Krupski, Dawson, and Rosenberg (1977) conducted a study on the spontaneous language of retarded teenagers, and found they were successful in describing solutions to daily life problems. These authors make a strong argument that IQ scores and laboratory memory tasks do not reflect the cognitive competence required in daily language. This study was flawed, however, by its failure to include a comparison group.

Thus the literature suggested a viable investigation would be a comparative study of reason giving in spontaneous interaction by mentally retarded and normal children. The investigation of the mentally retarded was conducted by one of our collaborators (Yanagisawa, 1985).

The participants were 30 mildly to moderately retarded individuals, 10 at each MA of 3, 5, and 8 years. In the "3"-year group the mean mental age was 3;4 years (mean CA, 5;2 years), the "5"-year group had a mean MA of 5;4 (mean CA, 9;8 years), and the "8"-year group had a mean MA of 8;5 (mean CA, 15;9 years). All retarded participants had normal hearing and verbal language at least equal to their MAs. These participants were matched by mean MAs to the mean CAs of the normal children in the original study.

The study was conducted using the witch story in exact duplication of the data elicitation and data analyses chosen for the normal children. The results of the comparison (of the reasons given by frequency of occurrence) between mentally retarded participants and normal participants are presented in Table 4.

In general, the mentally retarded functioned like their normal counterparts in reason giving. The Mann-Whitney U Test was used to measure the level of confidence in the differences between the normal and mentally retarded participants. Table 4 shows that 81% of the categories (11 reason-giving and total utterances) showed no significant difference. Age-level differences between the retarded participants' reason giving were measured by one-way analysis of variance, the Scheffé test (Sharp, 1979). These results showed that because was used significantly more by the retarded 3-year-olds and moral obligation was used significantly more by retarded 8-year-olds. The same results were reported with the normal subjects. When the mentally retarded are matched using MA and language age to the normals' CAs, we would expect the reason giving to be similar, assuming the reason giving is related to mental and language abilities. These results agree with pragmatic studies of earlier-stage children that have also shown little difference in pragmatic development (Coggins et al., 1983; Owens & Mac-Donald, 1982).

We need, however, to consider differences between these populations as well. The first difference is that those in the retarded population who had the MA of 8 years differed more (in reason categories) from the normal group than the others. We can speculate that some retarded individuals plateau at different cognitive levels (Inhelder, 1968), and the giving of reasons may reflect this. For example, by the time they reach a mental age of 8, the retarded showed clear differences in their use of power authority, own authority, and bribes. They do not plateau in their use—they quit using them. We can think of two reasons to account for this. First, we expected normal children to be more assertive than the mentally retarded (Cimorell-Strong & Kreiling, 1981). Since the use of power authority, own authority, and bribes seems to require a willingness to be assertive, perhaps the absence of these reasons is explained by an expected reluctance to be assertive on the part of the mentally retarded. Second, it is possible that in order to control the behavior of the mentally retarded the persons responsible for them have systematically discouraged the use of power authority, own authority, and bribes.

The category labeled "other" yielded results that showed differences between the normal and retarded populations. In the study with normal participants, other

TABLE 4
Total Response Frequency of Mentally Retarded and Normal Participants in
Categories of Reason Giving

Category	3 Years		5 Years		8 years	
	Normal Subjects	*Mentally Retarded Subjects*	*Normal Subjects*	*Mentally Retarded Subjects*	*Normal Subjects*	*Mentally Retarded Subjects*
Power authority	10	7	56	9	41	0*
Own authority	77	71	75	17**	22	2*
Bribes	0	0	7	11	28	1*
Moral obligation	28	32	38	60	105	129
Social pressure	11	7	23	20	19	12
Alternative	0	0	6	2	7	11
Switch burden	1	9	42	51	28	22
Closure attempt	0	1	1	4	11	11
Because	51	100*	26	30	1	0
Stall	36	4	29	24	28	32
Other	29	35	7	27*	0	19***
Total Responses	210	266	310	265	279	239

$*p < .05; **p = .09; ***p = .06.$

was used for off-topic comments, comments that had no apparent relationship to the topic, such as "I lost my piggy bank." While the retarded participants had off-topic comments as well, they also used utterances that were descriptions, greetings, questions, or make-believe incidents concerning the captive or the power figure that had no discernible connection to why the witch should let the animal go. Examples included the following: "The bear's looking out the door" (3 years); "We say witch go, 'ah ah ah' " (5 years); "How old is the bear?" (8 years). These were considered a subcategory of other. Table 3 shows that at 5 years the mentally retarded used significantly more "other" comments and at 8 years the frequency approached significance ($p < .06$).

In summary, when mentally retarded individuals are matched by MA and language age to normal children by chronological age, there are more similarities than differences. The most similar is the group at 3 years. The more advanced the MA becomes, the more differences appear.

Autistic

The second group of people with disorders that we studied were high-functioning autistic adolescents. Autism is a behaviorally defined syndrome consisting of a cluster of characteristics that includes onset before 30 months, pervasive lack of responsiveness to other people, gross deficit in language development, peculiar speech patterns, bizarre responses to various aspects of the environment, and absence of delusions or hallucinations (American Psychiatric Association, 1980).

Many researchers have hypothesized that the language disorder in autism is the primary abnormality of the syndrome (Bartak, Rutter, & Cox, 1975; Churchill, 1972; Rutter, Bartak, & Newman, 1971). The group that has provided the most insight into the language impairment of autism has been the small percentage of autistic children labeled as high functioning, because this group is less governed by severe developmental delay and mental retardation.

The delay in acquisition of phonology, semantics, and syntax among the autistic has been widely reported since the 1970s. More recently, the pragmatic deficits have been investigated. One of the major connections of autism to pragmatics is the inability to relate to people and social situations in a normal way (Kanner, 1943; Rimland, 1964; Rutter et al., 1971; Wing, 1981). Bartak et al. (1975) conclude that autistic persons' language usage is characterized by concreteness, repetitiveness, recognition without analysis, and a mechanical noncommunicative approach. This usage pattern holds true even among high-functioning autistic persons. Hermelin (1982) states that the autistic child who develops good language skills rarely uses language for sharing and exchanging ideas. Baker, Cantwell, Rutter, and Bartak (1976) state that the language of the autistic is ambiguous, contextually inappropriate, or uninterpretable. Others have found among the autistic an inability to form abstractions necessary in using language for symbolic or conceptual purposes (Ricks & Wing, 1975; Scheerer, Rothman, & Goldstein, 1945). However, Needleman, Ritvo, and Freeman (1980) found that a significant number of verbal autistic children use language communicatively. These investigators studied interaction between autistic individuals and a linguist and analyzed the spontaneous requests, expressions of needs, and comments to others. This study suggests that the high-functioning autistic might respond in a reason-giving task.

The reason-giving study of autistic adolescents that was part of our research program was conducted by Thomas (1988). The participants were three high-functioning verbal autistic adolescents ranging in age from 12 to 16 years. All participants had intellectual functioning within the normal range (IQ = 85-115).

The autistic adolescents were presented a discourse situation exactly like that presented to normal adolescents: the terrorist holding students hostage in a school. The comparison of the mean number of reasons in each category of the normal and autistic adolescents is displayed in Table 5. It is important to remember that there were 10 participants in each normal group and only 3 autistic participants. However, of all the ways of analyzing the data, this seemed to be the best way to present the results.

Our autistic participants were able to respond in the supplication situation even though our research review suggested that they would be limited in social functions. Even more remarkable is the fact that our task required unplanned interaction

TABLE 5
Mean Number of Reasons in Each Category by Normal 12-Year-Old, Normal
16-Year-Olds, and Autistic Adolescents

Category	12-Year-Olds	16-Year-Olds	Austistic Adolescents
Power authority	4.6	3.6	1.6
Own authority	7.7	6.1	8.0
Bribes	0.0	0.6	3.0
Moral obligation	6.8	6.1	2.0
Social pressure	1.0	2.6	1.3
Listener benefit	1.0	1.0	0.3
Alternative	1.0	0.6	1.0
Switch burden	0.7	1.2	3.3
Closure attempt	0.0	0.0	0.0
Because	0.0	0.0	0.0
Other	0.0	0.0	3.7
Stall	0.9	1.2	1.0
Mean number of categories	5.5	7.2	6.0

in an imaginary, hypothetical, and abstract communication situation when the literature had predicted impairment among the autistic in abstraction and symbolic, conceptual functioning. We do not claim, on the basis of our results, that predictions of impairment are incorrect. We do claim, however, that these high-functioning autistic adolescents were able to understand an abstract, hypothetical situation and give reasons even when the reasons they gave were rejected.

The mean number of utterances for the autistic group did not vary significantly from the mean number used by normal adolescents. If the autistic participants had been uncommunicative or remote, this result would not have been the case. It is likewise surprising to note that they used a similar variety of categories, including emphasis on own authority and use of listener benefit and switch burden, both defined as mature reason giving.

There were obvious differences, however. Two categories were quite different. Moral obligation was used considerably less by the autistic participants and the distribution of types of moral reason used varied substantially. Normal participants used individual rights, group rights, species rights, sustaining life, and equity. Autistic adolescents used only individual rights and group rights. Autistic adolescents relied on what they perceived to be their rights or those of their peer group. They gave no recognition of the rights of society. Both Kohlberg (1986) and Piaget (1967) have discussed social rules consequences as advanced stages of reasoning development.

The category of other showed decreasing frequency with maturity in children, was not used at all by adolescents and rarely used by adults. The autistic adolescents, on the other hand, used off-topic, bizarre comments such as "I will sing 'Beat it.' " Normal children and the mentally retarded also had off-topic comments, however.

French Children's Reasons

Comparison of language knowledge and use in differing cultures is not only of academic interest; it leads to better intercultural understanding and communication as well. Each culture has rules that govern social interaction (Coulthard, 1978), and little is known about how these rules may be similar or different. Givon (1985) uses observations of Ute Indians and the Spanish population in the southwestern United States to point out that their language use in social interaction is quite different from that of the White middle class. Clark (1985) discusses a variety of studies on the acquisition of syntactic structures and spatial and temporal terms in French. She points out that there has been only brief mention of the discourse itself. As a consequence, French discourse strategies remain uninvestigated.

A few studies (although now somewhat dated) mention characteristics of the French culture that might suggest effects on oral reasoning. French children are expected to be passive (de Gramont, 1969), to be silent in the presence of adults (Coulthard, 1978), and to cultivate personal thoughts and feelings in private (Bishop, 1969). In general, the French are characterized as not believing in the basic goodness of people, although they do have a strong reverence for authority (Sharman, 1984). In France, teachers are authority figures who punish children for answering incorrectly (Scarangello, 1967).

The study of the French children was an exact replica of the initial supplication study using the witch story.[3] The participants were 20 normal French children; half were 4-year-olds and half were 8-year-olds. The children lived in Paris suburbs.

Before we discuss the types of reasons used by the French children, we must explain a remarkable difference. Participants volunteered from a pool of suitable children. The person (witch) who interacted with them was an adult who was a fluent speaker of French as a second language. Another adult who was present was native to France. Despite having volunteered, 30 children sat throughout the entire process and either said nothing or used stalls such as "I don't know." They did not leave, cry, express fear, or act disinterested. They listened. They said nothing. This response never occurred in any of the studies in the United States.

It seems most likely that the major difference between French and American children is the orientation of the French toward authority, silent children, the "right answer," and suspicion of others, while Americans reward children who speak up and respond to what they are asked. However, in retrospect, the fact that there were two adults present could have created part of the problem. In a pilot study, we found that the French native was leading the children with reasons and was asking questions that led to certain responses, instead of just asking, "Why?" The decision was made to have the trained examiner who spoke French as a second language do the eliciting and have the native present to reduce the mistrust of outsiders, to help establish rapport, and to handle any problems. As we study other cultures, we will

TABLE 6
A Comparison of the Responses of American and French Children

Category	4-Year-Olds		8-Year-Olds	
	American	French	American	French
Power authority	61	17	41	60
Own authority	44	12	22	22
Bribes	1	0	28	5
Moral obligation	60	86	105	43
Social pressure	17	0	19	3
Alternative	4	9	7	1
Switch burden	30	1	28	8
Closure attempt	6	0	1	1
Because	14	26	1	0
Stall	27	64	28	24
Other	19	8	0	5
Methods query		2	0	17
Total	283	225	280	189

spend all the time necessary to train the native person and have only that person present.

Only those who actually interacted with the witch were included in the data. Table 6 shows the comparison of the French and American children. The problems we had in eliciting responses rendered statistical analysis moot. The differences shown in the table, however, plus the 30 children who did not talk, point to the conclusion that French children are reluctant communicators or that Americans are, comparatively, loquacious.

In terms of the reasoning categories, the French children used all the same types of reasons as the American children, with one exception. Table 6 shows that the new category, labeled "methods query," appeared at both ages but increased remarkably after the children were in school. Utterances in this category appeared at various positions in the discourse and included comments such as "How do I give reasons?" "One can find it in several tries, the reason?" "You have to guess and when one guesses . . .?" Power authority increased remarkably by 8 years, but switch burden was rarely used. These results reflect the comments in the literature (Scarangello, 1967; Sharman, 1984) that the French have a respect for authority and children are punished in school for answering questions incorrectly. One other category, own authority, increased in the French children between 4 and 8 years. A possible explanation is that with French children encouraged to remain silent, own authority may take time to become salient.

By 8 years there is a decrease in moral obligation, alternative, and stall. The decrease in moral obligation is notable. The subcategories of moral obligation included individual rights, group rights, species rights, sustaining life, and equity.

Recalling the reports that the French are ill disposed toward people (Sharman, 1984), this may directly affect the use of these moral reasons. Furthermore, there were no other types of moral reasons included.

The comparison of the developmental changes between 4 and 8 years in American children and 4 and 8 years in French children revealed opposite results. Power authority reasons decrease with age in American children and increase with age in French children; own authority decreases in American children and increases in French; and moral obligation increases in American children and decreases in French. Other cultural differences noted are that social pressure and switch burden are commonly used categories for American children and rarely used categories for French children. Children acquire language that is in the environment. While the repertoire is basically the same, the frequency of use is not. In both cultures the conspicuous change that occurs between 4 and 8 years is that the children go to school. It seems likely that schools in the two cultures are working in opposite directions in terms of what is supported. These cultural differences in reason giving could have serious impact on cross-cultural communication. This study is only a beginning, but it suggests the need to compare discourse strategies across various cultures for practical as well as intellectual purposes.

CONCLUSIONS

At this stage in the research program some conclusions seem justified. We will set them out as conservatively as possible, but we will not hesitate to describe what we have come to believe during the course of this work that has extended for almost 10 years.

We claim that we have developed a new approach to the study of reason giving. No other research of which we are aware has captured spontaneous discourse within a reason-giving situation and analyzed it from a grounded theoretical posture with no explicit preconceptions. One consequence of this new approach is the data base of actual unplanned discourse from many participants. We have found reasoned discourse where, predictably, with participants such as very young children, the retarded, and the autistic, it should not have appeared. A second consequence of this new approach is the development of data-generated categories. We have worked inductively building this taxonomy, without being driven by prior theories.

The category system or taxonomy developed from our studies has proven to be discrete and stable. While it is a living thing, constantly responding to new data, its essence has been tested in both dyadic and group interaction across situations involving efforts to free others or oneself from the grip of a powerful party and efforts to discuss and understand a story that has been read in common with fellow students.

The category system has been tested across ages ranging from 3 through adolescence to adulthood. It has described the reason giving of American children and adults both sophisticated in argumentation and those untrained, French children, and those diagnosed as either mentally retarded or autistic. We claim, therefore, that we have produced a taxonomy that is sensitive to a broad spectrum of spontaneous reasoning communication.

Oral reasoning in unplanned discourse may be defined as the use of *authority* (your own or a powerful other's), *values* assumed to be shared (moral, social, or bribes), and the *interests* of the interlocutor (listener benefit, switch burden, or alternatives). The definition of reasoning is derived from the common core of reasons given by all participants.

This definition is distinguished by its contrast to traditional characterizations of reasoning, logic, or persuasion. We find that the scope of reasoning is broader than the tradition would have suggested. While moral appeal and perspective taking were expected, power authority, switch burden, alternative, social pressure, own authority, and bribes were not. Some, if not all, of these unexpected strategies seem related to reasoning in an ongoing interaction, in contrast to the static models traditionally advanced.

Further, nothing in our data gives support to the value of formal logic as the rationale of spontaneous reason giving. There was no evidence, however subtle, of our participants' communications being directed by anything that resembled the rules of logic as traditionally described.

Finally, in the various taxonomies of compliance gaining, there are persuasion strategies that did not appear in our discourse at all, and we found people using power authority and switch burden, which do not appear in compliance-gaining taxonomies. Furthermore, the role of moral obligation reasons is more prominent in our reason-giving data than it is in the compliance-gaining or persuasion literature. We believe reason giving is not a completely different process from persuasion, but when people perceive themselves in a reason-giving situation, they tend to select a cluster of categories that makes use of those we have identified as reasoning.

We have drawn conclusions on the development of communicative competence in unplanned oral reasoning. We will now discuss both the pattern of development evidenced in our data and the changes that occur over time. While it has been traditional to view language development as a series of transitory stages that are replaced as one becomes more competent, we are led to accept Ochs's (1979) hypothesis that a retention model provides a better explanation. Ochs uses bits of data from various sources to argue that retention of strategies would best be demonstrated in unplanned discourse. The idea of retention is that development is characterized by overlapping patterns in which previously developed strategies coexist with newly developed ones and thus are retained as one becomes more competent. Oral reasoning in unplanned discourse clearly demonstrates a retention model. The strategies developed by 4 years of age are retained throughout childhood, adolescence, and adulthood.

While the overall theoretical model that explains discourse reasoning development is retention, we can also point to changes over time. At 3 years of age, and probably before, children can participate in reason giving, but they use few categories and demonstrate their immaturity in the use of "because" alone. This usage may represent simple knowledge of the syntactic marker that often accompanies reasons or it may be a bona fide reason for young children.

The important age for reason giving is 4. At this age most of the categories are present and there is little change in distribution until 8 years, when the use of moral reasons peaks. At about 9 years, listener benefit reasons emerge and remain infrequently used through adolescence. The next real change comes in the adult years, and the difference is not in the repertoire of categories but in the types of reasons used most frequently. Adults most frequently use listener benefit, switch burden, and social pressure.

To argue that oral reasoning is completely developmental would mean that human beings would progress merely by virtue of increasing age or maturity. We believe there is much more involved. Oral reasoning in unplanned discourse demonstrates language use that is dependent in part on interaction with the environment. There are clearly personal styles in frequency of reasons chosen that result in strategies that cross ages and separate groups of adults. And one child introduced a category no other person used. Retarded children decreased frequency of certain strategies they had already acquired and in which normal children did not decrease. An academic discussion resulted in a greater frequency of use of one category and a new subcategory of reason that had been given in a story children read. Adolescents arguing for themselves as well as for others changed the frequency of use of a category. The French and American children showed markedly different frequencies of reason types chosen, and French children presented us with a new reason type. In all these cases, environmental influences seem obvious.

In the search for what aspects of the environment influence oral reasoning, some speculations are possible. Personal style might be influenced by individual personality or by prior interactions with parents, peers, and significant others. The different strategy groups indicate that some people tend to use certain categories of reasons more frequently, while others choose different clusters to use frequently. The repertoire of reasons was constant, but the frequency of use varied. It seems likely that people would tend to emphasize the types of reasons they think are salient or the types of reasons they hear most frequently. It is also probable that speakers would emphasize the types of reasons their listeners usually respond to positively. An interesting area for further research might be to explore what types of reasons listeners are most likely to respond to negatively or positively.

One type of environmental influence that might be important is education. Wilson (1986) raises the issue of what would happen to the development of types of reasons if children were not "firmly and decisively taught otherwise" (p. 223). Since our research began with preschool children, we have data relevant to that question. Only one type of reason appeared to have been instilled by education.

This was the courage/fear subcategory that appeared in the Great Books discussion. Overall, we can point to very little that education does to different types of reasons. The one new reason added primarily in adult years was explained developmentally, and adults trained in debate did not differ from adults without such training.

While types of reasons are not influenced, the frequency with which certain reasons are used is likely influenced by schooling. The decreasing responses of the oldest retarded participants and the opposite direction in the pattern of change over time in the French and American children strongly implicate the schools. While education may influence the frequency of types of reasons, the influence of the culture certainly seems to be an environmental factor to consider. The children in the French culture used one type of reason the children in the American culture did not use. Variations in other cultures might be predictable. While culture is relevant, the changes in frequency noted in the American and French children and in the retarded population may be due to other environmental influences.

Cognition is another aspect of development. Cognition and language are reciprocal in some manner. While this is a discourse study and not a cognitive study, one aspect of cognition may be inferred. Piaget and Inhelder (1969) specify that, cognitively, perspective taking is not present until 9 or 10 years, and we found the stating of listener benefit reasons to occur first at 9 years of age. Delia and his associates have reported perspective taking to relate to cognitive complexity (Delia & Clark, 1977; Hale & Delia, 1976). Other possible cognitive inferences may be made from the prominent use of "other" comments by young children and by the retarded and the autistic participants, and from the limited use of moral reasons by the retarded and the autistic.

Of course, this investigation is not complete. Further research might specify what reasons are the most salient, most accepted, or judged most impressive by listeners. The data could be studied from a cognitive perspective, or cognitive data could be compared to discourse data. Research with other populations with language problems and research with other cultures might yield valuable results.

APPENDIX

Power authority: These reasons include propositions that involve the use of some basis for the claim outside the speaker. The word *claim* is used to indicate the thesis (e.g., freeing an animal or hostage). The word *power* is used to demonstrate that the person indicates the outside source has greater strength than he or she does. Subcategories include threat, action threat, desire, and law.

Own authority: These reasons rely on the speaker's ethos as the basis of the claim. Subcategories include threat, action threat, desire, and demand.

Bribes: These include utterances that state an offer of a specific positive desirable reward to the addressee in return for granting the claim. Subcategories include tangible and social bribes.

Moral obligation: These reasons take the form of a proposition involving a value that would justify granting the claim. Subcategories include personal property, individual rights, group rights, species rights, sustaining life, equity, and courage/fear.

Social pressure: These reasons include propositions that provide justification for the claim on the basis of perceived norms of a society and imply the results of compliance or noncompliance with those norms. Subcategories include general, positive personal, negative personal, positive group, and negative group.

Alternative: These reasons include propositions that present a different approach that might serve as a negotiated compromise of the two positions.

Switch burden: In the tradition of argumentation, these propositions include charges or challenges to get another person to reason in order to debate that reason. Subcategories include invitation to switch and assertion to switch.

Closure attempt: These include proposals, in declarative or interrogative form, for the addressee to accept the claim. These efforts of closure may appear at various places in the discourse and thus do not necessarily close the topic.

Listener benefit: These reasons specifically assert the interests or perspective of the addressee.

Comparison/contrast: These propositions suggest similarity or differences of the animate or inanimate (as in an analogy or metaphor).

Methods query: These propositions are utterances that ask how to proceed or what to say. These utterances appear at various places in the discourse, and do not come during the regular explanation period.

Because: These reasons involve the use of the single word *because*, not followed by any proposition.

Stall: These propositions include efforts to withdraw from the discourse or insertions to delay.

Other: Utterances that are off the topic are coded here.

NOTES

1. Willbrand (1981, 1982) discusses how the intent to give reasons is indicated overall by responses to requests for reasons and by specific utterances such as, "I already gave you some reasons" or "Wait. I'm thinking of a reason." Rieke (1980) reports that after the discourse was collected, adults were questioned about their intent. All adults reported they were giving reasons or were being reasonable.

2. Our research is an investigation of discourse reasoning, not perspective taking. For a reason to be labeled "listener benefit," the speaker actually had to state such in the discourse. Clearly, many of the reasons we coded in other categories would be similar to what Delia and Clark (1977) report as listener adaptation in communication in their developmental study of changes between 6 and 12 years of age. In general, their notion of developmental changes would be supported by our research. However, they tested listener adaptation by asking children to give a single message to different people in pictures. There was no real or simulated discourse interaction. In a related study, Hale and Delia (1976) reported college students imagining what the other person was thinking or how they were viewing the situation. But the researchers asked specifically for that information, and they did not use discourse. Thus our data compare to theirs in only the most general way, and we provide new information from quite a different viewpoint.

3. The French study was conducted by our research associate, Nancy Guillerm.

REFERENCES

Allwood, J. (1986). Logic and spoken interaction. In T. Myers, K. Brown, & B. McGonigle (Eds.), *Reasoning and discourse processes* (pp. 67-94). Orlando, FL: Academic Press.

American Psychiatric Association. (1980). *Diagnostic and statistic manual of mental disorders* (3rd ed.). Washington, DC: Author.

Austin, J. L. (1962). *How to do things with words.* Cambridge, MA: Harvard University Press.

Baker, L., Cantwell, D. P., Rutter, M., & Bartak, L. (1976). Language and autism. In E. R. Ritvo (Ed.), *Autism: Diagnosis, current research and management* (pp. 121-149). New York: Spectrum.

Baker, W., & Derwing, B. (1982). Response coincidence analysis as evidence for language acquisition strategies. *Applied Psycholinguistics, 3,* 193-221.

Bartak, L., Rutter, M., & Cox, A. (1975). A comparative study of infantile autism and specific developmental receptive language disorder. *British Journal of Psychiatry, 126,* 127-145.

Benoit, P. (1981). Production of rules for winning arguments. In G. Ziegelmueller & J. Rhodes (Eds.), *Dimensions of argument* (pp. 624-642). Annandale, VA: Speech Communication Association.

Benoit, P. (1983). Extended arguments in children's discourse. *Journal of the American Forensic Association, 20,* 72-89.

Bishop, C. H. (1969). *Here is France.* New York: Farrar, Straus & Giroux.

Brainerd, C. (1978). *Piaget's theory of intelligence.* Englewood Cliffs, NJ: Prentice-Hall.

Bray, J. N. (1987). *Reason giving in children's academic arguments.* Unpublished master's thesis, University of Utah, Salt Lake City.

Brown, R., & Herrnstein, R. (1974). *Psychology.* Boston: Little, Brown.

Churchill, D. W. (1972). The relation of infantile autism and early childhood schizophrenia to developmental language disorders of childhood. *Journal of Autism and Childhood Schizophrenia, 8,* 221-230.

Cimorell-Strong, J., & Kreiling, I. L. (1981, November). *Speech act behavior in normal and mentally handicapped children.* Paper presented at the annual meeting of the American Speech-Language-Hearing Association, Los Angeles.

Clark, E. (1985). The acquisition of romance, with special reference to French. In D. Slobin (Ed.), *The crosslinguistic study of language acquisition: Vol. 1. The data* (pp. 687-782). Hillsdale, NJ: Lawrence Erlbaum.

Coggins, T. E., Carpenter, R. L., & Owings, N. O. (1983). Examining early intentional communication in Down's syndrome and nonretarded children. *British Journal of Disorders of Communication, 18,* 98-106.

Congalton, J. (1988). *The history of early 20th century argumentation theory and practice.* Unpublished doctoral dissertation, University of Utah, Salt Lake City.

Coulthard, M. (1978). *An introduction to discourse analysis.* London: Longman.

Cox, J. R., & Willard, C. A. (Eds.). (1982). *Advances in argumentation theory and research.* Carbondale: Southern Illinois University Press.

de Gramont, S. (1969). *The French-portrait of a people.* New York: G. P. Putnam's Sons.

Delia, J., & Clark, R. (1977). Cognitive complexity, social perception and the development of listener-adapted communication in six, eight, ten, and twelve year old boys. *Communication Monographs, 44,* 326-345.

Fisher, W. (1987). *Human communication as narration: Toward a philosophy of reason, value, and action.* Columbia: University of South Carolina Press.

Flavell, J. H. (1977). *Cognitive development.* Englewood Cliffs, NJ: Prentice-Hall.

Friedman, M., Krupski, A., Dawson, E. T., & Rosenberg, P. (1977). Metamemory and mental retardation. In P. Mittler (Ed.), *Research to practice in mental retardation: Education and training* (Vol. 2, pp. 99-104). Baltimore: University Park Press.

Garbarino, J. (1985). *Adolescent development: An ecological perspective.* Columbus, OH: Charles E. Merrill.

Givon, T. (1985). Function, structure and language acquisition. In D. Slobin (Ed.), *The crosslinguistic study of language acquisition: Vol. 2. Theoretical issues* (pp. 1005-1028). Hillsdale, NJ: Lawrence Erlbaum.

Hale, C., & Delia, J. (1976). Cognitive complexity and social perspective-taking. *Communication Monographs, 43*, 195-203.

Hample, D. (1986). Argumentation and the unconscious. *Journal of the American Forensic Association, 23*, 82-95.

Haslett, B. (1983). Preschoolers' communicative strategies in gaining compliance from peers: A developmental study. *Quarterly Journal of Speech, 69*, 84-99.

Hermelin, B. (1982). Thoughts and feelings. *Australian Autism Review, 1*, 10-19.

Inhelder, B. (1968). *The diagnosis of reasoning in the mentally retarded.* New York: John Day.

Jackson, S., Jacobs, S., Burrell, N., & Allen, M. (1986). Characterizing ordinary argument: Substantive and methodological issues. *Journal of the American Forensic Association, 23*, 42-57.

Jacobs, S., Allen, M., Jackson, S., & Petrel, D. (1985). Can ordinary arguers recognize a valid conclusion if it walks up and bites them on the butt? In C. J. Cox, M. Sillars, & G. Walker (Eds.), *Argument and social practice.* (pp. 665-674). Annandale, VA: Speech Communication Association.

Jacobs, S., & Jackson, S. (1982). Conversational argument: A discourse analytic approach. In R. Cox & C. Willard (Eds.), *Advances in argumentation theory and research* (pp. 205-237). Carbondale: Southern Illinois University Press.

Kahn, J. V. (1976). Moral and cognitive development of moderately retarded, mildly retarded and nonretarded individuals. *American Journal of Mental Deficiency, 81*, 209-214.

Kanner, L. (1943). Autistic disturbances of affective contact. *Nervous Child, 2*, 217-250.

Kohlberg, L. (1986). A current statement on theoretical issues. In S. Modgil & C. Modgil (Eds.), *Lawrence Kohlberg consensus and controversy* (pp. 485-546). Philadelphia: Falmer.

Lerner, R., & Galambos, N. (Eds.). (1984). *Experiencing adolescents: A source book for parents, teachers and adolescents.* New York: Garland.

Modgil, S., & Modgil, C. (Eds.). (1986). *Lawrence Kohlberg consensus and controversy.* Philadelphia: Falmer.

Myers, T., Brown, K., & McGonigle, B. (Eds.). (1986). *Reasoning and discourse processes.* Orlando, FL: Academic Press.

Needleman, R., Ritvo, E., & Freeman, B. (1980). Objectively defined linguistic parameters in children with autism and other developmental disabilities. *Journal of Autism and Developmental Disorders, 10*, 389-398.

Nelson, K. (1986). *Event knowledge.* Hillsdale, NJ: Lawrence Erlbaum.

Ochs, E. (1979). Planned and unplanned discourse. In T. Givon (Ed.), *Syntax and semantics: Discourse and syntax* (pp. 51-80). New York: Academic Press.

O'Keefe, B., & Benoit, P. (1982). Children's arguments. In J. Cox & C. Willard (Eds.), *Advances in argumentation theory and research* (pp. 154-183). Carbondale: Southern Illinois University Press.

O'Keefe, D. J. (1977). Two concepts of argument. *Journal of the American Forensic Association, 13*, 121-128.

O'Keefe, D. J. (1982). The concepts of argument and arguing. In J. R. Cox & C. A. Willard (Eds.), *Advances in argumentation theory and research* (pp. 3-23). Carbondale: Southern Illinois University Press.

Owens, R. E., & MacDonald, J. D. (1982). Communicative uses of the early speech of nondelayed and Down's syndrome children. *American Journal of Mental Deficiency, 86*, 503-510.

Perelman, C., & Olbrechts-Tyteca, L. (1971). *The new rhetoric.* Notre Dame, IN: University of Notre Dame Press.

Piaget, J. (1967). *Six psychological studies.* New York: Random House.

Piaget, J., & Inhelder, B. (1969). *The psychology of the child.* New York: Basic Books.

Ricks, D. M., & Wing, L. (1975). Language, communication, and the use of symbols in normal and autistic children. *Journal of Autism and Childhood Schizophrenia, 5*, 191-221.

Rieke, R. D. (1980, December). *Modern reasoning theory for communication.* Paper presented at the East-West Communication Conference, Honolulu.

Rimland, B. (1964). *Infantile autism: The syndrome and its implications for a neural theory of behavior.* New York: Appleton-Crofts.

Rutter, M., Bartak, L., & Newman, S. (1971). A central disorder of cognition and language. In M. Rutter (Ed.), *Infantile autism: Concepts, characteristics, and treatment* (pp. 148-172). Edinburgh, Scotland: Churchill Livingstone.

Scarangello, A. (1967). *American education through foreign eyes.* New York: Hobbs, Dorman.

Scheerer, M., Rothman, E., & Goldstein, K. (1945). A case of "idiot savant." *Psychological Monographs, 4.*

Searle, J. (1969). *Speech acts: An essay in the philosophy of language.* New York: Cambridge University Press.

Sharman, F. (1984). *Coping with France.* Oxford: Basil Blackwell.

Sharp, V. F. (1979). *Statistics for social sciences.* Boston: Little, Brown.

Thomas, R. J. (1988). *An investigation of the reason giving performances of autistic adolescents and normal adolescents.* Unpublished master's thesis, University of Utah, Salt Lake City.

Toulmin, S. (1958). *The uses of argument.* Cambridge, MA: University Press.

Toulmin, S. (1972). *Human understanding.* Princeton, NJ: Princeton University Press.

Trapp, R. (1983). Generic characteristics of argumentation in everyday discourse. In D. Zarefsky, M. Sillars, & J. Rhodes (Eds.), *Argument in transition: Proceedings of the Third Summer Conference on Argumentation* (pp. 516-530). Annandale, VA: Speech Communication Association.

Trapp, R. (1986). The role of disagreement in interactional argument. *Journal of the American Forensic Association, 23*, 23-41.

Wheeless, L., Barraclough, R., & Stewart, R. (1983). Compliance-gaining and power in persuasion. In R. Bostrom (Ed.), *Communication yearbook 7* (pp. 105-145). Beverly Hills, CA: Sage.

Willbrand, M. L. (1981). The other witchy-poos won't like you. In M. Henderson (Ed.), *1980 mid-American linguistics conference papers* (pp. 505-516). Lawrence: University of Kansas Press.

Willbrand, M. L. (1982, November). *Contributions from linguistics for the study of argumentation: Competence, speech acts and discourse.* Position paper for argumentation seminar presented at the annual meeting of the Speech Communication Association.

Willbrand, M. L. (1987). A pragmatic perspective for reason giving across ages and situations. In F. van Eemeren, R. Grootendorst, A. Blair, & C. Willard (Eds.), *Argumentation: Perspectives and approaches* (pp. 195-204). Dordrecht, The Netherlands: Forbis.

Willbrand, M. L., & Rieke, R. (1986). Reason giving in children's supplicatory compliance gaining. *Communication Monographs, 53*, 47-60.

Wilson, J. (1986). First steps in moral education: Understanding and using reasons. In. S. Modgil & C. Modgil (Eds.), *Lawrence Kohlberg consensus and controversy* (pp. 223-242). Philadelphia: Falmer.

Wing, L. (1981). Language, social, and cognitive impairments in autism and severe mental retardation. *Journal of Autism and Developmental Disorders, 11*(1), 31-44.

Yanagisawa, E. M. (1985). *A comparative study of reason-giving by mentally retarded and normal children.* Unpublished master's thesis, University of Utah, Salt Lake City.

Reasoning as a Critical Thinking Skill

DONALD F. TIBBITS
Central Missouri State University

N EW ground has certainly been broken by Willbrand and Rieke concerning strategies of reasoning in spontaneous discourse. By setting aside assumptions that reasoning must be logically relevant, cognitively relevant, disagreement relevant, or planned, they have offered the reader a study of unplanned discourse that captures "what is being said for the first time with no preparation or forethought of either content or structure" (p. 416). Their method of collecting the data, through a series of discourse studies from which they would develop their theory, was also novel in that it allowed the subjects to respond to a request for reasons on a subject for which they had received no prior warning. In this way, the investigators obtained unplanned reasoning in spontaneous discourse.

Previous research methods have not accomplished reason giving through this type of discourse. For example, in their Test of Problem Solving, Zachman, Jorgensen, Huisingh, and Barrett (1984) presented pictured situations and told subjects about the situation before asking for reasons; Wiig and Secord (1985) also presented a specific situation to their subjects and, in addition, supplied two plausible and two implausible reasons from which their subjects were asked to restate the two plausible ones. Willbrand and Rieke have gone a step further by developing a taxonomy of reason categories, whereas other researchers have ended their inquiries by being content to report that subjects at various age levels either could or could not give reasons.

"Reason giving," as defined by Willbrand and Rieke, fits well into current research in the area of critical thinking. The major thrust of this commentary is to examine the research of Willbrand and Rieke in relation to the critical thinking research that has flourished during the last decade. What follows is an attempt to tie Willbrand and Rieke's research to the broader context of critical thinking. This

Correspondence and requests for reprints: Donald F. Tibbits, Department of Speech—Language Pathology and Audiology, Central Missouri State University, Warrensburg, MO 64093.

Communication Yearbook 14, pp. 441-444

attempt will undoubtedly cast additional insight for the reader's consideration on the topic of reasoned discourse.

REASONING AND CRITICAL THINKING

A vast amount of information has accumulated during the last decade in the area of thinking in general and in the area of critical thinking in particular (Costa, 1985; Heiman & Slomianko, 1985; Link, 1985; Maxwell, 1983; Paul, 1987; Perkins, Lochhead, & Bishop, 1987; Presseisen, 1986; Segal, Chipman, & Glasar, 1985; Whimbey & Lochhead, 1979). Critical thinking is one of the various kinds of thinking that have been influenced during the last few decades by the subject of cognitive psychological research. Presseisen (1985) states that "the current emphasis on thinking skills emphasizes *reasoning* as a major cognitive focus" (p. 43).

Critical thinking is viewed as a higher-order cognitive process involving the basic thinking skills to analyze arguments and to generate insight into particular meanings and interpretations. According to Costa (1985), critical thinking relies heavily on the processes of vertical thinking (thinking that is logical and straight-forward) and divergent thinking (thinking that is required to generate many different responses to the same problem). Adler (1987) asserts that reasoning, as a cognitive process, is rapid, nonconscious, and ubiquitous in revealing that it underlies such pervasive activities as comprehension, perception, and the explanation of action. His epistemological approach to critical thinking instruction emphasizes the importance of giving reasons and of being open to objections. Sternberg (1985) has described three taxonomies of critical thinking skills, all of which stress the importance of both deductive and inductive reasoning skills.

Strategic reasoning is also placed by Costa (1985) under the category of thinking strategies, which he defines as the tactics people employ when faced with situations for which resolutions or answers are not immediately known. Reasons have also been referred to as the notable products of thinking (Presseisen, 1985).

Presseisen (1986) includes the development of cohesive, logical reasoning patterns in her definition of critical thinking. Nickerson (1981) states that reasoning is one of the basic abilities that constitute thinking. Lipman (1985) argues that thinking involves reasoning in various ways. Critical thinking involves both dispositions and abilities, according to Ennis (1985), in which he views the seeking of reasons as a disposition and the giving of reasons as an ability. Researchers such as these make it clear that reasoning and thinking are directly linked together. The definition of *reason giving* as stated by Willbrand and Rieke appears to place their work within the child's broader cognitive domain.

Willbrand and Rieke's taxonomy contains 13 different types of reasons, and the majority (10) of these were observed in children between the ages of 3 and 8. This finding supports the previous position that, if reasoning is a critical thinking skill, the development of reasoning begins early as an overall process and that age simply adds the dimension of sophistication or refinement to its use in the cognitive system as revealed through the linguistic channel. Sadler and Whimbey (1985) state that thinking originates and develops through the verbalizing of one's experiences. Lowery (1985), who feels that there is a biological foundation for all human thinking, states that thinking capabilities develop sequentially over time. The developmental changes reported by Willbrand and Rieke in terms of age appear to be a significant addition to what we know about the sophistication and refinement demonstrated as a result of age in other areas of both language and thinking. Apparently, frequency of occurrence within the taxonomy of reason giving allows for differences to occur within a given area, but the given area remains relatively stable over time.

In addition, the inclusion of two groups typically described in research as nonnormal language learners (mentally retarded and autistic subjects) allows the investigators to develop their theory further and, at the same time, to add a significant dimension to previous investigations of the linguistic and cognitive abilities (or the lack of them) in these two groups. It may even lead to remedial strategies: Link (1985) feels that, by having students verbalize reasons, one may expect an increase in their abilities to verbalize their thinking, which he feels is a goal of any cognitive skills program.

Finally, the data from Willbrand and Rieke's French subjects are presented with carefully considered speculations that may prove to be significant in terms of multicultural issues in both language and cognition. In particular, the data suggest some rather provoking inquiry into the possible effects of educational practices on multicultural differences. This speculation is also important if one accepts the theoretical positions of researchers such as Feuerstein (1979) that critical thinking can be taught. Willbrand and Rieke's taxonomy could provide sequential steps in the development and teaching of reasoning skills in children. Because of the emphasis on the teaching of critical thinking, several researchers have suggested specific strategies for such endeavors (Beyer, 1987; Chance, 1986; Heiman & Slomianko, 1987; Tiedt, Carlson, Howard, & Watanabe, 1989).

SUMMARY

The Willbrand and Rieke claim that "we have developed a new approach to the study of reason giving" (p. 433) is supported. Spontaneous discourse, although time-consuming and tedious to collect, appears to capture the essence of reason giving and, though at times it may appear to be less precise and more subjective than previous research methodology, it does yield the richness of reasoning ability as this is demonstrated in oral discourse. The results of this richness are evident in the taxonomy built by Willbrand and Rieke without their "being driven by prior theories" (p. 433). They have thus provided a category system that is not only discrete and stable but also is sensitive to change over a broad spectrum, based on frequency of use of strategies within a system rather than systemwide changes in the process of reasoning.

REFERENCES

Adler, J. E. (1987). On resistance to critical thinking. In D. N. Perkins, J. Lochhead, & J. C. Bishop (Eds.), *Thinking: The second international conference.* Hillsdale, NJ: Laurence Erlbaum.

Beyer, B. K. (1987). *Practical strategies for the teaching of thinking.* Boston: Allyn & Bacon.

Chance, P. (1986). *Thinking in the classroom: A survey of programs.* New York: Teachers College Press, Columbia University.

Costa, A. L. (Ed.). (1985). *Developing minds: A resource book for teaching thinking.* Alexandria, VA: Association for Supervision and Curriculum Development.

Ennis, R. H. (1985). Goals for a critical thinking curriculum. In A. L. Costa (Ed.), *Developing minds: A resource book for teaching thinking.* Alexandria, VA: Association for Supervision and Curriculum Development.

Feuerstein, R. (1979). *The dynamic assessment of retarded performers.* Baltimore: University Park Press.

Heiman, M., & Slomianko, J. (1985). *Critical thinking skills.* Washington, DC: National Education Association.

Heiman, M., & Slomianko, J. (Eds.). (1987). *Thinking skills instruction: Concepts and techniques.* Washington, DC: National Education Association.

Link, F. R. (1985). *Essays on the intellect.* Alexandria, VA: Association for Supervision and Curriculum Development.

Lipman, M. (1985). Philosophy for children and critical thinking. *National Forum, 65*(1), 18-23.

Lowery, L. F. (1985). The biological basis for thinking. In A. L. Costa (Ed.), *Developing minds: A resource book for teaching thinking.* Alexandria, VA: Association for Supervision and Curriculum Development.

Maxwell, W. (Ed.). (1983). *Thinking: The expanding frontier.* Philadelphia: Franklin Institute Press.

Nickerson, R. S. (1981). Thoughts on teaching thinking. *Educational Leadership, 39*(1), 21-24.

Paul, R. W. (1987). Critical thinking and the critical person. In D. N. Perkins, J. Lochhead, & J. C. Bishop (Eds.), *Thinking: The second international conference.* Hillsdale, NJ: Lawrence Erlbaum.

Perkins, D. N., Lochhead, J., & Bishop, J. C. (Eds.). (1987). *Thinking: The second international conference.* Hillsdale, NJ: Lawrence Erlbaum.

Presseisen, B. L. (1985). Thinking skills: Meanings and models. In A. L. Costa (Ed.), *Developing minds: A resource book for teaching thinking.* Alexandria, VA: Association for Supervision and Curriculum Development.

Presseisen, B. L. (1986). *Thinking skills: Research and practice.* Washington, DC: National Education Association.

Sadler, W. A., & Whimbey, A. (1985, November). A holistic approach to improving thinking skills. *Phi Delta Kappan, 70.*

Segal, J. W., Chipman, S. F., & Glasar R. (Eds.). (1985). *Thinking and learning skills.* Hillsdale, NJ: Lawrence Erlbaum.

Sternberg, R. J. (1985). Critical thinking: Its nature, measurement, and improvement. In F. R. Link (Ed.), *Essays on the intellect.* Alexandria, VA: Association for Supervision and Curriculum Development.

Tiedt, I., Carlson, J., Howard, B., & Watanabe, K. (1989). *Teaching thinking in K-12 classrooms.* Boston: Allyn & Bacon.

Whimbey, A., & Lochhead, J. (1979). *Problem solving and comprehension.* Philadelphia: Franklin Institute Press.

Wiig, E. H., & Secord, W. (1985). *Test of language competence.* San Antonio, TX: Psychological Corporation.

Zachman, L., Jorgensen, C., Huisingh, R., & Barrett, M. (1984). *Test of problem solving.* Moline, IL: LinguiSystems.

Strategies of Reasoning

S T E P H E N   T O U L M I N
Northwestern University

T HE systematic and thorough work reported in Willbrand and Rieke's chapter is a useful pilot study for a larger subject. The outcome of their work, however, illustrates not merely the power of their questionnaires, but also the limited capacity of such procedures to penetrate behind the "language games" that children and adults employ in answering questions, and reach deeper ("mental") levels of thought or feeling. The central aims of this comment are to place their inquiry in a broader framework and to ask why the significance of their results is so hard to assess. To summarize: It is not clear what weight we can put on the answers they report and analyze — whether these come from American or French people, adults or children — without "unbracketing" the contextual factors that they have chosen to "bracket off" in their present study.

To back up, historically, by way of preface: The activity of "giving reasons" is a focal example of the kinds of human activity that Wilhelm Wundt (1920) classified as objects of study for *Volkpsychologie* — that is, the *non*experimental, *non*physiological half of psychology, as he conceived it. The very name Wundt used for this field (in particular, his reliance on the suspect word *Volk*) has led Americans to overlook the importance of his distinction between psychological activities and mental processes that can be studied by extending the experimental procedures of physics and physiology and those that must be approached from another direction, such as by way of history and cultural anthropology. We can grasp the force of Wundt's distinction better if we interpret it as the contrast between "individual" and "cultural" psychology, where the latter subject overlaps the areas nowadays studied by Eleanor Rosch (1975a, 1975b, 1976) and others under the title of "cross-cultural psychology."

The distinctive feature of the activities to be studied in the latter case is that they are generated or mastered in the course of, and as the outcomes of, an individual's *enculturation.* Any experimental studies we undertake on them must, therefore, be designed with a prior eye to their culturally conditioned contexts and meanings.

Correspondence and requests for reprints: Stephen Toulmin, 1818 Hinman Avenue Evanston, IL 60208.

Communication Yearbook 14, pp. 445-450

This fact at least calls into question Willbrand and Rieke's use of the word *spontaneous* in their title. Any activity that is, in significant measure, shaped by enculturation is spontaneous only in a partial sense. Insofar as it is the reenactment of learned procedures, it may be done spontaneously (i.e., not "to order"), but the *content* that is reenacted can scarcely be spontaneous in the parallel sense, of being shaped wholly by the agent's inner motivations. If Wundt is even halfway right in drawing the distinction he does, then studies of such activities can be fully effective only if they use a *mixed* procedure: placing the results of the kinds of experiment or questionnaire reported on here in the context of the cultural/historical background information that alone puts us in a position to read their "meanings."

That was the methodological conclusion drawn from Wundt's work by such Russian scientists as L. S. Vygotsky (1962, 1978; see also Kozulin, 1990) and A. R. Luria (1966, 1979). The different ways in which Wundt is understood in the United States and the Soviet Union, respectively, are well worth reflecting on: They throw light on a pervasive contrast between the individualism of Western thought in this field and the care and attention to collective and cultural factors that comes naturally to people working in the Soviet Union. That attention is partly associated with the influence of Marxism, but it was already evident in the work of Pavlov, which is often misread in the West, where his speculations about the "second signaling system" are largely untranslated, and so ignored. From the beginning, the field of "cognition" was seen in the Soviet Union as *uniting* the facts about individual and collective life and activity. In their work, Vygotsky and Luria never divorced the cultural significance of the things they investigated from their prior cultural/educational frames: Instead, they saw the learning of language (and even the neurophysiological bases of psycholinguistics) as evidence of how we "make" the cultures in which we grow up into "our own" cultures. The mastery of language games was, to them, a process by which a child *internalizes* culture. As a result, their experimental studies threw light, at one and the same time, on both sides of the crucial intersection between individual and culture.

THE EXAMPLE OF KOHLBERG

It is not for nothing that Willbrand and Rieke compare their work to that of Lawrence Kohlberg. Kohlberg's (1976) work on children's expressions of moral approval and "reason giving" are classic examples of exaggerated individualism in Western developmental psychology. Kohlberg followed the example of Piaget's (1923, 1924) early work, before he had conceded the force of Vygotsky's attack on the idea of "egocentrism." Piaget himself moved part way toward the Russians, by acknowledging the cultural frame to which the child has to adapt his or her activities, but Kohlberg went on taking children's words as direct evidence of their inner mental attitudes — and even generalized them across cultural boundaries — without independent studies to confirm the legitimacy of those steps.

Sometimes, as in his studies of children's dream reports, Kohlberg's procedures led him into plain mistakes. At other times, as in his work on children's moral development, they encouraged him to treat observations of their moral *language games* as implying conclusions about their moral *feelings.* In doing so, he ignored the independent tradition of research on the expression of the emotions in children and adults, by ethnographers, physical anthropologists, and cultural psychologists from Charles Darwin to Paul Eckman. From this research, it has long been clear that children respond affectively to typical "emotion-arousing" situations in ways independent of what they have yet learned to *say,* to say nothing of the ways in which they have yet learned to *answer questions.* Arguably, then, the subject of Kohlberg's work on children's moral talk is not a series of "stages" in the development of their internal moral feelings about the acceptability of various actions, but the sequence of steps by which they progressively master the art of answering the questions adults put to them about this acceptability. How they *answer adult questions* about the moral quality of the actions is one thing; how they *perceive or feel about* those actions can be quite another.

In their prefatory discussion of "cognitive relevance" and the like, Willbrand and Rieke refer to the contrast between language learning and "cognitive" development, in particular to a widely assumed "correlation between the mental process leading to the support of [a] claim and the social process of presenting and justifying it" (p. 415), and they give credit to Piaget and Kohlberg for recognizing the significance of that contrast. In doing so, they speak too generously about Piaget and even more so of Kohlberg, most notably when they echo Piaget's hope that "investigation may even prove ultimately that the language patterns in reasoning are isomorphic with cognitive activity, and both of them are adequately described by the principles of [formal] logic" (p. 415). Piaget's vision of systematic isomorphisms between mental activities on every level is one of the most bizarre hypotheses about "thinking" since Leibniz (1714/1840) dreamed up the "preestablished harmonies" between the monads of his monadology. If such formal correspondences can be found among speech, inner thought, and neurophysiology, they *must have been put there* (presumably, in enculturation) by the internalization of cultural patterns. Accordingly, we can no longer ignore Vygotsky's fundamental question: "How does this internalization take place?"

CHALLENGES, REASONS, AND REHEARSALS

What is the relevance of this general point to Willbrand and Rieke's own investigations? It relates by way of facts that we well understand, but usually take for granted when we focus in on the human activity of "reason giving" in isolation. At the outset, they declare that "the concept 'reasoning,' as applied to spontaneous spoken discourse, is an unusually foggy one" (p. 414). This comment is at first sight disingenuous. In actual practice, we have little difficulty in recognizing when someone is "giving reasons"; so why do they call this notion "unusually foggy"? It begins to appear so only at the point at which we bracket off the *culture* that is in practice taken for granted and try to give a theoretical definition that refers only to facts about the *individual*. At that point, we find ourselves in some difficulty, but that is because — like the fly in Wittgenstein's fly bottle — we are unwilling to turn around and go out by the way we went in.

Yet it is not hard to "unbracket" the things that an individualistic account conceals. In practice, for instance, we all know a lot about the contexts in which, the purposes for which, and the manner in which our children are introduced, in their upbringing, to the arts of reason giving. To be more precise, there is a lot that we all "lived through" in practice, provided that we were involved in the upbringing of at least one child, and were responsible for spotting when the child had "caught on" to these arts. To begin with, children begin "giving reasons" in response not to naked factual inquiries, but to *challenges*: Initially, the request for a "reason" does not typically have neutral force — "What *happened to be* the target or destination, when you acted as you did?" Rather, the child is usually asked for justification of an action that is perceived as more or less out of line — "What on earth *were you up to* in doing what you did?" From early on, children "rehearse" responses to such challenges, foreseeing possible objections to their actions, and preparing to counter them.

In a word, there is a family of "language games" that forms part of the activity of socialization and is familiar in our everyday lives (e.g., the language game of "challenging and countering challenges"). Taken out of context, and removed from all possible challenges, our actions cease to have *reasons* in any obvious sense of the term: "What reason had I for doing that? I didn't *have to have* a 'reason' — it was something I just did!" It is not merely an incidental fact that "learning to give reasons" is part of our enculturation, which has to be discovered empirically. In addition, the contexts of enculturation are constitutive elements in determining the "meanings" (i.e., force and effect) both of *requests* for reasons in any given context and of the reasons available *in response*.

To begin by following up Wilhelm Wundt's arguments, studies like those reported by Willbrand and Rieke are intelligible only as one wing of a double inquiry, the other wing of which — the ethnographic, or cultural wing — is indispensable if we are to draw meaningful conclusions from *either* half. Willbrand and Rieke rightly seek to guard against prompting: "To obtain unplanned reasoning, all respondents were tape-recorded as they responded to a request for reasons *on a subject for which they had received no prior warning*" (p. 417; emphasis added). But this precaution is insufficient to ensure that the responses were spontaneous in the sense of "culture independent." Although all of the respondents — American or French, children or adult — were free to reply *without prompting*, they could only construe "requests for reasons" as an invitation to reapply the language games they had learned previously in other more typical situations, where more was at stake. What we get by way of answers from respondents of different ages, or from different cultures, is thus evidence about the stage of their enculturation and the content of their native culture as much as about development.

Here again, the authors excuse the inconclusive character of their results by claiming that the state of general human ignorance is greater than it surely is:

> Comparison of language knowledge and use in differing cultures is not only of academic interest; it leads to better intercultural understanding and communication as well. Each culture has rules that govern social interaction (Coulthard, 1978), and little is known about how these rules may be similar or different. (p. 431)

In this connection, a single reference to a book on discourse analysis is hardly enough: Cross-cultural study of the "rules for social interaction" was one of the founding fields of social anthropology, and it is scarcely kind to turn a blind eye to the work of generations of ethnographers and anthropologists who have made this their field of interest.

True, some of the early generalizations to which this ethnographic work led (e.g., those in Westermarck's famous 1932 work *Ethical Relativity*) appear in retrospect premature and dated, but much has been done since Westermarck's day, and students of communication can find much better thought-out schemas to guide and complement their own investigations in the work of (say) Clifford Geertz (1973) and his colleagues.

CONCLUSION

The burden of this comment is easily stated. The greatest obstacle to serious progress in the human sciences at the present time lies in the administrative and intellectual fragmentation of those disciplines. What Wilhelm Wundt recognized was the *interdependence* of all the behavioral, social, and human sciences — that it is impossible to arrive at a definitive understanding of (say) the ways in which children speak and act by relying on the methods of a single discipline alone. Indeed, it is even impossible to frame an inquiry that is capable of yielding definitive results unless from the start one plans several complementary research projects, using methods drawn from several disciplines.

Every human activity — linguistic as much as any other — represents the intersection of neurophysiological, developmental, linguistic, social, familial, cultural, and a dozen other kinds of processes. Piaget's (1973, pp. 14-21, sections 3, 4) dream of a general isomorphism among the processes on all these levels was a wish-fulfillment dream that allowed him to present his conclusions in more definitive-sounding terms than a proper understanding of the issues involved can justify. That is why, since Piaget's departure, scholars and scientists in the West have been paying more attention than before to the ideas and methods of their counterparts in the Soviet Union, where behavioral and social scientists are never as fragmented as they are in the West — to Bakhtin (1981) in the study of literature and language, and to Vygotsky (1962, 1978) and Luria (1966, 1979) in the study of clinical neurology, child development, enculturation, and the like.

Students of communication do, in general, pay better attention to neighboring disciplines than, for example, the radical behaviorists and experimental psychologists studying animal behavior. Few writers on communication, for example, would leap to the kinds of exaggerated conclusions that are characteristic of the popular books of B. F. Skinner or E. O. Wilson. All the same, we still have much to learn in developing our methods of study further and giving ourselves a better chance of reaching the truly informed understanding we want about the human activities in which we are most interested. My friends and colleagues, Mary Louise Willbrand and Richard Rieke, will therefore excuse me for taking their fine — but carefully limited — chapter as an occasion to preach on a text of continuing importance.

REFERENCES

Bakhtin, M. (1981). *The dialogic imagination* (M. Holquist, Ed.). Austin: University of Texas Press.
Coulthard, M. (1978). *An introduction to discourse analysis.* London: Longman.
Geertz, C. (1973). *Interpretation of cultures.* New York: Basic Books.
Kohlberg, L. (1976). Moral stages and moralization. In T. Lickona (Ed.), *Moral development and behavior.* New York: Holt.
Kozulin, A. (1990). *Vygotsky's psychology.* New York: Harvester Wheatsheaf.
Leibniz, G. W. (1840). *La monadologie.* Berlin: J. E. Erdmann. (Original work written 1714)
Luria, A. R. (1966). *Higher cortical functions in man.* New York: Basic Books.
Luria, A. R. (1979). *The making of mind.* Cambridge, MA: Harvard University Press.
Piaget, J. (1923). *Le langage et la pensée chez l'enfant.* Neuchâtel-Paris: Delachaux & Niestlé.
Piaget, J. (1924). *Le jugement et le raisonnement chez l'enfant.* Neuchâtel-Paris: Delachaux & Niestlé.
Piaget, J. (1973). *Main trends in interdisciplinary research.* New York: Harper.
Rosch, E. (1975a). Cognitive reference points. *Cognitive Psychology, 7,* 532-547.
Rosch, E. (1975b). Family resemblances. *Cognitive Psychology, 7,* 573-605.
Rosch, E. (1976). Basic objects in natural categories. *Cognitive Psychology, 8,* 382-439.
Vygotsky, L. S. (1962). *Thought and language.* Cambridge: MIT Press.
Vygotsky, L. S. (1978). *Mind in society: The development of higher psychological processes* (M. Cole et al., Eds.). Cambridge, MA: Harvard University Press.
Wundt, W. (1910-1920). *Völkerpsychologie* (Vols. 1-10). Leipzig: Engelmann.

10 Interpersonal Attraction and Attitude Similarity: A Communication-Based Assessment

MICHAEL SUNNAFRANK
University of Minnesota, Duluth

Critically reviewing and synthesizing a century's worth of accumulated research, this chapter demonstrates that there is little evidence to support the generally held "scientific" belief that attitude similarity increases attraction. To the contrary, the great preponderance of evidence indicates that attitude similarity is *not* a motivating force in most types and stages of relationships. Explanations for the development of this erroneous belief are suggested and the theoretical attempts to reinterpret the research literature are examined. Influences of, and on, communication are featured throughout the chapter. The chapter concludes with an examination of several key communication issues arising from this iconoclastic perspective.

... and everyone willingly enjoyeth peace, and loveth those best that agree with him. (Thomas a Kempis, c. 1427/1980, p. 95)

And they are friends who have come to regard the same things as good and the same things as evil ...

We like those who resemble us, and are engaged in the same pursuits, provided they do not get in the way. (Aristotle, c. 330 B.C./1932, pp. 103-105)

Conventional wisdom traditionally agrees with Aristotle's observation that friends are similar to one another in several respects. With only a few notable exceptions, folklore further portrays similarity as an important determinant of both friendship and mating choices.

Scientific findings frequently support this commonsense view. Persons consistently show an inclination to be in or attracted to relationships with others who resemble them in several diverse ways, such as in their activity preferences (Werner & Parmelee, 1979), physical attractiveness (Berscheid & Walster, 1974), intelligence (Richardson, 1939), and various demographic characteristics (Kandel, 1978).

One of the most studied forms of similarity in this research has been the similarity of individuals' attitudes. The positive association between attitude

Correspondence and requests for reprints: Michael Sunnafrank, Department of Communication, University of Minnesota, Duluth, MN 55812.

Communication Yearbook 14, pp. 451-483

similarity and interpersonal attraction is frequently cited as one of the most examined and widely accepted relationships in the social sciences (De Wolfe & Jackson, 1984; Parks & Adelman, 1983). There is general agreement with Berscheid and Walster's (1983) conclusion that "people are attracted to those who share their attitudes" (p. 88). However, a growing body of contrary research evidence (Condon & Crano, 1988; Rosenbaum, 1986; Sunnafrank & Miller, 1981; Sykes, 1983) indicates that the lawlike status of this relationship is unjustified. An examination of the issues raised by this controversy provides the central theme of the work presented in this chapter.

The view of attitude similarity as a positive attraction influence is contingent upon the assumption that individuals acquire at least somewhat accurate perceptions of others' attitudes. In the similarity-attraction literature, the attitude construct has typically been defined as representing "an orientation along a positive-negative continuum with respect to any object or event" (Byrne, 1971, p. 24). Distinctions are seldom drawn among attitudes, values, opinions, and other like constructs. Given this nature, another's attitudes are not directly observable, and must be inferred from available information. Such inferences can be based on several sources of information, including attitude-relevant communication with others, observations of behaviors associated with attitude topics, and information provided by mutual acquaintances. The communication processes involved in generating such perceptions require much more study. However, it is clear that while perceptions of partners' attitudes are usually low in accuracy during beginning acquaintance, these perceptions do become increasingly accurate as relationships develop (Newcomb, 1961).

Whether and why such perceptions produce a positive attitude similarity effect on attraction is the focus of several theoretical interpretations, with most offering balance (Brewer & Brewer, 1968; Newcomb, 1961, 1963) or reinforcement (Byrne, 1971; Lott & Lott, 1974) explanations. For example, Newcomb's balance perspective is frequently employed to explain attraction and relational development processes. This perspective is derived from Heider (1958), and assumes that individuals prefer psychologically balanced states among their own attitude toward an object, their perception of a relational partner's attitude toward the same object, and their attraction toward the partner. Balance exists in this system when attraction is positive and attitude similarity is perceived, and balance or nonbalance (indifference) exists when negative attraction is associated with perceived dissimilarity. All other combinations produce imbalance, which is associated with changes in one or more elements of the system, or simply nonbalance. For these balance processes to result, the attitude object must have relatively high importance, and must be mutually relevant to the relational partners. Under these conditions, the actual attitude similarity state between partners will eventually influence the perceived similarity state as observations and communication related to the attitude topic occur. Therefore, actual attitude similarity would become positively related to attraction as relationships develop.

Byrne's effectance-arousal perspective (Byrne, 1961, 1971; Byrne & Clore, 1970; Byrne & Nelson, 1965) provides the most studied and supported reinforcement explanation of the attitude similarity-attraction relationship. Byrne argues that a key reinforcement property of attitude similarity stems from an individual's motive to be logical and accurate in interpreting the environment (Festinger, 1954). From this perspective, attitudinal similarity with another provides consensual validation for one's attitudes. Such validation is positively reinforcing, which through conditioning produces attraction to the individual as the source of this reinforcement. Social invalidation, negative reinforcement, and repulsion would result from attitudinal dissimilarity. Since several reinforcement sources are present in relationships involving acquainted individuals, most research testing this explanation has isolated the attitude similarity variable through experimentally revealing information about a stranger's attitudes.

During the last decade researchers have increasingly questioned these traditional perspectives, particularly with regard to Byrne's explanation of attraction between relative strangers. Some of this research indicates that while attitude dissimilarity in strangers may be repulsive, similarity does not increase attraction (Rosenbaum, 1986). Other research demonstrates that individuals believe attitudinally similar strangers will evaluate them more positively than will dissimilars, and that it is this anticipated difference in evaluation that produces most of the attraction differences (Aronson & Worchel, 1966; Condon & Crano, 1988). Several perspectives indicate that familiarity and certainty are key attraction influences, and that the positive attitude similarity-attraction may be related to a tendency to be more certain about or feel more familiar with others who appear similar (Berger & Calabrese, 1975; Moreland & Zajonc, 1982). Bochner (1984) suggests that the influence of attitude similarity on attraction association may be substantially reduced by the opportunity to communicate with relative strangers. This view is supported by recent research on the influence of communication processes in early acquaintance (Sunnafrank, 1983, 1984; Sunnafrank & Miller, 1981) that indicates that the pursuit of interpersonal goals in conversations between relative strangers may eliminate the similarity-attraction effect.

These findings regarding the apparent ephemeral influence of attitude similarity in early-acquaintance conversations, along with questions raised by recent interpretations of the attitude similarity-attraction association, call for a comprehensive reexamination of theory and research in this area. The goal of this chapter is to provide just such a critical review. During this review, an attempt will be made to assess whether research results justify the lawlike status of the attitude similarity-attraction relationship, and to appraise alternative explanations of these results.

This review begins with an examination of research on attitude similarity in naturally occurring relationships. Early research on spouses and friends provided the first scientific documentation of a positive association between the attitudes of partners in existing intimate relationships, and led to theoretical speculation and tests concerning the causes of this association. Some of these tests continued to examine attitude similarity in existing and developing "real-world" relationships. However, most subsequent theoretical tests have involved laboratory examinations of attraction to strangers. This research has overwhelmingly demonstrated that individuals are more attracted to strangers when they are depicted as attitudinally similar than when they are depicted as dissimilar (Byrne, 1961; Cappella & Palmer, 1988; Gormly & Gormly, 1984; Jamieson, Lydon, & Zanna, 1987). Theory and research that explore various explanations for this finding are reviewed in the second section below. The literature review then concludes with an examination of research on how this positive preacquaintance similarity-attraction association is influenced by various beginning communicative transactions. In the final portion of the chapter I will attempt to examine various implications of the research reviewed for understanding the interrelationship of communication processes, similarity, attraction, and relational change.

ATTITUDE SIMILARITY IN
NATURALLY OCCURRING RELATIONSHIPS

Many studies concerning similarity between partners in existing relationships have appeared since the early part of the century, several of which report results relevant to the degree of attitudinal resemblance between partners. The earliest research on existing relationships examined various similarities between spouses (Galton, 1870/1952; Pearson & Lee, 1903). Research on similarity between friends (Vreeland & Corey, 1935; Winslow, 1937) and roommates (Schellenberg, 1957) was subsequently added to the continuing work on homogamy (Farber, 1957; Hunt, 1935; Newcomb & Svehla, 1937). Romantic, friend, and roommate relations differ in several important respects that might well be associated with processes involving attitude similarity (though a single relationship might involve all three types of relation). Given this, research on each is reviewed separately below.

Early research on attitude similarity in marriage focused on simply determining if marriage partners' attitudes were related. Most such studies proceeded by obtaining measures of individuals' attitudes on various topics for comparison with attitudes reported by their spouses. Researchers employing this method consistently found a positive association between partners' attitudes (Byrne & Blaylock, 1963; Kirkpatrick & Stone, 1935; Newcomb & Svehla, 1937; Schooley, 1936).

While findings from these studies generally demonstrated a high degree of attitude similarity between spouses, they provided little information about the cause of this association. Various explanations of this attitudinal homogamy were nevertheless proposed, with assortative mating and attitudinal convergence most prominently mentioned. Assortative mating interpretations propose that the discovery of attitude similarity with potential marriage partners increases attraction and fosters the development of highly committed romantic relationships; attitudinal convergence explanations argue that individuals exert mutual persuasive influences that lead to their becoming attitudinally similar in these long-term relationships.

Little evidence of attitudinal convergence can be found in the literature on attitude similarity in marriage or in other types of long-term relations. However, indirect support for assortative mating regarding attitudes is provided by some sources. For example, Byrne and Blaylock (1963), Newcomb and Svehla (1937), and Schooley (1936) found that individuals who had been married for a relatively short period were as attitudinally similar as couples who had been married for much longer periods. These results are frequently regarded as indicating that marriage partners do not become more attitudinally similar in relationships of greater duration, but that they decide to marry others who are found to have similar attitudes. However, the lack of meaningful comparison groups in these studies renders any such conclusions highly speculative. As one illustration, in any society socialization processes would produce consensus on a variety of attitude topics. If so, then the reported attitude similarity of spouses might be at least partially due to such societal consensus rather than assortative mating.

Research that compares attitude similarity exhibited by spouses with similarity found between random pairs supports this position. For example, Hunt (1935) and Schiller (1932) found that spouses were highly similar with respect to their attitudes on various topics, and that married couples were more attitudinally similar than random pairs. However, the attitudes of these random pairs of individuals were also found to be moderately and positively associated. It should be noted that Hunt's and Schiller's methods of randomly pairing unacquainted individuals likely produced pairs that were more demographically heterogeneous than the married couples in these studies. It seems reasonable to assume that random pairs that were more representative of this demographic homogamy might well have exhibited even greater attitude similarity levels, thus further reducing the unique attitude similarity level associated with married couples. Even so, the most obvious conclusion to be drawn from these early studies is that married partners tend to be attitudinally similar. It also appears that some form of assortative mating is influencing this outcome, though it is not clear the degree to which this represents attitudinal, demographic, or some other form of assorting.

Later studies offered more direct evidence regarding the possible causes of attitude similarity in marriage by attempting to discover if attitude similarity was related to such variables as relational satisfaction and development. For example, Kirkpatrick and Hobart (1954) and Hobart (1956) found that couples exhibited greater attitude similarity concerning marriage-related topics when in exclusive relationships (going steady, engaged, married) than when in less committed romantic relationships (favorite date). However, in only one of four comparisons did married couples demonstrate greater attitude similarity than couples in the other types of exclusive relationships. This finding suggests that any influence of and on attitude similarity may be limited to relatively early stages of development in romantic relations, as expected in assortative mating explanations. This interpretation is further supported by Kerckhoff and Davis's (1962) longitudinal study, which found value agreement was related to progress toward marriage in the first 18 months of courtship, but not thereafter. However, Levinger, Senn, and Jorgensen's (1970) failed attempt to replicate Kerckhoff and Davis's findings regarding the positive influence of value agreement during the beginning months of relationships casts doubt on this interpretation.

Research on marriage provides further evidence that attitude similarity and relational satisfaction may be unrelated in such relationships. Levinger and Breedlove's (1966) research on the association between marital satisfaction and actual and assumed attitude similarity supports such an interpretation. Levinger and Breedlove found that while spouses were attitudinally similar to one another, they assumed even greater similarity to their partners than actually existed. It was also found that amount of assumed similarity and marital satisfaction were positively related. However, *actual* attitude similarity and marital satisfaction were unrelated. In a more recent study, Hendrick (1981) found that attitude similarity was positively associated with marital adjustment, but was unrelated to spouses' assessment of their marriage or marriage partner. Apparently, general attitude similarity levels may be related to problems experienced in marital relationships, but not to the extent of influencing spouses' perception of the marriage or one another.

Overall, the research on courtship and marriage leaves little doubt that partners in these relationships are generally attitudinally similar to one another, though how or why this occurs remains unclear. There is good evidence that some of this similarity can be attributed to societal consensus. However, assortative mating processes appear to result in additional attitude similarity between couples. The degree to which this assortative mating influence might be explained by demographic matching tendencies or other factors is an open question. If assortative mating related to attitude similarity does occur, it appears to exert most of its influence relatively early in the development of relationships. Satisfaction in more enduring relationships appears to have little association with attitude similarity.

Findings regarding the relationship between the attitudes of friends are less supportive of a positive association than those reported for romantic relationships. Some studies report that friends' attitudes are unrelated (Reilly, Commins, & Stefic, 1960; Vreeland & Corey, 1935; Werner & Parmelee, 1979; Wright & Crawford, 1971), while those that do find evidence of attitude similarity report associations of generally low magnitude (Kandel, 1978; Precker, 1952; Richardson, 1940; Winslow, 1937).

Vreeland and Corey's (1935) initial study of attitude similarity in friendship was also the first to indicate that work supporting attitudinal homogamy might not generalize straightforwardly to friend relationships. They found that while close friends were similar on some characteristics, this similarity did not extend to attitudes measured. In a similar pattern, Richardson (1940) found a significant positive correlation between friends' values in only one of six value areas studied, while Reilly et al. (1960) found that the values of friends were unrelated.

A few studies report results that are slightly more supportive of an association between friends' attitudes. Both Winslow (1937) and Kandel (1978) found weak positive correlations between friends' opinions on several issues. Given the methods employed in these studies, it is possible that these weak attitudinal associations simply reflect general similarity levels in the population. However, Precker (1952) did make relevant comparisons and found that while random pairs were similar, mutual friendship pairs were slightly more so.

In addition to assessing whether friends are attitudinally similar, a few studies have attempted to determine if the degree of attitude similarity between friends influences the quality of their friendship. In a study addressing both of these questions, Werner and Parmelee (1979) found that friends were no more attitudinally similar than random pairs of individuals, and that attitude similarity was unrelated to attraction between friends. Wright and Crawford (1971) supply further evidence that attitude similarity is unrelated to quality of friendship. They assessed five components related to friendship quality in a series of studies aimed at determining how these components were related to various types of similarity. Their results demonstrated that level of composite attitude similarity on several potentially relevant topics was unrelated to any of the friendship components.

Overall, studies of attitude similarity in existing friendships provide inconsistent and weak support for the view that friends are attitudinally similar, and no support for a relationship between attitude similarity and friendship quality. Some studies indicate that friends' attitudes are unrelated, while other studies report very low levels of association that may partially reflect relevant population similarity levels. Just why attitude similarity levels in friend relations would be different from those in romantic relations is unclear. One interesting possibility is that greater attitudinal coordination is required for progress in romantic than in friend relations. More attitudes may be mutually relevant to spouses or partners seriously contemplating marriage than for friendship pairs. Agreement or acquiescence on several topics could be instrumental to progress in such romantic relations, while friends may be more likely to succeed through "agreeing to disagree" with respect to most topics. Another possible explanation is that individuals may choose more demographically similar partners for long-term romantic relationships than for friendships, which might well result in greater attitudinal consensus in the population of likely romantic partners than in the population of potential friends.

The research reviewed above provides little support for an association between attitude similarity and satisfaction or attraction in marriage, and no support for such an association in friendship. In contrast, research on roommate relations provides some evidence that satisfaction and attraction may be weakly related to attitude similarity, although even this support is inconsistent.

At the outset, it should be noted that research on roommate relations differs from work on friend and romantic relations in several important respects. First, almost all roommate research examines relations between individuals in a forced proxemic situation. This research focuses on relations formed in various types of communal living arrangements where individuals share a residence, though not necessarily a room. Individuals are generally unacquainted prior to taking up residence in these units, and consequently do not choose one another as residence partners. While friend and romantic relations are certainly formed in such situations, membership in these relations is voluntary.

Second, all studies regarding attitude similarity between roommates examine similarity in relation to attraction, satisfaction, or some other measure of relational quality. Studies of romantic and friend relations have frequently made the assumption, not always justified, that since individuals choose partners in these relationships they are highly attracted to one another. Given this assumption, the existence of attitude similarity in romantic and friend relations has often been taken as implicit evidence of a similarity-attraction association even when no measure of attraction or satisfaction is reported. Since relational quality is measured in research on roommate relations, its association to attitude similarity and other interrelated variables can be more directly assessed.

Finally, many studies of attitude similarity between roommates are longitudinal. These longitudinal studies are frequently motivated by a theoretical desire to determine the causal connections between variables such as attitude similarity and attraction, while much of the work on friend and romantic relations is atheoretical in nature.

Prior to examining these more theoretical longitudinal studies of roommate relations, it would be instructive to review briefly a few one-shot studies of roommate attraction and similarity. Schellenberg (1957) examined housemates' sociometric choices for four different situations, and found that in all situations chosen persons were more similar on a composite assessment of value similarity than was the average house member. Conversely, Perkins (1977) studied the value similarity of living mates in several residence hall sections, and found similarity to be unrelated to either satisfaction with the living unit or attraction between unit members. Nudd (1965) compared satisfied and dissatisfied residence hall roommates on various dimensions. Of greatest relevance to the present analysis, Nudd found that dissatisfied roommates were more likely to disagree regarding religious and economic values than satisfied roommates, though there were no differences between the two groups in four other value areas.

The inconsistencies in the above findings can perhaps be explained by differences in the measures of similarity employed. The studies supporting an association between value similarity and relational quality employed a scale of Spranger Values (Allport & Vernon, 1931), while Perkins utilized a measure of values developed by Newcomb (1961). Newcomb assessed the similarity-attraction association with both scales, and found that the measure of Spranger Values was more strongly associated with attraction than his own scale. An examination of these scales demonstrates that the Spranger Values may be more mutually relevant to college roommates than the values measured in Newcomb's scale. If mutual relevance of attitude topics is assumed to be necessary to a similarity-attraction association (Newcomb, 1961, 1963), then this difference could well explain the contradictory results obtained in these studies.

Newcomb's (1961, 1963) classic longitudinal studies of acquaintance in a college residence house employed the above value measures, as well as attitude topics assumed to have a high likelihood of mutual relevance in the population examined. Newcomb studied semester-long acquaintance processes in two successive groups of previously unacquainted males, and found support for several predictions from his balance perspective. As expected, Newcomb found that perceived attitude similarity and attraction were positively associated throughout the semester. In addition, perceived attitude similarity more closely approximated actual similarity levels as the semester proceeded, and as housemates' opportunities to discuss their attitudes increased. Finally, Newcomb found that preacquaintance attitude similarity was positively related to attraction observed between pairs late in the semester.

Newcomb did report one finding that was inconsistent with this general similarity-attraction pattern. In the second group of housemates, Newcomb placed pairs of highly similar and highly dissimilar individuals together as roommates, and found no attraction differences between these pairs. Levinger's (1972) 18-month investigation of developing roommate relationships produced similar unsupportive results. Levinger assigned entering freshmen to two-person dormitory rooms with a roommate who had either highly similar values or whose values were unsimilar. Measures of attraction taken at 3 weeks, 3 months, 5 months, and 18 months demonstrated no consistent differences attributable to value similarity.

Other research attempting to replicate and extend Newcomb's (1961, 1963) work has produced results that partially conflict with his finding of a positive relationship between preacquaintance attitude similarity and attraction. Curry and Emerson (1970) found that the strongest associate of attraction in developing roommate relations was individuals' perception of their roommates' attraction to them, followed by perceived agreement on attitudes toward other residents, and a relatively weak association with perceived value similarity. In contrast to Newcomb's findings, actual value similarity was unrelated to attraction.

In a reanalysis of these data, Curry and Kenny (1974) report a trend suggesting an increasing correlation between actual value similarity and attraction between the first and fourth week of the eight-week study, with no change thereafter. Curry and Kenny do not report significance levels for these correlations, but the associations they reflect, if real, are very weak. It is possible that the different lengths of time involved in Curry and Emerson's (8 weeks) and Newcomb's studies (15 weeks) is responsible for these conflicting findings. However, the lack of change in the association of similarity and attraction between weeks 4 and 8 in the Curry and Kenny study suggests that further change was unlikely. Moreover, attraction between pairs in Newcomb's studies was highly stable from week 5 onward.

A recent examination of acquaintance in U.S. Navy apprentice training units continues this pattern of mixed support for an attitude similarity-attraction relationship. Sykes (1983) examined off-duty interaction patterns in these units and found that the strongest determinant of interaction partners was previous acquaintance. Proximity was the next largest contributor, followed by various demographic similarities. After these variables were statistically controlled, attitude similarities on relevant topics were found to be unrelated or only weakly related to choice of interaction partners. Even when summed across topic areas, the amount of additional variance explained by attitude similarity on relevant topics was very low.

Overall, the results of research on roommate relations provide inconsistent support for a weak association between attraction and attitude similarity. If associations between attitude similarity and attraction occur, they appear to take place relatively early in the formation of roommate relationships. The sequence of events suggests that relevant communication and observations during this time lead roommates to become more accurate in perceiving the attitudes held by one another. Such perceived attitude similarity is consistently and positively associated with relational quality between roommates. Some of this association appears to be due to a tendency to overestimate the attitudinal similarity of attractive roommates. A relatively small portion may result from attraction changes produced by actual attitude similarity acting on perceived similarity. How, why, and even whether such an effect of actual attitude similarity occurs is still unclear.

In summary, research on romantic, friend, and roommate relations demonstrates interesting consistencies and contradictions regarding associations involving the attitude similarity variable. Spouses and individuals in relatively enduring romantic relations certainly exhibit a weak to moderate degree of attitude similarity. A significant portion of this similarity may be due to general societal similarity levels. The degree to which this association is influenced by attitude similarity increasing attraction between romantic partners is unknown. Some evidence suggests that a weak influence may exist, but that it is limited to relatively early stages of development. Once romantic relations achieve greater commitment levels, attitude similarity appears to lose influence. In addition, some research on roommate relations supports a weak association between actual attitude similarity and relational quality. As in the case of romantic relations, this possible association appears to have an influence relatively early in relationship formation.

Research on friend relations is less supportive of an attitude similarity- attraction association. Friends are much less likely to be attitudinally similar than romantic partners, with several studies finding that the attitudes of friends are unrelated. The weak associations reported in other studies may largely be accounted for by processes other than that of attitude similarity producing attraction or relational development. The quality of friend relations and attraction between friends appear to be uninfluenced by attitude similarity.

It has been suggested that the discrepancy between friend and romantic relations might be due to a greater need to coordinate on attitude topics in successful romantic relations. This same argument might explain the possible difference between friend and roommate relations. Individuals who share living units are more likely to find that they are influenced by one another's attitudes than are friends who do not live together. This increased mutual relevance might well explain why the quality of roommate relations would exhibit a slight association to attitude similarity that is not apparent in friend relations. Certainly, there is abundant anecdotal evidence indicating that friends who become roommates frequently experience difficulties in adjusting to this new facet of their relationship. It seems reasonable that this might be partially related to the increased relevance of some attitude topics.

This issue concerning topic relevance, along with the issue of topic importance, may help explain the pattern of inconsistent findings reported above. Newcomb proposes that attraction is influenced by similarity on attitude topics that are mutually relevant to partners and of high importance to the individual member. Byrne (1971) has subsequently shown that attitude similarity influences attraction regardless of, or in addition to, topic importance and relevance. However, these demonstrations have involved attraction between relative strangers, not between partners in ongoing relationships. It would seem that importance and relevance would be much more critical to attitude similarity influences in existing relationships. While many of the above studies attempted to employ mutually relevant and important attitude topics, variations between studies on these variables undoubtedly occurred. It is possible that differences in the degree of successfully choosing relevant and important topics may account for some of the inconsistent findings. Even if partially accurate, this speculation cannot explain the inconsistencies among studies employing the same attitude measures and types of relationships.

The research on existing relationships reveals variables that are more consistently related to the likelihood of relationship formation and relational quality than is attitude similarity. It may be that some of these variables would also partially explain how attitude similarity is associated with apparent attraction. Proximity, similarity on various demographic characteristics, and activity preference similarity all appear to be associated with the development of positive relationships. Associations involving demographic and activity preference similarity may be largely due to proximity. That is, individuals generally find themselves in social environments with others who have common demographic characteristics and activity preferences. This proximity increases the opportunity to communicate and associate with these similar persons, and the likelihood that relationships will develop. Of course, individuals may choose certain social environments because of these opportunities, so the relationship of proximity and such similarities may be reciprocal.

If certain attitudinal constellations are associated with specific demographic groups or groups who share activity preferences, then some attitude similarity in these intragroup associations would be expected. A positive association between the attitudes of existing relational partners could occur as a by-product of such tendencies. The degree to which attitude similarity may have an additional influence on relational development, or its possible motivational role in choosing partners who are similar with respect to demographic characteristics and activity preferences, is still unclear.

Given these findings, no general laws concerning an attitude similarity-attraction relationship emerge. Partners in romantic relations tend to be attitudinally similar, but there is only limited and indirect evidence to indicate that this is due to attitude similarity acting on attraction. There is no consistent evidence to indicate that friends are attitudinally similar, or that friend similarity is related to attraction. The quality of roommate relations appears to be influenced weakly by attitude similarity, but even the findings regarding this association are inconsistent.

Where, then, does the general perception concerning a positive influence of attitude similarity on attraction arise? Certainly Newcomb's (1961) classic study is a factor in this perception. However, the main support has been generated through research on attraction between relative strangers conducted by Donn Byrne and his associates. We now turn to an examination of this research program. Given that Byrne's research is the pivotal work on attitude similarity and attraction, considerable attention will be devoted to alternative interpretations of his findings.

ATTITUDE SIMILARITY
AND ATTRACTION TO STRANGERS

While investigations into the attitude similarity-attraction association have examined various types of relationships, studies of attraction to relative strangers have lately predominated. Theory testing has been the central concern of these studies, with Byrne's effectance-arousal perspective (Byrne, 1971; Byrne & Clore, 1970; Byrne & Nelson, 1965) forming the basis for the vast majority of tests. The results of numerous studies conducted by Byrne and his colleagues provide support for his reinforcement explanation of attraction, especially regarding the predicted influence of reinforcements provided by the social validation or invalidation of attitudes. This work is consistent with the view that consensual validation received through the discovery of attitude similarity with a stranger is positively reinforcing, and that such reinforcement leads to attraction. Conversely, invalidation produced through attitude dissimilarity may be negatively reinforcing, leading to rejection.

Byrne's (1971) perspective specifies that attitude similarity is only one of many potential sources of reinforcement that may influence attraction. Certainly in the complex social and communicative environment in which relationships are formed many such reinforcement sources are likely. Given these other reinforcement sources, the influence of attitude similarity on attraction may be weak in naturally occurring relationships. Indeed, the actual contribution of any given source of reinforcement to attraction in these relationships would be difficult to determine.

In order to control these sources of reinforcement and test his theory, Byrne (1961, 1971) adapted and extended a method introduced by Smith (1957) that involved examining attraction to simulated strangers. Byrne's bogus stranger method has been employed to examine the influence of various reinforcement sources, but the influence of attitude similarity on attraction is the central focus of this program. Researchers using this technique normally measure individuals' attitudes concerning various topics. Attitude similarity is manipulated by presenting research participants with the attitudes of a stranger toward these same topics. This stranger is typically portrayed as someone who filled out the attitude scale at a prior time, and who they will never meet. The stranger's responses are actually manufactured by the experimenter to agree or disagree at some preset level with the respondent's attitudes, thus the label "bogus stranger." After receiving this attitude similarity manipulation, the participants respond to Byrne's (1961) Interpersonal Judgment Scale, which includes an estimate of how much they would like the stranger and how much they would like working with the stranger. The responses to these two items are summed to produce the attraction measure. The use of this technique and variations on it consistently demonstrate that such methods lead participants to report greater attraction to attitudinally similar strangers than dissimilar strangers (Byrne & Clore, 1970; Byrne & Griffitt, 1966; Byrne & Nelson, 1965; Clore & Baldridge, 1968; Griffitt, 1969).

There appears to be little question that in most situations individuals are more attracted to strangers who are perceived to be attitudinally similar than to those perceived to be dissimilar. However, there is no lack of controversy concerning the theoretical explanation of this phenomenon. In fact, several alternative explanations propose that the discovery of attitude similarity per se does not enhance attraction to strangers (Fishbein & Ajzen, 1972; Jellison & Oliver, 1983; Kaplan & Anderson, 1973). Since almost all of the research evidence directly supporting attitude similarity as an attraction influence comes from bogus stranger studies, it would be useful to examine some of these alternative interpretations further. Two current examples are discussed in detail below, and several more will be considered in the following section.

Rosenbaum's (1986) repulsion hypothesis provides a novel explanation of the attitude similarity-attraction association. Rosenbaum rightly argues that the great preponderance of support for attitude similarity as a positive influence on attraction is based on the works of Newcomb and of Byrne and his colleagues. He further contends that the findings from both of these research programs can be credibly interpreted as indicating that attitude dissimilarity leads to repulsion, but that similarity does not generally produce attraction.

Rosenbaum critiques Byrne's bogus stranger studies primarily on the basis of their lack of adequate no-attitude control conditions. He argues that information indicating attitude similarity would not enhance attraction to an anonymous stranger beyond normal levels, but that dissimilarity would produce repulsion. Rosenbaum (1986) tested these proposals in a series of studies that attempted to provide the necessary control conditions. As expected, participants were no more attracted to attitudinally similar strangers than to strangers representing no-attitude controls, but they were indeed repulsed by attitudinally dissimilar strangers.

Rosenbaum's explanation for these results rests on a combination of Helson's (1959, 1964) adaptation level theory and cognitive consistency theories (Festinger, 1957; Heider, 1958; Newcomb, 1953; Osgood & Tannenbaum, 1955). From this perspective, consistency, balance, congruity, and consonance are all adaptation level or stable states. It is their opposites that create motivation to change. Rosenbaum views information indicating attitude similarity in a stranger as generally a "consistent event lacking in affective or motivational potency" (p. 1164), but he views information indicating dissimilarity as inconsistent and aversive. There-fore, no change or increase in attraction should result from attitude similarity with a stranger (unless such similarity is inconsistent with past information), but repulsion should result from the aversive state produced through dissimilarity.

Another explanation of the attitude similarity-attraction association concerns the possible influence of information indicating stranger similarity on individuals' expectations about the stranger's likely evaluations of them (Aronson & Worchel, 1966). This inferred evaluation position claims that individuals expect that similar others will like them, and that this presumed evaluation produces reciprocal attraction. The inferred evaluation explanation was first proposed and examined more than 20 years ago (Aronson & Worchel, 1966; Byrne & Griffitt, 1966; Byrne & Rhamey, 1965; McWhirter & Jecker, 1967; Nelson, 1966). Since this initial debate, only limited work has investigated these contrasting proposals (Erwin, 1981; Gonzales, Davis, Loney, Lukens, & Junghans, 1983; Insko, Thompson, Stroebe, Shand, Pinner, & Layton, 1973; Stroebe, 1971).

Condon and Crano (1988) have recently suggested that the apparent rejection of the inferred evaluation perspective may have been premature, and largely due to methodological and interpretive problems in the research. They attempted to address these problems in a partial replication and extension of Byrne and Rhamey's (1965) original investigation into the role of inferred evaluation. Con-don and Crano's results support the claim that the bogus stranger association between attitude similarity and attraction is largely attributable to the effect of inferred evaluation. Their findings further indicate that social validation plays, at most, a minor role in producing the similarity-attraction relationship.

Rosenbaum's (1986) repulsion hypothesis provides an alternative perspective on the inferred evaluation findings. It may be that the primary factor in inferred evaluation is potential rejection by an attitudinally dissimilar other, and that anticipated liking from an attitudinally similar stranger is an unmotivating circum-stance. If we assume that individuals normally expect new acquaintances to have a mildly positive reaction to them, and that rejection from relative strangers is generally unexpected, then such an interpretation of Condon and Crano's (1988) results seems reasonable. Research employing an adequate no-attitude control condition from which "normal" levels of inferred evaluation could be determined is needed to examine this possibility.

Several other viable interpretations of Byrne's findings have been offered. For example, Jellison and Oliver (1983) provide evidence that individuals' attraction responses to similar and dissimilar others may be due to image-management processes (Goffman, 1959; Jones & Wortman, 1973; Schlenker, 1980; Tedeschi, 1981). Jellison and Oliver propose that individuals believe they are expected to respond in such ways, and do so to conform to others' expectations, thereby creating favorable impressions of themselves in others. Fishbein and Ajzen (1972) and Kaplan and Anderson (1973) offer information-integration explanations that argue that the social desirability of traits has been confounded with attitude similarity in past research, and that it is the social desirability variable that is largely responsible for attraction differences. Wetzel and Insko (1982) demonstrate that previous research has confounded similarity to the individual with similarity to the ideal self, and that similarity to the ideal is a much more powerful attraction influence than similarity to self. As a final example, Davis (1981) and Werner and Parmelee (1979) propose and find that similarity on topics that have implications for the quality of future interactions is of primary importance in producing the similarity-attraction relationship. This "rewards of interaction" interpretation (Berscheid & Walster, 1983) indicates that when communicative contact is involved, it is the relevance of similarity to future interactions rather than consensual validation that motivates attraction responses.

While there is much theoretical disagreement over explanations of the positive attitude similarity-attraction association in bogus stranger research, there is no doubt that such an association exists. Whether this association might be observed in normal beginning communicative relationships, as suggested by Davis's and Werner and Parmelee's findings, has not been a primary concern of this basic research. Indeed, Byrne indicates that attitude similarity would be unlikely to influence attraction in most initial encounters, because individuals would normally be unaware of one another's attitudes. He also suggests that even if attitudes were revealed, other reinforcements operating in the situation would certainly reduce the attitude similarity influence (Byrne, 1971; Byrne, Ervin, & Lamberth, 1970).

Even so, the consistent results from Byrne's program are one of the primary reasons for the general acceptance of attitude similarity as an attraction influence in existing relationships. Moreover, research from this program has demonstrated that these findings may generalize to somewhat normal beginning relationships (Byrne et al., 1970) in which attitude similarity levels are revealed and various other reinforcement sources are controlled or minimized. Several other studies have focused on theoretical concerns arising from questions about how the attitude similarity variable might operate in situations involving real or anticipated beginning communicative contact. It is to these and related questions that we now turn.

COMMUNICATION AND ATTITUDE SIMILARITY
IN BEGINNING ACQUAINTANCE

Longitudinal research clearly indicates that any association between actual attitude similarity and attraction may take weeks to emerge in normally developing relationships (Curry & Kenny, 1974; Newcomb, 1961). Newcomb (1961) assumes that actual attitude similarity comes to exert an influence on attraction through changes in perceived similarity. These changes are expected to occur through communication that provides information related to individuals' attitudes on mutually relevant topics. Since communication concerning many attitudes occurs only after relationships are well under way, it seems reasonable to assume that a considerable amount of relational time would be required before general attitude similarity level could exert attraction influences.

General attitude similarity level might normally be related to attraction only after an extended period of acquaintance, if at all. However, the work of Byrne and his colleagues makes it clear that preacquaintance attraction can be influenced by information indicating specific attitudinal similarities and dissimilarities (Byrne, 1961, 1971; Byrne & Clore, 1970; Byrne & Griffitt, 1966). Information indicating attitude similarity level is one of only a few pieces of information normally made available regarding strangers in this research. This experimental control allows an assessment of whether similarity is related to attraction and other variables in an informationally simple environment. The reported attitude similarity effect is, as expected, both more consistent and much stronger when isolated in this manner than in research on existing relations. It is also the case that the methods generally employed in these studies have required isolating attitude similarity from the important influences of interpersonal communication and communication-related variables.

Experimental control and isolation are undeniably useful in generating knowledge about processes involved in first impressions and initial attraction. However, the key role of communication in possibly linking attitude similarity and attraction in existing relationships makes it clear that an adequate understanding of this association will require examination of communication processes. Relatively few studies have given this serious consideration. As Bochner (1984) indicates, this tendency frequently reflects a failure to recognize the central role of communication in developing attraction, as well as in generating perceptions of attitude similarity.

While few studies have directly examined the influence of early-acquaintance communication processes on the attitude similarity-attraction relationship, some studies have provided limited initial interaction between participants. Most of these studies manipulate attitude similarity through some form of communicative contact that restricts interlocutors to the revelation of their attitudes on selected topics. The results of these studies indicate that even such unusual initial communicative contact substantially reduces or eliminates the attraction influence of attitude similarity. The following review begins with an examination of research employing these attitudinal exchanges, and then proceeds to studies involving more normal beginning acquaintance conversations.

One of the most unusual communication environments is provided by research on speaking in reply to the attitudes expressed by relative strangers (Brink, 1977; Lombardo, Weiss, & Stich, 1973). In this research, unseen strangers (experimental accomplices) express attitudes that are known to be dissimilar to those held by research participants. The participants are then given various opportunities to respond to these expressions. Research employing this method has shown that when individuals respond by stating their attitudes they are more attracted to strangers than when given no opportunity to reply, and that this effect is greatest for individuals who respond in their own words (Brink, 1977; Lombardo et al., 1973). This line of research has further demonstrated that attraction to strangers expressing dissimilar attitudes is as great as to those expressing similar attitudes when individuals are given the opportunity to reply in their own words, and that this elimination of the attitude similarity effect may be primarily due to elevated attraction to dissimilar strangers.

Research on the inferred evaluation explanation of the attitude similarity-attraction association provides further support for this possibility. Aronson and Worchel (1966) attempted to examine this explanation in a study involving face-to-face interaction. Participants expressed and elaborated on their attitudes regarding several topics, followed by an agreeing or a disagreeing accomplice who did the same. Individuals next exchanged written messages in which the accomplice indicated having either a very positive or negative affective reaction toward the research participant. Aronson and Worchel found that expressed liking strongly influenced attraction, but attitude similarity had no effect. In the context of the current chapter, it is possible that the opportunity to engage in limited communication with the accomplice is partly responsible for these results. As in the research on speaking in reply, individuals were allowed to express the reasons for their attitudes in their own words, with the same attraction result.

Byrne and Griffitt's (1966) partial replication of Aronson and Worchel's experiment is consistent with this explanation. Byrne and Griffitt provided a stronger manipulation of attitude similarity, and found that both expressed liking and attitude similarity influenced attraction. However, rather than allowing subjects to discuss their attitudes in their own words, as did Aronson and Worchel, Byrne and Griffitt asked participants simply to read responses from an attitude questionnaire that the participants had previously completed. As the work of Lombardo et al. (1973) and Brink (1977) demonstrates, these two methods of communicating result in different attraction responses. Responding in one's own words appears to result in a considerable reduction of the attitude similarity influence, while reading responses from a questionnaire strongly mitigates this effect of communication. The findings of Aronson and Worchel, as well as those of Byrne and Griffitt, are certainly compatible with such an interpretation.

Gormly and Gormly (1984) provide further support for the position that attitudinal self-expression reduces the attraction influence of the attitude similarity variable. Participants in this study communicated their attitudes to either a similar or dissimilar partner (an accomplice) by way of an intercom. In one condition, the participant and the accomplice read their attitudes to several items in turn, with the participant going first each time. In a second condition, this expression of attitudes was followed by a two-minute discussion. Gormly and Gormly report that individuals were more attracted to their partners when they discussed their attitudes than when they only read attitude statements, and that they were also more attracted to similar than to dissimilar partners. However, these reported main effects for communication format and attitude similarity should be interpreted cautiously in light of an apparent borderline interaction involving these two variables. The pattern of means reported by Gormly and Gormly indicates that attitude similarity positively influenced attraction when individuals read their attitudes, but was only slightly related to attraction when individuals had the opportunity to discuss their opinions. In addition, the increase in attraction to dissimilars between the reading and the discussion conditions was three times as large as for similars. These results are again consistent with the view that communicating about attitudinal topics in one's own words reduces the influence of attitude similarity through increasing attraction to dissimilar others.

While generally consistent, the results from the above research approaches that produce early-acquaintance attitudinal discussions are not directly comparable because of several methodological differences. Perhaps the most important difference concerns a distinction between attitude similarity and agreement. Let us loosely define *attitude similarity* as the degree of correspondence between the attitudes of individuals, and *agreement* as expressing concurrence with another's stated view. Much of the attitude similarity research involving communicative contact confounds the agreement and similarity variables. For example, the inferred evaluation research manipulates attitude similarity through the accomplice's agreement or disagreement with the participant's attitude statements. Given this, both similarity and agreement level are simultaneously varied. In contrast, research on speaking in reply manipulates similarity through accomplices' initiating attitude statements. In this situation, the accomplice does not agree or disagree with the participants' attitudes, because the participants' attitudes have yet to be expressed.

It should be obvious that the influences of agreement and similarity may differ. Expressions of agreement and avoidance of disagreement are normative in conversation, particularly in conversations between relative strangers (Brown & Levinson, 1978; Jackson & Jacobs, 1980; McLaughlin, Cody, & Rosenstein, 1983; Pomerantz, 1978). Unusual levels of disagreement in beginning conversations might generally be considered rude, and would likely result in a strong negative attraction influence. Research relating attraction to the degree of attitudinal agreement and disagreement expressed during conversations between relative strangers certainly appears to support this conclusion (Brewer & Brewer, 1968; Jones, 1964; Jones & Wortman, 1973), although the findings of Aronson and Worchel suggest that expressed liking can overcome this effect. In contrast, conversations that lead to the discovery of dissimilarity in the absence of disagreement should produce much weaker attraction influences (Rosenbaum, 1986). Research that examines attitude similarity through manipulation or measures of agreement should be carefully interpreted with this distinction in mind. It is also clear that an understanding of the attitude similarity-attraction relationship in early acquaintance will require more normal conversational conditions that do not promote abnormal levels of attitudinal disagreement.

Research by Storms and Thomas (1977) provides evidence that communication that is unrelated to attitudes or to attitudinal agreement may reduce the magnitude of the attitude similarity-attraction association. In their research, Storms and Thomas followed the usual bogus stranger method of manipulating participants' perceptions of their partners' attitudes. Each participant then met his or her partner (an experimental accomplice) and engaged in a brief communication exchange in which first the participant and then the accomplice provided some autobiographical information. Storms and Thomas found that individuals were more attracted to both similar and dissimilar partners after interacting with them. As in the previous research involving attitudinal discussions, these autobiographical exchanges produced greater increases in attraction to dissimilar partners than to similar partners.

Levinger (1972) found similar results regarding the influence of attitude similarity on attraction in a somewhat more representative communication situation. Levinger manipulated attitude similarity through a variation on bogus stranger methods. Each participant subsequently met and conversed with his or her partner (an experimental accomplice) as they worked together on an experimental task. Both attitude similarity and communication stage influenced attraction in this research. Individuals were more attracted to similar partners than to dissimilar partners, and were more attracted to partners after talking with them than before conversing. In addition, Levinger reports a statistical interaction between similarity and communication stage. This interaction reflects a greater increase in attraction to dissimilar partners than to similar partners subsequent to the conversation, again suggesting that communication mitigates the influence of attitude similarity.

Byrne et al. (1970) report results that are inconsistent with this general pattern. They examined the attitude similarity-attraction relationship in a computer dating study that provided participants with the opportunity to engage in an extended initial conversation. Participants were sent on a 30-minute "Coke date" with partners who had previously given either primarily similar or dissimilar responses to a questionnaire containing personality and attitude measures. In one variation, partners were informed that they had either similar or dissimilar responses to the questionnaire, while in another condition they were asked to imagine this. Measures of attraction obtained subsequent to the date were found to be positively associated with this manipulation of attitude similarity level. Although this research lacked an appropriate control condition that would allow a direct assessment of attraction changes attributable to the dating interaction, somewhat comparable no-interaction conditions were included. The results from these conditions suggest that attraction may have been uninfluenced by the dating interaction.

The results from this study appear to conflict with most of the previously reviewed research in which individuals were allowed to communicate with one another. In contrast to these works, Byrne et al. provide no evidence of a communication influence on either attraction or the attitude similarity-attraction relationship. There are several possible explanations for these different results. One possibility is that as initial communicative contact becomes less constrained and more normal, the influence of communication on attraction processes is reduced. This is an unlikely explanation on several counts. Many attraction influences are present during normal conversations that would be unavailable in more controlled interactions. As Byrne et al. (1970) suggest, the additional reinforcements in these more normal interactions would likely overwhelm or substantially reduce the attraction influence of attitude similarity. A decreased attraction influence of communication in Byrne et al. seems an implausible explanation.

Several aspects of the unique research environment in this study suggest explanations for these conflicting findings. First, Byrne et al. indicate that the computer dating study was widely discussed in their student population, with the result that almost all of the subjects had heard something about the study prior to participating. Such subject awareness would have unpredictable attraction effects that could provide a partial explanation of the unusual findings. Second, the similarity examined and manipulated in this study was only partially concerned with attitude. The majority of items on which the similarity manipulation was based were personality related. Since the previous studies discussed were limited to similarity of attitudes, this difference in type of similarity could partially account for the contradictory results.

The manner of manipulating similarity combined with the computer dating nature of the study provides another plausible interpretation. Byrne et al. informed their participants that computer dating and the variables that influence individuals' reactions to one another were being investigated. Assuming that individuals perceive that computer dating services attempt to match compatible people, it seems likely that many participants suspected that variables were being manipulated to produce variations in compatibility. If so, then partners in the high-similarity condition may have perceived that they were compatible, while those in the low-similarity condition suspected incompatibility. This would suggest that similarity and compatibility were confounded by the similarity manipulation.

Finally, participants were instructed to learn as much as possible about one another during their date in order to respond to postinteraction questions about their partners. Interlocutors who followed these instructions may have attempted to acquire much more information about one another than normal. Given that partners were aware that their pairing was based on responses to the attitude questionnaire, they may have focused their conversation on these issues. It is quite possible that an unusually high number of exchanges of attitudinal information may have consequently occurred in these dyads. In dissimilar dyads these exchanges would have been more likely to result in norm-violating disagreement than in similar dyads, with potential negative repercussions for attraction.

Taken together, these possibilities indicate that a conclusion about the influence of attitude similarity on attraction in Byrne et al.'s research is unwarranted. In the research discussed below, an experimental approach to studying the interrelationship of type of conversation, attitude similarity, and attraction that overcomes these alternative possibilities is presented. As will be seen, the findings from this approach are again consistent with research showing a communication-produced reduction in or elimination of the attitude similarity-attraction relationship.

Sunnafrank and Miller (1981) propose that a reduced influence of attitude similarity in typical early-acquaintance conversations would derive from interlocutors' goals of achieving stable, predictable, and controllable communicative environments (Heider, 1958). To obtain these goals, individuals engage in phatic communication and avoid potentially controversial topics. Sunnafrank and Miller further posit that the degree to which these goals are achieved is the primary determinant of attraction in beginning acquaintance. This communication-based perspective on initial attraction suggests that past research that mandated or encouraged attitudinal exchanges during initial communicative contact is not informative about this process. Moreover, this perspective indicates that an adequate understanding of the attitude similarity-attraction association in acquaintance requires research that realizes more normal communicative processes.

Sunnafrank and Miller suggest that during normal early-acquaintance and preacquaintance situations individuals might seek information about a few attitudes of relative strangers if those attitudes are perceived to have implications for or to be relevant to future interactions (Davis, 1981; Newcomb, 1961). Such information might be acquired from mutual acquaintances, inferred from the social context of the initial encounter, or deduced from limited demographic information about the stranger. If this information indicates that the relevant attitudes are similar, then in most cases individuals would perceive that the stability, predictability, and control goals would be satisfied in future interactions, thereby increasing attraction. Conversely, information indicating attitude dissimilarity on interaction-relevant attitudes would likely threaten these goals, leading to lower levels of attraction. Sunnafrank and Miller propose that these differences in goal satisfaction states, combined with consensual validation influences, would produce the usual bogus stranger attraction results in such preacquaintance situations.

Once individuals meet and engage in normal initial conversations, the goal-related influence of preacquaintance attitude similarity should be overcome. Sunnafrank and Miller suggest that the phatic communication occurring in these get-acquainted conversations would provide goal satisfaction. This function of initial conversations should have little influence on attraction between preacquaintance similars, since they already expect these goals to be satisfied. In fact, it may be that individuals anticipate relatively stable, predictable, and controllable interactions during initial acquaintance, even in the absence of preacquaintance information. Normally proceeding get-acquainted conversations would simply confirm expectations in such cases, and produce only mildly positive attraction influences. Goal satisfaction generated during nonthreatening, conflict-free initial conversations would have rather different consequences for preacquaintance dissimilars. This reduction in the threat to goals should lead to substantial increases in attraction between these partners.

Sunnafrank and Miller tested this perspective through an extension of Byrne's (1971) methods. Partners were selected on the basis of their similarity/dissimilarity regarding two controversial topics. In order to assure the mutual relevance of attitude topics, participants were informed that they and their partners would meet and work together on a project involving both topics. Partners' attitudinal responses were then exchanged. Participants in a no-interaction condition next responded to a questionnaire containing an attraction measure, while participants in an initial-interaction condition responded to this questionnaire after spending five minutes getting acquainted with their partners. Participants in both of these conditions continued to expect that the next phase of the study would involve the attitude-relevant project.

Sunnafrank and Miller found that get-acquainted conversations overcame the influence of preacquaintance similarity by producing a large increase in attraction to dissimilar partners combined with no change in attraction to similars. My own further investigation of this phenomenon has demonstrated that get-acquainted conversations followed by discussions of relevant attitude topics continue to result in equal attraction between similar and dissimilar partners (Sunnafrank, 1983); that get-acquainted conversations influence perceived attitude similarity, but that perceived attitude similarity is unrelated or weakly related to attraction in these circumstances (Sunnafrank, 1986); and that only atypical initial conversations focused entirely on attitude topics produce a positive similarity-attraction association, though even this association is substantially reduced from preacquaintance levels (Sunnafrank, 1984). In all of these subsequent studies, conversation has continued to increase attraction to preacquaintance dissimilars, but not to similars.

These findings are again consistent with the general pattern of communication influence documented above. It should be noted that my use of only two attitudes may produce a relatively weak similarity manipulation. However, this manipulation has been sufficient to produce large attraction differences in preacquaintance, as well as in perceived similarity on a variety of other attitude topics. The apparent strength of my manipulation is consistent with Byrne's research, which demonstrates that it is the proportion of similar attitudes and not the number that produces the attraction influence (Byrne, 1971; Byrne & Nelson, 1965; Griffitt, 1974).

Wright and Crawford (1971) report further results that bear on this issue. They manipulated attitudinal agreement level on 10 discussion topics, and also allowed participants to interact in a mildly pleasant, attitudinally neutral context. Wright and Crawford found that individuals were equally attracted to agreeing and disagreeing partners. These findings suggest that even when a relatively large number of relevant attitudes are revealed, attraction between partners who have engaged in goal-satisfying conversations is uninfluenced by similarity.

Several limitations of the overall research on initial acquaintance are addressed above, but a few other concerns merit mention. First, in most of these studies participants were unlikely to perceive that they would continue to interact with their partners outside of the research environment. Certainly future contact was possible in studies involving face-to-face interaction. Suggestions of, or provisions for, such contact could even have been made in studies involving relatively free discussion. In fact, Byrne et al. (1970) report that some dating partners did continue their relationships. With these few possible exceptions, participants in initial-acquaintance studies likely expected that their relationships would begin and end in the laboratory. Given this, even dissimilarity on topics relevant to their laboratory interaction may have been more easily dealt with than in situations involving the expectation of continuing contact. Research is needed to investigate this possibility.

Second, the importance of attitude topics to research participants, their interest in the topics, and the implications of the topics for interactions have not been systematically varied and examined in this research. Previous work has demonstrated the potential attraction influence of these variables in bogus stranger settings (Byrne, 1971; Davis, 1981). Such influences could conceivably continue or even strengthen once individuals meet and begin to converse. Again, further research is needed.

Despite these limitations, studies of initial communicative contact have produced remarkably consistent results regarding the relationship of attitude similarity and attraction. Research demonstrates that initial contact involving attitudinal discussions or even the simple expression of attitudes in one's own words eliminates or sharply reduces the strength of the attitude similarity-attraction association. Initial exchanges of nonattitudinal information in highly restricted communicative environments, as well as in more normal initial conversations, produce similar results. Even when attitudes are relevant to future interactions, get-acquainted conversations serve to eliminate the influence of similarity on attraction. This effect of communication contact has almost universally involved a relatively large increase in attraction to attitudinally dissimilar strangers, and no change or little change in attraction to similars — findings that strongly support Rosenbaum's (1986) repulsion hypothesis. While these results regarding the relationship of attitude similarity and attraction in beginning acquaintance appear to be highly dependable, many questions regarding the role of communication processes in the similarity-attraction association obviously remain.

SUMMARY

Do the research results justify lawlike status for the propositions that attitude similarity and attraction are positively associated, that attitude similarity increases attraction, and that attitude similarity produces this influence, at least in part, through consensual validation? Support for these claims is largely limited to findings from bogus stranger research. The first proposition is clearly affirmed in these instances. However, doubt remains concerning the cause of the association. It is beginning to appear increasingly likely that a stranger's dissimilarity may produce repulsion (Rosenbaum, 1986), rather than similarity causing attraction. The proposal that consensual validation accounts for this attraction influence is being questioned by several other viable explanations. Research continues to investigate these alternatives, and will for the foreseeable future.

None of these propositions qualifies as lawlike or even as an empirical generalization when attraction between initial acquaintances is considered. With one possible exception (Byrne et al., 1970), research demonstrates that the opportunity to communicate with a relative stranger in one's own words reduces the strength of the attitude similarity-attraction relationship through increasing attraction to dissimilar others. In several studies this reduction eliminates the similarity-attraction association (Brink, 1977; Sunnafrank, 1983, 1985, 1986; Sunnafrank & Miller, 1981; Wright & Crawford, 1971). As Byrne (1971; Byrne et al., 1970) suggests, other factors operating in initial acquaintance are likely to mitigate or overwhelm the attitude similarity influence. Research is just beginning to examine the communication factors that may be responsible for this result.

Findings from research on existing and developing relationships are frequently unsupportive of a positive association between attitude similarity and attraction. Individuals in committed romantic relationships have consistently been found to be attitudinally similar. However, a significant portion of this similarity appears to be due to attitudinal consensus in the population of potential partners. Indirect evidence suggests that attitude similarity may influence attraction between romantic partners in the early stages of relationship development, but no such association is evident in subsequent relational stages. Research on friend relationships provides little evidence of attitude similarity among friendship pairs, and no support for an attitude similarity-attraction association. Finally, research on roommate relationships provides highly inconsistent support for a weak attraction influence attributable to attitude similarity.

It would appear from this review that reports regarding the attitude similarity-attraction association have been greatly exaggerated. These variables are only clearly associated in preacquaintance. Once communication contact takes place in primarily social relationships, attitude similarity level appears to play a relatively minor and inconsistent role in attraction. In the following closing remarks, I would like to indicate some directions for future thought and research on attitude similarity that may be especially amenable to a communication focus. Perhaps such a focus will eventually affirm age-old views regarding the attitude similarity-attraction relationship.

COMMUNICATION AND SIMILARITY:
SOME FURTHER CONSIDERATIONS

The above findings might lead one to question the wisdom of further pursuing the attitude similarity-attraction relationship from a communication perspective. If research demonstrates that attitude similarity is unrelated or only weakly related to attraction and relational development in communicative relationships, then aren't there much more important and relevant communication issues with which to be concerned? The answer to this question will obviously depend on one's personal and theoretical interests. My own view is that attitude similarity and related processes may play a central role in illuminating the functions of communication in developing attraction and changing relationships. Whether or not they do will hinge on the questions we ask. Let me end this essay by suggesting a few unresolved issues from the above literature that might prove useful in formulating these questions.

One important issue with implications for ongoing programs of communication research concerns Rosenbaum's repulsion hypothesis. It is becoming increasingly clear that a key to understanding the attitude similarity-attraction association in early acquaintance is to focus on dissimilarity as repulsive rather than similarity as attractive. Rosenbaum's hypothesis is supported by his own data, his reinterpretation of findings from Newcomb's and Byrne's programs, and almost all of the relevant research on beginning communicative contact. In addition, Byrne, Clore, and Smeaton (1986) have acknowledged that repulsion due to attitude dissimilarity may be a much more powerful attraction influence then similarity in the early stages of relationship formation.

Individuals' typical conversational strategy of avoiding controversial topics and disagreement during early acquaintance may function to reduce or eliminate the potential for repulsion. This strategy may allow one to achieve various interpersonal goals (Brown & Levinson, 1978: Sunnafrank & Miller, 1981). However, the unintended discovery of some dissimilarity during early acquaintance may occur or even be probable. McLaughlin et al. (1983) have attempted to delineate the conversational strategies individuals employ when confronted with the discovery of such dissimilarity or disagreement in initial conversations. The communicative strategy one employs when this occurs would very likely be the key factor in determining the degree of repulsion, if any, that would result. For example, research on message openness (Broome, 1983) indicates that the more open-minded one appears in stating dissimilar attitudes, the more positive are the resulting attraction influences. Further investigations on the discovery of dissimilarity in typical initial interactions, and the attraction effect of resulting conversational strategies, may well lead to a better understanding of the weak or nonexistent similarity-attraction association in such interactions.

Aside from initial-interaction situations in which dissimilarity is unintentionally discovered, there are certainly situations in which discussion of topics involving potential dissimilarity and disagreement would be necessary. For example, decision-making situations in organizations frequently involve the expression of, and disagreement with, members' attitudes. In such situations, the communicative strategy one employs could be critical in determining one's degree of success in influencing both organizational decisions and maintaining interpersonal goals. O'Keefe and Shepherd (1987) have directly addressed situations involving attitudinal disagreement in which these multiple goals of achieving interpersonal success and persuasive success were involved. Their findings indicate that individuals who employ integration message strategies designed to advance both aims are the most interpersonally successful, and are as likely as other strategists to be successful persuaders. Future research that compares attraction resulting from these strategies to attraction levels from comparable conversations involving agreement is needed to determine the degree to which such strategies overcome repulsion responses.

Aronson and Worchel's (1966) and Condon and Crano's (1988) findings that messages indicating liking from another reduce the negative effects of attitude disagreement suggests other areas for communication research. Broome's (1983) research demonstrates that messages that simply increase the expectations of positive evaluations from strangers reduce the negative effects of dissimilarity. It may be that messages that generate such positive expectations are common in beginning conversations, which could partially explain the consistent finding that initial interactions overcome the negative influence of revealed attitude dissimilarity (Levinger, 1972; Sunnafrank & Miller, 1981; Wright & Crawford, 1971). Research in such areas as affinity seeking (Bell & Daly, 1984; Bell, Tremblay, & Buerkel-Rothfuss, 1987), relational messages (Burgoon, Buller, Hale, & deTurck, 1984; Burgoon & Hale, 1984, 1988), and rhetorical sensitivity (Hart & Burks, 1972; Hart, Carlson, & Eadie, 1980) may help illuminate the communicative strategies individuals employ to produce perceptions that they like another while disagreeing with or revealing potential areas of dissimilarity to the other.

On a related issue, the general tendency to avoid controversial topics and disagreement and to focus on topics of agreement during early acquaintance may lead to both intended and unintended consequences. Interlocutors who employ this strategy may succeed in getting their partners to like them, and to think this liking is reciprocal (Jones, 1964; Jones & Wortman, 1973). They would also be likely to cause their partners to perceive that a high degree of attitude similarity exists between them (Sunnafrank, 1986). This would partially explain the relatively strong correlation typically observed between perceived attitude similarity and attraction (Duck, 1976). It would also explain the consistent finding that individuals perceive greater attitude similarity with others than actually exists (Sillars & Scott, 1983). Of course, both the degree of perceived similarity and the discrepancy between perceived and actual similarity will vary greatly. Individual differences in tendencies to use agreement strategies would partly account for these variations. Individuals who engage in such conversational patterns as producing high levels of reciprocal interpersonal exchanges (Altman, 1973) and other methods of speech accommodation (Giles & Powesland, 1975; Giles & Street, 1985) may also increase partner perceptions of attitude similarity levels. Moreover, certain reinforcement properties of others (e.g., physical attractiveness, status) that make them desirable partners may lead to greater use of these conversational tactics. The successful use of such strategies should produce high levels of perceived attitude similarity, as well as increase the likelihood of relational development. In some cases, relationships containing members with highly discrepant perceived and actual attitude similarity levels will successfully progress beyond casual acquaintance through these conversational processes.

When high perceived attitude similarity is combined with very discrepant perceived and actual similarity levels, the likelihood of future relational strain and problems may increase dramatically. High levels of perceived attitude similarity may eventually lead individuals to make relatively bald and unguarded attitude statements. Blunt revelation of attitudes in the presence of actual dissimilarity may lead to several potentially negative conversational and relational consequences. These embarrassing occurrences might produce anger and destructive conflict in some cases, particularly when the attitude in question is important to, or intensely held by, one or both partners. Even when surprising dissimilarities are discovered less directly, an individual may suspect that his or her former perception of similarity was generated by partner deception or disingenuousness. Such discoveries would likely have negative consequences for several key relational variables, including trust, perceptions of partner credibility, self-disclosure level, intimacy of communication content, and attraction.

Studies focusing on analogous surprises (Planalp & Honeycutt, 1985) have shown that such negative events may increase uncertainty (Berger & Bradac, 1982; Berger & Calabrese, 1975) and result in relational conflict and dissolution. Obviously, the likelihood of these attitudinal surprises occurring should increase as the discrepancy between perceived and actual similarity widens. I am suggesting that early-acquaintance conversation strategies, which give rise to erroneously high perceptions of similarity, may sow the seeds of relational discontent. Research on communication in deescalating relationships (Baxter, 1985; Cody, 1982; Cupach & Metts, 1986; Duck, 1982; Miller & Parks, 1982) could bear directly on these issues.

Another seemingly crucial issue for understanding an attitude similarity-attraction association in communicative relationships concerns the mutual relevance of attitude objects. From Newcomb's (1961) perspective, mutual relevance is necessary before attraction-related processes would be engaged. Newcomb considers an object to have mutual relevance when one or both partners perceive that they have a common fate with respect to the object: that each one's own consequences regarding it are bound to his or her partner's. In noncompetitive situations, attitudinal similarity on such relevant objects would normally aid individuals in achieving relational and individual goals regarding these consequences, while dissimilarity would thwart goal achievement.

It is clear that topic relevance has not been adequately considered in most studies of existing and developing relationships. The most common research approach to relevance is simply ignoring the issue, followed closely by research in which topics are chosen for their assumed relevance. Obviously, the former approach is ineffective, and the latter depends entirely on the insightfulness of the particular researcher. Experimentally inducing relevance is possible in studies of initial acquaintance, but would generally be inappropriate in research on naturally occurring relationships. At a minimum, adequate measures of topic relevance need to be employed to allow a serious examination of the relevance variable in these ongoing relationships.

In developing such measures, it will be necessary to understand that the topics that may be highly relevant in one type or stage of relationship may be irrelevant in another. It also seems likely that the topics that are most relevant in many ongoing relationships will prove idiographic. If so, then studies of individual cases may be necessary to unravel interrelationships involving attitude similarity, topic relevance, relational quality, and related issues. Research that focuses on the content and themes (Owen, 1984) of communicative transactions may produce an understanding of some of the topic categories that are likely to have greater relevance in varying phases and classes of relationships, as well as in individual relationships. An assessment of the goals individuals attempt to serve in and through particular relationships would also provide important information concerning topic relevance.

An approach to relevance suggested by Lea and Duck (1982) may prove useful in this analysis. They propose that both the importance of a value to an individual and the uncommonness of similarity with respect to this value increase its relevance. In more general terms, if an individual has an unusual attitude on an important topic, then the discovery of similarity with another should make that topic more relevant to their relationship. Presumably, the rarer the attitudinal support received, the more partners would focus on the topic in their conversations and in evaluating their relationship.

Another promising approach related to the relevance issue that may be particularly useful in communication research is provided by Davis's (1981) work on implications for interactions. From this perspective, those topics that are perceived to have greater implications for the quality of future interactions would be more likely to influence attraction responses and relational trajectories. Attitudinal similarity on such topics would generally be perceived as increasing the quality of future interactions and positively influencing attraction and the relationship. Davis's research suggests that activity preferences have the strongest implications for interaction in early acquaintance. As in the previous discussion of topic relevance, topics that have implications for interaction will likely vary across types and stages of relationships, as well as across individual relationships as they move beyond initial acquaintance.

This consideration of topic relevance and interaction implications leads to the inevitable conclusion that past research on naturally occurring relations has generally taken an overly gross approach to the attitude similarity variable. It may well be that in most such relationships only a few pivotal and relatively idiosyncratic attitudinal similarities or dissimilarities will have sufficient relevance and importance to influence partner attraction and relationship quality. A few attitudes reflecting activity preference or interest similarities, in the absence of other important and relevant attitudinal dissimilarities, may be enough to begin and maintain many positive relationships. Conversely, one or a few relevant attitudinal dissimilarities may be a source of continued conflict and tension.

These few critical similarities and dissimilarities would go undetected with most current measures of attitude and value similarity. Even if attitudes concerning these critical topics were tapped by general measures, they would have a relatively small impact on the overall level of similarity reported. The inconsistent and weak support for an attitude similarity-attraction association in existing and developing relationships is unsurprising given this analysis. Future research that employs methods capable of detecting such critical attitudinal similarities and dissimilarities may well find that similarity and attraction are strongly related when highly relevant attitude topics with strong implications for interaction are considered.

While there are several other communication questions that arise from a consideration of the attitude similarity-attraction literature, perhaps it is appropriate to end on the above optimistic note concerning the future potential for investigations in this area. I began this chapter by noting the generally accepted view that attitude similarity positively influences attraction. With the exception of attraction between unacquainted individuals, the research evidence generally indicates otherwise. However, the jury is still out. A continuing focus on communication processes will allow the deliberations to proceed. As always, research is needed.

REFERENCES

a Kempis, T. (1980). *The imitation of Christ* (P. M. Beehtel, Ed.). Chicago: Moody. (Original work written c. 1427)

Allport, G. W., & Vernon, P. E. (1931). *A study of values.* Boston: Houghton Mifflin.

Altman, I. (1973). Reciprocity in interpersonal exchange. *Journal for the Theory of Social Behavior, 3,* 249-261.

Aristotle (1932). *The rhetoric.* New York: Appleton-Century-Crofts. (Original work written c. 330 B.C.)

Aronson, E., & Worchel, S. (1966). Similarity versus liking as determinants of interpersonal attractiveness. *Psychonomic Science, 5,* 157-158.

Baxter, L. A. (1985). Accomplishing relational disengagement. In S. Duck & D. Perlman (Eds.), *Understanding personal relationships: An interdisciplinary approach* (pp. 243-266). Beverly Hills, CA: Sage.

Bell, R. A., & Daly, J. A. (1984). The affinity-seeking function of communication. *Communication Monographs, 51,* 91-115.

Bell, R. A., Tremblay, S. W., & Buerkel-Rothfuss, N. L. (1987). Interpersonal attraction as a communication accomplishment: Development of a measure of affinity-seeking competence. *Western Journal of Speech Communication, 51,* 1-18.

Berger, C. R., & Bradac, J. J. (1982). *Language and social knowledge: Uncertainty in interpersonal relations.* London: Edward Arnold.

Berger, C. R., & Calabrese, R. (1975). Some explorations in initial interactions and beyond: Toward a developmental theory of interpersonal communication. *Human Communication Research, 1,* 99-112.

Berscheid, E., & Walster, E. (1974). Physical attractiveness. In L. Berkowitz (Ed.), *Advances in experimental social psychology* (pp. 158-216). New York: Academic Press.

Berscheid, E., & Walster, E. (1983). *Interpersonal attraction.* Reading, MA: Addison-Wesley.

Bochner, A. P. (1984). The functions of human communication in interpersonal bonding. In C. C. Arnold & J. W. Bowers (Eds.), *Handbook of rhetorical and communication theory* (pp. 544-621). Boston: Allyn & Bacon.

Brink, J. H. (1977). Effect of interpersonal communication on attraction. *Journal of Personality and Social Psychology, 35,* 783-790.

Brewer, R. E., & Brewer, M. B. (1968). Attraction and accuracy of perception in dyads. *Journal of Personality and Social Psychology, 8,* 188-193.

Broome, B. J. (1983). The attraction paradigm revisited: Responses to dissimilar others. *Human Communication Research, 10,* 137-151.

Brown, P., & Levinson, S. (1978). Universals in language usage: Politeness phenomena. In E. N. Goody (Ed.), *Questions and politeness* (pp. 56-289). Cambridge: Cambridge University Press.

Burgoon, J. K., Buller, D. B., Hale, J. L., & deTurck, M. A. (1984). Relational messages associated with nonverbal behaviors. *Human Communication Research, 10,* 351-378.

Burgoon, J. K., & Hale, J. L. (1984). The fundamental topoi of relational communication. *Communication Monographs, 51,* 193-214.

Burgoon, J. K., & Hale, J. L. (1988). Nonverbal expectancy violations: Model elaboration and application to immediacy behaviors. *Communication Monographs, 55*, 58-79.

Byrne, D. (1961). Interpersonal attraction and attitude similarity. *Journal of Abnormal and Social Psychology, 62*, 713-715.

Byrne, D. (1971). *The attraction paradigm.* New York: Academic Press.

Byrne, D., & Blaylock, B. (1963). Similarity and assumed similarity of attitudes between husbands and wives. *Journal of Abnormal and Social Psychology, 67*, 636-640.

Byrne, D., & Clore, G. L. (1970). A reinforcement model of evaluative responses. *Personality: An International Journal, 1*, 103-128.

Byrne, D., Clore, G. L., & Smeaton, G. (1986). The attraction hypothesis: Do similar attitudes affect anything? *Journal of Personality and Social Psychology, 51*, 1167-1170.

Byrne, D., Ervin, C. R., & Lamberth, J. (1970). Continuity between the experimental study of attraction and real-life computer dating. *Journal of Personality and Social Psychology, 16*, 157-165.

Byrne, D., & Griffitt, W. (1966). Similarity versus liking: A clarification. *Psychonomic Science, 6*, 295-296.

Byrne, D., & Nelson, D. (1965). Attraction as a linear function of proportion of positive reinforcements. *Journal of Personality and Social Psychology, 1*, 659-663.

Byrne, D., & Rhamey, R. (1965). Magnitude of positive and negative reinforcements as a determinant of attraction. *Journal of Personality and Social Psychology, 2*, 884-889.

Cappella, J. N., & Palmer, M. T. (1988, May). *Attitude similarity and attraction: The mediating effects of kinesic and vocal behaviors.* Paper presented at the annual meeting of the International Communication Association, New Orleans.

Clore, G. L., & Baldridge, B. (1968). Interpersonal attraction: The role of agreement and topic interest. *Journal of Personality and Social Psychology, 9*, 340-346.

Cody, M. J. (1982). A typology of disengagement strategies and an examination of the role intimacy, reactions to inequity and relational problems play in strategy selection. *Communication Monographs, 49*, 148-170.

Condon, J. W., & Crano, W. D. (1988). Inferred evaluation and the relation between attitude similarity and interpersonal attraction. *Journal of Personality and Social Psychology, 54*, 789-797.

Cupach, W. R., & Metts, S. (1986). Accounts of relational dissolution: A comparison of marital and non-marital relationships. *Communication Monographs, 53*, 311-334.

Curry, T. J., & Emerson, R. M. (1970). Balance theory: A theory of interpersonal attraction? *Sociometry, 33*, 216-238.

Curry, T. J., & Kenny, D. A. (1974). The effects of perceived and actual similarity in values and personality in the process of interpersonal attraction. *Quality and Quantity, 8*, 27-44.

Davis, D. (1981). Implications for interaction versus effectance as mediators of the similarity-attraction relationship. *Journal of Experimental Social Psychology, 17*, 96-116.

De Wolfe, T. E., & Jackson, L. A. (1984). Birds of a brighter feather: Level of moral reasoning and similarity of attitude as determinants of interpersonal attraction. *Psychological Reports, 54*, 303-308.

Duck, S. (1976). Interpersonal communication in developing acquaintance. In G. R. Miller (Ed.), *Explorations in interpersonal communication* (pp. 127-148). Beverly Hills, CA: Sage.

Duck, S. (1982). A topography of relationship disengagement and dissolution. In S. Duck (Ed.), *Personal relationships 4: Dissolving personal relationships* (pp. 1-30). London: Academic Press.

Erwin, P. G. (1981). The role of attitudinal similarity and perceived acceptance evaluation in interpersonal attraction. *Journal of Psychology, 109*, 133-136.

Erwin, P. G. (1982). The role of attitudinal similarity and direct acceptance-evaluation in attraction. *Journal of Psychology, 111*, 97-100.

Farber, B. (1957). An index of marital integration. *Sociometry, 20*, 117-134.

Festinger, L. (1954). A theory of social comparison processes. *Human Relations, 7*, 117-140.

Festinger, L. (1957). *A theory of cognitive dissonance.* Stanford, CA: Stanford University Press.

Fishbein, M., & Ajzen, I. (1972). Attitudes and opinions. *Annual Review of Psychology, 23*, 487-544.

Galton, F. (1952). *Hereditary genius: An inquiry into its laws and consequences.* New York: Horizon. (Original work published 1870)

Giles, H., & Powesland, P. F. (1975). *Speech style and social evaluation.* London: Academic Press.

Giles, H., & Street, R. L., Jr. (1985). Communicator characteristics and behavior. In M. L. Knapp & G. R. Miller (Eds.), *Handbook of interpersonal communication* (pp. 205-262). Beverly Hills, CA: Sage.

Goffman, E. (1959). *The presentation of self in everyday life.* Garden City, NY: Doubleday.

Gonzales, M. H., Davis, J. M., Loney, G. L., Lukens, C. K., & Junghans, C. M. (1983). Interactional approach to interpersonal attraction. *Journal of Personality and Social Psychology, 44,* 1192-1197.

Gormly, A. V., & Gormly, J. B. (1984). The impact of discussion on interpersonal attraction. *Bulletin of the Psychonomic Society, 22,* 45-48.

Griffitt, W. (1969). Attitude evoked anticipatory responses and attraction. *Psychonomic Science, 14,* 153-155.

Griffitt, W. (1974). Attitude similarity and attraction. In T. L. Huston (Ed.), *Foundations of interpersonal attraction* (pp. 285-308). New York: Academic Press.

Hart, R. P., & Burks, D. M. (1972). Rhetorical sensitivity and social interaction. *Speech Monographs, 39,* 75-91.

Hart, R. P., Carlson, R. E., & Eadie, W. F. (1980). Attitudes toward communication and the assessment of rhetorical sensitivity. *Communication Monographs, 47,* 1-22.

Heider, F. (1958). *The psychology of interpersonal relations.* New York: John Wiley.

Helson, H. (1959). Adaptation level theory. In S. Koch (Ed.), *Psychology: A study of a science* (Vol. 1, pp. 565-621). New York: McGraw-Hill.

Helson, H. (1964). *Adaptation level theory: An experimental and systematic approach to behavior.* New York: Harper & Row.

Hendrick, S. S. (1981). Self-disclosure and marital satisfaction. *Journal of Personality and Social Psychology, 40,* 1150-1159.

Hobart, C. W. (1956). Disagreement and non-empathy during courtship: A restudy. *Marriage and Family Living, 18,* 317-322.

Hunt, A. M. (1935). A study of the relative value of certain ideals. *Journal of Abnormal and Social Psychology, 30,* 222-228.

Insko, C. A., Nacoste, R. W., & Moe, J. L. (1983). Belief congruence and racial discrimination: Review of the evidence and critical evaluation. *European Journal of Social Psychology, 13,* 153-174.

Inskoe, C. A., Thompson, V. D., Stroebe, W., Shand, K. F., Pinner, B. F., & Layton, B. D. (1973). Implied evaluation and the similarity-attraction effect. *Journal of Personality and Social Psychology, 25,* 297-308.

Jackson, S., & Jacobs, S. (1980). Structure of conversational argument: Pragmatic bases for the enthymeme. *Quarterly Journal of Speech, 66,* 251-265.

Jamieson, D. W., Lydon, J. E., Zanna, M. P. (1987). Attitude and activity preference similarity: Differential bases of interpersonal attraction for low and high self-monitors. *Journal of Personality and Social Psychology, 53,* 1052-1060.

Jellison, J. M., & Oliver, D. F. (1983). Attitude similarity and attraction: An impression management approach. *Personality and Social Psychology Bulletin, 9,* 111-115.

Jones, E. E. (1964). *Ingratiation.* New York: Appleton-Century-Crofts.

Jones, E. E., & Wortman, C. (1973). *Ingratiation: An attributional approach.* Morristown, NJ: General Learning Press.

Kandel, D. B. (1978). Similarity in real-life adolescent friendship pairs. *Journal of Personality and Social Psychology, 36,* 306-312.

Kaplan, M. F., & Anderson, N. H. (1973). Comparison of information integration and reinforcement models for interpersonal attraction. *Journal of Personality and Social Psychology, 28,* 301-312.

Kerckhoff, A. C., & Davis, K. E. (1962). Value consensus and need complementarity in mate selection. *American Sociological Review, 27,* 295-303.

Kirkpatrick, C., & Hobart, C. (1954). Disagreement, disagreement estimate, and nonempathetic imputations for intimacy groups varying from favorite date to married. *American Sociological Review, 19,* 10-19.

Kirkpatrick, C., & Stone, S. (1935). Attitude measurement and the comparison of generations. *Journal of Applied Psychology, 19,* 564-582.

Lea, M., & Duck, S. (1982). A model for the role of similarity of values in friendship development. *British Journal of Social Psychology, 21*, 301-310.

Levinger, G. (1972). Little sand box and big quarry: Comments on Byrne's paradigmatic spade for research on interpersonal attraction. *Representative Research in Social Psychology, 3*, 3-19.

Levinger, G., & Breedlove, J. (1966). Interpersonal attraction and agreement: A study of marriage partners. *Journal of Personality and Social Psychology, 3*, 367-372.

Levinger, G., Senn, D. J., & Jorgensen, B. W. (1970). Progress toward permanence in courtship: A test of the Kerckhoff-Davis hypotheses. *Sociometry, 33*, 427-443.

Lombardo, J. P., Weiss, R. F., & Stich, M. H. (1973). Effectance reduction through speaking in reply and its relation to attraction. *Journal of Personality and Social Psychology, 28*, 325-332.

Lott, A. J., & Lott, B. E. (1974). The role of reward in the formation of positive interpersonal attitudes. In T. E. Huston (Ed.), *Foundations of interpersonal attraction* (pp. 171-192). New York: Academic Press.

McLaughlin, M. L., Cody, M. J., & Rosenstein, N. E. (1983). Account sequences in conversations between strangers. *Communication Monographs, 50*, 102-125.

McWhirter, R. M., & Jecker, J. D. (1967). Attitude similarity and inferred attraction. *Psychonomic Science, 7*, 225-226.

Miller, G. R., & Parks, M. R. (1982). Communication in dissolving relationships. In S. Duck (Ed.), *Personal relationships 4: Dissolving personal relationships* (pp. 127-154). London: Academic Press.

Moreland, R. L., & Zajonc, R. B. (1982). Exposure effect in person perception: Familiarity, similarity, and attraction. *Journal of Experimental Social Psychology, 18*, 395-415.

Nelson, D. (1966). *Attitude similarity and interpersonal attraction: The approval-cue hypothesis*. Paper presented at the annual meeting of the Southwestern Psychological Association, Arlington, VA.

Newcomb, T. M. (1953). An approach to the study of communicative acts. *Psychological Review, 60*, 393-404.

Newcomb, T. M. (1961). *The acquaintance process*. New York: Holt, Rinehart & Winston.

Newcomb, T. M. (1963). Stabilities underlying changes in interpersonal attraction. *Journal of Abnormal and Social Psychology, 66*, 376-386.

Newcomb, T. M., & Svehla, G. (1937). Intra-family relationships in attitudes. *Sociometry, 1*, 180-205.

Nudd, T. R. (1965). Satisfied and dissatisfied college roommates. *Journal of College Student Personnel, 6*, 161-164.

O'Keefe, B. J., & Shepherd, G. J. (1987). The pursuit of multiple objectives in face-to-face persuasive interactions: Effects of construct differentiation on message organization. *Communication Monographs, 54*, 396-419.

Osgood, C. E., & Tannenbaum, P. H. (1955). The principle of congruity in the prediction of attitude change. *Psychological Review, 62*, 42-55.

Owen, W. F. (1984). Interpretive themes in relational communication. *Quarterly Journal of Speech, 70*, 274-287.

Parks, M. R., & Adelman, M. B. (1983). Communication networks and the development of romantic relationships: An expansion of uncertainty reduction theory. *Human Communication Research, 10*, 55-79.

Pearson, K., & Lee, A. (1903). On the laws of inheritance in man: I. *Biometrika, 2*, 357-462.

Perkins, K. A. (1977). The effect of value similarity on satisfaction with college residence hall living groups. *Journal of College Student Personnel, 18*, 491-495.

Planalp, S., & Honeycutt, J. (1985). Events that increase uncertainty in interpersonal relationships. *Human Communication Research, 11*, 593-604.

Pomerantz, A. (1978). Compliment responses: Notes on the co-operation of multiple constraints. In J. Schenkein (Ed.), *Studies in the organization of conversational interaction*. New York: Academic Press.

Precker, J. A. (1952). Similarity of valuings as a factor in selection of peers and near authority figures. *Journal of Abnormal and Social Psychology, 47*, 406-414.

Reilly, M. S. A., Commins, W. D., & Stefic, E. C. (1960). The complementarity of personality needs in friendship choice. *Journal of Abnormal and Social Psychology, 61*, 292-294.

Richardson, H. M. (1939). Studies of mental resemblance between husbands and wives and between friends. *Psychological Bulletin, 36*, 104-120.

Richardson, H. M. (1940). Community of values as a factor in friendships of college and adult women. *Journal of Social Psychology, 11*, 303-312.

Rosenbaum, M. E. (1986). The repulsion hypothesis: On the nondevelopment of relationships. *Journal of Personality and Social Psychology, 51*, 1156-1166.

Schellenberg, J. A. (1957). Social choice and similarity of personal values. *Sociology and Social Research, 41*, 270-273.

Schiller, B. (1932). A quantitative analysis of marriage selection in a small group. *Journal of Social Psychology, 3*, 297-318.

Schlenker, B. R. (1980). *Impression management: The self-concept, social identity and interpersonal relations.* Monterey, CA: Brooks/Cole.

Schooley, M. (1936). Personality resemblances among married couples. *Journal of Abnormal and Social Psychology, 31*, 340-347.

Sillars, A. L., & Scott, M. D. (1983). Interpersonal perception between intimates: An integrative review. *Human Communication Research, 10*, 153-176.

Smith, A. J. (1957). Similarity of values and its relation to acceptance and the projection of similarity. *Journal of Psychology, 43*, 251-260.

Storms, M. D., & Thomas, G. C. (1977). Reactions to physical closeness. *Journal of Personallty and Social Psychology, 35*, 412-418.

Stroebe, W. (1971). Self-esteem and interpersonal attraction. In S. W. Duck (Ed.), *Theory and practice in interpersonal attraction* (pp. 79-104). London: Academic Press.

Sunnafrank, M. (1983). Attitude similarity and interpersonal attraction in communication processes: In pursuit of an ephemeral influence. *Communication Monographs, 50*, 273-284.

Sunnafrank, M. (1984). A communication-based perspective on attitude similarity and interpersonal attraction in early acquaintance. *Communication Monographs, 51*, 372-380.

Sunnafrank, M. (1985). Attitude similarity and interpersonal attraction during early communicative relationships: A research note on the generalizability of findings to opposite-sex relationships. *Western Journal of Speech Communication, 49*, 73-80.

Sunnafrank, M. (1986). Communicative influences on perceived similarity and attraction: An expansion of the interpersonal goals perspective. *Western Journal of Speech Communication, 50*, 158-170.

Sunnafrank, M., & Miller, G. R. (1981). The role of initial conversations in determining attraction to similar and dissimilar strangers. *Human Communication Research, 8*, 16-25.

Sykes, R. E. (1983). Initial interaction between strangers and acquaintances: A multivariate analysis of factors affecting choice of communication partners. *Human Communication Research, 10*, 27-53.

Tedeschi, J. T. (1981). *Impression management theory and social psychological research.* New York: Academic Press.

Vreeland, F. M., & Corey, S. M. (1935). A study of college friendships. *Journal of Abnormal Social Psychology, 30*, 229-236.

Werner, C., & Parmelee, P. (1979). Similarity of activity preferences among friends: Those who play together stay together. *Social Psychology Quarterly, 42*, 62-66.

Wetzel, C. G., & Insko, C. A. (1982). The similarity-attraction relationship: Is there an ideal one? *Journal of Experimental Social Psychology, 18*, 253-276.

Winslow, C. N. (1937). A study of the extent of agreement between friends' opinions and their ability to estimate the opinions of each other. *Journal of Social Psychology, 8*, 433-442.

Wright, P. H., & Crawford, A. C. (1971). Agreement and friendship: A close look and some second thoughts. *Representative Research in Social Psychology, 2*, 52-69.

On the Paradigm
That Would Not Die

ARTHUR P. BOCHNER
University of South Florida

ICHAEL Sunnafrank's review of the literature on attitude similarity
and interpersonal attraction is a story about a paradigm that will not
die. It has been more than 20 years since Byrne (1969) wrote the first
chapter of the story by proposing that similarity leads to attraction. In the beginning, the empirical relation between attitudinal similarity and attraction seemed so
conclusively supported by experimental evidence that there was, in Fishbein and
Ajzen's (1975) words, "little question about [it]" (p. 263). Eventually Byrne
(1971) attributed paradigmatic status to his hypothesis. The importance of the
"attraction paradigm" was reinforced by Berger (1975), who claimed that "one of
the most robust relationships in all of the behavioral sciences is that which exists
between perceived attitudinal similarity and interpersonal attraction" (p. 281), and
by Berscheid and Walster's (1983) unqualified conclusion that "people are
attracted to those who share their attitudes" (p. 88).

As time passed, however, some doubt began to be raised about the "robust"
connection between similarity and attraction (Bochner, 1984). Under what conditions does this connection hold, and to what forms of relationship can it be
generalized? The applicability of the attraction paradigm was never a prime
concern for Byrne and his colleagues, but for scholars whose work centers on
personal relationships this issue is crucial. If the limiting conditions of the attraction paradigm preclude application to long-term relationships — relationships that
have a historical context and in which the individuals have something psychologically significant to gain or lose — then the premise that similarity causes attraction
has little, if any, pragmatic value.

Sunnafrank's interpretation of the evidence is largely destructive. His well-sup-
ported conclusion is that "reports regarding the attitude similarity-attraction association have been greatly exaggerated" (p. 474). As he tells it, there are no

Correspondence and requests for reprints: Arthur P. Bochner, Department of Communication, University of South Florida, Tampa, FL 33620-5550.

Communication Yearbook 14, pp. 484-491

empirical grounds for concluding that similarity leads to attraction in romantic relationships. The weak to moderate attitudinal similarity reported by marriage partners can be attributed, in his opinion, to "general societal similarity levels" associated with demographic and proxemic factors. Once a romantic relationship evolves beyond its initial stages the association between attitude similarity and attraction weakens or loses its influence entirely. Indeed, as Sunnafrank keenly observes, couples who begin with perceptions of high attitudinal similarity may "sow the seeds of relational discontent" (p. 477), because they will find out eventually that they are not as similar as they thought they were.

Among friends and roommates the link between similarity of attitudes and attraction is either weaker or more muddled. Attitude similarity appears to be entirely unconnected to the likelihood of developing or sustaining a friendship. For roommates there appears to be some initial association between attitude similarity and attractions, but, as in romantic relationships, there is some support for the proposition that "familiarity breeds contempt" (Altman & Taylor, 1973; Taylor, 1968).

One would assume that the data on marriage, friendship, and other long-term interpersonal bonds would be more than sufficient to kill the attraction paradigm. But this is a paradigm that will not die. Sunnafrank suggests that the primary reason for the continued acceptance of the link between attitude similarity and attraction, in the face of so much contrary evidence from studies of "real-life" relationships, is the impressive support mounted by Byrne and his associates mainly from laboratory studies using the "bogus stranger" stimulus.

Sunnafrank's critical assessment of this research echoes many of the concerns I raised about Byrne's research in an earlier review of this literature (Bochner, 1984). These points are worth repeating here, I think, because they make it clear that Byrne's research program cannot be meaningfully generalized to the initiation and development of interpersonal relationships.

In the experiments that provided the foundation for the attraction paradigm, the information received by the subject about the other person (the bogus stranger) was confined to a questionnaire reporting the other's opinions, attitudes, or self-reported personality traits. All of the information acquired about the stranger is written, the attitudinal data are provided *before* a judgment is made about the other's attractiveness, and no commitment to do anything is implied by the subject's attractiveness ratings. These crucial informational constraints establish clear boundary conditions for limiting the conditions under which the attraction paradigm can be generalized.

First, the attraction paradigm deals only with *noninterpersonal* relationships and hence with what Miller and Steinberg (1975) would call noninterpersonal attraction. Awareness of the other is unilateral and there is no interdependence between the individuals (subject and bogus stranger). Clearly, these studies of noninteractive relationships do not generalize to relationships "in progress."

Second, the attraction paradigm focuses only on a global measure of attraction — an assessment of liking and/or working on a task with a person. This kind of reported attraction — assuming it measures "attraction" at all — is certainly very different from the romantic, passionate, or emotional attractions associated with interpersonal bonding. Furthermore, the prospective hypothetical relationship proposed by the attraction paradigm is exceptional, not typical: the relation of subject with subject in a laboratory experiment.

Third, the attraction paradigm offers a basis for making attitudinal attributions that is neither typical nor natural. People usually meet and interact with each other *before* they have direct knowledge of each other's attitudes (Touhey, 1975). Written messages only rarely form the basis for initial evaluational attributions. Moreover, the flow of attributional information is rarely one-way (Williams, 1975), and reporting that one feels attracted for the purposes of a hypothetical, unusual task is not the same as making a commitment to interact for one's own personal interest — for example, to go out on a date (Duck, 1977).

These limiting conditions imply that the causal connection between attitude similarity and attraction, even in a laboratory setting, will be considerably different when (a) information is acquired via other channels or forms of communication, (b) subjects expect to interact with one another, (c) subjects can see one another, (d) two-way exchanges of messages take place, and (e) face-to-face communication is permitted (Bochner, 1984). As Sunnafrank points out, the more closely experimental conditions mirror the contexts of more naturally occurring initial interactions, the more "other factors operating in initial acquaintance are likely to mitigate or overwhelm the attitude similarity influence" (p. 465). Previous research strongly suggests that all five of the above-mentioned conditions mediate, alter, dampen, or reverse the hypothesized relationship between attitude similarity and interpersonal attraction (Bochner, 1984). What people say and do to each other — their communicative actions — seems considerably more important than the similarity of their attitudes as a basis for attraction. As Brink (1977) has observed, "It should be recognized that the relationship between attitudinal similarity and attraction may be extremely complex in the context of the multiple responses and counterresponses of real life interactions" (p. 789). Indeed, Sunnafrank's own research program offers strong evidence that attraction between attitudinally dissimilar individuals can be significantly enhanced by natural conversation (Sunnafrank, 1983, 1984, 1985, 1986; Sunnafrank & Miller, 1981).

Nevertheless, Sunnafrank resists the temptation to end the story. Apparently, he does not think the jury has sufficient evidence to reach a verdict (to use his metaphor). He remains open to the possibility that research focusing on relationally salient attitudes and relationally relevant topics may yet produce support for the incriminated hypothesis linking attitude similarity and attraction.

I want to say, on the other hand, that it is time to write the final chapter of the story. The attraction paradigm is dead. Let it go. Give it up. There is no longer any reason to let it speak. The limiting conditions of Byrne's studies preclude generalizing the results of his studies to relationships in progress. In fact, relationships in progress provide little or no support for the attraction paradigm's main hypothesis. How much more evidence is needed to silence the attraction paradigm? When we act as empiricists our claims are supposed to be governed by rules of evidence and principles of falsification. Whether we reach a verdict from empirical evidence or from reflective analysis, the unmistakable conclusion is that when the central hypothesis of the attraction paradigm is generalized to long-term interpersonal relationships it becomes irrelevant, trivial, or false.

Before we close the book on similarity and attraction, however, it may be useful to reflect on several lessons that could be learned from this subject's stifling mountain of truth, to use Ernest Becker's famous phrase. My comments shall focus on two issues: the temporal ordering of the similarity/attraction connection, and the ideological biases of the attraction paradigm.

SIMILARITY/ATTRACTION
OR ATTRACTION/SIMILARITY?

I have never been able to understand why the attraction paradigm presumed that similarity *precedes* attraction, making it tenable, therefore, to hypothesize that similarity *causes* attraction. Since persons rarely learn about each other's attitudes prior to interacting with each other, it seems far more reasonable to assume that attraction *precedes* similarity and to hypothesize, instead, that attraction *causes* similarity (or at least perceived similarity). The communication research reported and reviewed by Sunnafrank adds greater force to my earlier argument (Bochner, 1984) about the causal ordering of these variables. Face-to-face communication has substantial functional significance because it precedes or is the basis for attitudinal attributions. It is unlikely that a person's attitudinal similarity/dissimilarity can be sized up before any interaction with the person takes place.

The results of an experiment conducted by Insko and Wilson (1977) suggest that the largest differences in attraction resulting from initial interactions of an informal nature are in perceived similarity of personality and beliefs or attitudes, and in ratings of the other as an interesting person with whom to talk. In this experiment, persons were arranged in three-person groups that permitted two of the possible pairs to interact verbally while preventing the other one from doing so. The results of this study, considered in conjunction with studies on anticipated interaction and expected topic of discussion (Layton & Insko, 1974; Sutherland & Insko, 1973), suggest that *one of the main functions of communication in early and perhaps even in later encounters is to foster perceptions of attitudinal and personality similarity and also to create the impression of being an interesting and stimulating person.*

Whether individuals actually have similar or dissimilar attitudes is not as important as the assumption shared by most individuals that they should have something important in common with the other (e.g., attitudes) if they are to form a relationship together. Most of us probably assume that we should have something in common and, if we want the other to be attracted to us, we should show the other that we have something in common. Thus attraction to the other probably motivates an individual to foster the impression of similarity.

Sunnafrank lifts the veil covering the pitfalls of this interaction ritual of impression management when he alludes to the potentially devastating unintended consequences of fostering impressions of greater similarity than actually exists. The irony is that if one resists the impulse to foster the impression that "we have a lot in common," one may never be able to form a solid foundation for an interpersonal relationship, but if one does foster this impression, the foundation on which the relationship is built may be too weak to withstand the acid test of experience. Pineo (1961, 1969) has argued that marriage is characterized by a natural process of deterioration involving, in most cases, the growing awareness that the other is not as similar to oneself as one assumed initially. One conclusion that can be drawn from an understanding of this paradoxical situation is that the development of a relationship is a problem in its own right and that efforts to reduce a relationship to the status of an object of contemplation or the product of cognition will most likely be irrelevant, trivial, or false.

If communication scholars want to make the process by which persons form interpersonal bonds more intelligible, then we need to adopt or create a different language for describing the development of a relationship, one that differs radically from the vocabulary offered by the attraction paradigm. Most of the descriptions offered by social psychologists share the premise that interpersonal bonds are largely the product of the personal or psychological characteristics that individuals bring to the relationship. In the case of attraction, attitudes are construed as the most important characteristic that an individual brings to a relationship, and the success or failure of the relationship is made dependent upon whether there is sufficient attitudinal matching. Interpersonal communication is ignored, taken for granted, or reduced to an information-seeking operation. Apparently the main or only purpose of interpersonal communication is to produce data (knowledge) about the other on the basis of which the individual perceiver can decide whether the cognitive match is sufficient to sustain a developing relationship. Interpersonal communication becomes the instrument for determining attractiveness (by providing information about similarity of attitudes). Generally, the problem of building a relationship is construed as a problem of acquiring knowledge about the other; thus relationship development is reduced to cognitive and epistemic determinations.

My preference is for a vocabulary that focuses on the activities that go on between individuals — what they say and do to each other — as they create an interpersonal bond. As a student of communication, I find a description that focuses on action and interaction more useful than one that emphasizes knowledge and information acquisition. In my opinion, the functions of communication come into sharper focus when it is assumed that attraction leads to relationships (instead of relationships leading to attraction). My premise is that interpersonal bonding is a problem in its own right and that individuals communicate with each other for reasons other than or in addition to the need to acquire information about each other's attitudes. Given some initial attraction between two persons, the course of a relationship is affected by the individuals' strategic management of sentiments, their success at securing commitments, their ability to exert or resist subtle pressures, and the functioning of private and public symbols that grow out of their involvement with each other and in turn affect it.

One of the main deficiencies of the attraction paradigm is that it tells us virtually nothing about what people must say or do to develop and sustain a relationship. Many social and psychological factors may predispose attraction between individuals. Nonetheless, an interpersonal bond cannot progress without overt communication. Friendship, marriage, and other long-term relationships are, in this sense, communicative accomplishments that evolve from interactive experiences in which individuals are able to attract, form, keep, and cement their relationship to each other.

THE ATTRACTION PARADIGM AS IDEOLOGY

In the past, most discussions of social and communication theories have focused on criteria such as empirical validity, predictive power, verifiability, and capacity to organize and account for existing facts. More recently, however, the conversation about social and communication theories has begun to address the ways in which theories influence, extend, or alter cultural norms and ideals. It is no longer safe to assume that theories, even those cast in rigorous scientific jargon, are merely neutral descriptions of "the way things are" (Gergen, 1978, 1982). Social and communication theories portray an image of communicative functioning, and the decision to embrace a particular theoretical perspective is an implicit endorsement of the values that the theory embodies. This was one of the lessons we learned when Skinner (1971) overtly extrapolated behaviorism into a conception of an ideal world. We frowned at the terms he offered for predicting and controlling human behavior, not because we were certain he was wrong, but because we did not want to think he could be right (Rorty, 1982).

Hogan and Emler (1978) have correctly placed the research on interpersonal attraction into ideological perspective. Not unlike the major currents of social psychological theory, the literature on interpersonal attraction takes the autonomous individual as the unit of analysis. It is the individual who "chooses" or "decides" whether the degree of cognitive matching is sufficient to sustain a relationship. This "deeply rationalist" and individualist account casts the individual mainly into the role of the perceiver rather than the role of interactive participant (Hogan & Emler, 1978), and the only communicative problem faced by the individual is, as mentioned above, the need to acquire sufficient information on which to base the decision about forming a relationship.

Why would we want to embrace the characterization of attraction and relationship formation promoted by this theory? Perhaps it is comforting to be protected from the realization that the formation of relationships requires some degree of interpersonal competence; or perhaps we have so much invested in the ideal of autonomous and rational choice that we do not want to confront the possibility that "choices" may, in fact, be made collectively or relationally through a process of mutual influence and on the basis of nonrational or emotional factors.

Sunnafrank's research shows that communicative action can make a difference. Obviously, individuals can and do change, modify, misrepresent, and/or misperceive each other's attitudes. These are the risks that one takes when entering interpersonal encounters. Some of us may believe that interpersonal life is made easier by manufacturing evidence supportive of individualist and rationalist biases, but by most reasonable accounts the development of an interpersonal bond is not an orderly process. As interactants proceed, they tend to form idealized images of each other, publicly symbolize their involvement, initiate stabilizing rituals, and stay close to supportive third parties (Bochner, 1984). These communicative activities and functions significantly affect the course of a relationship and probably mitigate or ameliorate attitude similarities or differences.

Sunnafrank concludes that there is a need to conduct individual case studies of relationship formation for the purpose of unraveling some of the unsolved mysteries of relationship development. I think it is fitting to end this commentary by quoting from one of the few existing research investigations of relationships that have been based on intensive case interviews. In *Habits of the Heart*, Bellah, Madsen, Sullivan, Swindler, and Tipton (1985) poignantly champion the cause of an interdependent and interactional worldview that diverges radically from the premises and ideals of the social psychological worldview from which the attraction paradigm emerged:

> We find ourselves not independently of other people and institutions but through them. We never get to the bottom of ourselves on our own. We discover who we are face to face and side by side with others in work, love, and learning. All of our activity goes on in relationships, groups, associations, and communities ordered by institutional structures and interpreted by cultural patterns of meaning. And the positive side of our individualism, our sense of the dignity, worth, and moral autonomy of the individual, is dependent in a thousand ways on a social, cultural, and institutional context that keeps us afloat even when we can not very well describe it. There is much in our life that we do not control, that we are not even "responsible" for, that we receive as grace or face as tragedy, things Americans habitually prefer not to think about. Finally, we are not simply ends in ourselves, either as individuals or as a society. We are part of a larger whole that we can neither forget nor imagine in our own image without paying a high price. If we are not to have a self that hangs in the void, slowly twisting in the wind, these are issues we cannot ignore. (p. 84)

REFERENCES

Altman, I., & Taylor, D. A. (1973). *Social penetration: The development of interpersonal relationships.* New York: Holt, Rinehart & Winston.

Bellah, R. N., Madsen, R., Sullivan, W. M., Swindler, A., & Tipton, S. M. (1985). *Habits of the heart.* Berkeley: University of California Press.

Berger, C. R. (1975). Task performance and attributional communication as determinants of interpersonal attraction. *Speech Monographs, 40*, 280-286.

Berscheid, E., & Walster, E. (1983). *Interpersonal attraction.* Reading, MA: Addison-Wesley.

Bochner, A. P. (1984). The functions of communication in interpersonal bonding. In C. C. Arnold & J. W. Bowers (Eds.), *Handbook of rhetorical and communication theory* (pp. 544-621). Boston: Allyn & Bacon.

Brink, J. H. (1977). Effect of interpersonal communication on attraction. *Journal of Personality and Social Psychology, 35*, 783-790.

Byrne, D. (1969). Attitudes and attraction. In L. Berkowitz (Ed.), *Advances in experimental social psychology* (Vol. 4). New York: Academic Press.

Byrne, D. (1971). *The attraction paradigm.* New York: Academic Press.

Duck, S. W. (1977). Similarity, interpersonal attitudes and attraction: Right answers and wrong reasons. *British Journal of Social and Clinical Psychology, 16*, 15-21.

Fishbein, M., & Ajzen, I. (1975). *Belief, attitude, intention, and behavior: An introduction to theory and research.* Reading, MA: Addison-Wesley.

Gergen, K. (1978). Toward generative theory. *Journal of Personality and Social Psychology, 36*, 1344-1360.

Gergen, K. (1982). *Toward transformation in social knowledge.* New York: Springer-Verlag.

Hogan, R. T., & Embler, N. P. (1978). The biases in contemporary social psychology. *Social Research, 45*, 478-534.

Insko, C. A., & Wilson, M. (1977). Interpersonal attraction as a function of social interaction. *Journal of Personality and Social Psychology, 35*, 903-911.

Layton, B. D., & Insko, C. A. (1974). Anticipated interaction and the similarity-attraction effect. *Sociometry, 37*, 149-162.

Miller, G. R., & Steinberg, M. (1975). *Between people: A new analysis of interpersonal communication.* Palo Alto, CA: Science Research Associates.

Pineo, P. C. (1961). Disenchantment in the later years of marriage. *Journal of Marriage and Family Living, 23*, 3-11.

Pineo, P. C. (1969). Developmental patterns in marriage. *Family Coordinator, 18*, 135-140.

Rorty, R. (1982). *Consequences of pragmatism.* Minneapolis: University of Minnesota Press.

Skinner, B. F. (1971). *Beyond freedom and dignity.* New York: Random House.

Sunnafrank, M. (1983). Attitude similarity and interpersonal attraction in communication processes: In pursuit of an ephemeral influence. *Communication Monographs, 50*, 273-284.

Sunnafrank, M. (1984). A communication-based perspective on attitude similarity and interpersonal attraction in early acquaintance. *Communication Monographs, 51*, 372-380.

Sunnafrank, M. (1985). Attitude similarity and interpersonal attraction during early communicative relationships: A research note on the generalizability of findings to opposite-sex relationships. *Western Journal of Speech Communication, 49*, 73-80.

Sunnafrank, M. (1986). Communicative influences on perceived similarity and attraction: An expansion of the interpersonal goals perspective. *Western Journal of Speech Communication, 50*, 158-170.

Sunnafrank, M., & Miller, G. R. (1981). The role of initial conversations in determining attraction to similar and dissimilar strangers. *Human Communication Research, 8*, 16-25.

Sutherland, A. E., & Insko, C. A. (1973). Attraction and interestingness of anticipated interaction. *Journal of Personality, 41*, 234-243.

Taylor, D. A. (1968). The development of interpersonal relationships: Social penetration process. *Journal of Social Psychology, 75*, 79-90.

Touhey, J. C. (1975). Interpersonal congruency, attitude similarity, and interpersonal attraction. *Journal of Research in Personality, 9*, 66-73.

Williams, E. (1975). Medium or message: Communications medium as a determinant of interpersonal evaluation. *Sociometry, 38*, 119-130.

The Generalizability of the Communication to Attraction Relationship to Intercultural Communication: Repulsion or Attraction?

STEVEN T. McDERMOTT
California Polytechnic State University

> The acceptability of a theory will in any case be a matter of degree — more or less weight will be assigned to it, and it will always have a more or less limited range of justified application. (Kaplan, 1964, p. 312)

Sunnafrank's review clearly demonstrates that the repulsion hypothesis (Rosenbaum, 1986) should be considered as a rival hypothesis to the historically accepted attraction one (see Byrne, 1971; Byrne, Clore, & Smeaton, 1986) *in INTRAcultural communication.* Sunnafrank also aptly demonstrates that certain methodological problems need to be resolved before a crucial test of the rival hypotheses can be satisfactorily completed. Plowing over old measurement issues may help resolve the Rosenbaum/Byrne feud, but it may be equally easy for both advocates of their hypotheses to end up the way the Festinger/Bem feud between dissonance and self-perception has evolved: Kuhn's observation about the role of conviction and institutionalized paradigms in the advocacy of covering laws has certainly played out in that controversy, and may again appear in this one.

But Sunnafrank has carved out an area for this research that helps us evaluate the current dispute by pointing us in the direction of communication. In doing so, he allows us to apply different criteria for evaluating the seeming contradictions between the repulsion and attraction hypotheses — and their associated theoretical positions — by placing the evaluation of the utility of the general hypothesis in *communication contexts.* He thus permits us to apply an additional theoretical worthiness test by asking if communication contexts make a difference. It is clear

Correspondence and requests for reprints: Steven T. McDermott, Department of Speech Communication, California Polytechnic State University, San Luis Obispo, CA 93407.

Communication Yearbook 14, pp. 492-497

from his analysis that communication does make a difference, as he demonstrates not only in his review, but also in his own programmatic, empirical research.

Moreover, by examining the similarity-attraction hypothesis from a communication perspective, Sunnafrank allows us to use another criterion of theoretical worth: *How much* does the theory or hypothesis explain? Roughly speaking, this criterion for establishing theoretical worth has been referred to as theoretical extension (Kaplan, 1964), increasing the domain (Dubin, 1969), abstraction (Blalock, 1969, p. 141), scope (Merton, 1957), and richness (Reynolds, 1971).

Thus, with the goal of exploring theoretical extension in mind, let me take Sunnafrank's interpretation as it stands for *intra*cultural communication—that is, that people are more likely to use dissimilarities to be repulsed than similarities to be attracted, especially after communication. However, I want to follow his path by outlining a future for research on *inter*cultural communication by way of attempting to explore how and if the Byrne hypothesis or the Rosenbaum hypothesis might be properly applied in that domain. In doing so, I hope to address whether there is utility in expanding research on the similarity-attraction hypothesis in contexts broader than the typical interaction between college sophomores or between White American couples.

To complete this task, this essay will (a) describe the purpose of communication interaction for *inter*cultural communicants compared with *intra*cultural ones as they relate to attraction, (b) examine the normative factors involved in communicating interculturally and that may or may not lead to attraction, and (c) suggest the way similarity and attraction may work in intercultural contexts by noting the generalizability of the current communication and attraction or repulsion hypotheses.

COMMUNICATING FOR ATTRACTION PURPOSES

To start the discussion, let me examine what it means to be attracted. A hybrid of operationalizations has been posited, perhaps because of the vagueness of Sunnafrank's conceptualization of attraction as "an inclination to be in or attracted to relationships with others" (p. 451). Measurements have ranged from a partial use of Byrne's (1961) Interpersonal Judgment Scale (IJS) that assesses the evaluation of how much the individual likes his or her partner combined with how much he or she would like working with that partner (see Gonzales, Davis, Loney, Lukens, & Junghans, 1983; Sunnafrank & Miller, 1981); to use of the whole IJS (e.g., Condon & Crano, 1988) that includes feelings about a stranger's intelligence, knowledge of current events, morality, adjustment, likability, and desirability as a work partner; to estimates based on multi-item scales of liking (e.g., Rosenbaum, 1986). Besides the lack of comparability for intracultural studies, this salad bar variety of operationalizations is more troublesome when one considers the key elements in intercultural communication. Let me examine the key differences.

Although communicators in intracultural communication contexts communicate for a variety of reasons (e.g., to get acquainted, task purposes), an essential outcome for intercultural strangers is adaptation and acculturation (Gudykunst & Kim, 1984). Communicating for adaptation purposes involves sifting out the appropriate and functional *norms* for behaving within a culture for the foreigner, and cultivating (either passively or actively) the foreigner's acculturation by the host culture (Kim, 1988; McGuire & McDermott, 1987). Acculturation occurs after the norms of the old culture come into conflict with the norms of the new culture. When this conflict arises, the participants take on the new cultural norms or reject (or do not accept) the norms expressed by the other communicator (McDermott & McGuire, 1988). In the former case, they are in essence *becoming more similar*; in the latter, they are *remaining* or *becoming dissimilar.*

THE IMPORTANCE OF NORMS

Two communication problems have their roots between the furrows of becoming more similar and remaining dissimilar: deciding whether one wants to be attracted, to communicate, or to adapt, and figuring out which information is essential for doing each. If similarity is essential for adaptation and acculturation, communicators who wish to adapt should seek information that can allow them to do so. But trying to become more similar requires that the interactants estimate the similarity or nonsimilarity of the essential norms that each interactant may have for interacting. After all, the initial differences in norms are what culturally distinguish the interactants. Thus, because these norms are so important (McGuire & McDermott, 1988), intercultural interactants, unlike intracultural ones, must chance across congruent norms or figure out the behavioral norms of their interaction partners early in a relationship. Once this is done, these communicators may estimate the extent of similarity/dissimilarity and then be attracted or repulsed. They may also select certain normative differences (even if trivial) that help them to maximize dissimilarities psychologically (and presumably thus find their interaction partners repulsive). After either of these estimations, they may then decide whether they are or want to become more similar or remain dissimilar. This process is generally *not* the same as it is in intracultural communication.

But where is the information about norms? Which normative similarities are the most functionally important? If we plow back through the IJS, it is not easy to tell which similarities would be functional: intelligence? knowledge of current events? Perhaps morality is most important? What about adjustments that specifically address adaptation and norms?

If functional, adaptive intercultural communication is inextricably tied to estimates of the similarities and nonsimilarities between interactants, the most fertile questions are these: Which similarities and nonsimilarities are essential for deciding on attraction? Which are most likely to bring about repulsion? Unfortunately, the answers are not known (although there are hints, to be discussed later).

Tangentially, the "desire" to engage in adaptive activities by a foreigner or host-culture member should be a predictor of the importance of generalized similarity and uncertainty reduction. Presumably, a person who does not want to adapt will select dissimilarities to emphasize. I believe this is in line with Sunnafrank's (1988) other theoretical research on predicted outcome value.

SIMILARITY AND ATTRACTION
IN THE INTERCULTURAL CONTEXT

Byrne et al. (1986) examined Byrne's hypothesis in five different cultural groups. They found that general similarity was related to attraction (remember the methodological problems, however), but they also found that culture influenced the level of attraction. This finding is not surprising, given that culture influences expectations and perceptions of desirable characteristics in others (Oddou & Mendenhall, 1984). For instance, when Korten (1974) asked Ethiopian and American students to describe people they knew (descriptions that presumably contain the most salient/important criteria for evaluation), the Ethiopians' descriptions included interpersonal relations, opinions, and beliefs as main categories. American students, on the other hand, evaluated their friends in categories that can be described as cognitive-emotional style, interpersonal style, abilities, and knowledge. Thus to expand the similarity-attraction research to intercultural communication might be a mistake unless one standardizes the frame of reference for the intercultural communicators — a move that would ruin the generalizability of the intracultural results.

The perceived cultural similarities of categories evaluation and generalized stereotyping also related to interpersonal attraction. Triandis (1960) found that the more similar the categories people use for evaluating others, the more attractive they will be to others in intracultural communication situations. More recently, intercultural researchers have found that in-group and out-group identification is important in communication and attraction (see Gudykunst & Hammer, 1987). Stereotyping and selective perception play a part in initial interaction among foreigners and host-culture members. Kim (1978) found that new Korean immigrants in the United States identified dissimilarities between themselves and Americans more often than they identified similarities. An extensive study of racism and communication by van Dijk (1987) supports this line of reasoning. He found that most people report that they rarely have contact with foreigners — so, presumably, stereotypes should predominate. Moreover, he found that when people within a culture talk about foreigners, nearly *all* the conversation is negative, and the talk contains the same categories of information about foreigners. His study demonstrates that most often in the intercultural context, people reinforce each other to maximize the dissimilarities among cultures. It thus seems that it is more likely for repulsion to occur, even after communication, or that people will use the stereotypical dissimilarities as criteria for negative evaluation.

Where are we then? I believe that Sunnafrank's review has taken us to a starting point, perhaps with a push, to explore the very nature of the kind of information people use *and* communicate in order to establish attraction or repulsion. Much of the intercultural research and theory suggests that repulsion may be common, especially when one considers the information that is used to make such judgments. However, the exact nature of the data people use when communicating interculturally and deciding on attraction and determining friendships is not now known. Attempting to determine if the attraction (repulsion) and similarity hypothesis generalizes to intercultural communication should present some exciting challenges and some fruitful results.

REFERENCES

Blalock, H. M., Jr. (1969). *Theory construction: From verbal to mathematical formulations.* Englewood Cliffs, NJ: Prentice-Hall.

Byrne, D. (1961). Interpersonal attraction and attitude similarity. *Journal of Abnormal and Social Psychology, 62,* 713-715.

Byrne, D. (1971). *The attraction paradigm.* New York: Academic Press.

Byrne, D., Clore, G. L., & Smeaton, G. (1986). The attraction hypothesis: Do similar attitudes affect anything? *Journal of Personality and Social Psychology, 51*(6), 1167-1170.

Condon, J. W., & Crano, W. D. (1988). Inferred evaluation and the relation between attitude similarity and interpersonal attraction. *Journal of Personality and Social Psychology, 54,* 789-797.

Dubin, R. (1969). *Theory building.* New York: Free Press.

Gonzales, M. H., Davis, J. M., Loney, G. L., Lukens, C. K., & Junghans, C. M. (1983). Interactional approach to interpersonal attraction. *Journal of Personality and Social Psychology, 44,* 1192-1197.

Gudykunst, W. B., & Hammer, M. R. (1987). Strangers and hosts: An uncertainty reduction based theory of intercultural adaptation. In Y. Y. Kim & W. B. Gudykunst (Eds.), *Cross-cultural adaptation: Current approaches.* Newbury Park, CA: Sage.

Gudykunst, W. B., & Kim, Y. Y. (1984). *Communicating with strangers: An approach to intercultural communication.* New York: Random House.

Kaplan, A. (1964). *The conduct of inquiry.* Scranton, PA: Chandler.

Kim, Y. (1978). A communication approach to the acculturation process: A study of Korean immigrants in Chicago. *International Journal of Intercultural Relations, 2,* 197-223.

Kim, Y. (1988). *Communication and cross-cultural adaptation.* Clevedon, England: Multilingual Matters.

Korten, F. (1974). The influence of culture and sex on the perception of persons. *International Journal of Psychology, 9,* 31-44.

McDermott, S. T., & McGuire, M. (1988, November). *The relationship of host member and foreigner communication to alienation and assimilation states in acculturation.* Paper presented at the annual meeting of the Speech Communication Association, New Orleans.

McGuire, M., & McDermott, S. (1987). Communication in assimilation, deviance, and alienation states. In Y. Y. Kim & W. B. Gudykunst (Eds.), *Cross-cultural adaptation: Current approaches* (pp. 90-105). Newbury Park, CA: Sage.

McGuire, M. & McDermott, S. (1988). Identifying communication in acculturation. In J. Lehtonen (Ed.), *The future of speech* (pp. 15-83). Jyvaskyla, Finland: University of Jyvaskyla.

Merton, R. K. (1957). *Social theory and social structure.* New York: Free Press.

Oddou, G., & Mendenhall, M. (1984). Person perception in cross-cultural settings. *International Journal of Intercultural Relations, 8,* 77-96.

Reynolds, P. D. (1971). *A primer in theory construction.* New York: Bobbs-Merrill.

Rosenbaum, M. E. (1986). The repulsion hypothesis: On the nondevelopment of relationships. *Journal of Personality and Social Psychology, 51*(6), 1156-1166.

Sunnafrank, M. (1988). Predicted outcome value in initial conversations. *Communication Research Reports, 2,* 169-172.

Sunnafrank, M., & Miller, G. R. (1981). The role of initial conversations in determining attraction to similar and dissimilar strangers. *Human Communication Research, 8,* 16-25.

Triandis, H. (1960). Some determinants of interpersonal communication. *Human Relations, 13,* 279-287.

van Dijk, T. A. (1987). *Communicating racism.* London: Sage.

SECTION 4

LEADERSHIP
AND
RELATIONSHIPS

11 Cognitive Processes in Leadership: Interpreting and Handling Events in an Organizational Context

MARK F. PETERSON
RITCH L. SORENSON
Texas Tech University

Research concerning the antecedents of leadership is reviewed using a cognitive-contextual model that focuses on factors affecting conscious, script-driven, and programmed behavioral choice. Causal relationships are suggested among several categories of contextual variables that affect behavioral choice and enacted leadership through their effects on cognitive processes. The model recognizes that leadership involves intervening in a social situation by affecting the meaning that other parties give to specific events, and as a way of fulfilling organizational functions. The review identifies gaps in current knowledge about cognitive and social processes that intervene among events that occur, problems that require management, and the leading activities of organization members. Implications for senior management strategies to influence leadership at all levels of an organization are discussed from cognitive, role, and symbolic interaction perspectives.

L EADERSHIP has long been given an important place in organization theory. Several reviews have summarized and integrated research about how leadership, variously conceived, contributes to individual, group, or organizational effectiveness (e.g., Bass, 1981, 1985; House, 1988; Hunt, Baliga, & Peterson, 1988; Jacobs, 1970; Kerr, Schriesheim, Murphy, & Stogdill, 1974; Smith & Peterson, 1988; Yukl, 1989). However, very limited emphasis has been placed on the strategy and tactics an individual adopts when attempting to enact leadership. The present review moves toward a model that identifies why and how an individual might attempt to initiate leadership. This model is used to anchor a set of propositions that provide a new look at how cognition may mediate the effects of context on a given person's leadership.

Correspondence and requests for reprints: Mark F. Peterson, Area of Management, College of Business Administration, Texas Tech University, P.O. Box 4320, Lubbock, TX 79409-4320.

Communication Yearbook 14, pp. 501-534

The propositions developed below are based on recent publications in psychology, management, and communication, as well as more classic work. Our intent is to use recent research addressing cognitive and interactionist themes to reinterpret traditional research with a role theory flavor (i.e., studies of behavior by occupants of "formal leadership roles"). The disparate theoretical bases for our reinterpretation require certain compromises and some creative sense making. Constructs such as individual cognition, an organization's environment, group characteristics, and organization characteristics are treated as independently describable, whereas a more theoretically pure interaction model would treat them as mutually defining.

On the other hand, studies devoted to the "objective" behavior (e.g., Halpin & Winer, 1957) aspects of leadership processes — the communication acts and interactions driven by conscious and nonconscious cognitions and directed toward influencing the beliefs and actions of others — are now broadly understood to reflect the way that respondents reconstruct and give meaning to leadership (Lord, 1985). Our reinterpretation, then, is to discuss these studies as relating to "experienced" leadership. *Experienced leadership* is the meaning given by other parties to specific acts or patterns of behavior. Although the aspects of leadership receiving the greatest empirical attention are those displayed by formal "superiors" as experienced by "subordinates," *leadership* will be broadly understood here to include implicit and explicit negotiations within a diverse role set (Smith & Peterson, 1988). Basically, our interest is in communication episodes and interactions that can be analytically characterized as leadership, and we see them as being affected by (a) prior exchanges among the communicating parties and others who have held similar *roles* in the communication network, (b) the history of communication patterns among larger collectivities modeled as *systems*, and (c) the individual communicators' personal interaction histories modeled as *cognition*.

The model used to structure our review provides a framework for understanding leadership in organizations as it emanates from *anyone* (called herein the "focal individual," or FI) an analyst chooses to consider. The model includes a strong cognitive element to represent personal interaction histories, follows Stryker and Statham's (1985) initiative by drawing on role theory to describe socially structured meaning frameworks, and uses symbolic interaction theory to describe social processes. By recognizing the distinctive forms of interdependence, differentiation, and boundedness of the individuals, groups, and organizations that shape organizational events and problems, the model is also consistent with general systems theory (Buckley, 1967; Cooke & Rousseau, 1981; Krone, Jablin, & Putnam, 1987).

Researchers have identified many variables that are modeled as predicting or being associated with leadership behavior and its consequences. The model illustrated in Figure 1 clusters these predictors and identifies frequently studied relationships among them. Variables are clustered into nine categories: (a) FI's environment, (b) FI's characteristics, (c) FI's attitudes and beliefs about their context, (d) group's and organization's environment, (e) group characteristics, (f)

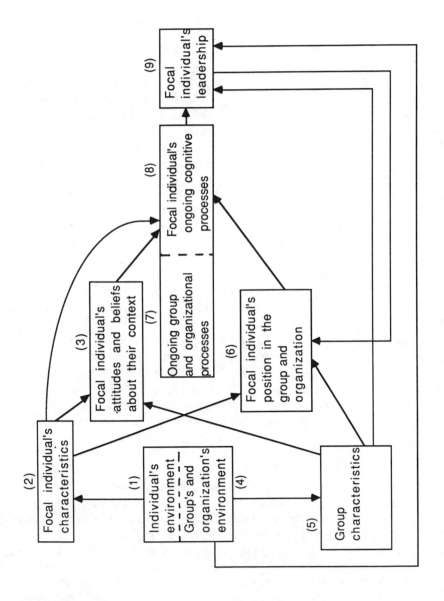

Figure 1. A cognitive-contextual model of leadership processes.

503

FI's position in the group, (g) ongoing group processes, (h) FI's ongoing cognitive processes, and (i) FI's leadership.

The present review emphasizes the context within which group and organizational leadership occurs (cells 4 through 7) and treats cognitive processes (cell 8) as a central mediating site. We had to make some choice of focus within the domain of leadership antecedents, given space constraints. We have, therefore, limited comment on cells 1 and 3 and offer the following as our thoughts on cell 2, the FI's characteristics.

Prior reviews of the individual antecedents of leadership have covered such relatively stable characteristics as personality, expressed attitude, and background characteristics. Cognitive psychology is recasting personality formation as the development of cognitive structures. As cognitive psychology pursues this task, it should become increasingly possible to link the personality components of Figure 1 directly with the cognitive themes developed in our review.

For the present, then, we will begin with a set of propositions that suggest possible cognitive processes through which particular contextual characteristics and events affect leadership. Similar models are found in other applications of communications theory (Cody & McLaughlin, 1985). Since cognitive processes mediate the effects of all other variables on leadership behavior, a cognitive model of leadership behavior choice is a useful point of departure for reviewing and interpreting studies of leadership antecedents.

ONGOING COGNITIVE PROCESSES AND LEADERSHIP (8,9)

Important progress in understanding human behavior in organizations (e.g., Lord & Kernan, 1987; Walsh, 1988) and in interpersonal communication (Cody & McLaughlin, 1985; Giles & Street, 1985) has recently been made by applying cognitive information-processing models to social interaction. These models identify ways in which people interpret events based on their personal predispositions and previous experiences to arrive at behavioral "choices." Smith and Peterson (1988, p. 49) summarize the cognitive antecedents of leadership in a model that suggests that the events a person experiences via perceptual processes, schemata, attributions, and salient values influence motivated, script-driven, or programmed choice processes. Choices, in turn, drive action. The model indicates that behavioral intentions, whether conscious or not, depend most immediately upon a motivated choice process, a "programmed" (March & Simon, 1958) process, or a script-driven hybrid of the two (Abelson, 1976). Cognitive social psychologists have tended to focus on only one or two of these elements in any one study. This chapter provides a more complete, but speculative, direction of extending such links in the context of leadership processes by considering perception and attention, schemata, attributions, salience, and motivated, programmed, and script-driven choice.

Perception and Attention

Although context impinges on social perception, perception filters and interprets context even at the initial point of awareness (Kiesler & Sproull, 1982; Walsh, 1988). Typically, attention is directed toward goal-relevant information, but extraordinary events also cause attention interrupts (Bettman, 1979). Mintzberg (1973), for example, has observed that an executive's work consists of disruptions requiring immediate short-term attention.

Schemata

The closest counterpart of schemata in leadership research are "implicit leadership theories" (Phillips, 1984; Phillips & Lord, 1981, 1982; Rush & Beauvais, 1981; Rush, Phillips, & Lord, 1981; Rush, Thomas, & Lord, 1977). Implicit leadership theories have been studied as cognitive structures used to interpret interactions with authority figures, but might also be viewed as knowledge structures that directly affect the leadership process.

Attributions

Closely tied to social perceptions are processes that link perceived events to a framework of causal relationships (Kelley, 1973; Ross & Fletcher, 1985). Several leadership models describe causal attributions and their consequences for leadership behavior and especially for conscious, self-reported behavioral intentions about how to respond to good or bad subordinate performance (e.g., Green & Mitchell, 1979; Lord & Smith, 1983; Podsakoff, 1982). A small amount of research addresses attributional processes for interpreting discrete situations other than subordinate performance. For example, upon reaching the conclusion that a request is legitimate, warranted, and justified, individuals increase assertiveness toward (Kipnis & Cohen, 1980) and pressure (Dillard & Burgoon, 1984) on others. The belief that an influence target will benefit from persuasion also results in applying pressure (Williams & Boster, 1981).

Salience Processes

Salience processes highlight the experience that some perceptual goals, schemata, and attribution frameworks are more readily available at particular moments than are others. Salience processes have received little direct attention in leadership research, but are postulated to mediate the effects of short-term context features on leadership.

Motivated Choice

The cognitive model developed by Smith and Peterson (1988) suggests that the implicit decision to attempt leadership and the choice of specific leadership behaviors depends most directly on motivated choice processes, programmed responses, or scripts. Deliberative, motivated choice processes noted are those that are typically included in expectancy models (e.g., Vroom's, 1964, expectancy/instrumentality/valence model). However, such a highly rationalized formulation has been recognized to be, at best, a limiting extreme of even the few relatively deliberate, conscious choices that people make (Mitchell, 1974). Elements of rationality are noted below as occurring infrequently, but under potentially important circumstances.

Programmed Choice

The total capacity of a human information-processing system is certainly limited. However, the limits of the conscious, resource-intensive, short-term deliberative processor of motivated choices may be the most constrained. Under many circumstances, deliberative processes will be simplified or replaced in part by habitual, programmed responses (March & Simon, 1958). Internalized programs held by individuals, both separately and as part of a stylized set of interactions, may develop through deliberate organization socialization "policies" (Green & Mitchell, 1979) as well as through nonwork personal experience.

Script-Driven Choice

Script theory (Abelson, 1976; Markus & Zajonc, 1985) integrates quasi-rational choice processes and programmed processes. Script theory and a related model, control theory (Carver & Scheier, 1982) suggest that situations affect the salience of integrated deliberative and programmed processes. Based on script theory, leadership behavior is seen as a series of integrated actions and cognitions rather than as either discrete behaviors or generalized behavior styles (Lord & Kernan, 1987; Martinko & Gardner, 1987).

Summary

A cognitive perspective on leadership must combine the customary emphasis on the way a focal person affects the meanings given to events by other parties (e.g., Bennis & Nanus, 1985; Burns, 1978; Hunt et al., 1988; Martin, Feldman, Hatch, & Sitkin, 1983) with the way a focal person's cognitions are affected by the meanings given to events by other parties. In order to remedy the present overemphasis in the literature on the leader as an "independent variable" shaping the cognitions of others, the propositions and review presented below emphasize factors that affect a focal person's actions by affecting the person's cognitions.

GROUPS, ORGANIZATIONS, AND EVENTS

Group and organizational variables in Figure 1 affect the events a focal person perceives, the context in which events are encountered, and the interpretive frameworks within which events are given meaning. The different kinds of groups in organizational settings include the basic work-performing groups in an organization's operating core, the middle-line groups that supervise and manage them, and the upper-level "strategic apex" groups that influence the basic patterns of interaction with external parties. In addition, organizations contain support staff and technostructure groups that (respectively) serve and design controls for other components (Mintzberg, 1979).[1]

Effects of Group's and Organization's Environment (4)

Proposition 1: Organizations provide explicit and implicit role performance and information-processing rules through various socialization processes. These rules can be internalized with personal modifications to structure elements of a focal person's cognition and thus shape his or her leadership.

Behavior typically is enacted in the presence of group members, or with the anticipation that actions will become known to other parties. In an organization, an FI's interaction history and subsequent sources of role expectations can be specified in more precise terms than by the general idea of "role sender" used in classic organizational psychology (Kahn, Wolfe, Quinn, Snoek, & Rosenthal, 1964). A focal person does indeed have a role set made up of people who exert influence through social information-processing mechanisms (Salancik & Pfeffer, 1978). However, this role set is augmented by collective rules, norms, or "cultures" (Smith & Peterson, 1988, chaps. 5, 6) and by any preexisting cognitive structures that an FI brings to a new work situation. This augmented role set provides alternative information-processing structures that compete with one another. Established norms and role expectations for an FI can be expressed in overt attempts to guide the interpretation of events (e.g., why a group was unable to complete a task on time). Even in the absence of overt attempts, stories and personal experiences that veterans share will have a broad effect on the meanings that an FI will learn to give to particular happenings (Martin et al., 1983).

Classic, grand leadership theories are well known for their preoccupation with the interplay of formally programmed information processing and individual choice (e.g., Perrow, 1970). The recent literature addressing leadership effectiveness suggests that leaders, especially senior executives, behave symbolically to affect the scripts, programs, and motivations throughout an organization (e.g., Bennis & Nanus, 1985; Burns, 1978; Hunt et al., 1988; Martin et al., 1983). Other recent models of senior management leadership have treated organization culture as a different, less explicit, but no less powerful source of individual programming (Hunt et al., 1988). For example, supervisors whose superiors maintain a management philosophy supporting autocratic decision making report that they themselves tend to treat subordinates punitively (Hammer & Turk, 1987).

Some recent contingency theories of organization treat the degree of formalization imposed on people in formal leadership roles as dependent upon organization size (large), technology (repetitive), or some other characteristic that contributes to the mixed virtue of being able to document consistent behavior (Mintzberg, 1979). Such organizations are viewed as "tightly coupled systems" (Weick, 1976).

Implicitly, models of formalization suggest that formal organization rules provide a template that programs many elements of cognitive structure. A rule-based template is designed and implemented to produce a cognitive replica of itself, a replica that not only exists but carries with it a motivational force to promote its use. For example, rules in the form of union contracts are associated with supervisors' reports that their interactions with subordinates are guided by written rules and regulations (Hammer & Turk, 1987). March and Simon (1958) emphasize the intended, and often successful, function of bureaucratic rules for generating a fixed interpretation and response by organization members, formal leaders included, to the events they encounter. Nonetheless, rules can have unanticipated consequences. For example, formal reward systems governing managers' compensation are typically designed to increase the salience of those rules that have particular organizational value. Ilgen, Mitchell, and Fredrickson (1981), however, in their laboratory study, found that supervisors whose own rewards depended on their subordinates' performance provided greater financial rewards for poor performers than did other supervisors, an apparent violation of traditional organizational values.

Katz and Kahn (1978) recognize the effects of organizational rules on cognitive programming by redefining leadership as those initiatives taken by managers that are *not* rule-driven. Stewart (1976, 1982) makes a similar point when describing the process by which managers learn to behave according to job *demands* as distinct from external *constraints* and more effortful *individual choices*.

Green and Mitchell (1979), however, show a confusion in their analysis of leadership and cognition that is encouraged by March and Simon's language of "programmed" versus "nonprogrammed" activity. These terms are applied both to rules of an organization *designed* to program behavior, and to cognitive structures that *directly* program behavior. A distinction is needed between deliberately deciding to follow a rule or policy and habitually enacting an established pattern of behavior that may or may not have its origin in organizational rules. For example, "programming" in the sense of following a managerially prescribed sequence of activities when reviewing a subordinate's performance is different from habitually following an implicit, personally developed program for the same purpose.

Proposition 2: The social climate or culture surrounding an FI affects the triggering of rule-based, programmed cognitive structures, and the use of scripts and deliberative processes.

A few early studies may be reinterpreted to suggest how group and organizational environments affect leadership by affecting bureaucratically programmed versus more creative cognition. The quality of group process in superordinate groups (part of the environment of a subordinate group) may affect subsequent organizational climate, managerial leadership, peer leadership, and the overall quality of group process in subordinate groups (Franklin, 1975a). Organizational climate may also affect experienced managerial leadership, which in turn may affect experienced peer leadership, and finally group process (Franklin, 1975b).

Peterson and Cooke (1983) interpret data from a cross-sectional study to indicate that the supportive and participative leadership that community college students experience from a professor is affected by the extent to which teachers are encouraged to participate in college decision making. Qualitative documentation of People Express further supports the conclusion that even an intentionally created, formally legitimated culture can sometimes militate against the extensive application of narrowly constraining organization rules (Hackman, 1984). In other words, leaders at a corporate level can intentionally create a culture and work system that can either increase or reduce the extent to which leaders at lower organization levels follow highly specific organizational rules (Manz & Sims, 1987). Some element of a group's organizational context that has been identified as a "supportive" or "participative" culture appears to reduce the triggering of bureaucratically programmed action and encourages action driven by other cognitive processes. It is premature to speculate whether the action patterns triggered are equally highly structured "participative leadership" scripts or more rationally adaptive problem-solving cognitive processes.

Mischel's (1968) critique of personality-based predictions of behavior suggests that situational characteristics, such as a person's role in a particular social setting, condition the attitudes that a person considers when faced with a behavior choice. Salancik and Pfeffer's (1978) social information-processing perspective implies that organizational norms as well as the values and beliefs of peers and subordinates have the potential to affect the outcomes an FI evaluates as well as the needs that are salient when assigning values to outcomes. Thus a variety of personal characteristics (e.g., typical need satisfaction levels) and situational characteristics (e.g., past associations with a particular context and social forces) may affect those leadership behavior choices that are relatively rational by affecting outcome valences.

Proposition 3: An organizational context will affect which of an FI's cognitive structures are brought into play by affecting the overall level and particular task domain within which the person's augmented role set communicates expectations for leadership.

As in emergent groups, an organization member's role set includes individuals with whom the person interacts. In organizations, this role set is augmented by the depersonalized expectations reflected in systems of organizational rules, procedures, and norms (Kahn et al., 1964; Smith & Peterson, 1988, chap. 6). "Position power" is a concept popularized by Fiedler (1967, 1971, 1972) that refers to expectations that various role set members have for various sources regarding an FI's role combined with formalized role requirements. The concept traditionally includes organizational factors that can affect a formal leader's behavior by affecting the degree and source of the leader's power. Yukl (1989) suggests that power sources (Cartwright, 1965; French & Raven, 1968) affect a formal leader's behavior by affecting shared norms about acceptable leader behavior. Power source studies have included a leader's abilities to reward and coerce, as well as the amount of group-relevant organizational information and formally recognized or legitimated control the person possesses.

One effect of position power was demonstrated in a field experiment in which a supervisor's ability to reward good performance was removed (Greene & Podsakoff, 1981). When control of rewards was removed, subordinates subsequently reported not only that rewards were used less, but that punishments increased. Influence based on liking for the supervisor and on organizationally supported power were also viewed as being used less. Other research indicates that subordinates' expectations about appropriate behavior by a formal leader are affected by the personal and position power of the person's role set members, notably his or her subordinates and superordinates (Lee, 1977). As noted above in connection with the often assumed determining effects of formal rules, the efficacy of appointing someone as a formal leader on his or her leadership initiative has generally been taken for granted. Studies noted below in connection with the effects of an FI's role typically assume the efficacy of appointment.

A moderate amount of attention has been devoted to a kind of semiformal leadership role — the role of "mentor" (e.g. Hunt & Michael, 1983; Kram, 1983). However, the empirical literature about this leadership role has not developed very far. A person's status outside a particular organizational group can place the person in the position of being sought as mentor by junior group members seeking socialization into upper organizational levels. More generally, the mentor idea highlights the possibility that any organization member can experience role expectations to fulfill specific leadership functions. Broad categorizations of group member roles as "task leader," "socioemotive leader," and "follower" have the advantage of being general enough to be applied in many social settings. However, for understanding organizational leadership, more specific functional characterizations might be better. For example, measures such as the observational scheme developed by Bales (1950) are not easily adaptable to, say, distinguishing task-related behaviors directed toward procuring resources from task-related behaviors directed toward coordinating the activities of group members. If such behavior goals were distinguishable, a more realistic picture of the structures of organizational groups might be provided. For example, an adequate representation of leadership in an organizational group composed of an MBA-trained manager with formal authority over a diversified group of professional scientists, engineers, and technicians would require that quite complex forms of differentiated leadership roles be identified.

Other Mediated Effects on Behavior

As direct relationships between organizational variables and behavior are increasingly clarified, indirect relationships that use group characteristics as intervening variables will need to be modeled as well. Relationships between variables in a group's environment and leadership behavior in the group can reflect two alternative causal paths. Environmental variables could either directly affect individual-level variables such as an FI's cognitions or affect group-level variables that in turn affect those cognitions. Leadership research seeking effects of organizational context on leadership behavior faces two difficult tasks. First, it must interpret the implicit operation of individual and group-level intervening variables. Second, it must identify causal forces strong enough to overcome inertia and alternative forces that simultaneously affect the individual- and group-level mediating variables.

Effects of Group Characteristics (5)

The three propositions presented above refer to the implications of organization context as a simplified representation of interaction history at a rather "macro" level. Other aspects of interaction history indicated in Figure 1 are typically modeled as "group" characteristics. Enduring social system characteristics are relatively stable characteristics of a group (e.g., communication networks, control structure, role structure). Prevailing characteristics are commonly recurring, but less stable variables (e.g., repeated work events that make coordination difficult). The construction of these two sets of variables reflects a partial acceptance of the role theory structuralist position that people construct social systems as having properties of stability. Studies reviewed here as indicating the consequences of enduring group characteristics deal with variables that members and observers view as being quite stable. Other studies are discussed below that deal with more transient situational characteristics in connection with ongoing group processes.

The group and organizational environment together with group characteristics are likely to affect ongoing group processes (i.e., the events that occur and the problems that become acute in a group at various times). Since these relationships fall outside the traditional domain of leadership research, no propositions will be provided. Group problems can be categorized in several ways. A common division arising from group process theories distinguishes broadly between production and maintenance problems (e.g., Bales, 1950; Cartwright & Zander, 1968; Misumi, 1985). More refined ways to categorize problems clearly place groups and the leadership provided for them into an organizational context. One such model distinguishes among coordination, integration, maintenance, resource allocation, strain and tension management, and adaptation (Georgopoulos, 1972). The leadership provided is likely to depend on members' beliefs about what particular events indicate about how well various problem areas are being managed.

Direct Relationships
of Group Characteristics to Behavior

Proposition 4: Leadership scripts are triggered and reinforced by salient schemata about self and others associated with (a) an FI's cognitive structures linked to group composition, and (b) other members' actions reflecting group composition.

Researchers have studied group composition according to the distribution of individual difference and demographic characteristics. Many studies have used aggregated group member personality and attitudinal characteristics to predict the behavior of formal leaders. Most studies reflect the belief that a formal leader will respond to a group's composition based on the leader's stereotypes, person perceptions, and "other" schemata. A few studies imply that actions by members in groups having certain characteristics reflect particular role expectations for a leader. For example, it has been argued that formal leaders behave more autocratically within groups of autocratic or authoritarian members than within groups of democratically oriented members (Bass, Valenzi, Farrow, & Solomon, 1975; Crowe, Bochner, & Clark, 1972; Haythorn, Couch, Haefner, Langham, & Carter, 1956). Bass et al. (1975) also found supervisors to be more consultative, participative, and delegative, but less negotiative and directive, in making decisions in groups composed of subordinates who believe that "people act and are treated fairly" (p. 722) than with other groups. Following a similar logic, Ford (1981) found that department managers display less initiating structure and less consideration (based on LBDQ-Form XII scores) in departments of more highly educated employees than in those of less highly educated employees.

Other studies have identified relationships between group demographic composition and the leadership provided by formal leaders. Demographically based expectations for subordinates have the potential to affect several aspects of cognitive information processing. If a subordinate, due perhaps to his or her race or sex, is expected to perform poorly but in fact performs distinctly well, attributions to special effort or unique ability can occur and may result in particularly positive rewards (Terborg & Ilgen, 1975). Bartol and Wortman (1975) indicate that supervisors are more likely to exhibit leadership behaviors when working with female rather than male subordinates. Baker, DiMarco, and Scott (1975) found that supervisors rewarded blind workers more highly than sighted workers for the same level of performance. Parker (1976) found "the behavior of supervisors toward their subordinates to be a complex function of (a) the supervisor's own race and role in combination with (b) the race of subordinates and (c) the majority or minority positions of racial groups within the groups supervised" (p. 140). Kipnis, Silverman, and Copeland (1973) report that first-line supervisors used coercion more often with Black than White and with union than nonunion subordinates. Hill and Hughes (1974), however, found no direct effect of group racial composition on leader behavior, although a difficult-to-interpret interaction of racial composition and task type on behavior did appear.

In sum, group demographic composition is more apparent to a focal member than is a group's psychological composition. Consequently, group demographics are likely to have direct effects on a focal member's attitudes and beliefs about their context apart from indirect effects mediated by members' expectations for leadership.

Many other examples of the effects of group personality or demographic composition on a supervisor's behavior could be cited (Stogdill, 1974). Proposition 4 suggests that further research should distinguish explanations based on group expectations for and actions toward a leader from those based on the leader's expectations for people having certain characteristics.

Proposition 5: Unclear goals, lack of task structure, or lack of other behavioral cues will increase (a) the focal member's goal-directed attention to task-related information from external sources, (b) the salience of extraorganizational schemata and scripts, and (c) the deliberateness or conscious rationality of interpretation and choice processes.

Task characteristics, particularly task structure, have remained important in leadership effectiveness research, particularly in path-goal theory and substitutes for leadership theory (e.g., Fiedler, 1967; House, 1971; Howell, Dorfman, & Kerr, 1986; Kerr et al., 1974), but have been studied less often as variables affecting leadership behavior. Effectiveness-oriented researchers may be reluctant to face the interpretational problems that would be underlined if what have been treated as moderators and intervening variables were pointedly demonstrated to affect what are usually treated as predictors. Unfortunately, unless formal leaders are systematically unobservant, they are likely to realize, along with path-goal and substitutes for leadership researchers, that they should seek to be more directive when subordinates experience task ambiguity. Of course, if appointed leaders and subordinates experience equal uncertainty, as sometimes occurs when uncertainty has an extraorganizational origin (Ford, 1981), leaders may not be able to provide the guidance their subordinates desire.

Research on task characteristics that affect leadership has a long history. Carter, Haythorn, Shriver, and Lanzetta (1950) experimentally studied the effects of qualitatively different tasks on various behaviors. Regardless of task type, recognized leaders, whether emergent or appointed, collected information for interpreting the events that occurred and solving group problems. The specific activities involved in information gathering and problem solving, however, varied somewhat across tasks. In another study, supervisors in groups whose members were working toward a common goal were found to behave differently from supervisors in groups where there was some internal conflict of interest (Richards & Cuffe, 1972).

Fiedler used a "situation favorability" dimension to indicate the ease with which a formal leader can exert influence in a group. This dimension is constructed in part from a task structure index that itself collapses a number of more specific task dimensions (Fiedler, 1967; see also Shaw, 1963). Research on Fiedler's model typically has not dealt with task structure in isolation from other situational variables. Consequently, its independent effect on behavior is not known, although it appears to have some interactive effect on a formal leader's behavior in conjunction with other variables.

Heller and Yukl (1969) studied the associations between a number of situational variables and the use of decentralized decision making by formal leaders. One variable related to a group's task was managerial specialty. From the specialty in which the most centralization was used to the one in which the least was used, the ranking was as follows: production, finance, sales, purchasing, general, and personnel. The authors linked task characteristics to formalization by speculating that this order could be accounted for by the greater external constraints and work procedure programming in the specialties in which decisions are most centralized.

Several task-related variables were included in a study that Ford (1981) conducted to assess the relationship that departmental characteristics had with (LBDQ-Form XII) measures of consideration and initiating structure. The study involved 25 departments in a book publishing company, a bank branch, and a university. Department manager initiating structure was negatively associated with external uncertainty and positively associated with experienced task routineness and internal uncertainty.

Thompson's (1967) classification of technology types was applied to classify sections in a manufacturing plant as long-linked, mediating, or intensive technologies. Of the three technology types, supervisors in long-linked technologies, those technologies in which machine-paced work is prevalent, indicated spending the most time with subordinates on matters of group maintenance. Supervisors in mediating technologies, those technologies that mediate between two other departments, reported spending more time networking with other units.

The above examples indicate that task characteristics can be associated with subordinates' perceptions of a leader's behavior patterns. The work remains of systematically categorizing task dimensions at individual (Hackman & Oldham, 1975), group (Shaw, 1963), and organizational (Thompson, 1967) levels of analysis and determining whether and in what way each is associated with various kinds of leadership behaviors by people in various roles. Ford (1981) and Hammer and Turk (1987) have suggested that formal leaders may change their behavior patterns when they perceive task or other potential substitutes for personally engaging in leadership. The impact of task characteristics is probably on the frequency with which a group encounters certain problematic events (aspects of the "ongoing group and organizational processes" cell) and, consequently, the information to which managers give most attention. Thus the effects suggested in Proposition 5 are generally assumed to be mediated by short-term group events.

Proposition 6: Increased group size will increase a formal leader's use of highly structured cognitions to conserve information processing when interpreting a given event or selecting an action.

Large groups, or large "spans of control," have the potential to require a great deal of a manager's time. The larger the group being supervised, the more managers try to reduce the time pressure that is placed on them by their groups. Supervisors of large groups have been found to be more directive (Skinner, 1969), less considerate (Ford, 1981), and more autocratic (Blankenship & Miles, 1968; Heller & Yukl, 1969) than supervisors of smaller groups. When considering senior managers (as distinguished from first- or second-line supervisors), however, Heller and Yukl (1969) found that many would delegate decisions in response to the time demands placed on them by large subordinate groups. However, Ford (1981) found no relationship between size and initiating structure. Still, senior managers used participative decision methods that require the supervisor's active involvement less often than they used less time-consuming autocratic or delegative methods. Mahoney, Frost, Crandall, and Weitzel (1972) also found that delegation is used more in large than in small units. In another vein, Goodstadt and Kipnis (1970) found that supervisors of larger groups used more official warnings and less expert power than did supervisors of small groups. The increasing awareness of the full range of demands on a manager suggests that future research concerning the effects of group size will take into account other time-consuming duties besides just managing many subordinates (Mintzberg, 1979).

Variables such as group size that determine the time available for dealing with subordinates may affect behavior by encouraging the use of programmed responses that require little information-processing time. Thus, under conditions of time constraints, an action that requires little information gathering from subordinates or other sources (either autocratic or delegative) is immediately selected. Alternatively, time considerations may enter into a more complex deliberative process so that behavioral alternatives that are likely to require considerable time to implement successfully are judged to be negatively valent themselves or to have a low probability of successful enactment. Since both processes are likely to result in the same decision, however, the difference in process may be of little importance. A more important problem is the situational determinants (perhaps group norms) and personal determinants (perhaps generalized autocratic attitudes) that determine which of the several alternative behaviors a formal leader uses to respond to a large group under conditions of time pressures (Vroom & Jago, 1988).

Proposition 7: The salience, priority, and ease of access of relevant cognitive structures increase as similar problems and events within a group recur. A group's hierarchical level, the group's function in relation to a larger system, and the typical performance problems of individual group members and of the group as a whole are among the factors affecting typical problems and recurring events. Recurrence increases the salience of events, which in turn triggers the frequent enactment and strengthening of related scripts.

While hierarchical structure is a characteristic of the larger organization in which a group operates, the hierarchical level of a particular group is better seen as a complex variable having implications for group task variables and for a group's functional relationships to other organizational subunits. A field study by Dowell and Wexley (1978) indicated that supervisory jobs were similar enough across a variety of subsidiaries of one corporation to indicate that hierarchical level has important implications for first-line supervisor behavior regardless of organization technology or functional specialty. In a study of several factors affecting decision-making style, Blankenship and Miles (1968) found hierarchical level to be the best predictor of leadership behavior. In general, upper-level managers appeared to use more participative methods than did lower-level managers. The difference between managers' decision methods at higher and lower levels was accentuated in large organizations and reduced in small ones. Jago and Vroom (1977), using both self-descriptions and subordinate descriptions at four hierarchical levels, found that upper-echelon managers used more participative decision methods than did lower-level managers. Following Vroom's (1974) decision-making model, a variety of cognitive intervening processes may account for these findings. Whether hierarchical level predicts behavior because of its association with task variables or with interunit-relations variables and what other variables intervene between it and behavior are issues deserving more research attention than they have received.

Reasonably strong evidence suggests that the typical performance levels of a group or of individual members affect subsequent leadership behavior. In an experimental study, Ashour and England (1972) found that the amount of discretion given to subordinates was proportionally related to descriptions of the subordinates' previous performance. Using cross-lagged correlations (Pelz & Andrews, 1964), Farris (1966) found that the scientific contributions (performance) of engineers were more closely related to nine subsequent supervisory functions (e.g., showing enthusiasm, providing a neutral "sounding board," providing clear instructions, showing appreciation) than were these leadership practices to subsequent performance. In another longitudinal study, Greene (1975) found that prior subordinate performance was positively related to subordinates' later experiences of the leader's emphasis on consideration and negatively to experiences of initiating structure. The opposite causal direction, however, was found in a study of machine workers based on the path-goal leadership model (House, 1971) conducted by Downey, Sheridan, and Slocum (1975).

Research concerning performance-contingent rewards and punishments (e.g., Sims, 1977) has begun to address the question of why supervisors reward (or punish) subordinates for good (or poor) performance under some conditions, but not under others. Mitchell and his coworkers have reviewed the research literature and conducted additional studies to determine the basis for attributional responses to instances of good and poor performance and the behavioral implications of these attributions (see, e.g., Green & Mitchell, 1979; Mitchell & Kalb, 1981, 1982; Mitchell & Wood, 1980). The importance of interaction history is indicated by their findings that an "internal attribution" to characteristics of a subordinate is promoted by a *history* of poor performance on the same task as well as on other tasks, good performance on the task by other subordinates, and knowledge that the poor performance had negative consequences. Internal attributions of poor performance are responded to by punitive actions by a supervisor. Speculative models indicating possible cognitive mediators of links between attributions and behaviors are becoming quite well developed (e.g., Lord & Smith, 1983; Smith & Peterson, 1988, chap. 4).

The general implication of the group interaction history elements of performance attribution research is that typical or repeated events affect a leader's interpretation of subsequent occurrences. Research remains to determine whether this general result can be applied to events that do not fall into distinct good performance/bad performance categories. For example, would repeated resource inadequacies result in a tendency to attribute new instances of interpersonal conflict or poor group performance to a new resource deficiency?

A potentially useful approach based on social information-processing theory (Salancik & Pfeffer, 1978) and role theory (Kahn et al., 1964) might be to ask about role expectations from various sources (context) concerning expectations for response (action) toward particular problems that may arise in the work activities of a particular organizational group (target).

Effects of Group Characteristics on a Focal Member's Position in the Group

Proposition 8: A group's demographic composition will affect the salience of an FI's role-related self-schemata. Self-schemata that are consistent with internalized cultural stereotypes and personal beliefs about the relationship between people with backgrounds similar to the focal person and people having backgrounds similar to those of group members will be particularly accessible.

The effects of an FI's demographic characteristics are outside the present discussion's focus on effects that context has on an FI's cognition. However, some attention to an FI's background is necessary because the focal person's interpretation of a group's demographic composition is likely to be affected by his or her own background. The demographic characteristics of leader and group members can also affect members' leadership expectations for one another and for a formal leader. Determining whether leader-group demographic differences generate highly structured, stereotyped responses or fastidious, highly deliberative social information processing will be a difficult task.

For example, if male managers generally expect working women to behave differently from men (Bass, Krusell, & Alexander, 1971), these expectations have the potential to contribute to differences between men and women in subjective probabilities that their leadership attempts will be constructive. Consistent with studies of competence, conformity, and status, Bass (1981, chap. 30) argues from a review of research concerning sex differences in social status that the probability of leader emergence is affected by any tendencies of an organization to give women lower status compared with men.

Reviews of the implications of supervisor and subordinate gender for leader emergence and leadership behavior (Bartol, 1978; Bass, 1981, chap. 30; Terborg, 1977) indicate that gender-based expectations by role set members may be more potent factors affecting gender differences in leadership than are gender-linked attitudes or skills. Numerous laboratory and field studies have been conducted to identify gender-based expectations and to document their effects. In general, little evidence indicates that female leaders are appraised differently from male leaders by subordinates in situations outside of the laboratory (Bartol, 1978). Jacobson and Effertz (1974) did find that males are expected to exhibit more leadership behavior than females. Adams (1976) reports that subordinates claimed that White female supervisors exhibited more consideration than White male supervisors. No significant differences based on the gender of the manager were found in perceptions of authority in any subordinate group. Bartol and Wortman (1975) found that females in their study were reported by subordinates to exhibit more initiating structure than males. No other differences based on leader gender were found.

Bartol (1978), in an extensive review, concludes that the relatively small numbers of gender-based leader perception differences may well be attributable more to chance or to characteristics of a given job situation than to bona fide gender differences in the way leaders are perceived. Bartol does not exclude the possibility that gender may combine with other variables to influence how a leader is perceived, and, in this vein, found that dominating women were viewed more positively by subordinates than were passive women (Bartol, 1974). Bartol concludes that dominant behavior is more in keeping with general expectations for a formal leader than is passivity.

In contrast, a subordinate's gender does seem to have an impact upon responses to male and female leaders. Bartol and Wortman (1975) found that females perceived leaders of both sexes to be significantly higher on demand reconciliation, persuasiveness, initiating structure, consideration, and predictive accuracy than did males. Adams (1976) found that female subordinates reported that their managers allowed them more self-determination, but also showed more initiating structure than did male subordinates. Bartol and Butterfield (1974) report that females rated hypothetical leaders who structured group work activities more positively than did males.

Haccoun, Haccoun, and Sallay (1978) found that male superiors were perceived more favorably than female supervisors by nonmanagement employees. Although these results are assumed to be the result of gender role or minority stereotyping employed by subordinates, such findings could in fact be due to actual characteristics of male and female leaders. Sex composition of a group may interact with the sex of a leader to influence the position of that person in the group. Haccoun et al. (1978) found that male subordinates rated directive leadership by females as less effective than a friendly strategy employed by a female or either type of strategy employed by a male. This effect was not found in female subordinates.

Racially based expectations about appropriate behavior in general and appropriate leadership behavior in particular have the potential to affect leadership. Bass (1981, chap. 31) outlines some of the sociological research concerning stereotypic expectations for blacks and reviews studies of various combinations of black and white leaders and subordinates. Studies of black leaders with primarily black subordinates showed that tensions arose when the black leaders needed to deal with whites in authority (Delbecq & Kaplan, 1968; King & Bass, 1974; Kochman, 1969). Black supervisors were expected by white subordinates to avoid close supervision and to be more reactive than proactive (King & Bass, 1974). Depending on the people involved, however, racial biases by one group for another may be directly reflected in leadership expectations or neutralized or even reversed as a function of organizational or subcultural norms (Fenelon & Megargee, 1971).

Adams (1976) found that black male managers were perceived to be higher in consideration by subordinates than white male managers. No differences were reported in perceptions of work sensitivity, personal sensitivity, self-determination, or negotiating latitude, or on items other than consideration. Subordinate race interacted with leader race to influence subordinate perceptions of managers. Black subordinates reported that black managers exhibited the highest degree of consideration when compared with white subordinates or with subordinates of either race reporting upon white managers.

As a set, studies focusing on group demographics are likely to be particularly time and culture bound (Tait, Padgett, & Baldwin, 1989). The meanings of "male" and "female" and of race and ethnicity are unlikely to remain fixed. Although Proposition 8 suggests that demographic distributions will affect leadership role expectations, it is unlikely that *particular* expectations for *particular* demographic combinations will be identified with much stability.

Proposition 9: Enduring and prevailing group characteristics affect an FI's role-related self-schemata by eliciting setting-specific expectations from the FI's role set members.

Enduring and prevailing group characteristics imply that certain events or problems have had repeated salience to group members. The shared, repeated salience of events is likely to generate regularities in interaction patterns, including those that involve leadership. Questionnaire studies during the 1970s of leadership ideals indicated that situational variables affect member expectations for a formal supervisor. Hunt and Liebscher (1973) found that supervisors were expected to show greater consideration and tolerance of freedom in design than in production bureaus of a state highway department. No differences were found for initiating structure or for production emphasis expectations. In a follow-up reanalysis based on the Hunt and Liebscher study and another study by Stogdill and Coady (1970), Kavanagh (1975) concluded that people with employment experience (i.e., professional managers) expected more initiating structure and less tolerance of freedom from their superiors than did high school and college students. Kavanagh (1972) found that subordinate competence was inversely related to subordinate expectations for leader structuring, but task complexity had no similar effects.

Proposition 10: The functional specialty of an FI's department will have a modest effect on the cognitive structures used to process problem-solving information under conditions that call for deliberative judgment.

Two studies have sought to address the question of whether the kind of department in which a manager is working restricts the ability to take a broad perspective on multifaceted management problems (Dearborn & Simon, 1958; Walsh, 1988). Both studies asked managers in training programs to identify the key issues in a written case analysis. Although Dearborn and Simon (1958) interpret their findings to indicate functionally biased, selective perception by managers, Walsh's (1988) results encouraged him to reinterpret the earlier study. Although Walsh found a tendency for managers to be particularly attentive to issues related to their departments' specialties, managers also used information related to other departments. Walsh argues that a careful reanalysis of Dearborn and Simon's data yields the same conclusion. These studies suggest that managers in any functional department will open their "perceptual filters" to seek information from many role senders about many organization problems, at least when sufficient time is available, and they are called upon by a legitimate party to comment upon an unfamiliar, uncertain problem. The question remains open of the extent to which department characteristics besides technical specialty, like department norms or subcultures, restrict managers' creative, deliberative diagnosis of interpersonal situations.

Summary

Research dealing with group characteristics has been fairly successful in predicting the perceived behavior of formal leaders. The greatest inadequacy in this area has been the meager empirical work to develop and test cognitive explanations for the relationships that have been found. Group characteristics may increase the salience of setting-specific cognitive structures and provide a shared, cognitively based group culture that affects how all role set members interpret events. However, empirical support for such speculation is lacking.

Effects of Focal Member's Position in the Group and Organization (6)

Factors affecting group expectations for the leadership contribution of a particular member have received a great deal of research attention under the heading "leader emergence." Belief in the strong effect of holding a formal leadership position is reflected in the continued, nearly universal practice of using hierarchy in an attempt to control activities in work organizations. Different factors may affect the amount of leadership each member is expected to provide as well as the area in which each person is expected to provide leadership. The "vertical dyad linkage" approach to leadership (Dansereau, Graen, & Haga, 1975; Graen, 1976; Wakabayashi, Graen, Graen, & Graen, 1988) also brings out a point made earlier by Homans (1950), that one group may have several echelons of informal leadership. Different areas for leadership are reflected in Bales's (1950) distinction between task and socioemotive leadership roles. As noted above, leadership roles may also develop for managing different categories of events in ways that satisfy needs in different problem areas.

Direct Effects on Behavior and Experienced Behavior

Proposition 11: Expectations for leadership from the augmented role set will activate an FI's goal-directed search for cues about how to provide that leadership, and will increase leadership attempts by increasing the salience of cognitive structures associated with the leadership role.

A focal member's position in the group's role structure is probably the most important "position in the group" antecedent of leadership behavior identified in previous research. Most researchers differentiate between a member expected by the group to fulfill leadership functions and other members expected to behave as followers (e.g., Carter et al., 1950). More often than not, the recognized leader is the only person whose leadership behavior is considered to be worth studying.

In a modern work organization, appointment to a position as a formal leader carries several ingredients that also encourage group acceptance as an emergent leader. Appointment often conveys status, provides access to resources needed to contribute competently, and indicates norm conformity in the opinion of at least some powerful constituencies in the larger system. Michels's (1949) "iron law of oligarchy" suggests that much less than these bases for control will affect the initiatives emergent leaders take and the functions they fulfill in symbolic exchanges with other parties.

Many examples indicating the effects of particular kinds of leadership status are known. Heller and Yukl (1969) compared centralization in decision making by student leaders (least centralized), senior managers, second-line supervisors, and first-line supervisors (most centralized). Putnam and Wilson (1982) found that managers use more "control strategies" (impersonal rules, formalized procedures, and persuasion) than did subordinates, while low-level employees use more "non-confrontational" (avoiding, smoothing, or trivializing differences) strategies, and first-line supervisors use more solution-oriented strategies. Kipnis and Schmidt (1983) found that people placed in a less dominant position use more direct requests, supporting evidence, and offers of reciprocity than do dominant parties. Supervisors also use direct, coercive tactics on resistant subordinates (Kipnis & Cohen, 1980). Being in a peer status leads to a contingent diagnosis of exchange tactic (Cody et al., 1985). Rim and Erez (1980; Erez & Rim, 1982) found that individuals use rational strategies when influencing their bosses, and use clandestine, exchange, or administrative sanctions to influence subordinates. In a study of managers from the United States, the United Kingdom, and Australia, Kipnis, Schmidt, Swaffin-Smith, and Wilkinson (1984) found more self-reported use of "reason," "coalition," or "bargaining" than other strategies when influencing superiors, and more use of "reason" when influencing subordinates.

Morris and Hackman (1969) indicate that two-thirds of the experimental subjects who were assigned to be leaders in three-person experimental groups received above-average scores on leadership ratings. A few researchers have distinguished among leaders, "lieutenants" (key subordinates), and followers (e.g., Dansereau et al., 1975; Homans, 1950) or between task leaders and socioemotive leaders (e.g., Bales, 1950). Research making these structural distinctions indicates that people take more leadership initiative in interpreting and managing particular events the more they are expected to provide leadership by their supervisors, peers, and subordinates in dealing with these events.

Particular aspects of an appointed leader's managerial role also affect behavior. For example, participation in hiring decisions is sometimes part of a supervisor's role. In such cases, a supervisor's original opinion about a prospective employee can shape the subsequent performance evaluations by the supervisor after the employee is hired (Schoorman, 1988). The initial opinion is likely to direct the supervisor's attention to incidents that justify that opinion.

A focal member's position in the group should affect several aspects of cognitive information processing. When people see themselves as being expected to behave in certain ways or to contribute to solving certain problems, they are likely to believe that their leadership will be considered appropriate and responded to positively by others. Perceptions of other group members' expectations should increase a person's expectations that his or her leadership attempts will not be resisted, and that he or she will be rewarded if leadership is attempted but punished if it is not. Leadership expectation may also stimulate a greater amount of information-processing activity of all kinds—including information search, causal analysis, generation of behavior alternatives, and evaluation of alternatives—for the person in the leadership role than for others.

Proposition 12: A focal person's centrality in a communication structure increases (a) the perception of cues indicating needs and opportunities, (b) the probability that the leadership scripts elicited fit with the social context, and (c) the tendency for a central person to emerge into a generalized leader role.

A focal member's location in group structures other than the leadership structure has been found to affect leadership behavior. Shaw (1976, pp. 140-148) reports that the consequences of physically constructed communication networks come about because of the consequences of these networks for a group's actual information flows. His results also imply that the individual most central to the group's communication structure is the one likely to provide the most leadership. The central individual is likely to be the first one to learn of events requiring concerted group effort. If communication structures depend upon the possession of information critical to key constituencies (Hickson, Hinnings, Lee, Schneck, & Pennings, 1971), then possessing critical information is likely to promote leader emergence by affecting communication patterns. To the extent that the social as well as physical structuring of communication patterns affect information flows, people high in the group's status and control structures will tend to make more leadership attempts than will others (Bass, 1963; Hollander, 1964; Knapp & Knapp, cited in House & Baetz, 1979, p. 57; Shiflett & Nealey, 1972).

Effects of Ongoing
Group and Organizational Processes (7)

Ongoing group and organizational processes are analogous to the portion of a situation that is modeled in Figure 1 as being outside the focal individual. Cody and McLaughlin (1985) define the situation as circumscribed by the physical and temporal boundaries within which two or more people interact. The dashed line in Figure 1 separating ongoing group and organization processes from ongoing psychological processes avoids a more radical separation. At the point of interaction, Cody and McLaughlin are correct in treating person-in-context as a unitary situation. The disparity in historical context and future of various parties and situational elements, indicated by the more enduring variables toward the left of Figure 1, requires the present analytic separation and reintegration of person and context. The present treatment is consistent with general analytic models of situation as person-in-context found in various communication applications.

An enlargement of the "ongoing group and organizational processes" cell would entail an analysis that repeats the integrated description of cognitive process, behavior, and individual context for each person in a focal individual's role set. In effect, the entirety of the model shown in Figure 1 could be constructed for each person. Pragmatics require both simplification and some recognition of the implicit dynamics hidden beneath a focus on one focal individual at a time.

Direct Effects on Behavior and Experienced Behavior

Proposition 13: A focal person's cognitive structures interpret physical external conditions to notice/construct events and initiate leadership behavior choice.

Evidence has been accumulating that leadership behavior varies with transient events that arise out of the group's tasks and problems. During the years of classic group dynamics laboratory research, Lanzetta (1955) found experimentally that observed task-facilitating behaviors were more frequent when a group was faced with stress (i.e., time constraints, space limitations, verbal harassment) from an external source than when it was not. Hill (1973a, 1973b) has demonstrated that subordinates perceive their supervisors as exhibiting different task-oriented and interpersonally oriented behaviors when faced with different kinds of problems. Hill and Hughes (1974), in an experimental study, found that undergraduate leaders varied their behavior according to task differences, although the correspondence between specific tasks and specific behavior was not reported. In a similar subsequent experiment, Barrow (1976) found that complex tasks resulted in greater task emphasis (based on subordinate descriptions) than did less complex tasks. Task complexity had no effect on rated supportive-consideration behavior.

The influence attempts used in situations of cooperativeness and resistance have received a good deal of attention in communication research. Cody and Mc-Laughlin (1985) report that on occasions when people perceive resistance to their influence attempts, self-benefit tactics were used most when resistance was low and personal benefits were high. Self-benefit tactics were used least when personal beliefs were low, resistance was high, and the target was dominant. Other-benefit tactics were used to overcome higher levels of perceived resistance. Exchange tactics were used when the target was expected to show low resistance. Although it is difficult to decode the behavior constructs used here in traditional leadership terms, the *content* of the influence attempts is likely to include the higher task component, and the tactics used to achieve tasks are likely to have the higher social system function component. When people perceive cooperativeness in others, they use integrative strategies of influence and avoid passive and distributive strategies (Sillars, 1980). Kipnis and Cohen (1980) found that when targets demonstrated resistance by refusing to comply with requests, people were persistent and increased the use of personal negative sanctions. When people perceive resistance, they tend to offer supporting evidence to overcome resistance (Cody et al., 1985).

Vroom and Yetton (1973) and Hill and Schmitt (1977) provide evidence that transient characteristics of decision situations affect a manager's intended decision-making style. Vroom and Yetton's (1973) descriptive model of leadership in decision making identifies several variables that determine whether formal leaders intend to make decisions by themselves or to involve their subordinates by requesting information and advice, by collaborating fully in decision making, or by delegating a decision. The conditions that affect these intentions include (a) the presence of a quality requirement (i.e., if a bad decision is possible), (b) the supervisor's knowledge, (c) the subordinates' knowledge, (d) the supervisor's ability to structure the problem, (e) the extent to which subordinates share organizational goals, (f) the probability of disagreements among subordinates, (g) whether or not subordinates could resist decision implementation, (h) the probability the leader's autocratic decision would be accepted, and (i) the time available to make the decision (Vroom & Jago, 1988).

Other experimental studies indicate that the quality of subordinate performance during a short period positively affects supervisor consideration, support, and certain goal emphasis, work facilitation, and interaction facilitation behaviors, but affects initiating structure inversely (Farris & Lim, 1969; Lowin & Craig, 1968). Herold (1977) demonstrated that undergraduates assigned as experimental leaders gave positive evaluative messages to subordinates in response to good performance and negative messages to poor performers. Supervisors in laboratory studies (Farris & Lim, 1969) and field studies (Dansereau et al., 1975) have also been observed to give subordinates more discretion or influence when subordinates perform well than when they do not. McFillen and New's (1979) experimental findings indicate that supervisors view successful performers as more trustworthy than others and treat them very favorably while allowing them considerable autonomy. Successful performers were also given greater rewards than less successful performers. In the study noted above in which task complexity was manipulated, Barrow (1976) also included subordinate performance levels as experimental conditions. He found that leaders exhibited more supportive-considerate behavior toward high-performing subjects than toward low-performing subjects. A change in performance from low to high resulted in increased subordinate descriptions of leader supportive-consideration behavior, although a change from high to low mainly brought about increases in autocratic and punitive performance-oriented behavior. Task complexity, as noted above, was substantially more important in promoting task-emphasis behavior than was subordinate performance. These results indicate that internal attributions of poor performance to subordinate motivation may be typical in the absence of other information (Jones & Nisbett, 1971). However, an initial experience of good performance by a subordinate seems to affect leader attributions of the cause of subsequent poor performance.

Summary: Links to Ongoing Cognitive Processes

Studies concerning ongoing group and organizational processes can be separated into two sets. One set identifies particular events that a focal member responds to with particular behaviors (e.g., Vroom & Yetton, 1973). The other set identifies more general situational variables that may produce or be associated with unspecified, more specific events to which a focal member responds (e.g., Farris & Lim, 1969; Lowin & Craig, 1968). While leadership responses to particular events may be more interpretable than overall leadership "style," variability in the context within which even single events, such as instances of poor performance, occur affects behavior through cognitive information processing.

IMPLICATIONS FOR SHAPING ORGANIZATIONAL LEADERSHIP

Thus far, this chapter has discussed how an FI's cognitive processes and behaviors are influenced by organizational and environmental antecedents. Organizational leaders can and do apply similar ideas when they attempt to shape one another's leadership by manipulating these antecedents. From a symbolic interactionist perspective, manipulating antecedents may be a form of communication in which antecedents elicit desired cognitions. However, a multiple-party, interactionist perspective must recognize that people assigned to leadership roles will view themselves as "independent variables" and can be analytically treated as such, although even CEOs are embedded in and influenced by their social context. Below we suggest how people attempting leadership might influence cognitions by altering antecedents. Those of our 13 propositions that are related to different portions of the discussion are indicated in parentheses.

Top-Level Leadership

If leader behavior is affected by contextual antecedents as outlined in Figure 1, then top-level leaders can exhibit considerable influence on leadership at other levels (Manz & Sims, 1987). Schein (1983), for example, argues that when founders initiate organizations, they create organizing mechanisms that reflect their own assumptions and values. These assumptions and values become embedded in the organization itself so that implicit and explicit messages are sent about the way the organization should function (Proposition 1).

From a symbolic interactionist perspective, in order for top-level leaders to use organizational antecedents as a form of influence, they must (a) treat their actions and organization as symbols, (b) be sensitive to the cognitions of organization members, and (c) promote common understanding on key issues. First, leaders must treat their actions and organizations as symbols — objects whose meanings may be shared (Hall, 1980). Top-level leaders may or may not have frequent interpersonal communication with subordinates at other levels. Even without personal contact, top leaders may use formal rules, socialization processes, structures, recurring events, and role expectations to elicit desired leadership schemata and scripts from lower-level managers (Propositions 1 and 2) — symbolically using these antecedents as a form of communication (Smith & Peterson, 1988, chap. 8).

Second, top leaders must be sensitive to the cognitions of lower-level leaders. They need feedback mechanisms to understand the schemata and scripts actually elicited by the antecedents they seek to control. They will be most successful when they are not only sensitive to subordinate managers' cognitions, but can shape antecedents to elicit desired schemata and scripts (Proposition 4).

Third, top-level leaders must be able to promote common understandings. We assume that top-level leaders can obtain a measure of control by using the communication process to engender common orientations among lower-level leaders (Goffman, 1959). Basically, leaders must draw attention to words, acts, objects, and events (Morgan, Frost, & Pondy, 1983) and promote consensus on their value and meaning (Proposition 7). Numerous strategies may be used to create common cognitions: Training and education can provide appropriate scripts, evaluation and reward systems focus attention on desired behavior patterns and goals, information systems define corporate reality by selectively highlighting certain kinds of data and organizational answers to questions so that members rely less on personal information sources and decision rules, and meetings help create common mind sets (Propositions 7 and 13; Smith & Peterson, 1988, chaps. 6, 8, 9).

The model of leadership for managing events and problems shown in Figure 1 offers senior leaders some strategies for eliciting desired leadership at other levels. The model suggests that the most long-term characteristics of a person's context will have the greatest effect on cognitions and behavior. Therefore, top leaders should give attention to enduring antecedents such as definitions of the environment, organizational culture, patterned organizational processes, and group structure in their efforts to elicit desired cognitions (Propositions 1, 2, 5, and 8). The key to making the cognitions endure is to wed them to symbols that endure.

The long-term characteristics of an FI's context are the variables to the extreme left in Figure 1, the organization and its environment. Although some conditions of the general environment are volatile, many environmental factors, especially national cultural variables, are relatively stable (Proposition 4; Smith & Peterson, 1988, chap. 11). Senior leaders can sometimes shape their external environment, and can even more often draw attention to, label, and define a limited set of environmental characteristics (Proposition 13). For example, leaders might use symbols to identify and characterize their views of competing organizations ("We Try Harder") and customers ("Customer Satisfaction Always"). When appropriate, leaders should make enduring desired cognitions by using stories, legends, myths, and metaphors about key people and events (Propositions 7 and 13; Deal & Kennedy, 1982; Martin et al., 1983).

Senior leaders should give considerable attention to creating enduring definitions of the organization by employing slogans, logos, philosophies, charters, and creeds, and promote their meaning through rites, rituals, training, publications, group meetings, and presentations (Proposition 1; Schein, 1983). They may also use actual physical facilities, including buildings and physical spaces, to elicit cognitions of desired forms of interaction, for example, of openness, professionalism, and progressiveness (or the converse) (Proposition 2).

Organizational structure and design are often viewed as the most concrete characteristics of organizations. The organizational chart, the nature of work groups, technological design, and functional divisions all symbolize desired relationships within an organization. Care should be taken to ensure they are mutually understood and elicit desired cognitions from relevant parties (Propositions 6, 8, 9, 10, and 12).

Top leaders may also use enduring social system characteristics to elicit desired cognitions, such as the use of large groups to suggest a desire for limited input (Proposition 6). The symbol works if it makes salient the desired script. However, prevailing characteristics such as dissatisfaction with working conditions could make other scripts salient, resulting in more input than the leader desired (Proposition 9). Thus leaders should be sensitive to contexts and cognitions associated with various actions, especially in times of uncertainty and change (Proposition 5). Change in structure creates considerable uncertainty, and top-level leaders should expend the energy necessary to ensure that adequate symbols are created to represent new structures and that significant stakeholders hold desired cognitions (Proposition 1; Quinn & Andersen, 1984).

In some situations, long-term characteristics such as enduring cultural schemata may not agree with the schemata top-level leaders desire in their employees. Leaders should be highly attuned to differences that may exist about such things as role relations and stereotypes about sex, race, and leadership (Proposition 4). In these cases, leaders may influence behavior by formally imposing language requirements and highly explicit rules about desired behavior and relationships (Proposition 1). Use of highly explicit strategies *may* alter both cognitive structures and behavior. Making explicit the expected roles of leaders through some set of enduring antecedents should also aid role transitions (Proposition 11). Symbolic representations of roles should help new leaders adopt cognitions desired by top-level leaders instead of cognitions from competing sources.

Research Issues

The discussion about leaders' use of antecedent influence provided here is suggestive. The relationships among symbols, cognitions, and actions need further exploration (Deetz & Kersten, 1983; Stablein & Nord, 1985). A number of recent articles address issues of symbolic interaction and suggest the importance of making the link between symbols and meanings in organizations (Eisenberg & Riley, 1988; Hall, 1980; Tompkins, 1987). They also summarize some limitations relevant to our discussion. Schein (1985) notes that people are limited in their ability to change material reality (or a person's perception of reality) and bend it to their interpretations. Weick (1979) argues that in some cases coordination of action is more important than coordinations of beliefs and attitudes, and that attempts at developing shared cognitions can lead to dysfunctional conflicts. Furthermore, research suggests that people can hold allegiance to abstract symbols without agreeing on the specific interpretation of the symbol (Becher, 1981). Even though there is disagreement on the symbols, they can create a sense of community.

Both leaders and researchers need to distinguish among those situations in which it is desirable and possible to create common symbols, common meanings, and common beliefs and attitudes. They need to determine when symbols should be used to trigger rule-based cognitive structures, to create common cognitions, and to create a sense of community within which leaders may use non-rule-based, personally developed scripts. We hope that a reinterpretation of research concerning leadership antecedents can contribute something to an understanding of the dynamics underlying emerging theories of charisma and culture-shaping leadership (e.g., Bass, 1985; Burns, 1978; Schein, 1985).

NOTE

1. Such differentiation highlights the need for caution in those studies noted below that use laboratory methods to understand interaction processes in organizations. Organizations structure the interactions of members and affect the cognition of formal leaders and followers alike through information control and social control processes that simply do not occur in emergent groups.

REFERENCES

Adams, E. F. (1976). *Influences of minority supervisors on subordinate attitudes.* Unpublished manuscript.
Abelson, R. P. (1976). Script processing in attitude formation and decision making. In J. S. Carroll & J. W. Payne (Eds.), *Condition and social behavior* (pp. 33-45). Hillsdale, NJ: Lawrence Erlbaum.
Ashour, A. S., & England, G. (1972). Subordinate's assigned level of discretion as a function of leader's personality and situational variables. *Journal of Applied Psychology, 56,* 120-123.
Baker, L., DiMarco, N., & Scott, W. (1975). Effects of supervisor's sex and level of authoritarianism on evaluation and reinforcement of blind and sighted workers. *Journal of Applied Psychology, 60,* 28-32.
Bales, R. F. (1950). *Interaction process analysis.* Cambridge, MA: Addison-Wesley.
Barrow, J. C. (1976). Worker performance and task complexity as causal determinants of leader behavior, style, and flexibility. *Journal of Applied Psychology, 61,* 433-440.
Bartol, K. M. (1974). Male vs. female leaders: The effect of leader dominance on follower satisfaction. *Academy of Management Journal, 17,* 225-233.
Bartol, K. M. (1978). The sex structuring of organizations: A search for possible causes. *Academy of Management Review, 3,* 805-815.
Bartol, K. M., & Butterfield, D. A. (1976). Sex effects in evaluating leaders. *Journal of Applied Psychology, 61,* 446-454.
Bartol, K. M., & Wortman, M. S. (1975). Male versus female leaders: Effects on perceived leader behavior and satisfaction in a hospital. *Personnel Psychology, 28,* 533-547.
Bass, B. M. (1963). Amount of participation, coalescence, and probability of decision making discussions. *Journal of Abnormal and Social Psychology, 67,* 92-94.
Bass, B. M. (1981). *Stogdill's handbook of leadership.* New York: Free Press.
Bass, B. M. (1985). *Leadership and performance beyond expectations.* New York: Free Press.
Bass, B. M., Krusell, J., & Alexander, R. A. (1971). Male managers' attitudes toward working women. *American Behavioral Scientist, 15,* 221-236.

Bass, B. M., Valenzi, E. R., Farrow, D. L., & Solomon, R. J. (1975). Management styles associated with organizational, task, personal, and interpersonal contingencies. *Journal of Applied Psychology, 60*, 720-729.

Becher, T. (1981). Towards a definition of disciplinary cultures. *Studies in Higher Education, 6*, 109-122.

Bennis, W. G., & Nanus, B. (1985). *Leaders: The strategies for taking charge.* New York: Harper & Row.

Bettman, J. R. (1979). *An information processing theory of consumer choice.* Reading, MA: Addison-Wesley.

Blankenship, L. V., & Miles, R. E. (1968). Organizational structure and managerial decision behavior. *Administrative Science Quarterly, 13*, 106-120.

Buckley, W. (1967). *Sociology and modern systems theory.* Englewood Cliffs, NJ: Prentice-Hall.

Burns, J. M. (1978). *Leadership.* New York: Harper & Row.

Carter, L., Haythorn, W., Shriver, B., & Lanzetta, J. (1950). The behavior of leaders and other group members. *Journal of Abnormal and Social Psychology, 46*, 589-595.

Cartwright, D. (1965). Influence, leadership and control. In J. G. March (Ed.), *Handbook of organizations* (pp. 1-47). Chicago: Rand McNally.

Cartwright, D., & Zander, A. (1968). Leadership and performance of group functions. In D. Cartwright & A. Zander (Eds.), *Group dynamics: Research and theory* (pp. 301-317). New York: Harper & Row.

Carver, C. S., & Scheier, M. F. (1982). Control theory: A useful conceptual framework for personality — social, clinical and health psychology. *Psychological Bulletin, 92*(1), 111-135.

Cody, M. J., Greene, J. O., Marston, P., Baaske, E., O'Hair, H. D., & Schneider, J. I. (1985). Situation-perception and the selection of message strategies. In M. L. McLaughlin (Ed.), *Communication yearbook 9* (pp. 390-420). Beverly Hills, CA: Sage.

Cody, M. J., & McLaughlin, M. L. (1985). The situation as a construct in interpersonal communication research. In M. L. Knapp & G. R. Miller (Eds.), *Handbook of interpersonal communication* (263-312). Beverly Hills, CA: Sage.

Cooke, R. A., & Rousseau, D. M. (1981). Problems of complex systems: A model of system problem solving applied to schools. *Education Administration Quarterly, 17*, 15-41.

Crowe, B. T., Bochner, S., & Clark, A. W. (1972). The effects of subordinate's behavior on managerial style. *Human Relations, 25*, 215-237.

Dansereau, F., Graen, G., & Haga, W. J. (1975). A vertical dyad linkage approach to leadership within formal organizations. *Organizational Behavior and Human Performance, 13*, 46-78.

Deal, T. E., & Kennedy, A. A. (1982). *Corporate cultures.* Reading, MA: Addison-Wesley.

Dearborn, D. C., & Simon, H. A. (1958). Selective perception: A note on the department identification of executives. *Sociometry, 21*, 140-144.

Deetz, S. A., & Kersten, A. (1983). Critical models of interpretive research. In L. Putnam & M. Pacanowsky (Eds.), *Communication and organization* (pp. 147-172). Beverly Hills, CA: Sage.

Delbecq, A. L., & Kaplan, S. J. (1968). The myth of the indigenous community leader: A case study of managerial effectiveness within the "War on Poverty." *Academy of Management Journal, 11*, 11-25.

Dillard, J. P., & Burgoon, M. (1984). *Situational influences on the selection of compliance-gaining messages: Two tests of the Cody-Laughlin typology.* Unpublished manuscript, University of Wisconsin.

Dowell, B. E., & Wexley, K. N. (1978). Development of a work behavior taxonomy for the first-line supervisors. *Journal of Applied Psychology, 63*, 563-572.

Downey, H., Sheridan, J., & Slocum, J. (1975). Analysis of relationships among leader behavior, subordinate job performance and satisfaction: A path-goal approach. *Academy of Management Journal, 18*, 253-262.

Eisenberg, E. M., & Riley, P. R. (1988). Organizational symbols and sense-making. In G. M. Goldhaber & G. A. Barnett (Eds.), *Handbook of organizational communication* (pp. 131-150). Norwood, NJ: Ablex.

Erez, M., & Rim, Y. (1982). The relationships between goals, influence tactics, and personal and organizational variables. *Human Relations, 35*, 871-878.

Farris, G. (1966). *A causal analysis of scientific performance.* Unpublished doctoral dissertation, University of Michigan, Ann Arbor.

Farris, G., & Lim, F. (1969). Effects of performance on leadership, cohesiveness, influence, satisfaction, and subsequent performance. *Journal of Applied Psychology, 53*, 490-497.

Fenelon, I. R., & Megargee, E. I. (1971). The influence of race on the manifestation of leadership. *Experimental Publication System, American Psychological Association, 10*(380-412).

Fiedler, F. E. (1967). *A theory of leadership effectiveness.* New York: McGraw-Hill.

Fiedler, F. E. (1971). Note on the methodology of the Graen, Orris, and Alvares studies testing the contingency model. *Journal of Applied Psychology, 55*, 202-204.

Fiedler, F. E. (1972). Personality, motivational systems, and behavior of high and low LPC persons. *Human Relations, 25*, 391-412.

Ford, J. D. (1981). Departmental context and formal structure as constraints on leader behavior. *Academy of Management Journal, 24*, 274-288.

Franklin, J. L. (1975a). Down the organization: Influence processes across levels of hierarchy. *Administrative Science Quarterly, 20*, 153-164.

Franklin, J. L. (1975b). Relations among four social-psychological aspects of organization. *Administrative Science Quarterly, 20*, 422-433.

French, J. R. P., & Raven, B. (1968). The bases of social power. In D. Cartwright & A. Zander (Eds.), *Group dynamics* (pp. 259-269). New York: Harper & Row.

Georgopoulos, B. A. (1972). The hospital as an organization and problem-solving system. In B. S. Georgopoulos (Ed.), *Organizational research on health institutions* (pp. 9-48). Ann Arbor: University of Michigan, Institute for Social Research.

Giles, H., & Street, R. L. (1985). Communicator characteristics and behavior. In M. L. Knapp & G. R. Miller (Eds.), *Handbook of interpersonal communication* (pp. 205-262). Beverly Hills, CA: Sage.

Goffman, E. (1959). *The presentation of self in everyday life.* Garden City, NY: Doubleday.

Goodstadt, B., & Kipnis, D. (1970). Situational influences on the use of power. *Journal of Applied Psychology, 54*, 201-207.

Graen, G. (1976). Role making processes within complex organizations. In M. D. Dunnette (Ed.), *Handbook of industrial and organizational psychology* (pp. 1201-1245). Chicago: Rand McNally.

Green, S. G., & Mitchell, T. R. (1979). Attributional processes of leaders in leader-member interactions. *Organizational Behavior and Human Performance, 23*, 429-458.

Greene, C. N. (1975). The reciprocal nature of influence between leader and subordinate. *Journal of Applied Psychology, 60*, 187-192.

Greene, C. N., & Podsakoff, P. M. (1981). Effects of withdrawal of a performance-contingent reward on supervisory influence and power. *Academy of Management Journal, 24*, 242-244.

Haccoun, D. M., Haccoun, R. R., & Sallay, G. (1978). Sex differences in the appropriateness of supervisory styles: A nonmanagement view. *Journal of Applied Psychology, 63*, 124-127.

Hackman, J. R. (1984). The transition that hasn't happened. In J. R. Kimberly & R. E. Quinn (Eds.), *Managing organizational transitions* (pp. 29-59). Homewood, IL: Irwin.

Hackman, J. R., & Oldham, G. R. (1975). Development of the job diagnostic survey. *Journal of Applied Psychology, 60*, 159-170.

Hall, P. M. (1980). Structuring symbolic interaction: Communication and power. In D. Nimmo (Ed.), *Communication yearbook 4* (pp. 49-60). New Brunswick, NJ: Transaction.

Halpin, A. W., & Winer, B. J. (1957). A factorial study of the leader behavior descriptions. In R. M. Stogdill & A. Coons (Eds.), *Leader behavior: Its description and measurement* (pp. 6-38). Columbus: Ohio State University, College of Administrative Science.

Hammer, T. H., & Turk, J. M. (1987). Organizational determinants of leader behavior and authority. *Journal of Applied Psychology, 72*, 515-521.

Haythorn, W. W., Couch, A., Haefner, D., Langham, P., & Carter, L. F. (1956). The effects of varying combinations of authoritarian and egalitarian leaders and followers. *Journal of Abnormal and Social Psychology, 53*, 210-219.

Heller, F. A., & Yukl, G. (1969). Participation, managerial decision-making, and situational variables. *Organizational Behavior and Human Performance, 4*, 227-241.

Herold, D. M. (1977). Two way influence processes in leader-follower dyads. *Academy of Management Journal, 20*, 224-237.

Hickson, D. J., Hinnings, C. R., Lee, C. A., Schneck, R. E., & Pennings, J. M. (1971). A strategic contingencies theory of interorganizational power. *Administrative Science Quarterly, 16*, 216-229.

Hill, T. E., & Schmitt, N. (1977). Individual differences in leadership decision making. *Organizational Behavior and Human Performance, 19*, 353-367.

Hill, W. A. (1973a). Leadership style: Rigid or flexible. *Organizational Behavior and Human Performance, 9*, 35-47.

Hill, W. A. (1973b). Leadership style flexibility, satisfaction, and performance. In E. A. Fleishman & J. G. Hunt (Eds.), *Current developments in the study of leadership* (pp. 62-85). Carbondale: Southern Illinois University Press.

Hill, W. A., & Hughes, D. (1974). Variations in leader behavior as a function of task type. *Organizational Behavior and Human Performance, 11*, 83-96.

Hollander, E. P. (1964). *Leaders, groups, and influence.* New York: Oxford University Press.

Homans, G. C. (1950). *The human group.* New York: Harcourt, Brace.

House, R. J. (1971). A path-goal theory of leader effectiveness. *Administrative Science Quarterly, 16*, 321-338.

House, R. J. (1988). Leadership research: Some forgotten, ignored, or overlooked findings. In J. G. Hunt, B. R. Baliga, H. P. Dachler, & C. A. Schriesheim (Eds.), *Emerging leadership vistas* (pp. 245-260). Lexington, MA: Lexington.

House, R. J., & Baetz, M. L. (1979). Leadership: Some empirical generalizations and new research directions. In B. M. Staw (Ed.), *Research on organizational behavior* (Vol. 1). Greenwich, CT: JAI.

Howell, J. P., Dorfman, P. W., & Kerr, S. (1986). Moderator variable in leadership research. *Academy of Management Review, 11*, 88-102.

Hunt, D. M., & Michael, C. (1983). Mentorship: A career training and development tool. *Academy of Management Review, 8*, 475-485.

Hunt, J. G., Baliga, B. R., & Peterson, M. F. (1988). Strategic apex leader scripts and an organizational life cycle approach to leadership excellence. *Journal of Management Development, 7*, 61-83.

Hunt, J. G., & Liebscher, V. K. C. (1973). Leadership preference, leadership behavior, and employee satisfaction. *Organizational Behavior and Human Performance, 9*, 59-77.

Ilgen, D. R., Mitchell, T. R., & Fredrickson, J. W. (1981). Poor performers: Supervisors' and subordinates' responses. *Organizational Behavior and Human Performance, 27*, 386-410.

Jacobs, T. O. (1970). *Leadership and exchange in formal organizations.* Alexandria, VA: Human Resources Research Organization.

Jacobson, M. B., & Effertz, J. (1974). Sex roles and leadership: Perceptions of the leaders and the led. *Organizational Behavior and Human Performance, 12*, 383-396.

Jago, A. G., & Vroom, V. H. (1977). Hierarchical level and leadership style. *Organizational Behavior and Human Performance, 19*, 131-145.

Jones, E. E., & Nisbett, R. E. (1971). *The actor and the observer: Divergent perceptions of the causes of behavior.* New York: General Learning Press.

Kahn, R. L., Wolfe, D. M., Quinn, R. P., Snoek, J. D., & Rosenthal, R. A. (1964). *Organizational stress: Studies in role conflict and ambiguity.* New York: John Wiley.

Katz, D., & Kahn, R. L. (1978). *The social psychology of organizations* (2nd ed.). New York: John Wiley.

Kavanagh, M. J. (1972). Leadership behavior as a function of subordinate competence and task complexity. *Administrative Science Quarterly, 17*, 591-600.

Kavanagh, M. J. (1975). Expected supervisory behavior, interpersonal trust, and environmental preferences: Some relationships based on a dyadic model of leadership. *Organizational Behavior and Human Performance, 13*, 17-30.

Kelley, H. H. (1973). The processes of causal attribution. *American Psychologist, 28*, 107-128.

Kerr, S., Schriesheim, C. A., Murphy, C. J., & Stogdill, R. M. (1974). Toward a contingency theory of leadership based on the consideration and initiating structure literature. *Organizational Behavior and Human Performance, 12*, 62-82.

Kiesler, S., & Sproull, L. (1982). Managerial response to changing environments: Perspectives on problem sensing from social cognition. *Administrative Science Quarterly, 27*, 548-570.

King, D. C., & Bass, B. M. (1974). Leadership, power and influence. In H. L. Fromkin & J. J. Sherwood (Eds.), *Integrating the organization* (pp. 247-268). New York: Free Press.

Kipnis, D., & Cohen, E. S. (1980). *Power tactics and affection.* Paper presented at the annual meeting of the Eastern Psychological Association, Philadelphia.

Kipnis, D., & Schmidt, S. M. (1983). An influence perspective on bargaining within organizations. In M. J. Bazerman & R. J. Lewicki (Eds.), *Bargaining inside organizations* (pp. 303-319). Beverly Hills, CA: Sage.

Kipnis, D., Schmidt, S. M., Swaffin-Smith, C., & Wilkinson, I. (1984). Patterns of managerial influence: Shotgun managers, tacticians, and bystanders. *Organizational Dynamics, 12*, 56-67.

Kipnis, D., Silverman, A., & Copeland, C. (1973). Effects of emotional arousal on the use of supervised coercion with black and union employees. *Journal of Applied Psychology, 57*, 38-46.

Kochman, T. (1969). "Rapping" in the black ghetto. *Trans-action, 6*, 26-34.

Kram, K. E. (1983). Phases in the mentor relationship. *Academy of Management Journal, 26*, 608-625.

Krone, K. J., Jablin, F. M., & Putnam, L. L. (1987). Communication theory and organizational communication: Multiple perspectives. In F. M. Jablin, L. L. Putnam, K. H. Roberts, & L. W. Porter (Eds.), *Handbook of organizational communication: An interdisciplinary perspective* (pp. 18-40). Newbury Park, CA: Sage.

Lanzetta, J. T. (1955). Group behavior under stress. *Human Relations, 9*, 29-52.

Lee, J. A. (1977). Leader power for managing change. *Academy of Management Review, 2*, 73-80.

Lord, R. G. (1985). An information processing approach to social perceptions, leadership, and behavioral measurement in organizations. In L. L. Cummings & B. M. Staw (Eds.), *Research on organizational behavior* (Vol. 7, pp. 87-128). Greenwich, CT: JAI.

Lord, R. G., & Kernan, M. C. (1987). Scripts as determinants of purposive behavior in organizations. *Academy of Management Review, 12*, 265-277.

Lord, R. G., & Smith, J. E. (1983). Theoretical, information processing, and situational factors affecting attribution theory models of organizational behavior. *Academy of Management Review, 8*, 50-60.

Lowin, A., & Craig, J. R. (1968). The influence of level of performance on managerial style: An experimental object-lesson in the ambiguity of correlational data. *Organizational Behavior and Human Performance, 3*, 440-458.

Mahoney, T. A., Frost, P., Crandall, N. F., & Weitzel, W. (1972). The conditioning influence of organization size upon managerial practice. *Organizational Behavior and Human Performance, 8*, 230-241.

Manz, C. C., & Sims, H. P. (1987). Leading workers to lead themselves: The external leadership of self-managing work teams. *Administrative Science Quarterly, 32*, 106-129.

March, J. G., & Simon, H. A. (1958). *Organizations.* New York: John Wiley.

Markus, H., & Zajonc, R. B. (1985). The cognitive perspective in social psychology. In G. Lindzey & E. Aronson (Eds.), *Handbook of social psychology* (Vol. 1, pp. 137-230). New York: Random House.

Martin, J., Feldman, M. S., Hatch, M. J., & Sitkin, S. B. (1983). The uniqueness paradox in organizational stories. *Administrative Science Quarterly, 28*, 438-453.

Martinko, M. J., & Gardner, W. L. (1987). The leader/member attribution process. *Academy of Management Review, 12*, 235-249.

McFillen, J. M., & New, J. R. (1979). Situational determinants of supervisor attributions and behavior. *Academy of Management Journal, 22*, 793-809.

Michels, R. (1949). *Political parties: A sociological study of the oligarchical tendencies of modern democracy.* New York: Free Press.

Mintzberg, H. (1973). *The nature of managerial work.* New York: Harper & Row.

Mintzberg, H. (1979). *The structuring of organizations.* Englewood Cliffs, NJ: Prentice-Hall.

Mischel, W. (1968). *Personality and assessment.* New York: John Wiley.

Misumi, J. (1985). *The behavioral science of leadership.* Ann Arbor: University of Michigan Press.

Mitchell, T. R. (1974). Expectancy models of job satisfaction, occupational preference, and effort: A theoretical, methodological, and empirical appraisal. *Psychological Bulletin, 81*, 1053-1077.

Mitchell, T. R., & Kalb, L. S. (1981). Effects of outcome knowledge and outcome valence on supervisors' evaluations. *Journal of Applied Psychology, 66*, 604-612.

Mitchell, T. R., & Kalb, L. S. (1982). Effects of job experience on supervisor attributions for a subordinate's poor performance. *Journal of Applied Psychology, 67*, 181-188.

Mitchell, T. R., & Wood, R. E. (1980). Supervisor's responses to subordinate poor performance: A test of an attributional model. *Organizational Behavior and Human Performance, 25*, 123-138.

Morgan, G., Frost, P., & Pondy, L. (1983). Organizational symbolism. In L. Pondy, P. Frost, G. Morgan, & T. Dandridge (Eds.), *Organizational symbolism* (pp. 3-37). Greenwich, CT: JAI.

Morris, C. G., & Hackman, J. R. (1969). Behavioral correlates of perceived leadership. *Journal of Personality and Social Psychology, 13*, 350-361.

Parker, W. S., Jr. (1976). Black-white differences in leader behavior related to subordinates' reactions. *Journal of Applied Psychology, 61*, 140-147.

Pelz, D. C., & Andrews, F. M. (1964). Detecting causal priorities in panel study data. *American Sociological Review, 29*, 836-848.

Perrow, C. (1970). *Organizational analysis: A sociological view.* Monterey, CA: Brooks/Cole.

Peterson, M. F., & Cooke, R. A. (1983). Attitudinal and contextual variables explaining teachers' leadership behavior. *Journal of Educational Psychology, 75*, 50-62.

Phillips, J. S. (1984). The accuracy of leadership ratings: A cognitive categorization perspective. *Organizational Behavior and Human Performance, 33*, 125-138.

Phillips, J. S., & Lord, R. G. (1981). Causal attributions and perceptions of leadership. *Organizational Behavior and Human Performance, 28*, 143-163.

Phillips, J. S., & Lord, R. G. (1982). Schematic information processing and perceptions of leadership in problem-solving groups. *Journal of Applied Psychology, 67*, 486-492.

Podsakoff, P. M. (1982). Determinants of a supervisor's use of rewards and punishments: A literature review and suggestions for further research. *Organizational Behavior and Human Performance, 29*, 58-83.

Putnam, L. L., & Wilson, D. E. (1982). Communicative strategies in organizational conflicts: Reliability and validity of a measurement scale. In M. Burgoon (Ed.), *Communication yearbook 6* (pp. 629-652). Beverly Hills, CA: Sage.

Quinn, R. E., & Andersen, D. F. (1984). Formalization as crisis: Transition planning for a young organization. In J. R. Kimberly & R. E. Quinn (Eds.), *Managing organizational transitions* (pp. 11-28). Homewood, IL: Irwin.

Richards, S. A., & Cuffe, J. U. (1972). Behavioral correlates of leadership effectiveness in interacting and counteracting groups. *Journal of Applied Psychology, 56*, 377-381.

Rim, Y., & Erez, M. (1980). A note about tactics used to influence superiors, co-workers and subordinates. *Journal of Occupational Psychology, 53*, 319-321.

Ross, M., & Fletcher, G. J. O. (1985). Attribution and social perception. In G. Lindzey & E. Aronson (Eds.), *Handbook of social psychology* (Vol. 2, pp. 73-122). New York: Random House.

Rush, M. C., & Beauvais, L. L. (1981). A critical analysis of format-induced versus subject-imposed bias in leadership ratings. *Journal of Applied Psychology, 66*, 722-727.

Rush, M. C., Phillips, J. S., & Lord, R. G. (1981). Effects of a temporal delay in rating on leader behavior descriptions: A laboratory investigation. *Journal of Applied Psychology, 66*, 442-450.

Rush, M. D., Thomas, J. C., & Lord, R. G. (1977). Implicit leadership theory: A potential threat to the internal validity of leader behavior questionnaires. *Organizational Behavior and Human Performance, 18*, 154-268.

Salancik, G. R., & Pfeffer, J. (1978). A social information processing approach to job attitudes and task design. *Administrative Science Quarterly, 23*, 224-253.

Schein, E. H. (1983). The role of the founder in creating organizational culture. *Organizational Dynamics, 11*, 13-28.

Schein, E. H. (1985). *Organizational culture and leadership.* San Francisco: Jossey-Bass.

Schoorman, F. D. (1988). Escalation bias in performance appraisals: An unintended consequence of supervisor participation in hiring decisions. *Journal of Applied Psychology, 73*, 58-62.

Shaw, M. E. (1963). Some effects of varying amounts of information exclusively possessed by a group member upon his behavior in the group. *Journal of General Psychology, 68*, 71-79.

Shaw, M. E. (1976). *Group dynamics: The psychology of small group behavior* (2nd ed.). New York: McGraw-Hill.

Shiflett, S. C., & Nealey, S. M. (1972). The effects of changing leader power: A test of "situational engineering." *Organizational Behavior and Human Performance, 7,* 371-382.

Sillars, A. L. (1980). Attributions and communication in roommate conflicts. *Communication Monographs, 47,* 180-200.

Sims, H. P. (1977). The leader as a manager of reinforcement contingencies: An empirical example and a model. In J. G. Hunt & L. L. Larson (Eds.), *Leadership: The cutting edge* (pp. 121-137). Carbondale: Southern Illinois University Press.

Skinner, E. W. (1969). Relationships between leadership behavior patterns and organizational-situational variables. *Personnel Psychology, 22,* 489-494.

Smith, P. B., & Peterson, M. F. (1988). *Leadership, organizations and culture: An event management model.* London: Sage.

Stablein, R., & Nord, W. (1985). Practical and emancipatory interests in organizational symbolism: A review and evaluation. *Journal of Management, 11,* 13-28.

Stewart, R. (1976). *Contrasts in management: A study of the different types of management jobs, their demands and choices.* London: McGraw-Hill.

Stewart, R. (1982). A model for understanding managerial jobs and behavior. *Academy of Management Review, 7,* 7-13.

Stogdill, R. M. (1974). *Handbook of leadership.* New York: Macmillan.

Stogdill, R. M., & Coady, N. P. (1970). Preferences of vocational students for different styles of supervisory behavior. *Personnel Psychology, 23,* 309-312.

Stryker, S., & Statham, A. (1985). Symbolic interaction and role theory. In G. Lindzey & E. Aronson (Eds.), *Handbook of social psychology* (3rd ed., Vol. 1, pp. 311-378). New York: Random House.

Tait, M., Padgett, M. Y., & Baldwin, T. T. (1989). Job and life satisfaction: A reevaluation of the strength of the relationship and gender effects as a function of the date of the study. *Journal of Applied Psychology, 74,* 502-507.

Terborg, J. R. (1977). Women in management: A research review. *Journal of Applied Psychology, 62,* 647-664.

Terborg, J. R., & Ilgen, D. R. (1975). A theoretical approach to sex discrimination in traditionally masculine occupations. *Organizational Behavior and Human Performance, 13,* 352-376.

Thompson, J. D. (1967). *Organizations in action.* New York: McGraw-Hill.

Tompkins, P. K. (1987). Translating organizational theory: Symbolism over substance. In F. M. Jablin, L. L. Putnam, K. H. Roberts, & L. W. Porter (Eds.), *Handbook of organizational communication* (pp. 70-96). Newbury Park, CA: Sage.

Vroom, V. H. (1964). *Work and motivation.* New York: John Wiley.

Vroom, V. H. (1974). Decision making and the leadership process. *Journal of Contemporary Business, 3,* 47-64.

Vroom, V. H., & Jago, A. G. (1988). *The new leadership: Managing participation in organizations.* Englewood Cliffs, NJ: Prentice-Hall.

Vroom, V. H., & Yetton, P. W. (1973). *Leadership and decision making.* Pittsburgh: Pittsburgh Press.

Wakabayashi, M., Graen, G., Graen, M., & Graen, M. (1988). Japanese management progress: Mobility into middle management. *Journal of Applied Psychology, 73,* 217-227.

Walsh, J. P. (1988). Selectivity and selective perception: An investigation of managers' belief structures and information processing. *Academy of Management Journal, 31,* 873-896.

Weick, K. E. (1976). Educational organizations as loosely coupled systems. *Administrative Science Quarterly, 21,* 1-19.

Weick, K. E. (1979). *The social psychology of organizing* (2nd ed.). Reading, MA: Addison-Wesley.

Williams, D., & Boster, F. (1981, May). *The effects of beneficial situational characteristics, negativism, and dogmatism on compliance-gaining message selection.* Paper presented at the annual meeting of the International Communication Association, Minneapolis, MN.

Yukl, G. A. (1981). *Leadership* (2nd ed.). Englewood Cliffs, NJ: Prentice-Hall.

Leadership Research:
Some Issues

G. LLOYD DRECKSEL
University of Utah

PETERSON and Sorenson's chapter, in which they provide a "new look at how cognition may mediate the effects of context on a given person's leadership" (p. 501), is a valuable contribution to the dialogue about these issues in the study of leadership. Their ambitious review and reinterpretation of the literature concerning the antecedents of leadership integrates a number of variables that traditionally are not combined (e.g., Fiedler, 1967). Further, their model suggests an alternative way to interpret the relationships among contextual contingencies and a leader's behavior. As a stimulus to future research, these authors identify the gaps in the current knowledge about the elements of their model and suggest that the disparate theoretical bases of their reinterpretation require certain compromises and some creative sense making. The implication for future research efforts is challenging.

My goal in this commentary is to join these authors in the quest to suggest directions for research and to engage in the dialogue about the issues surrounding the study of the leadership phenomenon. The following discussion addresses two basic issues deemed central to leadership theory and research: what constitutes leadership and where leadership is located. These issues merit attention because our position toward them influences the way we think about, understand, and study leadership. I will address four specific questions that are relevant to these two issues: What is leadership? Where is leadership located? Is leadership an individual property or a group property? Where might metaphors of leadership take the process of inquiry? My ultimate goal is to identify and discuss some alternative approaches to the study of leadership.

Correspondence and requests for reprints: G. Lloyd Drecksel, Department of Communication, University of Utah, Salt Lake City, UT 84112.

Communication Yearbook 14, pp. 535-546

ISSUE 1: WHAT IS LEADERSHIP?

The assumption that a grand theory of leadership is possible and useful is apparent in descriptions that combine, into a single explanation of leadership, studies of CEOs, managers, administrators, military leaders, political leaders, group leadership, and so forth. Such explanations may be more typical of conventional wisdom and myths of leadership than they are typical of academic research. A problem, however, emanates from the tendency to apply findings of context-specific studies to the understanding, analysis, and explanation of the phenomenon of leadership across a wide variety of contexts.

Scheidel (1987) argues that these categories of leadership may be disparate phenomena, not merely context-specific varieties of a single phenomenon. He points to the inherent confusion that results when "almost every act of prominence is seen as leadership and every prominent person in almost every kind of group is seen as leader" (pp. 4-5). Scheidel suggests that when such disparate phenomena as Amundsen leading a five-man team to the South Pole, Churchill exhorting his fellow Britishers to their "finest hour," a manager whose special task it is to coordinate and facilitate the work of others, the foreman on an assembly line in a manufacturing plant, and an anonymous sophomore assigned to chair a 20-minute discussion on a rank-ordering task are all explained under a single heading as a single phenomenon, the explanation cannot be very discriminating. The ability to understand these phenomena is reduced by combining them into a single concept, leadership (p. 8).

If our goal is to enhance the understanding of leadership, our quest is to differentiate these phenomena. Scheidel and other leadership scholars (e.g., Cartwright & Zander, 1968; Fisher, 1986; Gibb, 1969; Holloman, 1968; Shaw, 1981) recommend beginning this quest by differentiating leadership from headship and studying these as separate concepts. *Headship*, these scholars claim, refers to a person who is appointed by some agency outside the group to a formal position within that group. The authority and influence of the person who occupies that position, therefore, derives from a source outside the group. The members of the group (who cannot meaningfully be called *followers*) accept the head's domination "on pain of punishment, rather than follow" (Gibb, 1969, p. 213).

Leadership, on the other hand, emerges from within the group. It is achieved status or status that emerges through communication. That is, the group awards this status on the basis of a person's ongoing behaviors within that group. Status is earned, then, in the active context of group effort. Leadership, these scholars claim, emanates from the leader-follower relationship within which the group willingly delegates the leadership role and followers spontaneously accord authority to the leader. Leadership, therefore, is a process, not a position, and this process can be described as emergent leadership. This distinction, of course, does not suggest the person appointed to the headship position is precluded from earning leadership and emerging as leader. This distinction does suggest, however, that headship and leadership are not equivalent phenomena.

A number of leadership scholars have lamented the state of our knowledge about leadership (e.g., Fisher, 1985; Lombardo & McCall, 1978; Melcher, 1977; Stogdill, 1974) and have suggested that a grand theory of leadership may not be feasible or desirable (e.g., Dubin, 1979; Greene, 1977; Hunt, Sekaran, & Schriesheim, 1982; Lord, Foti, & Phillips 1982; Pondy, 1978). Indeed, the search for a grand theory may confound our knowledge.

Perhaps our failure to understand this phenomenon derives from our failure to question our taken-for-granted assumptions and conventional wisdom about leadership. The indiscriminate use of this term may lead researchers to overlook differences that make a difference. We may be attaching unwarranted meaning and characteristics to a variety of differentiated activities that may be worthy of study in their own right. Worse yet, we may be creating unrealistic expectations for incumbents when we attach the label of leadership to every form of hierarchical status. Worst of all, we may be limiting our potential to improve our understanding of leadership itself when we tolerate the use of the term *leadership* as an all-inclusive concept incorporating a variety of phenomena that may not be equivalent.

To enhance our understanding of the variety of phenomena traditionally labeled *leadership*, each form of hierarchical status should be studied and documented separately. Rather than assume these phenomena can be understood as one, researchers should devise studies that explore and document the central features and characteristics of each form of hierarchical status (identifying the differences as well as the similarities). Distinguishing and identifying the central features constituting each form of hierarchical status is a useful step toward understanding leadership. Another step toward improving our understanding of this concept is to address the locus issue: Where do leadership studies locate the leadership phenomenon?

ISSUE 2: WHERE IS LEADERSHIP LOCATED?

Studies of leadership employ a variety of loci. Each locus identifies a place to observe and interpret the leadership phenomenon. I will describe two that are most relevant to this commentary: individual cognition and external behavior.

Peterson and Sorenson's model locates the leadership phenomenon in an individual's cognitive processes as it strives to explain "how cognition may mediate the effects of context on a given person's leadership" (p. 501). Their model treats the leader's cognitive processes as the central mediating site, while emphasizing the context within which group and organizational leadership occurs (p. 502). Maintaining their assumption that "cognitive processes mediate the effects of all other variables on leadership behavior" (p. 504), they identify characteristics and events that affect a leader's cognitive choice of behavior (i.e., intentions and attempts to enact leadership), and this choice, in turn, drives the leader's actions (p. 504). Clearly, the locus of leadership in their chapter is the focal person's cognitive processes. Within this cognitive locus, group interaction history may be viewed as one of the events that may mediate a leader's cognitions as that leader diagnoses interpersonal situations and chooses a leadership behavior. Leadership, however, is located, observed, and interpreted as a cognitive process.

For others, however, the locus of leadership is found in the ongoing enactment of leadership (i.e., the ongoing group or system interaction). Such studies observe externalized and directly observable leadership behavior as it appears in leader-follower interactions and describe emergent patterns of a leader's behavior or emergent patterns of the leader-follower interaction (Drecksel, 1985; Ellis, 1979; Husband, 1985; Nydegger, 1975; Pepinsky, Hemphill, & Shevitz, 1958; Stein, Hoffman, Cooley, & Pearce, 1979). Within the external behavior locus, group or system interaction constitutes the phenomenon. This locus assumes that leadership emerges (i.e., is constructed, created, and maintained) through communication. Leadership is located, observed, and interpreted as a communicative process comprising externalized and directly observable behaviors.

The foregoing descriptions, although not exhaustive of all leadership loci, demonstrate that various studies locate the leadership phenomenon in various places, hence they explore different empirical phenomena and provide different explanations. The point of the locus issue, however, is not which is correct and which is mistaken, but that the loci are incommensurable.

The careful and thoughtful selection of locus is crucial to leadership research. This selection reflects assumptions about leadership and guides observation, interpretation, explanation, and understanding of leadership. It is, for example, the locus issue that leads us to question whether leadership is an individual property or a group property.

ISSUE 3: IS LEADERSHIP
AN INDIVIDUAL OR GROUP PROPERTY?

Traditionally, leadership studies assume this phenomenon is an individual property. Numerous studies suggest that leadership comprises behaviors of specific individuals who are identified as leader (e.g., Baird, 1977; Jaffee & Lucas, 1969; Knutson & Holdridge, 1975; Mortensen, 1966; Russell, 1970; Schultz, 1974). Some of these studies observe behaviors manifested in group interaction, whereas others observe group member perceptions or cognitions of behaviors manifested in group interaction. Their assumption about leadership, however, is the same: Leadership is an individual property, the property of an individual who has emerged as leader, has been identified as leader, or has been appointed as leader.

Studies exploring an individual's leadership style and studies exploring the contingencies of an individual's leadership style and situational components employ this assumption (e.g., Bales, 1950; Blake & Mouton, 1984; Fiedler & Chemers, 1974; Hage, 1974; House & Mitchell, 1974; March & Simon, 1958; Moment & Zalenznick, 1963; Sargent & Miller, 1971; Strube & Garcia, 1981; Van de Ven, Delbecq, & Koenig, 1976). Contingency research assumes that leadership comprises an individual's style, which may or may not be appropriate to the particular contingencies of the context.

On the other hand, Fisher (1985) proposes reconceptualizing leadership as a group property, suggesting this view may provide useful insight into this phenomenon. This view assumes leadership is a social influence process created through the reciprocal relationship between leader and follower (Fisher, 1986, pp. 212-213). Within this view, the description of leadership must reflect the *interdependence* of the communicative behaviors performed by both leaders and followers during the process of group interaction, not merely the isolated behavior of the leader or operant reinforcement of leader or follower behavior. Studies conceptualizing leadership as a group property, therefore, must observe and analyze all of the interaction of all participants. Gibb (1969) suggests that conceptualized as a group property "it is possible for leadership to be nominal only" (p. 271). Hence leadership would be an emergent property of a group that names one component of the system *leader* — a leader in name only. Advancing this argument, Fisher (1985) provides the implication for future leadership research:

> Perhaps we should dismiss entirely the importance of "leader" and focus exclusively on the process of leadership. We may find ourselves discussing the presence or absence of leadership in a group without ever needing to identify one or more of the members as the leader. (p. 177)

Reconceptualizing a concept, however, requires researchers to step outside the boundaries of conventional thinking and, therefore, may require the help of some tools for creative thinking. Metaphors (the topic of the following section) provide a rich resource to stimulate innovative thinking and to guide the process of inquiry.

ISSUE 4: WHERE MIGHT METAPHORS
OF LEADERSHIP TAKE THE PROCESS OF INQUIRY?

Metaphors guide the way we look at a phenomenon. Leadership metaphors share some common assumptions: Leadership is an influence process directed toward goal achievement, and communication is the process through which influence occurs. Different explanations of the nature of the influence process, however, lead to several recognizable metaphors (Fisher, 1985). I will describe the two metaphors that illuminate the present discussion: the physics metaphor and the leader-as-medium metaphor.

The physics metaphor characterizes the relationship between leader and follower as act-react. A force or source of energy (a leader) directs that energy (a message) on some object (a follower), which then reacts to the force. This activity involves a conveyor of energy (communication). The physics metaphor thus

characterizes communication as a mechanistic conveyer of energy and characterizes leadership acts as messages that direct and control others. The central features
of this metaphor are leader, followers, messages carried on channels, and control.

The locus of this metaphor is the message carried on the channel (i.e., an external
channel such as the telephone or a memo, an internal channel such as cognitive
processes, or a combination of internal and external channels). The features are
related to one another by "transportation or conveyance" (i.e., messages are
transported on the channel from the leader to the follower) and the nature of the
leader-follower relationship is act-react (director-directee, controller-controllee).

According to the physics metaphor of leadership, then, ineffective leadership
implies ineffective messages. If a desired reaction (control) is not elicited from
followers, the problem lies in the message. Therefore, the leader must devise a
"better" message (i.e., one that elicits the desired behavior) and, perhaps, transport
the message on multiple channels (e.g., face-to-face, memo, bulletin board).

Although I am aware of no leadership studies explicitly claiming employment
of the physics metaphor, its employment is implicit in much of the literature.
Where might the physics metaphor of leadership take the process of inquiry? This
metaphor might generate models designed to explore the several categories of
contextual variables that affect a leader's choice of messages and channels through
their effects on cognitive processes — a model that provides suggestions for manipulating antecedents to shape and elicit desired cognitions, which, in turn, elicit the
desired behaviors (e.g., Peterson & Sorenson).

The leader-as-medium metaphor (introduced by Weick, 1978), on the other
hand, locates leadership within the social information-processing system (i.e., the
communication system) and focuses on the interdependence of the leader-follower
relationship. Within the information-processing system, "leadership functions as a
mediator between events or actions by the group in terms of outcomes. The 'stuff'
that is mediated is, of course, information" (Fisher, 1985, p. 182).

This metaphor assumes that social information processing (as opposed to individual information processing) is extremely complex, comprising, for example, a
variety of information sources, a variety of possible interpretations, a variety of
rules for interpreting information, and a variety of ways to act on the information.
Thus the information being processed by the system is characterized by equivocality (i.e., uncertainty).

The system's goal is to reduce the informational equivocality to a manageable
level, and group leadership interaction contributes to this goal through providing
(e.g., registering or enacting) the required variety of information, the required
variety of ways to interpret the information, and the required variety of ways to act
on the information. The degree of variety required and the level of equivocality
reduction deemed "manageable" will, of course, vary from one system to another.

The notion of contributing variety to reduce variety may appear counterintuitive. However, the law of requisite variety (explicated by Ashby, 1968; Buckley,
1968) indicates "the variety within a system must be at least as great as the
environmental variety against which it is attempting to regulate itself. . . . only

variety can regulate variety" (Buckley, 1968, p. 495). In other words, the greater the variety of information in the system's environment, the greater the variety of information and ways to interpret and act on the information the system must provide. The amount of complexity must be registered before it can be reduced (i.e., made sense of).

Consequently, the more nearly the complexity of the leader-as-medium is appropriate to the amount of complexity in the information-processing system's environment, the more effective the leadership. According to this metaphor, then, if the desired goal (equivocality registration and reduction) is elusive, the information-processing agent (the leader-as-medium — the group system) strives to develop a greater degree of complexity.

Where might the leader-as-medium metaphor take the process of inquiry? This metaphor is beginning to generate research activity (e.g., Barge 1989; Drecksel, 1985). Barge (1989) has identified and compared two models of leadership. The first is the group leader influence (GLI) model, which is similar to the physics metaphor. This model, Barge states, equates leadership with a formal authority position and portrays leadership as an active and directive influence process. The goal of leadership activity is to gain the compliance of followers and to dominate the group's activity. Leadership thus comprises commanding and controlling behaviors. This model assumes that the leader's personal action directed toward the group is what influences group outcomes. Therefore, the model assumes that "leaders are more effective when they are active within the group and that this activity level is positively associated with group productivity" (Barge, 1989, p. 237).

The second model is the leaderless group discussion (LGD) model, which invokes the leader-as-medium metaphor. This model portrays leadership as a process and as a form of mediation. The major purpose of leadership, according to this model, is to mediate among group action, the group's information environment, and performance outcomes. "Viewing leadership as mediation suggests that leadership occurs when actions are performed that help the group adjust to environmental, social, or procedural obstacles" (Barge, 1989, pp. 239-240). Thus when the group's informational environment is complex, the information-processing system needs to reduce the equivocality to manageable levels of sense making and action. This model assumes effective leadership is more docile (i.e., a leader mediates — a leader does not control) and "that the group's overall leadership activity versus the activity of an individual leader is a better predictor of group productivity" (p. 237).

Using these two models, Barge tested the relationship between leadership performance and group productivity. The results of his study suggest that the leader-as-medium metaphor provides a better explanation of the relationship between leadership behavior and group outcomes. That is, group leadership is a better predictor of group productivity than is the amount of the leader's activity. Barge concludes that "an individual leader's behavior does not necessarily aid groups in achieving their goals but that group leadership behavior does" (p. 245).

Invoking the leadership-as-medium metaphor, in my own study I sought to describe the interaction characteristics of emergent group leadership (Drecksel, 1985). The theoretical framework for this study was the interact system model (Fisher & Hawes, 1971). This study was based on the assumption that leadership emerges through the communication occurring in the group context and, therefore, the characteristics of group leadership can be empirically identified through analyzing the external and directly observable interaction of all group participants. The data of this study comprised the entire interaction history (from the initial group meeting through the end of group history) of 15 initially leaderless discussion groups. Of the original groups in the study, those remaining were the groups that named emergent leaders at the end of their group histories.

To identify the characteristics of group leadership interaction, I compared the interaction patterns characterizing leader-follower dyads (i.e., group leadership) within a specific group to the interaction patterns characterizing nonleader-nonleader dyads within that group and then identified the similarities and differences in these interaction patterns within each group and across the 15 groups. The observed differences and similarities in interaction were interpreted and explained within the assumptions of the leader-as-medium metaphor.

The results of this study suggest group leadership interaction was characterized by complexity (i.e., variety, diversity, and distinctiveness). That is, group leadership interaction reflected the qualities of a "good" medium: a variety of ways to register, interpret, and act on the information in the group system's environment rather than a preponderance of specific functions, behaviors, interpretations, or ways to act on the information. On the other hand, nonleadership interaction was characterized by simplicity: routine and habitual ways to register, interpret, and act on the information (e.g., tightly coupled and rigid views, functions, and behaviors). Clearly, the data of this study supported and were illuminated by the leader-as-medium metaphor.

The two leadership metaphors described above suggest disparate ways to conceptualize, study, and understand this phenomenon. The implication is that metaphors hold the potential to provide fresh insight, and to organize and enhance our thinking about this concept. Each metaphor provides a useful alternative for understanding leadership. Taken together, the alternative views provided throughout this commentary suggest other implications for leadership theory and research.

IMPLICATIONS FOR
LEADERSHIP THEORY AND RESEARCH

Scholars have identified a variety of ways to understand and explain the leadership phenomenon. In this commentary I have briefly reviewed some of the issues that differentiate some of these views. These issues merit attention because they influence the way we think about and study leadership. This brief review is, of course, not exhaustive of the relevant views and issues but attempts, instead, to stimulate a dialogue about leadership.

The views discussed can be classified (rather loosely) into two categories: a more nearly traditional view of leadership and a less traditional view of leadership. Each view incorporates a set of assumptions about leadership (i.e., what is leadership) and a distinctive leadership locus (i.e., where is leadership).

The traditional view of leadership is more likely to assume that leadership is a single phenomenon observable in nearly every form of hierarchical status and that leadership is a position occupied by a person. Hence leadership is an individual property located and observable in individual behavior (e.g., cognitions). This view assumes, further, that a leader's actions are directed toward controlling followers (e.g., eliciting desirable follower behaviors).

A less traditional view of leadership, on the other hand, is likely to question the taken-for-granted assumptions surrounding the leadership concept. For example, this view is more likely to question the use of the term *leadership* (i.e., How discriminating or meaningful is this term?) and to suggest abandoning it for a variety of terms identifying empirically documented phenomena. That is, this view is more likely to reframe the question, What is leadership? as an empirical one.

Awaiting this research, however, present nontraditional studies are more likely to assume that leadership is not a position but a process that is created through communication. This view assumes leadership emerges through, and therefore is located in, externalized and directly observable interaction. Further, this view is more likely to assume leadership is a group property (i.e., a system property comprising interdependent leader-follower interaction) and to assume group leadership interaction is aimed toward registering the information in the communication system's environment, acting toward that information, and making sense of it.

Neither the traditional nor the less traditional view is without limitations, of course. For example, the less traditional view is not mainstream, and it requires a rather dramatic reconceptualization of the leadership phenomenon. Although understandable, because it is relatively new, this view lacks the body of evidence generated by the conventional view, and it has fewer adherents. This way of thinking about and studying leadership, therefore, is quite foreign to most scholars, practitioners, and students, and it may seem counterintuitive to some of them. Certainly its philosophical and theoretical foundations are at variance with the more traditional view.

The less traditional approach differs from conventional research expectations, too. For example, it may require data gathering over a relatively long period of time (e.g., to allow the researcher to observe whether and how leadership emerges and interaction patterns emerge; whether and how the system registers information equivocality, acts toward that equivocality, and makes sense of it).

The notion of interdependence among system components (e.g., leader-followers) precludes conceptualizing strategies for controlling others and precludes holding one person accountable for problems in the system. The less traditional view assumes all participants create and, therefore, are responsible for the system. Further, problems are viewed as problems of the system itself and are dealt with as such. These limitations become particularly problematic for people whose interests center on behavioral control. Perhaps the most severe limitation for some people is the fact that this approach centers on understanding the system (i.e., interdependent relationships between leaders and followers) rather than the individual.

As stated earlier, the traditional view of leadership may be limited by the basic physics metaphor that underlies this view and may be too simple to explain the complex phenomena of leadership adequately. To compensate for this oversimplicity, researchers generate complex models that incorporate moderating, mediating, and intervening variables with direct and indirect effects. The complexity of some of the models generated within this view, however, may render interpretation and application difficult if not virtually impossible.

Partially because of the large body of research generated by this view, some of the research findings are contradictory and conflicting. Often, this discovery leads to the search for additional intervening variables, which may lead to more complicated research designs, which may compound the problems involved in interpreting and applying the new results.

Although I have identified differences between the more traditional and less traditional views of leadership throughout this commentary, my goal is not to determine which view is correct and which is mistaken. Rather, my goal is to point to some of the options available to prospective research. This commentary is intended to engage in a dialogue about the issues, not to engage in argument based on synonymy. Contributing, to some degree, to the understanding and appreciation of the alternative views is my ultimate goal.

REFERENCES

Ashby, W. R. (1968). Variety, constraint, and the law of requisite variety. In W. Buckley (Ed.), *Modern systems research for the behavioral scientist* (pp. 129-136). Chicago: Aldine.

Baird, J. E. (1977). Some nonverbal elements of leadership emergence. *Southern Speech Communication Journal, 42*, 352-361.

Bales, R. (1950). *Interaction process analysis*. Reading, MA: Addison-Wesley.

Barge, K. (1989). Leadership as medium: A leaderless group discussion model. *Communication Quarterly, 37*, 237-247.

Blake, R., & Mouton, J. (1984). *The managerial grid*. Houston: Gulf.

Buckley, W. (1968). Society as a complex adaptive system. In W. Buckley (Ed.), *Modern systems research for the behavioral scientist* (pp. 490-512). Chicago: Aldine.

Cartwright, D., & Zander, A. (1968). *Group dynamics*. New York: Harper & Row.

Drecksel, G. L. (1985, May). *Interaction characteristics of emergent leadership*. Paper presented at the annual meeting of the International Communication Association, Honolulu.

Dubin, R. (1979). Metaphors of leadership: An overview. In J. Hunt & L. Larson (Eds.), *Crosscurrents in leadership* (pp. 225-238). London: Feffer & Simons.

Ellis, D. (1979). Relational control in two group systems. *Communication Monographs, 46*, 153-166.

Fiedler, F. (1967). *A theory of leadership effectiveness*. New York: McGraw-Hill.

Fiedler, F., & Chemers, M. (1974). *Leadership and effective management.* Glenview, IL: Scott, Foresman.

Fisher, B. A. (1985). Leadership as medium: Treating complexity in group communication research. *Small Group Behavior, 16,* 167-196.

Fisher, B. A. (1986). Leadership: When does the difference make a difference? In R. Hirokawa & M. Poole (Eds.), *Communication and group decision-making* (pp. 197-215). Beverly Hills, CA: Sage.

Fisher, B. A., & Hawes, L. (1971). An interact system model: Generating grounded theory of small groups. *Quarterly Journal of Speech, 57,* 444-453.

Gibb, C. (1969). Leadership. In G. Lindzey & E. Aronson (Eds.), *The handbook of social psychology* (2nd ed., Vol. 4, pp. 205-282). Reading, MA: Addison-Wesley.

Greene, C. (1977). Disenchantment with leadership research: Some causes, recommendations and alternative directions. In J. Hunt & L. Larson (Eds.), *Leadership: The cutting edge* (pp. 57-67). Carbondale: Southern Illinois University Press.

Hage, J. (1974). *Communication and organizational control.* New York: John Wiley.

Holloman, C. (1968). Leadership and headship: There is a difference. *Personnel Administration, 31,* 38-44.

House, R., & Mitchell, T. (1974). Path-goal theory of leadership. *Journal of Contemporary Business, 3,* 81-97.

Hunt, J., Sekaran, U., & Schriesheim, C. (1982). Beyond establishment views: Introduction. In J. Hunt, U. Sekaran, & C. Schriesheim (Eds.), *Leadership: Beyond establishment views* (pp. 1-6). Carbondale: Southern Illinois University Press.

Husband, R. (1985). Toward a grounded typology of organizational leadership behavior. *Quarterly Journal of Speech, 71,* 103-118.

Jaffee, C., & Lucas, R. (1969). Effects of rates of talking and correctness of decision on leader choice in small groups. *Journal of Social Psychology, 79,* 247-254.

Knutson, R., & Holdridge, W. (1975). Orientation behavior, leadership and consensus: A possible functional relationship. *Speech Monographs, 42,* 107-114.

Lombardo. M., & McCall, M. (1978). Leadership. In M. McCall & M. Lombardo (Eds.), *Leadership: Where else can we go?* (pp. 1-11). Durham, NC: Duke University Press.

Lord, R., Foti, R., & Phillips, J. (1982). A theory of leadership categorization. In J. Hunt, U. Sekaran, & C. Schriesheim (Eds.), *Leadership: Beyond establishment views* (pp. 104-121). Carbondale: Southern Illinois University Press.

March, J., & Simon, H. (1958). *Organization.* New York: John Wiley.

Melcher, A. (1977). Leadership models and research approaches. In J. Hunt & L. Larson (Eds.), *Leadership: The cutting edge.* (pp. 94-108). Carbondale: Southern Illinois University Press.

Moment, D., & Zalenznick, A. (1963). *Role development and interpersonal competence.* Cambridge, MA: Harvard University.

Mortensen, C. (1966). Should the discussion group have an assigned leader? *Speech Teacher, 15,* 34-41.

Nydegger, R. (1975). Leadership in small groups: A rewards-costs analysis. *Small Group Behavior, 6,* 353-368.

Pepinsky, P., Hemphill, J., & Shevitz, R. (1958). Attempts to lead, group productivity and morale under conditions of acceptance and rejection. *Journal of Abnormal and Social Psychology, 57,* 47-54.

Pondy, L. (1978). Leadership is a language game. In M. McCall & M. Lombardo (Eds.), *Leadership: Where else can we go?* (pp. 87-99). Durham, NC: Duke University Press.

Russell, H. (1970). *Dimensions of the communication behavior of discussion leaders.* Paper presented at the annual meeting of the Central States Speech Association, Chicago.

Sargent, J., & Miller, G. (1971). Some differences in certain communicative behaviors of autocratic and democratic leaders. *Journal of Communication, 21,* 233-252.

Scheidel, T. (1987, April 23). *The study of leadership.* B. Aubrey Fisher Memorial Lecture, University of Utah, Salt Lake City.

Schultz, B. (1974). Characteristics of emergent leaders of continuing problem-solving groups. *Journal of Psychology, 88,* 167-173.

Shaw, M. (1981). *Group dynamics: The psychology of small group behavior* (3rd ed.). New York: McGraw-Hill.
Stein, R., Hoffman, R., Cooley, S., & Pearce, R. (1979). Leadership valence: Modeling and measuring the process of emergent leadership. In J. Hunt & L. Larson (Eds.), *Crosscurrents in leadership* (pp. 126-147). London: Feffer & Simons.
Stogdill, R. (1974). *Handbook of leadership.* New York: Free Press.
Strube, M., & Garcia, J. (1981). A meta-analytic investigation of Fiedler's contingency model of leadership effectiveness. *Psychological Bulletin, 90*, 307-321.
Van de Ven, A., Delbecq, A., & Koenig, R. (1976). Determinants of coordination modes within organizations. *American Sociological Review, 41*, 322-337.
Weick, K. (1978). The spines of leaders. In M. McCall & M. Lombardo (Eds.), *Leadership: Where else can we go?* (pp. 37-61). Durham, NC: Duke University Press.

A Message-Centered Approach to Leadership

BEVERLY DAVENPORT SYPHER
University of Kansas

L EADERSHIP, of all organizational performances, is fundamentally a communicative accomplishment. It is certainly one that is imbued with cognitive and emotional life. However much of leadership is scripted and seemingly automatic, surely just as much is irrational and unpredictable. Moreover, conscious information processing is necessary to meet the problematic demands of the situations organizational members create. For it is responses to problematic instances, the why and how of enacting influence and social order, that make the greatest differences to organizations and members. The position adopted in this commentary is that social situations are created through communication. In a somewhat different view, Peterson and Sorenson adopt a more structuralist position, implying that action and meaning are inherent in the organizational situations themselves. The position advocated here is that leadership messages, rather than objectified social action, provide the greatest opportunity for increasing our understanding, critiquing, and teaching of leaders' influence attempts. In short, it is communication that makes leadership possible.

While generally agreeing with the philosophical underpinnings of a cognitive and contextual approach to leadership, I consider in this commentary alternative ways of casting the relationship between cognition and leadership by focusing particularly on individual differences in the cognitive makeup of leaders and followers, the seemingly ethical and philosophical considerations raised when influence is cast in terms of "eliciting desired cognitions," and the emotional or affective aspect of such cognitions.

What follows is an interpretation of Peterson and Sorenson's approach, a suggestion to consider the ethics of the language and/or approach that is offered, a brief overview of alternatives for studying leadership messages, an elaboration of how a social constructionist orientation can guide our thinking in terms of leader

Correspondence and requests for reprints: Beverly Davenport Sypher, Communication Studies, 3090 Wescoe Hall, University of Kansas, Lawrence, KS 66045.

Communication Yearbook 14, pp. 547-559

communication, and a conclusion that suggests perhaps the fundamental differences in cognitive approaches to leadership lie in how communication is construed. A final call is made to consider the emotional or affective aspects of leadership, communication, and organization.

PETERSON AND SORENSEN'S MODEL

The propositions undergirding Peterson and Sorenson's model generally suggest that leaders act the way they do because of various contextual demands; individual interpretations notwithstanding, most of their 13 propositions are couched in terms of the effects of context on leadership. In their first set of propositions, they address macrocontextual factors as intervening variables that "need to be modeled" and that reflect "causal paths." By focusing on how cognitive structures are affected by others, they point out how organizational rules, culture (or "social climate," as they call it), and the person's augmented role set "program" individual cognitive structures. While I wholeheartedly agree that "a distinction is needed between deliberately deciding to follow a rule or policy and habitually enacting an established pattern of behavior that may or may not have its origins in organizational rules" (p. 508), an interactionist approach is somewhat at odds with a focus on "programming" and "structuring" of cognitions, since it tends to underplay important questions about leaders' active, conscious participation in organizational life. Peterson and Sorenson address this concern somewhat by recognizing that leadership research "must identify causal forces strong enough to overcome inertia and alternative forces that simultaneously affect the individual- and group-level mediating variables" (p. 511). For Peterson and Sorenson, however, these causal forces are not directly tied to communication. This disconnection eschews somewhat individuals' role in creating and negotiating social selves and situations, including the more enduring, stable characteristics of a group.

The focus on organizational rules as a major predictor of leader behavior also suggests a blurring of the distinction between leaders and managers. An organizational rules-based approach to cognitive structuring may, for example, more closely capture the behavior of managers than of leaders; managers are generally cast as more rule bound, while leaders are generally thought to be more creative and risk taking in their enactments. For a recognition of the importance in distinguishing between the two, one is better informed by Smith and Peterson (1988), who refer to Dachler's (1984) distinction that "management is an attribute not of individuals but of social systems" (Smith & Peterson, 1988, p. 113). Without clarification in the present text, Peterson and Sorenson lead us to question whether the views in their chapter do not suggest the same about leadership. To be sure, Smith and Peterson suggest in much more detail the reciprocal relationship between leaders and social systems when they introduce "the possibility that leaders and their context constantly redefine one another" (p. 165).

In general, Peterson and Sorenson's model seems driven more by systems theory and an implicit determinism than by symbolic interactionism. Symbolic interactionism directs our attention toward role enactments themselves. Here, causal explanations of why leaders do what they do seem to take precedence over questions regarding what leaders do and, more important, why they are able, versus programmed, to act as they do. It seems that explanations of interpretation give way to explanations of causation. As Peterson and Sorenson describe it, theirs is a model of "leadership research seeking effects of organizational context on leadership behavior" that "reflects a partial acceptance of the role theory structuralist position that people construct social systems as having properties of stability" (p. 511). While there is little question that context affects behavior, Peterson and Sorenson's model leaves us wanting to know more about how individuals shape the context and interpret it the way they do through the persuasive messages that are produced. We cannot deny that organizations affect how we think and act; they are in fact social creations. But organizations do not limit us to only one way of thinking and acting; social consensus can always be renegotiated. It would be helpful to see more attention paid to individual differences in members' creation of organizational reality.

The second set of propositions in the Peterson and Sorenson model includes characteristics of the group that affect leader cognition. Here and throughout, the authors review an impressive number of leadership studies, but, as they point out, some findings are confusing and not easily incorporated into a cognitive model of leadership. While factors such as leader and member demographics, task ambiguity, group size, and functional specialty are no doubt important dimensions in the leadership process, the propositions regarding their role in affecting leaders' cognitive structures seem rather straightforwardly derived from the studies they review. The set of propositions regarding group influences on leader behavior (especially demographics) seems to account less for interaction history than their discussion alleges.

The philosophical anthropology of this model is implicit in the discussion of strategies to create "common cognitions." Peterson and Sorenson suggest various ways in which "desired cognitions" may be attained. In essence, they suggest leaders should use all available means to influence employees' cognitive processes, including manipulating antecedents, choosing typical cultural forms (stories, legends, myths, and metaphors), imposing language requirements, enforcing highly explicit rules about desired behavior and relationships, ensuring that adequate symbols are created, and engineering the physical space and facilities to produce desired forms of interaction. They conclude that "the symbol works if it makes salient the desired script" (p. 527). In this way, individual interpretation seems to be considered some type of error variance.

What Peterson and Sorenson seem to suggest is a view of people who are to be "acted on" much like machines: In a computerlike fashion, they can be "programmed" to respond properly. Their language of "manipulating," "eliciting," "ensuring," and "imposing" seems at odds with a cognitive reinterpretation as well as with much of the recent work that recasts leadership as "acting with" people to enable (Dupree, 1989), restore (Demming, 1989), transform (Bass, 1985), and empower (Albrecht, 1989; Kanter, 1977; Pacanowsky, 1989; Zuboff, 1988). While their propositions inform us of the various and competing forces on cognitions, their proposed communication strategies call into question the likelihood of attaining desired cognitions even if what is considered to be the right strategy is employed. Implicit in this line of reasoning is the notion that the "right" strategy is the one that gets the desired response. One is left to wonder if implicit in their talk of "eliciting desired cognitions" is the conscious attempt to submerge the unpredictable dimensions of personality and solve problems solely by individual effort or some authority figure.

Such a view calls into question various ethical considerations of just whose and which cognitions are most desirable. In their defense, Peterson and Sorenson point out that "both leaders and researchers need to distinguish among those situations in which it is desirable and possible to create common symbols, common meanings, and common beliefs and attitudes" (p. 528). A recognition of the difficulties of creating desired cognition notwithstanding, one is still left to wonder whose desires are being met. Such a context-determined perspective belies the complexity of cognitive processing, the potential of communication, and the achievement of outcomes based on either of these.

THE ETHICS OF DESIRED COGNITIONS

Deetz (1988), among others, reminds us that not all organizational members contribute equally, in part because they do not have equal opportunities or abilities. Peterson and Sorenson remind us that leaders more than anyone have the opportunity to contribute in ways many others do not, in particular by influencing the thoughts, actions, and feelings of others. If we are to believe that leading others is, for the most part, the act of eliciting desired cognitions, then we are faced with the question of whose cognitions are the most desirable. Peterson and Sorenson conclude that "symbolic representations of roles should help new leaders adopt cognitions desired by top-level leaders instead of cognitions from competing sources" (p. 527). Such a conclusion makes Deetz's (1985, 1988) concerns and those of others (Cameron & Whetton, 1983; Keeley, 1984) even more relevant to this discussion, given Deetz's (1988) demand that " 'whose' and 'what' interests are being served must be a central question in studying all aspects of organizational life" (p. 338).

If, in their propositions, Peterson and Sorenson accounted for the content of influence strategies and their interpretation, one might feel less compelled to question the ethical and perhaps pragmatic dimensions of eliciting desired cognitions. They review a series of message content studies that provide direction for such propositions, and they do in fact concede that eliciting desired cognitions may not always be possible (Schein, 1985), constructive (Weick, 1979), or necessary (Becher, 1981). And while it is not very reasonable to deny that leaders attempt and succeed in controlling or managing the impressions or cognitions of members (as a matter of fact, we would say they were unsuccessful if they did not), the ways in which influence is attempted and the explanations for why and what kind of influence is accomplished seem more important avenues of inquiry from a cognitive approach to leadership.

SOCIAL COGNITIVE AND
COMMUNICATIVE BASES OF LEADERSHIP

The study of leadership leads naturally to questions of influence. A cognitive and, moreover, social cognitive approach leads to an examination of persuasive message content in ways compatible with ethnomethodological, constructivist, symbolic interactionist, hermeneutic, critical, or rules-based approaches. Certainly general systems theory leads us to focus less on message content than do more interpretive theories. The relative lack of focus on the content of leader messages in Peterson and Sorenson's model is rather disappointing, given the overall focus on perception that characterizes research on social cognition and their propositions regarding leadership.

The process that Peterson and Sorenson offer relies heavily upon "eliciting desired cognition" in others, but the vehicle through which this is to occur — namely, communication — is discussed mainly in terms of the forms messages may take (stories, myths, rituals, slogans, rules, and so on). The content of such messages is perhaps more important when examining leadership from contextual, interpretive approaches. And while organizational ethnographers have begun to provide some examples of message content in natural contexts, an alternative approach is to explore the deep structure of message content, in particular by focusing on the "message design logics" (O'Keefe, 1988) embedded in messages (the researchers' and organizational members' alike) and the cognitive processing abilities reflected in the messages leaders produce. Such message-centered approaches can provide insight into the social cognitive processes ignored in most leadership research and can increase our understanding of how organizational events are interpreted and manifested in messages leaders produce. In other words, a focus on messages themselves gives us a another way of viewing context, cognition, and leadership.

A social cognitive orientation places interpretation at the center of explanation in communication research. In communication, *social cognition* refers to the thoughts about oneself and others that influence message strategies and their interpretation (Roloff & Berger, 1982). From this view, cognitions are not merely an outcome; they are central to construction, interpretation, and message reception.

MESSAGE-CENTERED APPROACHES
TO COMMUNICATION AND LEADERSHIP

Since influence is accomplished through messages, it is surprising that there is such a dearth of detailed examinations of leader messages, their content, the social cognitive abilities of their constructors, and the interpretation of them by the intended receivers. While Peterson and Sorenson review a number of studies focusing on message content, the following discussion provides three distinctively different avenues of research that could be pursued from a message-centered approach to leadership and cognition.

Zorn (1988), for example, found that cognitive differentiation (the degree of complexity one uses in construing others in interpersonal situations) and person-centered messages (ones that take into account the subjective interpretations and psychological characteristics of the receiver) were positively correlated with Bass's (1985) operationalization of transformational leadership. In fact, cognitive differentiation correlated most strongly with charisma, individual consideration, and inspiration — the more other-oriented dimensions of transformational leadership. Employees in this study also thought that the messages of the transformational leaders were more person-centered, better adapted, and more sensitive to their individual needs (Zorn, 1988). In a somewhat similar study, Husband (1981) also found that cognitively differentiated leaders were considered more effective.

In a theoretically unrelated effort, Fairhurst and Chandler (1989) have also argued for an individual differences approach to leadership by focusing on how language choices or "conversational resources" reflect power and social distance in leader-member interactions. One of the refreshing developments in this leadership study was the relational versus the individual unit of analysis. This study also pointed out rather clearly that the espoused leadership style varied a great deal from the leader's actual style as displayed in conversations with subordinates. Studies such as this, while necessarily limited to small samples, make it very clear why self-report data are troublesome, particularly in communication research (for an elaboration of such difficulties, see Burleson et al., 1988; Sypher & Sypher, 1984).

Perhaps more important was that Fairhurst and Chandler found both consistency and differentiation embedded in the leader's conversational forms. What this says in terms of the Peterson and Sorenson model is that there are indeed differences in how context is created, and such differences are made evident in what leaders and members say to one another. Once again, perhaps the most fruitful place for exploring the contextual and cognitive aspects of leadership in the actual messages they produce.

Barge, Downs, and Johnson (1989) offer yet a third, and theoretically distinct, approach to studying leadership and communication. From an interpretive, rules-based approach (Pearce & Cronen, 1980), their message-centered study examined conversations between leaders and members and revealed, from admittedly retro-spective accounts of talk, that structurally similar conversational forms result in perceptions of leadership effectiveness. While overall they found that effective conversations by leaders were viewed as positively valenced, coherent, and as facilitating the accomplishment of work-related and personal goals, they also found that what was positively valenced differed between organizations, even though they were both engaged in the same enterprise. Perhaps such differences can be attributed to the contextual features reviewed by Peterson and Sorenson, namely, the interaction history of the leaders and members and the specific characteristics of the group.

Barge et al.'s (1989) findings also point to the role of individual differences in understanding just how influence is accomplished. They draw on Weick's (1979) suggestion that to create meaning and influence for followers, leaders need both cognitive and behavioral skills. Future leadership research, Barge et al. (1989) conclude, "should focus not only upon documenting the variety of conversational structures that exist but also on the skills needed to produce them" (p. 383).

Constructivist research (as outlined by Delia, O'Keefe, & O'Keefe, 1982), in particular, sheds light on the kinds of social cognitive skills that influence the messages leaders produce (see also Sypher, 1984). The bulk of constructivist research has focused on persuasion and, more specifically, on the relationship between interpersonal construct system development, which is most often operationalized as cognitive differentiation (for a discussion of measurement issues, see O'Keefe & Sypher, 1981), and person-centered persuasive strategies. Findings indicate that more complex, abstract, interpersonal construct systems generally suggest a more developed set of schemata for understanding persons and social relations (for a review, see Applegate, 1990; Burleson, 1987).

However, construct system development ought to be considered a necessary but not sufficient path to ensuring person-centered, adaptive communication behavior. Of equal importance in this research is behavioral complexity, the use of strategies that reflect a more sophisticated integration of individuals' multiple goals. In short, construct system development and multiple goal integration are considered the major factors contributing to the construction of messages that "do more work" in social situations (for examples, see O'Keefe, 1984; O'Keefe & Delia, 1982; O'Keefe & Shepherd, 1987).

This research helps us to understand leadership because it helps us understand how messages work. What it says is that some leaders may be able to influence others, in part, because they have the ability to construe their followers in more complex, abstract, and psychologically centered ways, which enables them to produce messages that are more sensitive to the interpersonal aspects of the situations and address multiple aims and obstacles (for more details, see O'Keefe & Delia, 1982).

There are a wealth of studies that lend support to this assumption, and they have recently been reviewed by Burleson (1987), O'Keefe (1988), and Applegate (1990). In addition to the general conclusion about how construct system development and person-centeredness get played out in message design, there have also been a number of studies in the organizational context that are particularly relevant to this commentary. Specifically, more cognitively differentiated employees were perceived as more effective leaders by their subordinates (Husband, 1981) and more "transformational" in their leadership enactments, especially more charismatic, inspirational, and individualized in their consideration of others (Zorn, 1988). They also were rated as more persuasive by their peers and supervisors (Sypher, 1981), were located in higher levels of the organization (Haas, 1989; Roberts, 1987; Sypher, 1981; Sypher & Zorn, 1986), were more upwardly mobile (Haas, 1989; Sypher & Zorn, 1986), were higher self-monitors (Sypher & Zorn, 1986), and consistently received more positive performance evaluations (Haas, 1989) than their less differentiated coworkers.

Admittedly, control is important to this conception of communication, just as influence is the focus of leadership. Communication is designed primarily to do something and, from a constructivist orientation, it is designed in part to influence the impressions of others. However, research produced from this position suggests that influence or control is best achieved by accommodating to situational and relational demands and employing message strategies that integrate multiple goals, including relational and persuasive. The most consistent and central research in this vein concludes that person-centered messages hold the most promise for achieving multiple goals. Person-centered messages, which are sometimes referred to as "other-oriented," are those that are responsive to the other's aims and utterances, adapted to meet the specific characteristics or needs of the other, deal with the other's psychological or affective qualities, move the other to reflect on his or her circumstance or situation, and, *most important*, enhance the interpersonal relationship or create positive interpersonal identities (Applegate, 1990, p. 208).

Recently, O'Keefe (1988) has advocated a move from a more functional view of messages (i.e., looking at what they do) to a more rational goal-based model that suggests messages are designed to meet the demands of social situations and not to meet an individually selected and consciously recognized set of goals. She acknowledges, however, that representations of situational objectives may vary. She distinguishes among expressive, conventional, and rhetorical "message design logics" as fundamental premises in reasoning about communication, with each one subsuming the other and each one showing more concern for context. The expressive logic considers language a medium for expressing thoughts and feelings, the conventional logic characterizes action and meaning as context determined, and the rhetorical logic assumes that the communication process creates context.

Perhaps these distinctions best capture differences suggested by Peterson and Sorenson's model and the alternative represented by a message-centered approach. Peterson and Sorenson's focus on "contextual antecedents" in many ways suggests a conventional message design logic. In other words, they seem to say that the function of communication is to secure a desired response, and that action and meaning are determined by context. Constructivism is a rhetorical theory that construes communication as the "creation and negotiation of social selves and situations." The communication process itself creates context, and its function is to negotiate social consensus.

Moreover, O'Keefe (1988) suggests that people are socialized into communication systems with particular "logics" for designing messages:

> To the extent that negotiability is a clear possibility within the social situations people face, they will come more quickly and securely to a Rhetorical view of communication. . . . By contrast, persons who live in a world where power and resource control are used to fix meaning and social arrangements . . . will find it difficult to develop a belief in the social constitution of reality and the power of language to reorder social life. (p. 89)

In this way, an individual's view of communication is fundamentally tied to his or her view of leadership and organization.

This reasoning focuses our attention on the kinds of message design logics (a type of knowledge organization, and not a personality trait) leaders use and the kind of social order they make possible by their messages. That women tend to produce more powerful rhetorical messages than men (O'Keefe, 1988) also suggests that we begin to explore leadership in terms of the kinds of communities made possible by those who enact leadership roles. While relevant to Peterson and Sorenson's position, this notion certainly provides a different slant on the role of gender in leadership studies.

Taken together, these findings also suggest that power is more likely to be dispersed when a relatively large number of organizational members are more interpersonally centered and more capable of producing rhetorical messages. In cultural terms, people accommodate to the demands of the situations inasmuch as they contribute to the creation of it. While Peterson and Sorenson give us a great deal of detail about the organizational context that determines action and meaning, an interpretive social cognitive and, more specifically, a constructivist orientation provides information on how communication creates the context. Both acknowledge the reflexivity involved in accommodation and creation. Both perhaps could do more elaboration of situations that are enigmatic and require, as well as encourage, creative solutions and those that are rule bound and require only rule-following behavior. However, the key to such elaborations lies in understanding how communication is conceived and used.

A final concern about cognitive approaches to leadership is the relative lack of attention paid to the role of emotion or affect (for a recent anthropological exception, see Jones, 1990). Collins (1981) reminds us that organizations are "markets" where cultural and emotional resources are exchanged. Adams and Ingersoll (1983) suggest that "sentiment, attachment and affection are words one rarely hears in the context of conducting social science research. Likewise, one seldom reads reports of hatred, passion, or anger in the work of those who study organization [or leadership]" (p. 224). Organizations, they contend, are dramas that include and evoke a wide range of emotions, dreams, and dark desires. Pacanowsky and O'Donnell-Trujillo (1983) pursue the same theme. Leaders, likewise, have emotions, seek to arouse emotional responses in their followers, and are certainly subject to a wide variety of emotional responses and emotive behavior.

The ways these emotions affect the way we communicate and organize have recently been rediscovered and are just beginning to receive considerable attention in cognitive psychology and communication. And while this lack of previous attention might seem puzzling, it exists in part because cognitive research has been heavily influenced by work in artificial intelligence and human factors engineering, where affect has not been considered a relevant issue. More recently, psychologists and communication scholars have begun to explore the interrelationships of cognition, affect, and behavior (see, e.g., Clark & Fiske, 1982; Donohew, Sypher, & Higgins, 1988; Sorentino & Higgins, 1986). Developments in this area should add another piece to the leadership puzzle. Since cognitions are thought to be affectively tagged, the study of cognition and communication stripped of affect could be considered a sterile and unrealistic task (Donohew et al., 1988; Sypher & Donohew, 1988). Moreover, the focus on cognition and emotion may directly contribute to the study of leadership because of its potential to increase our understanding of the renewed interest in charisma and individualized consideration (Bass, 1985) in predicting leadership potential.

CONCLUSION

From an understanding of person-centeredness that is captured in the work reviewed in this commentary, one could conclude that those who take into account others' needs and aspirations (who generally have a more developed knowledge structure of others) when trying to influence those others are often the ones who may move more quickly into legitimated and informal positions of influence. They also may seek leadership as well by creating opportunities to influence members in terms of their view of communication and what is possible for all organizational members because of it.

More developed social cognitive abilities certainly do not preclude the communicator, and in this case the leader, from using all of the knowledge he or she has to achieve goals that are self-serving or Machiavellian. However, a close reading of constructivist research, and a deep understanding of how closely tied cognitive development in this sense is tied to person-centeredness, should make it clear that messages which are *only* self-serving are unlikely to be the most persuasive or effective.

What we see here is evidence suggesting that leadership may be best enacted through person-centered communication that accommodates to the needs of the followers and the demands of the situations they have conjointly created. Those who lead the best, and perhaps those who choose to lead, may often be those who have an extensive repertoire of rhetorical strategies to influence others, to articulate their visions, to empower followers, to capture task demands in terms of performance opportunities (and actually create them), to comfort others when they make mistakes, to avoid face-threatening communication, and to restore the dignity of followers by protecting their identities. This position at least holds forth the possibility that people will have a say in what they become. I have hope in this possibility perhaps because "when we do organizational research, we can't avoid telling the world something about who we are and the kind of organizational life we would choose for ourselves" (Adams & Ingersoll, 1983, p. 225).

It is through person-centered communication—more specifically, multifunctional, goal-integrated, rhetorical messages—that these accomplishments are possible, and our task as researchers is to examine these accomplishments in terms of how and why they work. Like many others, Peterson and Sorenson seem to agree that leadership is a symbolic activity, but they provide little direction for studying meaning in leadership messages. They do suggest that we have to look at the social demands that influence individual interpretations, but as communication researchers, we also have to look at how interpretations create the social situations by examining the messages produced, the deep structure embedded in them, and the effects they have.

REFERENCES

Adams, G. B., & Ingersoll, V. H. (1983). The difficulty of framing a perspective on organizational culture. In P. Frost, L. Moore, M. Louis, C. Lundberg, & J. Martin (Eds.), *Organizational culture* (pp. 223-235). Beverly Hills, CA: Sage.

Albrecht, T. L. (1989). Communication and personal control in empowering organizations. In J. A. Anderson (Eds.), *Communication yearbook 11* (pp. 380-391). Newbury Park, CA: Sage.

Applegate, J. L. (1990). Constructs and communication: A pragmatic integration. In G. Neimeyer & R. Neimeyer (Ed.), *Advances in personal construct psychology* (Vol. 1, pp. 203-230). Greenwich, CT: JAI.

Barge, J. K., Downs, C. W., & Johnson, K. M. (1989). An analysis of effective and ineffective leader conversation. *Management Communication Quarterly, 2*, 357-386.

Bass, B. M. (1985). *Leadership and performance beyond expectations.* New York: Free Press.

Becher, T. (1981). Towards a definition of disciplinary cultures. *Studies in Higher Education, 6*, 109-122.

Burleson, B. R. (1987). Cognitive complexity. In J. C. McCroskey & J. A. Daly (Eds.), *Personality and interpersonal communication* (pp. 305-349). Newbury Park, CA: Sage.

Burleson, B., Ely, T., Goering, E., Waltman, M., Whaley, B., & Wilson, S. (1988). Item desirability effects in compliance-gaining research. *Human Communication Research, 14*, 429-486.

Cameron, K., & Whetton, D. (1983). Organizational effectiveness: One model or several? In K. Cameron & D. Whetton (Eds.), *Organizational effectiveness: A comparison of multiple models* (pp. 1-24). New York: Academic Press.

Clark, M. S., & Fiske, S. T. (Eds.). (1982). *Affect and cognition.* Hillsdale, NJ: Lawrence Erlbaum.

Collins, R. (1981). On the microfoundations of macrosociology. *American Journal of Sociology, 86*, 984-1014.

Dachler, H. P. (1984). On refocusing leadership from a social systems perspective of management. In J. G. Hunt, D. M. Hosking, C. A. Schriesheim, & R. Stewart (Eds.), *Leaders and managers: International perspectives on managerial behavior and leadership* (pp. 100-108). Oxford: Pergamon.

Deetz, S. (1983). Critical-cultural research: New sensibility and old realities. *Journal of Management, II*, 121-136.

Deetz, S. (1985). Ethical considerations in cultural research in organizations. In P. Frost, L. Moore, M. Louis, C. Lundberg, & J. Martin (Eds.), *Organizational culture* (pp. 251-269). Beverly Hills, CA: Sage.

Deetz, S. (1988). Cultural studies: Studying meaning and action in organizations. In J. A. Anderson (Ed.), *Communication yearbook 11* (pp. 335-346). Newbury Park, CA: Sage.

Delia, J. G., O'Keefe, B. J., & O'Keefe, D. J. (1982). The constructivist approach to communication. F. E. X. Dance (Ed.), *Human communication theory* (pp. 147-191). New York: Harper & Row.

Demming, E. (1989, October). *Restoring the individual.* Invited address given at the University of Kansas, Lawrence.

Donohew, L., Sypher, H. E., & Higgins, E. T. (Eds.). (1988). *Communication, social cognition and affect.* Hillsdale, NJ: Lawrence Erlbaum.

Dupree, M. (1989). *Leadership is an art.* Garden City, NY: Doubleday.

Fairhurst, G. J., & Chandler, T. A. (1989). Serial structure in leader-member interaction. *Communication Monographs, 56,* 215-240.

Haas, J. W. (1989). *The impact of communication abilities on individual success in organizational settings: A replication and extension.* Unpublished doctoral dissertation, University of Kentucky, Lexington.

Husband, R. L. (1981). *Leadership: A case study, phenomenology and social-cognitive correlates.* Unpublished doctoral dissertation, University of Illinois, Urbana-Champaign.

Jones, M. O. (Ed.). (1990). Emotions in work: A folklore approach [Special issue]. *American Behavioral Scientist, 33*(3).

Kanter, R. M. (1977). *Men and women of the corporation.* New York: Basic Books.

Keeley, R. M. (1984). Impartiality and participant-interest theories of organizational effectiveness. *Administrative Science Quarterly, 29,* 1-25.

O'Keefe, B. J. (1984). The evolution of impressions of small working groups: Effects of construct differentiation. In H. E. Sypher & J. L. Applegate (Eds.), *Communication by children and adults* (pp. 262-291). Beverly Hills, CA: Sage.

O'Keefe, B. J. (1988). The logic of message design: Individual differences in reasoning about communication. *Communication Monographs, 55,* 80-104.

O'Keefe, B. J., & Delia, J. G. (1982). Impression formation and message production. In M. E. Roloff & C. R. Berger (Eds.), *Social cognition and communication* (pp. 33-72). Beverly Hills, CA: Sage.

O'Keefe, B. J., & Shepherd, G. J. (1987). The pursuit of multiple objectives in face-to-face persuasive interactions: Effects of construct differentiation on message organization. *Communication Monographs, 64,* 396-419.

O'Keefe, D. J., & Sypher, H. E. (1981). Cognitive complexity measures and the relationship of cognitive complexity to communication: A critical review. *Human Communication Research, 8,* 72-92.

Pacanowsky, M. (1989). Communication in the empowering organization. In J. A. Anderson (Ed.), *Communication yearbook 11* (pp. 356-380). Newbury Park, CA: Sage.

Pacanowsky, M., & O'Donnell-Trujillo, N. (1983). Organizational communication as cultural performance. *Communication Monographs, 50,* 126-147.

Pearce, W. B., & Cronen, V. (1980). *Communication, action and meaning.* New York: Praeger.

Roberts, R. (1987). *Communication elements in newcomer enculturation.* Unpublished doctoral dissertation, University of Kentucky, Lexington.

Roloff, M. E., & Berger, C. R. (Eds.). (1982). *Social cognition and communication.* Beverly Hills, CA: Sage.

Schein, E. G. (1985). *Organizational culture and leadership.* San Francisco: Jossey-Bass.

Smith, P. B., & Peterson, M. F. (1988). *Leadership, organizations and culture: An event management model.* London: Sage.

Sorentino, R. M., & Higgins, E. T. (Eds.). (1986). *Handbook of motivation and cognition.* New York: Guilford.

Sypher, B. D. (1981). *A multimethod investigation of employee communication abilities, communication satisfaction and job satisfaction.* Unpublished doctoral dissertation, University of Michigan, Ann Arbor.

Sypher, B. D. (1984). The importance of social cognitive abilities in organizations. In R. N. Bostrom (Ed.), *Competence in communication* (pp. 103-129). Beverly Hills, CA: Sage.

Sypher, B. D., & Sypher, H. E. (1984). Seeing ourselves as others see us: Convergence and divergence in assessments of communication behavior. *Communication Research, 11,* 97-115.

Sypher, B. D., & Zorn, T. E. (1986). Communication abilities and upward mobility: A longitudinal investigation. *Human Communication Research, 12,* 420-431.

Sypher, H. E., & Donohew, L. (Eds.). (1988). Communication and affect [Special issue]. *American Behavioral Scientist, 31*(3).

Weick, K. E. (1979). *The social psychology of organizing* (2nd ed.). Reading, MA: Addison-Wesley.

Zorn, T. E. (1988, November). *Construct system development, transformational leadership and leadership messages among small business owners.* Paper presented at the annual meeting of the Speech Communication Association, New Orleans.

Zuboff, S. (1988). *In the age of the smart machine: The future of work and power.* New York: Basic Books.

AUTHOR INDEX

SUBJECT INDEX

ABOUT THE EDITOR

JAMES A. ANDERSON (Ph.D., University of Iowa) is Department Chair and Professor of Communication at the University of Utah. A Past President of the International Communication Association, he currently edits the ICA's prestigious *Communication Yearbook* series. Author of *Mediated Communication: A Social Action Perspective* and *Communication Research: Issues and Methods*, he has been concerned in his recent works with the constitution of audience in critical and empirical inquiry. His research interests focus on the communication structures and practices of social action routines, political campaigns, media literacy, and family ethnographies.

ABOUT THE AUTHORS

LEE B. BECKER (Ph.D., University of Wisconsin – Madison, 1974) is Professor in the School of Journalism and Department of Communication at The Ohio State University. His research has examined uses and effects of the mass media as well as media personnel practices.

DOUGLAS BIRKHEAD (Ph.D., University of Iowa, 1982) is Associate Professor of Communication at the University of Utah. His scholarly interests include media ethics and criticism, communication theory, and cultural studies. His commentaries and research have appeared in professional and academic journals as well as in newspapers.

ARTHUR P. BOCHNER (Ph.D., Bowling Green University, 1971) is Professor and Chairperson of the Department of Communication at the University of South Florida in Tampa. He has contributed more than 25 articles to both national and international journals and has authored several books, monographs, and book chapters on interpersonal relationships. He is currently studying processes of redescription in scholarly discourse and biographical ethnography.

MIHALY CSIKSZENTMIHALYI is Professor of Sociology at the University of Chicago.

JAMES A. DANOWSKI (Ph.D., Michigan State University, 1975) is Associate Professor and Director of Graduate Studies in Communication, University of Illinois at Chicago. Currently, he serves as a Trustee of the Education Foundation of the National Investor Relations Institute and is on the Board of Directors of the International Communication Association as Chair of the Information Systems Division. His research activities investigate how organizational communication management, media, and messages affect people's meanings for corporate symbols. He has also been developing semantic network methods for content analysis and automatic message creation.

G. LLOYD DRECKSEL (Ph.D., University of Utah, 1984) is Assistant Professor of Communication at the University of Utah. Her areas of interest include interpersonal, group, and organizational communication.

JOHN FISKE was educated at Cambridge University in England and has held appointments at universities in the United Kingdom, Australia, and the United States. He is currently Professor of Communication Arts at the University of Wisconsin – Madison. He is author of *Reading Television* (with John Hartley), *Introduction to Communication Studies, Key Concepts in Communication* (with

T. O'Sullivan et al.), *Television Culture, Understanding Popular Culture*, and *Reading the Popular.* He edits a book series, Studies in Culture and Communication, for Routledge and is general editor of *Cultural Studies.*

JOSEPH P. FOLGER (Ph.D., University of Wisconsin—Madison, 1978) is Associate Professor and Chair of the Department of Rhetoric and Communication at Temple University in Philadelphia. His work focuses on the development of representational validity procedures, influences on conflict interaction, and the role of third parties in alternative dispute resolution settings. His research has been published in *Human Communication Research, Communication Monographs,* the *Communication Yearbook, Mediation Quarterly,* and the *Harvard Negotiation Journal.* He is coauthor of *Working Through Conflict: A Communication Perspective.*

KLAUS BRUHN JENSEN is Assistant Professor in the Department of Film, TV, and Communication, University of Copenhagen, Denmark, and received the European second doctorate (Dr. Phil.) from the University of Aarhus, Denmark, in 1986. He is chair of the working group of the Network on Qualitative Audience Research (NEQTAR) at conferences of the International Association for Mass Communication Research. He was Fellow of the American Council of Learned Societies at the Annenberg School of Communications, Los Angeles, 1988-1989, and is a member of the Board of the Danish Association for Mass Communication Research. His publications include *Making Sense of the News* (Aarhus University Press, 1986), *A Handbook of Qualitative Methodologies for Mass Communication Research* (coedited volume, in preparation, Routledge), and contributions to *Critical Studies in Mass Communication, European Journal of Communication, Journal of Communication,* and *Media, Culture & Society,* as well as edited works. His current research examines mass media history and international communications from the perspective of communication theory and qualitative methodology.

GARTH S. JOWETT (Ph.D., University of Pennsylvania) is currently Professor in the School of Communication, University of Houston. He is the author of *Film: The Democratic Art,* the standard history of moviegoing in America. His next major project is a social history of television. His interest in the history of propaganda was outlined in his book *Propaganda and Persuasion* (with Victoria O'Donnell; Sage, 1986).

STEVEN T. McDERMOTT (Ph.D., Michigan State University, 1982) is Assistant Professor of Speech Communication at California Polytechnic State University, San Luis Obispo. He is the 1987 recipient of the distinguished research award from the Intercultural Division of the Speech Communication Association for his coauthored theory of acculturation and 1988 recipient of the Ralph Cooley Award for his empirical research on the theory.

RAYMIE E. McKERROW (Ph.D, University of Iowa, 1974) is Professor of Communication Studies in the Department of Speech Communication at the University of Maine. His research areas include the study of nineteenth-century rhetorical history, contemporary argumentation, and critical theory. He edited *Explorations in Rhetoric*, and is coauthor of *Principles and Types of Speech Communication*. His published work has appeared in several journals, including the *Journal of the History of Ideas, Church History, Rhetorica, Philosophy and Rhetoric, Quarterly Journal of Speech*, and *Communication Monographs*, and in several conference proceedings and edited collections on argument theory and criticism.

DENIS McQUAIL (Ph.D., University of Leeds, 1976) is Professor of Mass Communication at the University of Amsterdam, Netherlands (since 1977). Prior to that, he was Professor of Sociology at the University of Southampton, England. He has held visiting posts at the University of Pennsylvania and the Gannett Center for Studies, Columbia University, New York. His chapter in this volume in part reflects his experience as adviser to the British Royal Commission on the Press (1974-1977). His main publications include *Television and the Political Image* (with J. Trenamen), *Television in Politics* (with J. Blumler), *Analysis of Newspaper Content, Mass Communication Theory,* and *New Politics* (with Karen Siune). He is a founding editor of the *European Journal of Communication.*

G. H. MORRIS (Ph.D., University of Texas at Austin, 1980) is Associate Professor and Graduate Director in the Department of Communication Studies, Texas Tech University. His research focuses on how people converse for action, find fault, and give accounts to explain themselves. His current projects include editing a collection of papers about talk within clinics, exploring new contexts of accounts, and examining the offering and receipt of instructions. His articles have appeared in *Quarterly Journal of Speech, Journal of Language and Social Psychology, Management Communication Quarterly, Research on Language and Social Interaction,* and *Southern Communication Journal.*

SERGE MOSCOVICI is Director of Studies and Professor of Social Psychology at l'Ecole des Hautes Etudes en Sciences Sociales in Paris. He was one of the founders of the European Association of Experimental Social Psychology. He has published many books, including *La machine à faire des dieux* (Fayard, 1988), *The Age of the Crowd* (Cambridge University Press, 1985), *Social Influence and Social Change* (Academic Press, 1977), and *Society Against Nature* (Harvester, 1976), and numerous articles on social representations, minority influence, language, and scientific epistemology.

JOHN P. MURRAY (Ph.D., Catholic University of America, 1970) is Department Head and Professor in Human Development and Family Studies at Kansas State University. He began his professional career more than 20 years ago as a scientist-administrator at the National Institute of Mental Health, where he served as a research coordinator for the Surgeon General's Scientific Advisory Committee on Television and Social Behavior. He has maintained an interest in television's impact on children from the mid-1960s to the present. He has published 11 books and more than 100 articles and reports on various aspects of child and family development. He was elected a Fellow of the American Psychological Association in 1982, presented an award for outstanding service to troubled and neglected youth by Boys Town in 1985, and appointed a member of the National Board of Trustees of Dr. Karl Menninger's Villages of Kansas and Indiana from 1986 to the present.

HORACE M. NEWCOMB (Ph.D., University of Chicago, 1969) is currently F. J. Heyne Centennial Professor of Communication in the Department of Radio-Television-Film at the University of Texas at Austin. He is the author of *TV: The Most Popular Art* (1974), coauthor (with Robert Alley) of *The Producer's Medium* (1984), and editor of four editions of *Television: The Critical View.*

SARA E. NEWELL (Ph.D., University of Utah, 1982) is Assistant Professor in the Department of Speech Communication and Theatre at West Chester University in West Chester, Pennsylvania. Complementing her work in conflict processes, her research interests include communication theory, argumentation, and qualitative approaches to the study of social interaction. She is currently completing a book on confrontation and conflict processes with R. K. Stutman.

ELISABETH NOELLE-NEUMANN (Ph.D., Berlin, 1940) is Founder and Director of the Institut für Demoskopie Allensbach, West Germany. She is also Founding Director and Professor Emeritus, Institut für Publizistik (Communications Research) and Visiting Professor, University of Chicago (Department of Political Science) since 1978. She is Past President of WAPOR, and her research interests include methods of survey research, international comparative analyses of value systems, psychological well-being, public opinion theory, and the effects of mass media. She has served as public opinion analyst since 1978 for the German newspaper *Frankfurter Allgemeine Zeitung*, and as coeditor for the *International Journal of Public Opinion Research.*

MARK F. PETERSON (Ph.D., University of Michigan) is Professor of Management at Texas Tech University. He currently serves on editorial boards of *Group and Organization Studies* and the *Journal of Management.* He is coauthor (with Peter B. Smith) of *Leadership, Organizations and Culture* (Sage, 1988). His current research focuses on comparative and intercultural studies of decision making and leadership.

STEPHEN D. REESE (Ph.D., University of Wisconsin—Madison) is Associate Professor and Graduate Adviser in the Department of Journalism at the University of Texas. He has been head of the Radio-TV Journalism Division of the Association of Education in Journalism and Mass Communication and edits the book review section of *Journalism Quarterly*. His research, as published in book chapters and articles in *Journalism Quarterly, Communication Research, Journal of Communication, Journal of Broadcasting and Electronic Media,* and *Public Opinion Quarterly,* has focused on the news media, including audience learning from television news, media reliance, attitudes toward both conventional and high-tech news media, and factors affecting network news coverage. His media sociology theory text, coauthored with Pamela Shoemaker, has recently been published (Longman). His present research interests include the process of intermedia influence within the mainstream press and the relationship between journalistic occupational ideology and hegemony.

RICHARD D. RIEKE (Ph.D., The Ohio State University, 1964) is Professor of Communication at the University of Utah. He specializes in argumentation, reasoning, persuasion, and decision making both theoretically and as applied in a variety of situations. His most recent work has been a book on communication in trial advocacy and a series of articles explaining U.S. Supreme Court decision making in terms of small group communication theory. He is the coauthor of seven books and numerous articles.

KARL ERIK ROSENGREN (Fil. Dr., University of Lund, 1968) is Professor of Sociology at the University of Lund in Lund, Sweden. For a time he was also Professor of Mass Communication (University of Gothenburg, 1982-1986). His main research interests cover primarily the sociology of culture and communication. His book-length publications in English include *Sociological Aspects of the Literary System* (1968), *Advances in Content Analysis* (1981), *Communication and Equality* (with A. M. Thunberg, K. Nowak, and B. Sigurd; 1982), *The Climate of Literature* (1983), *Media Gratifications Research* (with L. A. Wenner and P. Palmgreen; 1985), and *Media Matter* (with S. Windahl et al.; 1989). He is a founding coeditor of *European Journal of Communication.*

JAN SERVAES (Ph.D., Leuven University, Belgium) is working on international communications at the Department of Mass Communications, Catholic University of Nijmegen, the Netherlands. In 1987-1988 he was in the United States as a Fulbright scholar. He has taught at the Catholic University of Leuven, Belgium, and Thammasat University, Thailand. He is the author of six books in Dutch and two in English, and has written numerous articles for international journals.

RITCH L. SORENSON (Ph.D., Purdue University, 1979) is Associate Professor of Management at Texas Tech University. His research interests include leadership, conflict management, and interpersonal communication in organizations. His work has appeared in several communication and management journals, including *Human Communication Research, Communication Education,* and *Communication Quarterly.*

J. MICHAEL SPROULE (Ph.D., The Ohio State University, 1973) is Associate Professor of Communication Studies at San Jose State University. Trained in rhetoric, public address, and broadcasting, he has merged these interests in recent studies of twentieth-century American propaganda.

RANDALL K. STUTMAN (Ph.D., University of Utah, 1985) is Assistant Professor and Director of the Applied Communication Graduate Program in the Department of Rhetoric and Communication at Temple University in Philadelphia. His research interests include social influence processes, conflict management, and discourse analysis. He is the author of two books on communication theory and maintains an active consulting practice in applied communication.

MICHAEL SUNNAFRANK (Ph.D., Michigan State University, 1979) is Associate Professor of Communication at the University of Minnesota, Duluth. His research interests in interpersonal communication include communication behavior and influences during early acquaintance, and dynamics in personal relationships. His research has been published in *Communication Monographs, Human Communication Research, Quarterly Journal of Speech,* and several other journals.

BEVERLY DAVENPORT SYPHER (Ph.D., University of Michigan, 1981) is Associate Professor of Communication Studies at the University of Kansas. She has been a Visiting Fellow at Chisholm Institute for Technology, Melbourne, Australia, and on the business administration and communication faculties at the University of Kentucky, where she was named a Great Teacher in 1986. She has published in a variety of communication, psychology, and business journals, and has authored several book chapters on the relationship between social cognitive abilities and organizational behavior. She recently edited *Case Studies in Organizational Communication* (Guilford Press).

DONALD F. TIBBITS (Ph.D., University of Missouri, Columbia, 1973) is Professor of Speech-Language Pathology at Central Missouri State University in Warrensburg, where he is a recipient of the Byler Distinguished Faculty Award. He holds the Certificate of Clinical Competence from the American Speech-Language-Hearing Association and a license for the practice of speech-language pathology from the State Board for the Healing Arts in Missouri. His research is in the areas of both linguistic acquisition and linguistic disabilities. He is particularly interested in the relationship between thinking processes and the use of language as an academic tool for students between the ages of 10 and 16 years. He has published in the *Journal of Psycholinguistic Research* and is the author of *Language Disorders in Adolescents.* He is currently writing a chapter on the relationship of critical thinking and language to academic success for a book that he is editing, titled *Linguistic Disabilities in Schools: Beyond the Primary Grades.*

STEPHEN TOULMIN has the Avalon Foundation Chair in the Humanities at Northwestern University. Trained as a physicist during World War II, he did graduate work at Cambridge in philosophy under Wittgenstein, and has published books on ethics, epistemology, and the history of thought. His best-known book on communication is *The Uses of Argument* (1958).

JEREMY TUNSTALL (M.A., Cambridge University) has been Professor of Sociology at City University in Central London since 1974. He has written numerous books, including *The Fishermen* (1962), *Journalists at Work* (1971), *The Media Are American* (1977), *Media Made in California*, and *Communications Deregulation*. More recently, he has authored (with Michael Palmer) *Liberating Communications: Policy Making in France and Britain*. With the same coauthor, he is publishing a second volume, part of which deals with European media moguls. He is currently engaged in a funded study about media executives that involves interviewing 100 TV executive producers and 100 national newspaper executives. He hopes to write a book on the media industries.

CECILIA VON FEILITZEN (Ph.D., Stockholm University, 1971) is Senior Researcher in the Department of Journalism, Media, and Communication, Unit of Media and Cultural Theory, Stockholm University, and the Audience Programme Research Department, Swedish Broadcasting Corporation (since 1964). She has published many reports, articles, and books. She is Past President of the Swedish Association of Mass Communication Researchers (1979-1981), has worked as Film Inspector at the Board of Film for Children (1983-1988), and is coeditor of international journals on communication research. Her research interests include the relationships among individuals, culture, and society; the role of media in the socialization process; power relations and oppression; and psychological, cultural, and social scientific perspectives on mass communication.

D. CHARLES WHITNEY (Ph.D., University of Minnesota, 1978) is Research Associate Professor in the Institute of Communications Research and Associate Professor in the Department of Journalism at the University of Illinois at Urbana-Campaign. He was coeditor, with Ellen Wartella, of the Sage *Mass Communication Review Yearbook*, volumes 3 and 4, and of *Individuals in Mass Media Organizations*, with James Ettema. He is completing a book on public attitudes toward the U.S. news media for Columbia University Press.

MARY LOUISE WILLBRAND (Ph.D., University of Missouri, 1972) is Professor of Communication Disorders at the University of Utah. She specializes in normal language behavior and in language disorders. Her recent research has been concentrated in a variety of studies on discourse interaction. She has published in communication, communication disorders, psychology, and linguistics. She is the author or coauthor of three books, numerous articles, and several convention presentations.

Continuing the innovative format developed for Volume 11, **Communication Yearbook 14** delves into the latest research concerned with: audiences — their effect on the mass media and how the mass media effect them; the quality of mass media performance and public opinion; the study of contemporary media from an organization studies approach; the implications of propaganda; the pressure of public opinion; and media agenda setting, among other issues. Commentaries provide refreshing viewpoints to each chapter, enhancing each chapter with complementary or, sometimes competing, perspectives. Once again Anderson has brought together an internationally distinguished team of contributors who have created a forum for discussing cutting-edge topics in the field.